T0191651

Lecture Notes in Computer Science   12486

More information about this series at http://www.springer.com/series/7410

Xiaofeng Chen · Hongyang Yan ·
Qiben Yan · Xiangliang Zhang (Eds.)

Machine Learning for Cyber Security

Third International Conference, ML4CS 2020
Guangzhou, China, October 8–10, 2020
Proceedings, Part I

Springer

Editors
Xiaofeng Chen
Xidian University
Xi'an, China

Hongyang Yan
Guangzhou University
Guangzhou, China

Qiben Yan
Michigan State University
East Lansing, MI, USA

Xiangliang Zhang
Division of Computer, Electrical
and Mathematical Sciences and Engineering
King Abdullah University of Science
Thuwal, Saudi Arabia

ISSN 0302-9743   ISSN 1611-3349   (electronic)
Lecture Notes in Computer Science
ISBN 978-3-030-62222-0   ISBN 978-3-030-62223-7   (eBook)
https://doi.org/10.1007/978-3-030-62223-7

LNCS Sublibrary: SL4 – Security and Cryptology

This Springer imprint is published by the registered company Springer Nature Switzerland AG
The registered company address is: Gewerbestrasse 11, 6330 Cham, Switzerland

Preface

The Third International Conference on Machine Learning for Cyber Security (ML4CS 2020) was held in Guangzhou, China, during October 8–10, 2020. ML4CS is a well-recognized annual international forum for AI-driven security researchers to exchange ideas and present their works. This volume contains papers presented at ML4CS 2020.

The conference received 360 submissions. The committee accepted 118 regular papers and 40 short papers to be included in the conference program. The proceedings contain revised versions of the accepted papers. While revisions are expected to take the referees comments into account, this was not enforced and the authors bear full responsibility for the content of their papers.

ML4CS 2020 was organized by the Institute of Artificial Intelligence and Blockchain, Guangzhou University, China. Furthermore, ML4CS 2020 was supported by the Peng Cheng Laboratory, Shenzhen, China. The conference would not have been such a success without the support of these organizations, and we sincerely thank them for their continued assistance and support.

We would also like to thank the authors who submitted their papers to ML4CS 2020, and the conference attendees for their interest and support. We thank the Organizing Committee for their time and effort dedicated to arranging the conference. This allowed us to focus on the paper selection and deal with the scientific program. We thank the Program Committee members and the external reviewers for their hard work in reviewing the submissions; the conference would not have been possible without their expert reviews. Finally, we thank the EasyChair system and its operators, for making the entire process of managing the conference convenient.

September 2020   Fengwei Zhang
                                                                        Jin Li

Preface

The Third International Conference on Materials Sciences on CyberSecurity (MMX/ACS 2020) was held in Guangzhou, China during October 5-10, 2020. MEACS is a well-recognized annual international forum for Academic Security researchers to exchange ideas and present their works. This volume contains papers presented at MEACS 2020.

The conference received 360 submissions. The committee accepted 218 regular papers and allowed panel to be included in the conference program. The proceedings contain revised versions of the accepted papers. While revisions were expected to take into the reviewers into account, the authors take full responsibility for the content of their papers.

MEACS 2020 was organized by the Institute of Artificial Intelligence and Block-chain, Guangzhou University, China. Furthermore, MEACS 2020 was supported by the Peng Cheng Laboratory, Shenzhen, China. The conference would not have been such a success without the support of these organizers, and we sincerely thank them for their continuous assistance and support.

We would also like to thank the authors who submitted their papers to MEACS 2020 and the participants who attended the conference and provided support. We thank the Organizing Committee for their time and effort in organizing the conference. This allowed us to focus on the paper selection and ensure a smooth scientific program. We thank the Program Committee members and the external reviewers for their hard work in reviewing the submissions. The conference would not have been possible without their expert reviews. Finally, we thank the EasyChair system and its operators, for making the entire process of managing the conference convenient.

September 2020

Fengwei Zhang
Jin Li

Organization

General Chairs

Fengwei Zhang	Southern University of Science and Technology, China
Jin Li	Guangzhou University, China

Program Chairs

Xiaofeng Chen	Xidian University, China
Qiben Yan	Michigan State University, USA
Xiangliang Zhang	King Abdullah University of Science and Technology, Saudi Arabia

Track Chairs

Hao Wang	Shandong Normal University, China
Xianmin Wang	Guangzhou University, China
Yinghui Zhang	Xi'an University of Posts and Telecommunications, China
Wei Zhou	Yunnan University, China

Workshop Chairs

Sheng Hong	Beihang University, China
Ting Hu	Queen's University, Canada
Nan Jiang	East China Jiaotong University, China
Liangqun Li	Shenzhen University, China
Jungang Lou	Hunan Normal University, China
Hui Tian	Huaqiao University, China
Feng Wang	Wuhan University, China
Zhi Wang	Nankai University, China
Tao Xiang	Chongqing University, China

Publication Chairs

Hongyang Yan	Guangzhou University, China
Yu Wang	Guangzhou University, China

Publicity Chair

Lianyong Qi	Qufu Normal University, China

Steering Committee

Xiaofeng Chen	Xidian University, China
Iqbal Gondal	Federation University Australia, Australia
Ryan Ko	University of Waikato, New Zealand
Jonathan Oliver	Trend Micro, USA
Islam Rafiqul	Charles Sturt University, Australia
Vijay Varadharajan	The University of Newcastle, Australia
Ian Welch	Victoria University of Wellington, New Zealand
Yang Xiang	Swinburne University of Technology, Australia
Jun Zhang	Swinburne University of Technology, Australia
Wanlei Zhou	Deakin University, Australia

Program Committee

Silvio Barra	University of Salerno, Italy
M. Z. Alam Bhuiyan	Guangzhou University, China
Carlo Blundo	University of Salerno, Italy
Yiqiao Cai	Huaqiao University, China
Luigi Catuogno	University of Salerno, Italy
Lorenzo Cavallaro	King's College London, UK
Liang Chang	Guilin University of Electronic Technology, China
Fei Chen	Shenzhen University, China
Xiaofeng Chen	Xidian University, China
Zhe Chen	Singapore Management University, Singapore
Xiaochun Cheng	Middlesex University, UK
Frédéric Cuppens	Télécom Bretagne, France
Changyu Dong	Newcastle University, UK
Guangjie Dong	East China Jiaotong University, China
Mohammed EI-Abd	American University of Kuwait, Kuwait
Wei Gao	Yunnan Normal University, China
Dieter Gollmann	Hamburg University of Technology, Germany
Zheng Gong	South China Normal University, China
Zhitao Guan	North China Electric Power University, China
Zhaolu Guo	Chinese Academy of Sciences, China
Jinguang Han	Queen's University Belfast, UK
Saeid Hosseini	Singapore University of Technology and Design Singapore
Chingfang Hsu	Huazhong University of Science and Technology, China
Haibo Hu	The Hong Kong Polytechnic University, Hong Kong
Teng Huang	Guangzhou University, China
Xinyi Huang	Fujian Normal University, China
Wenchao Jiang	Guangdong University of Technology, China
Lutful Karim	Seneca College of Applied Arts and Technology, Canada

Hadis Karimipour	University of Guelph, Canada
Sokratis Katsikas	Open University of Cyprus, Cyprus
Neeraj Kumar	Thapar Institute of Engineering and Technology, India
Ping Li	South China Normal University, China
Tong Li	Guangzhou University, China
Wei Li	Jiangxi University of Science and Technology, China
Xuejun Li	Anhui University, China
Kaitai Liang	University of Surrey, UK
Hui Liu	University of Calgary, Canada
Wei Lu	Sun Yat-sen University, China
Xiaobo Ma	Xi'an Jiaotong University, China
Fabio Martinelli	IIT-CNR, Italy
Ficco Massimo	Second University of Naples, Italy
Weizhi Meng	Technical University of Denmark, Denmark
Vincenzo Moscato	University of Naples, Italy
Francesco Palmieri	University of Salerno, Italy
Fei Peng	Hunan University, China
Hu Peng	Wuhan University, China
Lizhi Peng	Jinan University, China
Umberto Petrillo	Sapienza University of Rome, Italy
Lianyong Qi	Qufu Normal University, China
Shahryar Rahnamayan	Ontario Tech University, Canada
Khaled Riad	Guangzhou University, China
Yu Sun	Guangxi University, China
Yu-An Tan	Beijing Institute of Technology, China
Zhiyuan Tan	Edinburgh Napier University, UK
Ming Tao	Dongguan University of Technology, China
Donghai Tian	Beijing Institute of Technology, China
Chundong Wang	Tianjin University of Technology, China
Ding Wang	Peking University, China
Hui Wang	Nanchang Institute of Technology, China
Jianfeng Wang	Xidian University, China
Jin Wang	Soochow University, China
Licheng Wang	Beijing University of Posts and Telecommunications, China
Lingyu Wang	Concordia University, Canada
Tianyin Wang	Luoyang Normal University, China
Wei Wang	Beijing Jiaotong University, China
Sheng Wen	Swinburne University of Technology, Australia
Yang Xiang	Swinburne University of Technology, Australia
Run Xie	Yibin University, China
Xiaolong Xu	Nanjing University of Information Science and Technology, China
Li Yang	Xidian University, China
ShaoJun Yang	Fujian Normal University, China
Zhe Yang	Northwestern Polytechnical University, China

Yanqing Yao   Beihang University, China
Xu Yuan   University of Louisiana at Lafayette, USA
Qikun Zhang   Beijing Institute of Technology, China
Xiao Zhang   Beihang University, China
Xiaosong Zhang   Tangshan University, China
Xuyun Zhang   Macquarie University, Australia
Yuan Zhang   Nanjing University, China
Xianfeng Zhao   Chinese Academy of Sciences, China
Lei Zhu   Huazhong University of Science and Technology,
                                 China
Tianqing Zhu   China University of Geosciences, China

Track Committee

Jin Cao   Xidian University, China
Hui Cui   Murdoch University, Australia
Rui Guo   Xi'an University of Posts and Telecommunications,
                                 China
Qi Li   Nanjing University of Posts and Telecommunications,
                                 China
Muhammad Baqer Mollah   Nanyang Technological University, Singapore
Ben Niu   Chinese Academy of Sciences, China
Fatemeh Rezaeibagha   Murdoch University, Australia

Contents – Part I

Contents – Part II

Contents – Part III

Dynamic Adjusting ABC-SVM Anomaly Detection Based on Weighted Function Code Correlation

Ming Wan[1], Jinfang Li[1], Hao Luo[1], Kai Wang[2,3(✉)] (iD),
Yingjie Wang[4], and Bailing Wang[2,3]

[1] School of Information, Liaoning University, Shenyang 110036, China
{wanming, luohao}@lnu.edu.cn,
lijinfang_lnu@hotmail.com
[2] School of Computer Science and Technology, Harbin Institute of Technology,
Weihai 264209, China
{dr.wangkai, wbl}@hit.edu.cn
[3] Research Institute of Cyberspace Security, Harbin Institute of Technology,
Weihai 264209, Shandong, China
[4] School of Computer and Control Engineering, Yantai University,
Yantai 264005, China
towangyingjie@163.com

Abstract. Under the tendency of interconnection and interoperability in Industrial Internet, anomaly detection, which has been widely recognized, has achieved modest accomplishments in industrial cyber security. However, a significant issue is how to effectively extract industrial control features which can accurately and comprehensively describe industrial control operations. Aiming at the function code field in industrial Modbus/TCP communication protocol, this paper proposes a novel feature extraction algorithm based on weighted function code correlation, which not only indicates the contribution of single function code in the whole function code sequence, but also analyzes the correlation of different function codes. In order to establish a serviceable detection engine, a dynamic adjusting ABC-SVM (Artificial Bee Colony - Support Vector Machine) anomaly detection model is also developed. The experimental results show that the proposed feature extraction algorithm can effectively reflect the changes of functional control behavior in process operations, and the improved ABC-SVM anomaly detection model can improve the detection ability by comparing with other anomaly detection engines.

Keywords: Anomaly detection · Function code weight · Correlation analysis · Dynamic adjusting ABC-SVM

1 Introduction

With the information-based development of intelligent manufacturing, today's industrial control systems have become a complicated tangle of hardware and software components, which are gradually connected to public network [1]. As a result, they are

X. Chen et al. (Eds.): ML4CS 2020, LNCS 12486, pp. 1–11, 2020.
https://doi.org/10.1007/978-3-030-62223-7_1

gradually evolved from stand-alone automation to interconnected intelligence. In view of this, the hidden industrial cyber vulnerabilities have been revealed by various viruses and Trojans, and industrial security incidents all over the world have occurred frequently [2, 3]. Especially, targeted and sophisticated attacks have the huge destructive power to industrial control systems in recent years. For example, in 2010, Stuxnet destroyed Iran's nuclear power plant, and this virus exploited multiple vulnerabilities in Windows and Siemens software to maliciously manipulate the centrifuges controlled by the PLC (Programmable Logic Controller) [4]. Different from the spying task, it aims to destroy industrial controllers according to the preset instructions. Additionally, it can also infect industrial-oriented software of core operation computers, and camouflage to send malicious instructions to other computers in the whole automatic system.

Under normal circumstances, when industrial communication protocols (such as Modbus/TCP and Siemens S7) are applied to industrial control services, the master station can send an instruction to the slave station, where the corresponding control operation is performed by using the specified function field in industrial communication protocols [1, 5]. Although industrial communication protocols facilitate various communications of industrial devices, they are also easy to be parsed and utilized for devastating attacks [6]. To cite a simple example: one attacker can intercept normal Modbus/TCP traffic through the camouflage, and insert arbitrary control commands due to the plaintext transmission. Due to the specific industrial control protocols, industrial security problems are still different from the ones of traditional IT network.

Although many methods have been developed to defend against unknown cyber threats in industrial control systems, anomaly detection is still a valuable and promising approach by learning hidden communication features to identify industrial attacks or intrusion behaviors [7–9]. However, a significant problem is how to effectively extract industrial control features from the captured communication packets. From the perspective of function control behavior [10], this paper proposes a novel feature extraction algorithm based on weighted function code correlation, and designs an improved ABC-SVM anomaly detection model to detect abnormal behaviors in industrial control communications. More specially, in the aspect of feature extraction, the proposed algorithm performs the weight analysis on the extracted Modbus/TCP function code sequences, and the function code correlation is analyzed to describe the dependency between industrial control operations; in the aspect of anomaly detection, the SVM anomaly detection model is established as an applicable detection engine, and the dynamic adjusting ABC algorithm based on double mutations is presented to optimize SVM's parameters, which can further strengthen its detection performance.

2   Feature Extraction Based on Weighted Function Code Correlation

In industrial Modbus/TCP networks, malicious attackers can perform command-based control operations on industrial control devices [11], including opening or closing the coils, reading and writing register data, and even changing the control logic, etc. Actually, the change of function codes in Modbus/TCP packets can be indirectly mapped to different function control behaviors, and the probability of function codes is one of the most critical influences on the behavior feature calculation. From this point of view, the proposed feature extraction algorithm is designed as follows:

Step 1: function code sequence construction.

By extracting function codes in Modbus/TCP packets at the same time interval, we can obtain different functional code sequences $A_i = a_1^i a_2^i a_3^i \cdots a_n^i, \forall i \in [1, m]$, and further form the function code sequence set $A = \{A_1, A_2, A_3, \cdots, A_m\}$. Here, m is the number of function code sequences, and n is the number of function codes in each function code sequence. Additionally, we construct and label all function code sequences in A to two categories: normal and abnormal, and each sequence belonging to the abnormal class contains some malicious function codes through the simulated attack.

Step 2: function code weight calculation.

In practice, different function codes can reflect different command-based control operations, and the corresponding function code weights in any function code sequence are not the same. The different function code weights can be calculated as follows:

Firstly, we compute the frequency of each function code in $A_i(i \in [1, m])$, and obtain the function code frequency set $F = \{F_1, F_2, F_3, \cdots, F_m\}$, in which each $F_i(i \in [1, m])$ consists of all frequencies of different function codes in $A_i(i \in [1, m])$.

Secondly, according to Relief algorithm [12], we can further calculate the function code weight. Moreover, we randomly select a sample $F_i(i \in [1, m])$ from F, and decide its category by using its classification label. If F_i belongs to the normal category, we find k nearest neighboring samples $N_j, \forall j \in [1, k]$ from all normal samples of F by computing the distances between these samples and F_i, and also find k nearest neighboring samples $M_j, \forall j \in [1, k]$ from all abnormal samples of F by computing the corresponding distances, or vice versa. After that, we can update the function code weight of function code by

$$W(a) = W(a) - \left[\sum_{j=1}^{k} \textit{diff}(a, F_i, N_j) * |H(F_i) - H(N_j)| \right] / (m \cdot k)$$

$$+ \sum_{C \neq Class(F_i)} \left[\frac{p(C)}{1 - p(Class(F_i))} \sum_{j=1}^{k} \textit{diff}(a, F_i, M_j(C)) * |H(F_i) - H(M_j(C))| \right] / (m \cdot k)$$

$$(1)$$

Here, $W(a)$ represents the weight of function code a, and its initial value is set to 0; $\textit{diff}(a, F_i, N_j)$ represents the distance of function code a between the samples F_i and N_j, and it is actually a frequency difference calculated by Formula (2); $H(F_i)$ represents the information entropy of function code a in F_i, and $H(N_j)$ represents the information entropy of function code a in N_j; $Class(F_i)$ represents the category to which F_i belongs, and $M_j(C)$ represents the j - th neighboring sample which belongs to the category C.

$$diff(a, R_1, R_2) = R_1[a] - R_2[a] \qquad (2)$$

Here, R_1 and R_2 are two samples belonging to F.

Step 3: Function code correlation analysis.

The characteristics of function control behavior appear finite and regular, and some strong dependencies can exist between different control operations. On this basis, we perform the function code correlation analysis by creating the function code itemsets and short sequences:

Firstly, we obtain all function code itemsets and short sequence patterns by parsing the set A: on the one hand, by scanning the set A, we find all different single function codes to form 1-itemset, and continue to construct 2-itemset and 3-itemset by using all combinations of two and three function codes in 1-itemset, respectively; on the other hand, for each function code sequence in A, we search all 2-length and 3-length function codes to form the corresponding short sequences by using 2-length and 3-length sliding windows, respectively.

Secondly, for each item in 2-itemset, we calculate its number in all 2-length short sequences of each function code sequence. Also, for each item in 3-itemset, we calculate its number in all 3-length short sequences of each function code sequence.

Finally, we can define the function code correlation rule, and calculate the function code correlation degree. Because the high feature dimension can result in the considerable computational complexity, we select the items in 2-itemset to exploit correlation rules of different function codes. Furthermore, we suppose that one item in 2-itemset is $a_x a_y$ and its next function code is a_z, who can be regarded as any item in 1-itemset. In practice, $a_x a_y a_z$ is an item in 3-itemset, which can represent three possible continuous control operations in industrial activities. After that, we can define one function code correlation rule as $a_x a_y \rightarrow a_z$, and calculate its correlation degree $S(a_x a_y \rightarrow a_z)$ by

$$\begin{cases} S(a_x a_y \rightarrow a_z) = p(a_x a_y a_z)/p(a_x a_y) \\ p(a_x a_y a_z) = N(a_x a_y a_z)/(n-2) \\ p(a_x a_y) = N(a_x a_y)/(n-1) \end{cases} \qquad (3)$$

Here, $N(\bullet)$ represents the statistical number in the second procedure, and n is the number of function codes in each A_i $(i \in [1, m])$.

Step 4: Feature value calculation.

For each item in 2-itemset, we can further calculate its feature value x_j^i by integrating the function code weight with the function code correlation degree:

$$x_j^i = \sum_{a_z} W(a_z) * S(a_x a_y \rightarrow a_z) \qquad (4)$$

According to the above steps, we can calculate all feature values to obtain the feature vector $X_i = (x_1^i, x_2^i, x_3^i, \cdots, x_d^i)$ for each $A_i (i \in [1, m])$, and generate the final function sample set $X = \{X_1, X_2, X_3, \cdots, X_m\}$. Here, d represents the dimension of feature vector, which also equates with the number of items in 2-itemset (Fig. 1).

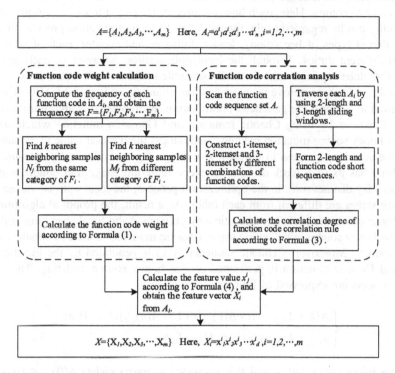

Fig. 1. Feature extraction algorithm based on weighted function code correlation.

3 Dynamic Adjusting ABC-SVM Anomaly Detection Model Based on Double Mutations

Attacks on command-based control operations can be implemented by changing adverse function codes in the normal function code sequence, and different types of attack sequences can be easily constructed. In order to locate anomalies, many machine learning methods have been successfully applied in intrusion detection, because they have obvious advantages in scientific predictions or judgments [13, 14]. In our model, binary classification becomes an appropriate method, and SVM is introduced as an applicable detection engine due to its high availability to solve small sample problems [15, 16]. However, in practical applications, SVM's classification performance can be largely affected by some factors, such as the penalty factor C and the parameters of kernel function. Therefore, we design a dynamic adjusting ABC-SVM anomaly detection model, which optimizes the SVM's parameters by using the improved artificial bee colony algorithm.

Nowadays, different optimization algorithms have been widely used to improve the model's performance, and each algorithm has its own principles and characteristics

[17–20]. The typical artificial bee colony algorithm is an optimization algorithm based on the intelligent searching behaviors of honey bee swarm, and it is a specific application of swarm intelligence [21]. Moreover, this algorithm has two elements: honey source and bee colony. Here, each honey source represents a feasible solution, and its profitability can be regarded as the fitness value. In the optimization process, there are three different types of bee colony: leader, follower and scouter, each of which can perform different duties. Through the local optimization behavior of each bee individual, the global optimal value is finally generated in the whole bee colony.

In order to further improve the classification accuracy, an improved ABC algorithm is designed to perform the parameter optimization. Moreover, this algorithm produces double mutations by using Chaotic mutation and Gaussian mutation which are two different honey source mutation methods, and adopts the optimal value to dynamically adjust the searching process in different searching stages. Additionally, because each bee colony has its own work division in every searching stage and double mutation operators play distinct roles in the optimization process, the local optimal values in all searching stages are different from each other. As a result, the proposed algorithm can evidently improve the global optimization by enhancing the local searching ability.

In the honey source initialization stage, Chaotic mutation is used to obtain N initial honey sources. Moreover, a chaotic sequence $A(k)$ is generated by the logistic mapping, and Chaotic mutation is performed on the honey source updating. The initialization process are expressed as follows:

$$\begin{cases} A(k+1)_{i,d} = u * A(k)_{i,d} * (1 - A(k)_{i,d}), k \in [0,n] \\ x_{i,d} = L_d + A(n)_{i,d} * (U_d - L_d) \end{cases} \tag{5}$$

Here, the initial value $A(0)_{i,d}$ and the parameter u must satisfies $A(0)_{i,d} \in (0,1)$ and $u \in (3.5699456, 4]$, and we set $u = 4$.

In the leader searching stage, the multivariate Gaussian mutation is performed on the honey source updating, and the association between different dimensions of honey sources can be automatically captured by covariance matrix during the mutation process. Then, based on the Gbest searching strategy, the global optimal value is used to perform the dynamic adjusting searching, and the dynamic factor can affect the variation degree of honey sources. The multivariate Gaussian mutation function is depicted by

$$p = \frac{1}{\sqrt{|\sum|(2\pi)^v}} \exp\left(-\frac{1}{2}(x-\mu)^T \sum^{-1}(x-\mu)\right) \tag{6}$$

Here, $x = \{x_{1,d}, x_{2,d}, \cdots x_{N,d}\}$ represent all honey sources before the mutation; $p = \{p_{1,d}, p_{2,d}, \cdots p_{N,d}\}$ represent new honey sources after the mutation; μ and $\sum$ are the mean and covariance matrixes of x; v is the dimension of $\sum$; $\sum^{-1}$ is the matrix inversion of $\sum$.

By using the multivariate Gaussian mutation, we can update new honey sources by:

$$v_{i,d} = f_i * p_{i,d} + \frac{1}{D}\left(p_{i,d} * f_i - p_{k,d} * f_k\right)$$
$$+ \frac{1}{D}\left(x_{GlobalBestInd} - p_{i,d} * f_i\right) \tag{7}$$

Here, $\frac{1}{D}$ is the dynamic factor, whose D can be set to the iteration number; $p_{k,d}$ is a different neighboring honey source of $p_{i,d}$ in all honey sources by using the random selection; $x_{GlobalBestInd}$ is the current global optimal value.

In the follower searching stage, instead of the roulette selection, the optimal value in the leader searching stage and the dynamic factor are used to dynamically adjust the searching process, and new honey source can be updated by:

$$v_{i,d} = x_{LeaderBestInd} + \frac{1}{D}\left(x_{i,d} - x_{k,d}\right) \tag{8}$$

Here, $x_{LeaderBestInd}$ is the optimal value in the leader searching stage.

The penalty factor C and the parameter σ of RBF kernel function are optimized by the improved ABC algorithm, and the process of dynamic adjusting ABC-SVM anomaly detection model is built as follows:

Step 1: Initialize the honey sources through Chaotic mutation.

Step 2: In the leader searching stage, Gaussian mutation is performed on the honey source updating, and neighborhoods of all honey sources are searched by (7). After that, the fitness values are calculated by the profitability of honey source, and a better honey source is selected through the greedy algorithm.

Step 3: In the follower searching stage, the neighborhoods of current honey sources are searched according to (8). Then, the corresponding fitness values are calculated by the profitability of honey source, and a better honey source is selected through the greedy algorithm.

Step 4: Determine whether a discarded honey source exists, if so, the leaders turn into the scouters, and the scouters randomly search for a new honey source.

Step 5: Record current best honey source, and determine whether the iteration is successfully completed, if so, the optimal SVM parameters C and σ can be obtained, otherwise return to Step 2.

4 Comparison and Analysis of Experimental Results

4.1 Experiment Environment

In order to carry out the feasibility analysis of the proposed approach, we design and build a Modbus/TCP control system. As shown in Fig. 2, the whole control system is divided into three layers: monitoring layer, process control layer and field device layer, and its key components include an operator workstation, three PLCs, an attacker, and a traffic capture computer. Additionally, the communication packets are captured from the monitoring port of industrial switch by using Libpcap. The specific process is listed as follows: in the first stage, after opening the valve 1, material 1 flows into the middle tank 2 to produce materials 2 and 3; in the second stage, after opening the valves 2 and 3, materials 2 and 3 flow into the middle tank 3 to produce materials 4 and 5; in the third stage, after opening valves 4 and 5, material 4 flows the last tank, and material 5 is discarded. Throughout the process, an operator station performs command-based control operations by sending Modbus/TCP control commands to three PLCs. The whole process is repeated every minute, and coils and registers are read once per second.

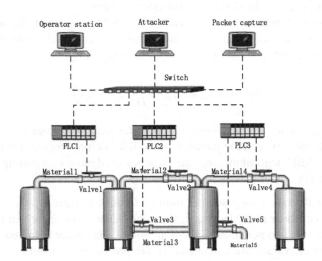

Fig. 2. Network structure of Modbus/TCP control system.

4.2 Experimental Result Analysis

The above technical process mainly includes six different function codes: function code 01, function code 03, function code 05, function code 06, function code 15, and function code 16. According to the proposed feature extraction algorithm, we further process the captured communication data, and obtain the 36-dimension feature vector and 185 function samples. Additionally, we set 50 normal samples and 50 abnormal samples as the SVM's training samples.

In order to illustrate the detection advantages of SVM, we introduce the classification accuracy and the consuming time as two important indicators to compare different detection engines, including SVM optimized by Grid, standard RBF neural network [22], BP neural network [23], and decision tree (DT) [24], and the compared results are shown in Table 1.

As shown in Table 1, although the average training accuracy of Grid-SVM for 10 different experiments is slightly lower than the one of RBF, its average test accuracy is the highest, and its average consuming time is the shortest. Additionally, its offline training and parameter optimization can indirectly save time and online resources. In other words, due to the strong generalization ability, SVM has a better detection performance, and is more appropriate for the proposed feature extraction algorithm.

Table 1. Detection performance of different detection engines.

	Grid-SVM	RBF	BP	DT
Average training accuracy	97.40%	100%	90.44%	94%
Average test accuracy	87.30%	83.38%	81.83%	77.31%
Average consuming time	0.0419 s	0.4237 s	0.2572 s	0.8762 s

In order to demonstrate the advantages of the improved ABC algorithm, we compare different classification accuracies of SVM under the typical ABC and the improved ABC. The experimental results are shown in Table 2, and the fitness comparisons of typical ABC and improved ABC (IABC) is depicted in Fig. 3.

Table 2. Average accuracy of ABC and IABC for different sample types.

Type	ABC-SVM		IABC-SVM	
	Accuracy	Time	Accuracy	Time
1	57.06%	0.0070 s	59.29%	0.0102 s
2	79.76%	0.0064 s	81.18%	0.0066 s
3	87.06%	0.0240 s	88.82%	0.0058 s
4	92.24%	0.0075 s	93.06%	0.0098 s
5	94.35%	0.0065 s	94.35%	0.0056 s
6	95.53%	0.0063 s	96.24%	0.0058 s
Average	84.33%	0.0096 s	85.49%	0.0073 s

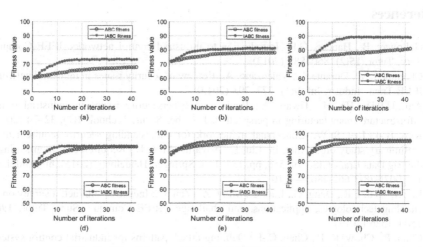

Fig. 3. Fitness curves of typical ABC and improve ABC.

In our experiments, there are six different types of samples in Table 2, which represent different numbers of malicious function codes. After 10 experiments for each type, the average classification accuracy of typical ABC algorithm is 84.33%, and the average classification accuracy of improved ABC algorithm is 85.49%. Furthermore, the classification accuracy of IABC-SVM is higher than the one of ABC-SVM, and ABC-SVM is more suitable to detect the above attack behaviors. Obviously, the dynamic adjusting ABC-SVM anomaly detection model based on double mutations has an optimal effect in improving SVM's classification performance.

5 Conclusion

Aiming at detecting abnormal behaviors in industrial Modbus/TCP communications, this paper proposes a dynamic adjusting ABC-SVM anomaly detection approach. Firstly, based on the weighted function control correlation, feature extraction is performed through the correlation analysis of process operations, and functional code sequences with different lengths are converted into feature vectors with the same dimension. Secondly, by improving the typical ABC algorithm, a dynamic adjusting ABC-SVM anomaly detection model based on double mutations is established to detect abnormal behaviors in industrial control operations. Finally, lots of experiments are conducted to evaluate the proposed approach, and the compared results and analysis can demonstrate its outstanding effectiveness.

Acknowledgment. This work is supported by the National Natural Science Foundation of China (Grant Nos. 61702439, 51704138), and the Natural Science Foundation of Liaoning Province (Grant No. 2019-MS-149).

References

1. Galloway, B., Hancke, G.P.: Introduction to industrial control networks. IEEE Commun. Surv. Tutor. **15**(2), 860–880 (2013)
2. Cheminod, M., Durante, L., Valenzano, A.: Review of security issues in industrial networks. IEEE Trans. Industr. Inf. **9**(1), 277–293 (2013)
3. Ani, U.P.D., He, H., Tiwari, A.: Review of cybersecurity issues in industrial critical infrastructure: manufacturing in perspective. J. Cyber Secur. Technol. **1**(1), 32–74 (2017)
4. Kim, B.-J., Lee, S.-W.: Conceptual framework for understanding security requirements: a preliminary study on stuxnet. In: Liu, L., Aoyama, M. (eds.) Requirements Engineering in the Big Data Era. CCIS, vol. 558, pp. 135–146. Springer, Heidelberg (2015). https://doi.org/10.1007/978-3-662-48634-4_10
5. Li, J.Q., Yu, F.R., Deng, G., Luo, C., Ming, Z., Yan, Q.: Industrial internet: a survey on the enabling technologies, applications, and challenges. IEEE Commun. Surv. Tutor. **19**(3), 1504–1526 (2017)
6. Chan, R., Chow, K.-P., Chan, C.-F.: Defining attack patterns for industrial control systems. In: Staggs, J., Shenoi, S. (eds.) ICCIP 2019. IAICT, vol. 570, pp. 289–309. Springer, Cham (2019). https://doi.org/10.1007/978-3-030-34647-8_15

7. Han, S., Xie, M., Chen, H.H., Ling, Y.: Intrusion detection in cyber-physical systems: techniques and challenges. IEEE Syst. J. **8**(4), 1049–1059 (2014)
8. Yang, J., Zhou, C., Yang, S., Xu, H., Hu, B.: Anomaly detection based on zone partition for security protection of industrial cyber-physical systems. IEEE Trans. Industr. Electron. **65**(5), 4257–4267 (2018)
9. Ponomarev, S., Atkison, T.: Industrial control system network intrusion detection by telemetry analysis. IEEE Trans. Dependable Secure Comput. **13**(2), 252–260 (2016)
10. Wan, M., Shang, W., Zeng, P.: Double behavior characteristics for one-class classification anomaly detection in networked control systems. IEEE Trans. Inf. Forensics Secur. **12**(12), 3011–3023 (2017)
11. Fachkha, C.: Cyber threat investigation of SCADA modbus activities. In: 2019 IFIP-NTMS, Canary Islands, Spain, pp. 1–7. IEEE (2019)
12. Deng, Z., Chung, F.L., Wang, S.: Robust relief-feature weighting, margin maximization, and fuzzy optimization. IEEE Trans. Fuzzy Syst. **18**(4), 726–744 (2010)
13. Jiang, N., Tian, F., Li, J., Yuan, X., Zheng, J.Q.: MAN: mutual attention neural networks model for aspect-level sentiment classification in SIoT. IEEE Internet Things J. **7**(4), 2901–2913 (2020)
14. Mishra, P., Varadharajan, V., Tupakula, U., Pilli, E.S.: A detailed investigation and analysis of using machine learning techniques for intrusion detection. IEEE Commun. Surv. Tutor. **21**(1), 686–728 (2019)
15. Boutaba, R., et al.: A comprehensive survey on machine learning for networking: evolution, applications and research opportunities. J. Internet Serv. Appl. **9**(1), 1–99 (2018). https://doi.org/10.1186/s13174-018-0087-2
16. Esmalifalak, M., Liu, L., Nguyen, N., Zheng, R., Han, Z.: Detecting stealthy false data injection using machine learning in smart grid. IEEE Syst. J. **11**(3), 1644–1652 (2017)
17. El-Abd, M.: Performance assessment of foraging algorithms vs. evolutionary algorithms. Inf. Sci. **182**(1), 243–263 (2012)
18. Jiang, N., Xu, D., Zhou, J., Yan, H.Y., Wan, T., Zheng, J.Q.: Toward optimal participant decisions with voting-based incentive model for crowd sensing. Inf. Sci. **512**, 1–17 (2020)
19. Wang, Y.J., Cai, Z.P., Zhan, Z.H., Gong, Y.J., Tong, X.R.: An optimization and auction-based incentive mechanism to maximize social welfare for mobile crowdsourcing. IEEE Trans. Comput. Soc. Syst. **6**(3), 414–429 (2019)
20. Wang, Y.J., Gao, Y., Li, Y.S., Tong, X.R.: A worker-selection incentive mechanism for optimizing platform-centric mobile crowdsourcing systems. Comput. Netw. **171**, 107–144 (2020)
21. Gao, W., Huang, L., Luo, Y., Wei, Z., Liu, S.: Constrained optimization by artificial bee colony framework. IEEE Access **6**, 73829–73845 (2018)
22. Bi, J., Zhang, K., Cheng, X.J.: Intrusion detection based on RBF neural network. In: 2009 International Symposium on Information Engineering and Electronic Commerce, Ternopil, Ukraine, pp. 357–360. IEEE (2009)
23. Zhao, Z.: Study and application of BP neural network in intrusion detection. In: Zhong, S. (ed.) Proceedings of the 2012 International Conference on Cybernetics and Informatics. LNEE, vol. 163, pp. 379–385. Springer, New York (2014). https://doi.org/10.1007/978-1-4614-3872-4_49
24. Jeldi, S.B.: A review of intrusion detection system using various decision tree algorithm optimize challenges issues. In: 2018 CTEMS, Belgaum, India, pp. 272–275. IEEE (2018)

AndrOpGAN: An Opcode GAN for Android Malware Obfuscations

Xuetao Zhang, Jinshuang Wang$^{(\boxtimes)}$, Meng Sun, and Yao Feng

Institute of Command Control Engineering, Army Engineering University
of PLA, Nanjing 210007, Jiangsu, China
siyezhishuang@163.com

Abstract. With the rapid development of Android platform, the number of Android malwares is growing rapidly. Due to the limitations of traditional static and runtime Android malware analysis methods, machine learning based approaches are widely adopted recently. Whereas, evading methods are also emerging, e.g. data set pollution, feature modification. Current feature modifications are mainly based on high-level features such as API calls or sensitive permissions. Our contribution is to show it is also feasible to deceive the detectors by modifying underlying features. Through this confusion, detector deceiving can be achieved. An Android malware opcode distribution feature modification system AndrOpGAN was proposed. To adjust the opcode distribution of malware, Deep Convolution Generative Adversarial Networks (DCGAN) was proposed to generate opcodes distribution features, and opcodes would be inserted through an Opcode Frequency Optimal Adjustment algorithm (OFOA). OFOA module can keep the APK running normally after insertion with a low modification cost. Test results against four detectors show that more than 99% APKs processed by AndrOpGAN could bypass detections successfully. Test results against VirusTotal shows that, the number of successful detection engines decreased 20%–44%. AndrOpGAN validates the feasibility of such attacks based on underlying feature modifications and provides a prototype system for researchers to improve detector's performance.

Keywords: Characteristics adjustment · DCGAN · Insertion · Obfuscation · Opcode

1 Introduction

The number of Android malwares is growing rapidly. 360 reports showed that there were more than 18 million new malwares on Android platforms in 2019 [1]. Traditional detection methods are difficult to meet the requirements in accuracy and efficiency. Therefore, machine learning methods are introduced. Features commonly used in malware detections include API calls, sensitive permissions, opcodes, and control flow graphs etc. [2, 3]. However, obfuscations are also developing rapidly. Comparing with extracting limited characteristics of features from benign samples and applying them to make malwares, adversarial learning can provide better feature obfuscations. Generative Adversarial Networks (GAN) was proposed by Goodfellow in 2014 [4], which can learn the distribution of target data sets. Therefore, it is also possible to generate adversarial

© Springer Nature Switzerland AG 2020
X. Chen et al. (Eds.): ML4CS 2020, LNCS 12486, pp. 12–25, 2020.
https://doi.org/10.1007/978-3-030-62223-7_2

features of APK with GAN, e.g. API and permission obfuscation based on GAN [5, 6]. However, high level feature modifications can be detected easily by underlying feature based detectors. To the best of our knowledge, there is still no underlying feature modification available in the academic and industrial area [7–10]. To show the feasibility of underlying feature obfuscations, we proposed an Android Opcode Modification GAN (AndrOpGAN) which implemented evasion attack by modifying the statistical distributions of opcode features. The main contributions are as follows:

1) The DCGAN was improved towards generating meaningful opcode distributions, which was originally used on image generation. And a new loss function was designed to exclude infeasible opcode distributions during optimization.
2) An Opcode Frequency Optimal Adjustment algorithm (OFOA) module was proposed to guarantee the feature modifications being both syntactically and semantically correct. In this way, the modified APKs can not only evade malware detection but also be installed and operated correctly.
3) Test results show that AndrOpGAN can achieve a high evasion success rate on opcode distribution-based detectors and can also impact online detection engines significantly.

The source code of AndrOpGAN is available on github[1].

2 Related Work

Android malware detection can be divided into static detection and dynamic detection. Yildiz et al. [11] used genetic algorithms to filter sensitive permissions for Android malware detection. Fan et al. analyzed the FCG based on graph embedding [12], which can extract behavior patterns of malicious code with a detection accuracy over 90%. Acarman et al. used LSTM to perform malware mining on opcode sequences and instruction call graphs [13], reached detection accuracy of 91%. Singh et al. detected Android malware behavior patterns based on API calls and sensitive permissions [14].

Attackers usually protect apps' code and evade detection from three aspects, namely, hiding Dex files, impeding the dumping of Dex files in memory, hindering the reverse-engineering of Dex files. However, these protection methods mainly improve the difficulty of manually analyzations. It can hardly mislead machine learning detectors. Therefore, attacks toward machine learning models have emerged. Training set pollution [15] method disturbed the classifier by constructing adversarial training samples. Gradient attack in Kathrin Grosse et al. [16] constructed such samples to deceive classifiers. However, this attack requires the white-box understanding of the target machine learning system, which is not available in many situations. Based on benign APK characteristics, researchers have implemented several attack methods against detection models, e.g. Weiwei Hu et al. used generative models to produce adversarial permissions [17] and API calls features [18]. Hyrum et al. [19] used reinforcement learning to change PE features.

---

[1] https://github.com/tianwaifeidie/AndrOpGAN.

Existing evasion methods are difficult to modify the underlying opcode distribution features, i.e. the malicious signature based on opcode are hard to change. Therefore, detectors based on opcode features have obtained good performance [20–22]. However, this paper shows that the opcode level obfuscation attack is feasible. The feature vector generated by AndrOpGAN can be labeled as malware features for future detector retraining [17].

3   AndrOpGAN

3.1   AndrOpGAN Overview

AndrOpGAN was assumed as a grey-box model which means that the model could only obtain the feature type used in detection model through testing. The framework was shown in Fig. 1, which include two main parts. DCGAN was used to learn and generate fake benign APKs' opcode distribution features. OFOA module was used to change the opcode distribution features, insert opcodes into the original APK and then repackage it.

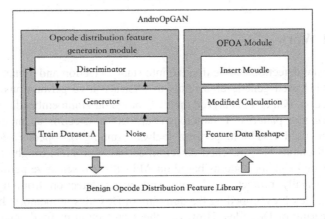

Fig. 1. AndrOpGAN Overview. It includes a generation module, an OFOA module, and a generation feature database for storing generated features.

3.2   Opcode Frequency Feature

There are more than 200 kinds of opcodes in the Dalvik instruction set. However, many instructions are similar to each other. In order to reduce feature space dimensions and achieve more efficient detections, similar opcodes were divide into the same class. [22] Ignoring data types and register differences, all opcodes were eventually divided into 44 classes in our work. Part of opcode classes were listed in Table 1.

Table 1. Examples of opcode classes.

Serial number	Opcode	Class
1	if-eq, if-ne, if-lt, if-ge, if-gt, if-le, if-eqz, if-nez, if-ltz, if-gez, if-gtz, if-lez	if
2	move, move/from16, move/16, move-wide, move-wide/from16, move-wide/16, move-object, move-object/from16, move-object/16, move-result, move-result-wide, move-result-object, move-exception	move
......	......	......
44	rsub-int, rsub-int/lit8	rsub

The opcode set can be expressed as $A = \{a_1, a_2, a_3, \ldots, a_{44}\}$, where the element $a \in A$ of each dimension contains normalized values of each opcode type which showed as (2). Each Android software sample x was expressed with vector $\varphi(x)$.

$$\varphi(x) = \frac{count(x, a)_{a \in A}}{\sum_{a \in A} count(x, a)} \qquad (1)$$

Each APK can be mapped to a vector with 44 dimensions according to (1).

$$\varphi(x) \mapsto \begin{cases} a_1 : move, move_{from16}, move_{16} \cdots \\ a_2 : return\_void, return \qquad \cdots \\ a_3 : const\_16, const\_14, const \cdots \\ \qquad \ldots \ldots \\ a_{43} : if\_eq, if\_ne, if\_lt, if\_ge \cdots \\ a_{44} : add\_int, add\_long, add \quad \cdots \end{cases} \qquad (2)$$

3.3   Opcode Distribution Feature Generation Module

The opcode distribution feature generation module was constructed based on a modified DCGAN, which uses random noise as input and generate fake benign opcode distribution feature as output.

Training Process. This section shows the training and generation process of AndrOpGAN. The training process is illustrated in Fig. 2.

Features extracted from real APKs were used as benign features. The data produced by the generator is characterized as false sample features. These two kinds of data are first used to train the discriminator. After finishing the discriminator training, the generator would be trained with the discriminator together. Besides, to ensure the generated data fit the rules of opcode distribution feature, a loss function was proposed.

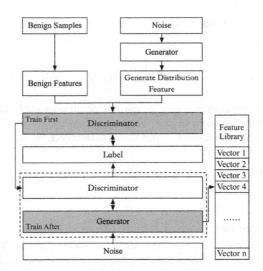

Fig. 2. Generator model training process. The discriminator is trained first, then the generator is connected to the discriminator for training.

Loss Function. To keep the generated feature be nonnegative, we added an additional penalty item based on the original GAN's loss function.

$G(z)$ represents the generator. $D(x)$ represents the discriminator. z is the random input vector of generator. x is the opcode distribution feature of real benign APKs. The overall loss function can be expressed as:

$$min_G\ max_D\ V(D,G) = E_{x \sim p_{data}}[log(D(x))] + E_{z \sim p_{random}}[1 - log(D(G(z)) - \alpha f(G(z))]$$

(3)

As is shown in (3), penalty $f(G(z))$ was added to control the data format produced by generator. It can be represented as:

$$f(G(z)) = sum(\|sig(G(z))\| - sig(G(z)))$$

(4)

$f(G(z))$ can extract symbols from each dimension. All negative values will be represented by -1. Positive values will be represented by 1. The value of α was a weight, which was set as 0.01 according to test results.

DCGAN Based Model Structure. The model structure is shown in Fig. 3:

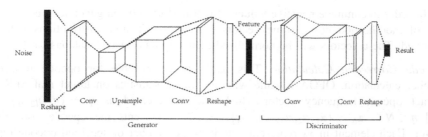

Fig. 3. Model Structure. The feature generation module contains a generator and a discriminator. Features generated in the middle are what we need.

As shown in Fig. 3, the generator uses 200 dimension random noises as inputs and includes convolution layers, up-sample layers, full-connect layers and reshape processes. The output of generator is a feature vector with a length of 44. Each dimension represented the frequency of one kind of opcode.

OFOA Module. OFOA module was designed to calculate opcode insertion number and repack it into APK. The whole process was shown in Fig. 4.

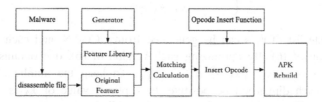

Fig. 4. OFOA Overview. This module contains feature data processing, correction value calculation, and opcode insertion of three functional modules.

Data Processing. It was necessary to perform back-end data processing on the generated data to keep the opcode distribution feature meet the requirement strictly.

Function Trans_data after Generation
1: Function **Trans**:
2:   **Read** data
3:   **For** i **From** data[start] **To** data[end]
4:   data[i]←**abs**(data[i])
5:   **If** data[i] > Threshhold **Then**
6:     drop data[i]
7:     data←data/**sum**(data)
8:     **save**(data)
9: End

In order to eliminate negative values, it will perform *abs* on generated vectors. To control modification costs, some vectors that with infeasible distributions will be removed. These vectors will be normalized then formed a feature database at last.

Opcode Correction Calculation. This part was responsible for opcode insertion number calculation. OFOA module will first make statistics on target mal-APK to extract opcode frequency vector which was represented as $\boldsymbol{\eta}_x = \{\eta_1, \eta_2, \eta_3, \ldots, \eta_{44}\}, \eta \in N^+$. $\boldsymbol{\alpha}_\Delta = \{\alpha_1, \alpha_2, \alpha_3, \ldots, \alpha_{44}\}, \alpha \in N^+$ represents the opcode correction vector. Each element in $\boldsymbol{\alpha}_\Delta$ represents the increase number of specified opcode type. $\emptyset_y = \{\emptyset_1, \emptyset_2, \emptyset_3, \ldots, \emptyset_{44}\}, \emptyset \in [0, 1)$ represents a certain vector in the feature database. These variables should satisfy (5).

$$\frac{\boldsymbol{\eta}_x + \boldsymbol{\alpha}_\Delta}{\sum_{n=1}^{44}(\boldsymbol{\eta}_x + \boldsymbol{\alpha}_\Delta)} = \emptyset_y \tag{5}$$

Our goal is to get the APK modification value $\boldsymbol{\alpha}_\Delta$. By reversing the formula, the process of obtaining $\boldsymbol{\alpha}_\Delta$ can be formulated in (6),

$$\begin{cases} min_{\boldsymbol{\alpha}_\Delta} \ \emptyset_y \sum_{n=1}^{44}(\boldsymbol{\eta}_x + \boldsymbol{\alpha}_\Delta) - \boldsymbol{\eta}_x \\ s.t. \ \boldsymbol{\alpha}_\Delta \geq 0 \end{cases} \tag{6}$$

A candidate list of $\emptyset_y$'s can be generated from DCGAN, and each $\emptyset_y$ defines a specific version of (6). By optimizing each version of (6), one obtains a group of optimized $\boldsymbol{\alpha}_\Delta$'s, say $A = \{\alpha_\Delta^1, \alpha_\Delta^2, \alpha_\Delta^3, \ldots, \alpha_\Delta^n\}$. To keep the numbers of insertion opcodes and each dimension be positive, the optimal value of $\boldsymbol{\alpha}_\Delta$ is subsequently chosen from A. The pseudo code is presented as follows.

Function OFOA Feature Selection
1: Function **OFOA**:
2:   Lib←**Read** Generate Feature Database
3:   Feat←**Get** APK Opcode Distribution
4:   **For** i **From** Lib[start] **To** Lib[end]
5:   Result[i]←**Get** α_Δ(Feat , Lib[i])
6:   **If** Result[i] < 0 **Then**
7:     **Drop** Result[i]
8:   **If** Result[i] < Result[i-1] **Then**
9:     Result[i-1]←Result[i]
10:   Final $\boldsymbol{\alpha}_\Delta$ ←Result[i-1]
11: End

Opcode Insertion. In order to ensure that the inserted opcodes didn't crash the original program, OFOA constructed a function dictionary which would never be called. It will be used as basic units to carry opcodes into smali files. There are 44 functions in this dictionary, one of functions in the insertion dictionary were listed below.

```
.method private nonesense()V
    .locals 3
    .prologue
    .line 31
    check-cast v0, Lcn/woblog/markdowndiary/domain/Note;
.end method
```

To improve the anti-detection capability of AndrOpGAN, the insertion positions were randomly selected in all smali files.

4 Target Detection Models

In order to verify the effectiveness of AndrOpGAN, four state-of-the-art Android malware detection systems based on opcode distribution features were selected. The detection process is shown in Fig. 5:

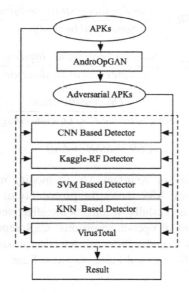

Fig. 5. Detection process. There are four target detectors to be attacked, based on CNN, random forest, SVM, and KNN.

The CNN based detector performs feature extraction through one-dimensional convolution layers. Kaggle-RF detector is a random-forest malware detection framework [23]. The SVM-based detector is constructed based on a linear kernel function. The KNN based detector was implemented with K-Neighbors Classifier in Sklearn. VirusTotal includes multiple malware detection engines, therefore it was also adopted to verify the impact of AndrOpGAN.

5 Experiments

5.1 Dataset

Training datasets of AndrOpGAN are independent from target detection models. Training set contains 10,021 benign and 10,035 malicious samples. The dataset for AndrOpGAN contains 5,003 benign samples and 5,017 malicious samples. All malicious APK samples were downloaded from VirusShare [24]. Benign samples were crawled from XiaoMi app store. We use VirusTotal to scan all the benign APKs to ensure that no malicious samples were contained in the benign dataset. The experiment was conducted on Intel E5 CPU, GTX1080Ti GPU, with 120 GB SSD, 16 GB memory.

5.2 Evaluation Method

All malwares in the AndrOpGAN dataset are used for test. These samples will be processed by AndrOpGAN then re-sent into target attack models. Four parameters were proposed for model evaluation.

$$MSR = \frac{Samples\ successfully\ modified}{Samples\ to\ be\ modified} \tag{7}$$

$$ASR = \frac{Samples\ successfully\ bypassed}{Samples\ sent\ to\ the\ detector} \tag{8}$$

$$AMC = \frac{Opcode\ insertions}{Sample\ amount \times Opcode\ categories} \tag{9}$$

$$CSR = MSR \times ASR \tag{10}$$

MSR reflects the ability of AndrOpGAN to modify malwares under different benign feature database sizes. ASR shows the probability of a modified malware can deceive detection models successfully. It reflects the effectiveness of an attack system. AMC evaluates the amount of opcode insertions. CSR represents the final evasion success rate of AndrOpGAN under different detection models. The test results also include Precision, Recall, F-score and False Negative Rate.

5.3 Evaluation

In order to verify the effectiveness of evasion, four detection models with ten-fold cross-validation were performed. Test results are listed in Table 2.

Table 2. Detection results

Model	Precision	Recall	FNR	F-Score
CNN	0.9694	0.9694	0.0306	0.9694
Kaggle-RF	0.9989	0.9922	0.0078	0.9956
KNN	0.9779	0.9889	0.0111	0.9834
SVM	0.8639	0.9900	0.0100	0.9227

It was shown that all these detection models can detect malwares effectively. It means that the attack system is valid if most of the modified malwares are falsely reported as benign APKs.

All 5,017 malwares in the test dataset were sent to AndrOpGAN for modification. The MSR was recorded in Table 3.

Table 3. Modification success rates.

Database size	Success modified number	MSR
1000	1877	37.41%
3000	3047	60.73%
5000	4667	93.02%
7000	4805	95.77%
9000	5010	99.86%
10000	5017	100.00%
11000	5017	100.00%
13000	5017	100.00%

Modified APK samples were also sent to the above detectors. The CSR was shown in Table 4.

Table 4. Evasion success rates.

Database size	MSR	KNN	SVM	Kaggle-RF	CNN	ACS
1000	37.41%	99.95%	100.00%	99.84%	100.00%	37.39%
3000	60.73%	100.00%	100.00%	99.45%	99.80%	60.62%
5000	93.02%	99.96%	100.00%	100.00%	100.00%	93.01%
7000	95.77%	99.77%	100.00%	99.98%	100.00%	95.71%
9000	99.86%	99.84%	100.00%	98.80%	99.90%	99.50%
10000	100.00%	99.27%	100.00%	98.16%	100.00%	99.36%
11000	100.00%	99.82%	100.00%	99.20%	100.00%	99.76%
13000	100.00%	99.92%	100.00%	98.50%	100.00%	99.61%

Figure 6 shows the MSR of modification under different dataset sizes. Figure 7 illustrated the success rate and CSR with different detection models. It shows that the dataset size is helpful for the evasion success rate.

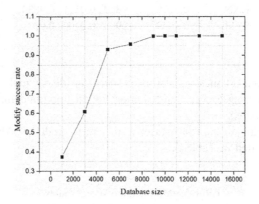

Fig. 6. Modification success rate. As the size of the sample database continues to expand, the success rate of revisions is gradually increasing.

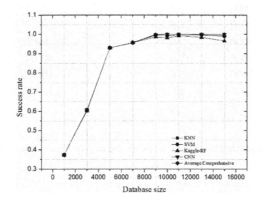

Fig. 7. Evasion success rate comparison. As the size of the sample database continues to expand, the evasion success rate for different models are rising.

When the sample size is larger than 10,000, the success rate for both detection models can reach 0.99 or higher. Besides, the test results show that the comprehensive success rate can rise to 0.98, which indicates that the system can successfully modify most of APKs, i.e. bypass the detection successfully.

The modification cost is defined as the average inserted number of each type opcodes. The average insertion amount of each type of operation code is about 28,000. The value will decrease with the increase of the feature database size (Fig. 8).

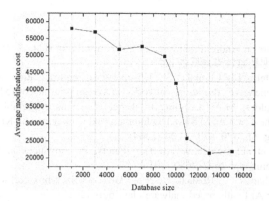

Fig. 8. The average modification cost. The possibilities for APK corrections is proportional to the size of the sample dataset.

We chose all the 5,017 malicious APKs to verify the effectiveness of AndrOpGAN, results were listed in Table 5.

Table 5. VirusTotal test results.

APK number	Alarm engines/Total engines (before AndrOpGAN)	Alarm engines/Total engines (after AndrOpGAN)
1	36/62	20/60
2	35/63	19/62
3	36/62	29/60
4	32/58	29/50
5	37/61	28/62
6	38/61	28/60
7	37/63	19/62

The results show that after processing by AndrOpGAN, the number of successful malware alarms decreases 20%–44%. This means that AndrOpGAN can deceive some detection engines in VirusTotal especially those based on opcodes.

6 Conclusion

AndrOpGAN deceives malware detectors based on the opcode frequency feature generations and feature insertions. Evaluation on four commonly used classification models and VirusTotal show that most of the modified samples could successfully bypass those detectors. It means that this attack method might pose a serious threat to the existing Android malware detection systems. AndrOpGAN provides a prototype system for further researches, i.e. the adversarial APKs generated by AndrOpGAN can be used for the re-training of existing detectors, so that the discriminator can detect this kind of malwares effectively.

References

1. The special report on Android malwares of 2019. http://pub-shbt.s3.360.cn/cert-public-file/ 2019年Android恶意软件专题报告.pdf
2. Radford, A., Metz, L., Chintala, S.: Unsupervised representation learning with deep convolutional generative adversarial networks. arXiv preprint arXiv:1511.06434 (2015)
3. Kolter, J.Z., Maloof, M.A.: Learning to detect malicious executables in the wild. In: Proceedings of the Tenth ACM SIGKDD International Conference on Knowledge Discovery and Data Mining, pp. 470–478. ACM (2004)
4. Goodfellow, I., et al.: Generative adversarial nets. In: Advances in Neural Information Processing Systems, pp. 2672–2680 (2014)
5. Rosenberg, I., Shabtai, A., Rokach, L., et al.: Generic black-box end-to-end attack against RNNs and other API calls based malware classifiers (2017)
6. Chen, S., Xue, M., Fan, L., et al.: Automated poisoning attacks and defenses in malware detection systems: an adversarial machine learning approach. Comput. Secur. (2017). S01674048173302444
7. Chen, L., Hou, S., Ye, Y.: Securedroid: enhancing security of machine learning-based detection against adversarial android malware attacks. In: Proceedings of the 33rd Annual Computer Security Applications Conference, ACSAC 2017, pp. 362–372 (2017)
8. Grosse, K., Papernot, N., Manoharan, P., Backes, M., McDaniel, P.: Adversarial examples for malware detection. In: Foley, S.N., Gollmann, D., Snekkenes, E. (eds.) ESORICS 2017. LNCS, vol. 10493, pp. 62–79. Springer, Cham (2017). https://doi.org/10.1007/978-3-319-66399-9_4
9. Chen, S., et al.: Automated poisoning attacks and defenses in malware detection systems: an adversarial machine learning approach. Comput. Secur. **73**, 326–344 (2018)
10. Yang, W., Kong, D., Xie, T., Gunter, C.A.: Malware detection in adversarial settings: exploiting feature evolutions and confusions in android apps. In: Proceedings of the 33rd Annual Computer Security Applications Conference, pp. 288–302. ACM (2017)
11. Yildiz, O., Doğru, I.A.: Permission-based android malware detection system using feature selection with genetic algorithm. Int. J. Softw. Eng. Knowl. Eng. **29**(02), 245–262 (2019)
12. Fan, M., Luo, X., Liu, J., et al.: Graph embedding based familial analysis of android malware using unsupervised learning. In: Proceedings of the 41st International Conference on Software Engineering, pp. 771–782. IEEE Press (2019)
13. Pektaş, A., Acarman, T.: Learning to detect android malware via opcode sequences. Neurocomputing **396**, 599–608 (2019)
14. Singh, A.K., Jaidhar, C.D., Kumara, M.A.A.: Experimental analysis of android malware detection based on combinations of permissions and API-calls. J. Comput. Virol. Hacking Tech. **15**, 1–10 (2019)
15. Kovacheva, A.: Efficient code obfuscation for android. In: Papasratorn, B., Charoenkitkarn, N., Vanijja, V., Chongsuphajaisiddhi, V. (eds.) IAIT 2013. CCIS, vol. 409, pp. 104–119. Springer, Cham (2013). https://doi.org/10.1007/978-3-319-03783-7_10
16. Chen, S., Xue, M., Fan, L., et al.: Automated poisoning attacks and defenses in malware detection systems: an adversarial machine learning approach. Comput. Secur. (2017). S01674048173302444
17. Grosse, K., Papernot, N., Manoharan, P., et al.: Adversarial perturbations against deep neural networks for malware classification (2016)
18. Hu, W., Tan, Y.: Generating adversarial malware examples for black-box attacks based on GAN (2017)
19. Hu, W., Tan, Y.: Black-box attacks against RNN based malware detection algorithms (2017)

20. Anderson, H.S., Kharkar, A., Filar, B., et al.: Learning to evade static PE machine learning malware models via reinforcement learning (2018)
21. Guen Kim, T., Joong Kang, B., Rho, M., Sezer, S., Im, E.G.: A multimodal deep learning method for android malware detection using various features. IEEE Trans. Inf. Forensics Secur. **14**(3), 773–788 (2018). https://doi.org/10.1109/TIFS.2018.2866319
22. Kang, B.J., Yerima, S.Y., Mclaughlin, K., et al.: N-opcode analysis for android malware classification and categorization (2016)
23. Chen, T., Mao, Q., Yang, Y., et al.: TinyDroid: a lightweight and efficient model for android malware detection and classification. Mob. Inf. Syst. **2018**, 1–9 (2018)
24. Microsoft Malware. https://www.kaggle.com/c/malware-classification
25. https://virusshare.com/. Accessed 2018

An Anomalous Traffic Detection Approach for the Private Network Based on Self-learning Model

Weijie Han[1,2(✉)], Jingfeng Xue[1], Fuquan Zhang[3],
and Yingfeng Zhang[4]

[1] School of Computer Science and Technology, Beijing Institute of Technology,
Beijing, China
bit_hwj2016@126.com
[2] School of Space Information, Space Engineering University, Beijing, China
[3] Fujian Provincial Key Laboratory of Information Processing and Intelligent
Control, Minjiang University, Fuzhou, China
[4] Equipment Development Department, Beijing 100071, China

Abstract. Although being isolated from the external network, the private network is still faced with some security threats, such as violations communications, malware attacks, and illegal operations. It is an attractive approach to recognize these security threats by discovering the underlying anomalous traffic. By studying the anomalous traffic detection technologies, an anomalous traffic detection approach is developed by capturing and analyzing the network packets, detecting the anomaly traffic that occurs in the network, and then detects anomalous behaviors of the network timely. In order to enhance its effectiveness and efficiency, a self-learning model is proposed and deployed in the detection approach. Finally, we conduct necessary evaluations about the proposed approach. The test results show that the approach can reach a good effect for detecting the unknown anomalous traffic.

Keywords: Private network · Anomalous traffic detection · Network anomalous behavior · Self-learning model

1 Introduction

The private network is physical isolated from the Internet and often used to construct the internal office environment. Because of being built by the IP technology, the private network is also faced with some typical security issues, such as some hosts communicating with each other against regulation, the external Trojan virus invading via mobile storage medium indirectly [1]. These anomalous behaviors of networks often cause anomalous reaction of network traffic. Therefore, how to detect the anomalous traffic appearing in the network, effectively detect the network anomalous behavior, and accurately locate the source of network attacks, is very important to ensure the security and reliability of the private network.

Up to now, the researchers have carried out various kinds of anomalies detection methods to discover the attacks underlying in the huge network traffic. However, most

X. Chen et al. (Eds.): ML4CS 2020, LNCS 12486, pp. 26–34, 2020.
https://doi.org/10.1007/978-3-030-62223-7_3

of the public methods are aiming at the usual network environment, their performance may fail when being applied in the domain of the private network [2].

In order to satisfy the detection requirements of the private network, an anomalous traffic detection approach is designed and implemented by the paper aiming for capturing and analyzing the network packet, and detecting the anomalous behaviors and delivering alarm to the manager. In summary, we make the following contributions in this paper:

(1) We employ the sniffer technology to capture the network traffic and conduct traffic statistical analysis in order to avoid disturbing the normal network communication.
(2) We design a self-learning model for training. The self-learning model can improve the effectiveness and efficiency by updating database and building traffic compliance templates.

2 Related Work

For different network environments and problem requirements, the researchers proposed a number of methods to detect anomalies in the network. According to its processing object, the literatures can be mainly divided into the following three categories: statistical technology based detection, signal processing based detection, and machine learning based detection [2].

Vijayasarathy et al. [3] optimized the Naive Bayesian classification by assigning different initial weights by weighting the naive Bayesian algorithm according to the differences between attributes.

Swarnkar et al. [4] proposed a method, which detect the anomalous traffic based on the polynomial naive Bayesian classifier by conducting in-depth analysis about each network packet and obtaining the current data packet in the flag field information to calculate the possibility of a packet being anomalous behavior.

Wei Li et al. [5] enhanced the weak classifier based on naive Bayesian by introducing the Adaboost iterative algorithm to enhance the training speed and detection accuracy of the network intrusion detection system and reduce the false alarm rate.

Ahirwar et al. [6] combined the Naïve Bayesian network with the RBF neural network to improve the detection accuracy based on the RBF neural network to determine the network traffic class.

Tao Peng et al. [7] improved the local least squares support vector machine algorithm by selecting and predicting the closer set of training samples to the data set, reducing the computational complexity of the high-dimensional transpose matrix in the training phase.

Catania et al. [8] prepared the training sample set to overcome the requirements of the support vector machine classifier training, and greatly improve the accuracy of the classifier through a filtering function based on SNORT.

Ji et al. [9] designed a two-layer detection mechanism to classify and detect anomalous traffic. The model first uses CART to determine the occurrence of anomalies, and then analyzes the types of anomalies by SVM.

Li Shicong et al. [10] proposed a Trojan horse communication behavior detection model based on hierarchical clustering method. By studying the characteristics of Trojan communication, the similarity degree is calculated by logarithmic likelihood value, and finally different categories are clustered.

Yu Bing et al. [11] clustered the top 16 bits of the IP address in the netflow stream record to get the traffic characteristics of the different network segments and performed the anomaly detection.

Wang Xuesong et al. [12] proposed a network flow forecasting model for inverse learning particle swarm optimization neural network, and optimized the relevant parameters of RBF neural network by using the inverse learning mechanism in particle swarm optimization to improve the prediction accuracy.

Ravale et al. [13] first extracted the eigenvectors of different attacks and trained RBF-SVM by K-MEANS clustering algorithm, and then used the eigenvectors generated by the unknown network traffic type in RBF-SVM to perform classification detection.

The state-of-the-art methods mainly aim at the conventional network environment, and can obtain satisfactory detection effects. However, most of them are not suitable for the private network environment. So, we design a novel detection approach in this paper for the private network based on these literature.

3   Framework of the Approach

The approach adopts a hierarchical architecture which is divided into data collection layer, data management layer, data statistical analysis layer and data presentation layer from the bottom to the top as illustrated in Fig. 1.

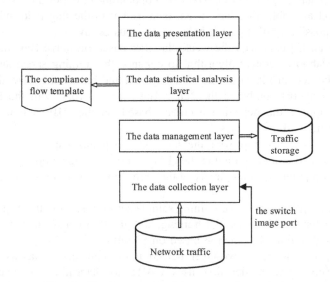

Fig. 1. The framework of the proposed approach.

(1) The data collection layer collects the network traffic of the switch image port. The acquisition mode can be set to sample model or the whole collection model. This layer provides original network traffic for the upper layer.
(2) The data management layer is responsible for storing the captured packet, and the traffic must be selectively stored so as to save the disk space.
(3) The data statistical analysis layer analyses the IP data flow statistically and gains the bandwidth threshold and the flow distribution of characteristic parameters, etc. It stored the traffic statistical analysis results as a compliance flow template in the training session which is used to achieve the real-time detection of IP measurement and detect the anomalous traffic in anomalous traffic detection stage.
(4) The data presentation layer is the interaction interface between the user and the approach. The layer shows the flow analysis results and anomalous flow test results for the user.

4 Key Technologies

4.1 Capturing Network Packet

In order to avoid disturbing the normal network communication, the approach uses the sniffer technology to capture the network traffic. The packet capturing program is realized by the open source SharpPcap library to collect the IP data flow of the switch imaging port. SharpPcap is encapsulated by two libraries for capturing network packet that are LibPcap and WinPcap, which can be used to develop the network monitoring program under the Windows.NET environment efficiently.

4.2 Analysing Statistical Traffic

Traffic statistical analysis is used to realize the interpretation of the network protocol, the statistics of traffic profile information and the acquisition of the traffic characteristic parameters distribution. The acquired parameters mainly include: (1) Traffic summary statistics information including the total flow, the total uplink flow, the total downward flow, the starting time of capturing packets, the duration, and the link speed so on. (2) Traffic characteristic parameter distribution including the distribution of packet length, the distribution of the transport layer protocol, the distribution of the business domain, etc.

4.3 Self-study Training

The purpose of the training phase is to establish a compliance traffic model of the private network. The self-learning model includes the legal IP address database, the legal IP session database and the compliance traffic IP template as illustrated in Fig. 2. Its involved main technologies include database update and the building of compliance traffic templates.

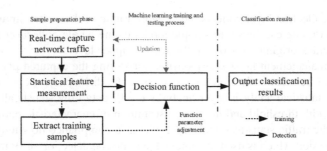

Fig. 2. Machine learning network traffic classification application process

(1) Database Update

The database update operations include the update of the legal IP address database and the legal IP session database.

(2) Compliance Flow Templates

In the period of the self-learning training, the flow statistical analysis is stored in the document form, namely to form a compliance flow template. The template is the description of the characteristics of normal network traffic and a standard of detecting anomalous traffic. The compliance flow templates are stored in XML format file.

4.4   Anomalous Traffic Detection

The methods of anomalous traffic detection include the method of threshold decision, the validity testing of IP address, the validity testing of IP session and the way of the relative entropy anomalous flow [2].

The validity inspection of IP address and IP session is the key important methods to realize anomalous traffic detection. The process of IP address validation is divided into the following steps:

(1) When starting the anomalous flow threads, the approach loads the legal IP address database, and converts it into memory hash array structure;

(2) Real-time analysis of the network traffic data. Extract the IP address in the packets. Calculate the hash value of the IP address, and look for it in the memory hash array structure;

(3) If there is no hash value in array, it is indicated that the IP is an illegal IP address. Otherwise compare it with the IP address hash in chain. If not existing, it shows that the IP of the hash chain is an illegal IP address, or is a legal IP address. In the process of relative entropy anomaly traffic detection, the approach load the compliance flow template file which generated in the training phase, use it as an empirical distribution of the flow characteristic parameters in a normal state, test the relative entropy to the parameters sample distribution of the real-time traffic characteristics and the experience distribution, and judge the anomalous flow according to the relative entropy.

5 Experimental Evaluations

5.1 Experimental Environment

According to the characteristics of the private network, a simulation testing environment is built as Fig. 3. The flow in the testing environment is classified by the business domain types which mainly include video, voice and data. The total bandwidth demand is about 2368 KBPS to 3200 KBPS.

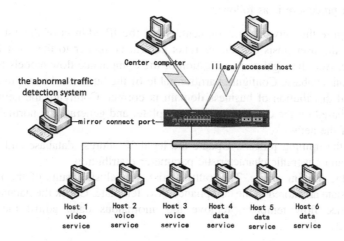

Fig. 3. Configuration of the experiment environment

The detailed deployment of the environment is as Table 1.

Table 1. Configuration of the user host access point

Host id	Access point	IP address	Comment
1	E0/1	146.111.100.246	Intranet user
2	E0/2	146.111.100.247	Intranet user
3	E0/3	146.111.100.248	Intranet user
4	E0/4	146.111.100.249	Intranet user
5	E0/5	146.111.100.250	Intranet user
6	E0/6	146.111.100.251	Intranet user
Anomalous traffic detection approach	E0/8		Mirroring port connection
Extranet center computer		21.146.222.108	A legal user of extranet
An illegal access host of extranet		21.146.222.109	An illegal user of extranet

5.2   Testing Case

Anomalous behaviors in the network include: the illegal network access, the illegal session of the legal user, the network attacks and some unknown types of anomalous flow. These are defined by the approaches as four unusual events: occupied bandwidth, illegal IP address, illegal IP session, anomalous relative entropy, where the relative entropy anomaly can set multiple threshold level based on the empirical data. The test cases use the normal traffic of the network as the background traffic for comparing with the anomalous traffic events.

The test procedure is as follows:

①Configure the network environment. Store the IP address of the 1st to the 6th hosts of the user hosts and the extranet central computer to the legal IP address database. Add the legal communication of the compliance flow models to the legal IP session database. Configure partition table of the business domain to ensure the statistical distribution of business domain is correct. Configure the network compliance based on the compliance flow template, and generate the normal condition traffic of the network.

②Start the training process. Update the legal IP address database and IP session library, and get traffic characteristic parameter distribution.

③End the training phase. The traffic statistics analysis results of the network in normal state are stored in the compliance flow template. Check the database and the compliance flow template, remove the anomalous data, adjust the threshold parameter.

5.3   Test Results Analysis

The indexes for evaluating the detection approach include the detection rate and the false alarm rate. The definition of the indexes is as follows:

$$\text{detection rate} = \frac{\text{The number of correctly detect abnormal events}}{\text{The total number of abnormal events}}$$

$$\text{false alarm rate} = \frac{\text{Total mistakenly identified abnormalities}}{\text{The total number of detection}}$$

Anomalous traffic detection method is based on the time window, detecting point by point, but the illegal traffic impact of anomalous events will continue for a period of time. So one exception event will produce more alarm. The alarm is still defined as a correct detection of anomalous events. During the approach training, network monitoring lasts for two hours. Template file of compliance flow is generated. The average bandwidth is 2.945 Mbps. Bandwidth threshold is set to 3.5 Mbps. The first test use case continuous monitoring network for two hours. The test results are shown as Table 2.

The second test use case continuous monitoring network for two hours. According to the relative entropy data output, a ROC curve is drawn as Fig. 4. The ROC curve accurately reflects the relationship of detection rate and false alarm rate in the way of

Table 2. The experiment results

Anomalous event type	Detection rate	False alarm rates
bandwidth	100% (20/20)	0
Illegal IP address	100% (20/20)	0
Illegal IP session	100% (20/20)	0

the relative entropy anomalous flow. By weighing the detection rate and the false alarm rate, the appropriate threshold is selected. When the relative entropy is set to 39.6, the detection rate is 84.36% and the false alarm rate is 3.86%. It shows that approach for detecting unknown anomalous flow has a good effect.

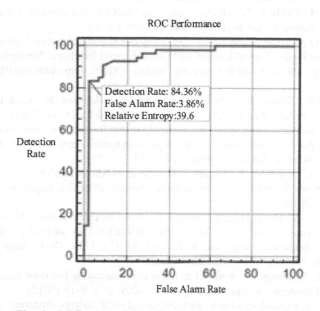

Fig. 4. ROC curve of the relative entropy anomalous flow

6 Conclusion

The private network has different characteristics from the conventional network. It is necessary for the researchers to design new methods to handle with the security problems due to its unique features. In this paper, we propose an anomalous traffic detection approach for the private network based on a self-learning model. The proposed approach can reach satisfactory detection performance compared with other methods. In the future, we will furthermore study the distributed detection method and realize distributed security detection in a larger scope and collaboratively [14, 15].

Acknowledgments. This work was supported by the National Key Research and Development Program of China under Grant 2016QY06X1205.

References

1. Hasan, M.S., ElShakankiry, A., Dean, T., Zulkernine, M.: Intrusion detection in a private network by satisfying constraints. In: 2016 14th Annual Conference on Privacy, Security and Trust. Auckland, New Zealand, 12–14 December 2016. https://doi.org/10.1109/PST.2016.7906997
2. Han, W., Xue, J., Yan, H.: Detecting anomalous traffic in the controlled network based on cross entropy and support vector machine. IET Inf. Secur. 13(2), 109–116 (2019). https://doi.org/10.1049/iet-ifs.2018.5186
3. Vijayasarathy, R., Raghavan, S.V., Ravindran, B.: A system approach to network modeling for DDoS detection using a Naive Bayesian classifier. In: Proceedings of 2011 Third International Conference on Communication Systems and Networks, Bangalore, India, 4–8 January 2011. https://doi.org/10.1109/COMSNETS.2011.5716474
4. Swarnkar, M., Hubballi, N.: OCPAD: one class Naive Bayes classifier for payload based anomaly detection. Expert Syst. Appl. 64, 330–339 (2016)
5. Li, W., Li, Q.X.: Using Naive Bayes with AdaBoost to enhance network anomaly intrusion detection. In: Proceedings of International Conference on Intelligent Networks & Intelligent Systems, pp. 486–489. IEEE Computer Society (2010). https://doi.org/10.1109/ICINIS.2010.133
6. Ahirwar, D.K., Saxena, S.K., Sisodia, M.S.: Anomaly detection by Naive Bayes & RBF network. Int. J. Adv. Res. Comput. Sci. Electron. Eng. 1(1), 14–18 (2012)
7. Peng, T., Tang, Z.: A small scale forecasting algorithm for network traffic based on relevant local least squares support vector machine regression model. Appl. Math. Inf. Sci. 9(2), 653–659 (2015). https://doi.org/10.12785/amis/092L41
8. Catania, C.A., Bromberg, F., Garino, C.G.: An autonomous labeling approach to support vector machines algorithms for network traffic anomaly detection. Expert Syst. Appl. 39(2), 1822–1829 (2010)
9. Ji, S.Y., Choi, S., Dong, H.J.: Designing a two-level monitoring method to detect network anomalous behaviors. In: Proceedings of the 2014 IEEE 15th International Conference on Information Reuse and Integration, Redwood City, CA, USA, 13–15 August 2014. IEEE (2014). https://doi.org/10.1109/IRI.2014.7051958
10. Li, S., Yun, X., Zhang, Y.: A model of trojan communication behavior detection based on hierarchical clustering technique. Comput. Res. Dev. (s2), 9–16 (2012)
11. Yu, H., Wang, J.: Analysis of network traffic based on IP address clustering. J. Ocean Univ. China Nat. Sci. Ed. (s1), 196–199 (2008)
12. Wang, X., Liang, X.: Network traffic prediction model based on BPSO-RBFNN. Comput. Appl. Softw. (9), 102–105 (2014)
13. Ravale, U., Marathe, N., Padiya, P.: Feature selection based hybrid anomaly intrusion detection system using k means and RBF kernel function. Procedia Comput. Sci. 45(39), 428–435 (2015)
14. Lykov, S., Asakura, Y.: Anomalous traffic pattern detection in large urban areas: tensor-based approach with continuum modeling of traffic flow. Int. J. Intell. Transp. Syst. Res. 18(1), 13–21 (2018). https://doi.org/10.1007/s13177-018-0167-5
15. Hou, E., Yılmaz, Y., Hero, A.O.: Anomaly detection in partially observed traffic networks. IEEE Trans. Signal Process. 67(6), 1461–1476 (2019). https://doi.org/10.1109/TSP.2019.2892026

A Malware Classification Method Based on the Capsule Network

Ziyu Wang[1], Weijie Han[1,2(✉)], Yue Lu[3], and Jingfeng Xue[1]

[1] School of Computer Science and Technology, Beijing Institute of Technology,
Beijing, China
`bit_hwj2016@126.com`
[2] School of Space Information, Space Engineering University, Beijing, China
[3] ByteDance Ltd., Beijing, China

Abstract. Malware has become a serious threat to network security. Traditional static analysis methods usually cannot effectively detect packers, obfuscations, and variants. Dynamic analysis is not efficient when dealing with large amounts of malware. Aiming at the shortcomings of the existing methods, this paper proposes a method for analyzing malware based on the capsule network. It uses a supervised learning method to train the capsule network with a large number of malware samples with existing category labels. In the process of constructing features, this paper adopts a method of combining static features and dynamic features to extract the operation code information based on static analysis, and extract the API call sequence information based on general analysis. Both characteristics can well represent the structure and behavior of malware. Then use N-Gram to construct sequence features, visualize the N-Gram sequence, generate malware images, and finally use the capsule network for classification detection. In addition, this paper improves the original capsule network and verifies the effect of the improved model.

Keywords: Malware · Capsule network · N-Gram · API

1 Introduction

The current analysis methods of malware are mainly divided into signature-based methods, traditional machine learning-based methods, and deep learning-based methods [1]. The signature-based analysis of malware is the traditional detection method adopted by most anti-virus software. It implements the detection of malware by establishing a feature library. However, with the increasing number of malware and their variants, the number of signature codes has increased dramatically. Since the signature database needs to be continuously updated as the number of malware increases, the delay in updating will lead to a decrease in detection efficiency, which also leads to the inability to detect malware effectively when the new malware features do not exist in the code feature database. The traditional machine learning-based method has a good performance in solving massive malware, and can detect unknown malware variants. However, since machine learning needs to be artificially affected when extracting features, the accuracy rate during detection will be affected by artificial

X. Chen et al. (Eds.): ML4CS 2020, LNCS 12486, pp. 35–49, 2020.
https://doi.org/10.1007/978-3-030-62223-7_4

factors. The method based on deep learning can automatically extract the characteristics of malware through the model, and can improve the accuracy of malware classification to a certain extent.

In the analysis method of malware based on deep learning, Convolution Neural Network (CNN) is a more popular classification model [2]. CNN is a kind of deep feed-forward artificial neural network. Its main parts are Convolution Layer and Pooling Layer, which are used to extract features and select features, respectively. However, in CNN, there is only a simple weight relationship between features, and Pooling Layer reduces the size of the space by extracting the maximum or average value of a certain area to achieve the effect of size reduction. This operation has no positional relationship between high-level and low-level features in CNN. Because the internal data representation of CNN does not take into account the important spatial hierarchy between simple and complex objects, the maximum pooling or average pooling causes some valuable information to be lost.

Capsule network is a new type of neural network proposed by Geoffrey Hinton, the father of deep learning, based on CNN. This kind of network proposes the concept of "capsule", which can save the relative position, angle and other information of important features of the image. It prevents important features in the capsule network model from being lost with the pooling, just like CNN [3]. The paper proposed by Hinton also shows that the implementation effect of the capsule network on the recognition of handwritten digit data sets is indeed better than that of CNN. Therefore, this paper proposes the use of a capsule network to optimize the accuracy of malware analysis. Through sufficient analysis and positioning of malware sequences, the accuracy of malware analysis is improved.

The main contributions of this paper include:

(1) The malware executable file is converted into a dense matrix according to the feature sequence, and it is converted into an image, which is used as the input of CNN to implement the classification of the malware based on the CNN model.
(2) Using an improved capsule network model based on CNN, taking the visualization model from the previous step as input, and fully considering the spatial, angular, and directional relationships of the characteristics of the malware to further improve the accuracy of the malware classification.

2 Related Work

At present, most analysis methods focus on feature code detection [4]. Traditional malware analysis methods are divided into static analysis and dynamic analysis. In recent years, artificial intelligence technology represented by machine learning has gradually been widely used in the field of security. The combination of artificial intelligence and malware analysis provides a new idea for automated analysis of malware [5, 6], so dynamic and static detection methods based on machine learning have gradually emerged.

Static analysis usually refers to analyzing the code structure of different levels without executing the code. Static analysis first needs to use the disassembly tools such as IDA-Pro to reverse process the malware to obtain the corresponding machine instructions, and then extract its useful feature information based on this. Because static analysis does not require the actual execution of malware, it is relatively fast and does not cause malicious behavior that harms the operating system. Merkel R. and Martin J. et al. presents a static malware detection system for the detection of unknown malicious programs which is based on combination of the weighted k-nearest neighbors classifier and the statistical scoring technique from [7, 8]. Han W. et al. used the longest common sub-strings of unknown samples and known samples as features [9], and the longest common sub-strings usually take a long time to calculate. It proposes a method of reducing the number of special instructions to reduce the calculation time. Wang W., et al. used the clustering algorithm to cluster malware into different malware families by extracting the behavioral characteristics of malware, using code function control flowcharts and function calls as similarity measures [10].

Dynamic analysis requires the actual execution of code in the sandbox, dynamic monitoring and collection of various characteristic information during the recording of the program. It is an analysis technology based on the behavior characteristics of malware. Han et al. used the feature of taint dynamic propagation to find the dependency between control and data, make full use of the correlation of malware behavior, and compare the similarity of malware [11]. Ye et al. obtained dynamic behavior fingerprints of malware through API, strings, and registry changes, and compared the fingerprint database with the fingerprint matching algorithm to determine whether the sample was a variant [12]. Imran constructs a Hidden Markov Model by dynamically executing the dynamic features obtained from known samples, and comparing them with classifiers in various machine learning fields [13]. Experiments show that the random forest method works best. Tan et al. proposed extracting API call sequences based on the behavior of specific malware fragments and using SVM to implement malware classification [14]. This model implements classification based on the function of malware, but its classification performance mainly depends on the selection of the kernel function. Ding et al. proposed a method of extracting API call sequences through a dynamic tracking system to generate behavior patterns, a method of extracting API call sequence information, and combining data mining and machine learning to further improve classification accuracy [15]. Dynamic analysis can only detect a specific running path during the running process, so certain behaviors may only occur when the user does a specific operation. Therefore, there may be cases where dynamic analysis is incomplete or if malware is judged to be benign.

Deep learning has become popular in various fields in the last two years. In general, deep learning is very good at processing massive single types of data without the need for artificial features. These properties also make deep learning very suitable for the field of binary virus sample classification. Therefore, in the past two years, methods for detecting and analyzing malware based on deep learning have been gradually proposed [16]. Park et al. proposed a malware detection method based on deep learning of Operation Code behavior [17]. This method is based on static analysis. First, the N-Gram algorithm is used to construct sequence pairs for Operation Code, and then two feature selection methods, information gain and document frequency, are used to select the appropriate Operation Code sequence characteristics. It uses restricted Boltzmann machine adjustment, feedback adjustment of deep belief network, and feedback fine-tuning of error back propagation, and finally uses deep belief network for classification detection. Meng et al. proposed a method for classifying malware images and text features based on deep learning [18]. It uses binary files for visual display in the form of grayscale images, and then classifies the images. It also combines high-order CNN and fusion models to improve the accuracy. Sewak et al. used N-Gram window sliding to obtain features and used information gain to select features based on static analysis [19]. The deep belief network module uses Deep Belief Network (DBN) to train on the training set to generate a deep learning network, and then uses the trained network to classify and detect samples. Compared with the traditional malware detection method, this method has greatly improved the detection speed and efficiency.

3   Classification of Malware Based on Capsule Network

3.1   Capsule Network Model

Capsule network is one of the most advanced technologies for current image classification and recognition. It is developed on the basis of CNN to solve the two shortcomings of the poor recognition of the space between the objects by CNN and the low recognition ability after the object is rotated greatly. In the capsule network structure, each feature is a vector, which represents the result after the network model corresponding to the structure is trained. The capsule network model uses capsules to extract images, advances through clustering, and combines features. In the malware classification model based on the capsule network constructed in this paper, the malware image is used as input, and the classification results are obtained after training through Convolution Layer, Primary Capsule Layer and Graph Capsule Layer. The structure of a malware classification model based on capsule network is shown in Fig. 1.

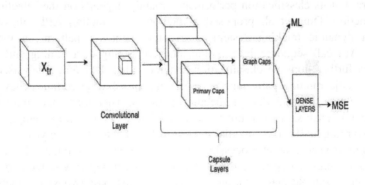

Fig. 1. Malware classification model based on capsule network

3.2   Capsule Structure

Capsules in a capsule network are composed of multiple neurons, and capsule networks are composed of multiple capsules. The capsule is the most important part of the capsule network. It is a vector composed of neurons, which can represent the instantiate parameters and existence of multidimensional entities of the detection type. The structure of the capsule is shown in Fig. 2.

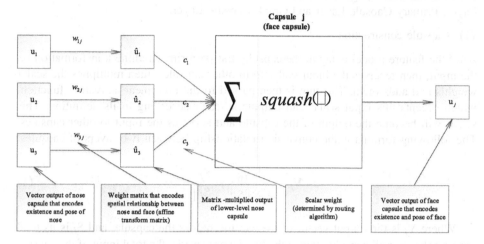

Fig. 2. Schematic diagram of capsule structure

The pose information of the target is stored in the capsule, and the target is identified by calculating the probability of a feature point on the target image at a certain position in the image. When the predicted location and state of the low-level features are the same as the target's position and state, then the target must exist. Taking the human face as an example, the method of capsule recognition target is shown in Fig. 3.

Fig. 3. Capsule recognition target

3.3 Training Process

The structure of the capsule network is relatively shallow. In the model training process, the malware image is first taken as input, and then trained through Convolution Layer, Primary Capsule Layer and Graph Capsule Layer.

(1) Capsule construction

After the feature model is input, the capsule first performs an affine transformation on the input, then receives the input scalar from other capsules, then multiplies the scalar weights and adds them. The sum is then passed to the non-linear activation function, which accepts this input scalar and outputs a scalar according to its definition. This scalar will become the output of the capsule and serve as the input to other capsules. The following formula is the conversion relationship between two layers of capsules:

$$V_j = \frac{\|S_j\|^2}{1 + \|S_j\|^2} \frac{S_j}{\|S_j\|} \tag{1}$$

Where V_j is the output vector of the capsule before the capsule, and S_j is its total input vector. For all capsules except the first layer capsule, the total input of the capsule S_j is a weighted sum of all "prediction vectors" $\hat{u}_{j|i}$ from the capsules in the lower layer, and is generated by multiplying the output $\hat{u}_{j|i}$ of the capsules in the layer. Here is a weight matrix W_{ij}:

$$S_j = \sum_i c_{ij}\hat{u}_{j|i} \tag{2}$$

$$\hat{u}_{j|i} = W_{ij}u_i \tag{3}$$

Where c_{ij} is the coupling coefficient determined by the iterative dynamic routing process. The sum of the coupling coefficients between capsule i and all capsules in the layer is 1 and is determined by "routing softmax". Its initial b_{ij} is the probability that the logarithmic prior capsule i should be coupled with capsule j.

$$c_{ij} = \frac{\exp(b_{ij})}{\sum_k \exp(b_{ik})} \tag{4}$$

Log priors can be learned simultaneously and distinctly from all other weights. They depend on the position and type of the two capsules, but not on the current input image. The initial coupling coefficient is refined by measuring the consistency between the current output v_j of each capsule j in the upper layer and the prediction $U_{j|i}$ made by capsule i. Among them, i represents the position of the feature in the image, and j represents any neuron. If $\hat{u}_{1|2}$ and $\hat{u}_{2|1}$ both point to the same image, it means that they are pointing to the same object. But if we encounter objects with similar targets, errors will occur. Therefore, we need to multiply the input vector with the coupling coefficient we get to form a weighted input vector.

$$N_{j|i} = c_{ij} \cdot U_{j|i} \tag{5}$$

$U_{j|i}$ is the prediction vector of the bottom capsule to the upper capsule. Multiplying the prediction vectors of all the capsules in the lower layer and the capsules in the upper layer to get the weight of the lower layer S_j.

$$S_j = \sum_i N_{j|i} \tag{6}$$

The activation value v_j of capsule S_j is obtained by a non-linear compression function (squash function):

$$v_j = Squash(S_j) = \frac{\|S_j\|}{\left(1 + \|S_j\|^2\right)} \cdot \frac{S_j}{\|S_j\|} \tag{7}$$

The key of the capsule network is to measure the feature saliency with the vector modulus length, and the squash function makes the length of v_j no more than 1. If S_j is long, the length of v_j tends to 1; If S_j is short, the length of v_j tends to 0. In compression, the vector S_j is unitized, so that the length of the function output vector v_j is between 0 and 1. This length can also be interpreted as the probability value that a vector neuron has a given feature.

In order to highlight the meaning of the mold length, it also needs to be associated with it when designing the model. As shown in Fig. 4, although the class length of the feature vector u_1, u_2, u_4, u_8 included in the class represented by v_1 is relatively small, the module length of v_1 can also be dominant because there are many members. This shows that whether a class stands out is related to the number of vectors in the class and the module length of the vector in each class.

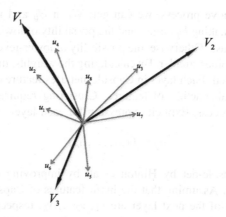

Fig. 4. Clustering combination of feature vectors

(2) Dynamic routing

The capsule network first defines the feature image as a low-level routing node and the overall target as a high-level routing node, and then adjusts the weights so that the low-level routing node connects to the corresponding high-level routing node. Each weight is a non-negative value. For each low-level routing node, the total weight is 1. The number of weights is equal to the number of high-level routing nodes, and the weights are determined by the iterative dynamic routing algorithm. The iterative dynamic routing algorithm is as follows:

Algorithm1 Dynamic routing algorithm

1: procedure routing($\hat{u}_{j|i}$,r,l)
2:   for all capsule i in layer l and capsule j in layer (l+1) : bij ← 0
3:   for r iterations do
4:   for all capsule i in layer l : ci ← **softmax(bi)**
5:   for all capsule j in layer (l+1) : Sj ← $\sum_i c_{ij}\hat{u}_{j|i}$
6:   for all capsule j in layer (l+1) : vi ← **squash(Sj)**
7:   for all capsule i in layer l and capsule j in layer (l+1) : bij ← bij + $\hat{u}_{j|i}$. vj
8: return vj

For the layer i, calculate the weight probability by Formula 8:

$$c_i = softmax(b_i) \tag{8}$$

Where c_i is the probability, b_i is the weight, and the initialization of b_i is 0. Then use the formula 8 to perform weighted summation on the upper node j to obtain S_j, and then compress S_j to obtain v_j by formula 7. Finally, update b_{ij} according to the relationship between U_{ij} and v_j obtained by Formula 9 as follows:

$$b_{ij} = U_{ij} \cdot v_j + b_{ij} \tag{9}$$

By iterating the above process, we can get: When U_{ij} and v_j are similar, the dot product will increase, making b_{ij} larger, and the possibility of lower nodes connecting to higher nodes will increase. Otherwise, the possibility of lower-level nodes connecting to higher-level nodes becomes smaller. By calculating the weights, the probability of target recognition can be routed. Each layer in Capsule-net uses feature clustering to complete the combination and abstraction of features. Clustering requires repeated iterations, which is an implicit process. Explicit expression for each layer of the network is:

$$v_j = f_j(u_1, \ldots, u_n) \tag{10}$$

We improved Capsule-net by Hinton et al. by improving dynamic routing and compression functions. Assuming that the input features of Capsule-net are u_1, u_2, ... u_n, the feature vectors of the next layer are v_1, v_2 ... v_k, respectively. The clustering centers of the n layers in the previous layer can be obtained, and the measure of clustering can be obtained by normalizing the inner product. This paper believes that gradient descent is the only way to find other parameters of the model. In order to solve this problem, this paper does not take the limit of k-> positive infinity. This paper takes a constant K > 0 and change the routing algorithm to:

Algorithm2 Improved routing algorithm
1: procedure softmax(x, axis = -1)
2: ex = exp(x – max(x, axis = axis, keepdims = True))
3: return ex/sum(sum(ex, axis = axis, keepdims = True))
1: procedure routing(a, V)
2: for r iterations do
3:   v1=v1/$\|v_1\|$
4:   cij=softmax(<ui,Kvj >)
5:   vj=$\Sigma_i c_{ij} u_i$
6: return squash(vj)

The definition of the *softmax* function in the above routing algorithm is based on formulas 8, 9 and the probability value c_{ij} is the output of the *softmax* function. The main purpose of the *softmax* function is to normalize b_{ij}. The *softmax* function is defined as follows:

$$c_{ij} = \frac{e^{b_{ij}}}{\sum_k e^{b_{ij}}} \tag{11}$$

The improved model differs from Hinton's model. The most obvious difference is that squash (v_j) is replaced by $\frac{S_j}{\|S_j\|}$ during the iteration, and squash is executed only at the last output. Based on the above discussion, this paper improved formula 7 as follows:

$$squashing(x) = \frac{\|x\|^2 + epsilon()}{0.5 + \|x\|^2} \cdot \frac{x}{\|x\|} \tag{12}$$

Epsilon in the formula represents a constant value, usually between [0, 1], this paper will set it to 10-8, mainly to prevent the output from being 0; The process of using 0.5 instead of 1 is mainly to enlarge the vector norm. According to Capsule-net, the magnitude of the modulus of a vector is used to measure the probability of the occurrence of an entity. If the magnitude of the modulus is larger, the probability is greater. Using formula 12 as the compression function, the output vector modulus may be greater than 1, which can improve the accuracy of identifying an entity.

Dynamic routing can be seen as a process similar to clustering. Generally speaking, the number of iterations in dynamic routing is 3. According to the above process, in this paper, the size of the first layer input image is set to 32 * 32 * 3; The second layer is Convolution Layer, which uses a convolution kernel size of 9 * 9 * 3 * 256 for VAILD convolution with a step size of 1. This layer converts pixels into local feature detection; The third layer is Primary Capsule Layer. It is still convolved first. The convolution kernel is 9 * 9 * 3 * 256 and the VAILD convolution with a step size of 2. This step combines the results into 32 * 6 * 6 capsules, each of which is an 8-dimensional vector; The fourth Graph Capsule Layer is a total of n capsules (n is the malicious family type), and each capsule has a dimension of 16. We get the output of the fourth layer through the static conversion matrix and dynamic routing process of the output of the third layer. Finally, we use the fully connected layer to output the results.

4 Experiment Verification

4.1 Experiment Environment

(1) Parameter Setting

The classification model of this paper's malware is implemented under the Pycharm compiler in the Linux environment. It was developed via IDAPRO 7.2 SDK, Python3.5, and OpenCv Library.

The classification method of malware based on capsule network includes three steps, data pre-processing, feature extraction and training of classification model. Data preprocessing is implemented under Windows platform. First, VMUNPACKER is used to strip malicious samples and normal samples, then Cuckoos Sandbox is used to generate a dynamic running report. Sample features and visualization is to use IDA pro to disassemble and analyze the samples, and use IDA script to extract the operation code to obtain a sequence of dynamic and static features. Finally, this paper uses N-Gram to build a comparison experiment, uses this as input, then uses OpenCv for visualization. The training of the classification model consists of two parts, a classification model based on CNN and a capsule network model, both of which are based on the TensorFlow framework and implemented via Python. The specific experimental environment is shown in Table 1.

Table 1. Experimental environment configuration

Software/Hardware name	Configuration
CPU	Intel(R) Xeon(R) E5-2643
RAM	64G
GPU	NVIDIA Tesla K40 m × 2
VRAM	12G * 2
Hard Disk	2T
Operating System	Ubuntu14.04
Framework	TensorFlow1.1.0, OpenCv
Language	Python3.5, IDA Python

(2) Data Set

In this experiment, a total of 8123 malicious samples were used for experiments, which were divided into six families, and the samples were all executable files. The data set selected in the experiment is mostly selected from malicious samples provided by the laboratory, and the rest are from VX Heaven. The samples contain obfuscated malware. In addition, in order to verify the detection effect of malware, a benign data set is also set up. The normal samples come from the windows system files and some other normal files. Table 2 shows the specific family names and sample numbers.

Table 2. Sample size and family name

Family name	Number of samples
Trojan-GameThief	963
Baixiang	1001
Trojan-Clicker	1309
Trojan-Downloader	1795
Worm-spy	1448
Backdoor-broker	1607
Sum	8123

(3) Classification model evaluation criteria

During the training and verification of the malware classification model, the model evaluation criteria selected in this paper are the classification accuracy rate and the cross-entropy loss function value, respectively.

The classification accuracy rate is used to judge the accuracy rate of the model for malware classification. The formula is as follows:

$$accuracy = \frac{TP + TN}{TP + TN + FP + FN} \tag{13}$$

Among them, N represents the total number of malicious samples, and N_i represents the number of malware samples correctly classified by the classification model. Cross-entropy loss function is used to describe the error function between the actual output calculated by the model and the standard output. The smaller the function value, the closer the actual output value is to the standard output value. The cross-entropy loss function is:

$$J = -\frac{1}{m} \sum_{i=1}^{m} \left[y^{(i)} \log \hat{y}^{(i)} + \left(1 - y^{(i)}\right) \log\left(1 - \hat{y}^{(i)}\right) \right] \tag{14}$$

Cross entropy loss function is often used in classification problems, especially when using neural networks for classification problems, cross entropy is often used as a loss function. In addition, because cross-entropy involves calculating the probability of each category, cross-entropy appears with the *softmax* function almost every time. *softmax* function formula is as follows:

$$\sigma(z) = \frac{e^{z_j}}{\sum_{k=1}^{K} e^{z_k}} \tag{15}$$

4.2 Experiment Design

Traffic statistical analysis is used to realize the interpretation of the network protocol, the statistics of traffic profile information and the acquisition of the traffic characteristic parameters distribution. The acquired parameters mainly include:

(1) Traffic summary statistics information including the total flow, the total uplink flow, the total downward flow, the starting time of capturing packets, the duration, and the link speed so on.
(2) Traffic characteristic parameter distribution including the distribution of packet length, the distribution of the transport layer protocol, the distribution of the business domain, etc.

In this section, a set of controlled experiments are performed to compare the improved and unimproved capsule network models. The parameters of the two types of models are the same, as shown in Table 3:

Table 3. Model parameters

Parameters	Configuration
Batch_size	32
Num_epoch	100
Num_capsul	100
Routings	3
Dropout	0.5

In the classification experiment using the capsule network as the training model, as the structure of the capsule network is shallow, this paper uses 32 * 32 * 3 images as input. During training, in order to balance memory efficiency and memory capacity, a batch size of 16 was used for training, and a total of 100 rounds of training were set with the number of capsules set to 100. To improve the training efficiency, the times of iterations is set to 3 during dynamic routing.

4.3 Experiment Result

(1) Visualization of malware characteristics

In this experiment, malware images with a size of 32 * 32 * 3 is used as the input feature. There are 7 categories in total, and tags are placed in the image files. The visualization representation of malware features is shown in Fig. 5.

(2) Classification model based on unimproved capsule network

First, the original capsule network was used for experiments. The classification experiment effect is shown in Fig. 6.

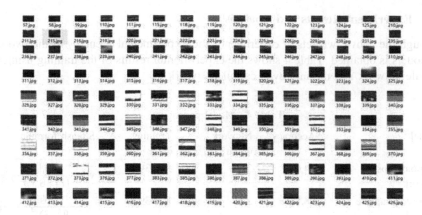

Fig. 5. Visualization of malware characteristics

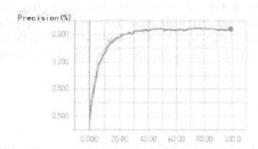

Fig. 6. Classification experiment results based on the original capsule network model

(3) Classification model based on improved capsule network

Then, we use the improved capsule network model for classification. The experimental results are shown in Fig. 7.

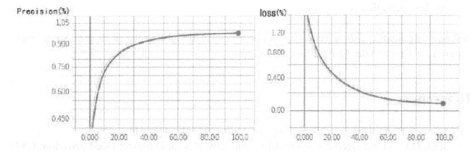

Fig. 7. Classification experiment results based on the improved capsule network model

4.4 Experiment Results and Analysis

Through the above two sets of experiments, the experimental accuracy of the two sets of models is obtained. Table 4 shows the experimental results of the training using the capsule network and the improved capsule network.

Table 4. Model parameters

Model	Accuracy	Network depth	Training cycle	Squash formula
Original capsule network	94.63%	3	100/390	$v_j = \dfrac{\|S_j\|}{\left(1+\|S_j\|^2\right)} \cdot \dfrac{S_j}{\|S_j\|}$
Improved capsule network	98.84%	3	100/390	$= \dfrac{\|x\|^2 + \mathrm{epsilon}()}{0.5 + \|x\|^2} \cdot \dfrac{x}{\|x\|}$

In the experiment on the capsule network, this paper uses the original capsule network and the capsule network with improved compression function. According to the experimental results, the improved capsule network model is better than the original capsule network. Therefore, we know that there is room for improvement in the capsule network.

5 Conclusion

Aiming at the new problems of malware detection, this paper studies the detection method based on the capsule network, and effectively applies the deep learning model of the capsule network to the field of malware detection. The experimental results prove that the classification accuracy rate can reach 94.63% when using the original capsule network model, and the accuracy rate of improved capsule network can reach 98.84%. The experimental results prove that the capsule network has a good performance when dealing with malware classification. When the number of samples is small, the model of the improved capsule network has better training effect and has higher classification accuracy. Capsule network could supply an appealing choice for classification in the case of less samples.

Acknowledgments. This work was supported by the National Key Research and Development Program of China under Grant 2016QY06X1205.

References

1. Yann, Y.B., Geoffrey, H.: Deep learning. Nature **521**(4), 436–444 (2015)
2. Shin, H.C., et al.: Deep convolutional neural networks for computer-aided detection: CNN architectures, dataset characteristics and transfer learning. IEEE Trans. Med. Imaging **35**(5), 1 (2016)

3. Nikitha, R., Vedhapriyavadhana, R., Anubala, V.P.: Video saliency detection using weight based spatio-temporal features. In: 2018 International Conference on Smart Systems and Inventive Technology (ICSSIT), Tirunelveli, pp. 343–347. IEEE (2018)
4. Han, W., Xue, J., Wang, Y., Zhu, S., Kong, Z.: Review: build a roadmap for stepping into the field of anti-malware research smoothly. IEEE Access 7, 143573–143596 (2019)
5. Liu, L., et al.: A static tagging method of malicious code family based on multi-feature. J. Inf. Secur. Res. 4(4), 322–328 (2018)
6. Song, Y., et al.: Structure and properties of shapememory polyurethane block copolymers. Mach. Learn. 81(2), 179–205 (2017)
7. Merkel, R., Hoppe, T., Kraetzer, C., Dittmann, J.: Statistical detection of malicious PE-executables for fast offline analysis. In: De Decker, B., Schaumüller-Bichl, I. (eds.) CMS 2010. LNCS, vol. 6109, pp. 93–105. Springer, Heidelberg (2010). https://doi.org/10.1007/978-3-642-13241-4_10
8. Martin, J., Lórencz, R.: Malware detection using a heterogeneous distance function. Comput. Inform. 37(3), 759–780 (2018)
9. Han, W., et al.: MalInsight: a systematic profiling based malware detection framework. J. Netw. Comput. Appl. 125(1), 236–250 (2019)
10. Wang, W., et al.: Detecting Android malicious apps and categorizing benign apps with ensemble of classifiers. Future Gener. Comput. Syst. 78(3), 987–994 (2018)
11. Han, W., et al.: MalDAE: detecting and explaining malware based on correlation and fusion of static and dynamic characteristics. Comput. Secur. 83, 208–233 (2019)
12. Ye, Y., et al.: An intelligent PE-malware detection system based on association mining. J. Comput. Virol. 4, 323–334 (2008)
13. Imran, M., Afzal, M.T., Qadir, M.A.: Using hidden markov model for dynamic malware analysis: first impressions. In: International Conference on Fuzzy Systems and Knowledge Discovery, Zhangjiajie, pp. 816–821. IEEE (2016)
14. Tan, L.N., et al.: Dynamic time warping and sparse representation classification for birdsong phrase classification using limited training data. J. Acoust. Soc. Am. 173(3), 1069–1080 (2015)
15. Ding, J., et al.: MGeT: malware gene-based malware dynamic analyses. In: Proceedings of the 2017 International Conference on Cryptography, Security and Privacy, Wuhan, pp. 96–101. ACM (2017)
16. Stokes, J.W., et al.: Detection of prevalent malware families with deep learning. In: 2019 IEEE Military Communications Conference (MILCOM), Norfolk, pp. 1–8, IEEE (2019)
17. Park, S., et al.: Generative malware outbreak detection. In: 2019 IEEE International Conference on Industrial Technology (ICIT), Melbourne, pp. 1149–1154. IEEE (2019)
18. Meng, X., et al.: MCSMGS: malware classification model based on deep learning. In: 2017 International Conference on Cyber-Enabled Distributed Computing and Knowledge Discovery (CyberC), Nanjing, pp. 272–275. IEEE (2017)
19. Sewak, M., et al.: Comparison of deep learning and the classical machine learning algorithm for the malware detection. In: 19th IEEE/ACIS International Conference on Software Engineering, Artificial Intelligence, Networking and Parallel/Distributed Computing (SNPD), Busan, pp. 293–296. IEEE (2018)

A Novel Intrusion Detection System for Malware Based on Time-Series Meta-learning

Fangwei Wang[1,2], Shaojie Yang[2], Changguang Wang[1,2], and Qingru Li[1,2(✉)]

[1] Lab of Network and Information Security of Hebei Province,
Hebei Normal University, Shijiazhuang 050024, China
{fw_wang,wangcg}@hebtu.edu.cn
[2] College of Computer and Cyber Security, Hebei Normal University,
Shijiazhuang 050024, China
1657392397@qq.com, liqingru2006@163.com

Abstract. In recent years, frequent occurrence of network security incidents indicates that host security is more and more fragile. However, current protection tools leads to reduce the efficiency of CPU or GPU. Meanwhile, they give up active defense and increase the security risk. Unfortunately, the existing intrusion detection systems seldom adjust the defense policy according to the host's performance and the time when the attack might occur. Thus, different from traditional intrusion detection systems, our system is capable of intelligently detecting and predicting threats. Firstly, our system converts the malware into gray-scale images according to the instruction execution logic. Secondly, the system uses a computer vision method to identify the signature of the gray-scale images. Finally, the proposed system classifies malware family. Specifically, the system can also predict the time when a host faces a severe threat using time-series datasets and create a multi-neural network task for defending the threat. Then, a meta-learning framework is utilized to improve malware detection accuracy and defend against attacks effectively. The experimental results show that our system can accurately classify 15 malware families, and we compare our detection results with that of other IDSs, which proves that our system achieves a better performance.

Keywords: Malware classification · Malware detection · Meta-learning · Neural network

1 Introduction

With the continuous improvement of bandwidth, the amount of data exchange between clients and service providers increases, malicious attacks are easily hide in normal traffic and softare, which makes them difficult to be detected in time.

X. Chen et al. (Eds.): ML4CS 2020, LNCS 12486, pp. 50–64, 2020.
https://doi.org/10.1007/978-3-030-62223-7_5

How to efficiently detect and identify the malware signatures in the received data has become an urgent problem to be solved. Machine learning and neural network techniques have been widely applied to develop intrusion detection systems (IDS) to protect timely and automatically host and network from cyber attacks [1]. An IDS provides a secure policy by detecting abnormal traffic and illegal behaviour, so it reduces the risk that users interact with malware signatures. However, IDS is trained on massive and unbalanced datasets, which faces the complicated data processing problem [2]. In particular, the selection of the appropriate datasets for analysis is particularly important during the outbreak of malware attacks. Therefore, we apply a malicious attack dataset of nearly three years as training samples through the Virustotal website to test and verify our proposal's persuasive power.

In computer vision and Natural Language Processing (NLP) areas, meta-learning is a promising methodology with low-resource requirements [3]. In particular, the model-independent meta-learning framework can quickly adapt to a variety of neural network models to solve different learning tasks [4]. Because IDS is compatible with any gradient descent algorithm, the existing IDS based on the Neural Network (NN) can be efficiently utilized with a small number of training samples to solve new neural network learning task. Based on this idea, we also include the outbreak time of malware within the training range, so the system can predict the time during which the host will face a severe intrusion threat. Similar to the research of time-related network intrusion detection systems [5], temporal correlation is considered throughout the defending process. When a malicious attack is predicted to occur, the defense policy of the IDS system can be adjusted to make better use of the limited performance resources of the host. Specifically, when the IDS considers the host to be in a relatively safe stage, it only employs the low host resources to scan the local files and the incoming and outgoing traffic. On the contrary, when the IDS predicts the host will be in risk, it creates multiple neural network tasks to scan and identify whether malware signatures are contained in the local files and traffic sequences.

In order to propose a more intelligent intrusion detection method to improve the malware detection accuracy with few samples, we present a novel intrusion detection system based on time-series meta-learning. The main contributions of this paper are summarised as follows:

- We use the time-series labels in the malicious attack data set provided by Virustotal for training, use the LSTM neural network to predict the time when the malicious attack might occur, and assign training tasks to other neural networks according to the predicted time.
- The guard neural network mentioned in this paper can accurately grasp malicious attacks' characteristics after large-scale malicious attack data training. The guard neural network transmits the acquired optimal gradient values to the MoE neural network using the meta-learning framework so that the MoE can continue to be trained.

- The MoE neural network mentioned in this paper can accurately classify various kinds of malicious attacks with relatively low resources, which proves that our scheme is feasible.

This paper is organized as follows. Section 2 compares the proposal against related work. Section 3 presents the system design of IDS. Section 4 presents the method of main neural network algorithms. Section 5 analyzes the experiment results. Section 6 concludes this paper.

2   Related Work

The design of IDS has become one of the most attention in the field of network security. However, existing solutions cannot successfully solve the problem of identifying all types of attacks [6], so a combination with a machine learning model for designing a perfect function of IDS is becoming an issue for cyber security researchers. This section discusses the current research status of network-based intrusion detection systems (NIDS) and host-based intrusion detection systems (HIDS) derived from IDS and how they are integrated in the background of machine learning and deep learning. Finally, our intrusion detection scheme is proposed.

The network-based intrusion detection system was proposed by Vigna et al. [7]. In order to adapt to the complex network environment, a security model NetSTAT was initially proposed to identify the type of network security events. With the coming of big data circumstances, this method cannot meet the requirements of large-scale log auditing any longer, so a new approach is urgently needed to improve the NIDS's defense efficiency. Bivens et al. [8] presents a network intrusion system based on the neural network model, which focuses on analyzing TCP traffic to defend against malicious network attacks. Compared with modern neural networks, the neural network model used in this method has low performance and cannot deal with the malicious attacks of polymorphic worms. Therefore, the host and network security still needs to be improved, the combination of the neural network model and NIDS provides researchers with new ideas. Karatas et al. [9] proposed a network intrusion detection system based on multi-layer artificial neural network, which aims to defend against distributed denial-of-service (DDoS) attack. And the system is achieved by adjusting several training functions. Labonne et al. [10] proposed a cascaded meta-specialists neural network intrusion detection system. Experimental shows that this integrated learning intrusion detection method is more accurate than the previous NIDS model.

To solve the problem of host protection, Yeung et al. [11] applied hidden Markov models and maximum likelihood estimation in their dynamic model, and used the minimum cross entropy in their static model approach. Rahmatian et al. [12] proposed an embedded HIDS. An embedded HIDS is used to assist hardware devices in observing system behavior to identify inappropriate activities. However, the main disadvantage of the HIDS is the delay between the occurrence attack and the detection attack. The time required for generating and analyzing audit documents also leads to the contradiction that improved HIDS monitoring performance comes at the expense of system resources, while low-resource HIDS is not be able to take defensive measures timely. Chawla et al. [13] describes an efficient anomaly IDS based on recurrent neural network. Replacing LSTM network with gated recurrent units, the IDS obtained a comparable set of results in less training time. Besharati et al. [14] proposed a HIDS based on logistic regression. Firstly, the logistic regression algorithm is used to select the essential features of the datasets. Secondly, regular matching is used to improve the values of important features. Finally, the virtual machine security problem in the cloud server is solved by using neural network, decision tree, and linear discrimination.

Most IDSs have some issues during training. For example, Convolutional Neural Network (CNN) and Recurrent Neural Network (RNN) need a large number of datasets, and in the process of training datasets will occupy a large number of operating system resources. The meta-learning framework in neural networks is used to improve the speed of training and reduce the cost of deploying IDS in the operating system. Lake et al. [15] proposed a method that makes the neural network complete the training quickly with few samples. Sun et al. [16] proposed a meta-transfer learning method by combining meta-learning with few-shot training. This method significantly improves the training speed of the neural network and has a better performance in the field of computer vision. Bao et al. [3] also demonstrated that the combination of a few samples and meta-learning, which could be applied to the field of NLP.

Different from previous IDSs, where basic IDS needs the support of huge datasets and occupies a lot of operating system resources, we propose a more reasonable intrusion detection system, which utilizes the meta-learning framework and combines with the time predict of malware attack. Our system can not only generate traffic signatures of polymorphic worms, but also quickly traverse local directories, identify malware files and classify them. Our system can predict the time of attack occurrence combined with the time-series information.

3   System Design

To protect hosts from malware, we design a system to identify the malware family by quickly traversing the network traffic log files and executable system files in the local disks. The flow chart of our intrusion detection system is shown in Fig. 1. The system consists of four modules: data collection and pre-processing module, task distribution center, guard module and classification module of malware family. First, time-series datasets after pre-processing are put into LSTM neural network in the distribution center to predict the attack time and generate a task scheduling table. Then, according to the task scheduling table, datasets are assigned to guard module and classification module of malware family to allocate reasonably system resources. Finally, the attack time obtained by classification module is fed back to the LSTM neural network in task distribution center to adjust its defending strategy in time. In the following sections, we will describe the functions of each part.

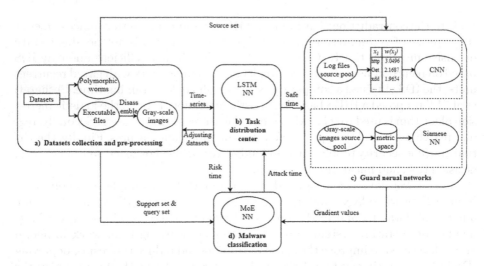

Fig. 1. Flow chart of the intrusion detection system

3.1 Dataset Collection and Preprocessing

The function of this module is mainly to collect the data. It contains polymorphic worms and other malware executable files. After that, this module disassembles these executable files to binary ones, then converts them to gray-scale images with "PGM" file format. The preprocessed datasets are compressed to reduce the capacity.

3.2 Task Distribution Center

The function of distribution center is to distribute datasets to guard module and classification module according to the host risk. First, the module a) separates time-series labels from executable files and transfers them to the module b). Long Short-Term Memory (LSTM) [17] neural network in module b) predict the attack time by training the time-series datasets. Then the predicted time are written in the task scheduling table. And module a) distributes datasets to modules c) and d) according to the task scheduling table. When the host is secure, module c) is activated, and the module a) distributes the datasets to the module c). When the host is in risk, the module a) distributes the datasets to the module d), which is keep active to protect the host against attack.

3.3 Guard Neural Network

Guard Neural Network is responsible for training the datasets over source pool, and generating the minimum gradient loss values in combination with the meta-learning framework. There are two neural networks in module c). One is the CNN, which is used to generate polymorphic worm signatures. The other is the

Siamese neural network (Siamese NN), which generates executable signatures over gray-scale image datasets.

Specifically, module c) relies on a large number of datasets to improve model accuracy. Therefore, module c) can only be awakened on the premise that attacks do not threaten the host. In the meantime, the current CPU or GPU utilization is low.

3.4   Malware Classification

The classification module classifies the attack type based on signatures. First, the Mixture of Experts (MoE) neural network gets the gradient value of neural networks in module c) using a meta-learning framework [18]. Then, the module generates malware signatures based on the support set and query set from module a). Therefore, when new attacks coming, module d) could identify the attacks type based on the acknowledged signatures. Compared with the module c), the module d) can learn to learn using meta-learning with training the support set and query set.

Module d) keeps the host's active monitoring because it can achieves significant performance with few samples and low resource. Specifically, module d) uses the MoE [19] neural network, so it can create multiple tasks to continuously protect the host according to the current situation of the host.

Section 4 introduces the main algorithms of implementing the neural network of module b), c) and d).

4   Function Implementation

LSTM is an improved neural network of RNN, which could process sequence datasets. The LSTM is useful to train time-series datasets [20], using the existing LSTM model is sufficient to meet our need for time prediction. Thus, we designed an LSTM concerning [17]:

$$
\begin{cases}
g^1 = \sigma \left(w^1 h_{i-1} + I^1 t_i + b \right), \\
g^2 = \sigma \left(w^2 h_{i-1} + I^2 t_i + b \right), \\
g^3 = \sigma \left(w^3 h_{i-1} + I^3 t_i + b \right), \\
g^4 = \tanh \left(w^4 h_{i-1} + I^4 t_i + b \right), \\
m_i = g^2 \odot m_{i-1} + g^1 \odot g^4, \\
h_i = \tanh \left(g^3 \odot m_i \right),
\end{cases}
\tag{1}
$$

where, w^1, w^2, w^3, w^4 are weight matrices, and I^1, I^2, I^3, I^4 are projection matrices. h is a hidden vector and m is a memory vector for controlling state update and outputs. Parameter t is a time-series feature vector and time step $i > 0$, b is a random value of bias.

4.1   Implementation of Guard Neural Networks

We use Guard NN as pre-trained networks for meta-learning framework. The Guard NN consists of two neural networks. One is CNN, which generates signatures of polymorphic worms. The other is Siamese NN, which deals with malware behavior signatures by means of gray-scale images datasets. CNN converts the sequences from polymorphic worms into weight matrices using the Term Frequency–Inverse Document Frequency (TF-IDF) [21] algorithm. Thus, the sequences of polymorphic worm could increase rare words and decrease frequent words.

However, TF-IDF is not enough to improve the neural network training accuracy after translating words into weight matrices. Polymorphic worm has its own unique fixed semantics (payloads), and the semantics in sequences should not be disrupted during training process. Therefore, we use bi-gram [22] as an embedding algorithm in neural network training:

$$S\left(x_j\right) = \frac{V}{V + P\left(x_j\right)}. \tag{2}$$

In Eq. (2), V is a random value in the range of 0.0001 to 1. $P\left(x_j\right)$ is the bi-gram likelihood values of x_j over the log polymorphic worms, x_j is the jth word of input example x from sequences. Next, we use the CNN [23] to train the word matrix vector.

Siamese neural network [24] is used to train gray-scale image datasets. CNN and Siamese NN, which work as pre-trained neural networks in the meta-learning framework, are implemented by Pytorch, Scikit-learn, and Keras.

4.2   MoE Neural Network

The module of malware classification is composed of a MoE neural network, which can create multiple tasks according to the usage of CPU and GPU to train the datasets quickly. MoE NN is described as follows [25,26]:

$$y = \sum_{z=1}^{n} p\left(e_z|x\right) p\left(c|e_z, x\right) = p(c|x). \tag{3}$$

In Eq. (3), x denotes input samples of polymorphic worms or gray-scale image files, which comes from support set and query set. z is the number of task and $z = 1, 2, 3, \ldots, n$, e_z is intermediate variables between the hidden layers and the full connection layers in MOE neural network, $p(c|x)$ utilizes activation function Softmax. Next section describes the details of activation function and gradient descent algorithm.

4.3   Activation Function and Gradient Descent Algorithm

Both Guard neural networks and malware classification neural network need activation functions to improve the expression ability of neural networks model.

In our IDS, we use Relu and Softmax as activation function to enhance the accuracy of neural networks training. Relu activation function can be written as follows [27]:

$$y_j^{(relu)} = \begin{cases} x_j, \text{ if } x_j \geq 0, \\ 0, \text{ if } x_j < 0. \end{cases} \tag{4}$$

To make the neural network achieve better classification performance, the Softmax activation function can be used as the output of classification module, and Softmax activation function can be expressed as [28]:

$$y_j^{(softmax)} = \max \left(\widehat{y}_j = \frac{\exp(R_j)}{\sum_{i=1}^{\max(j)} \exp(R_i)} \right). \tag{5}$$

In Eq. (5), R_j consists of multiple linear regression equations.

To finetune the new neural network (that is, MoE NN), which uses support set and query set through the meta-learning framework, the gradient descent algorithm transfers gradient value θ_i from pre-trained neural networks (that is, Guard NN) to the MoE NN. In this paper, we use Stochastic Gradient Descent (SGD) as neural networks optimizer [29] to get the optimal θ. The SGD algorithm is as following:

$$\theta(x_j) = \frac{1}{2 \max(j)} \sum_{i=1}^{\max(j)} \left(y_i^{(pre)} - y_i^{(tru)} \right)^2 + \varepsilon_{(time)}. \tag{6}$$

In Eq. (6), $y_i^{(pre)}$ is predict label of activation functions, $y_i^{(tru)}$ is true label of polymorphic worms or gray-scale image files. $\varepsilon_{(time)}$ is a random bias based on the time step.

5   Experimental Results and Analysis

5.1   Datasets

In this section, we use Microsoft malware (BIG 2015) and 2019 virustotal malware[1] as host-based datasets, and use 10,000 polymorphic worm sequences from a real-world as training datasets. We use BIG 2015 of 0.5TB malware datasets and 9,000 polymorphic worm datasets to train the Guard neural network, 40 GB virustotal executable malware files and 1000 polymorphic worm datasets as support set and query set for training MoE neural network. Our experimental settings are shown:

- CPU: Inter core i7-6700HQ CPU @ 2.60 GHz.
- GPU: NVIDIA GeForce GTX 960M 8G.
- RAM: 8 GB.
- OS: Windows 10.

---

[1] Datastes available at https://www.kaggle.com/c/malware-classification and https://www.virustotal.com/.

5.2 Task Distribution Based on Time-Series

In module b) in Fig. 1, we use LSTM NN to train time-series datasets, the results are shown as Fig. 2 and Fig. 3. Specifically, we use the real time-series of virustotal's attacks behavior on May 10, 2019 and November 29, 2019 to simulate the practice environment, and the results are shown in the following.

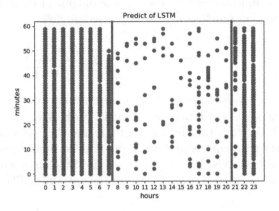

Fig. 2. LSTM neural network predicts time-series (May 10, 2019)

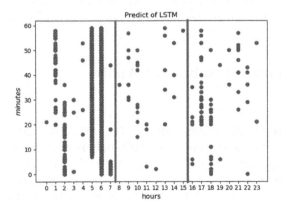

Fig. 3. LSTM neural network predicts time-series (November 19, 2019)

In Fig. 2 and Fig. 3, the space between the two red lines is regarded as the safe time by LSTM NN. The rest of the space is considered as the period when the host is in the risk of attacks. Thus, module b) sets the safe time as 8:00 AM–3:00 PM, during which module b) activates the Guard NN to train the datasets and collects the data from the host for training. At this time, the MoE NN is in a state of low occupancy of resources to deal with external attacks. When the host is in a risk time, module b) stops the Guard NN's training tasks. At this time, the Guard NN has passed the learned parameters to the MoE NN through the meta-learning framework. When the host is in risk, the MoE NN creates multiple neural network tasks based on the host's performance to detect malicious attacks quickly.

In Sect. 5.4, we focus on how the Guard NN are trained on the polymorphic and malware datasets.

5.3   Signature Generation from Guard NN

Guard NN is composed of two different networks (CNN and Siamese NN) to train Polymorphic worms and gray-scale image files. To get the different signatures, in this paper we use three types of polymorphic worms and normal data traffic, totaling 12,000 pieces of datasets.

For the BIG 2015 dataset, we first convert the 0.5T dataset and 200 MB benign software into gray-scale images in the format of ".pgm" according to the binary executable file, with the size of each image being 11 Kb and then compress the gray-scale images in the format of "7z". In this way, we only need to train 30 MB of malware gray-scale images, which significantly saves the cost of computer resources. The CNN is trained by 4-way 10-shot to generate polymorphic worm and normal traffic signatures. The Siamese NN uses 2-way 10-shot to get behavior signatures of malware and benign files.

In CNN, there are three steps to generate the signatures of the polymorphic worms and normal traffic sequences. First, the polymorphic worm and normal traffic sequences arc reloaded from the files and converted into weight matrices through the TF-IDF algorithm. Then the bi-gram algorithm embedded in CNN is used to transform the weight matrices into the word vector matrices. Finally, the word vector matrices are input to the CNN hidden layer and SGD optimizer is utilized to generate different signatures of polymorphic worms and normal traffic sequences. Take Apache-Knacker worm signatures as an example, the generated signatures are as shown in Table 1:

Table 1. Generated signatures with CNN

Type	Signatures
Apache-Knacker worms	'GET', 'HTTP/1.1 \ r\ n', '\ r\ nHost', 'xff\ xbf'
Normal traffic	'GET', 'POST', 'PUT', '\ $\sim$ms', 'referer='

From Table 1, we find that CNN can effectively generate the signatures of the polymorphic worms and normal traffic sequences. Moreover, it can also be seen from Table 1 that significant difference between normal traffic sequences and polymorphic worms. We stored the optimal θ_{worm} values of the SGD optimizer in CNN and passed it to the MoE NN through the meta-learning framework.

The Siamese NN aims to analyze the different logical structures in the gray-scale images of malware and benign software, so it can learn to distinguish the distribution of malicious behaviour from benign behaviour. The results are shown in Fig. 4 and Table 2.

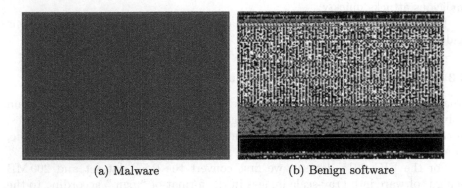

(a) Malware   (b) Benign software

Fig. 4. Difference between malware and benign behaviour

Table 2. Performance of Siamese neural network

Method	Total time	Accuracy	Used GPU
Saimese NN	3 h	92.38%	50%

From Fig. 4, Siamese NN can obviously distinguish the gray-scale images of malware from that of benign behavior. Figure 4(b) shows that the gray-scale images of the benign software have more pixel domains. Like CNN, SGD algorithm are also used as the optimizer of neural network, and the result is passed to the MoE NN .

5.4   Malware Classification Results

The module d) is composed of MoE NN. During the host is in safe time, the MoE neural network only creates two tasks that are trained through a meta-learning framework to generate network-based polymorphic worm signatures and host-based malicious family signatures. By using learned θ_{worm}, 1,000 polymorphic worms and 500 normal traffic sequences were divided into support set and query set, and MoE is trained by the 4-way 10-shot. Compared with the reference [30], the accuracy of polymorphic worm signature by MoE meta-learning is shown in Table 3.

It can be seen from Table 3 that our method can accurately identify the signatures of polymorphic worms.

Table 3. Accuracy comparison of three systems

Method	Apache-Kancker worm	BIND-tsig worm
SRE	83.5%	Null
ERES	99.6%	100%
MoE meta-learning	100%	100%

In safe time, the second task of MoE is to train malware family classification. We extract 30,000 malware files from the virustotal datasets and mix them with 2,000 benign software, and the mixture are input to the system as interference. The meta-learning framework uses θ_{gray} to train the MoE NN. Compared with the reference [31] from the perspective of malware behavior and benign behavior, the results are shown in Table 4.

Table 4. Performance results

Method	Accuracy
PCA k-means	0.8667
Extra tree classifier k-means	0.8149
VAE k-means	0.7075
DEC	0.8644
EDEC	0.9045
MoE meta-learning	0.9432

Table 4 shows that our algorithm has a better performance and can distinguish malware behavior from benign behavior more accurately than those of other methods. To further study the effectiveness of our proposed IDS scheme, we compare the MoE meta-learning with 15-way 20-shot and 4-way 10-shot under different tasks. Suppose the host is in risk time initially, module b) will assign different number of tasks to the neural network according to the CPU usage, and train the MoE NN on the polymorphic worm datasets and the malware datasets at a ratio of 1:2. The datasets consists of 30,000 malware files from the virustotal datasets and 1,000 polymorphic worm sequences, with 2,000 benign software and 2,000 normal traffic as interference. The results are shown in Table 5 and Fig. 5.

Table 5 shows that when the number of tasks of MoE meta-learning is 2 or 6, the performance is the best, and the family classification of malware is relatively accurate, and the polymorphic worm classification is accurate. The reason for accurately classifying polymorphic worms is that there are few kinds of worms used for classification, so the MoE meta-learning can generate signatures accurately in the training process of different tasks. When MoE meta-learning task is 12, MoE uses 100% CPU to train malware classification, this situation could make host lead to memory error, which effects training accuracy.

Table 5. MoE meta-learning performance in risk time

Number of tasks	Worm family	Malware family	CPU	Used time
2	100%	87.32%	10%	60 min
6	100%	86.41%	45%	10 min
12	100%	52.76%	100%	3 min

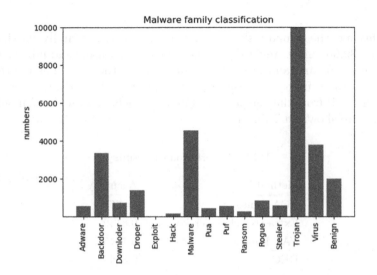

Fig. 5. Malware family classification by MoE meta-learning with 6 Tasks

6 Conclusion

We put forward a more comprehensive system of IDS in the paper. In our proposed system, the defense strategy can be allocated more reasonably by LSTM neural network training time-series datasets, then malicious attacks can be defended rapidly. The experiment results show that 15 different kinds of malicious attacks can be classified accurately.

However, the system still some disadvantages. Because there are too many types of malicious attacks, the classification accuracy and program execution efficiency can be improved further. Our future work will focus on improving the classification accuracy of multiple types of malware and exploring new and better solutions.

Acknowledgments. This work was supported by the National Natural Science Foundation of China under Grants No. 61572170, Program for Hundreds of Outstanding Innovative Talents in Higher Education Institutions of Hebei Province (III) under Grant No. SLRC2017042, and Natural Science Foundation of Hebei Province of China under Grant No. F2019205163, and department of Human Resoueces and Social Security of Hebei Province under Grant No. 201901028.

References

1. Vinayakumar, R., Alazab, M., Soman, K.P., Poornachandran, P., Al-Nemrat, A., Venkatraman, S.: Deep learning approach for intelligent intrusion detection system. IEEE Access **7**(10), 41525–41550 (2019)
2. Mazini, M., Shirazi, B., Mahdavi, I.: Anomaly network-based intrusion detection system using a reliable hybrid artificial bee colony and AdaBoost algorithms. J. King Saud Univ.-Comput. Inf. Scie. **31**(4), 541–553 (2019). https://doi.org/0.1016/j.jksuci.2018.03.011
3. Bao, Y., Wu, M., Chang, S., Barzilay, R.: Few-shot text classification with distributional signatures. In: International Conference on Learning Representations 2020, Addis Ababa, Ethiopia. IEEE Press (2020). http://arxiv.org/abs/1908.06039
4. Finn, C., Abbeel, P., Levine, S.: Model-agnostic meta-learning for fast adaptation of deep networks. In: Proceedings of the 34th International Conference on Machine Learning, Sydney, NSW, Australia, pp. 1126–1135. IEEE Press (2017)
5. Lin, Y., Wang, J., Tu, Y., Chen, L., Dou, Z.: Time-related network intrusion detection model: a deep learning method. In: 2019 IEEE Global Communications Conference (GLOBECOM), Waikoloa, pp. 1–6. IEEE Press (2019)
6. Mishra, P., Varadharajan, V., Tupakula, U.: A detailed investigation and analysis of using machine learning techniques for intrusion detection. IEEE Commun. Surv. Tutor. **21**(1), 686–728 (2018)
7. Vigna, G., Kemmerer, R.A.: NetSTAT: a network-based intrusion detection approach. In: Proceedings 14th Annual Computer Security Applications Conference, Phoenix, pp. 25–34. IEEE Press (1998)
8. Bivens, A., Palagiri, C., Smith, R.: Network-based intrusion detection using neural networks. Intell. Eng. Syst. Artif. Neural Netw. **12**(1), 579–584 (2002)
9. Karatas, G., Sahingoz, O.K.: Neural network based intrusion detection systems with different training functions. In: 2018 6th International Symposium on Digital Forensic and Security (ISDFS), Antalya, Turkey, pp. 1–6. IEEE Press (2018)
10. Labonne, M., Olivereau, A., Polve, B., Zeghlache, D.: A Cascade-structured meta-specialists approach for neural network-based intrusion detection. In: 2019 16th IEEE Annual Consumer Communications & Networking Conference (CCNC), Las Vegas, pp. 1–6. IEEE Press (2019)
11. Yeung, D.Y., Ding, Y.: Host-based intrusion detection using dynamic and static behavioral models. Pattern Recogn. **36**(1), 229–243 (2003)
12. Rahmatian, M., Kooti, H., Harris, I.G., Bozorgzadeh, E.: Hardware-assisted detection of malicious software in embedded systems. IEEE Embed. Syst. Lett. **4**(4), 94–97 (2012)
13. Chawla, A., Lee, B., Fallon, S., Jacob, P.: Host based intrusion detection system with combined CNN/RNN model. In: Alzate, C., et al. (eds.) ECML PKDD 2018. LNCS (LNAI), vol. 11329, pp. 149–158. Springer, Cham (2019). https://doi.org/10.1007/978-3-030-13453-2_12
14. Besharati, E., Naderan, M., Namjoo, E.: LR-HIDS: logistic regression host-based intrusion detection system for cloud environments. J. Ambient Intell. Humaniz. Comput. **10**(9), 3669–3692 (2018). https://doi.org/10.1007/s12652-018-1093-8
15. Lake, B.M., Salakhutdinov, R., Tenenbaum, J.B.: Human-level concept learning through probabilistic program induction. Science **350**(6266), 1332–1338 (2015)
16. Sun, Q., Liu, Y., Chua, T.S., et al.: Meta-transfer learning for few-shot learning. In: The IEEE Conference on Computer Vision and Pattern Recognition (CVPR), Long Beach, pp. 403–412. IEEE Press (2019)

17. Adam, K., Smagulova, K., James, A.: Memristive LSTM network hardware architecture for time-series predictive modeling problems. In: 2018 IEEE Asia Pacific Conference on Circuits and Systems (APCCAS), Chengdu, pp. 459–462. IEEE Press (2018)
18. Fei, N., Lu, Z., Gao, Y., Xiang, T., Wen J.: Meta-learning across meta-tasks for few-shot learning. arXiv preprint arXiv:2002.04274 (2020)
19. Ma, J., Zhao, Z., Yi, X., Chen, J., Hong, L., Chi, E.H.: Modeling task relationships in multi-task learning with multi-gate mixture-of-experts. In: The 24th ACM SIGKDD International Conference, London, pp. 1930–1939. ACM Press (2018)
20. Gers, F.A., Eck, D., Schmidhuber, J.: Applying LSTM to time series predictable through time-window approaches. In: Tagliaferri, R., Marinaro, M. (eds.) International Conference on Artificial Neural Networks, pp. 193–200. Springer, Berlin (2001). https://doi.org/10.1007/978-1-4471-0219-9_20
21. Ramos, J.: Using TF-IDF to determine word relevance in document queries. In: Proceedings of the First Instructional Conference on Machine Learning, Washington DC, pp. 133–142. IEEE Press (2013)
22. Pagliardini, M., Gupta, P., Jaggi, M.: Unsupervised learning of sentence embeddings using compositional n-gram features. arXiv preprint arXiv:1703.02507 (2017)
23. Aloysius, N., Geetha, M.: A review on deep convolutional neural networks. In: 2017 International Conference on Communication and Signal Processing (ICCSP), Chennai, pp. 588–592. IEEE Press (2017)
24. Koch, G., Zemel, R., Salakhutdinov, R.: Siamese neural networks for one-shot image recognition. In: ICML Deep Learning Workshop, Lille, pp. 1–27. Elsevier Press (2015)
25. Shazeer, N., Mirhoseini, A., Maziarz, K., David A.: Outrageously large neural networks: the sparsely-gated mixture-of-experts layer. arXiv preprint arXiv:1701.06538 (2017)
26. Eigen, D., Ranzato, M.A., Sutskever, I.: Learning factored representations in a deep mixture of experts. arXiv preprint arXiv:1312.4314 (2013)
27. Nair, V., Hinton, G.E.: Rectified linear units improve restricted Boltzmann machines. In: Proceedings of the 27th International Conference on Machine Learning (ICML 2010), Haifa, pp. 807–814. IEEE Press (2010)
28. Asadi, K., Littman, M.L.: An alternative softmax operator for reinforcement learning. In: Proceedings of the 34th International Conference on Machine Learning-Volume, Sydney, Australia, vol. 79, pp. 243–252. JMLR Press (2017)
29. Bottou, L.: Stochastic gradient descent tricks. In: Montavon, G., Orr, G.B., Müller, K.-R. (eds.) Neural Networks: Tricks of the Trade. LNCS, vol. 7700, pp. 421–436. Springer, Heidelberg (2012). https://doi.org/10.1007/978-3-642-35289-8_25
30. Eskandari, R., Shajari, M., Ghahfarokhi, M.M.: ERES: an extended regular expression signature for polymorphic worm detection. J. Comput. Virol. Hacking Tech. **15**(3), 177–194 (2019). https://doi.org/10.1007/s11416-019-00330-1
31. Ng, C.K., Jiang, F., Zhang, L., Zhou, W.: Static malware clustering using enhanced deep embedding method. Concurr. Comput.: Pract. Exp. **31**(19), 1–16 (2019)

DAD: Deep Anomaly Detection for Intelligent Monitoring of Expressway Network

Juan Wang[1], Meng Wang[1], Guanxiang Yin[1,2], and Yuejin Zhang[1(✉)]

[1] School of Information Engineering, East China Jiaotong University,
Nanchang 330013, China
zyjecjtu@foxmail.com
[2] College of Computer and Control Engineering, Nankai University,
Tianjin 300071, China

Abstract. In order to improve the real-time efficiency of expressway operation monitoring and management, the anomaly detection in intelligent monitoring network (IMN) of expressway based on edge computing and deep learning is studied. The video data collected by the camera equipment in the IMN structure of the expressway is transmitted to the edge processing server for screening and then sent to the convolution neural network. Then video data was preprocessed after the edge calculation to generate the training sample set, then send it to the AlexNet model for feature extraction. SVM classifier model is used to train the feature data set and input the features of the test samples into the trained SVM classifier model to realize the anomaly detection in the IMN of expressway. The experimental results showed that the method has better detection effect than the machine learning method and the small block learning method, and the detection time is greatly shortened.

Keywords: Edge computing · Anomaly detection · AlexNet network

1 Introduction

Building a highly intelligent highway video surveillance network and network video anomaly detection are important components of future intelligent transportation systems [1]. They aid traffic monitoring, counting, and surveillance, which are necessary for tracking the performance of traffic operations [2]. Now cities are basically installing field devices such as fixed-position cameras or motion sensors on traffic lights to monitor vehicles [3]. However, the image or video of the vehicle target will inevitably change due to factors such as light, viewing angle and vehicle interior. With the rapid development of deep learning theory and practice in recent years, researchers at home and abroad have found that deep convolutional neural networks have a certain degree of invariance to geometric transformation, deformation and lighting, and can effectively overcome the variability of vehicle appearance, in addition, the feature description is adapted to the training data to provide greater flexibility and versatility [4, 5]. This makes it possible for monitoring equipment to operate at high speed and high accuracy in complex road traffic conditions.

© Springer Nature Switzerland AG 2020
X. Chen et al. (Eds.): ML4CS 2020, LNCS 12486, pp. 65–72, 2020.
https://doi.org/10.1007/978-3-030-62223-7_6

But with the advent of the 5G era, the number of mobile devices at the edge of road networks is rapidly increasing, which will inevitably lead to a large number of data processing problems. Large-scale centralized computing with cloud computing as the core obviously cannot effectively handle the large amount of data generated from edge devices [6]. A feasible approach is to use edge computing. Researchers use edge computing microdata centers as a bridge between mobile devices and IMNs, and put a small amount of data in advance into the network edge for processing [7, 8]. Although edge computing has potential advantages, its application in vehicle anomaly detection has not been explored.

Based on the above analysis, our starting point should be the speed and accuracy of vehicle detection. Therefore, we propose a vehicle anomaly detection method based on edge computing and deep learning. We first designed the edge processing layer to filter out unwanted parts from the image. Then use the AlexNet to extract image features, at the classification stage, we choose the "parallel + voting" method to train the classifier. Finally, a voting decision is made.

2 Anomaly Detection Method for IMN of Expressway

2.1 Edge Processing

The expressway IMN collects the traffic video of the expressway through the camera, monitors the road condition of the expressway in real time, and provides support for the management of the traffic department [9]. Images without complete expressway is obviously useless, in order to reduce the consumption of resources and time, the edge data processing layer is designed. When the layer receives the expressway image information from the camera equipment, it temporarily saves it for screening, selects the image data containing the expressway panorama, and sends it to the IMN to detect the vehicle driving anomaly on expressway. In fact, it is "computing migration", which is the key idea of edge computing [10]. After the edge processing, the information is sent to convolutional neural network to extract image features.

2.2 Anomaly Detection Method Based on Deep Learning

Data Preprocessing
Video is a dynamic data composed of multiple interrelated images, with two dimensions of time and space [11]. However, in the practical anomaly detection process, the video is generally transformed into a multi-frame image. Therefore, how to effectively obtain the spatiotemporal characteristics of vehicles from the image data becomes a key problem [12].

This paper uses the AlexNet network to automatically learn the spatiotemporal features of moving objects from the original video input. In order to better combine the network with the anomaly detection problem, the input sample set was preprocessed. Firstly, the color image data in the sample set is grayed out, and then the image size is normalized. Finally, time sampling is carried out. Considering that the vehicle motion state changes unevenly, to avoid ignoring details, different time intervals M_a are selected for sampling. The i-th frame expressway image of the input video is set as y_i. The i-th data of sample one is $Y1_i = \{y_{i-2}, y_{i-1}, y_i\}$, and the i-th data of sample two is $Y2_i = \{y_{i-4}, y_{i-2}, y_i\}$, the i-th data of sample three is $Y3_i = \{y_{i-6}, y_{i-3}, y_i\}$, so that it can get three sample sets $Y1 = \{Y1_i\}$, $Y2 = \{Y2_i\}$, $Y3 = \{Y3_i\}$.

Feature Extraction

ImageNet data set is a widely recognized data set in the field of deep learning and computer vision, which has a wide range of image sources [13]. AlexNet model is a classification and recognition network model trained on this data set, which has strong expansibility and good generalization when migrating to other image data. Therefore, we performed transfer learning based on the trained AlexNet model, use the trained weight as the initial weight, and fine tune the network model during retraining process. This method can accelerate the convergence speed of the network, and effectively extract the features of the abnormal detection data set. Note that with the deepening of network level, feature representation becomes more and more abstract, and a lot of details will be lost. Therefore, this paper selects the first k convolution layers of AlexNet to act on the input sample data to achieve the function of feature extraction. In feature extraction, Y1, Y2 and Y3 were input into the same AlexNet network in turn, and the output of the k-th layer of the network is taken as the extracted feature, so as to get three sets of feature data sets F1, F2, F3 in turn.

SVM Classifier Model Training

When it comes to improving the recognition rate of the model, we can choose to train the classification model with the combination of multiple classifiers. The common combinations are cascade and parallel. When cascade is used, only the scores of the previous classifier are needed. Class results are used as auxiliary information input of the latter classifier to guide its training process [14, 15]. Considering that in parallel, each classifier training is based on different features, has different recognition performance and certain complementarity. Therefore, based on the principle of "one person, one vote", the parallel + voting method is selected to train the classifier. A class of support vector machine model based on Libsvm3.2 toolbox is implemented under MATLAB2019a, the steps are shown in Fig. 1.

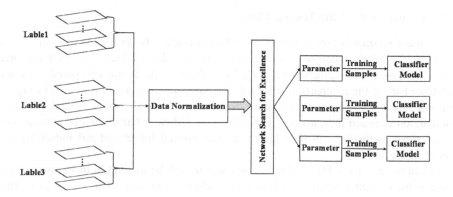

Fig. 1. Steps of using Libsvm

Anomaly Detection Stage

The features of the test samples are input into SVM classifier trained in the previous section for anomaly detection, and the classification tag values of the three test samples are output, which are recorded as L1, L2 and L3 respectively. If the value of the classification tag is equal to 1, it means that the frame image is a normal frame; if the value of the classification tag is equal to −1, it means that the frame image in the IMN of expressway is an abnormal frame. Finally, the abnormal judgment is carried out by voting. the final label output result is calculated as formula (1):

$$L = \begin{cases} -1 & if \quad \text{sum}\,(L_1, L_2, L_3) \leq -1 \\ 1 & if \quad \text{sum}\,(L_1, L_2, L_3) > -1 \end{cases} \tag{1}$$

3   Experimental Results

Taking an expressway as the experimental object, the method proposed in this paper, machine learning method and small block learning method are used to detect the anomaly in the IMN of the expressway. The effectiveness of the proposed method is verified by comparing the detection effect, accuracy and efficiency of each method in the actual detection process.

In this paper we built an expressway data set which includes the motion video data of vehicles on the expressway in three different scenes: sunny day, night and rainy day. The normal behavior of the data set is that the vehicle drives normally according to the traffic regulations in the expressway scene, and the abnormal behavior is that the vehicle violates the traffic regulations or accidents at a certain time.

The experiments were based on MATLAB2019a software under Windows 10 platform. The computer configuration parameters are as follows:

CPU: Intel Core i7 processor
GPU: NVIDA GTX 1080Ti
Running memory: 16 GB

3.1   Comparison of the Testing Effect

The three abnormal behavior videos as test data contain 6400 frames in total, which represent the whole video sequence in the form of indicator bars. The indicator bars corresponding to the detection results of the three methods are compared with the indicator bars of the comparison standard. The specific comparison is shown in Fig. 2. Among them, Fig. 2(a) is an example diagram of three abnormal behaviors and a comparison standard indicator bar, Fig. 2(b) is an indicator bar of the detection results of the three methods, with blue indicating the normal frame and red indicating the abnormal frame.

It can be seen from Fig. 2 that the indicator bar of the method in this paper is very close to the reference standard indicator bar, while the indicator bars of the other two

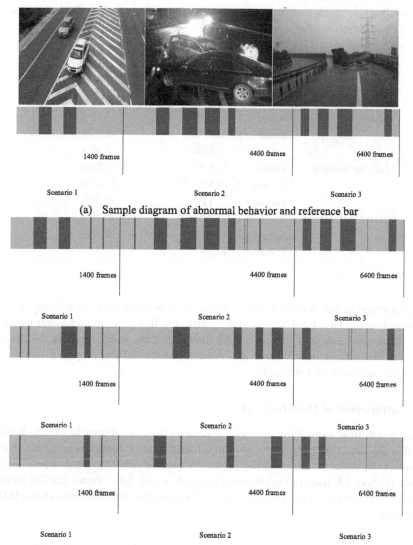

(a) Sample diagram of abnormal behavior and reference bar

(b) Indicator bar of proposed method, machine learning and small block learning

Fig. 2. Comparison of detection results

methods have different degrees of errors, which shows that the method in this paper has better detection effect in the practical application of detecting the abnormalities in the IMN of the expressway.

3.2 Accuracy Comparison

The missed detection rate and false positive rate of three abnormal scenes detected by three methods in the experiment 3.1 are recorded to make statistics. Accuracy of the three methods is compared according to the statistical results. Table 1 shows the specific comparison results.

Table 1. Comparison results of missed detection rate and false positive rate

		Missed detection rate	False positive rate
Proposed method	Scenario 1	1.21%	7.13%
	Scenario 2	0.98%	6.27%
	Scenario 3	1.34%	6.39%
Machine learning	Scenario 1	23.57%	33.86%
	Scenario 2	19.86%	36.41%
	Scenario 3	21.12%	32.51%
Small block learning	Scenario 1	43.27%	25.69%
	Scenario 2	42.15%	27.86%
	Scenario 3	40.38%	31.55%

By comparing the data in Table 1, it can be concluded that the missing detection rate as well as the false positive rate of the method in this paper are far lower than those of the other two methods under all the different scenarios, indicating that the detection results of the method in this paper are more accurate, and the proposed method outperformed the traditional methods.

3.3   Comparison of Detection Efficiency

The detection time using three methods was compared, as shown in Fig. 3. It can be seen that the detection time of the proposed method is the least, the machine learning method is more than 4 times of the proposed method, and the small block learning method is about 18 times of the proposed method, which fully shows that the proposed method is more time-saving and efficient in detecting the abnormalities in the IMN of expressway.

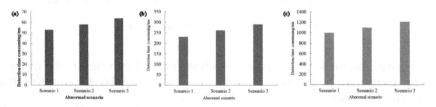

Fig. 3. Test time comparison: (a) Detection time of the method proposed in this paper; (b) Detection time of machine learning method; (c) Detection time of block learning method

4 Conclusions

This paper proposes a vehicle anomaly detection method based on edge computing and deep learning. An edge processing layer was first designed to screen out unwanted parts from the image in the device. Then extract the image features through the AlexNet network, and select the "parallel + voting" method to train the classifier. Through the voting decision method, all independent classifiers can be combined into a high-performance comprehensive classifier. Finally, the experimental results show that the method has better detection effect than the machine learning method and small block learning method. Compared with the machine learning method and the small block learning method, the missed detection rate and the false positive rate were significantly reduced, the detection time was also greatly shortened. Therefore, this method has superior practical application effect and accuracy. In the future, we would apply this method to IMNs of a more complicated anomaly detection problem, and the feasibility and application effect of this method can be further explored.

References

1. Li, Y., Wang, Z.W., Xu, S.F.: Image encryption algorithm based on multiple-parameter fractional fourier and Arnold transforms. J. China Acad. Electron. Inf. Technol. **11**(2), 164–168 (2016)
2. Zhou, Y., Nejati, H., Do, T.T., et al.: Image-based vehicle analysis using deep neural network: A systematic study. In: 2016 IEEE International Conference on Digital Signal Processing (DSP), Beijing, China, pp. 276–280. IEEE (2016)
3. Mansour, A., Hassan, A., Hussein, W.M.: Automated vehicle detection in satellite images using deep learning. IOP Conf. Ser. Mater. Sci. Eng. **610**(1), 012–027 (2019)
4. Jiang, N., Tian, F., Li, J., et al.: MAN: mutual attention neural networks model for aspect-level sentiment classification in SIoT. IEEE Internet Things J. **7**(4), 2901–2913 (2020)
5. Jiang, N., Chen, J., Zhou, R.G., et al.: PAN: pipeline assisted neural networks model for data-to-text generation in social internet of things. Inf. Sci. **530**, 167–179 (2020)
6. Zhang, R., Wang, J., Chen, Z.X.: wireless digital communication technology for parallel DC-DC converter. J. Power Supply **16**(3), 44–47 (2018)
7. Yuan, G., Zhong, F.Q.: On computing the edge-connectivity of an uncertain graph. IEEE Trans. Fuzzy Syst. **24**(4), 981–991 (2016)
8. Daniel, H., Jun, S., Taku, K.: A deep learning framework for character motion synthesis and editing. ACM Trans. Graph. **35**(4), 1–11 (2016)
9. Eric, L.F., Rishi, R., Stefan, B.W.: Deep learning approach to passive monitoring of the underwater acoustic environment. J. Acoust. Soc. Am. **140**(4), 3351 (2016)
10. Ruo, M.Y., Ling, S.: Blind image blur estimation via deep learning. IEEE Trans. Image Process. **25**(4), 1910–1921 (2016)
11. Nguyen, T., Bui, V., Lam, V.: Automatic phase aberration compensation for digital holographic microscopy based on deep learning background detection. Opt. Express **25**(13), 15043–15057 (2017)
12. Ji, Q.G., Lu, Z.M., Chi, R.: Real-time multi-feature based fire flame detection in video. Image Process. IET **11**(1), 31–37 (2016)

13. Xu, Yu., Li, D., Wang, Z., Guo, Q., Xiang, W.: A deep learning method based on convolutional neural network for automatic modulation classification of wireless signals. Wireless Netw. **25**(7), 3735–3746 (2018). https://doi.org/10.1007/s11276-018-1667-6
14. Jin, Y.F., Gao, Y.: Optimal piecewise real-time pricing strategy for smart grid. Comput Simul. **33**(4), 171–175 (2016)
15. Jiang, N., Xu, D., Zhou, J., et al.: Toward optimal participant decisions with voting-based incentive model for crowd sensing. Inf. Sci. **512**, 1–17 (2020)

A Two-Phase Cycle Algorithm Based on Multi-objective Genetic Algorithm and Modified BP Neural Network for Effective Cyber Intrusion Detection

Yiguang Gong[✉], Yunping Liu, Chuanyang Yin, and Zhiyong Fan

School of Automation, Nanjing University of Information Science
and Technology, Nanjing, China
yiguang-gong@nuist.edu.cn

Abstract. In this paper, a novel two-phase cycle training algorithm based on multi-objective genetic algorithm (MOGA) and modified back propagation neural network (MBPNN), namely TPC-MOGA-MBPNN, is proposed for effective intrusion detection based on benchmark datasets. In the first phase, the MOGA is employed to build multi-objective optimization model that tries to find Pareto optimal parameter set for MBPNN. The Pareto optimal parameter set is applied for simultaneous minimization of average false positive rate (Avg FPR), mean squared error (MSE), and negative average true positive rate (Avg TPR) in the dataset. In the second phase some MBPNNs are created based on the parameter set obtained by MOGA and are trained to search for more optimal parameter set locally. The parameter set obtained in the second phase is used as the input of the first phase, and the training process is repeated until the termination criteria are reached. Benchmark dataset namely KDD cup 1999 is used to demonstrate and validate the performance of the proposed approach for intrusion detection. The proposed approach can discover a pool of MBPNN based solutions. The MBPNN or MBPNN combination can be used to detect the intrusions accurately. The result shows that the proposed approach could reach an accuracy of 98.59% and a detection rate of 98.37%, which outperform most systems of previous works found in the literature. In addition, the proposed approach is a generalized classification approach that is applicable to the problem of any field having multiple conflicting objectives.

Keywords: Multi-objective genetic algorithm · Modified back propagation neural network · Intrusion detection · Pareto-optimality

1 Introduction

An intrusion is any set of actions intended to compromise the confidentiality, integrity, or availability of a resource [1]. Cyber intrusions are prevalent, increasingly sophisticated, and are adept at hiding from detection [2]. To counteract this ever-evolving threat, Network-based Intrusion Detection System (NIDS) has been considered to be one of the most promising methods.

© Springer Nature Switzerland AG 2020
X. Chen et al. (Eds.): ML4CS 2020, LNCS 12486, pp. 73–88, 2020.
https://doi.org/10.1007/978-3-030-62223-7_7

Intrusion detection techniques have become a significant topic of research in recent years. Many researchers propose different algorithms in different categories, such as Artificial Neural Networks (ANNs) [3], SVM [4], k-nearest neighbor [5], random forest [6], deep learning approaches [7], Bayesian approaches [8], decision trees [9]. As a result, the performance of detection techniques is getting better and stronger.

Artificial Neural Network (ANN), the computing paradigm that mimics the way neuron system of human brain work is widely used in cyber intrusion detection. Hodo E, Bellekens X, et al. [10]. presents a multi-level perceptron, a type of supervised Artificial Neural Network (ANN) to detect Distributed Denial of Service (DDoS/DoS) attacks. The experimental results demonstrate 99.4% accuracy and can successfully detect various DDoS/DoS attacks. A. Arul Anitha, L. Arockiam [11] propose an Artificial Neural Network based IDS (ANNIDS) technique based on Multilayer Perceptron (MLP) to detect the attacks initiated by the destination oriented direct acyclic graph information solicitation (DIS) attack and version attack in IoT environment. Zichao Sun, Peilin Lyu [12] uses the LSTM neural network with long and short memory function to train the KDD99 dataset, and identify the DOS according to the trained model. This is a research process of the planned adjustment for the hyperparameters to find the optimal solution after processing the data. Shenfield, Day and Ayesh [13] present a novel approach to detecting malicious cyber traffic using artificial neural networks suitable for use in deep packet inspection based IDS. Results presented show that this novel classification approach is capable of detecting shell code with extremely high accuracy and minimal numbers of false identifications. Amruta and Talha [14] present a Denial of Service Attack Detection system using ANN for wired LANs. The proposed ANN classifier gives ninety six percent accuracy for their training data-set. Most of the systems have produced promising classification accuracy.

ANN has the ability to approximate an arbitrary function mapping and learn from examples much like the human brain. In many cases, ANN surpasses the conventional statistical method for the classification task in various fields of applications [15]. However, designing an ANN is a difficult process. Its performance depends on the optimization of various design parameters such as choosing an optimal number of hidden nodes, suitable learning algorithm, learning rate and initial value of the weights, and some objectives are conflicting each other such as accuracy and complexity. Therefore, a multi-objective optimization (MOO) is considered to be a more realistic approach to the design of ANN, compared with the single-objective approach [16]. In addition, ANN has some shortcomings such as slow convergence speed, entrapment in local optimum, unstable network structure etc. [17]. In contrast, the genetic algorithm (GA) exhibits its characteristic of global search and quick convergence ability, and is the most widely used technique in data mining and knowledge discovery [18]. On the other hand the method of Pareto-optimality has been widely used in MOO [19]. It offers a pool of non-inferior individual solutions and ensemble solutions instead of a single optimum, accordingly provides more degrees of freedom in selection of proper solutions. The multi-objective genetic algorithm (MOGA) [20] and the non-dominated sorting genetic algorithm (NSGA II) [21] are two examples of GA based MOO which apply the concept of Pareto-optimality.

Some multi-objective genetic algorithms (MOGA) based approach is proposed for effective intrusion detection based on benchmark datasets. Elhag S, Altalhi A, et al.

[22]. propose a multi-objective evolutionary fuzzy system which can be trained using different metrics. The system obtains more accurate solutions, and allows the final user to decide which solution is better suited for the current network characteristics. M. Stehlík, A. Saleh, et al. [23]. propose multi-objective evolutionary algorithms (NSGA-II and SPEA2) for intrusion detection parametrization, which focus on the impact of an evolutionary algorithm (and its parameters) on the optimality of found solutions, the speed of convergence and the number of evaluations. Kumar G., Kumar K [18] proposes a three phase MOGA based Micro Genetic Algorithm2 (AMGA2) [24] which considers conflicting objectives simultaneously like detection rate of each attack type, error rate, accuracy, diversity etc. In first phase, a Pareto front of non-inferior individual solutions is approximated. In second phase, entire solution set is further refined, and another improved Pareto front of ensemble solutions over that of individual solutions is approximated. In third phase, a combination method like majority voting method is used to fuse the predictions of individual solutions for determining prediction of ensemble solution. The experiments conducted on two benchmark datasets demonstrate that the proposed approach can discover individual solutions and ensemble solutions for intrusion detection.

This paper aims to develop a novel two-phase cycle training algorithm for intrusion detection. The MOGA based approach is used to find the Pareto optimal parameter set for the neural networks. A MBPNN set is created based on Pareto optimal parameter set and trained to find more optimal parameter set locally. The proposed approach can discover a pool of MBPNN based solutions to detect the intrusions accurately.

The rest of this paper is organized as follows: Sect. 2 presents an overview of the proposed methodology. Experimental results and discussion is presented in Sect. 3. Finally, the concluding remarks of the study are provided in Sect. 4.

2   Proposed Methodology

2.1   The Proposed Approach

The TPC-MOGA-MBPNN includes training session and testing session, and them are described below.

1) The Training Session

The training session as illustrated in Fig. 1 is implemented by TPC-MOGA-MBPNN. In the first phase, a MOGA algorithm tries to find the Pareto optimal parameter set for the neural networks. The MOGA algorithm considers Avg TPR, Avg FPR and MSE on training dataset as the objectives to be minimized. Meanwhile, the weights, biases and gain factors of neural networks become the genotype to be evolved simultaneously by MOGA. In this phase we use the global search capability of MOGA to search for the initial parameter values of neural network, thereby avoid being trapped in local minima. In the second phase, neural network set is trained to find more optimal parameter set locally. The nondominated parameter set obtained from the first phase is considered as the input archive. A neural network set is generated by selecting excellent parameter set from the input archive, then back propagation is used to update the weights for the neurons, in order to bring the error function to a minimum. In this phase we use the local search and fast learning capabilities of the neural network to refine the parameter set from the first phase, and obtain a more optimal nondominated parameter set. The nondominated parameter set obtained in the second phase is used as the input of the first stage, and the training process of two-phase algorithm is repeated until the termination criteria are met. In addition, a new self-adaptive parameter adjustment strategy is also used in the training process of genetic algorithm and neural network.

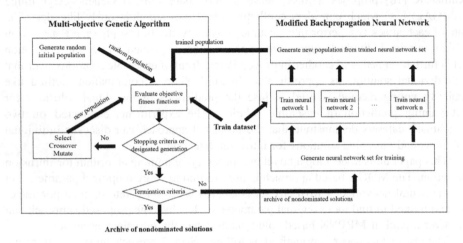

Fig. 1. Training session of the proposed methodology.

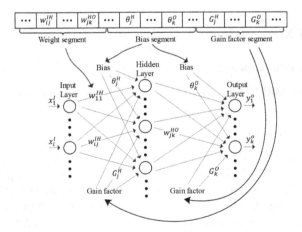

Fig. 2. The chromosome represents the parameters of neural network.

The detail implementation of the proposed algorithm is as follows:

Step 1: Generate Random Initial Population. Create random initial population, and maintains it in a solution archive. The structure of the chromosomes that make up the entire population is illustrated in Fig. 2. The weight segment in chromosomes represents the weights between input layer and hidden layer, and also includes the weights between hidden layer and output layer. The bias segment is dedicated to representing the biases of hidden nodes and output nodes. The gain factors of hidden nodes and output nodes are represented by the gain factor segment. After studying multiple training results of neural network, the numerical range of neural network parameters is estimated, and the initial value of neural network parameters is limited between - 1000 and 1000.

Step 2: Evaluate Objective Fitness Functions. Calculate the objective fitness function values for neural network corresponding to solution, then sort all solutions based on these values and update the solution archive.

First, create neural networks based on the parameters represented by all chromosomes in the MOGA population. Then, these neural networks are used to classify the samples in the training dataset one by one. Next, calculate and record TPR and FPR for five output types. The TRP and FPR are the most important criteria for the classifier, at the same time, MSE is an important criterion for evaluating the performance of neural network classification. MSE is record and is calculated as follows.

$$MSE = \frac{1}{n}\sum\nolimits_{l=1}^{n} \left(D_l - Y_l^o\right)^2 \qquad (1)$$

Where D_l and Y_l^o represent the desired output and actual output for the l-th sample of the neural network respectively, and n is the number of samples in the training dataset.

After that calculate Avg TPR and Avg FPR for the types, and they together with MSE constitute three objective fitness functions of the MOGA algorithm. Using Avg TRP instead of TRP as objective fitness function of the algorithm can avoid bias against specific attack types, especially those with less training samples such as R2L and U2R. For the same reason, Avg FRP is also used as objective fitness function.

Finally sort all chromosomes and update the solution archive. The chromosomes are sorted according to the following two rules [25]:

(1) First, chromosomes are sorted according to non-inferior order, and the chromosomes with small non-inferior order values are ranked at the top of the solution archive.
(2) Secondly, chromosomes with same non-inferior order are sorted according to crowded degree, and the less crowded chromosomes is closer to the top of the solution archive.

Among the above two rules, the first rule is made to find non-inferior solutions, and the second rule is set down to ensure that the distribution of non-inferior solutions is as dispersive as possible.

Step 3: Stopping Criteria or Designated Generation. MOGA uses two different criteria to determine when to stop the solver. MOGA detects if there is no change in the best fitness value for some number of generations (stall generation limit). MOGA also stops when the designated number of generations is reached, by default this number is 300. If either of the two stopping criteria is reached, the algorithm will stop and go to step 5, otherwise the algorithm will go to step 4.

Step 4: Select Crossover and Mutate. MOGA uses selection, crossover, and mutation operators in the solution archives to generate new population. Add the new population into the solution archive, go back to step 2 and repeat the above steps.

The MOGA used in this paper is a variant of Stud GA [26]. First, some best solutions in the archive obtained from step 2 are moved to a stallion archive, and the rest solutions were moved to the other temporary archive. Then, the linear ranking selection is used to select a solution from the stallion archive as a stallion, and select the other solution from the temporary archive. Next, the selected two solutions are particular randomly for crossover and create two offspring by arithmetic crossover operator. After that all the chromosomes resulted from the crossover operation will go through a mutation process and consequently. Finally, the selection, crossover, and mutation operators are used repeatedly to generate new population until the maximum population size is reached.

Step 5: Termination Criteria. The algorithm will terminate only if the following three conditions are met:

(1) The Avg TPR value is greater than the designated value.
(2) The Avg FPR value is smaller than the designated value.
(3) The number of non-inferior individual solutions is greater than the designated value.

If termination criteria are satisfied, the algorithm will terminate, otherwise the algorithm will go to step 6.

Step 6: Generate Neural Network Set for Training. Select some best solutions from archive of nondominated solutions, and generate neural networks using the parameters represented by the solutions.

The MBPNN [27] which is used in our approach adds gain factors G to change the steepness of neural network activation function. During the learning process, gain factors change with the change of weights and biases, so as to speed up the convergence. The main modifications of the algorithm are as follows:

(1) The neural network activation function is still sigmoid function, but the value range is changed to [−0.5, +0.5]. It can overcome the problem that the change of weights and biases does not change the calculation when learning zero value samples. The modified sigmoid is as follows:

$$f(x) = -0.5 + \frac{1}{1 + e^{-x}} \tag{2}$$

(2) Let f be the neural network activation function, add gain factor G_j to the net input I_j, which is computed as the sum of the input features multiplied by the weights, so the output y_j is defined as follows:

$$y_j = f(G_j I_j) \tag{3}$$

(3) The rule for gain factor update is the same as the rule for weights and biases, and the update value of gain factor ΔG_j can calculate as follows:

$$\Delta G_j = \eta \delta_j I_j / G_j \tag{4}$$

Where η is learning rate, δ_j represents error term at node j.

Step 7: Train Neural Network. Each created neural network from step 6 is trained on training dataset by back propagation algorithm, which reduces the error values and update weights, biases and gain factors, so that the actual output values and desired output values get close enough. The method to update gain factors is expressed as Eq. (4).

Step 8: Generate New Population from Trained Neural Network Set. When the learning process for neural networks is completed new chromosomes are constructed based on the parameters of each trained neural network, and then these chromosomes form a new population. Add the new population into the solution archive, go back to step 2 and repeated the above steps.

2) The Testing Session

The testing session is depicted in Fig. 3. The testing session of the proposed approach integrates the predictions of several MBPNN classifiers to get prediction of the final ensemble. The majority voting method is used to determine which attack type a test sample is finally classified into. The final attack type of a test sample is the one which gets the most votes.

The detail implementation of the testing session is as follows:

Step 1: Generate Neural Network Set for Testing. Select some non-inferior solutions from archive of nondominated solutions obtained by genetic algorithm, and generate neural networks using the parameters represented by the solutions.

The users can select several different solutions for combination prediction according to their own preferences. For example, choose a solution subset with large TPR values, or a solution subset with small FPR values, or a mixed solution subset with large TPR values and small FPR values.

Step 2: Neural Network Predicting. Each created neural network from step 1 is used to classify samples on test dataset by forward propagation algorithm of MBPNN, which is done and the neural network gives out prediction result.

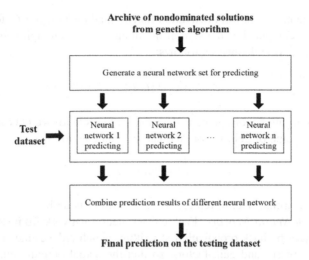

Fig. 3. Test session of the proposed methodology.

Step 3: Combine Prediction Results of Different Neural Network. The prediction results from different MBPNN are combined by the majority voting method to give the final output of the ensemble. For each individual sample, the prediction result of each MBPNN will get one vote, and the final attack type of this sample is the one which gets the largest number of votes.

2.2   The Intrusion Detection Dataset

The performance of the proposed approach is measured based on that KDD cup 1999 [28] dataset which is the most widely used for validation of an IDS. Each record of the KDD dataset contains 41 feature attributes and 1 label attribute. The dataset contains five major types: Normal, Probe, Denial of Service (DoS), User-to-Root (U2R) and Remote-to-Local (R2L) attacks. The last four are attack types which can be subdivided into 39 different attack types. The dataset is very large, including 5 million training records and 2 million test records, so it's practically very difficult to use the whole dataset. In this study, we firstly remove records which have the same value for all features, then randomly select different records to form subsets which contain different proportions of normal and attack instances. The selected subsets used in our experiments is as depicted in Table 1. Validation set is created by extracting 10% of the records (14,558) from the train set. The test set has the same number of records as validation set, and has never been exposed to training session.

Data Transformation. We use one-hot encoding scheme to transform the three categorical features: protocol, service and state. A dimension is added for each new feature value found in the train set. The added dimensions indicate the presence or absence of certain category, represented by binary [0, 1]. Following this scheme, the resulting datasets are extended into 123-dimensional features.

Table 1. Total instances of subsets of KDD cup 1999 dataset

Type	Train set	Test set	Validation set	Subtotal
Normal	79049	8783	8783	87832
Probe	1918	213	213	2131
DoS	49115	5457	5457	54572
U2R	47	5	5	52
R2L	899	100	100	999
Total	131028	14558	14558	145586

Data Normalization. We use min-max normalization to scale feature values, since the range of numerical features differ considerably from one another. We scale feature values linearly into the range of [−0.5, 0.5] by using the following equation.

$$x' = \frac{x - mim(x)}{\max(x) - \min(x)} - 0.5 \tag{5}$$

Where x' represents the normalized data, x represents the raw data, $mim(x)$ finds the minimum data value in the current feature values, and $max(x)$ searches for the maximum data value for the current feature.

2.3 Experimental Setup

To evaluate the proposed approach, an experimental application is implemented in C#. MBPNN is used as a basic classifier. The performance of the proposed technique is evaluated based on benchmark dataset of the KDD cup 1999 dataset. Avg TPR, Avg FPR and MSE are used as objective fitness functions of MOGA. Majority voting method is used to integrate the predictions of several basic classifiers to get combined prediction for the final ensemble. The results of experiments are computed on a Windows PC with Core i7-8550U, 1.80 GHz CPU and 16 GB RAM.

1) Performance Metrics

In order to evaluate the performance of the proposed IDS, we use the following widely known metrics: accuracy, true positive rate, false positive rate as defined as follows:

- True Positive (TP) is the number of attack records classified correctly;
- True Negative (TN) is the number of normal records classified correctly;
- False Positive (FP) is number of normal records classified incorrectly;
- False Negative (FN) is the number of attack records classified incorrectly.

True positive rate (TPR), also known as detection rate, recall or sensitivity, is the proportion of positive cases that are correctly identified and is calculated as follows:

$$TPR = \frac{TP}{TP + FN} \qquad (6)$$

False positive rate (FPR), also known as false alarm rate (FAR), is the proportion of positive cases that are incorrectly identified and is calculated as follows:

$$FPR = \frac{FP}{FP + TN} \qquad (7)$$

Accuracy is the proportion of the total number of predictions that is correct and is calculated as follows:

$$Accuracy = \frac{TN + TP}{TN + TP + FN + FP} \qquad (8)$$

The closer the value of these metrics (except for FPR) to one is, the better the network topology is. The values of FPR should be close to zero for better topologies.

2) Design of Experiments
The proposed approach involves two algorithms: MOGA and MBPNN. The implementation of MOGA algorithm takes some parameters as depicted in Table 2. Designated generation is used to set the maximum number of cycles for genetic algorithm. In order to find more solutions, the population size maintains a large value. Stallion population is created to keep few optimal solutions. Trained population size is the number of selected chromosomes which is used to created MBPNN for phase 2. The probability of crossover and mutation change with the quality of the obtained solutions, and bad solutions will increase the probability, but cannot exceed the set maximum value.

Table 2. Configuration of MOGA

Parameter	Values
Designated generation	400
Population size	300
Stallion population size	10
Trained population size	20
Maximum value of crossover probability	0.4
Maximum value of mutation probability	0.1

The parameters of MBPNN is depicted in Table 3. Designated training epochs number is used to set the maximum number of cycles. The number of input nodes is the number of cyber intrusion feature attributes after one-hot encoding. The number of hidden nodes keep small for less computation. The number of output nodes corresponds to five types of cyber intrusion. The learning rate increase when the network error is large, otherwise it will decrease. The learning rate cannot exceed the set maximum value. Maximum and minimum initial value is used to set the range of the initial parameter values.

Table 3. Configuration of MBPNN

Parameter	Values
Designated training epochs number	100
Input nodes number	123
Hidden nodes number	3
Output nodes number	5
Maximum value of learning rate	0.5
Maximum initial value of neural network parameters	1000
Minimum initial value of neural network parameters	−1000

3 Result and Discussion

Here, the two-phase cycle training algorithm is done to optimize parameter values for MBPNN. After that we select some non-inferior solutions obtained by the training algorithm to create MBPNN classifiers for the final ensemble. Finally, each created MBPNN is used to classify samples on test dataset, and the prediction results are combined by the majority voting method to give the final output of the ensemble.

The proposed approach is applied to KDD cup 1999 dataset that produces a set of non-inferior MBPNN based ensemble solutions. The performance of ensemble solutions for training data is depicted in Fig. 4, and for test data is shown in Fig. 5. A very clear Pareto front can be seen in Fig. 4 and Fig. 5, which exhibits the excellent optimization performance of the algorithm.

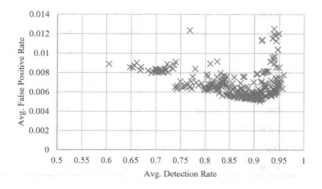

Fig. 4. Training performance of the proposed approach

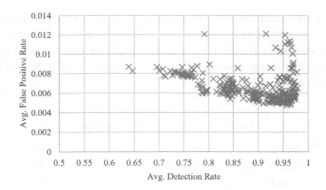

Fig. 5. Test performance of the proposed approach

It is worth noting that although some individual non-inferior solutions with high DR and low FAR have good performance, the combination of these solutions can still significantly improve their performance. We choose one solution with largest Avg TPR value, one solution with smallest Avg FPR value, and one solution with smallest MSE value to carry out prediction respectively. At the same time, an experiment called Mixed was performed, which classifies by combining the previous three solutions. The detection rate on test dataset is shown in Table 4. In the tables, for each major type, the highest DR and lowest FAR will be emphasized in bold. The shaded cells represent the methods that have good trade off of DR and FAR. Based on DR and FAR, best performing classifiers are selected for local experts as follow: Avg TPR for Probe Detector, and Mixed for Normal, DoS, U2R, and R2L Detectors. Obviously, the combined classification method performs better than the individual classification.

Table 4. Comparison of detection rate

Attack type		Avg TPR	Avg FPR	MSE	Mixed
Normal	DR	97.92	99.18	99.26	**99.32**
	FAR	2.68	**1.7**	1.97	1.8
DoS	DR	95.6	**98.41**	98.26	98.31
	FAR	0.11	0.18	0.19	**0.05**
Probe	DR	**97.65**	92.96	95.31	95.77
	FAR	0.82	0.35	**0.26**	0.32
U2R	DR	**100**	**100**	80	**100**
	FAR	0.66	0.07	0.07	**0.06**
R2L	DR	83	**88**	84	87
	FAR	0.46	0.08	**0.04**	0.06

Table 5. Comparison of overall accuracy, Detection rate, and false alarm rate

Attack type	Avg TPR	Avg FPR	MSE	Mixed
Accuracy	96.94	98.72	98.74	**98.8**
DR	97.27	**98.3**	98.02	98.16
FAR	3.26	1	0.8	**0.77**

Table 6. Comparison of proposed model with other methods by detection rate, accuracy, and false alarm rate

Method	Normal	DoS	Probe	U2R	R2	Accuracy	DR	FAR
Multi-level SVM-ELM [29]	98.13	99.54	87.22	21.93	31.39	95.75	95.17	1.87
NFC [29]	98.2	99.5	84.1	14.1	31.5	N/A	95.2	1.9
Genetical algorithm [29]	69.5	99.4	71.1	18.9	5.4	90	94.95	30.46
SVM + BIRCH clustering [29]	99.3	99.5	97.5	19.7	28.8	95.7	N/A	0.7
MOGFIDS [29]	98.36	97.2	88.6	15.79	11.01	93.2	91.96	1.6
Association rules [29]	99.47	96.6	74.8	3.8	1.21	92.4	N/A	0.53
Multiclass SVM [29]	99.6	96.8	75	5.3	4.2	92.46	90.74	**0.43**
Winning the KDD99 [29]	99.5	97.1	83.3	13.2	8.4	93.3	91.81	0.55
t-SNE SVM [30]	**99.85**	99.62	**98.89**	86.8	96.51	N/A	N/A	N/A
Hybrid classifier [31]	96.8	98.66	93.4	46.97	71.43	96.77	96.77	3
DT–SVM [32]	99.7	**99.92**	98.57	48	37.8	N/A	N/A	N/A
GA FPM [33]	N/A	98.85	98.05	78.7	**98.7**	N/A	N/A	N/A
Proposed approach (Mixed)	98.85	98.33	97.18	**100**	93	**98.59**	**98.37**	1.3

Table 5 compares the overall accuracy, detection rate and false alarm rate, and it also proves that the combination classification method is a feasible classification method with better performance for intrusion detection.

More experiments are done to validate the performance of the proposed approach. One of experimental results of TPC-MOGA-MBPNN are compared with the results of some well-known models reported in the literatures as shown in Table 6. It is evident that the proposed TPC-MOGA-MBPNN outperforms the cited approaches in case of consistently good overall accuracy and DR.

4 Conclusions

In this paper, a novel TPC-MOGA-MBPNN algorithm based on MOGA and MBPNN is proposed for effective intrusion detection. The proposed approach is capable of producing a pool of non-inferior individual solutions which exhibit classification trade-offs for the user. By using certain heuristics or prior domain knowledge, a user can select an ideal solution or combined solution as per application specific requirements. The proposed approach attempts to tackle the issues of low DR, high FPR and lack of classification trade-offs in the field of intrusion detection. The proposed approach consists of encoding of chromosomes that provides optimized parameter values of MBPNN. MOGA is employed to build multi-objective optimization model that generates Pareto optimal solutions with simultaneous consideration of Avg TPR, Avg FPR and MSE in the dataset. A two-phase cycle training algorithm based approach can rapidly generate numerous non-inferior solutions. In the first phase, a MOGA algorithm tries to find the Pareto optimal parameter set for the neural networks. In the next phase some selected MBPNN based on chromosomes obtained by MOGA are trained to find more optimal parameter set locally. The nondominated parameter set obtained in the second phase is used as the input of the first stage, and the training of two-phase algorithm is repeated until the termination criteria are reached.

KDD cup 1999 dataset for intrusion detection are used to demonstrate and validate the performance of the proposed approach. The proposed approach exhibits the excellent optimization performance of the algorithm and a very clear Pareto front has been obtained. The optimized set of MBPNN exhibits the classification tradeoffs for the users. The user may select an ideal solution as per application specific requirements. We also demonstrate that combining a few MBPNN to classify is a feasible classification method and has better performance than using an individual MBPNN to classify. The proposed approach can discover an optimized set of MBPNN with good accuracy and detection rate from benchmark datasets. The result shows that the proposed approach could reach an accuracy of 98.59% and a detection rate of 98.37%, which outperform most systems of previous works found in the literature. The result of this work has also provided an alternative in the issue of selecting an optimal solution among the non-dominated Pareto-optimal solutions.

The major issue in the proposed approach is that MOGA takes long time to compute fitness functions in various generations. It may be overcome by computing the function values in parallel, or limiting the population size. The proposed approach only uses a small subset of benchmark dataset for validation, and its applicability can be validated by more experiments on real cyber traffic in the field of intrusion detection.

References

1. Heady, R., Luger, G., Maccabe, A., Servilla, M.: The architecture of a network level intrusion detection system. Technical Report CS90-20, Department of Computer Science, University of New Mexico. Other Inf. PBD 15 Aug 1990 (1990)
2. F-Secure: The state of cyber security 2017 (2017)
3. Manzoor, I., Kumar, N.: A feature reduced intrusion detection system using ANN classifier. Expert Syst. Appl. **88**, 249–257 (2017)
4. Vijayanand, R., Devaraj, D., Kannapiran, B.: Intrusion detection system for wireless mesh network using multiple support vector machine classifiers with genetic-algorithm-based feature selection. Comput. Secur. **77**, 304–314 (2018)
5. Li, L., Yu, Y., Bai, S., Hou, Y., Chen, X.: An effective two-step intrusion detection approach based on binary classification and k-NN. IEEE Access **6**, 12060–12073 (2017)
6. Farnaaz, N., Jabbar, M.A.: Random forest modeling for network intrusion detection system. Proc. Comput. Sci. **89**, 213–217 (2016)

7. Vinayakumar, R., Alazab, M., Soman, K.P., Poornachandran, P., AlNemrat, A., Venkatraman, S.: Deep learning approach for intelligent intrusion detection system. IEEE Access **7**, 41525–41550 (2019)
8. Cemerlic, A., Yang, L., Kizza, J.M.: Network intrusion detection based on bayesian networks. In: Twentieth International Conference on Software Engineering & Knowledge Engineering. DBLP (2008)
9. Cataltepe, Z., Ekmekci, U., Cataltepe, T., et al.: Online feature selected semi-supervised decision trees for network intrusion detection. In: NOMS 2016 - 2016 IEEE/IFIP Network Operations and Management Symposium. IEEE (2016)
10. Hodo, E., Bellekens, X., Hamilton, A., Dubouilh, P.L., Atkinson, R.: Threat analysis of IoT networks using artificial neural network intrusion detection system. In: 3th International Symposium on Networks, Computers and Communications (ISNCC). IEEE (2016)
11. Anitha, A.A., Arockiam, L.: ANNIDS: artificial neural network based intrusion detection system for Internet of Things. Int. J. Innov. Technol. Explor. Eng. (2019)
12. Sun, Z., Lyu, P.: Network attack detection based on neural network LSTM (2019)
13. Shenfield, A., Day, D., Ayesh, A.: Intelligent intrusion detection systems using artificial neural networks. ICT Express **4**, 95–99 (2018). S2405959518300493
14. Amruta, M., Talhar, N.: Effective denial of service attack detection using artificial neural network for wired LAN. In: Proceedings 2016 International Conference on Signal Processing, Communication, Power and Embedded System (SCOPES), pp. 229–234 (2016). https://doi.org/10.1109/SCOPES.2016.7955826
15. Paliwal, M., Kumar, U.A.: Neural networks and statistical techniques: a review of applications. Expert Syst. Appl. **36**(1), 2–17 (2009)
16. Ahmad, F., Isa, N.A.M., Hussai, Z.: A genetic algorithm-based multi-objective optimization of an artificial neural network classifier for breast cancer diagnosis. Neural Comput. Appl. **23** (5), 1427–1435(2013). https://doi.org/10.1007/s00521-012-1092-1
17. Cao, X.Y., Yu, H.L., Zou, Y.Y.: Character recognition based on genetic algorithm and neural network. In: Lu, W., Cai, G., Liu, W., Xing, W. (eds.) Procceedings of the 2012 International Conference on Information Technology and Software Engineering. LNEE, vol. 211. Springer, Heidelberg (2013). https://doi.org/10.1007/978-3-642-34522-7_96
18. Kumar, G., Kumar, K.: A multi-objective genetic algorithm based approach for effective intrusion detection using neural networks. In: Yager, R.R., Reformat, M.Z., Alajlan, N. (eds.) Intelligent Methods for Cyber Warfare. SCI, vol. 563, pp. 173–200. Springer, Cham (2015). https://doi.org/10.1007/978-3-319-08624-8_8
19. Abbass, H.A.: Pareto neuro-evolution: constructing ensemble of neural networks using multi-objective optimization. In: Proceedings of the 2003 Congress on Evolutionary Computation, CEC 2003, 8–12 December 2003, vol. 2073, pp. 2074–2080 (2003)
20. Fonseca, C., Fleming, P.: Genetic algorithms for multiobjective optimization: formulation, discussion and generalization. In: Proceedings of the 5th International Conference on Genetic Algorithm, University of Illinois, 1993, pp. 416–423. Morgan Kaufmann (1993)
21. Deb, K., Pratap, A., Agarwal, S., Meyarivan, T.: A fast and elitist multiobjective genetic algorithm: NSGA-II. IEEE Trans. Evol. Comput. **6**(2), 182–197 (2002)
22. Elhag, S., Fernández, A., Altalhi, A., Alshomrani, S., Herrera, F.: A multi-objective evolutionary fuzzy system to obtain a broad and accurate set of solutions in intrusion detection systems. Soft. Comput. **23**(4), 1321–1336 (2017). https://doi.org/10.1007/s00500-017-2856-4
23. Stehlik, M., Saleh, A., Stetsko, A., Matyas, V.: Multi-objective optimization of intrusion detection systems for wireless sensor networks, pp. 569–576 (2013). https://doi.org/10.7551/978-0-262-31709-2-ch082

24. Tiwari, S., Fadel, G., Deb, K.: Amga2: improving the performance of the archive-based microgenetic algorithm for multi-objective optimization. Eng. Optim. **43**(4), 377–401 (2011)
25. Fei, Y., Li, N., et al.: Multiobjective optimization method based on Pareto solution and its application. Lift. Transp. Mach. **9**, 13–15 (2006)
26. Khatib, W., Fleming, P.J.: The stud GA: a mini revolution? In: Eiben, A.E., Bäck, T., Schoenauer, M., Schwefel, H.-P. (eds.) PPSN 1998. LNCS, vol. 1498, pp. 683–691. Springer, Heidelberg (1998). https://doi.org/10.1007/BFb0056910
27. Zhu, J.: Non-classical mathematical methods for intelligent systems (2001)
28. KDD: Kdd cup 1999 dataset (1999). http://kdd.ics.uci.edu/databases/kddcup99/kddcup99.html
29. Al-Yaseen, W.L., Othman, Z.A., Nazri, M.Z.A.: Multi-level hybrid support vector machine and extreme learning machine based on modified K-means for intrusion detection system. Expert Syst. Appl. **67**, 296–303 (2017)
30. Hamid, Y., Sugumaran, M.: A t-SNE based non linear dimension reduction for network intrusion detection. Int. J. Inf. Technol. **12**(1), 125–134 (2019). https://doi.org/10.1007/s41870-019-00323-9
31. Xiang, C., Yong, P.C., Meng, L.S.: Design of multiple-level hybrid classifier for intrusion detection system using bayesian clustering and decision trees. Pattern Recogn. Lett. **29**(7), 918–924 (2008)
32. Peddabachigari, S., Abraham, A., Grosan, C., Thomas, J.: Modeling intrusion detection system using hybrid intelligent systems. J. Netw. Comput. Appl. **30**(1), 114–132 (2007)
33. Kadam, P.U., Deshmukh, M.: Real-time intrusion detection with genetic, fuzzy, pattern matching algorithm. In: International Conference on Computing for Sustainable Global Development. IEEE (2016)

An Improved Localization Algorithm Based on Invasive Weed Optimization for WSNs

Yaming Zhang[1] and Yan Liu[2(✉)]

[1] Key Laboratory of Education Informalization for Nationalities,
Ministry of Education, Yunnan Normal University, Kunming 650500, China
[2] School of Information Science and Technology, Yunnan Normal University,
Kunming 650500, China
liuyan_xidian@163.com

Abstract. Wireless sensor network is regarded as one of the ten emerging technologies that will change the world in the 21st century. The related basic theories, key technologies and application models have been widely studied in the industry and academia. As one of its key supporting technologies, localization technology has attracted much attention. In this paper, an improved localization algorithm based on invasive weed optimization is presented and used for the field of localization in wireless sensor network. It uses two stages to complete the node location estimation. In the first stage, the region of nodes is estimated by proactive estimation method, and in the second stage, the location of nodes is estimated by search optimization. During the execution of the algorithm, several measures were taken to improve the performance of algorithm. The simulation results show that the proposed algorithm has higher localization accuracy and better stability under different ranging errors. Moreover, for the same accuracy requirement, the new algorithm needs fewer anchor nodes, which is more conducive to the cost control of the system.

Keywords: Wireless sensor networks · Intelligent computing · Invasive weed optimization · Node localization

1 Introduction

Wireless sensor networks have received continuous attention worldwide in recent years. It is listed as one of the 21 most influential technologies in the 21st century and one of the top 10 emerging technologies that changed the world in the report by the US "Business Weekly" and "MIT Technology Review". "MIT Technology Review" even lists wireless sensor networks as the first future emerging technology. The related basic theories, key technologies and application models have been widely studied in the industry and academia [1].

This research was supported by the Natural Science Basic Research Plan in Shaanxi Province of China (No. 2017JM6068), the Science Research Fund of Yunnan Education Department (No. 2020J0099, No. 2019J0072), and the PhD Early Development Program of Yunnan Normal University (No. 2017ZB014, No. 2017ZB012).

© Springer Nature Switzerland AG 2020
X. Chen et al. (Eds.): ML4CS 2020, LNCS 12486, pp. 89–99, 2020.
https://doi.org/10.1007/978-3-030-62223-7_8

As a new information acquisition and processing method, wireless sensor network technology is also an important part of the Internet of things technology. When the sensor equipment in the network detects the occurrence of an event, one of the important issues that people are concerned about is the location of the event, because the monitoring data without location information is often meaningless. Therefore, localization is a key support function for wireless sensor networks to determine the location of events or nodes to obtain messages.

At present, localization research has become a key technology in wireless sensor networks. Localization technology is an important prerequisite and powerful guarantee to promote the development of wireless sensor network applications. Many localization algorithms for WSNs have been proposed by researchers at home and abroad.

In this paper, an improved IWO-based localization algorithm (abbreviated as IIWO-LA) is presented and used for the field of wireless sensor network localization.

2 Related Work

According to whether it is necessary to directly measure the distance between nodes during the localization process, the traditional localization algorithm can be divided into two types [2]: range-based localization algorithms and range-free localization algorithms. The range-based algorithms use some ranging method to measure the distance or angle information between nodes, and then uses triangulation, triangulation or maximum likelihood estimation to estimate the coordinates of unknown nodes. It has higher positioning accuracy but usually requires additional hardware. The range-free algorithm does not need to measure the distance or angle between nodes directly. In many cases, it only depends on the connectivity between adjacent nodes to determine the region of the unknown node or the number of hops it reaches each anchor node. Then, the unknown node coordinates are estimated by centroid calculation, signal coverage, distance vector and so on, and the localization accuracy is slightly less.

In addition to the above traditional localization algorithms, many new localization algorithms have emerged in recent years. The intelligent location algorithm based on intelligent computing technology has attracted much attention. The classical intelligent computing methods, including simulated annealing algorithm (SA), particle swarm optimization algorithm (PSO), genetic algorithm (GA) and so on, are all used to localization in wireless sensor networks [3, 4].

An famous localization algorithm example based on simulated annealing is presented by Kannan and Mal et al. [5], which is one of the first attempts to discuss localization problem of wireless sensor networks as an optimization problem. Its disadvantage is that it has high calculation cost. Since then, Gopakumar, Jacob and other scholars have presented several PSO based localization algorithm [6, 7]. Compared with the SA-based localization algorithm, the PSO-based algorithm showed better localization performance. In addition, there are many others similar intelligent computing based localization algorithms [8, 9]. Invasive weed optimization (IWO) is a novel intelligent optimization algorithm [10, 11]. It shows better search performance in many engineering fields than PSO, GA and so on. It also shows good performance in the field of wireless sensor network positioning [12, 13]. On the basis of the above research, this paper makes a further research on the localization algorithm based on IWO, and proposed an improved IWO-based localization algorithm.

3 Problem Statement

Presume there is a wireless sensor network, which has a total of N sensor nodes. Among them, there are M anchor nodes (they know their position coordinates) and $N - M$ unknown nodes (i.e., target nodes, they don't know their position coordinates and need to calculate it by localization algorithm).

The key of localization problem is how to estimate the coordinates $N_i(\tilde{x}_i, \tilde{y}_i)$ of the rest $N - M$ unknown nodes use the coordinates $A_j(x_j, y_j)$ $(j = 1, 2, \cdots M)$ of M anchor nodes. Obviously, this problem can be transformed into an optimization problem to solve.

Suppose the real distance from the unknown node u to its neighbor anchor node A_i is:

$$d_i = \sqrt{(x_i - x_u)^2 + (y_i - y_u)^2} \tag{1}$$

where (x_u, y_u) is the coordinates of unknown node u. And the ranging distance between these two nodes obtained by ranging technology is $\hat{d}_i$ which including noise.

The objective function of this optimization problem for localization can be expressed by:

$$f(x, y) = \frac{1}{n} \sum_{i=1}^{n} |\hat{d}_i - d_i| \times \frac{1}{\hat{d}_i} \tag{2}$$

where, n is the number of adjacent anchor nodes, $1/\hat{d}_i$ is a weighted value, which can be used to adjust the function and constrain the estimated coordinates of target node into the vicinity of the true location.

4 The Presented Algorithm

The improved IWO-based localization algorithm proposed in this paper is called IIWO-LA. It uses two stages to complete the node location estimation. In the first stage, the region of nodes is estimated by proactive estimation method, and in the second stage, the location of nodes is estimated by search optimization. During the execution of the algorithm, several measures were taken to improve the performance of algorithm. Firstly, the uniform design method is used to improve the random distribution of the initial population, which helps to improve the search efficiency of the algorithm.

Then, an adaptive standard deviation (SD) is used to replace the constant SD in the original IWO, which helps to improve the convergence speed of the algorithm, and makes it more exploitive.

4.1   First Stage—Proactive Regional Estimation

Most intelligent computing based localization algorithms using entire monitor area as the feasible solution space. Based on this understanding, we try to reasonably estimate the area where the nodes are located use the proactive regional estimation method. It can greatly reduce the range of feasible solutions, improve the global search speed and reduce the amount of iterative computation. the proactive regional estimation method can be expressed by:

$$
\begin{cases}
x_l = \max(x_i - R) \\
x_r = \min(x_i + R) \\
y_b = \max(y_i - R) \\
y_t = \min(y_i + R)
\end{cases}
\tag{3}
$$

where, x_{left}, x_{right}, y_{bottom} and y_{top} are the four boundaries of the rectangular estimation region, (x_i, y_i) are the coordinates of neighbor anchor node of the unknown node u, R is the maximum transmission range of sensor nodes.

4.2   Second Stage—Search Optimization

At this stage, the rectangular estimation area in the previous stage is the search space, and the search for the optimal solution is performed. Its processing steps are as follows:

Step 1: Using the uniform distribution method to generate n weed individual within the feasible search space S to form the initial weed population $P(G) = \{p_i, i = 1, 2, \cdots, n, n \le p_{\max}\}$.

Step 2: Calculate the fitness value $f(x, y)$ of each individual weed in the initial weed population use formula (2), and get the minimum, maximum and average fitness value;

Step 3: Use formula (4) to calculate the number of seeds that each weed can reproduce:

$$
s_{num} = floor(\frac{F_{\max} - f(p_i)}{F_{\max} - F_{\min}}(s_{\max} - s_{\min}) + s_{\min})
\tag{4}
$$

$F_{\max}$ and $F_{\min}$ are the maximum and minimum fitness value, $s_{\max}$ and $s_{\min}$ are the maximum and minimum number of seeds.

Step 4: Use formula (5) to calculate the adaptive SD of each weed:

$$\sigma_{iter,i} = \begin{cases} (1 + \gamma \frac{f(p_{iter,i}) - F_{iter,a}}{F_{iter,max} - F_{iter,a}})\sigma_{iter} & f(p_{iter,i}) > F_{iter,a} \\ (1 - \gamma \frac{F_{iter,a} - f(p_{iter,i})}{F_{iter,a} - F_{iter,min}})\sigma_{iter} & f(p_{iter,i}) \leq F_{iter,a} \end{cases} \tag{5}$$

where $F_{iter,a}$ is the average fitness value, γ represents a scaling factor.

Step 5: Use formula (6) to complete the generation and diffusion of seeds, so that the seeds after diffusion and the parent weed form a new weed population $P(G+1)$.

$$P_{i,s} = P_i + N(0, \sigma^2)(s_{min} \leq s \leq s_{max}) \tag{6}$$

where P_i indicates the position of the previous generation of weeds.

Step 6: Use formula (2) to calculate the fitness value of each individual weed in the new weed population.

Step 7: Determine whether the current population size exceeds the maximum allowable population size. If it exceeds, the survival of the fittest will be carried out.

Step 8: Determine whether the search stop condition is met. If not, turn to step 2; otherwise, determine the best weed individual of the population according to the fitness value, and take it as the optimal solution.

Step 9: Take the optimal solution obtained in the previous step as the best location estimation of unknown nodes, and output the location results.

5 Simulation Experiment and Analysis

Matlab software was use to carry out the simulation experiments in this paper. To verify the effectiveness and feasibility of the presented algorithm, we compare the proposed IIWO-LA algorithm with the classical IWO based localization algorithm (i.e. IWO-LA) and the classical PSO based localization algorithm (i.e. PSO-LA). The three algorithms are all intelligent evolutionary algorithms based on population, and the same population size and evolutionary times were used in the experiment.

The network coverage area is set as a rectangular area of $100 \times 100 \, m^2$. A total of 100 sensor nodes were randomly deployed within this rectangular area. The average of 30 experiments was taken as the experimental result.

The main metric used to evaluate the performance of the localization algorithm is set as the average localization error.

5.1 Experiment of Proactive Regional Estimation Effect

The schematic diagram of the results of prospective area estimation is shown in Fig. 1.

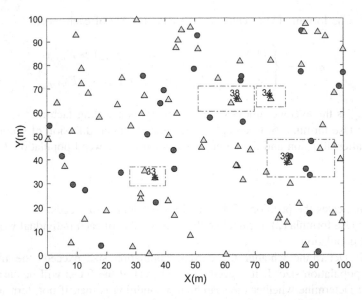

Fig. 1. Schematic diagram of regional estimation results

In Fig. 1, Circle represents anchor node, triangle represents unknown node, dashed rectangles represent the rectangular estimation area obtained in the first stage of the algorithm, and the star shape indicates the final location result of the unknown node. Because of the large number of unknown nodes, only a few unknown nodes are randomly selected in Fig. 1 to demonstrate the regional estimation effect and the final positioning effect. The numbers "33, 34, 36 and 38" in the figure are the unknown node numbers extracted.

As can be seen from Fig. 1, the proactive regional estimation method can reduce the feasible solution space of unknown nodes from the whole network area to the minimal range represented by each "dotted rectangle" in the graph, which makes the coverage of the search space can be completed with a smaller population size, and the search of the optimal solution can be completed with a smaller number of evolution times, which greatly accelerates the convergence rate, reduces the computational cost, and improves the feasibility and practicability of distributed applications.

5.2 Experiment of Uniform Design Effect

The schematic diagram of the uniform design (UD) method effect is shown in Fig. 2 and Fig. 3.

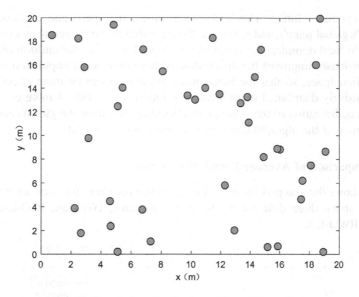

Fig. 2. Population distribution without UD method

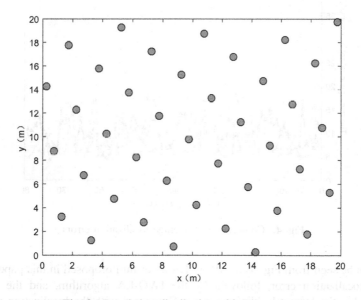

Fig. 3. Population distribution with UD method

Figure 2 indicates the initial population distribution when the UD is not used, and Fig. 3 indicates the initial population distribution after using the UD.

It can be seen from Fig. 2 that the randomly generated population does not guarantee uniform and effective coverage of the feasible solution space (there is a large-area blank phenomenon and individual overlap phenomenon), which is likely to deviate far from the optimal solution. This will directly affect the speed and efficiency of the algorithm's global search, and also make the algorithm prone to premature convergence and fall into local optimization. It can be seen from Fig. 3 that the uniform distribution method obviously improves the distribution of the initial weed population in the feasible solution space, so that the initial weed population can be more effectively and comprehensively distributed in the feasible solution space. This is more conducive to the search optimization of the subsequent algorithm, improves the global search speed and efficiency of the algorithm, and reduces the calculation cost.

5.3   Comparison of Average Localization Errors

Figure 4 shows the comparison of average localization errors for each unknown node using the above three different localization algorithms, IWO-LA, PSO-LA and the proposed IIWO-LA.

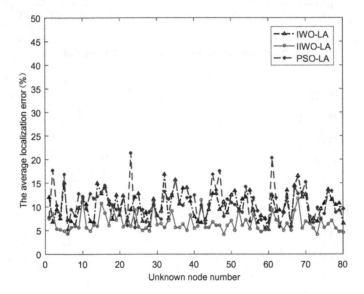

Fig. 4. Comparison of average localization errors

As can be seen from Fig. 4, the IIWO-LA algorithm proposed in this paper has the smallest localization error, followed by the IWO-LA algorithm, and the PSO-LA algorithm has the largest localization error. Compared with the localization results of the IWO-LA algorithm, the localization accuracy of the algorithm proposed in this paper is obviously improved, the maximum improvement accuracy is about 11.26%, and the average improvement accuracy is about 3.85%. This is mainly due to the adoption of several measures, such as regional estimation, uniform distribution and adaptive standard deviation.

5.4   Comparison of Localization in Different Situations

Figures 5 and Figs. 6 show the whole network average localization accuracy of the above three different algorithms under different ranging errors of 5% and 25%.

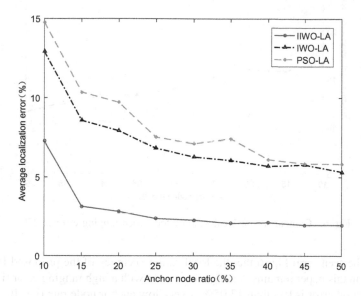

Fig. 5. Comparison of localization effect when ranging error is 5%

It can be seen from Fig. 5 that the localization error of IIWO-LA algorithm is kept at a low level when the ranging error is small. Even when the proportion of anchor nodes is 10%, the localization error is still less than 7.5%. Compared with IWO-LA and PSO-LA algorithms, the localization error of algorithm proposed in this paper is reduced by about 4.38% and 5.42% respectively.

As can be seen from Fig. 5 and 6, with the increase of the proportion of anchor nodes, the localization errors of the three algorithms are gradually reduced. This is mainly because unknown nodes can obtain more location reference information. Among them, the localization error of the IIWO-LA algorithm proposed in this paper is the smallest, it can maintain good stability under different ranging errors and shows that it is more suitable for complex environment. Otherwise, because the cost of anchor nodes is two orders of magnitude higher than that of ordinary nodes, the proportion of anchor nodes will directly affect the cost of the entire network. Under the same localization error requirements, the IIWO-LA algorithm requires the least number of anchor nodes, which can reduce the demand for the number of anchor nodes to the greatest extent, thereby greatly reducing the network cost.

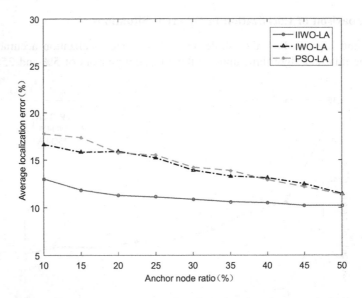

Fig. 6. Comparison of localization effect when ranging error is 25%

It can be seen form Fig. 6 that the localization accuracy of the proposed IIWO-LA algorithm in this paper remains at a high level even with a high ranging error (i.e. 25%). Its localization error is less than 13.05% at very low anchor node rate (i.e. 10%), and it is 3.14% less than that of IWO-LA algorithm and 3.48% less than that of PSO-LA algorithm on average.

6   Conclusion

As a key supporting technology of WSNs, localization research has attracted much attention. In this paper, an improved localization algorithm based on invasive weed optimization is presented. It uses two stages to complete the node location estimation. In the first stage, the region of nodes is estimated. In the second stage, the location of nodes is estimated. During the execution of the algorithm, several measures such as were taken to improve the performance of algorithm.

The experimental results show that the algorithm presented in this paper has higher localization accuracy and better stability under different ranging errors. This shows that the new algorithm is more suitable for node localization in complex environment with high ranging error. Moreover, for the same accuracy requirement, the new algorithm needs fewer anchor nodes, which is more conducive to the cost control of the system.

References

1. Rawat, P., Singh, K.D., Chaouchi, H., Bonnin, J.M.: Wireless sensor networks: a survey on recent developments and potential synergies. J. Supercomput. **68**(1), 1–48 (2013). https://doi.org/10.1007/s11227-013-1021-9
2. Khelifi, M., Moussaoui, S., Silmi, S., Benyahia, I.: Localisation algorithms for wireless sensor networks: a review. Int. J. Sensor Netw. **19**(2), 114–129 (2015)
3. Kulkarni, R.V., Forster, A., Venayagamoorthy, G.K.: Computational intelligence in wireless sensor networks: a survey. IEEE Commun. Surv. Tutorials **13**(1), 68–96 (2010)
4. Toral, S., Dobre, C., Dorronsoro, B., Gunes, M., Reina, D.G.: Computational intelligence in wireless sensor and ad hoc networks. Int. J. Distributed Sensor Netw. (2016)
5. Kannan, A.A., Mao, G., Vucetic, B.: Simulated annealing based wireless sensor network localization. JCP **1**(2), 15–22 (2016)
6. Gopakumar, A., Lillykutty, J.: Localization in wireless sensor networks using particle swarm optimization. In: IET Conference on Wireless, Mobile and Multimedia Networks, Mumbai, India, pp. 227–230 (2008)
7. Gumaida, B.F., Luo, J.: A hybrid particle swarm optimization with a variable neighborhood search for the localization enhancement in wireless sensor networks. Appl. Intell. **49**(10), 3539–3557 (2019). https://doi.org/10.1007/s10489-019-01467-8
8. Alomari, A., Phillips, W., Aslam, N., Comeau, F.: Swarm intelligence optimization techniques for obstacle-avoidance mobility-assisted localization in wireless sensor networks. IEEE Access **6**, 22368–22385 (2018)
9. Wang, W., Yang, Y., Wang, L., Lu, W.: PMDV-hop: An effective range-free 3D localization scheme based on the particle swarm optimization in wireless sensor network. KSII Trans. Internet Inf. Syst. **12**(1), 61–79 (2018)
10. Liu, Y., Jiao, Y.C., Zhang, Y.M., Tan, Y.Y.: Synthesis of phase-only reconfigurable linear arrays using multiobjective invasive weed optimization based on decomposition. Int. J. Antennas Propag. **2014**, 1–11 (2014)
11. Li, H., Jiao, Y.C., Zhang, L.: Hybrid differential evolution with a simplified quadratic approximation for constrained optimization problems. Eng. Optim. **43**(2), 115–134 (2011)
12. Zhang, Y., Liu, Y., Gan, J.: A novel localization algorithm based on invasive weed optimization in wireless sensor networks. In: 2018 26th International Conference on Geoinformatics, pp. 1–5. IEEE, Kunming, China, June 2018
13. Chen, Z., Zhang, L., Li, J., Sun, G.: Invasive weed optimization based localization algorithm for wireless sensor network. Comput. Eng. Appl. **50**(9), 77–82 (2014)

A Scientometric Analysis of Malware Detection Research Based on CiteSpace

Budong Xu[1], Yongqin Li[2(✉)], and Xiaomei Yu[3]

[1] Office of Information Technology, Shandong Normal University, Ji'nan, Shandong, China
[2] Faculty of Education, Shandong Normal University, Ji'nan, Shandong, China
976914572@qq.com
[3] School of Information Science and Engineering, Shandong Normal University, Ji'nan, China

Abstract. In recent years, the increasing number of malicious software has led to more and more serious security threats to computers or network. The researches have been devoting significant efforts to solve the numerous challenges in malware detection and a large amount of literature available which worthies deeply analyzing and sorting out to offer guidance for the developmental research on malicious code detection. In this paper, the visualized tool of CiteSpace is used to assess the current state and explore the trends of malware research based on the bibliographic records retrieved from the China National Knowledge Internet. We analyze the malware research in a scientific and systematic way and display the research status and possible development trend in this field concisely and intuitively, which provide the theoretical basis for the in-depth study of malware detection for the scientific research. Finally, the malware detection model is designed according to the analysis results of Mapping Knowledge Domain to achieve effective and efficient performance in malware detection.

Keywords: Malware detection · CiteSpace · Analysis · Visualization

1 Introduction

As an ever growing security threat, malware is one of the research hotspots and the malware detection remains an important area of research. In the last two decades, the computer security researchers invent a variety of new methods to detect malicious codes and protect computers and networks. The publications about malware research increase each year and involve an increasing number of subject categories. At present, malware research has acquired a great deal of harvest in scientific research and application. It is significantly necessary to summarize those studies and results with a scientometric analysis method and explore the potential development direction in the malware detection domain.

Taking the papers in the CNKI database as the research object, we use CiteSpace [1] to make quantitative statistics on the relevant documents in the past ten years. With the visualizations on Mapping Knowledge Domain including institutional cooperation,

X. Chen et al. (Eds.): ML4CS 2020, LNCS 12486, pp. 100–110, 2020.
https://doi.org/10.1007/978-3-030-62223-7_9

author cooperation, keyword co-occurrence, keyword clustering and time zone, the frontiers and research focuses on malware research are achieved, the development veins of malware detection is explored. Also, the distribution of research topics is obtained. Thus, the theoretical system of malware detection is preliminarily constructed. Finally, the malware detection model is designed according to the analysis results of mapping knowledge domain to achieve efficient performance.

The main contributions of this paper are summarized as follows:

- Knowledge mapping analysis on malware research is performed with the data derived from the CNKI database.
- Knowledge mapping analysis on the research hotspots and topic evolution of malware detection are achieved. The analysis results show the focused problems and corresponding strategies.
- A novel malware detection model is proposed according to the analysis results from the studies in the last decade.

The structure of this paper is as follow. In the second section, a brief overview of malware detection is reviewed and CiteSpace software is introduced. Afterwards, Knowledge mapping analysis on International papers about malware research are explored. And then, Knowledge mapping analysis on the research hotspots and topic evolution of malware detection are achieved., A still then, a novel malware detection model are presented. Finally, the paper is concluded and research directions are suggested.

2 Related Work

2.1 Malware Detection

There are several methods to deal with the threat brought by malware, including code analysis based and network features based malware detection [2]. With the program itself as the basis for malware detection, the code analysis based methods mainly extracts and explores the common features for following confirmatory analysis. On the other hand, the detection method based on network features mainly focuses on the host itself. With the comprehensive analysis of the network characteristics, behavior characteristics and basic attributes of the host, the network features based methods intend to find the susceptible hosts host and avoid the subsequent attacks.

At present, the code analysis methods attack most attention and obtain magnificent achievement in the past twenty years. Such methods have been widely used in real applications, such as management system in business, government and schools. The code analysis based methods focus on real-time protection and timely alarm. However, it is easy to be destroyed by the obfuscation and confusion technology, resulting in false negative and false positive results. As to the network features based malware detection, it is not received extensive attention and in-depth research though some publications are available here and there in International journals. Therefore, this paper mainly focuses on the publications on the code analysis based malware detection.

2.2 CiteSpace

The Bibliometric analysis is a generic process of domain analysis and visualization, which is a high-level analysis method to perform scientometric analysis on special research domains, such as educational technology, data science and so on. Several types of software are currently used including VOSViewer, CiteSpace, HistCite and SciMAT [3], in which CiteSpace is of particular concern in our malware research.

The CiteSpace is prevalently applied in many research fields including computer science engineering, information science and library science etc. As a visualization tool, it is competent for the task of assessing the current research state and exploring the trends of malware research based on the bibliographic records. In this way, these studies provide reference for the assessment of malware research, and it is helpful for the new researchers quickly integrate into the field. Furthermore, the analysis results are significant for the researchers to easily grasp the frontiers of malware research and obtain more valuable scientific information.

3 Data Analysis on Malware Research

With an advanced retrieval conducted on the subject of "malware", related data are collected from the CNKI database [4] covering the period from 2003 to 2020, and a total of 562 references are retrieved. The exported data mainly includes the topic, author, keywords, abstract, institution and other relevant information of each paper.

3.1 Analysis on Keyword in Malware Research

As shown in Fig. 1, there are keywords that appear frequently in malware research in the last 18 years, and the font size represents the frequencies of the keywords appearing in malware research. The larger the word, the more frequent the keyword appears. As we can see, high-frequency keywords include malware detection, machine learning, static analysis, dynamic analysis, deep learning and etc. According to the frequencies of the keywords, we discover that malware detection have been caused great interesting and notice in malware research. Furthermore, machine learning methods attack great attention in malware detection where static analysis and dynamic analysis play some roles. Moreover, a variety of publications focus on deep learning methods in malware research.

3.2 Analysis on Countries and Institutions in Malware Research

The countries and institutions have made outstanding contributions to the malware research are shown in Fig. 2. The size of the nodes reveals the importance that the countries contribute to the malware research. The top three countries with significant contribution are USA, China and India.

On the other hand, we discover the central position of some institutions presented in malware research. The larger the node is, the more centrality that appears to be. For example, Beijing University of posts and telecommunication shows some leading role

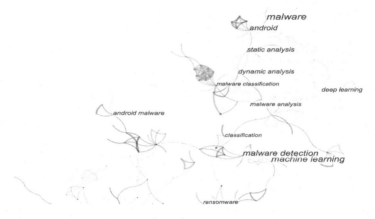

Fig. 1. Keywords in malware research

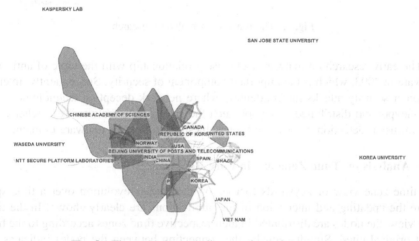

Fig. 2. The countries contribute to the malware research

in the malware research which can be seen by the centrality of the institutions. Overall, there is not much institutions which demonstrate significant leadership in malware research and cooperation between the institutions is relatively insufficient, and the research intensity needs to be strengthened.

3.3 Analysis on Time Line of Malware Research

In timeline view of CiteSpace, the whole network is to divide into several clusters, and the documents belonged to each cluster are arranged in chronological order. In this way, many phenomena can be observed about the development grain of malware research. From timeline view in Fig. 3, the development of malware research is clearly outlined during the year from 2003 to 2020.

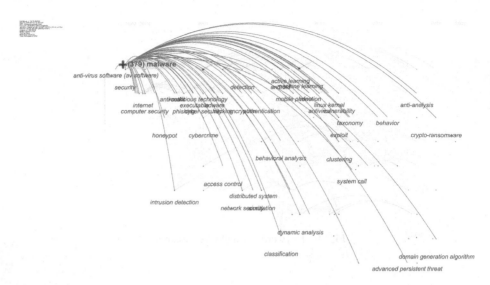

Fig. 3. The timeline of malware research

The early research on malware had closely relationship with the topic of anti-virus software in 2003, which is the important component of security. Subsequently, internet computer security attacks much attention where network deception technologies such as honeypot and distributed honeypot catch the sight of the malware researchers. and then intrusion detection comes a indispensable part in field of malware domain.

3.4   Analysis on Time Zone of Malware Research

The time zone view of keywords focuses on the studies evolution over a time span where the updating and interaction of the publications are clearly shown. In the time zone view, the nodes are distributed in their respective time zones according to the time point original cited. Simultaneously, the connection between the nodes indicates the inheritance relationship of topics under consideration.

Seen from time zone view in Fig. 4 and Fig. 5, the direction in malware research experiences the security and internet security in the beginning, and then information security as well as cyber security, still then mobile security around 2015. The research content on malware includes the early intrusion detection, to the malware detection, even the present android malware detection. The prevalent technologies applied in malware research focuses on data mining at first, and then advanced to machine learning, and gradually entered the prosperity of deep learning at present. During the evolution of malware research in timezone (shown more clearly in Fig. 5), we discover that malware detection is the most significant malware research context in the field of security domain, in which dynamic analysis based machine learning occupies the most important position for the scholars and researchers.

In the following section, we focus on the studies on malware detection, especially the methods based on machine learning and deep learning.

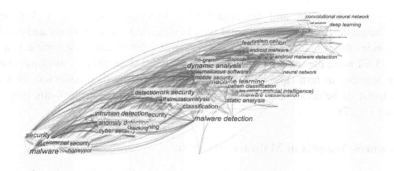

Fig. 4. The timezone of malware research

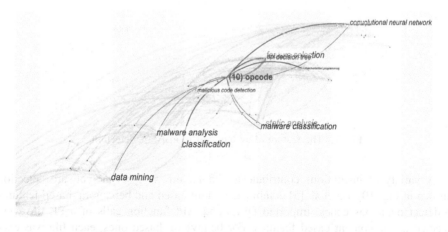

Fig. 5. The evolution of malware research in timezone

Fig. 6. The feature of OpCode in malware detection

4   Research on Malware Detection

Equipped with the knowledge of malware research, we confirm that the detection of malware is an area of major concern not only to the research community but also to the general public. The early techniques for malware detection are categorized broadly into signature-based detection and behavior-based detection. Since the techniques of signature-based detection are mature and widely used in real applications and products, it is no longer the research focus and is away from the vision of scientific research. From 2003 till now, the interesting techniques includes data mining, machine learning and deep learning in turn (Shown in Fig. 4). Moreover, the data collected for feature analysis insist of behavior analysis, static analysis and dynamic analysis (shown in Fig. 6 and Fig. 7).

4.1 Features Analysis in Malware Detection

There are static and dynamic features devote to an effective malware detection, which derived from the binary instructions and PE files (shown in Fig. 6, 7, 8 and 9). Generally, the static features consist of OpCodes, N-grams, system calls and so on (shown in Fig. 6, 7 and 8), while the dynamic features include call sequences (shown in Fig. 9) and etc. With the deep development of the research work on malware detection, the hybrid analysis on static, dynamic and behavior features are adopted jointly to perform efficient malware detection, especially in the machine learning and deep learning approaches (shown in Fig. 8).

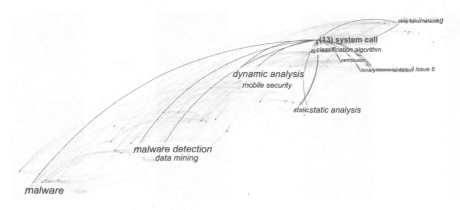

Fig. 7. The feature of system call in malware detection

A variety of institutions contribute to the feature analysis in malware detection (shown in Fig. 10). Lu et al. [5] combined content based and behavioral based features to detect malicious codes. Imported DLLs and API function calls of a PE file were selected as the content based features. For behavioral based ones, each file was executed with a VMware tool and the behaviors were recorded and represented as a vector. Elhadi et al. [6] built API call graph with API calls collecting from the executable file in which the operating system resources were used as nodes, and the references between the nodes were represented as edges. Hence the nodes have two attributes of API call and operating system resource, while the graph label is the API calls itself or the operating system resource. In the study of [7], the authors designed two schemes to incorporate the three single-view features of byte N-gram, OpCode N-gram and format

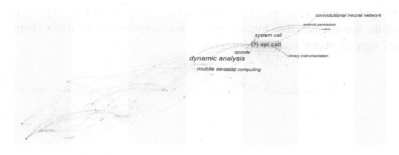

Fig. 8. The feature of api call in malware detection

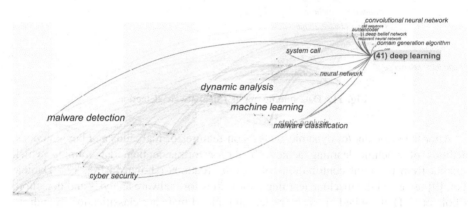

Fig. 9. The methods of deep learning applied in malware detection

information, and fully exploited complementary information of those features to discover the malicious codes in a program.

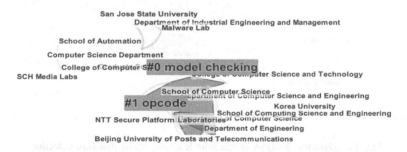

Fig. 10. Institutions contribute to feature analysis in malware detection

4.2   The Evolution of Approaches Applied in Malware Detection

After the step of feature extraction, various methods can be chosen to perform malware
detection. In the prosperous period of data mining, classification and clustering were

the two popular approaches attracted much attention (shown in Fig. 11). Ye et al. [8] surveyed the mainly used data mining techniques including decision tree, naive bayes classifier, support vector machine and so on.

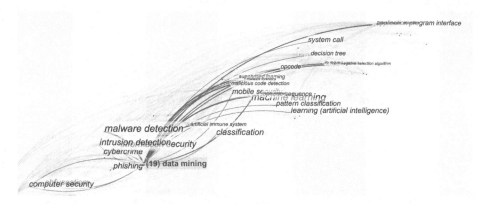

Fig. 11. Data mining applied in malware detection

After the static and/or dynamic analysis on features of malicious and benign codes, methods of machine learning achieve better performance than data mining which benefits from the joint contributions of various features (shown in Fig. 12). Daniele et al. [9] reviewed the machine learning approaches for malware analysis and detection. Nikola et al. [10] studied the machine learning aided malware classification in android applications.

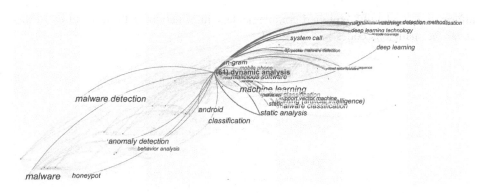

Fig. 12. Dynamic analysis in machine learning based malware detection

Without the participation of artificial expert knowledge, deep learning gains more and more favors in the recent several years (shown in Fig. 9), in which the models of convolutional neural network, recurrent neural network and deep belief network occupy the dominant position. However, in the latest research result, significant achievements in the fields of graph mining and natural language processing are introduced to gain improved performance in malware detection. Wang et al. [11] proposed a data-driven graph matching framework to learn the program representation and similarity metric via Graph Neural Network in malware detection. Yu et al. [12] presented a novel framework for binary code graph learning, in which BERT pre-training model is introduced to capture the semantic features, the Message Passing Neural Network (MPNN) is used to extract the structural information and a CNN-based model is applied to capture the node order information.

From the connection in the figures above, we can see that feature analysis runs basis role through the whole periods of malware detection. It indicates that malicious code detection is mainly based on valuable features extracted. Currently, the methods for malware detection research is based on the previous research results and are constantly adjusted and optimized. There is promising to be more achievements introduced into the field of malware detection and gain better performance in malware detection.

5   Conclusions and Future Work

In the paper, a visual tool of CiteSpace is introduced to analyze the research on malware with the data derived from the CNKI database. With a scientometric analysis method, the research hotspots and topic evolution of malware detection are studied in depth. The analysis results show the focused problems and corresponding strategies in malware detection. Finally, a possible malware detection model is proposed according to the analysis results from the studies in the last decade.

In the future work, a novel model for malware detection would be studied which merges the achievements of deep learning and knowledge graph.

Acknowledgment. This work is partly funded by the National Nature Science Foundation of China (No.61672329, No.61773246), Shandong Provincial Project of Graduate Education Quality Improvement (No. SDYY18058, No.SDYJG19171), Industry-University Cooperation and Education Project of Ministry of Education (No.201801165024, No. 201802002055, No.201901025009, No.201901140022, No.201902095002, No.201902173028, No.2019022-93009, No.201902009008).

References

1. Chen, C., Ibekwe-Sanjuan, F., Hou, J.: The structure and dynamics of cocitation clusters: a multiple-perspective cocitation analysis. J. Am. Soc. Inform. Sci. Technol. **61**(7), 1386–1409 (2010)
2. Demontis, A., Melis, M., Biggio, B., Maiorca, D., Arp, D., Rieck, K., et al.: Yes, machine learning can be more secure! a case study on android malware detection. IEEE Trans. Dependable Secure Comput. **16**, 711–724 (2017)
3. Chen, C., Song, M.: Visualizing a field of research: a methodology of systematic scientometric reviews. PLoS ONE **14**(10), e0223994 (2019)
4. CNKI. https://www.cnki.net/. Accessed 21 May 2020

5. Lu, Y., Din, S., Zheng, C., Gao, B.: Using multi-feature and classifier ensembles to improve malware detection. J. CCIT **39**(2), 57–72 (2010)
6. Elhadi, A.A., Maarof, M.A., Osman, A.H.: Malware detection based on hybrid signature behaviour application programming interface call graph. Am. J. Appl. Sci. **9**, 283–288 (2012)
7. Bai, J., Wang, J.: Improving malware detection using multi-view ensemble learning. Secu. Commun. Netw. **9**, 4227–4541 (2016)
8. Ye, Y., Li, T., Adjeroh, D., et al.: A survey on malware detection using data mining techniques. ACM Comput. Surv. **50**(3), 1–40 (2017)
9. Ucci, D., Aniello, L., Baldoni, R.: Survey of machine learning techniques for malware analysis. Comput. Secur. **81**, 123–147 (2017)
10. Milosevic, N., Dehghantanha, A., Choo, K.-K.R.: Machine learning aided android malware classification. Comput. Electric. Eng. **61**, 266–274 (2017). ISSN 0045-7906
11. Wang, S., Chen, Z., Yu, X., Li, D., et al.: Heterogeneous graph matching networks for unknown malware detection. In: Proceedings of the Twenty-Eighth International Joint Conference on Artificial Intelligence (IJCAI), pp. 3762–3770 (2019)
12. Yu, Z., Cao, R., Tang, Q., Nie, S., et al.: Order matters: semantic-aware neural networks for binary code similarity detection. In: Association for the Advancement of Artificial Intelligence (AAAI), pp. 1–8 (2020)

Malware Detection Based on Static and Dynamic Features Analysis

Budong Xu[1], Yongqin Li[2(✉)], and Xiaomei Yu[3]

[1] Office of Information Technology, Shandong Normal University, Ji'nan, Shandong, China
[2] Faculty of Education, Shandong Normal University, Ji'nan, Shandong, China
976914572@qq.com
[3] School of Information Science and Engineering, Shandong Normal University, Ji'nan, China

Abstract. Machine learning algorithms are widely used in malware detection where successful analysis on static and dynamic features plays a crucial role in process of detecting malicious samples. In this paper, the potential malicious features are summarized with their effectiveness in detection. Moreover, the machine learning approaches based on static and dynamic features analysis are studied with both merits and limitations. Finally, possible solutions are proposed and novel malware detection are put forward, which shows superiority in performance comparison.

Keywords: Malicious features · Static analysis · Dynamic analysis · Malware detection

1 Introduction

Malware detection is a highly concerned issue in computer security. Malicious features play a fundamental role in a successful detection for malware. The early signature-based methods rely on domain knowledge of malicious features manually extracted, while the behavior-based approaches identify malicious behavior from suspicious activity and potential patterns. However, signature-based methods are defeated by concealment techniques and behavior-based approaches confronted with challenging problems of resource cost and false detection.

To settle the problems mentioned above, machine learning based methods attract the most attention which rely on static and/or dynamic features artificially extracted. Suffering from the evolution of malware environments, the original well-designed features are not effective in detecting a new malware family. Therefore, heavy and inefficient feature engineering poses an enormous challenge for researchers to overcome.

In this paper, we summarize the significant features mainly used in detecting malicious samples and classify them according to static and dynamic analysis for machine learning. Meanwhile, related machine learning methods are studied with both advantages and disadvantages. Finally, novel malware detection methods are proposed to reduce the cost of artificial feature engineering and to achieve features of self-learning to improve the accuracy and efficiency in malware detection.

© Springer Nature Switzerland AG 2020
X. Chen et al. (Eds.): ML4CS 2020, LNCS 12486, pp. 111–124, 2020.
https://doi.org/10.1007/978-3-030-62223-7_10

The structure of this paper is outlined as follow. In the second section, a brief overview of malicious features is classified according to the detection mode. Afterwards, static and dynamic features are summarized for effective and efficient malware detection respectively. And then, novel intelligent methods are proposed and research results are presented. Finally, the paper is concluded and research directions are suggested.

2 Malicious Features

The signature-based malicious code detection is the standard technique in most commercial antivirus software. In signature-based methods, some techniques such as lexical analysis, parsing, control flow, and data flow analysis are always applied to analyze known static features, while lack their power on unknown malwares with new features. Behavior information collected from the execution environment plays important role in behavior-based malware detection, such as system calls traces, network access, as well as file and memory modifications. However, the behavior analysis on features during running time loses its superiority as it confronts with large database, since it is difficult to confirm the monitoring activity and determine the stop time.

Machine learning based malware detection achieves significant development in recent years due to its scalability, rapidity and flexibility. The stage of feature extraction is of great importance in successful malware detection where static analysis and dynamic analysis are mainly used to capture malicious feature representations. Static feature analysis learns statistical characteristics like API calls, N-grams, and so on, while dynamic behavior analysis relies heavily on the simulation in operation environment to arouse potential malware behaviors. In most malicious code detection tasks, several feature representations and behavior activities bend their efforts to reach a malware detection solution. Schultz et al. [1] used three static features of PE head, string sequence and byte sequence to detect malware. Kolter and Maloof [2] reached a better solution with N-gram instead of non-overlapping byte sequence features for malware detection.

In general, static features are received as OpCodes (execution operation codes) extracted from executable files, while dynamic features are obtained by monitoring system calls, operations and exceptions. In the following section, we summary the static and dynamic features for malware detection respectively, so as to explore effective solutions in detecting malicious executable codes without artificial supports from domain experts.

3 Static Features in Malware Detection

PE (Windows Portable Executable) is a common file format for Windows operating systems. As the aim of most attackers, PE files are the majority malware samples at present. In static analysis on features extracted, PE files (Portable Executable file) are always considered as the target of binary or source files. The PE files, which are used in Windows operating system, include comprehensive information about the segments of the program that forms the main part of the file. They mainly components are shown as follows.

- .text file is formed with the code and the entry point of the application, which constitutes the main part of the file and contains all the code to be analyzed
- .data file is made up of various type of data
- .idata file describes a Dynamic-Linking Library (DLL) or the list of imported APIs for an application
- .edata file represents a Dynamic-Linking Library (DLL) or the list of exported APIs for an application

Static features are always collected by disassembling the infected file without executing it. To translate an executable program into an equivalent high-level-language program, the disassemble tools (e.g., IDA Pro) and/or the memory dumper tools (e.g., OllyDump and LordPE) can be helpful. The former expresses malicious codes with Intel $\times86$ assembly instructions, while the later dumps protected codes in main memory into a file. With such tools, the binary codes are disassembled, and then the assembly codes are parsed, still then the syntax tree of program is generated. In this way, low-level information could be extracted for analysis, such as Windows API calls, byte N-grams, strings, OpCodes (operational codes), Control Flow Graphs (CFGs), Data-Flow Graphs (DFGs) and System calls.

3.1 API Calls/System Calls

A program is a sequence of instructions to manipulate information including creating, deleting, reading, writing, or computing new information, etc. With the intermediary of the APIs (application programming interface), these information is available which is done with the resources of a computer. Therefore, Windows API calls are used by almost all programs to send requests to the Windows Operating System, which reflects the behavior of a piece of code like malware. With the advantages of strong representations on documents and being easily extracted, Windows API calls are suitable to represent static features and describe the documents in malware detection tasks. For example, the associations among Windows APIs may capture the underlying semantics of malware's behaviors, which are essential features used in malware detection.

Hofmeyr et al. treated API call sequences as a kind of features of a malware. In [3], short sequences of system calls executed by running programs were used to distinguish normal operating characteristics from abnormal ones. And then the larger hamming distance of sequences than given threshold were reported as anomalies. With the representations of binary codes, an extensive research on API calls was under consideration which includes Bergeron et al. [4], Xu et al. [5], and Geng et al. [6].

In recently five years, Ye et al. [7] presented Intelligent Malware Detection System (IMDS) and later CIMDS which achieved effective malware detection with analysis on Windows API execution sequences called by Portable Executable (PE) files. And then an interpretable classifier based on the analysis of API calls by a PE file was developed to detect malware from large and imbalanced gray list [8]. Lee et al. built a code graph with system call sequences. In [9], they classified API calls to 128 groups and optimized the large graph for every binary program. Based on the comparison of malicious code graph with benign ones, metamorphic malware detection works well even though code obfuscation methods are available. Asha et al. [10] developed an efficient system to detect the malwares using API call sequences, and classified malicious type as worms, virus, Trojans, or normal.

Conceptually, a Windows application can be mapped to a stream of Windows API calls. And monitoring the call stream provides insights into the behavior of an application effectively. Therefore, most of the existing run-time malware detection methods use the information available in Windows Application Programming Interface (API) calls. They work well with code obfuscation and gain good performance in both detection ratio and accuracy.

3.2   OpCode

Generally, a program is formed with a series of ordered assembly instructions in which an OpCode (executable Operational Code) is a key component in a machine language instruction that identifies the operation to be executed. With the ability to reflect program functionality, the OpCodes reveal significant statistical differences between malware and benign codes. Moreover, the rare OpCodes have more effective detection abilities than the common ones.

In the past studies, scientific evidence shows that the malware samples derived from the same source code or belong to the same family often share a large number of instruction blocks. Bilar [11] et al. proposed a detection mechanism for malicious code through statistical analysis of OpCode distributions. In his remarkable research, malicious OpCode frequency distribution deviates significantly from benign ones, and rarer OpCodes seem to have more frequency variation than common ones. His work verified the ability of single OpCode in identifying and differentiating malware in detection tasks.

Santos et al. [12] developed a series of malware detection models based on the frequency of the appearance of OpCode sequences. They focused on detecting obfuscated malware variants with the appearance frequency of OpCode sequences. And then they calculated a weight for each operational code to measure the relevance of the OpCode to malicious and benign codes according to the frequency it appears in malware or in benign codes. Continually, they proposed Mutual Information to measure the statistical dependence of the OpCode frequency and the executable class. Finally, they used Weighted Term Frequency (WTF) [13] to make suitable feature vector extracted from files and calculated the Cosine similarity measure between two feature vectors.

As the text-based OpCode sequences extraction cannot represent the true behaviors of an executable. Runwal et al. [14] computed the similarity of executable files based on OpCode graphs and applied the technique to detect metamorphic malware families with a simple graph similarity measurement. Ding et al. [15] presented a control flow-based method to extract executable OpCode behaviors, which can fully represent the behavior characteristics of an executable. With OpCode behaviors represented as OpCode sequences, Duan et al. [16] developed an OpCode running tree to simulate the dynamic execution of a program, and OpCode N-grams are extracted to describe the features of an executable files. With two LSTM layers and one mean-pooling layer to obtain the feature representations of OpCode sequences in malicious files, Renjie Lu [17] performed static analysis for malware detection based on OpCode sequence patterns automatically learned.

These studies demonstrate the high reliability of OpCodes in determining the maliciousness of an executable files. It is proved that OpCodes can be used as a powerful representation for executable files and be used as reliable static features to achieve effective malware detection.

3.3   N-Gram

An N-gram is formed with n symbols in a given sequence and N-grams are all sub sequences of a larger sequence with a length of N. By treating a file as a sequence of bytes, bytes of N-gram are extracted by looking at the unique combination of every n consecutive bytes as an individual feature. Neither knowledge of the file format nor the dynamic analysis is required, bytes of N-gram attack particularly attention in malware detection. Besides, more information from both headers and the binary code sections of an executable file could also be available. And then N-grams which derive from code generators, compilers, and programming environments could be used to detect code features, even further to capture coding styles and behavioral features. Moreover, since the captured features are implicit in the extracted N-grams, it is difficult for the attackers to write deceptive software to fool N-gram analysis even being given full access to the detection algorithm.

Over the past decade, many researches have been conducted unknown malware detection based on the binary code content. Kephart et al. [18] provided one of the earliest instances of N-gram for malware analysis, using byte 3-gram to classify infected boot-sectors. Schultz et al. [19] considered DLL imports, Strings, and byte N-gram as features, evaluating them with a number of different classifiers. To some extent, N-gram based model had the highest rate in malware detection. Abou-Assaleh et al. [20] explored the idea to automatically detect new malicious code based on byte N-gram analysis. After collecting N-grams from training data, the most frequent N-grams with their normalized frequency represents a class profile. And the CNG method is applied to achieve effective detection relied on the profiles of class representations. Shafiq et al. [21] discovered that conditional N-gram exhibits more meaningful representation than traditional one in file's statistical properties. Hence, they captured and leveraged this correlation structure for embedded malware detection. Their work is the first anomaly based malware detection approach that has the capability to locate the position of the infection in a malicious file. Fang et al. [22] proposed an N-gram based malicious code feature extraction algorithm with statistical language model where the N-gram features of the sample set were extracted and the features of the malicious code were obtained exactly.

Considering that a short length N-gram is easily extracted, while the underlying characteristics in executable files are better represented in a long N-gram, Parvin et al. [23] presented an efficient feature extraction with both adjacent and non-adjacent bi-grams to gain more information and win better accuracy. Raff et al. [24] discovered significant unreported issues with byte N-gram features. Firstly, with N-grams learned mostly from string content in an executable and items obtained from the PE header (which also contains strings), a possible preference of 6-gram may be large enough to regularly capture a whole x86 instruction. To capture three sequential assembly instructions, N-gram of at least 12 bytes in length is necessary for most cases and up to 45 bytes for extreme cases. Secondly, N-grams are computationally expensive and exhibit diminishing returns with more data, are prone to over-fitting and do not seem to carry information much stronger than what is more readily available from the PE header and ASCII strings. Finally, as a limited portion of an executable code and with limited information to provide, N-gram can be in conjunction with other features to achieve more effective solution in malware detection. Zak et al. [25] also performed byte N-gram analysis on only specific sub-sections of the binary files. They discovered that byte N-gram can be learned from code regions, while no new information is necessarily learned. Moreover, they declared that assembly N-gram maybe not as effective as previously thought and that disambiguating instructions by their binary OpCode is critical for model generalization.

In the past several decades, N-gram is regarded as the basic features commonly used in sequence-based malicious code detection methods. The empirical results from previous work suggested that, while short length N-gram is easier to extract, the characteristics of the underlying executable file are better represented in lengthier N-gram. However, with increasing the length of N-gram, the feature space grows in an exponential manner and much space and computational resources are demanded. Therefore, feature selection turns to be the most challenging step in establishing an accurate detection system based on byte N-gram. At present, novel solutions suggest that N-gram should be in conjunction with other features to jointly achieve better performance in malware detection.

3.4 Control Flow Graph

Since a graph to represent the control flow of a program, Control Flow Graph (CFG) is widely used in analysis of software and has been deeply studied. CFG is a directed graph, where each node represents a statement of the program and each edge represents control flow between the statements. Here statements may be assignments, copy statements, branches, etc. Control-flow analysis detects control dependencies among different instructions, such as dominance relations, loops and recursive procedure calls.

In the past several years, some malware detection approaches have been proposed based on Control Flow Graph. Lo et al. [26] introduced CFG in the Malicious Code Filter (MCF) project. An executable program is cut into blocks while looking for key operations (such as network access events and file operations) in a program to determine malicious codes. Later, Bruschi et al. [27] built labeled inter-procedural control flow graph (CFGPN). The corresponding CFGPN is compared with the control flow graph of a normalized malware (CFGM) so as to verify whether CFGPN contains a sub-graph which is isomorphic to CFGM. In this way, the problem of detecting malware is reduced to the sub-graph isomorphism problem. Considering that a generic inter-procedural control flow graph has large but highly sparse nodes, the well-known NP-complete problem of isomorphism can be efficiently computed and effective malware detection is achieved.

Considering that the CFG is composed of nodes and edges where each assembler consists of four types of instruction: non-conditional jumps (jmp), conditional jumps (jcc), function calls (call) and function returns (ret), Bonfante et al. [28] built CFG based on six types of node, and then reduced the CFG which becomes a signature for each file to achieve effective malicious codes detection. Zhao [29] presented a malware detection based on features extracted from the control flow graph of PE files where the features are information about nodes, edges and sub-graphs in CFG from each executable file.

Shahid et al. [30] presented Annotated Control Flow Graph (ACFG) to efficiently detect metamorphic malware. Firstly, an ACFG for each function in the program was built by annotating CFG of a binary program. A program signature was then represented by the set of corresponding ACFGs which captures the control flow semantics of a program. Finally, a program signature was used for graph and pattern matching to analyze and detect metamorphic malware since a program which contains part of the control flow of a training malware sample could be classified as malware. Their work verified that an ACFG contains more information and hence provides more accuracy than a CFG. Nguyen et al. [31] proposed an enhanced form of CFG, known as lazy-binding CFG to reflect the malicious behaviors. With the recent advancement of deep learning techniques, they presented a method of producing image-based representation from the generated CFG. As deep learning is very popular to perform image classification on very large dataset, the proposed approach can be applied for malware detection on with very high accuracy. Ma et al. [32] constructed a control flow graph of the application from source code and obtained API information to build API data sets of Boolean, frequency and time-series data sets. And then three detection models were developed focusing on API calling, API frequency and API sequence respectively. Finally, an ensemble model was achieved for effective Android malware detection.

As an appealing representation model, CFG is always used to visualize the structure of executable files which reveals another semantic aspect of programs. CFG has been successfully applied in detection of simple malware. Moreover, to detect complex malware such as polymorphic or metamorphic ones, recent researches inclined to improve the simple CFG with beneficial information such as API calls on the CFG. Converting the resulted sparse graph to a vector to decrease the complexity of graph mining algorithms, a specific feature selection is utilized and different classification approaches have been qualified. The experimental results manifested the contribution of these approaches in both accuracy and false detection rate measurements in comparison with the simple graph modifications.

3.5 Hybrid of Static Features

The significant researches on malware detection show empirically that the combination of some features is always better than any single feature in terms of detection accuracy. Schultz et al. [33] first applied the data mining method to detect malware where three static features of PE head, string sequence and byte sequence are used respectively. Some studies focus on expanding features at different levels of abstraction, rather than using more features at a single level of abstraction. Masud et al. [34] developed a classifier based on a hybrid feature set with three different kinds of features from the executable files at different levels of abstraction. They are binary N-gram extracted from binary executable files and assembly instruction sequences obtained from the disassembled executable files.

Eskandari et al. [35] proposed machine learning method based on the simple CFG and API calls to detect metamorphic malware where CFG was used to understand semantic of malware. With API called in CFG, more semantic aspects of new malware were got to reach successful malware detection. In the following study [36], they presented a robust semantic based method to detect unknown malwares with combination of a visualize CFG and API calls. Extracting CFG from programs and combining it with extracted API calls, a new representation model of API-CFG was constructed with much information about executable files. To achieve significant improvement on time complexity, the control flow graphs were converted to a set of feature vectors. Finally, the new model made a definite improvement over N-gram based malware detection.

In the latest research from Yan et al. [37], the gray scale image was extracted from raw binary file and then CNN was used to get the structure features of a malware from its local image patterns. Moreover, OpCode sequences were extracted by decompilation tool where LSTM was applied to learn features about malicious code sequences and patterns. With CNN and LSTM networks to automatically learn features from the raw data and to capture the malicious file structure patterns as well as code sequence patterns, the new model greatly reduced the cost of artificial features engineering.

3.6 Some Newly Introduced Features

Considering that certain malicious behaviors appear in all variants of a certain malware, Christodorescu et al. [38] proposed semantics-aware malware detection framework where malicious behavior was described with templates. Since the algorithm is semantic rather than purely syntactic, the templates of instruction sequences consisting with variables and symbolic constants have abilities of resisting common obfuscations.

In studies of Kim and Moon [39], the VBScript malware was represented as a dependency graph where every script code was transformed to a semantic one. In this way, a directed graph representing the relationships among lines of the semantic code was generated and the detection was achieved based on finding maximum sub-graph isomorphism.

As the relationships among different file samples may imply their interdependence and can provide critical information about their properties and characteristics, Ye et al. [40] combined both file content and file relations as features to detect malware. The content in files are API calls extracted from the content of malicious and benign PE files, while the file relations refer to the co-presence or absence of files in the computer of all cloud users.

Besides, file-to-machine relation graphs and file-to-file relation graphs were also introduced as the features for malware detection. Chau et al. [41] inferred the file reputations by analyzing file-to-machine relations, and Tamersoy et al. [42] achieved effective malware detection with the features of file-to-file relation graphs.

Moreover, Yan et al. [43] insisted on ensemble methods where some simple metadata features were added as a description of global information. These metadata features are easy to obtain such as the size of malware source files, the starting address of the byte file, the size of decompiled file, number of rows and the length of different PE segments.

4 Dynamic Features in Malware Detection

With sophisticated techniques such as packing and obfuscation to avoid malware detection, zero-day attacks and false positives become the most challenging problems in detecting malware. Hence dynamic features play a crucial role in process of detecting malicious samples. Operating system events are valuable dynamic features mainly used in dynamic analysis based approaches, such as API calls, I/O requests, instruction traces, registry changes, memory writes, resource locks and battery consumption.

To obtain the valuable dynamic features, dynamic analysis is exerted on infected files in simulated environment (a debugger or a virtual machine or an emulator) to trace its malicious functions. By running in a virtual environment, Tian et al. [44] extracted API call sequences from executable files. In [45], Firdausi et al. extracted the behaviors of malware samples in a sandbox environment using Anubis [45]. Alberto et al. [46] automatically identified the sub-sequences of execution traces where malicious activity happened, hence made further manual analysis and understand malware more easily. Based on dynamic features concerning resources usage and system calls, which are jointly collected during executing the application, an execution trace is then split in shorter chunks that are analyzed with machine learning techniques to detect local malicious behaviors.

Donggao et al. [47] constructed a practical malware detection system where API call sequences were introduced to capture activities of a program. Based on the malicious behavior features of software, such as variable-length N-gram, API call order extracted from API call sequence, more new malware were discovered compared with the solution based on fixed-length N-gram features. Kakisim et al. [48] analyzed different dynamic features with common malware detection approaches. With separately different features obtained in dynamic analysis, such as API calls, usage system library and operations, they observed the contributions of these features to malware detection and evaluated the performance of some dynamic analysis based malware detection and classification approaches.

In dynamic feature analysis based malware detection, the simulated environment must be invisible to the malware since the malware writer may use tools like anti-virtual machine and Anti-emulation to hide their malware functions if they are under analysis. Dynamic analysis fails to detect activities of interest if the target changes since the behavior depending on trigger conditions such as the existence of a specific file or specific day is only a single execution path which may be examined for each attempt. Furthermore, since it takes time for a malware sample to expose all its behaviors while running, dynamic analysis is often more time consuming and requires more resources than static analysis.

5 Hybrid Feature Representations for Malware Detection

Hybrid feature representations combine both static and dynamic features to jointly achieve effective malware detection.

Some researchers focused on graphs (control flow graph, call graph, code graph) where different features were used to build the node graphs. Lee et al. [50] constructed call graph by transforming operations on PE file where the nodes were system calls and the edges were system call sequences. Then the call graph minimized into code graph to speed up the analysis and comparison on graphs. Guo et al. [51] proposed a hybrid framework which took advantage of both static and dynamic binary translation features to detect malicious functions. They applied behaviors in Control Flow Graph (CFG), and then critical API call graph based on CFG was generated to do sub-graph matching.

Table 1. Hybrid features for malware detection.

Author & Paper	Static Features	Dynamic Features
Lu et al. [49]	Imported DLLs, API function calls	Behavior vector
Lee et al. [50]	System call graph	System call sequence
Guo et al. [51]	API calls, Control Flow Graph	Behavior Control Flow Graph
Elhadi et al. [52]	API calls	Operating system resources
Santos et al. [53]	OpCodes	System calls, operations, and exceptions
Bai et al. [54]	Byte N-gram, OpCode N-gram	Format information
Zhang et al. [55]	OpCodes	API call sequence

Santos et al. [53] proposed a hybrid malware detection tool that utilized a set of features obtained from static and dynamic analysis of malicious codes. Static features were obtained by mining OpCodes from the executable files, and dynamic features were obtained by monitoring system calls, operations, and exceptions. Zhang et al. [55] proposed a hybrid feature based approach to detect variant malware based on multi-types of features obtained. Firsrly, OpCodes were represented as a bi-gram model and API calls were represented as a vector of frequency. And then principal component analysis was introduced to optimize the representations and improve the convergence speed. Still then a convolutional neural network was adopted for OpCode based feature embedding and a back-propagation neural network was applied for API based feature embedding respectively. Finally, these features were embedded to train a detection model.

In hybrid analysis, static features such as permission, API calls based on used-permission, reflection API, cryptographic API, dynamic loading of code are always combined with dynamic features such as file operations, network operations, phone events, data leaks, dynamically loaded code, dynamically registered broadcast receivers (Shown in Table 1). Moreover, as seen from previous studies, permissions are used mostly as a feature along with dynamic features like logged information, API call traces and network traffics in hybrid features analysis to achieve efficient malware detection. Generally, multi-features jointly achieve effective malware detection solution based on hybrid analysis on static and dynamic features.

6 Conclusions and Future Work

Malicious features play a vital foundational role in combating the rapidly growing number of malware variants. In this paper, we categorize available features into three groups, namely, static features, dynamic features and hybrid features. Additionally, the potential malicious features are summarized with their effectiveness in detection. We discuss solutions used in the recent studies and analyze evaluation measures utilized.

In the future work, with the deep learning methods concerned, we will explore novel solutions based on multi-features to obtain improved performance in malware detection.

Acknowledgment. This work is partly funded by the National Nature Science Foundation of China (No.61672329, No.61773246), Shandong Provincial Project of Graduate Education Quality Improvement (No. SDYY18058, No.SDYJG19171), Industry-University Cooperation and Education Project of Ministry of Education (No.201801165024, No. 201802002055, No.201901025009, No.201901140022, No.201902095002, No.201902173028, No.2019022-93009, No.201902009008).

References

1. Schultz, M.G., Eskin, E., Zadok, F., Stolfo, S.J.: Data mining methods for detection of new malicious executables. In: Proceedings 2001 IEEE Symposium on Security and Privacy. S&P 2001, pp. 38–49. IEEE (2000)
2. Kolter, J.Z., Maloof, M.A.: Learning to detect and classify malicious executables in the wild. J. Mach. Learn. Res. **7**, 2721–2744 (2006)
3. Hofmeyr, S., Forrest, S., Somayaji, A.: Itrusion detection using sequences of system calls. J. Comput. Secur. **6**, 151–180 (1998)
4. Bergeron, J., Debbabi, M., Desharnais, J.M., Erhioui, M., Tawbi, N.: Static detection of malicious code in executable programs. Int. J. Req. Eng. **2001**, 79 (2001)
5. Xu, X., Xie, T.: A reinforcement learning approach for host-based intrusion detection using sequences of system calls. In: Huang, D.-S., Zhang, X.-P., Huang, G.-B. (eds.) ICIC 2005. LNCS, vol. 3644, pp. 995–1003. Springer, Heidelberg (2005). https://doi.org/10.1007/11538059_103
6. Geng, L.Z., Jia, H.B.: A low-cost method to intrusion detection system using sequences of system calls. In: Second International Conference on Information & Computing Science. IEEE Computer Society (2009)
7. Ye, Y., Wang, D., Li, T., Ye, D.: IMDS: intelligent malware detection system. In: Proceedings ACM International Conference Knowledge Discovery Data Mining, pp. 1043–1047 (2007)

8. Ye, Y., Li, T., Huang, K., Jiang, Q., Chen, Y.: Hierarchical associative classifier (HAC) for malware detection from the large and imbalanced gray list. J. Intell. Inf. Syst. **35**(1), 1–20 (2010). https://doi.org/10.1007/s10844-009-0086-7
9. Lee, J., Jeong, K., Lee, H.: Detecting metamorphic malwares using code graphs. In: Proceedings of the ACM Symposium on Applied Computing, ser. New York, NY, USA, pp. 1970–1977. ACM (2010)
10. Jerlin, M.A., Marimuthu, K.: A new malware detection system using machine learning techniques for API call sequences. J. Appl. Secur. Res. **13**(1), 45–62 (2018)
11. Bilar, D.: OpCodes as predictor for malware. Int. J. Electron. Secur. Digit. Forensics **1**(2), 156 (2007)
12. Santos, I., et al.: Idea: Opcode-sequence-based malware detection. In: Massacci, F., Wallach, D., Zannone, N. (eds.) ESSoS 2010. LNCS, vol. 5965, pp. 35–43. Springer, Heidelberg (2010). https://doi.org/10.1007/978-3-642-11747-3_3
13. Santos, I., Brezo, F., Ugarte-Pedrero, X., Bringas, P.G.: OpCode sequences as representation of executables for data-mining-based unknown malware detection. Inf. Sci. **231**, 203–216 (2013)
14. Runwal, N., Low, R.M., Stamp, M.: OpCode graph similarity and metamorphic detection. J. Comput. Virol. **8**(1–2), 37–52 (2012). https://doi.org/10.1007/s11416-012-0160-5
15. Ding, Y., Dai, W., Yan, S., Zhang, Y.: Control flow-based OpCode behavior analysis for malware detection. Comput. Secur. **44**, 65–74 (2014)
16. Yuxin, D., Wei, D. Yibin, Z., Chenglong, X.: Malicious code detection using OpCode running tree representation. In: 2014 Ninth International Conference on P2P, Parallel, Grid, Cloud and Internet Computing, Guangdong, pp. 616–621 (2014)
17. Lu, R.: Malware detection with LSTM using OpCode language (2019)
18. Kephart, J.O., Sorkin, G.B., Arnold, W.C., Chess, D.M. Tesauro, G.J., White, S.R.: Biologically inspired defenses against computer viruses. In: Proceedings of the 14th International Joint Conference on Artificial Intelligence, vol. 1, pp. 985–996. Morgan Kaufmann (1995)
19. Schultz, M., Eskin, E., Zadok, F., Stolfo, S.: Data mining methods for detection of new malicious executables. In: Proceedings IEEE Symposium on Security and Privacy, pp. 38–49 (2001)
20. Abou-Assaleh, T., Cercone, N., Keselj, V., Sweidan, R.: N-gram-based detection of new malicious code. In: Proceedings of the 28th Annual International Computer Software and Applications Conference. IEEE (2004)
21. Shafiq, M.Z., Khayam, S.A., Farooq, M.: Embedded malware detection using markov *n*-grams. In: Zamboni, D. (ed.) DIMVA 2008. LNCS, vol. 5137, pp. 88–107. Springer, Heidelberg (2008). https://doi.org/10.1007/978-3-540-70542-0_5
22. Fang, L., Qingyu, O., Guoheng, W.: Research on N-gram-based malicious code feature extraction algorithm. In: International Conference on Computer Application & System Modeling. IEEE (2010)
23. Parvin, H., Minaei, B., Karshenas, H., Beigi, A.: A new N-gram feature extraction-selection method for malicious code. In: Dobnikar, A., Lotrič, U., Šter, B. (eds.) ICANNGA 2011. LNCS, vol. 6594, pp. 98–107. Springer, Heidelberg (2011). https://doi.org/10.1007/978-3-642-20267-4_11
24. Raff, E., et al.: An investigation of byte n-gram features for malware classification. J. Comput. Virol. Hacking Tech. **14**(1), 1–20 (2016). https://doi.org/10.1007/s11416-016-0283-1
25. Zak, R., Raff, E., Nicholas, C.: What can N-gram learn for malware detection? In: 2017 12th International Conference on Malicious and Unwanted Software. IEEE (2018)

26. Lo, R.W., Levitt, K.N., Olsson, R.A.: MCF: a malicious code filter. Comput. Secur. **14**(6), 541–566 (1995)
27. Bruschi, D., Martignoni, L., Monga, M.: Detecting self-mutating malware using control-flow graph matching. In: Büschkes, R., Laskov, P. (eds.) DIMVA 2006. LNCS, vol. 4064, pp. 129–143. Springer, Heidelberg (2006). https://doi.org/10.1007/11790754_8
28. Bonfante, G., Kaczmarek, M., Marion, J.Y.: Control flow graphs as malware signatures. WTCV, May 2007
29. Zhao, Z.: A virus detection scheme based on features of control flow graph. In: 2nd International Conference on Artificial Intelligence, Management Science and Electronic Commerce (AIMSEC), pp. 943–947 (2011)
30. Alam, S., Traore, I., Sogukpinar, I.: Annotated control flow graph for metamorphic malware detection. Comput. J. **58**(10), 2608–2621 (2015)
31. Nguyen, M.H., Le, N.D., Nguyen, X.M., Quan, T.T.: Auto-detection of sophisticated malware using lazy-binding control flow graph and deep learning. Comput. Secur. **76**, 128–155 (2018)
32. Ma, Z., Ge, H., Liu, Y., Zhao, M., Ma, J.: A combination method for android malware detection based on control flow graphs and machine learning algorithms. IEEE Access **7**, 1 (2019)
33. Schultz, M.G., Eskin, E., Zadok, F., Stolfo, S.J.: Data mining methods for detection of new malicious executables. In: Proceedings of the IEEE Symposium on Security and Privacy (2001)
34. Masud, M.M., Khan, L., Thuraisingham, B.: A scalable multi-level feature extraction technique to detect malicious executables. Inf. Syst. Frontiers **10**(1), 33–45 (2007). https://doi.org/10.1007/s10796-007-9054-3
35. Eskandari, M., Hashemi, S.: Metamorphic malware detection using control flow graph mining. Int. J. Compute Sci. Netw. Secur. **11**, 1–6 (2011)
36. Eskandari, M., Hashemi, S.: A graph mining approach for detecting unknown malwares. J. Visual Lang. Comput. **23**(3), 154–162 (2012)
37. Yan, J., Yong, Q., Qifan, R.: Detecting malware with an ensemble method based on deep neural network. Secur. Commun. Netw. **2018**, 1–16 (2018)
38. Christodorescu, M., Jha, S., Seshia, S.A., Semantics-aware malware detection. IEEE Computer Society (2005)
39. Kim, K., Moon, B.R.: Malware detection based on dependency graph using hybrid genetic algorithm. In: Proceedings of the 12th Annual Conference on Genetic and Evolutionary Computation, 07–11 July (2010)
40. Ye, Y., et al.: Combinig file content and file relations for cloud based malware detection. In: Proceedings of the 17th ACM SIGKDD International Conference on Knowledge Discovery and Data Mining (2011)
41. Duen, H.C., Carey, N., Jeffrey, W., Adam, W., Christos, F.: Polonium: tera-scale graph mining for malware detection. In: Proceedings of the SIAM International Conference on Data Mining (SDM) (2011)
42. Acar, T., Kevin, R., Duen, H.C.: Guilt by association: large scale malware detection by mining file-relation graphs. In: Proceedings of ACM International Conference on Knowledge Discovery and Data Mining (ACM SIGKDD) (2014)
43. Yan, J., Qi, Y., Roa, Q.: Detecting malware with an ensemble method based on deep neural network. Secur. Commun. Netw. **2018**, 1–16 (2018)
44. Tian, R., Islam, R., Batten, L. and Versteeg, S.: Differentiating malware from cleanwares using behavioral analysis. In: Proceedings of 5th International Conference on Malicious and Unwanted Software (2010)

45. Firdausi, I., Erwin, A., Nugroho, A.S.: Analysis of machine learning techniques used in behavior based malware detection. In: Proceedings of 2nd International Conference on Advances in Computing, Control and Telecommunication Technologies (2010)
46. Ferrante, A., Medvet, E., Mercaldo, F., Milosevic, J., Visaggio, C.A.: Spotting the malicious moment: characterizing malware behavior using dynamic features. In: 11th International Conference on Availability, Reliability and Security. IEEE (2016)
47. Donggao, D., Gaochao, L., Yan, M.: Variable-length sequential dynamic features-based malware detection. High tech Commun. English Version **022**(004), 362–367 (2016)
48. Kakisim, A.G., Nar, M., Carkaci, N., Sogukpinar, I.: Analysis and evaluation of dynamic feature-based malware detection methods. In: Lanet, J.-L., Toma, C. (eds.) SECITC 2018. LNCS, vol. 11359, pp. 247–258. Springer, Cham (2019). https://doi.org/10.1007/978-3-030-12942-2_19
49. Lu, Y., Din, S., Zheng, C., Gao, B.: Using multi-feature and classifier ensembles to improve malware detection. J. CCIT **39**(2), 57–72 (2010)
50. Lee, J., Jeong, K., Lee, H.: Detecting metamorphic malwares using code graphs. In: Proceedings of the ACM Symposium on Applied Computing, USA, pp. 1970–1977. ACM (2010)
51. Guo, H., Pang, J., Zhang, Y., Yue, F., Zhao, R.: HERO: a novel malware detection framework based on binary translation. In: Proceedings of the IEEE International Conference on Intelligent Computing and Intelligent Systems, pp. 411–415. IEEE Xplore Press, Xiamen (2010)
52. Elhadi, A., Maarof, M., Osman, A.H.: Malware detection based on hybrid signature behaviour application programming interface call graph. Am. J. Appl. Sci. **9**, 283–288 (2012)
53. Santos, I., Devesa, J., Brezo, F., Nieves, J., Bringas, P.G.: OPEM: a static-dynamic approach for machine-learningbased malware detection. In: Proceedings of the International Joint Conference CISIS 2012-ICEUTE12-SOCO12 Special Sessions, vol. 189, pp. 271–280 (2013)
54. Bai, J., Wang, J.: Improving malware detection using multi-view ensemble learning. Secur. Commun. Netw. **9**, 4227–4241 (2016)
55. Zhang, J., Qin, Z., Hui, Y., Lu, O., Zhang, K.: A feature-hybrid malware variants detection using CNN based OpCode embedding and BPNN based API embedding. Comput. Secur. **84**, 376–392 (2019)

Classification of Malware Variant Based on Ensemble Learning

Hui Guo[1]([✉])[iD], Shu-guang Huang[1], Min Zhang[1], Zu-lie Pan[1], Fan Shi[1],
Cheng Huang[2], and Beibei Li[2]

[1] College of Electronic Engineering, National University of Defense Technology,
Hefei 230011, China
vance_guo@outlook.com
[2] College of Cybersecurity, Sichuan University, Chengdu 610065, China

Abstract. To explore the classification of malware variants, a malware
variant detection method is proposed based on the code visualization
method and ensemble learning model. First, malware binary data was
transformed into a gray-scale image and the GIST texture feature of the
image was extracted. Then, KNN (K Nearest Neighbor) and RF (random
forest) method are used as base learners and a malware variant classification model was proposed based on the voting learning method. Finally,
the integration results were mapped to the final malware classification
result. To verify the accuracy of the method, a malware family classification experiment was performed. The results show that the method can
reach an accuracy rate of 98.95% and the AUC value of 0.9976, meaning
that it can effectively analyze and classify malware variants.

Keywords: Cyberspace security · Malware variant detection · Code
visualization · Texture feature · Ensemble learning

1 Introduction

With the rapid development of the Internet in recent decades, the number and
scale of malware are currently growing exponentially, and have become one of the
most harmful elements in cyberspace security. According to Symantec's report
[1], 246,002,762 new malware variants were monitored in 2018, and the number
of new malware variants exceeded a billion in the past three years. Due to the low
production threshold and low difficulty, the authors of malware writing are more
inclined to adopt the method of slight modification or use of packaging, encryption and other techniques to package the original malware and make malware to
circumvent the detection technology and spread the malware. Rapid identification of malware variant information can effectively assist the network security
personnel to grasp its functionality and harm, and has important research value.

Supported by laboratory of Network Security, College of Electronic Engineering,
National University of Defense Technology.

Currently, malware detection technologies are mainly divided into three categories: based on signatures, based on static features, and based on dynamic features. The signatures are the special codes in the malware that are different from other program codes. However, signature-based detection technology cannot detect new malware and malware variants that modify signatures. Hackers can usually modify malware signatures by equivalent code replacement and other methods to circumvent such detection methods.

The malware detection technology based on static characteristics mainly obtains the static characteristics of the malware by analyzing the file attributes of the malware file structure, binary code, and disassembled program assembly code. However, the malware detection technology based on static characteristics is generally difficult to counter the malware obfuscation technology. Malware authors modify the malware by using encryption, packing, and additional instructions to increase the reverse code difficulty, time, and space costs.

Malware detection technology based on dynamic features runs malware through a virtually real environment, extracts malware API operation sequences, system instruction sequences, network communications, file operations and other behavioral features to detect malware. A malware detection method based on dynamic features does not require reverse analysis of malware, reducing the impact of code obfuscation technology on malware detection. However, the malware dynamic feature extraction process consumes high time and space costs. To reduce the consumption of resources, this method usually analyzes the running time of the program only for a few minutes. malware writers increase the behavior triggering conditions, set the sleep time, detect the operating environment attributes, determine whether the malware is running in the real host, etc. to hide the malware behavior characteristics and avoid dynamic detection methods.

Given the malware is modified to avoid the dynamic and static detection of malware, the researchers proposed a malware detection technology based on texture features [2]. This method treats the malware as a whole, by converting the malware into an image, and extracting the texture features of the image, to detect the malware. This method does not require the extraction of malware signatures and does not require reverse malware programs, and at the same time does not have to spend a lot of time and space costs, simulating the actual operating environment. This method can effectively combat anti-detecting technologies such as signature modification and dynamic feature detection evasion. At the same time, for code obfuscation, such as shelling and other technologies, this method also has a certain ability to resist. For example, the malware variant files use the same packing or encryption technology, and the generated new malware files still have a high degree of similarity in image texture features. By extracting image texture features, they can still be classified. Whether the hacker reuses the malware function module or obfuscates the malware, the malware variant file and the ancestral malware file have many homologous parts. Therefore, by extracting the texture features of the malware files, the homology of the malware variants can be effectively utilized to classify the malware variants. In recent years, based on this research, Cui [2] and others have proposed a method of malware detection based on convolutional neural networks, which has achieved a certain improvement in the overall classification effect. However, the paper points out that for a relatively small number of malware families, the deep learning model does not have a good classification effect. In response to this problem, Neem [3,4] and others conducted further research in this field, combined with DSIFT, SIFT and other texture features, and proposed a new detection model. This method achieves a better classification effect of malware and improves the classification accuracy of malware variants to 98.4%.

To improve the classification effect of malware variants, we delve into the characteristics of image texture features, test the impact of different data preprocessing methods on global texture features, and propose a new classification method of malware variants based on the ensemble learning model. Through a large number of experimental evaluations, the accuracy and robustness of the classification of the malware family have been improved to a certain extent, the accuracy of the classification of malware variants can be increased to 98.95%, and the AUC value of the classification model can be increased to 0.9976.

In summary, the main contributions of this paper are as follows:

1) We propose a new classification method of malware variants based on the hybrid model. In experiments, the model shows better classification accuracy and robustness.

2) We deeply analyze the principle of GIST texture features and test the impact of different data preprocessing methods on the classification effect of malware based on GIST features, which provides a certain reference for further research in this field.

3) After testing, at the level of GIST texture features, two models with certain classification effects can effectively improve the classification effect of malware through the use of integrated learning algorithms, which provides new ideas for further research in related fields.

2 Basic Concepts and Related Work

This chapter mainly introduces related concepts and related research in the field of malware detection

2.1 Malware Classification and Naming Rules

The malware mainly includes computer viruses, worms, Trojans, rootkit tools, spyware, ransomware, logic bombs, botnets, phishing, and malicious scripts. In recent years, the Microsoft Security Center has proposed a naming rule for viruses [5]. The naming method contains five items: type, platform, family, variant, and supplementary information. Type refers to the type of malware and describes the functional differences of the malware. The platform mainly refers to the operating system, programming language, file format, etc. targeted by the malware. Family refers to the grouping of malware based on common characteristics. Variants refer to the sequential naming of different versions of malware in each family, from "A-Z" to "AA"-"ZZ", according to the number of variants.

2.2   Related Work

malware detection is mainly divided into signature-based detection, static feature-based detection, and dynamic feature-based detection. In recent years, malware detection techniques based on image texture features have emerged.

Signature-Based Detection. The signature-based detection of malware technology is one of the earliest malware detection technologies. It is still one of the most important malware detection technologies currently used by major security vendors. A piece of signature refers to the unique short code that exists in the malware, allowing researchers to determine whether the detected file is the target malicious file through the signature [6]. When the technology first appeared, signatures usually needed to be manually generated and updated based on expert experience. When a cybersecurity vendor got a new malware, it needed to analyze the malware, generate a signature, then add the signature database and deploy it. Moskovitch et al. [6] pointed out that signature-based detection consumes more resources and can only detect malware that has already appeared, which has a certain lag for the detection of new malware or variant files. And the time window for typical malware from appearing to being detected is about 54 days. Detecting malware based on signatures is no longer suitable for the current environment. In recent years, with the rapid development of data mining, machine learning and other fields, more and more researchers use data mining methods for malware detection, which mainly includes malware detection based on static features [7–10] and dynamic features malware detection [11,12].

Static Feature-Based Detection. Based on static features, malware detection technology mainly extracts static file features of malware files through certain technical means, including malware byte stream, disassembled opcode, static API sequence, CPU register characteristics, PE file header, import Export function table, file features including symbols, and static features such as special characters in malware [7]. And establish a classification model based on a learning algorithm to detect malware. Ahmadi et al. [8] used a variety of static features including an N-gram algorithm to process malware byte streams, decompiled opcodes, PE file features, and static API sequence streams. A classification model was established based on support vector machines and random forests, To detect the malware family. Chen et al. citech11chen2015intelligent implemented the detection of malware based on the relationship between malware files. However, this method is difficult to detect malware files with a relatively small spread or emerging. Ng et al. [10] proposed a new clustering method based on the characteristics of malware files, which can efficiently implement the clustering of malware and distinguish malware from normal software. The malware detection method based on static features does not need to run malware files, and will not cause malicious harm to the system. It is fast and efficient, but the static analysis is often difficult to resist various code obfuscation techniques, such as packing, encryption, deformation, and more Technology. Hackers can greatly increase the difficulty of extracting static features of files by packing malware files, and effectively counter the static detection technology of malware.

Dynamic Feature-Based Detection. In recent years, more and more researchers have detected based on the dynamic features of malware. The malware runs in the real environment, and in order to achieve its malicious purpose, a series of malicious operations will be performed. Based on the behavioral characteristics of malware, the current researchers put the malware into sandboxes, virtual machines and other simulated real environments to run, extract the behavioral characteristics of the malware runtime API sequence, network communication behavior, file operation behavior, etc. Establishing models for malware detection can effectively reduce the impact of code obfuscation on malware detection. Liang et al. [11] and Kim et al. [12] separately extracted behavioral features such as malware file operations and network communication, and performed malware detection based on the similarity calculation method. The malware detection technology based on dynamic features directly mines the behavior characteristics of the malware, which is closer to the essential characteristics of the malware and overcomes the anti-killing technology such as code obfuscation. However, the dynamic feature detection consumes more resources and has higher requirements for time and space. And at present, malware writers adopt countermeasures such as setting waiting time and running environment detection technology, so that network security personnel cannot normally extract the dynamic behavior features of malware.

Code Visualization. For malware writers to use code obfuscation and set a waiting time to generate malware variants to avoid detection technology, in recent years, researchers have proposed methods for using code visualization to detect malware. Nataraj et al. [13] proposed for the first time to convert malware into grayscale images, extracted image GIST texture features, and classified them based on machine learning algorithms. This method treats the malware executable file as an overall file, effectively reducing modification The influence of most anti-killing technologies such as signatures and waiting time settings, and at the same time, for the packaging and encryption technologies, it can also effectively achieve the classification of malware families to a certain extent. Cui [2] and others proposed a method of detecting malware families based on convolutional neural networks combined with malware images. The experimental results are better, but the paper points out that the deep learning model is not good for the classification of malware families with relatively small samples. At the same time, Kosmidis et al. [14] also detected the malware family based on the GIST texture feature of the malware image, and achieved certain results. Based on this research, Naeem et al. [3,4] and Hashemi et al. [15] proposed a family of detection algorithms for malware variants using various texture features such as LBP, SURF, DSIFT, etc., and achieved good results. From the current According to related research, it is an important detection method to detect malware family based on image texture features, and GIST global texture features are still one of the focuses of current research.

3 Approach

The research content of this paper is a malware variant detection technology based on global texture features, including malicious file binary data extraction, gray image mapping, global texture feature generation and ensemble learning algorithm research. As shown in Fig. 1, the method proposed in this paper first extracts the binary sequence data of the malware file, then maps the binary data to an uncompressed grayscale image, and generates an image global texture feature based on the grayscale image. Finally, based on the image texture feature, A hybrid model based on integrated learning algorithms is used to classify the malware variants.

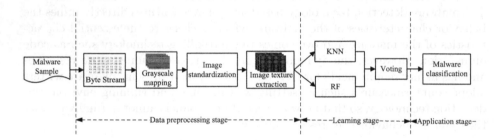

Fig. 1. Overview of methods

3.1 Binary Sequence Data Extraction

Most of the existing malware detection technologies usually extract some characteristics of malware files as the basis for detection, and we directly treat the malware file as a binary file consisting of 1, 0-bit data stream, containing each byte Te eight-bit data format extracts byte stream data of malware files.

3.2 Grayscale Mapping

Mapping grayscale images of malware files mainly involve two problems. First, how to convert the data in the malware files into pixel data of the image. Second, how to determine the height and width of the image. For the first problem, this paper treats each byte of data as an 8-bit unsigned integer data with a value range of [0,255]. The value range of each pixel in a binary grayscale image is also [0,255] (Where 0 corresponds to black and 255 corresponds to white), according to the one-to-one correspondence between each byte data and pixel points, all byte stream data is converted into gray image pixels.

In response to the second problem, the size range of malware files is large, ranging from KB level to MB level. In order to ensure that the aspect ratio of the grayscale image after the malware file is mapped is within a certain range, it is convenient for further feature processing. As shown in Table 1, this paper formulates different width standards according to the file size, combined with the file size, the image height can be calculated, and finally, the byte stream data is converted into a grayscale image.

Table 1. Gray scale image conversion width

File size(KB)	Image Length	File size(KB)	Image length
<10	32	100–200	384
<10–30	64	200–500	512
<30–60	128	500–1000	768
<60–100	256	>1000	1024

As shown in Fig. 2(a), several malware samples from different families are converted into gray-scale images, which show a series of features. As shown in Fig. 2(a) (1), gray-scale images from the same family of malware variants have strong similarities As shown in Fig. 2(a)(1) and Fig. 2(a)(2), grayscale images between different malware variants of similar families have certain similarities, but also have differences;

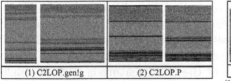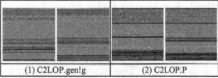
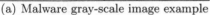

| (1) C2LOP.gen!g | (2) C2LOP.P | | (1) C2LOP.gen!g | (2) C2LOP.P |

(a) Malware gray-scale image example   (b) Malware gray-scale image standardization

Fig. 2. Malware gray-scale image

3.3 Image Standardization

As shown in Fig. 2(a), the files of different variants of the malware have large differences in size, and the size of the grayscale map is also different. When image feature processing is performed, it will cause some impact. In order to enhance the detection effect of the malware variants, we standardize the grayscale image and map the grayscale image of the malware file into a uniform size, for example, the image is standardized to the 256*256 format. As shown in Fig. 2(b), the normalized processing effect map of the grayscale map of the C2LOP.gen! G and C2LOP.P family of malware variants.

3.4   Image Texture Feature Extraction

GIST texture feature algorithm is a feature description method using wavelet transform and Gabor transform in combination. Use GIST global texture features to identify and classify the scenes in the image without the need to segment the image and extract local features, which can quickly and effectively realize the classification of the image and the classification accuracy is high. Numerous studies [16] and [3,4] have used this feature description method to extract image global texture features. Therefore, the GIST feature description method was selected in this study to extract global texture features of grayscale images of malware files.

The process of extracting image GIST features mainly includes: 1. Use Gabor filters of different scales and different directions to filter the image to obtain multiple filtered images; 2. After each filtering, the generated image is divided into several grid parts; 3. Calculate the average value of the internal values of the grid after each division; 4. Connect all the filter to generate the average value of the grid data of image segmentation, and combine to get the image GIST feature.

Combined with the method in the paper, the GIST texture feature of the grayscale image of the malware file is generated as shown in formula (1):

$$GIST = f_{gist}(M, R, F_n, N_i = (b_x, b_y)) \tag{1}$$

where M represents the input image data, R represents the standardized image format, F_n represents the number of parameters used in different directions and scales, $N = (b_x, b_y)$ represents the number of parameters in the horizontal and vertical directions of the filtered image segmentation grid, and $b_x * b_y$ is the number of grids after segmentation. For example,$F_n = (8, 8, 4)$, represents three directions, there are 8 directions, 8 directions and 4 directions, a total of 20 filters to filter the image,$n_b = (4, 4)$ represents the filtered image is divided into $4 * 4 = 16$ grid, The resulting dimension of the GIST feature is $20 * 16 = 320$ dimensions.

3.5   Ensemble Learn Strategy

Ensemble learning can improve the effectiveness of malware detection to a certain extent by synthesizing the results of multiple basic learning models. The overall overview of the Ensemble learning method proposed in this paper is shown in Fig. 3. The entire process can be divided into two stages. The first stage of learning is mainly the learning stage of the basic machine learning model, and the second stage is the result stage of the hybrid basic learning model.

In the first stage, two basic machine learning models are trained using the K nearest neighbor and random forest algorithm. Each basic learning model $M_i(i = 1, 2)$ makes predictions from a set of classes $F_1, F_2, \ldots, F_n$ (where N refers to the number of malware variant families). The output result $Result(x|h_i)$ of the input samples x in Learning model M_i is recorded as a vector $1 \times N$.

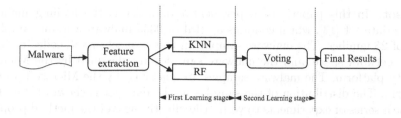

Fig. 3. Overview of malware variation detection

$$Result\_m(x|h_i) = \{h_i{}^1(x), h_i{}^2(x), \ldots\ldots, h_i{}^n(x)\} \tag{2}$$

Among them $h_i^j(x)$ refers to the probability that the learning model M_i detects the sample belongs to the family F_j, and its value range is [0,1]. The larger the value, the greater the possibility of judging that it belongs to the family.

In the second stage, the voting learning strategy is used for ensemble learning, where the voting learning output $Result(x|e)$ is defined as a vector of $1 \times N$.

$$Result\_e(x|e) = \{e^1(x), e^2(x), \ldots\ldots, e^n(x)\} \tag{3}$$

The element $e^i(x)$ of the vector refers to the probability that the output sample x is classified as the family F_i by the voting learning strategy, and its value range is [0,1], and its value is calculated using the voting strategy for each basic learning model. The classification of sample x is the average of h_1 and h_2 of family F_i. Finally, according to the output of each basic learner, the probability value of the sample x belonging to each family F_i is calculated comprehensively, and the family F with the largest probability value is output as the detection result of the sample x.

4   Evaluation

4.1   Evaluation Setup and Data Set

This paper implements the proposed method, which is mainly divided into three parts: gray image mapping part, image standardization and texture feature generation part, integrated learning model construction part. Gray-scale image mapping, image standardization and GIST global texture feature generation are all implemented through Python 2.7, and the ensemble learning model training part is implemented through the Scikit-learn library. The solution is deployed on a personal computer, the machine configuration: CPU Intel (R) Core (TM) i7-4790, 3.6Ghz, 20GB memory, 1TB hard drive.

Dataset. In this paper, the experimental data set is the malimg malicious sample data set [13], which contains a total of 9339 malware variant samples, a total of 25 families. The malware samples in the data set are all collected in the actual network space, and the malware samples are classified by the Microsoft security platform. The malware samples are classified by the Microsoft security platform. The distribution of the samples in the data set is shown in Fig. 6(a). We use a series of experiments to verify the effectiveness of the method proposed in this paper. In order to ensure the integrity and reliability of the experiment, this paper uses an 8-fold cross-validation experiment.

Evaluation Metric. The evaluation metric in this experiment includes correct rate, precision rate, recall rate, ROC curve and AUC value. The true positive samples involved are malware samples that are correctly classified into their corresponding family samples. False positive samples refer to samples where malware is misclassified into a specified family, and True negative samples refer to samples that are not a specified family but are classified into that family. False negative sample (False negative) refers to a malware sample of a specified family, but it is misclassified into other family categories. Other evaluation criteria are calculated as follows.

Accuracy: The ratio of the number of correct judgments of the malware sample family by the model to the total number of samples:

$$Acc = \frac{TP + TN}{TP + TN + FP + FN} \tag{4}$$

Recall: Regarding the positive examples judged by the model in the data set, the ratio of the correct sample (TP) to all positive examples in the data set.

$$Recall = \frac{TP}{TP + FN} \tag{5}$$

Precision: The proportion of true positives (TP) judged by the model among the positive examples judged by the model in the data set. The calculation formula is as follows:

$$Precision = \frac{TP}{TP + FP} \tag{6}$$

F1 measure (F1-measure): F1 measure is the harmonic average of recall rate and precision rate, which is defined as:

$$F1 = \frac{2 \times TP}{2 \times TP + FP + FN} \tag{7}$$

ROC curve and AUC area: The vertical coordinate of the ROC curve is the True Positive Rate, and the horizontal coordinate is the False Positive Rate. When judging the performance of the two learners, the criterion is usually based on comparing the AUC (Area Under ROC Curve) area.

4.2   Ensemble Learning Model Effect

Accuracy, Precision and Recall. Different basic learning models and GIST feature dimension selection have a certain impact on the experimental effect of the ensemble learning algorithm. In this section, the GIST feature dimension is temporarily set to 320, and the grayscale image is not standardized in the image format. Test the experimental classification effect of different machine learning models.

The parameter setting of each model is as follows. The K value in the KNN model is 2, and the remaining learning models use the default configuration parameters in sklearn. The experimental effect is shown in Fig. 4(a).

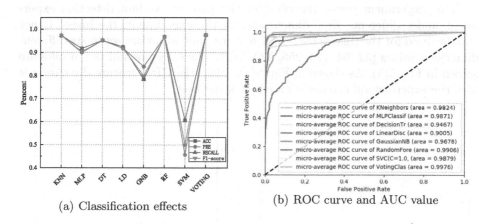

(a) Classification effects   (b) ROC curve and AUC value

Fig. 4. Effect of different model

As shown in Fig. 4(a), the classification accuracy rate of KNN is 0.972, and the classification accuracy rate of the random forest (RF) learning model is 0.965. These two models are the two learning models with the best experimental results among all the individual basic learning models. At the same time, the experiment using the ensemble strategy model proposed in this paper has better results, and the classification accuracy rate can reach 0.975.

ROC Curve and AUC Area. The generalization ability of the model is one of the important evaluation indicators of the quality of the model. In the actual environment, the robustness of the model is sometimes more important than the accuracy.

In order to test the model generalization ability, this paper tests the ROC curve of each model in the experiment, as shown in Fig. 4(b) is the ROC curve and AUC value of the model.

As can be seen from Fig. 4(b), the generalization ability of the ensemble strategy model is relatively best, and the AUC value can reach 0.9976, which is an increase of 0.1 compared to the KNN learning model and a certain improvement compared to the random forest learning model.

4.3   GIST Dimension and Image Format Experiment

In this section, the GIST feature dimension and image format standardization experiments are all tested using the ensemble learning model.

GIST Feature Dimension Test. In related studies, Nataraj et al. [13] used GIST feature dimensions of 320, and Naeem et al. [3, 4] used GIST feature dimensions of 256 and 512. In order to further explore the impact of different GIST feature dimensions on the classification effect of malware, this paper first studies the effect of different GIST dimension numbers on the detection of malware variants.

This experiment tested the effect of the malware variant detection experiment under different GIST dimensions. In the experiment, the image is not standardized for the time being, GIST feature dimensions are set in six different dimension values (32, 64, 128, 256, 320, 512). The experimental test results are shown in Fig. 5(a). As shown in Fig. 5(a), when the GIST feature dimension is 256, the experimental classification effect is the best.

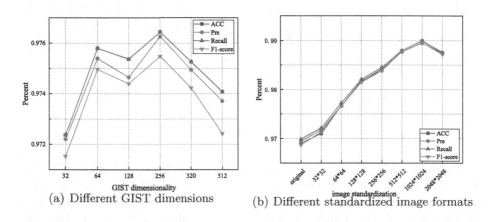

(a) Different GIST dimensions   (b) Different standardized image formats

Fig. 5. Experimental of different parameter

Comparison of Image Standardization Effects. The format of the image influences the texture characteristics of the image. This experiment tested the experimental classification effect of different image formats. In the experiment, the GIST feature dimension is set to 256, and the image format is set (unstandardized, 32 * 32, 64 * 64, 128 * 128, 256 * 256, 512 * 512, 1024 * 1024, 2048 * 2048) six formats. The experimental effect is shown in Fig. 5(b). As shown in Fig. 5(b), the standardization of the image format can improve the detection effect of malware, and in the data set, when the image format is standardized to 1024 * 1024, the classification accuracy rate can reach 0.9895(the best experimental effect).

4.4   Efficiency

To test the efficiency of the model, we counted the time spent on model training and testing experiments. The experiment set the image normalization format to 1024 * 1024 and the GIST feature dimension to 256. The effect is shown in Fig. 6(b).

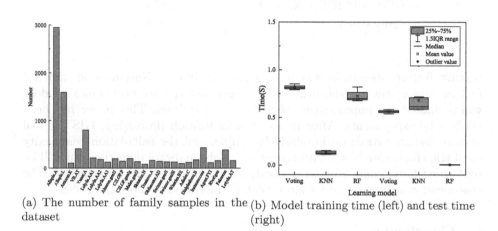

(a) The number of family samples in the dataset

(b) Model training time (left) and test time (right)

Fig. 6. Dataset samples and efficiency of model

As shown in Fig. 6(b), in the experiment, the training time of the mixed model is about 0.8 s, and the test time is about 0.5 s. In the experiment, the training and testing time of the K nearest neighbor learner and the random forest learner are also counted. Compared with the K nearest neighbor model and the random forest model, the training time of the ensemble model is relatively high, and the test time is centered, but overall the ensemble model has a shorter running time and is feasible in the actual environment.

4.5   Related Research Comparison

Combining all the experimental results, the model trained based on the ensemble learning strategy has a better classification effect of malware variants. To further verify the quality of the proposed method, we compared the proposed method with the four methods (GIST + KNN, GIST + RF, LBP + KNN, GIST + DSIFT + KNN). The result is shown in Table 2.

It can be seen from the comparison results that the method proposed in this paper exhibits better detection accuracy and effect than other methods. As shown in Table 2, the malware classification effect of GIST + DSIFT + KNN can be increased to 98.4%, showing that the use of more complex texture features will improve the detection effect of malware variants to a certain extent. But combined with image standardization processing, the complexity of complex

Table 2. Table captions should be placed above the tables.

Method	Accuracy	Recall	F1-score(%)
GIST + KNN	97.2	97.3	97.1
GIST + RF	96.7	96.8	96.6
LBP + KNN	97.8	97.9	97.9
GIST + DSIFT + KNN	98.4	98.2	97.1
Our method	98.9	99.0	98.9

texture feature operations will have a greater impact, Naeem et al. did not further explore the standardization of images and the use of complex models, which limited the improvement of malware recognition. This paper has been verified by experiments. After image standardization processing, GIST global texture feature extraction is relatively simple, and the calculation complexity has little effect. Combined with complex models, malware detection can still be performed faster, and a better malware detection effect can be achieved. The classification accuracy and F1 metric can be increased to more than 98.9%.

5   Conclusion

Based on the code visualization method, this paper deeply analyzes the principle of malware detection based on global texture features, and has designed a large number of experiments to test the effectiveness of the model in multiple dimensions, and proposed a classification method for malware variants based on complex models. From the perspective of the similarity of the binary data of the malware to detect the family of malware variants, it has good application value. At the same time, the research on malware detection based on the code visualization method also has great research prospects. We hope that the research content of this paper can be used as a paving stone for research in this field and provide some guidance and reference value for future research and development in this field. In the next step of research, we will further study the detection methods of malware variants that combine more complex texture features to achieve better classification results.

References

1. SYMANTEC: Internet security threat report, 16 May 2020. https://www.broadcom.com/support/security-center/publications/threat-report
2. Cui, Z., Xue, F., Cai, X., Cao, Y., Wang, G., Chen, J.: Detection of malicious code variants based on deep learning. IEEE Trans. Industr. Inf. **14**(7), 3187–3196 (2018)
3. Naeem, H., Guo, B., Ullah, F., Naeem, M.: A cross-platform malware variant classification based on image representation. Ksii Trans. Internet Inf. Syst. **13**(7), 3756–3777 (2019)

4. Naeem, H., Guo, B., Naeem, M.R., Ullah, F., Aldabbas, H., Javed, M.S.: Identification of malicious code variants based on image visualization. Comput. Electr. Eng. **76**, 225–237 (2019)
5. Microsoft Antivirus. Malware names, 10 May 2020. https://docs.microsoft.com/en-us/windows/security/threat-protection/intelligence/malware-naming
6. Moskovitch, R., Feher, C., Elovici, Y.: A chronological evaluation of unknown malcode detection. In: IEEE International Conference on Intelligence & Security Informatics (2009)
7. Raff, E., Nicholas, C.: An alternative to NCD for large sequences, Lempel-ZIV Jaccard distance, pp. 1007–1015 (2017)
8. Ahmadi, M., Ulyanov, D., Semenov, S., Trofimov, M., Giacinto, G.: Novel feature extraction, selection and fusion for effective malware family classification, pp. 183–194 (2016)
9. Chen, L., Li, T., Abdulhayoglu, M., Ye, Y.: Intelligent malware detection based on file relation graphs, pp. 85–92 (2015)
10. Ng, C.K., Jiang, F., Zhang, L.Y., Zhou, W.: Static malware clustering using enhanced deep embedding method. Concurrency Comput. Pract. Exp. **31**(19), 1–16 (2019)
11. Liang, G., Pang, J., Dai, C.: A behavior-based malware variant classification technique. Int. J. Inf. Educ. Technol. **6**(4), 291–295 (2016)
12. Kim, H., Kim, J., Kim, Y., Kim, I., Kim, K.J., Kim, H.: Improvement of malware detection and classification using API call sequence alignment and visualization. Cluster Comput. **22**(1), 921–929 (2017). https://doi.org/10.1007/s10586-017-1110-2
13. Nataraj, L., Karthikeyan, S., Jacob, G., Manjunath, B.S.: Malware images: visualization and automatic classification. In: Proceedings of the 8th International Symposium on Visualization for Cyber Security, pp. 1–7 (2011)
14. Kosmidis, K., Kalloniatis, C.: Machine learning and images for malware detection and classification, p. 5 (2017)
15. Hashemi, H., Hamzeh, A.: Visual malware detection using local malicious pattern. J. Comput. Virol. Hacking Tech. **15**(1), 1–14 (2018). https://doi.org/10.1007/s11416-018-0314-1
16. Li, Y., Zuo, Z.H.: An overview of object code obfuscation technologies. Comput. Technol. Dev. **17**, 124–127 (2007)

Detection of Malicious Domains in APT via Mining Massive DNS Logs

Lu Huang[1(⊠)], Jingfeng Xue[1], Weijie Han[1,2], Zixiao Kong[1], and Zequn Niu[1]

[1] School of Computer Science and Technology,
Beijing Institute of Technology, Beijing, China
hhuangluu@163.com
[2] School of Space Information, Space Engineering University, Beijing, China

Abstract. With the rise of network attack, advanced persistent threats (APT) imposes severe challenges to network security. Since APT attacker can easily hide inevitable C&C traffic in massive Web traffic, HTTP-based C&C communication has become the most preferred method, providing us with new ideas for detecting. Moreover, under the assumption that attackers have limited attack resources, the domains used in the same attack will show relevance. Although there has been a lot of works focused on APT detection, it is still a difficult task to detect the abnormal DNS activity from massive Web traffic. In this paper, we propose a new framework based belief propagation to identify suspicious domains and compromised hosts in APT. We extract the domains features and calculate the score of being malicious from the DNS logs with minimal ground truth. We implement and validate our framework on anonymous DNS logs released by LANL. The experiment shows that our approach identifies previously unknown malicious domains and achieves high detection rates.

Keywords: APT · DNS · C&C detection · Malicious domain detection

1 Introduction

With the development of network technology, more governments, institutions and companies are accelerating the development of their own services on the network. At the same time, the cyber-attack is becoming more targeted, professional and sophisticated than ever before and a new threat called Advanced Persistent Threat(APT) has emerged [1]. Differ from traditional network attacks, APT always driven by humans, customized for target organizations after intelligence analysis, through long-term implementation and using known or even unknown vulnerabilities to penetrate the target system. Due to its persistence and concealment [2], it brings great challenges to traditional intrusion detection systems.

Multi-stage APT attack can be divided into five stages: reconnaissance; compromise; lateral movement; access keeping; and data exfiltration [3]. Firstly, the attacker obtains detailed information about the target network system through open source intelligence, sociological engineering, etc. Later, the attacker attempts to deliver

X. Chen et al. (Eds.): ML4CS 2020, LNCS 12486, pp. 140–152, 2020.
https://doi.org/10.1007/978-3-030-62223-7_12

customized malicious code to the target host using phishing emails, malicious links, etc. In the lateral movement phase, the attacker will hind in the target system and uses the controlled host as a springboard to further obtain more favorable information. During the access keeping phase, the infected host will periodically initiate connections with the communication and control server to receive instructions. In data exfiltration stage, the APT attacker sends back the stolen confidential data to an external server to achieve the ultimate goal of his attack.

The APT attacker will hide in the target system for a long period of time, during which only low signals are generated to connect with external C&C server and get new instructions. The C&C communication tends to base on HTTP/HTTPS protocol, because most firewalls usually allow Web communication [4]. Compared with other traffic analysis, using DNS data for anomaly detection has many advantages. First, DNS data only occupies a small part of the entire network traffic. Second, DNS traffic contains many meaningful features that can be used to identify domains related to malicious activities. More importantly, malicious domains or malicious IPs used in the same attack activity are usually related. Security teams can utilize relationship between them to mine potential infected hosts in the organization and detect attacks at the early stage.

We find that infected hosts leave beacon [5] (some communication packets sent at regular intervals, which can be found in DNS requests or URLs) in log records when connecting C&C. At the same time, in order to combat blacklist detection or avoid single point of failure, attacker tends to use Domain-Flux or IP-Flux to move between multiple domains. The former refers to using domain generation algorithm (DGA) to generate multiple FQDN, which mapping to the same IP. The latter is just the opposite. Therefore, malicious domains and malicious IPs always related, we can use the characteristic to effectively mine the association between malicious domains. We propose a Belief Propagation method, starting a few malicious seeds (compromised hosts or malicious domains) to mine the association between unknown domains and seeds. The algorithm will be verified on the public data set provided by LANL.

The rest of the paper is organized as follows: In the second part,we introduce related work about attack detection based on DNS traffic. In the third part, we introduce the proposed model, the fourth part shows the experimental results, and the discussion and conclusion in the fifth part.

2   Related Work

The Domain Name System (DNS) is an important part of the Internet, which maps difficulty-remembered Internet IP addresses to domains that are easy to remember. Compared with other detection methods based on traffic analysis, analysis based on DNS data is a very worthy direction. Current attack detection methods based on DNS traffic analysis can generally be divided into two categories: machine learning-based methods and graph-based methods. Researchers usually use one or more methods to detect APT attacks, also known as hybrid methods.

The main points of the machine learning-based method are feature selection and extraction. Yan, G. [6] proposed an APT detection framework AULD, focusing on time-related DNS features, which analyzes a large amount of DNS log data and obtain a list of suspicious domains through automatic unsupervised machine learning. Wang. [7] believes that accesses to malicious domains are usually independent, so he proposes the concept of COncurrent Domainin DNS records (CODDs), and extracts the connection times between hosts and domains, the average number of CODDs and the highest confidence level of CODDs as features. Nadler, A. [8] uses an Isolation Forest model as a classifier (i.e. trained only legitimate data and output an anomaly model), which realize detection of low throughput data exfiltration. Unlike negative DNS reputation system, Kheir, N. [9] extracts content features and popular features of domains to characterize the possibility that the domain being benign. Their work used to filter out misclassified benign domains.

Local features of malicious DNS activities can be hidden easily, resulting in poor scalability of detection. In Intuition, researchers believe that there is a potential connection between malicious domains/IPs and unidentified compromised hosts in the same attack activity. Thereby, mining global features or performing malicious reasoning on DNS activity graphs can further discover the potential threats. Manadhata, P. K. [10] uses a few priori nodes as seeds, and iteratively calculates the edge probability of the unknown domains being attacked using the Belief Propagation algorithm. Zou, F. [11] also uses the BP algorithm, but unlike [10], which assigns the same score to benign domains, it assigns score values according to the ranking of benign domains in Alexa. Oprea, A. [12] proposed a unique method which combine unsupervised learning techniques (belief propagation in hosts-domains graph), with a supervised learning method (linear regression) when limited ground truth is available. Both Ma, Z. [13] and Issa Khalil [14] constructed domains-resolved IPs graph and converted them into domain-domain graph to mine the association between domains. The difference is that [13] is concerned with the degree of association between domains and malicious IP subnets, while [14] is concerned with the degree of association between domains and malicious domains.

It's one of current trends to combine multiple methods for detection. Combined with malicious DNS detection and intrusion detection technology, Zhao, G. [15] proposed a new APT detection system IDns located at the edge of the network. Ghafir, I. [16] combined multiple APT detection modules to realize the detection system MLAPT, which fully considers the life cycle of APT. Stevanovic, M. [18] combined features of domain-IPs graph with other local features.

Above, we described different APT detection methods. All methods have their own emphasis, and the detection results and key-points are also different. Although not all detection methods are covered, we can still find that these methods are common on identifying and generalizing normal activities to achieve attack detection.

3   Framework Design

In this section, we will introduce the proposed Framework and describe each part in detail in the subsections. The framework is based on belief propagation and it outputs the list of suspicious domains by computing the feature function values of domains. The framework consists of following parts: data preprocessing, feature extraction and belief propagation algorithms. We will analyze the behavior patterns of APT attack activities, summarize and describe common characteristics. Figure 1 shows the flow diagram of the framework.

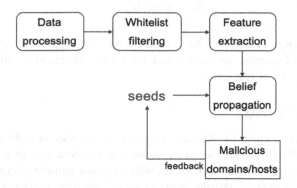

Fig. 1. The flow diagram of framework.

3.1 Raw Data

We use anonymous DNS logs from LANL, which includes DNS queries initiated by internal hosts and responses from the DNS servers. Each record contains the following data fields: timestamp, IP addresses of the sources and destinations, request domain, resolution information of domain, request type and other information.

3.2 Data Preprocessing

Data preprocessing includes four parts: converting (multi-level query), extracting valid fields, data normalizing.

Converting: We are only concerned with the A record type DNS log (A record translate given URLs into numerical addresses), which is the IP address type most frequently utilized by attackers. Records such as AAAA, TXT, PTR, SRV and other information are all deleted. Then, we merged the query and response records to eliminate DNS servers. The process of converting is shown in Fig. 2. The process of converting.

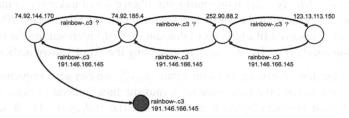

Fig. 2. The process of converting.

Extracting Valid Fields: We extracted the initiated host h_i, domain d_i and resolved IPs of it, timestamp T from the merged DNS records (standardizing the query times in seconds). Type-A record is expressed as follows:

$$R = (h_i, d_i, IP_{d_i}, T) \tag{1}$$

Data Normalizing: Traverse all Rs, for each internal host, store all queried domains and sequences of queried timestamps,and for each domain, store all internal hosts connected it and set of resolved IPs.

3.3 Whitelist Filtering

We collapsed the domain to 3LD and counted the number of individual hosts that visited each 3LD and the number of times the specific host queries it. We found the most popular internal domains (webb.bin) with the most number of connected hosts a removed all Rs about them. Popular domains are of little help to detection but consume computing resources,so we remove all Rs about top-100 popular 3LD.

Then, we apply customized filter rules on the remaining unique FQDNs. Due to the lack of training data, we use aggressive whitelist strategy: removing all domains with more than 10 connected hosts or queried by one host more than 100 times.

3.4 Feature Extraction

We define a feature extraction function $Fe(d_i)$ to transform a specific domain to a feature vector:

$$Fe(d_i) = (C\&C_{d_i}, Host_{d_i}, IP_{d_i}, Relation_{d_i}, Relation_{d_i}, TimeDis_{d_i}) \tag{2}$$

1. $C\&C_{d_i}$ corresponds to the automatic feature;
2. $Host_{d_i}$ correspond to the infected hosts ratio;
3. IP_{d_i} correspond to the resolve IPs similarity;
4. $Relation_{d_i}$ correspond to the query sequential correlation;
5. $TimeDis_{d_i}$ correspond to the query time similarity.

The description of these features and how to compute them are provided below.

Definition: $D = \{d_1, d_2 \ldots d_n\}$ representing the filtered set of unknown domains; $M = \{m_1, m_2 \ldots m_n\}$ representing the set of known malicious domain names; $IP(d_i)$ representing the set of resolved IP addresses of domain d_i; $C(d_i)$ representing the set of hosts accessing domain d_i; $H = \{h_1, h_2 \ldots h_n\}$ representing the set of known malicious hosts.

Automatic Feature: When we focus on a pair (h_i, d_i), we can get a sequence of query timestamps. We convert the time sequences into the time-interval vectors, which has length equal to the number of query times minus one (i.e. if d_i queried by h_i for n times, we will get a time-interval vector with length $n - 1$). Since the attacker will add random time to the fixed sleep interval to avoid detection, we consider all the approximate time interval to be the equal one. For example, if we allow 5 s variation, $[x - 5, x + 5]$ will be mapped to x. Finally, we use different letters to represent different time-intervals. The transformation sequence is depicted in Fig. 3.

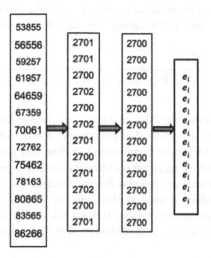

Fig. 3. Transformation of timestamps sequence.

We apply periodicity detection algorithm on the letter sequence S to get possible candidate periods p and we evaluate the confidence of all candidates. The confidence value is defined as follows:

$$\text{Confidence}_p = \frac{\text{frequence}(p, S)}{[S/p]}, \tag{3}$$

where is the number of occurrences of candidate p in S.

The feature is computed as follows:

$$C\&C_{d_i} = \begin{cases} 1, & if \ \max(\text{Confidence}_{p_i}) > \theta \\ 0, & otherwise \end{cases} \tag{4}$$

Infected Hosts Ratio: Generally, a domain queried by a large number of benign hosts has a low probability of being malicious, while one queried only by a malicious host has a high probability of being malicious. Therefore, we calculate the proportion of infected hosts for each domain. The feature is defined as follows:

$$Host_{d_i} = \frac{|C(d_i) \cap H|}{|C(d_i) \cup H|} \tag{5}$$

Resolved IPs Similarity: Due to resource limitations and the use of IP-flux and Domain-flux, the IPs and domains used in the same attack always be relevant. Generally speaking, different malicious domains may be mapped to the same IP or IP/24 subnet, or one malicious IP will be shared by multiple malicious domains. Therefore, we count the proportion of the unknown domain and malicious domains resolved to the same IP address or the same IP/24 subnet. The feature is defined as follows:

$$IP_{d_i} = 1 - \left(\frac{1}{1 + 10 |ip(d_i) \cap ip(M) + |ip(d_i) \cap ip(M)|_{24}|} \right) \tag{6}$$

Query Sequential Correlation: The attackers mostly use multiple domains in their attack activity (typically using DGA domain names) in order to avoid detection, which making their DNS activities more complicated in time and space. However, it is very difficult for a large number of malware on infected hosts to work alone without sharing any malicious domain names or common access patterns. The sequential correlation is proposed by Lee [17], which is used to represent the association relationship between two domains that are queried sequentially. If there is a strong order correlation between the unknown domain and malicious domains, then the unknown domain is likely to be a step in the APT.

Assuming that there is sequential access $(d_i \rightarrow m_i)$, the number of hosts is $C_{(d_i \rightarrow m_i)}$, the degree of sequential correlation is defined as follow:

$$\text{Relaition}_{(d_i, m_i)} = \frac{C_{d_i \rightarrow m_i}}{C_{d_i} \cap C_{m_i}} \tag{7}$$

In the case that the malicious domain set is empty, we only consider domains queried by known infected host sets, which are defined as follows:

$$\text{Relaition}_{(d_i, d_j)} = \frac{C_{d_i \rightarrow d_j}}{C_{d_i} \cap C_{d_i} \cap H} \tag{8}$$

Query Time Similarity: Different malicious domains involved in the same attack activity are usually used in each step. Therefore, the infected host usually accesses multiple malicious domains within a short time interval to carry out continuous attack activities. We use the minimum value of the access time interval between the unknown domain and malicious domains as feature, which is defined as follows:

$$minT = \min(|T_{d_i} - T_{m_{1,2...n}}|) \tag{9}$$

The feature is defined as follows:

$$\text{TimeDis}_{d_i} = \begin{cases} 1 - \log_{120} \min T + 1, & if \min T < 120\,s \\ 0, & otherwise \end{cases} \tag{10}$$

Malicious Score Calculation: For an input feature vector, we sort all the features from large to small and get

$$F_{d_i} = (f_1, f_2, f_3, f_4, f_5,), \text{ where } f_i \geq f_{i+1}, \text{ for } i = 1\ldots, 5.$$

The anomaly score is computed by:

$$\text{Malicious}_{d_i} = \left(\sum_{i=2\ldots5}^{i} \frac{1}{2^{i-1}} * f_i \right) \tag{11}$$

Belief Propagation Algorithm: Our approach is based on a simple intuition. If a host h_i or a domain d_i is known to be malicious, another domain with "strong association" with them is likely to be malicious as well. Therefore, we can discover unknown malicious ones from a small set of seeds.

Figure 4 shows an example of our algorithm. Starting from the seed host h_1, we calculate the malicious scores of all domains (filtered) visited by h_1. In the first iteration, we detected the domain d_3 with the highest anomaly score and added it into the malicious domain set M, as well as another hosts connecting M are added to the H. Iterate again until the maximum anomaly score is less than θ. The output of our method is the final set of malicious domains.

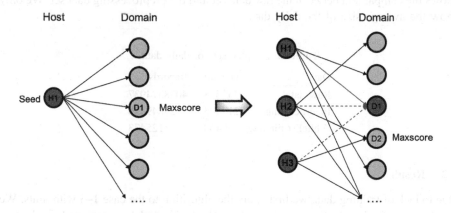

Fig. 4. Instance of belief propagation algorithm.

4   Evaluation

In this section, we introduce the details of the experiment' process and results. We first introduce our dataset and the situation of the data preprocessing and then analyze the results of our algorithm,

4.1   Experiment Dataset

We apply our methods to the data set of anonymous DNS logs including simulated APT sponsored by LANL [19]. They are real logs from a large web-site but concealed their origin and actual referenced host names. When we worked on this paper, only 16 days of data (more than 450G) were available, each day containing a simulated attack. The simulated attacks are divided into four cases, as shown in Table 1.

Table 1. The description of four cases in LANL.

Case	Seed	Task
1	One hint host	Detect contacted malicious domains
2	Three or four hint hosts	Detect contacted malicious domains
3	One hint host	Detect contacted malicious domains and other compromised hosts
4	No hint	Detect contacted malicious domains and other compromised hosts

For effective analysis, we processed the data (as described in Sect. 3.2). Table 2 shows the comparison between the raw data set and the preprocessing data set. We only show the average size of the daily data.

Table 2. Average size of daily data.

Data	Domains	Records
Raw data	357618	4038374937
Preprocessing	217603	23849438
Whitelist filtering	9463	125473

4.2   Result

Due to lack of training data, we first apply the algorithm to the case 1–3 with hints. We use three standard evaluation parameters to evaluate the model we designed. Evaluation parameters include: Precision Rate (TP/(TP + FP)), Recall Rate (TP/(TP + FN)) and False Negative Rate: FN/(TP + FN).

Table 3. The Results on different cases in LANL.

Case	Malicious domains	True positives	False positives	False negatives	APT detected
1	4	4	0	0	2 of 2
2	16	14	0	2	5 of 5
3	21	18	1	3	6 of 6
Total	41	36	1	5	13 of 13

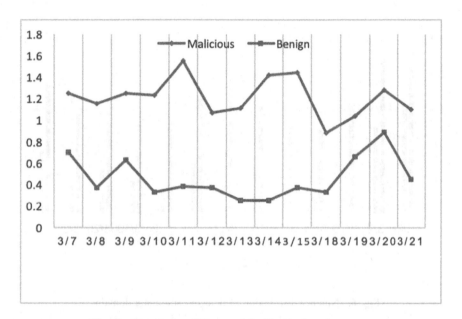

Fig. 5. Reported-malicious and legitimate domain scores.

As shown in Table 3, the precision rate of our model is 97.3%, the recall rate is 87.8%, and the false negative rate is 12.3%. It shows that our algorithm can detect related malicious domains and infected hosts under only a small amount of ground truth.

We counted the average malicious score of detected malicious domains and the maximum malicious score of Non-malicious domain per day, as shown in Fig. 5. Reported-malicious and legitimate domain scores. We can see the significant difference between malicious domains and benign domains, which shows that our feature functions can describe maliciousness accurately.

Through further analysis, we found that the undetected domain "rum.fibrous.wad" in case2 has a very common SLD, and it is queried by at least 1000 internal hosts, which lead us put it on the whitelist. In another day, the undetected domain "lisped.val" has been queried more than 500 times by one host. Our filtering rules believe that malicious domains will not generate such frequent access behaviors, so it was considered benign. But we found that all known hosts (3 hosts) query that domain using the same sleep interval. If we relax the filtering rules, "lisped.val" will be detected by the algorithm. Checking the undetected domains in case3, we found that they have almost no association with hints and known malicious domains, which brings difficulties to our detection. The observation shows that we still have a lot of work to do in finding unrelated malicious domains in same attack.

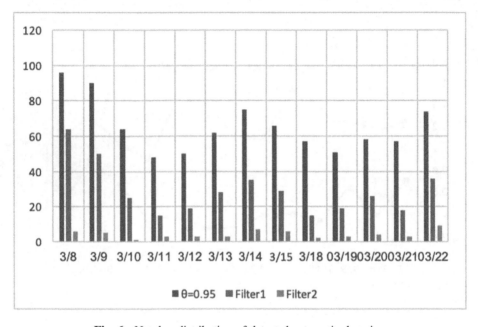

Fig. 6. Number distribution of detected automatic domains.

We use the data before 3/22 as the training set to verify our framework without hints. In order to avoid being affected by other legitimate program, we filter the legitimate automatic domains. We have adopted two kinds of filtering rules: Filter1: filter out the domains that have been automatic before; Filter2: filter out all the domains that have been queried before. The results are shown in the Fig. 6.

We finally discovered nine automatic domains on 3/22. Through further analysis, we found that only one malicious domain "otyugh.muck.don" was accessed by two hosts and the sleep interval both were 1800 s. We used this automatic domain as seed and successfully discover four other malicious domains with no false positives.

4.3   Experimental Discussion

Experimental results prove that our method performs well on the LANL dataset and can discover more unknown malicious domains given small-scale ground truth. One of the more prominent features of our method compared with others is that we can get an intuitive malicious explanation according to the feature vector during the iteration process. For example, the higher IP_{d_i}, the closer the unknown domain name and the malicious domain name, and the higher $Host_{d_i}$, the closer the unknown domain name is to the infected host, and this close relationship can largely indicate that they belong to the same kind.

5 Conclusion

We propose a detection framework based on belief propagation, which detect most of the malicious domains given small-scale seeds. But it's vulnerable to interference from other regular applications without reliable whitelist. At the same time, due to our aggressive filtering strategy, we will find it difficult to find those hijacked popular domains.

On the other hand, our method is more focused on discovering associated malicious domains in same attack activity. This helps the security team to further explore the potentially compromised hosts and potential malicious domains that have not yet been discovered. It is our shortcomings that we need to give some hints. In fact, our method can be used in combination with other detection mechanisms to improve performance. Furthermore, detect attacks without hints.

In this paper, we only propose a method for discovering associated domains, which will be difficult to achieve without beacons or hints. In future work, we will further analyze the APT attack and explore its deep-level behavior patterns to recover the entire APT attack process from scratch.

Acknowledgement. This work is supported by the National Key Research and Development Program of China under Grant 2016QY06X1205.

References

1. Bejtlich, R.: Air force cyberspace report (2007). http://taosecurity.blogspot.com/2007/10/air-force-cyberspace-report.html
2. Bohara, A., Noureddine, M.A., Fawaz, A., Sanders, W.H.: An unsupervised multi-detector approach for identifying malicious lateral movement. In: IEEE Symposium on Reliable Distributed Systems (2017)
3. Mavroeidis, V., Bromander, S.: Cyber threat intelligence model: an evaluation of taxonomies, sharing standards, and ontologies within cyber threat intelligence. In: European Intelligence and Security Informatics Conference (EISIC), pp. 91–98 (2017)
4. Sakib, M.N., Huang,C.T.: Using anomaly detection based techniques to detect HTTP-based botnet C&C traffic. In: IEEE International Conference on Communications, pp. 1–6 (2016)
5. Villeneuve, N., Bennett, J.: Detecting apt activity with network traffic analysis. Trend Micro Incorporated (2012)
6. Yan, G., Li, Q., Guo, D., Li, B.: AULD: Large scale suspicious DNS activities detection via unsupervised learning in advanced persistent threats. Sensors **19**, 3180 (2019)
7. Wang, X., Zheng, K.F., Niu, X.X., Wu, B., Wu, C.H.: Detection of command and control in advanced persistent threat based on independent access. In: IEEE International Conference on Communications (ICC) (2016)

8. Nadler, A., Aminov, A., Shabtai, A.: Detection of malicious and low throughput data exfiltration over the DNS protocol. Comput. Secur. **80**, 36–53 (2019)

9. Kheir, N., Tran, F., Caron, P., Deschamps, N.: Mentor: positive DNS reputation to skim-off benign domains in botnet C&C blacklists. In: Cuppens-Boulahia, N., Cuppens, F., Jajodia, S., Abou El Kalam, A., Sans, T. (eds.) SEC 2014. IAICT, vol. 428, pp. 1–14. Springer, Heidelberg (2014). https://doi.org/10.1007/978-3-642-55415-5_1

10. Manadhata, P.K., Yadav, S., Rao, P., Horne, W.: Detecting malicious domains via graph inference. In: Kutyłowski, M., Vaidya, J. (eds.) ESORICS 2014. LNCS, vol. 8712, pp. 1–18. Springer, Cham (2014). https://doi.org/10.1007/978-3-319-11203-9_1

11. Zou, F., Zhang, S., Rao, W., Yi, P.: Detecting malware based on DNS graph mining. Int. J. Distrib. Sens. Netw. **11**, 102687 (2015)

12. Oprea, A., Li, Z., Yen, T.-F., Chin.S. H., Alrwais, S.: Detection of early-stage enterprise infection by mining large-scale log data. In IEEE/IFIP International Conference on Dependable Systems and Networks (2015)

13. Ma, Z., Li, Q., Meng, X.: Discovering suspicious APT families through a large-scale domain graph in information-centric IoT. IEEE Access **7**, 13917–13926 (2019)

14. Khalil, I., Yu, T., Guan, B.: Discovering malicious domains through passive DNS data graph analysis. In: ACM on Asia Conference on Computer & Communications Security. ACM (2016)

15. Zhao, G., Xu, K., Xu, L., Wu, B.: Detecting APT malware infections based on malicious DNS and traffic analysis. IEEE Access **3**, 1132–1142 (2015)

16. Ghafir, I., Hammoudeh, M., Prenosil, V., Han, L., Hegarty, R., Rabie, K.: Detection of advanced persistent threat using machine-learning correlation analysis. Future Generation Comput. Syst. **89**, 349–359 (2018)

17. Lee, J., Lee, H.: GMAD: graph-based malware activity detection by DNS traffic analysis. Comput. Commun. **49**, 33–47 (2014)

18. Stevanovic, M., Pedersen, J.M., D'Alconzo, A., Ruehrup, S.: A method for identifying compromised clients based on DNS traffic analysis. Int. J. Inf. Secur. **16**(2), 115–132 (2016). https://doi.org/10.1007/s10207-016-0331-3

19. Ferrell, P.S.: Apt infection discovery using DNS data. Los Alamos National Laboratory (LANL), Technical report (2013)

Spatio-Temporal Graph Convolutional Networks for DDoS Attack Detecting

Qian Xie[1], Zheng Huang[1,2]($\boxtimes$), Jie Guo[1], and Weidong Qiu[1]

[1] Shanghai Jiao Tong University, Shanghai, China
{xieqian, huang-zheng, guojie, qiuwd}@sjtu.edu.cn
[2] Westone Cryptologic Research Center, Beijing, China

Abstract. Distributed Denial-of-Service (DDoS) attacks disrupts the availability of essential services, which are one of the most harmful threats in today's Internet. Many DDoS detection algorithms based on machine learning technology have emerged in recent years, for example, the LUCID algorithm, GNN model. But considering that DDoS attacks are based on both time and space, these algorithms only considered time and ignored space. Besides, by piece network traffic data is often difficult to obtain. The model we used in this paper is based on the Spatio-Temporal Graph Convolutional Network (STGCN) proposed by Yu B. et al. And on this basis, the model is improved for the unique characteristics of DDoS attacks. By considering the time-dependence of the network topology and network traffic, this model has a good recognition rate on the online DDoS data set, and can achieve detection of DDoS attacks under the premise of using only two-way traffic information.

Keywords: DDoS attack detecting · Machine learning · Graph convolutional network

1 Introduction

Distributed Denial-of-Service (DDoS) attacks disrupts the availability of essential services, which are one of the most harmful threats in today's Internet. According to the cisco vision network index, global IP traffic was 1.2ZB per year or 96 exabytes per month by 2016. By 2022, global IP will reach 3.3ZB per year or 278 exabytes per month [4]. DDoS attacks use a large number of zombie machines to attack the same server, and their traffic has certain characteristics in the space-time domain. Of course, with the development of attack technology, it is rarely effective to rely solely on a certain feature for DDoS attack detection. Newer DDoS attacks usually encrypt their data packets, change their control protocols and use peer-to-peer topology to improve their robustness [11]. Therefore, the traditionally used feature-based [12] methods to detect botnets become ineffective and less generalized, which makes detection becoming more difficult. While graph-based methods focus on the graphical structure of the communication using centrality-based graph measures. However, they require access to all the data at once to build the graph models while working [9].

In many cases, we cannot obtain detailed information about each traffic packet received by each node in the network, such as a monitoring system using a cloud server; or collecting all traffic information for each node and returning it is quite time-consuming And transmission bandwidth. Therefore, there is a need for a simpler DDoS attack detection tool that depends only on simple and easily obtained information such as the size of the traffic.

Based on the above reasons, this article attempts to use data with as few dimensions as possible for training. The main contributions are as follows:

- Detect DDoS attacks using graph networks based on both time and space;
- The model only depends on the 5-dimensional data to obtain the detection effect, which is suitable for the scenario without specific information of each network flow.

2   Related Works

Research on DDoS attacks has been developed for many years. Recently, with the continuous deepening of machine learning technology, many DDoS detection algorithms based on machine learning technology have emerged. For example, the LUCID algorithm proposed by R. Doriguzzi-Corin et al. [1], this algorithm has been able to perform a good detection function against DDoS attacks under certain conditions. However, considering that DDoS attacks are based on both time and space, the algorithm only considers time and ignores space, thus losing part of the information; in addition, Jiawei Zhou et al. Proposed using Graph Neural Networks (GNN) for attack detection Scheme [5], although there are no more restrictive conditions, but the detection effect is more general, the model also only considers the network space topology, and ignores the valid information in time. There is also the SDN-based DDoS attack detection method proposed by Gustavo A. Nunez Segura et al. [6], which has better detection performance under the premise that the number of attackers is limited. These methods often require more traffic information, such as IP Flags, ICMP Type, etc. Considering the widespread nature of DDoS attacks, there are also higher requirements for the performance of DDoS attack detection. Especially in some networks, we can't easily obtain detailed information of each traffic packet [10]. On the contrary, we may only get the flow size between two nodes in the network. Based on this assumption, we use Spatio-Temporal Graph Convolutional Network (STGCN), taking into account the correlation between DDoS attacks in network topology and network traffic in time, and can realize DDoS attacks under the premise of using only bidirectional traffic information Rapid detection.

3   Model

3.1   Overview

The model used in this paper is based on the Spatio-Temporal Graph Convolutional Network (STGCN) proposed by Yu B. et al. [2], and on this basis, the model is improved for the unique characteristics of DDoS attacks. As shown in Fig. 1, STGCN is mainly composed of three parts: two spatiotemporal convolution blocks and one output layer.

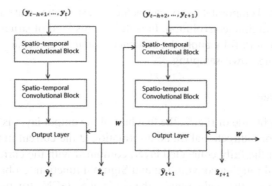

Fig. 1. Structure of STGCN.

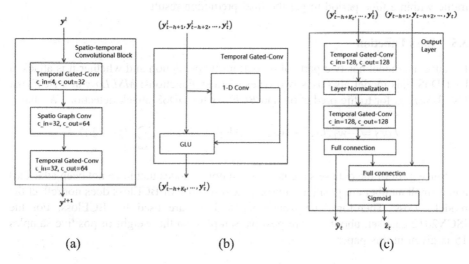

(a)   (b)   (c)

Fig. 2. Each part of STGCN. (a) Spatio-temporal Convolutional Block; (b) Temporal Gated Convolutional Block; (c) Output Layer.

3.2 Preprocessing for Input

Before the data enters the entire network, some adjustments are required. Chebyshev Polynomials Approximation is used here to help reduce the number of training parameters [2]. In addition, the input data needs to be normalized. Finally, the input data is the processed flow data flowing through each node.

3.3 Spatio-Temporal Convolutional Block

In order to fuse features from both time and space, Spatio-temporal Convolutional Block (ST-Conv Block) is used here to process graph-based time series data. As shown in the middle of Fig. 1, the Spatial Layer in the middle is used to bridge two Temporal

Layers. These two Temporal Layers can achieve fast spatial state propagation from graph convolution to time convolution. In addition, this kind of structured network can make the entire network fully apply the bottleneck strategy and change the feature ratio through up-sampling/down-sampling.

3.4 Output Layer

As shown in the right side of Fig. 2, the first half of the output layer is a fully connected layer that is used for bidirectional traffic information at the current moment. According to the prediction of the fully connected layer, combined with the current flow of a time window, and then through a convolution and Sigmoid function to obtain the prediction of the attack traffic for the node. Unlike the original STGCN structure [2], this model has been modified in the output layer in order to be able to predict whether the node is attacked: a fully connected layer has been added to use the known traffic and predicted traffic within a time period to get the final prediction result.

3.5 Loss Function

Because the model has two parts of output: traffic prediction and whether it is attacked by DDoS, this model also uses two types of Loss Functions: *MSELoss* and *BCEloss*. Use *MSELoss* for traffic prediction and *BCEloss* for DDoS attack detection. We have:

$$Loss = -w_T z log\hat{z} - w_F(1 - z) \log(1 - \hat{z}) + \sum_{i \in n_{feature}} (y_i - \hat{z}_i)^2 \qquad (1)$$

Since most of the data sets are negative samples (nodes that have not been attacked) and a small number are positive samples, the direct use of BCEloss does not reflect the model's Loss. Therefore, the weight w_T and w_F are used for BCEloss. For the ISCX2012 data set, about 7% are positive samples, so the weight of positive samples 15 is given in this paper.

4 Experiments

4.1 Dataset

The data set used in this article is ISCX2012 [3]. It contains network activity data from June 12 to June 17, 2010, with a total of about 5 million tagged traffic data (marking whether the network traffic flow is an attack traffic). It covers Inside Infiltrating, HTTP Denial of Service, IRC Botnet and other attack methods.

4.2 Data Preprocessing

A. Generate the network topology
Because the ISCX2012 data set does not provide the topology of the network between the servers, and there must be a topology in the computer network in reality. We first

use the traffic data and IP address to restore the network topology. We defines each network IP address as a node; the source IP and destination IP of each flow are directly connected between the two nodes; in addition, each LAN segment Node edges are directly connected (including each node and itself).

B. Traffic flow feature extraction

Because the data of ISCX2012 is a piece by piece network activity, including source IP and destination IP, but it does not have the characteristics based on network nodes. Therefore, this paper uses a sliding time window for sampling and extracts 518,400 flow data from the data set. Each piece of data contains 5 traffic characteristics of all nodes in the topology graph: *total source packets, total source bytes, total destination packets, total destination bytes* and *unknown app*. The *unknown app* is to mark whether unknown TCP traffic flows through the time window (unknown TCP traffic refers to traffic other than common types of traffic such as IMAP, POP, HTTP, RPC, SSH, etc.). In this paper, the length of the time window is 60 s, and the step size is 1 s. The flow data of each node is obtained by summing up the various flow characteristic values that flow through the node in the time window. In addition, if attack traffic flows through the node in the time window, the node is marked as an attacked label at this moment for later verification.

4.3 Evaluation Methodology

For the experimental results, we used Accuracy (ACC), False Positive Rate (FPR), True Positive Rate (TPR), F1 Score (F1) to reflect the experimental results.

$$ACC = \frac{TP+TN}{TP+TN+FP+FN} \tag{2}$$

$$FPR = \frac{FP}{FP+TN} \tag{3}$$

$$TPR = \frac{TP}{TP+FN} \tag{4}$$

$$F1 = \frac{2TP}{2TP+FP+FN} \tag{5}$$

Among them, TP, TN, FP, FN are True Positive, True Negative, False Positive, False Negative.

4.4 Results

As shown in Fig. 2, by adjusting the hyperparameters: time window size (T) and prediction period (h), the STGCN model can obtain a better detection capability. After many experiments, we found that when the time window size is 60 s and the prediction period is 10 s, a better prediction effect can be achieved (Fig. 3).

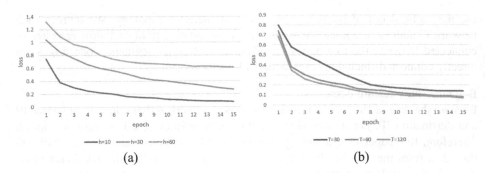

Fig. 3. Effects of hyper-parameters on training model; (a) prediction period (h); (b) time window size (T);

Although choosing a larger time window will have better training effect, but considering the time consumption and GPU memory consumption increased by increasing the time window, an appropriate time window size is more appropriate.

In the DDoS attack detection algorithm that also uses the data set ISCX2012, we combine the STGCN model with LUCID, 3LSTM [7] and TR-IDS [8] proposed in Deep Defense. The specific results are shown in Table 1. It can be seen that STGCN has no advantage in accuracy compared to other DDoS attack detection methods. However, considering that the STGCN network only uses flow information (considering that only flow information can be obtained in the network), this result is satisfactory.

Table 1. DDoS Attack detection results on ISCX2012

Model	ACC	FPR	TPR	F1
STGCN	0.983	0.005	0.837	0.882
LUCID	0.989	0.018	0.995	0.989
DeepDefense 3LSTM [7]	0.984	N/A	0.985	0.984
TR-IDS [8]	0.981	0.004	0.959	N/A

Considering that STGCN only uses traffic flow data as the basis for judgment, such a recognition rate is equally satisfactory.

5   Conclusion

From the results in the previous section, it is feasible to use STGCN for DDoS attack detection. Compared with other DDoS attack detection algorithms, STGCN can effectively learn the correlation both spatio and temporal features between network nodes. Because the traffic of DDoS attacks often comes from multiple meat machines, the attack path is variable and long, and even an attacker may use the machine on the intranet as a springboard to launch the attack. Therefore, the algorithm can address this situation to a certain extent and achieve effective DDoS attack detection. In addition, this algorithm does not require much information to make a judgment. It only needs the network packet traffic flowing through each node to achieve detection, which occupies less resources and is easier to deploy than other algorithms.

The data set used in this article does not contain the network topology, so the network topology used may differ from the actual topology. In the future, you can consider using SDN to build a network environment for testing to obtain a true network topology information verification model. accuracy.

In addition, in order to obtain better performance, we currently use only one layer of full connection to detect the DDoS attack. More complex and detailed classification methods can be considered to improve the accuracy of DDoS attack detection with a slight sacrifice in performance.

Acknowledgments. This study is supported by supported by The National Key Research and Development Program of China under grant 2017YFB0802704 and 2017YFB0802202.

References

1. Doriguzzi-Corin, R., Millar, S., Scott-Hayward, S., Martinez-del-Rincon, J., Siracusa, D.: LUCID: a practical, lightweight deep learning solution for DDoS attack detection. arXiv preprint, arXiv:2002.04902v1 (2020)
2. Yu, B., Yin, H., Zhu, Z. Spatio-temporal graph convolutional networks: a deep learning framework for traffic forecasting. arXiv preprint, arXiv:1709.04875 (2017)
3. ISCX2012," Intrusion detection evaluation dataset 2012" https://www.unb.ca/cic/datasets/ids.html. Accessed 15 May 2020
4. Cisco, VNI.: Cisco visual networking index: forecast and methodology 2016–2021. https://www.cisco.com/c/cn/us/solutions/collateral/service-provider/visual-networking-index-vni/completewhite-paper-c11-481360.pdf (2017)
5. Zhou, J., Xu, Z., Rush, A.M., Yu, M.: Automating botnet detection with graph neural networks. arXiv preprint, arXiv: arXiv:2003.06344 (2020)
6. Segura, G.A.N., Skaperas, S., Chorti, A., Mamatas, L., Margi, C.B.: Denial of service attacks detection in software-defined wireless sensor networks. arXiv preprint, arXiv: arXiv:2003.12027 (2020)
7. Yuan, X., Li, C., Li, X.: DeepDefense: identifying DDoS attack via deep learning. In: Proceedings of SMARTCOMP (2017)
8. Min, E., Long, J., Liu, Q., Cui, J., W.: Chen, TR-IDS: anomalybased intrusion detection through text-convolutional neural network and random forest. Security and Communication Networks (2018)
9. Warraich, S.H., Aziz, Z., Khurshid, H., Hameed, R.A., Awais, S.M.: SDN enabled and OpenFlow compatible network performance monitoring system. arXiv preprint, arXiv: arXiv:2005.07765 (2020)
10. Radware, "Memcached DDoS Attacks." https://security.radware.com/ddos-threats-attacks/threat-advisories-attack-reports/memcached-under-attack. Accessed 15 May 2020
11. Jaiswal, R., Bajgude, S.: Botnet technology. In: 3rd International Conference on Emerging Trends in Computer and Image Processing (ICETCIP 2013), pp. 169–175. (2013)
12. Perdisci, R., Lee, W., Feamster, N.: Behavioral clustering of http-based malware and signature generation using malicious network traces. In: Proceedings of the 7th USENIX Conference on Networked Systems Design and Implementation, NSDI 2010, pp. 26, Berkeley, CA, USA (2010)

Cerebral Microbleeds Detection Based on 3D Convolutional Neural Network

Meng Zhao[1], Chen Jin[1], Lingmin Jin[1], Shenghua Teng[1(✉)],
and Zuoyong Li[2(✉)]

[1] College of Electronic and Information Engineering,
Shandong University of Science and Technology, Qingdao 266590, China
zmzhaomeng1998@163.com, shteng@sdust.edu.cn
[2] Fujian Provincial Key Laboratory of Information Processing and Intelligent
Control, College of Computer and Control Engineering, Minjiang University,
Fuzhou 350121, China
fzulzytdq@126.com

Abstract. Cerebral microbleeds (CMBs) are important imaging and diagnostic biomarkers for cerebrovascular diseases and cognitive dysfunctions. Reliable detection of the location and amount of CMBs in brain tissue is crucial for the diagnosis, prevention and treatment of related diseases, where traditional Convolutional Neural Network (CNN) has been applied but may fail to achieve high enough detection accuracy. To alleviate this issue, we utilize 3D Fully Convolutional Networks (FCN) and 3D AlexNet to establish a cascade coarse-to-fine detection manner. Specifically, CMBs candidates are first screened out using 3D FCN, followed by 3D AlexNet which extracts the spatial features of CMBs and distinguishes the false positive samples from candidate regions. Experimental results show that the proposed method can realize precise detection of CMBs in magnetic resonance images (MRI) by improving detection sensitivity and reducing false positive samples.

Keywords: Cerebral microbleeds · 3D convolution neural network · High precision · 3D FCN · 3D AlexNet

1 Introduction

Cerebral microbleeds (CMBs) are important imaging and diagnostic biomarkers for cerebrovascular diseases and cognitive dysfunctions. Conventional CMB detection is time-consuming, laborious, and the results are poorly repeatable, due to manually labeling medical images by doctors or professional medical workers. To alleviate this issue, researchers have developed some computer-aided methods hoping to overcome the problem of manual segmentation. These methods are roughly divided into two categories, i.e., one is based on the combination of traditional image processing and machine learning [1–5], the other is based on deep learning [6, 7].

The detection methods based on the combination of traditional image processing and machine learning are mostly based on simple features such as shape, size, and intensity. These hand-crafted features are usually not enough to capture the complex

© Springer Nature Switzerland AG 2020
X. Chen et al. (Eds.): ML4CS 2020, LNCS 12486, pp. 160–169, 2020.
https://doi.org/10.1007/978-3-030-62223-7_14

features and spatial information of CMBs [1]. According to the research results of researchers [1–5], the cascaded random forest classifier or radial symmetry transformation is used to determine the position of CMBs. Then, it is used to improve the detection speed that methods such as supervised classification methods or support vector machine (SVM) classifiers.

The detection methods based on deep learning have been widely used in the field of medical image processing, through a data-driven way. The CMB automatic detection methods for three-dimensional feature representation can improve accuracy and maintain high sensitivity. For example, Chen et al. [6] proposed a CMB automatic detection method for three-dimensional feature representation based on deep learning. Its detection process includes three steps, i.e., step1 CMBs candidate region positioning, step 2 feature representation, and step 3 classification. Dou et al. [7] proposed to use deep learning theory to construct a cascade system using a three-dimensional convolutional neural network model to achieve automatic detection of CMBs.

After exploring existing methods of detecting cerebral microbleeds based on convolutional neural networks (CNNs), we found that they still have some problems. In the theorics of other researchers, they only focus on solving part of the problem, so they cannot achieve a balance between accuracy and efficiency. To alleviate these issues, we proposed a modified method for the detection of high cerebral microbleeds based on 3D convolutional neural network.

The remainder of this paper is organized as follows. Section 2 introduces the details of the proposed method. Experimental results are discussed in Sect. 3. Conclusion is drawn in Sect. 4.

2 Method

In most biomarker detection applications, the detected target is often discretely distributed among the 3D data and CMBs in MR images. If the traditional sliding window method of convolutional neural network (CNN) is used to process data, thousands of 3D block samples are analyzed. Especially when the input image collected at high resolution increases greatly the workload, and the 3D data also increases the processing time, which make the detection process spent more time. Therefore, it considers adopting a screening scheme to form a two-stage detection framework before detecting accurate targets.

In the first stage, as combining with 2D FCN, 3D fully convolutional network (3D FCN) is adopted as the first stage screening model to effectively screen out reliable candidate regions from 3D MR data [8]. The input of 3D FCN can be voxel data onto any size, and a 3D score can be generated within a single forward propagation, all of these can speed up the selection process of candidate regions without compromising sensitivity. In the second stage, 3D AlexNet is a wider and deeper convolutional neural network model, it can better capture the complex three-dimensional features of CMBs. At the same time, it can be avoided a problem that the gradient disappearance phenomenon caused by the saturated activation functions. Using the unsaturated linear activation function ReLU makes the training speed accelerate. The overall structure of the two-stage detection framework used is shown in Fig. 1.

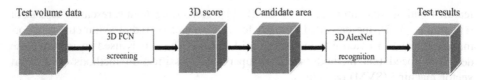

Fig. 1. Overview of CMB detection framework.

2.1 Candidate Selection Stage

At this stage, it is important to make the fully connected layer convert into a convolution method, so the fully-connected (FC) layer needs to be rewritten into a convolution form. As shown in the following formula:

$$h_i^l = \sigma\left(\sum_k h_k^{l-1} * W_{ki}^l + b_i^l\right)k, \tag{1}$$

in the above Eq. (1) [9], each neuron in the FC layer is regarded as a feature volume of size "$1 \times 1 \times 1$", $W_{pq}^l \in R^{1 \times 1 \times 1}$ is the 3D kernel, $*$ is the 3D convolution operation described in the Eq. (2) [9].

$$\mu_{ki}^l(x,y,z) = \sum_{m,n,t} h_k^{l-1}(x-m, y-n, z-t)W_{ki}^l(m,n,t). \tag{2}$$

In this way, the multiplication of the vector-matrix is expressed as a convolution operation of the convolution kernel, and the FC layer is converted into a convolution layer, so the network can support input of any size.

The workflow of the screening phase is shown in Fig. 2, including the training phase and the testing phase.

In training phrase, positive samples taken from the CMBs area achieve the data enhancement by translation, rotation, and mirroring to expand the training database. In the implementation process, the network is trained through three sub-steps. First, a non-CMB region randomly selected from the brain is used as a negative sample before the initial 3D CNN of the training. Next, it is added that false positive samples obtained by applying the initial model on the training set. Finally, the expanded and enhanced training database is used to adjust the initial model. The database includes 20.13% positive samples, 45.07% randomly selected negative samples, and 34.80% as supplementary false positive samples. In this way, the identification ability of the network is further enhanced. After the training is completed, the adjusted 3D CNN model is converted into a 3D FCN model by converting a convolution of the FC layer. In testing phase, the 3D FCN model takes the entire voxel data as input and generates a corresponding rough estimated score. The value on the score represents the probability of CMBs at the corresponding position in the original inputs.

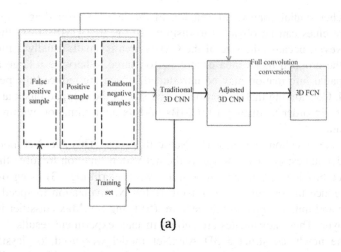

(a)

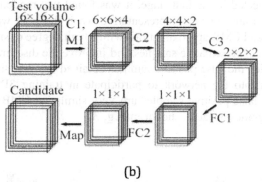

(b)

Fig. 2. Illustration of the workflow of the screening stage: (a) training stage, (b) testing stage.

The generated score may have a noise effect, the local non-maximum suppression is used for post-processing in 3D [10]. According to the mapping relationship in formula

$$x' = d \cdot x + \left[\frac{c-1}{2}\right], \tag{3}$$

the position on the score is mapped back to the corresponding coordinates of the original input space. Finally, the score is thresholding, and the threshold is the equal of 0.64 that it is selected to retrieve candidate regions with high probability.

2.2 Accurate Identification Stage

At this stage, the candidate positions selected in the first stage need to be divided into many small 3D blocks. The size of these massive areas needs to be carefully verified. We found that a training block of size $16 \times 16 \times 10$ produced many false positive results in the first stage. By appropriately expanding the size of the blocky area and using the richer spatial context information in the larger surrounding neighborhood, richer feature clues can be obtained to distinguish the true CMBs from the approximation. However, because the size of the CMBs area is small, usually 2 mm-10 mm, the size of the cropped block area cannot be too large, otherwise a large amount of redundant spatial information may be introduced, which are reduced the performance of the model. Considering that the reason, so the size of the cropped block area is set to $20 \times 20 \times 16$, in order to distinguish CMBs and its approximation within a suitable receptive field.

For accurate detection, we used AlexNet at this stage. This AlexNet model has the following advantages: (1) using ReLu as the activation function to solve the gradient disappearance problem; (2) using Dropout to avoid overfitting; (3) using overlapping pooling to reduce the output size; (4) using Batch Normalization to speed up model convergence and mitigate gradient dispersion; (5) using SoftMax classifier in the fully connected layer. These advantages are shown in later experiment results.

When the newly constructed 3D AlexNet model was used to classify the 3D candidate regions selected in the first stage, it was found that randomly selected non-CMB region samples are not very representative when the goal was to distinguish between true CMBs and CMB approximations with a high degree of similarity. In order to be able to generate representative samples and improve the discrimination ability of the 3D AlexNet model, the false-positive samples obtained from the first stage are used as negative samples into the network to participate in training 3D AlexNet in the second stage. These false-positive samples are very similar to CMBs. The schematic diagram of the recognition stage is shown in Fig. 3.

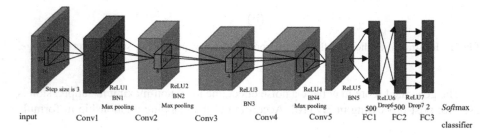

Fig. 3. Discrimination stage Diagram.

3   Experiments

In this article, the data sources are part of a large SWI dataset provided by researchers from the Chinese University Hong Kong School of Medicine and the department of a treatment research center for dementia prevention. In the experiment, the obtained data set is randomly divided into three parts, which are used for training, verification, and testing. The specific details are shown in Table 1.

Table 1. Details of datasets

Data-set	Training set	Testing set	Verification set
Subjects number	100	20	20
CMB number	403	57	62

Theano library is used to implement the network framework. In training phase, the following hyperparameters are used: learning rate = 0.03, momentum = 0.9, dropout rate = 0.5, batch size = 32. The trainable weights are randomly initialized by the Gaussian distribution ($\mu = 0$, $\sigma = 0.01$), and updated with the standard back-propagation. The entire model is spent about an hour. The 3D FCN will take about a minute to process an entire SWI voxel size of $512 \times 512 \times 150$. The stage of 3D AlexNet is faster, and it takes about 2 s to process each object.

3.1 Candidate Selection

In order to compare the time performance, the average time for 3D FCN to screen each subject is recorded and compared with other screening methods. The results are listed in Table 2. The method takes about one minute to process each input volume of size in this paper, which is faster than the method of calculating the local threshold using the sliding window of the traditional voxel method [11]. The screening method of Barnes et al. [5] is faster because it utilizes global thresholds based on size and intensity. But for the screening stage, the accuracy of the screening is the most important because the results affect the recognition process in the next stage. As can be seen from Table 2, the 3D FCN method has the highest sensitivity and effectively reduces the number of false-positive samples, thereby it can achieve a good balance between accuracy and time performance.

Table 2. Comparison of different screening methods

Method	Sensitivity	Number of false positive samples	Test time for each subject
SVM [5]	84.74%	2325.1	82.25
2D-CNN-SVM [12]	89.06%	827.6	13.70
3D FCN [7]	95.51%	253.2	66.90

In the experiment, local non-maximum suppression is performed in 3D. In order to show the results more clearly, the 3D score and its 3D suppression results are projected onto the visualization slice plane along the vertical axis. As shown in Fig. 4 is the comparison results of different screening methods.

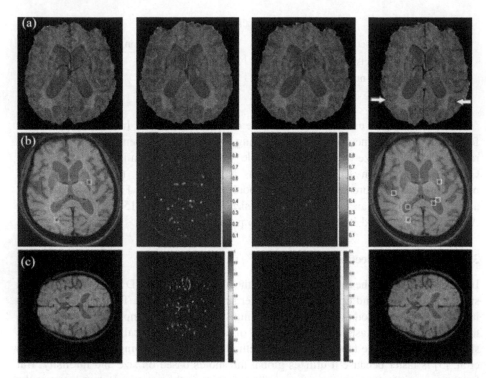

Fig. 4. Comparison results of different screening methods: (a) uses the SVM method with different thresholding, (b) uses the 3D FCN method, (c) uses the modified method based on 3D Convolutional Neural Network.

In Fig. 4(c), the first picture is the original data. The second picture is the 2D projection of the score generated after the first stage of screening. We can observe red small area distribution representing possible CMB candidate areas. The third picture is the projection of the post-processing score. After threshold processing, most low-probability areas have been excluded and left a few high-probability candidate areas. It can be observed that most of the high-probability areas on the score correspond to CMB lesions, and most of the background areas have been successfully compressed to zero. The fourth picture is the CMBs candidate that maps the screening results back to the original input volume. The location of the area is marked with a red circle in the figure. In this way, a large number of non-CMB regions are successfully eliminated, thereby greatly reducing the calculation workload in the subsequent recognition stage.

3.2   Accurate Identification

3D AlexNet needs a suitable receptive field to realize the recognition function. In order to find the input block sizes obtained the best detection effect, we verify a larger input block with more context information whether enhanced enough the identification ability of the model by testing a larger size than the input block size of the screening stage. In this experiment, three different configurations of input blocks with sizes

$16 \times 16 \times 10$, $20 \times 20 \times 16$ and $24 \times 24 \times 20$ are selected for testing, among which the size $16 \times 16 \times 10$ of the input block is the same size as the used training block in the screening stage. The test results are shown in Table 3.

Table 3. Detection results under different block sizes

3D block size	Sensitivity	Accuracy	Average false positive
$16 \times 16 \times 10$	83.13%	30.05%	5.60
$20 \times 20 \times 16$	**85.28%**	**39.17%**	**3.90**
$24 \times 24 \times 20$	84.02%	24.96%	6.18

It can be seen from Table 3 that the detection sensitivity reaches 83.13% and the average number of false positives is 5.60 when the block size is $16 \times 16 \times 10$. At a block size of $20 \times 20 \times 16$, the sensitivity is increased to 85.28% and the number of false positives is reduced to 3.90, which prove that it can enhance the recognition ability of 3D AlexNet by the appropriate increase of context information. When the block size is $24 \times 24 \times 20$, the detection sensitivity is reduced to 84.02%, and the average number of false positives per subject is also increased to 6.18. The reason that too much context information is introduced causes interference to the actual CMB signals, thereby reducing the detection performance.

In Fig. 5, the Free Response Operating Characteristic (FROC) [13] curves can also be clearly observed that the best detection effect can be obtained by using an input block of size $20 \times 20 \times 16$. Through this experiment, it can be concluded that the best performance can be obtained on 3D AlexNet when we set the input block size of $20 \times 20 \times 16$. In fact, regardless of the size of the used input block, the obtained results are better than using traditional CNNs or other methods.

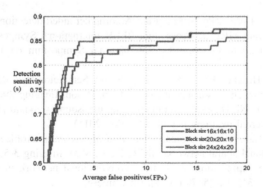

Fig. 5. FROC curves of 3D AlexNet with different block size.

4 Conclusion

After exploring the limitations of existing detection methods based on 3D convolution neural network, a modified method is presented in this paper. Contributions of the proposed method are as follows: (1) a two-stage CMBs detection model is built. In the first stage, the improved 3D FCN model is used for preliminary screening candidate regions. In the second stage, the 3D AlexNet model is used to accurately identify CMB, and they are distinguished between CMBs and similar high approximations. (2) By changing the input block size for comparative, the optional block size with the best performance can obtain. Several representatives experiment demonstrate that the proposed method can improve detection speed and accuracy and the disadvantage of traditional CNNs and making it possible to be used in practice.

Acknowledgements. This work is partially supported by National Natural Science Foundation of China (61972187, 61772254), Fujian Provincial Leading Project (2017H0030, 2019H0025), Government Guiding Regional Science and Technology Development (2019L3009), and Natural Science Foundation of Fujian Province (2017J01768 and 2019J01756).

References

1. Dou, Q., Chen, H., Yu, L., et al.: Automatic cerebral microbleeds detection from MR images via Independent Subspace Analysis based hierarchical features. In: Proceedings of Annual International IEEE Engineering in Medicine Biology Society, pp. 7933–7936 (2015)
2. Fazlollahi, A., Meriaudeau, F., Villemagne, V.L., et al.: Efficient machine learning framework for computer-aided detection of cerebral microbleeds using the Radon transform. In: 2014 IEEE 11th International Symposium on Biomedical Imaging (ISBI). IEEE (2014)
3. Kuijf, H.J., Bresser, J.D., Geerlings, M.I., et al.: Efficient detection of cerebral microbleeds on 7.0 T MR images using the radial symmetry transform. Neuroimage **59**(3), 2266–2273 (2012)
4. Ghafary, B., Lijn, F.V.D., Poels, M., et al.: A computer aided detection system for cerebral microbleeds in brain MRI. In: Proceedings/IEEE International Symposium on Biomedical Imaging: from nano to macro. IEEE International Symposium on Biomedical Imaging (2012)
5. Barnes, S.R.S., Haacke, E.M., Ayaz, M., et al.: Semiautomated detection of cerebral microbleeds in magnetic resonance images. Magn. Reson. Imaging **29**(6), 844–852 (2011)
6. Chen, H., Dou, Q., Ni, D., et al.: Automatic fetal ultrasound standard plane detection using knowledge transferred recurrent neural networks (2015)
7. Dou, Qi., Chen, Hao., et al.: Automatic detection of cerebral microbleeds from MR images via 3D convolutional neural networks. IEEE Trans. Med. Imaging **3**(5), 1182–1195 (2016)
8. Li, Xian, He, Jie: Application of 3D fully convolutional network in spine segmentation. Electron Technol. **31**(11), 75–79 (2018). (in Chinese)
9. Wang, K.: Research on medical image segmentation method based on deep learning. University of Science and Technology of China (2018). (in Chinese)
10. Li, Y.: CT image recognition of lung cancer based on three-dimensional convolutional neural network model. Shanxi Normal University (2018). (in Chinese)

11. Chen, H., Yu, L., Dou, Q., et al.: Automatic detection of cerebral microbleeds via deep learning based on 3D feature representation. In: 2015 IEEE 12th International Symposium on Biomedical Imaging (ISBI). IEEE (2015)
12. Zhu, Wei., Jingyi, Qu, Renbiao, Wu: Image classification algorithm of straight-through convolutional neural network combined with batch normalization. J. Comput. Aided Des. Graph. **29**(09), 1650–1657 (2017). (in Chinese)
13. Hillis, S.L., Chakraborty, D.P., Orton, C.G.: ROC or FROC? It depends on the research question. Med. Phys. **44**(5), 1603 (2017)

Liver Tumor Segmentation of CT Image by Using Deep Fully Convolutional Network

Lingmin Jin[1], Rui Ma[1], Meng Zhao[1], Shenghua Teng[1(✉)],
and Zuoyong Li[2(✉)]

[1] College of Electronic and Information Engineering,
Shandong University of Science and Technology, Qingdao 266590, China
lingmin_jin@163.com, shteng@sdust.edu.cn
[2] Fujian Provincial Key Laboratory of Information Processing and Intelligent
Control, College of Computer and Control Engineering, Minjiang University,
Fuzhou 350121, China
fzulzytdq@126.com

Abstract. Accurate segmentation of liver tumors is an important guarantee for the success of liver cancer surgery, where convolutional network has been a type of popular method. However, the performance of the traditional convolutional network is limited by the network depth. To improve the accuracy of liver tumor segmentation, we propose a cascaded deep fully convolutional network (DFCN) which uses ResNet as the basis network followed by side output layer in the upsampling stage to fuse multi-scale image features. For better localizing the liver tumors, the segmentation result is further refined by a fully connected conditional random field. Experimental results show that the proposed method achieves higher segmentation accuracy than several state-of-the-art methods.

Keywords: Liver tumor segmentation · Deep learning · Fully convolutional network · Fully connected conditional random field

1 Introduction

Accurate segmentation of liver tumors is an important guarantee for the success of liver cancer surgery. CT imaging technology is a common way for doctors to diagnose liver cancer. Comparing with other medical imaging technologies, CT images have the characteristics of clear imaging and high signal-to-noise ratio, playing an important role in the diagnosis and treatment of liver diseases. In the actual clinical diagnosis, doctors are required to manually segment liver tumors on CT images. The segmentation process requires a lot of time and effort, and the segmentation results are greatly affected by human subjectivity. To alleviate this issue, researchers have developed some computer-aided methods for liver tumor segmentation. These methods can be divided into three categories, namely traditional methods [1–4], machine learning-based methods [5, 6], and deep learning-based methods [7–11].

Traditional segmentation methods mainly include thresholding [1], region-based growth [2], level set and active contours [3, 4], and so on. Traditional methods mainly use manual extraction of features, resulting in inaccurate segmentation effects,

© Springer Nature Switzerland AG 2020
X. Chen et al. (Eds.): ML4CS 2020, LNCS 12486, pp. 170–179, 2020.
https://doi.org/10.1007/978-3-030-62223-7_15

especially the target of medical images to be segmented may not have obvious contours, etc. Machine learning based segmentation usually consist of feature extraction and classification or regression. Massoptier et al. [5] first segmented the liver in the CT image by the dynamic contour method, and then segmented the tumor on the liver using the K-means clustering method. Shi et al. [6] used the AdaBoost score Similar algorithm realizes the automatic segmentation of liver tumors. Machine learning-based methods need to manually set the features to be extracted and the features used could heavily affect the segmentation results, which are still affected by subjective experience and prior knowledge, and the segmentation efficiency needs to be improved.

Deep learning methods are widely used in the field of medical image processing. For example, Guo et al. [7] proposed ALexNet [8] liver tumor segmentation model based on the FCN structure. Ronneberger et al. [9] proposed U-Net for medical image segmentation. Christ et al. [10] proposed a method of segmenting liver tumors with a cascaded fully convolutional network. He [11] proposed that ResNet can directly pass the input information to the next layer by introducing the identity mapping structure to form a residual network. With the advent of ResNet, more and more deep convolutional networks are used in the field of medical image processing.

After exploring existing liver tumor segmentation methods based on convolutional neural networks, we can find that they still have two limitations. Firstly, the shallow convolutional neural network is plagued by the problem of deep network degradation, and the ability of the network to extract features is limited. Secondly, the output of the high-level convolutional layer tends to lose part of the detailed information like the number of layers increases and the pooling process, resulting in a rougher feature map obtained by upsampling, which affects the accuracy of liver tumor segmentation. To alleviate these issues, we proposed a modified method for liver tumor segmentation based on DFCN. Experimental results showed that the DFCN model had better feature expression capability and more generalization performance, which improved the segmentation accuracy of the model.

2 Method

To solve the problem of accurate segmentation of liver tumors, we proposed an improved method of liver tumor segmentation. First of all, this method overcomes the problem of deep network degradation and improves the rough expression of the fuzzy segmentation results of the fully convolutional network, and then introduces a balanced loss function to train the network. Finally, the fully connected conditional random field is used to optimize the liver tumor segmentation results of DFCN.

2.1 DFCN Segmentation Model

ResNet with the fully connected layer removed is used as the basic network of DFCN, where ResNet is formed by stacking residual units and has 24 layers in total. Each residual unit is composed of two convolutional layers with BN layers. The basic network is divided into 5 convolutional stages with the pooling layer as the demarcation point. The scale of the feature map generated at each stage is different: from shallow to deep, the original image size, 1/2 original image size, 1/4 original image size, 1/8 original image size, and 1/16 original image size. A side output layer is connected at the end of each convolution stage, and each side output layer is responsible for supervising the feature map generated by the convolution stage. The side output layer is composed of a convolution layer with a convolution kernel size of 3 × 3 and an output channel of 16 and a deconvolution layer. The deconvolution layer is responsible for upsampling feature maps of different scales to the original size. The feature maps with different scale information generated by each side output layer are superimposed and input into the fusion layer. The fusion layer linearly fuses the features of each scale through a convolution layer with a convolution kernel size of 1 × 1. Finally, the fused result is sent to the classifier as the output of DFCN for classification.

In this paper, when using DFCN for CT image liver tumor segmentation, we find that the receptive field in the first convolution stage is small, and it is easy to extract local image noise, which affects the entire tumor segmentation, so we only use feature maps for the last four convolution stages. In this paper, inspired by the structure of the cascaded full convolution network proposed by Christ et al. [10], the DFCN of the cascaded structure is designed. As shown in Fig. 1, two DFCNs with the same structure are trained to segment the liver and tumor respectively. The first DFCN focuses on segmenting the liver from the CT slices of the abdomen, and then the liver ROI was cut out from the original image through the liver segmentation results, and the second DFCN focuses on segmenting liver tumors from the liver ROI.

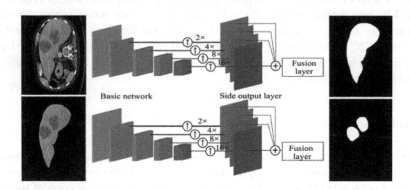

Fig. 1. Cascaded liver tumor segmentation network.

2.2 Training of DFCN Network

This article introduces the cost-sensitive loss objective function [12] in the process of calculating the network loss function, the loss function generated by all the side output layers in the DFCN network is:

$$L_{side}(W, w) = \sum_{m=1}^{M} \alpha_m l_{side}^{(m)}\left(W, w^{(m)}\right). \tag{1}$$

Because of the imbalance of the number of positive and negative sample pixels, this paper introduces the balance parameter β according to the cost-sensitive method. For each side output layer, the specific result of the loss function is:

$$L_{side}\left(W, w^{(m)}\right) = -\beta \sum_{j\in Y_+} logPr\left(y_i = 1|X; W, w^{(m)}\right)$$
$$- (1-\beta) \sum_{j\in Y_-} logPr\left(y_j = 0|X; W, w^{(m)}\right),$$

(2)

where $\beta = |Y_-|/Y$, $1 - \beta = |Y_+|/|Y|$, $|Y_-|$ represents the set of positive sample label pixels, and $|Y_+|$ represents the set of negative sample label pixels. The loss function of the network includes two parts: the loss function $L_{side}(W, w)$ generated by the output layer on all sides and the loss function $L_{side}(W, w, h)$ generated when the fusion layer predicts the final segmentation result, where h represents the weight parameter of the fusion layer.

In this paper, a stochastic gradient descent algorithm with momentum parameters is used to optimize the loss function of the network model. During the training process: the learning rate is set to 10^{-7} and the momentum parameter is 0.9. In order to prevent overfitting, the regular term coefficient is set to 0.0002, a total of 50000 iterations. In order to visualize the training process, this paper records the Loss generated by the network segmentation tumor every 100 iterations and draws a line graph.

The Loss line chart is shown in Fig. 2(a). In the training set and verification set, not all CT slices contain tumors, the Loss generated when there is no tumor is small, so it can be seen from the figure that the Loss fluctuates locally. But as the number of iterations increases, the overall trend of the Loss gradually declined and eventually stabilized in a lower range. The Dice line chart is shown in Fig. 2(b). Similarly, when recording the Dice similarity coefficient, the Dice similarity coefficient of CT slices that do not contain tumors will be 0. When drawing a line chart, this article discards the item whose Dice similarity coefficient is 0. As the number of iterations increases, the Dice similarity coefficient gradually increases, and finally stabilizes in the training set in the range of 70% ± 20%, and in the validation set in the range of 55% ± 20%.

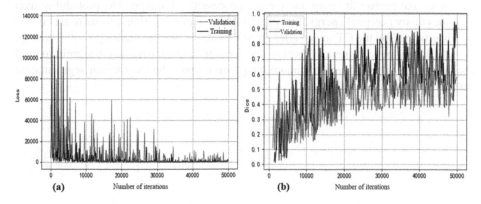

Fig. 2. Line charts during training: (a) Loss, (b) Dice.

2.3   FC-CRF Optimization Process

DFCN improved the roughness of segmentation results. However, it does not fully consider the relationship between pixels and lacks a priori constraints on context information, resulting in a lack of spatial consistency in segmentation results. To resolve this issue, we use fully FC-CRF [13] to further optimize the segmentation results.

The energy function $E(x)$ in the fully connected conditional random field is:

$$E(x) = \sum_i \varphi_u(x_i) + \sum_{i \neq j} \varphi_p(x_i, x_j), \tag{3}$$

where $\varphi_u(x_i)$ indicates the unary energy term, which represents the probability that the i-th pixel belongs to the category label x_i, and $\varphi_p(x_i, x_j)$ represents the binary energy term, which represents the probability that the pixel points i and j belong to the labels x_i and x_j at the same time. The binary energy term considers the interaction between adjacent pixels and uses spatial context information. Its expression is:

$$\varphi_p(x_i, x_j) = \mu(x_i, x_j) \left(w^{(1)} \exp \left(-\frac{\left\| p_i - p_j^2 \right\|}{2\sigma_\alpha^2} - \frac{\left\| I_i - I_j \right\|}{2\sigma_\beta^2} \right) + w^{(2)} \exp \left(-\frac{\left\| p_i - p_j^2 \right\|}{2\sigma_\gamma^2} \right) \right),$$

$$\tag{4}$$

$\mu(x_i, x_j) = [x_i \neq x_j]$ is the label compatibility function. When adjacent pixels are assigned different category labels, $\mu(x_i, x_j)$ is a penalty term, and it can be understood that similar pixels tend to be classified into the same category. The parameters σ_α, σ_β and σ_γ are used to control the scale of the Gaussian kernel function.

The solution of FC-CRF can be transformed into the energy function minimization problem. The average field approximation algorithm proposed by Krähenbühl [13] et al. is used to reduce computational complexity. First, the pre-processed abdominal CT image is input into the DFCN to predict the probability of each pixel being classified as a tumor and output a probability map, and then connect an FC-CRF to optimize the DFCN segmentation results. The input of FC-CRF includes two parts, which are the probability map and the pre-processed CT image. The probability map provides unary potential energy, and the color and spatial position information between pixels provided by the CT image after preprocessing is used as binary potential energy. Finally, it continuously iterates through the average field approximation algorithm until the energy function value is minimum, and then outputs the liver tumor segmentation results.

3   Experimental Results

3.1   Data Preprocessing

The experimental data use the data set officially provided by the CT Image Live Tumor Segmentation Challenge Competition (LiTS) [14]. Since the sponsor of LiTS does not disclose the label information of the liver and tumor of 70 patients in the data set, the data of 130 patients are used in the experiment. Among them, 100 patients' data are used for network training, 10 patients' data are used for verification, and 20 patients' data are used to test the trained network. Abdominal CT images need to be pre-processed before segmentation.

The pre-processing mainly includes: window technology processing [15], data enhancement, and normalization processing. K. Sahi et al. [16] have given that the window width of the liver is [−62,238]. To enhance the contrast of the liver in the abdominal CT image, the window of the abdominal CT is set to [−150,250] through the window technique. Since the density of liver lesions will decrease compared with normal liver tissue, the lower limit of the window is set to −150 to ensure that the liver lesions are not removed. Due to the lack of CT image data, this paper uses the way of data enhancement to expand the data. To solve the comparability between different data features, this paper uses the minimum-maximum standardized processing method. It processes the pixel matrix of the image, finds the minimum value X_{min} and maximum value X_{max} in the entire pixel matrix, and then we normalize these data by using Eq. (5). f is a coefficient in Eq. (5) that can control the range of normalization. If normalized to [0,1], the factor value is 1, normalized to [0,255], the factor value is 255.

$$X_{norm} = f * \frac{X - X_{min}}{X_{max} - X_{min}}. \tag{5}$$

3.2   Segmentation Results

To verify the superiority of the proposed liver tumor segmentation method over the counterparts including FCN [17] and DRIU [18], this article selected 30 photos in the test set for comparison. Figure 3 compares the similarities and differences between doctor marks and the results of DFCN, FCN, and DRIU. It can be seen that the segmentation result of FCN is relatively rough, the tumor contour is quite different from the tumor label image marked by the doctor, and when the tumor size is small and the grayscale is uneven, FCN cannot segment those tumors. The segmentation results of DRIU is more accurate than that of FCN, and the segmentation result is closer to the label map. However, when the tumor size is smaller and the grayscale is uneven, DRIU cannot also segment those tumors. The segmentation result of DFCN is more accurate than DRIU, and the segmentation result is closest to the tumor label map marked by the doctor. It can also be segmented if it encounters tumors with smaller grayscale unevenness and smaller size. The experimental environment is Ubuntu 16.04 + python2.7 + TensorFlow, the experimental equipment is a Dell computer with GPU, and its GPU model is TITAN X.

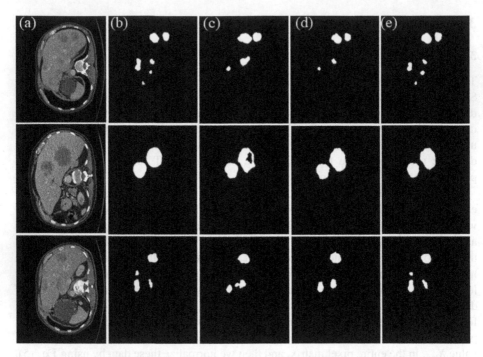

Fig. 3. Qualitative comparison of segmentation results obtained by different methods: (a) original CT image, (b) tumor label, (c) FCN [17], (d) DRIU [18], (e) DFCN.

Table 1. Quantitative comparison on liver tumor segmentation.

Method	Dice	Recall	Precision	F-measure
FCN [17]	0.7229	0.6919	0.7886	0.7653
DRIU [18]	0.7938	0.7243	0.8226	0.8057
DFCN	0.8234	0.7961	0.8705	0.8520

Table 1 lists the quantitative comparison of segmentation results. It can be seen from Table 1 that the liver tumor segmentation effect of the DFCN model is superior to the other two deep learning segmentation methods in the Dice similarity coefficient, Recall, Precision, and F-measure [19]. Regardless of FCN or DRIU, their network layers are relatively shallow, and they cannot learn the deep semantic features of liver tumors in CT images.

3.3   Optimization Results

To verify the optimization effect of the FC-CRF model on the DFCN tumor segmentation results, 100 CT images are selected in the test data set for comparative experiments. Part of tumor segmentation results is shown in Fig. 4, followed by the abdominal CT map, tumor labeling map, DFCN segmentation results and FC-CRF

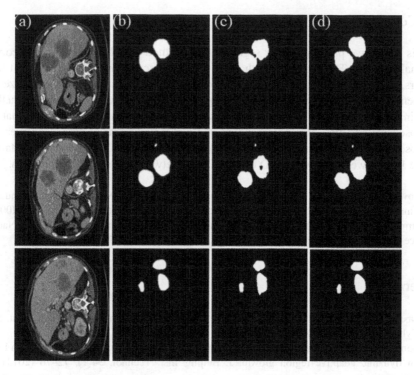

Fig. 4. FC-CRF optimization results: (a) original CT image, (b) tumor label, (c) DFCN, (d) DFCN + FC-CRF [13].

optimization results. It can be seen from Fig. 4 that the segmentation results of liver tumors optimized by FC-CRF add more detailed expression than the segmentation results before optimization, which is closer to the label diagram marked by the doctor. The experiment is conducted on the Ubuntu system, where FC-CRF is implemented using python's pydensecrf package. The densecrf interface provided by the program can solve FC-CRF using mean-field approximation algorithm.

Table 2. Segmentation accuracy comparison of DFCN without and with FC-CRF optimization.

Method	Dice	Recall	Precision	F-measure
DFCN	0.8431	0.8158	0.8802	0.8468
DFCN + FC-CRF [13]	0.8579	0.8318	0.8933	0.8615

It can be seen from Table 2 that after the DFCN liver tumor segmentation results are optimized by FC-CRF, all four indicators are improved, and the segmentation results are closer to the tumor label. Not only the prediction probability of each pixel is considered, but also the full use of the correlation between the gray value and position of all pixels in the CT image, which increases the constraints of context information, thereby improving the detailed expression and spatial consistency of the liver tumor segmentation results.

4   Conclusion

In this paper, we propose a liver segmentation method based on a deep fully convolutional network. The proposed method develops a cascaded network to segment liver tumors, and uses fully connected conditional random fields to further optimize the segmentation results. We qualitatively and quantitatively evaluate the proposed method on clinical data containing 30 sets of CT images. Experimental results show that the proposed method improves the accuracy of liver tumor segmentation. However, the proposed method does not use spatial information of liver tumors for the segmentation. In the future, we will develop 3D convolutional networks to solve this problem.

Acknowledgements. This work is partially supported by National Natural Science Foundation of China (61972187, 61772254), Fujian Provincial Leading Project (2017H0030, 2019H0025), Government Guiding Regional Science and Technology Development (2019L3009), and Natural Science Foundation of Fujian Province (2017J01768 and 2019J01756).

References

1. Otsu, N.: A threshold selection method from gray-level histograms. IEEE Trans. Syst. Man Cybern. **9**(1), 62–66 (2007)
2. Song, H., Wang, Y., Huang, X., et al.: Liver CT image tumor segmentation algorithm based on dynamic adaptive region growth. J. Beijing Inst. Technol. **34**(1), 72–76 (2014). (in Chinese)
3. Kass, M., Witkin, A., Terzopoulos, D.: Snakes: active contour models. Int. J. Comput. Vision **1**(4), 321–331 (1988)
4. Osher, S., Sethian, J.A.: Fronts propagation with curvature-dependent speed: algorithms based on Hamiton-Jacobi formulations. J. Comput. Phys. **79**(1), 12–49 (1988)
5. Massoptier, L., Casciaro, S.: A new fully automatic and robust algorithm for fast segmentation of liver tissue. In: Proceedings of the MICCAI Workshop on 3D Segmentation in the Clinic: A Grand Challenge II (2008)
6. Shimizu, A., Narihira, T., Furukawa, D., et al.: Ensemble segmentation using AdaBoost with application to liver lesion extraction from a CT volume. In: Proceedings of the MICCAI Workshop on 3D Segmentation in the Clinic: A Grand Challenge II (2008)
7. Guo, S., Ma, S., Li, J., et al.: Research on liver CT image segmentation based on fully convolutional neural network. Comput. Eng. Appl. **53**(18), 126–131 (2017). (in Chinese)
8. Krizhevsky, A., Sutskever, I., Hinton, G.E.: ImageNet classification with deep convolutional neural networks. In: International Conference on Neural Information Processing Systems, pp. 1097–1105. Curran Associates Inc. (2012)
9. Ronneberger, O., Fischer, P., Brox, T.: U-Net: convolutional networks for biomedical image segmentation. In: Navab, N., Hornegger, J., Wells, William M., Frangi, Alejandro F. (eds.) MICCAI 2015. LNCS, vol. 9351, pp. 234–241. Springer, Cham (2015). https://doi.org/10.1007/978-3-319-24574-4_28
10. Christ, P.F., Ettlinger, F., Grün, F., et al.: Automatic liver and tumor segmentation of CT and MRI volumes using cascaded fully convolutional neural networks. Medical Image Analysis (2017)

11. He, K., Zhang, X., Ren, S., Sun, J.: Deep residual learning for image recognition. In: Proceedings of the IEEE Conference on Computer Vision and Pattern Recognition, pp. 770–778 (2016)
12. Xie, S., Tu, Z.: Holistically-nested edge detection. In: Proceeding of IEEE International Conference on Computer Vision, vol. 1, pp. 1395–1403 (2015)
13. Krähenbühl, P., Koltum, V.: Efficient inference in fully connected CRFs with Gaussian edge potentials. In: Advances in Neural Information Processing System, pp. 109–117 (2011)
14. WWW: Web page of the Liver Tumor Segmentation Challenge. https://competitions. codalab.org/competitions/17094
15. Huaijun, L., Hua, Y., Pingyong, F., et al.: The value of window technology in CT diagnosis. J. Pract. Radiol. **2**, 109–110 (1992). (in Chinese)
16. Sahi, K., Jackson, S., Wiebe, E., et al.: The value of liver windows settings in the detection of small renal cell carcinomas on unenhanced computed tomography. Can. Assoc. Radiol. J. **65**, 71–76 (2014)
17. Long, J., Shelhamer, E., Darrell, T.: Fully convolutional networks for semantic segmentation. IEEE Trans. Pattern Anal. Mach. Intell. **39**(4), 640–651 (2014)
18. Bellver, M., Maninis, K.K., Pont-Tuset, J., et al.: Detection-aided liver lesion segmentation using deep learning (2017)
19. Dice, L.R.: Measures of the amount of ecologic association between species. Ecology **26**(3), 297–302 (1945)

Machine Learning Based SDN-enabled Distributed Denial-of-Services Attacks Detection and Mitigation System for Internet of Things

Muhammad Aslam[1]([✉]), Dengpan Ye[1], Muhammad Hanif[2],
and Muhammad Asad[3]

[1] School of Cyber Science and Engineering, Wuhan University, Wuhan, China
{aslamhayat,yedp}@whu.edu.cn
[2] School of Computer Science, COMSATS University Islamabad, Wah Campus,
Islamabad, Pakistan
hanif-cui@ciitwah.edu.pk
[3] Department of Computer Science, Nagoya Institute of Technology,
Nagoya, Aichi, Japan
m.asad@itolab.nitech.ac.jp

Abstract. Advancements of Internet of Things (IoT) enhance the application spectrum of smart networking and demand intelligent security measurements against cyber-attacks. Recent integration of Software Defined Networking (SDN) in IoT environments provides better network management by decoupling of control plane from forwarding plane. An advanced SDN based network management also utilize the machine learning models to classify IoT network traffic at OpenFlow Switches with the coordination of SDN controller. In this paper, we propose a novel SDN-enabled Distributed Denial-of-Services attacks Detection and Mitigation System (SDN-DMS) which utilize SDN enabled security mechanism for IoT devices with support of machine learning algorithms to develop Distributed Denial of Services (DDoS) detection and mitigation system. SDN-DMS integrates Floodlight and Pox SDN controllers to reconfigure the OpenFlow switches in order to mitigate the detected DDoS attacks by advanced Support Vector Machine (SVM) algorithms of Lagrangian Support Vector Machine (LSVM), Finite Newton Lagrangian Support Vector Machine (NLSVM), Smooth Support Vector Machine (SSVM) and Finite Newton Support Vector Machine (NSVM). SDN-DMS measures the network behaviour of IoT devices by collecting the network traffic and classifying the traffic as normal and DDoS attacks by using an environment-specific dataset.

Keywords: Cyber-attacks · Internet of Things · Distributed denial of services · Software defined networking · Machine learning · Detection · Mitigation

© Springer Nature Switzerland AG 2020
X. Chen et al. (Eds.): ML4CS 2020, LNCS 12486, pp. 180–194, 2020.
https://doi.org/10.1007/978-3-030-62223-7_16

1   Introduction

Industrial success of Internet of Things (IoT) provides many civilian and military applications and develop the connectivity of millions of new smart devices. These millions of insecure internet-connected smart devices pose a serious security risk in presence of countless cyber-attacks. These loosely guarded devices become the gateways for the hackers penetration and result into hurdle the industrial success of IoT [1,2]. These IoT equipped devices to formulate hotspot for attackers to launch volumetric attacks in the form of DoS, DDoS, brute force, and TCP SYN/UDP flooding. DDoS attacks are being experienced more frequently due to the progression of botnets which are infecting millions of IoT devices [3,4]. Flooding-based Distributed Denial-of-Service (DDoS) security attacks have been consistent threat towards the individual, organizations and enterprise service providers. DDoS attacks misuse the legitimate communication channels and protocols to launch expensive asymmetric penetration to the server's resources and result in exhausting of servers and individual hosts system capacity to respond to legitimate users. UDP Flood, PING Flood, SYN Flood and HTTP Flood are some of the consistently experienced DDoS attacks [5,6].

Network security attackers have achieved technical sophistication at many levels, which can trick the packet header fields and lunch legitimate extensive service requests on particular machine or servers in conventionally configured distributed networks [7]. In this regard, centrally coordinated SDN-enabled network can enable comprehensive traffic analysis and utilize the flexibility of system reconfigurations to gain appropriate response to these DDoS attacks [8–11]. The focus of recent research advancement of the centrally controlled architecture of Software Defined Networking (SDN) has diverted towards the enchantment of network security to achieve successful detection and mitigation of Distributed Denial-of-Services (DDoS) security attacks. Public web servers and individual network hosts face extensive DDoS attacks and designing an SDN-based security solution demand technical advancements to maintain quick and precise response towards abnormal network traffic [12–14].

In this paper, the proposed SDN-DMS is lightweight detection system where OpenFlow enabled switches to transfer new traffic entries towards SDN controller and SVMs algorithms. Furthermore, the SDN controller negotiates with advanced SVMs application algorithms over suspicions rate of requests among specific set hosts. In the results of SVM computations, the SDN controller recognized the attacker and victim hosts. In this way, proposed lightweight SDN-DMS achieve detection and Mitigation of DDoS attacks. In this paper, we implement our proposed model of SDN-DMS with advanced SVM algorithms of LSVM, NLSVM, SSVM and NSVM. Significant contributions to our proposed research work are the following:

1. Deploying and configurations of three custom topologies of SDN enabled IoT networks for experimentation in a virtual environment using Mininet, POX, Floodlight SDN controllers and Of switches using Open vSwitch. while IoT equipped devices are connected on forwarding plane OF switches.

2. Training the SVM classifier algorithms of LSVM, NLSVM, SSVM and NSVM to detect the normal and DDoS attacks using an environment-specific environment-specific dataset.
3. Running the SVMs applications on the edge switches so that the run-time data can be analyzed by extracting the flow table information or packets from the switch and classifying or performing a calculation to analyze the packets.
4. To monitor the usage and load on the switches, we utilize sFlow network flow analyzer. Host sFlow Daemon will be installed on the Linux machines which have been converted to switches. Sflow-RT will be running on the monitoring server which collects the real-time statistics of the switches.
5. Implement a complete DDoS detection solution which can be used in real-world SDN deployments by integrating multiple technologies.

2   Related Work

Few network-based mechanisms using SDN solutions have been proposed which have the lead foundational framework to move ahead to resolve the issue of DDoS attacks. In [6] A lightweight method for DDoS attacks detection based on traffic flow features has been proposed. This proposed model is divided into three modules; The flow collector module, feature extractor module, and classifier module. This solution shows the effective extraction of DDoS information in very low overhead compared to traditional approaches. But this solution is not suitable for dense network traffic which demands a more sophisticated system to provide a reliable security system. In [12], DDoS attacks detection is executed through content-based potential attackers, this solution is called Content-Oriented Networking Architecture (CONA). In CONA, the requests pattern face supervised accountability, and servers achieve the mitigation of DDoS outcomes with the help of controlled content based thresholds. In [14], a novel design is proposed based on the volume of traffic being requested per specific time. This DDoS defender detects DDoS to some extent by utilizing an OpenFlow-based intrusion prevention system. In [10], Cisco ONE SDN controller; Cisco switches and routers that are SDN enabled; DefenseFlow anti-DDoS SDN application; and DefensePro attack mitigation solution. All these DDoS attacks detection and mitigation systems use following modules; flow collector, feature extractor, anomaly detection, and attack mitigation [7, 8, 10].

These SDN-enabled DDoS detection systems can be further extended to secure the sensitive information IoT equipped devices. These IoT devices can be connected to SDN networks as end hosts to monitor the victim IoT devices by DDoS attacks [1, 2]. Our proposed model SDN-DMS is following the necessary footprints of the known state of the art solutions and having additional programmability of advanced SVMs algorithms which plays a critical role in the advancement of Proposed SDN-DMS solution.

3   Background

SDN-POX/OpenFlow Overview In this SDN-enabled DDoS attacks detection and mitigation configuration system, the network topology is launched by

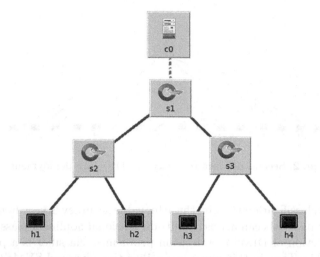

Fig. 1. First network topology of SDN-DMS deployment

Mininet emulator which are being coordinated to POX SDN controller. Deployed hosts are connected with OpenFlow enabled switches and theses OF Switches are primarily responsible for informing SDN controller about all new arrival communication requests. So practically, OF Switches delivers the reports of the DDoS attacks to SDN controller along with congestion rate over available communication links. SDN controller reactively performs the security measurements with the assistance of Support Vector Machines (SVMs) algorithms verdicts and enable DDoS detection and mitigation. In mitigation response, the SDN controller also manages the alternative path computation based on congestion statistics of link flows and operational ports for legitimate hosts request. OF switches react as intermediate devices and periodically perform path return with the flow rules and port statics in the form of bytes. Meanwhile, the controller maintains the network view and hash-table hierarchical structure of received statics. The controller also categorizes the computed alternative paths according to the network path congestion index of each path. The number of alternative paths installation of SDN controller over OF switches is inversely proportional to the computed network path congestion index of alternative paths. Figure 1 and Fig. 2 present the two network topologies used in the experimental section of this paper. In these network topologies, IoT equipped devices are supposed to be connected at forwarding plane.

Support Vector Machines (SVMs) Algorithms. Support Vector Machines (SVMs) algorithms are supervised algorithms used for classification and regression [15]. From a set of training data points, the SVMs algorithms represent them in a space, it maps them by categories and divides them by the separating Hyper-Planes. When new Data Points arrive based on the nature of the point, it categorizes the data into the clusters previously formed. Since SVMs algorithms

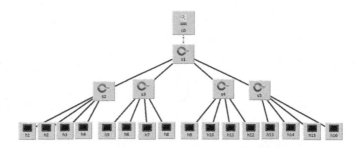

Fig. 2. Second network topology of SDN-DMS deployment

maximize the classification margin, the achievable accuracy is very high also using Kernel functions SVMs can act as a multi-dimensional nonlinear classifier.

Since detection of DDoS is a decision problem, a classifier is a perfect approach to do this. Thus in this paper, we utilize the advanced SVMs Classifier of by of LSVM, NLSVM, SSVM and NSVM to detect DDoS attacks Classifier on the Flow table entries of OpenFlow switches of SDN enabled IoT network. We first train the SVMs algorithms based on the network scenario and environment-specific datasets. Thus, these advanced SVMs algorithms can successfully differentiate the exact nature of the flow of traffic in both normal and DDoS scenarios. Northbound and Southbound Link Layer Data Protocol (LLDP) packets of OpenFlow protocol collect the network flow information and then deliver traffic to SVMs algorithms which classify the traffic into normal or attack traffic.

4   Poposed SDN-DMS

In the design of SDN-DMS, When the network is switched-on, Hello messages of Feature-Request, and Feature-Reply of OpenFlow protocol are exchanged between all OF switches and the controller to get the network view at the controller at a specific interval of 30 s. These hello messages also include the link layer discovery protocol (LLDP) packets to get the view of overall network topology. As controller and OF switches utilize OpenFlow protocols, so controller transmits OFP_PACKET_OUT including LLDP to every OF Switch. In this POX SDN controller IS attached to fully coordinated and authentic OF Switches. On another side, centralized controller of SDN-DMS request SVM for quick investigation based on these particular modules; data aggregation module, data features extraction module and data classification module.

Collecting Flows Using NOX/OpenFlow. During the actual communication phase, the different hosts generate the requests, and as requests data packet of a flow arrives at the OF switch, the OF switch looks for the matching entry in its forwarding table. If the matching is found, then the switch forwards the data packet according to the corresponding action of the flow table entry. Otherwise, the switch asks the controller to compute the response for the flow. According to pair of source and destinations hosts, the OF switches are attached

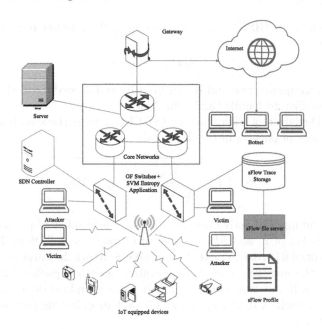

Fig. 3. Proposed SDN-DMS system prototype

with active communication flow and deliver the network topology of all engaged
OF Switches. Active group OF switches share the flow and port status including hosts information to controller OFP_PACKET_IN and OFP_PACKET_OUT
exchange. POX controller SDN-DMS delivers the collected data to SVM algorithm.

Selecting Traffic Features. In our proposed SDN-DMS solution, the SDN con-
troller is connected with SVMs application algorithms on northbound. LSVM,
NLSVM, SSVM and NSVM are the algorithms we utilize to test the accuracy
of DDoS attacks detection. SDN controller exchange the traffic attributes to
SVMS algorithms to discriminate legitimate network traffic and DDoS attacks.
The application layer SVMs algorithms construct the advanced trained traffic
model that utilizes hyperplane to divide the SVMs a high dimensional space.
The success rate of DDoS attacks detection and mitigation primarily depends
upon the quantitative ability of the trained SVMs algorithms. Extraction of particular characteristics values of the received flow tables is primary technical task
SVMs models.

As network flows reach SVMs algorithms, the flow inspection starts with a
selection of traffic features. The trend of DDoS attacks includes a large number of
IP addresses are forged to send packets of fixed size. This causes a regular pattern
in the network flows, and these can be characterized by monitoring relevant fields
of the flow table. Following characterizations features are collected as training
and test features:

1. Rate of Source IP (RSIP): This feature gives the number of source IPs per unit of time.

$$RSIP = \frac{\sum SIP}{T} \qquad (1)$$

where T is sampling time and it can be adjusted according to the SDN controller capability to handle the traffic flow.

2. Standard Deviation of Flow Packets (SDFP): This is the standard deviation of the number of packets in the T period:

$$SDFP = \sqrt{\frac{1}{F}\sum_{i=1}^{F}\sum_{j=1}^{P}(p_j - M_P)} \qquad (2)$$

where F is number of active network flows, P is number of packets per flow, p_j is jth packet of F_i and M_P is mean of all packets of F_i flow. This feature has high correlation to the event of a DDoS attack because in the case of an attack, the attacker sends large number of attack packets whose size is relatively small and this will have much lower standard deviation than the normal data packets resulting in a significant drop in this parameter during a DDoS attack.

3. Standard Deviation of Flow Bytes (SDFB): This is the standard deviation of the number of bytes in the T period:

$$SDFB = \sqrt{\frac{1}{P}\sum_{j=1}^{P}\sum_{k=1}^{B}(B_k - M_B)} \qquad (3)$$

where B is the number bytes per packets, and show the size of the packets P. Similar to SDFP, SDFB also has high correlation to the event of a DDoS attack and the expected value of this parameter is lower in case of an attack than in the case of normal traffic flows.

4. Rate of Flow Entries on Switch (RFES): This is the number of flow entries to the switch per unit of time:

$$RFES = \frac{\sum F}{T} \qquad (4)$$

This is a very relevant parameter of attack detection because the number of flows increases significantly in a fixed interval of time in case of an attack as compared to the SFE value in times of normal traffic flows.

5. Ratio of Pair-Flow Entries on Switch (RPFES): This is the number of flow entries in the switch which are interactive divided by the total number of flows in the T period:

$$RFES = \frac{IntIP}{N} \qquad (5)$$

where IntIP is the total number of interactive IPs in the flow and N is the total number of IPs. Thus there will be an abrupt decrease in the number of interactive flows as soon as the attack starts.

Using these parameters, we trained a SVMs algorithms to classify the incoming traffic to a switch as normal or malicious. Technical variation of tested LSVM, NLSVM, SSVM and NSVM algorithms is give next section.

4.1   Classifying Network Traffics

Collectively these features constitute an interactive flow is normal traffic or under DDoS attack. In DDoS attacks, flow entries to the destination host in time T increases sharply, and the destination host is unable to respond to them. Thus there will be an abrupt decrease in the number of interactive flows as soon as the attack starts. The total number of interactive flows is divided by the total number of flows so as make this detection parameter scalable to the network under different operating conditions. Using these parameters, we trained an SVM to classify the incoming traffic to a switch as normal or malicious. Designed of our proposed SDN-DMS prototype system is shown in Fig. 3.

5   Experiment Setup

Our approach included mixing different types of legitimate traffic and varying attack traffic parameters. As stated in the architecture for the demonstration purposes, we made use of two Linux machines as OpenFLow switches which had two hosts each in the form of virtual machines. The following software needs to be installed; Oracle VirtualBox, MiniNet, Open vSwitch, POX Controller, Floodlight Controller, Miniedit, tshark and sFlow RT.

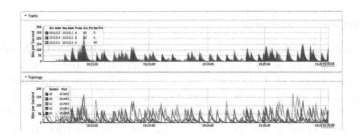

Fig. 4. Normal network traffic for first network topology

Dataset Description For detection, SDN-DMS use training environment specific dataset on which computation is performed and results are predicted. In case of SVM the environment specific dataset consists of the network statistics, which have been converted to a "csv" file with limited fields using a terminal-based tool "tshark".

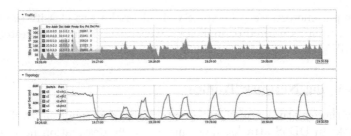

Fig. 5. DDoS attacks traffic for first network topology

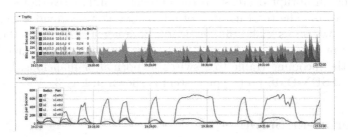

Fig. 6. Network traffic after implementation of SDN-DMS first network topology

This environment specific dataset is again categorized into attack traffic dataset and normal traffic dataset, which can be shown in Table 1 and Table 2, wherein the most standout variation is the packet interval field between normal traffic and attack traffic.

5.1   Experiments Results

Figure 4 shows the emulation performance of proposed SDN-DMS system for the network topology shown in Fig. 1. The forwarding plane of the network The network consists of 3 OF switches, which are further connected to 4 IoT devices. Outcome of this result evident the successful exchange of ICMP ping message protocols among all the hosts in the absence of any DoS attack. All network is categorized as normal traffic in this network scenario. All the network devices communicate through S1, S2, and S3 OF switches during communication phase and generate network traffic. The amount of overall network traffic can be observed from the upper graph of Fig. 4.

Table 1. Characteristics of normal traffic features

RSIP	SDFP	SDFB	RFES	RPFES
15	0.776327	320.0327	30	1
14	0.8231	313.7899	26	1
15	0.8675	329.7825	30	1

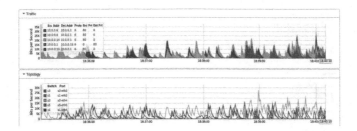

Fig. 7. Normal network traffic for second network topology

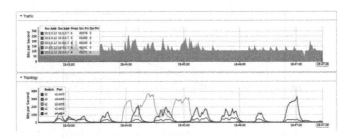

Fig. 8. DDoS attacks traffic for second network topology

Once we launch the DDoS attack through network devices to target other online hosts in the network, the Fig. 5 represents the accurate response of the network. This lower graph clearly indicates the disturbance of network traffic and drainage of communication resources for S1, S2 and S3. The request rate of attacked devices increases exponentially and overall network response decreases dramatically. The upper graph of Fig. 5 indicates the throughput of the network which is badly effected by the network.

When we implement our proposed DDoS detection and mitigation solution of SDN-DMS, the network response is shown in Fig. 6. The proposed model identifies the DDoS attacks and classify as abnormal network traffic and run the mitigation process to reallocate the network traffic. SDN-DMS reestablishes the network and increase the network throughput. With the passage of time SDN-DMS becomes more and more efficient and keep enhancing the network throughput. The lower graph indicates the participation of all networks hosts start improving. Moreover, the upper graph presents the increment of meaningful network traffic.

Table 2. Characteristic of abnormal traffic features

RSIP	SDFP	SDFB	RFES	RPFES
53	0.2688	88.328	53	0.5468
53	0.4675	119.754	53	0.5146
53	0.1276	56.1786	53	0.5197

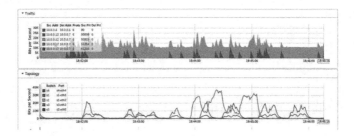

Fig. 9. Network traffic after implementation of SDN-DMS second network topology

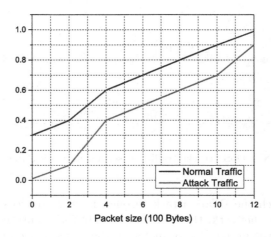

Fig. 10. DDoS anomaly detection from IoT traffic feature statistics according packet sizes

Figure 7 shows the emulation performance of proposed SDN-DMS system for the network topology shown in Fig. 2. This tree network topology consists of 5 OF Switches which are connected to 16 end hosts. In this network environment, nodes are exchanging ICMP ping message protocols to check the reachability of all the hosts connected over the network. This outcome indicates that all nodes are connected successfully in the whole network topology, and all nodes are generating normal network traffic. This outcome is evident that till this point of simulations, DDoS attacks have not been launched in the network.

Figure 8 indicates the fatal output results as DDoS attack have been launched, and SDN-DMS has not yet started the services of DDoS detection and Mitigation System. Until this point of the emulation SDN controller is conventionally dealing with Hping Flooding attacks by received from S1, S2, S3, S4 and S5. The throughput of the overall network topology is dramatically reduced from 35KBPS to 0KBPS. Due to extensive Hping Flooding attacks, the requested traffic jumped from 20KBPS to 80MBPS. The drastic volume of 80MBPS generated by DDoS attacks surpasses the network resources to respond effectively.

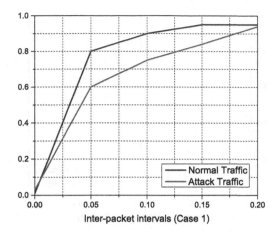

Fig. 11. DDoS anomaly detection from IoT traffic feature statistics according Inter-packet intervals of ΔT

Figure 9 shows the results when SVM logarithms are assisting SDN controller of SDN-DMS. This graph shows the resistance generated by the proposed solution and thought of the network gets improved quickly. The primary reason behind this improvement is the successful classification of normal and abnormal traffic and network resources are diverted to the legitimate network traffic. Performance of SDN-DMS gets better and better because initially, it takes computational overhead to sophisticate the detection and mitigation of DDoS attacks.

5.2   Features Engineering Results

In order to inspect the normal IoT traffic and anonymous DDoS attack traffic, we investigate the features of resulted traffic of the results of our simulations shown in the above figures. The pre-defined traffic features of expected normal and attack traffic successfully split the incoming traffic stream towards S-flow database. Figure 10 shows the difference between the size of normal traffic packets and attack packets. Almost 90% of attack packets size is under 100 bytes, and on the other hand, normal traffic packets size is varying between 100 to 1200 bytes. DDoS attacker tools usually try to flood the network with small size TCP, SYN requests to gain control available connections. Figure 11 and Fig. 12 indicate the traffic inter-packet interval feature to check the synchronous behaviour of requested traffic. Normally authorized IoT equipped devices to generate the traffic requests at assigned time-intervals while attacks are being launched at random manners. DDoS attacks have small packets size and minimum packet interval to block the traffic flow. These figures validate the effect of DDoS attacks traffic over ΔT and its first and second level derivatives of packet intervals. Similarly, $\frac{d\Delta T}{dt}$ inter-packet range features support classifier to identify the difference between normal and DDoS attack.

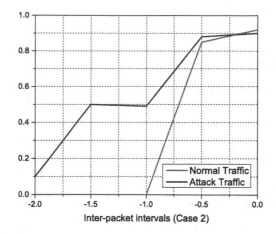

Fig. 12. DDoS anomaly detection from IoT traffic feature statistics according Inter-packet intervals of $\frac{d\Delta T}{dt}$

We also integrate and simulate the following algorithms of LSVM, NLSVM, SSVM and NSVM to analyze the proposed DDoS attacks detection and mitigation system.

In Fig. 13, we plot the F-score to measure the accuracy rate of SVMs algorithms classifications. This figure shows that NSVM performs the best while LSVM has least effective performance. This shows that NSVM is a fast, finitely terminating Newton methods for solving a fundamental classification problem of data mining and machine learning. The methods are simple and fast and can be applied to other problems such as linear programming. Although LSVM is faster than conventional SVM algorithm but provides lesser effective accuracy than NLSVM, SSVM and NSVM.

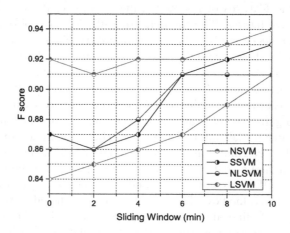

Fig. 13. Measure of accuracy in binary classification (F-Score)

6   Conclusion

In this paper, we propose SDN-enabled Distributed Denial-of-Services attacks Detection and Mitigation System (SDN-DMS) for Internet of Things (IoT) equipped devices connected through SDN distributed network. SDN-DMS utilize advanced SVM algorithms of LSVM, NLSVM, SSVM and NSVM to classify network traffic as normal and abnormal by using an environment-specific dataset. Implementation of SVM algorithms, classify the network traffic generated by two SDN frameworks and successfully discriminate the network traffic as normal or abnormal. The proposed model has excellent efficiency in detecting DDoS attack patterns in this type of a network, and it has reflected in its real-time performance. We also introduced a strategy for packet inspection box, though in its raw stage with directions for future improvements. DDoS detection and Mitigation by utilizing SDN framework is way forward to achieve commercial solutions for IoT devices which provide reliable network security solution against service disruption attacks.

Acknowledgement. This work was partially supported by the National Key Research Development Program of China (2019QY(Y)0206, 2016QY01W0200), the National Natural Science Foundation of China NSFC (U1736211)

References

1. Wu, H., Wang, W.: A game theory based collaborative security detection method for Internet of Things systems. IEEE Trans. Inf. Forensics Secur. **13**(6), 1432–1445 (2018)
2. da Costa, K.A., Papa, J.P., Lisboa, C.O., Munoz, R., de Albuquerque, V.II.C.: Internet of Things: a survey on machine learning-based intrusion detection approaches. Comput. Netw. **151**, 147–157 (2019)
3. Rathore, S., Kwon, B.W., Park, J.H.: BlockSecIoTNet: blockchain-based decentralized security architecture for IoT network. J. Netw. Comput. Appl. **143**, 167–177 (2019)
4. Lyu, M., Sherratt, D., Sivanathan, A., Gharakheili, H.H., Radford, A., Sivaraman, V.: Quantifying the reflective DDoS attack capability of household IoT devices. In: Proceedings of the 10th ACM Conference on Security and Privacy in Wireless and Mobile Networks, pp. 46–51. ACM, July 2017
5. Bhunia, S.S., Gurusamy, M.: Dynamic attack detection and mitigation in IoT using SDN. In 2017 27th International Telecommunication Networks and Applications Conference (ITNAC), pp. 1–6. IEEE, November 2017
6. Braga, R., de Souza Mota, E., Passito, A.: Lightweight DDoS flooding attack detection using NOX/OpenFlow. In LCN, vol. 10, pp. 408–415, October 2010
7. AlEroud, A., Alsmadi, I.: Identifying cyber-attacks on software defined networks: an inference-based intrusion detection approach. J. Netw. Comput. Appl. **80**, 152–164 (2017)
8. McKeown, N., et al.: Openow: enabling innovation in campus networks. SIGCOMM Comput. Commun. (2016)
9. Rawat, D.B., Reddy, S.R.: Software defined networking architecture, security and energy efficiency: a survey. IEEE Commun. Surv. Tutorials **19**(1), 325–346 (2016)

10. Xu, Y., Liu, Y.: DDoS attack detection under SDN context. In: IEEE INFOCOM 2016-The 35th Annual IEEE International Conference on Computer Communications, pp. 1–9. IEEE, April 2016
11. da Rocha Fonseca, P.C., Mota, E.S.: A survey on fault management in software-defined networks. IEEE Commun. Surv. Tutorials 19(4), 2284–2321 (2017)
12. Choi, Y.: Implementation of content-oriented networking architecture (CONA): a focus on DDoS countermeasure. In: Proceedings of European NetFPGA developers workshop, September 2010
13. Yan, Q., Yu, F.R., Gong, Q., Li, J.: Software-defined networking (SDN) and distributed denial of service (DDoS) attacks in cloud computing environments: a survey, some research issues, and challenges. IEEE Commun. Surv. Tutorials 18(1), 602–622 (2015)
14. Cui, L., Yu, F.R., Yan, Q.: When big data meets software-defined networking: SDN for big data and big data for SDN. IEEE Network 30(1), 58–65 (2016)
15. Lu, S.X., Wang, X.Z.: A comparison among four SVM classification methods: LSVM, NLSVM, SSVM and NSVM. In: Proceedings of 2004 International Conference on Machine Learning and Cybernetics (IEEE Cat. No. 04EX826), vol. 7, pp. 4277–4282, August 2004

A New Lightweight CRNN Model for Keyword Spotting with Edge Computing Devices

Yungen Wei[1], Zheng Gong[1], Shunzhi Yang[1], Kai Ye[1], and Yamin Wen[2](✉)

[1] School of Computer Science, South China Normal University, Guangzhou, China
genty1314@gmail.com, cis.gong@gmail.com
[2] School of Statistics and Mathematics,
Guangdong University of Finance and Economics, Guangzhou, China
wenyamin@gdufe.edu.cn

Abstract. Keyword Spotting (KWS) is a significant branch of Automatic Speech Recognition (ASR), which has been widely used in edge computing devices. The goal of KWS is to provide high accuracy at a low false alarm rate (FAR) while reducing the costs of memory, computation, and latency. However, limited resources are challenging for KWS applications on edge computing devices. Lightweight models and structures for deep learning have achieved good results in the KWS branch while maintaining high accuracy, low computational costs, and low latency. In this paper, we present a new Convolutional Recurrent Neural Network (CRNN) architecture named EdgeCRNN for edge computing devices. EdgeCRNN is based on a depthwise separable convolution (DSC) and residual structure, and it uses a feature enhancement method. The experimental results on Google Speech Commands Dataset depict that Edge-CRNN can test 11.1 audio data per second on Raspberry Pi 3B+, which are 2.2 times that of Tpool2. Compared with Tpool2, the accuracy of EdgeCRNN reaches 98.05% whilst its performance is also competitive.

Keywords: Edge computing · Keyword spotting · Convolutional recurrent neural network · Feature enhancement · Lightweight structure

1 Introduction

Keyword Spotting (KWS) is a branch of Automatic Speech Recognition, which focuses on detecting predefined keywords from a continuous audio stream. The wake-up words are the critical applications of KWS on edge computing devices, such as Apple's "Hey Siri" and Google's "OK Google". The device is awakened

This paper is supported by the National Natural Sciences Foundation of China (No. 61572028), National Cryptography Development Fund (No. MMJJ20180206), the Project of Science and Technology of Guangzhou (No. 201802010044) and Guangdong Basic and Applied Basic Research Foundation (No. 2019A1515011797).

© Springer Nature Switzerland AG 2020
X. Chen et al. (Eds.): ML4CS 2020, LNCS 12486, pp. 195–205, 2020.
https://doi.org/10.1007/978-3-030-62223-7_17

to execute the appropriate commands if the KWS system detects a predefined keyword in a dialogue.

Traditional methods of KWS usually use the Keyword/Filler Hidden Markov Model (HMM) [1,2]. However, depending on an HMM topology, these systems require Viterbi decoding and are computationally expensive. These approaches are not suitable for edge computing with limited resources. In KWS branch, Deep Neural Networks (DNN) has been shown to produce an efficient and reliable solution. DNN [3] was the first deep learning model to be applied to KWS with a model parameter size of 224M, which is smaller than the 373M of the GMM-HMM , and its performance exceeds that of the HMM model. However, these model parameters are still not suitable for edge computing devices.

In addition, the KWS system uses a server-client pattern, where the client collects data on the terminal and the cloud server processes it. With the rapid growth of data, pressures of computing and storage at the server will increase exponentially. Eventually, the user experience will become very bad. Moreover, there is a problem of user privacy leakage, which may lead to violations of law. Consequently, we adopt a new pattern that the client collects and processes data on the terminal. This model not only diminishes the burden of cloud servers and network bandwidth, but also provides positioning and high-quality services.

However, the model's high requirements for hardware resources and limited resources pose a challenge on applying KWS to edge computing devices. The hardware acceleration and designing lightweight models are used to solve this problem. In [4], Benelli et al. used a Neural Compute Stick (NCS) to accelerate and lower latency by 50%. Dinelli et al. [5] proposed a Convolutional Neural Network (CNN) based on a field-programmable gate array (FPGA), which is nearly 10 times faster than NCS. However, the hardware acceleration is costly and is not used in edge computing devices. So we choose the approach of designing lightweight model.

Various lightweight architectures for deep learning have been successfully applied to KWS problems, such as Tpool2 [6] and CNN [7]. Compared with DNN [3], CNN [7] offers a 27–44% relative improvement in false alarm rate (FAR). However, CNN ignores the global time and spectral correlation owing to the size of the convolution kernel. Recurrent Neural Network (RNN) could leverage a longer temporal context, which makes up for this question of CNN. Recently, RNN [8] and convolutional recurrent neural network (CRNN) [9] are used in KWS. CRNN is a hybrid of CNN and RNN. In CRNN, convolution layer extracts local temporal/spatial correlation and recurrent layer extracts global temporal features dependency in time sequence [9].

In this paper, we design a new CRNN model called EdgeCRNN. Its CNN adopts depthwise separable convolution (DSC) and residual structure. Besides, we propose two feature enhancement methods LFBE-Delta and first convolution feature enhancement, and use the LFBE-Delta feature instead of the Mel-Frequency Cepstrum Coefficient (MFCC) as input features. EdgeCRNN can recognize 12 class keywords by training on the Google Speech Commands Dataset [10]. The experiment results show that EdgeCRNN not only reduces model parameters and Floating-point Operations Per Second (FLOPs), but also decreases latency. The test cases can run normally and test 11.1 audio data per second on Raspberry Pi 3B+ without stuttering. Besides, accuracy rate is state of the art, reaches 98.05%. The source codes of EdgeCRNN and its test samples are available at GitHub repository[1].

This paper is organized as follows. Section 2 introduces the related work of the lightweight KWS model. We describe our approach and EdgeCRNN architecture in Sect. 3. In Sect. 4, we explain the experiment steps and results. Section 5 gives a conclusion.

2   Related Work

There are three main methods for designing lightweight KWS models: (1) model compression, (2) automatic neural network architecture design based on Neural Architecture Search (NAS), (3) artificial design of lightweight neural network.

The model compression is to further diminish the size of the model by removing redundant layers, quantizing high-precision weight parameters, and decomposing complex operations. In [11], George et al. use low-rank weight matrices throughout DNN, which obtains a 23.9% relative reduction in frame error rate.

The NAS can automatically design high-performance neural networks, which are gradually applied in the fields of speech recognition [12]. NAS is based on a search strategy to automatically design a model suitable for a specific application within a predefined search space [13].

The artificial design of lightweight neural network mainly reduces the amount of calculation by optimizing the calculation method of convolution and designing more efficient convolution operations. DS-CNN [14] proposes a lightweight model based on DSC and the accuracy rate reaches 95.4% with limited memory and compute capability.

The model compression and automatic design methods based on network architecture search consume resources and time costly. The artificial design of lightweight neural network requires designers to have professional knowledge, but it consumes fewer resources and is mature in technology. Therefore, we use the artificial neural network method to design a lightweight KWS model for edge computing devices.

3   EdgeCRNN

In this section, first we propose a Feature Enhancement approach. And then the architecture of EdgeCRNN is designed from EdgeCRNN Block.

3.1   Feature Enhancement

To extract acoustic features more efficiently, we propose two enhancement methods Input and First Convolution Layer Feature Enhancement.

---
[1] https://github.com/genty1314/KWS.git.

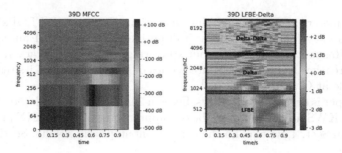

Fig. 1. Input Feature. 39 dimensions (39D) MFCC and 39D LFBE-Delta (LFBE-Delta denotes the concatenation of 13D LFBE, 13D Delta and 13D Delta-Delta).

Input Feature Enhancement. The traditional method MFCC only extracts the envelope information on spectrum and it loses sound details. However, the Log-Mel filterbank energies (LFBE) contains more features, such as low-frequency and spectral details. Many proposals have adopted LFBE as feature extract method [7,15]. Besides, the first derivative (Delta) and second derivative (Delta-Delta) features on the time axis of MFCC can better represent correlation among frames. We propose a new feature extraction method LFBE-Delta, which is 39 dimensions and computed every 30 ms with a 10 ms frame shift by LibROSA package [16]. LFBE-Delta contains three features with 13 dimensions, which include LFBE, Delta, and Delta-Delta (Fig. 1).

First Convolution Layer Feature Enhancement. The convolution kernel enhances features by multiplying input signals with sliding, then it outputs a small-size map feature. By setting convolution kernel stride = 1, the size of the output map remains the same. Therefore, repeating multiple convolution operation is equivalent to adding features. Compared to large-size inputs, small-size inputs could relatively save computational costs. Compared with the input data dimensions of $3 \times 224 \times 224$ in the computer vision [17,18], the acoustic feature of 39 dimensions LFBE-Delta is too small to effectively extract valid features. In the convolution layer, maintaining the output map size unchanged by setting stride could extract more efficient features. So we maintain the output map size by setting stride = 1 to achieve feature enhancement.

3.2 The Building Blocks of EdgeCRNN

In this section, we first describe the core approaches (i.e., DSC and residual structure), on which EdgeCRNN Block is built. We then describe the EdgeCRNN Block and RNN.

Depthwise Separable Convolution. According to Howard et al.'s research [18], the FLOPs of the DSC is $\frac{1}{N} + \frac{1}{D_k^2}$ times than the standard convolutional

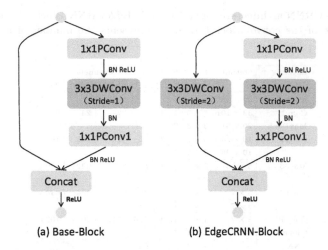

Fig. 2. EdgeCRNN Block. a) is the basic block, two branch outputs are "Concat" operation; b) is the downsampling module with the output operate by "Concat".

operation, where N is the number of output channels, D_k is the kernel size. The number of channels is usually large, so the $\frac{1}{N}$ value can be ignored. It consists of depthwise convolution (DWConv) and point convolution (PConv) and gradually replaces standard convolution kernels in many lightweight model studies. Most EdgeCRNN's convolution kernel sizes are 3×3 and 1×1, so the computation cost of EdgeCRNN can less about 9 times than full convolution layer. This proves that the DSC can reduce computational costs and model parameters.

Residual Structure. In theory, deeper networks are more capable of learning. However, with the number of network layers increases, the structure becomes more complicated and requires expensive computational cost. Therefore, He et al. [19] proposed ResNet based on the Residual Structure, which uses the identity mapping of shortcut connections, the input and output of different blocks are concatenated by an element-wise. It increases the training speed of the model. The Residual Structure was applied in the KWS task, and the accuracy rate was state-of-the-art at that time and reached 95.8% [20].

RNN. The RNN uses a loop structure to connect early state information to the later state, which can well extract sequence data context features. However, standard RNN has short-term memory problem. The long short-term memory (LSTM) [21] and gated recurrent unit (GRU) [22] of variant RNN were created as the solution to the problem. They have internal mechanisms called memory cells that can store the flow of information. BiLSTM can obtain time series features well and achieve the accuracy of 96.6% [23]. Hence, we use LSTM on EdgeCRNN model.

Table 1. EdgeCRNN architecture. Stage* include EdgeCRNN Block, K and S are the size and stride of the convolutions kernel, R represents the number of modules and padding = 1.

Layer	Output	K	S	R	Output channels			
					0.5x	1.0x	1.5x	2.0x
Audio	39 × 101	–	–	–	1			
Conv1	39 × 101	3 × 3	1	1	16	24	24	24
MaxPool	20 × 51	3 × 3	2					
Stage2	10 × 26	3 × 3	2	1	32	72	116	160
	10 × 26	3 × 3	1	1				
Stage3	5 × 13	3 × 3	2	1	64	144	232	320
	5 × 13	3 × 3	1	2				
Stage4	3 × 7	3 × 3	2	1	128	288	464	640
	3 × 7	3 × 3	1	1				
Conv5	3 × 7	1 × 1	1	1	256	512	1024	1024
GlobalPool	1 × 7	3 × 1	1					
RNN	–	–	–	–	64			
FC	–	–	–	–	12			
MFLOPs					4.10	14.54	34.89	57.65
MWeights					0.15	0.59	1.15	1.68

EdgeCRNN Block. We design EdgeCRNN Block based on DSC and residual structure, which is similar to the ShuffleNetV2 [24]. It includes Base-Block and EdgeCRNN-Block (Fig. 2). EdgeCRNN Block consists of two PConv layers and one DWConv layer, which selects the rectified linear unit (ReLU) nonlinearity and it uses Batch Normalization (BN) to normalize input data. EdgeCRNN-Block is used for downsampling to halve the input signal size by setting Stride = 2 on the DWConv layer, and then it uses the Concat operation to double the number of channels. Base-Block is the basic block and adding features by Concat operation, the input signal size and channels remain unchanged. EdgeCRNN-Block is on the first layer of each stage (see more detail in Session 3.3), and Base-Block follows it.

3.3   The Architecture of EdgeCRNN

The EdgeCRNN architecture is a hybrid model of CNN and RNN, where CNN is mainly composed of a stack of EdgeCRNN Block and the LSTM model which consists of one hidden layer with 64 nodes. Besides, CNN is divided into one first convolution layer feature enhancement layer called Conv1, three Stage, and one standard convolution layer named Conv5. Conv1 and Conv5 contain the variant Pool operator which is a sample-based discretization process with the goal of downsampling the input representation [8]. Conv1 is MaxPool and Conv5 uses GlobalPool. There are two units in each Stage. The first unit consists of a downsampling block EdgeCRNN-Block with a convolution kernel stride of 2. The second unit consists the Base-Block module, which is located behind the EdgeCRNN-Block and its number is determined by R in Table 1. The Edge-CRNN uses Width Multiplier α similar to MobilenetV1 [18]. The role of the α is to thin a network uniformly at each layer (Table 1).

4 Experiments on EdgeCRNN

In this section, we introduce the datasets, experiment steps, and how to train the model. We then investigate the effects of feature enhancement and EdgeCRNN Block. Finally, we compare performances between EdgeCRNN and popular KWS models.

4.1 Experimental Step on EdgeCRNN

We evaluate our models by using Google Speech Commands Dataset [10], which consists of 65,000 one-second utterances of 30 words by thousands of different people. The sampling frequency is 16 KHz. Our task is to discriminate among 12 classes "yes", "no", "up", "down", "left", "right", "on", "off", "stop", "go", unknown, and silence. The unknown class is used to simulate the model to learn the difference between keywords and non-keywords. The silence class represents background noise. The dataset is then randomly split into training, validation, and test sets in the ratio of 80:10:10. EdgeCRNN is trained in the training and validation set, and the experimental results are obtained from the test set.

We use the Tpool2 [6] as the baseline model, which consists of two convolutional layers and one DNN layer. In our experiment, the input features are 39 dimensions LFBE-Delta. The EdgeCRNN uses the Relu activation function, the Adam optimizer, and Cross Entropy loss function on each of the convolution layers.

4.2 Model Training on EdgeCRNN

Accuracy, FLOPs and model parameters are our primary metric of quality. We also plot receiver operating characteristic (ROC) curves, where the x and y axes denote FAR and false rejects rate (FRR), respectively. Curves for each of the keywords are computed and then averaged vertically to produce the overall ROC. The lower the curve, the better the model performance.

We compare the model performances that adopt feature enhancement and non-use. The accuracy of EdgeCRNN-Mel is 3% higher than EdgeCRNN-M for LFBE-Delta containing three features in Table 2. Meanwhile, EdgeCRNN-M-F and EdgeCRNN-Mel-F also have a similar relationship in accuracy. The Fig. 3(b) illustrates the EdgeCRNN-Mel-F gives a 69.5% relative improvement over the EdgeCRNN-M-F at the operating point of 0.1 FAR. This means that input features contain three feature types which can improve model accuracy more than containing one feature.

The first convolution layer feature enhancement can repeatedly extract features and improve accuracy. EdgeCRNN-Mel-F is 0.8% higher than EdgeCRNN-Mel. However, FLOPs of the EdgeCRNN-Mel-F is almost 10M more than that of EdgeCRNN-Mel. We have found that it is most appropriate to reuse it only once. So EdgeCRNN uses the first convolution layer feature enhancement only once. The EdgeCRNN-Mel-F curve is lower compared with the EdgeCRNN-Mel from Fig. 3(a), which depicts that EdgeCRNN extracts feature more robust by feature enhancement.

Table 2. Accuracy of features enhancement. Where M denotes MFCC as feature extraction and Mel represents LFBE-Delta, F represents first convolution layer feature enhancement, the α defaults to 1.0x.

Model	MFLOPs	Parameter	Accuracy(%)
EdgeCRNN-M	4.60M	0.59M	94.15
EdgeCRNN-M-F	14.54M	0.59M	94.97
EdgeCRNN-Mel	**4.60M**	0.59M	97.05
EdgeCRNN-Mel-F	14.54M	0.59M	**97.89**

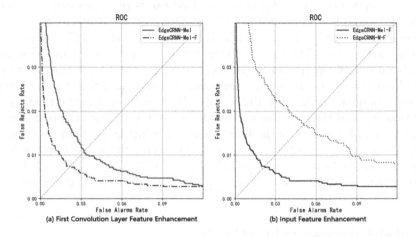

Fig. 3. ROC curves for feature enhancement.

4.3   Result on EdgeCRNN

First, we compare accuracy between previous KWS models [6,8,9,14,23] and EdgeCRNN (Table 3), these models are trained on the Google Speech Commands Dataset [10] (except CRNN [9], which uses a private TalkType dataset, and the data of LSTM from literature [14]). The parameter of EdgeCRNN 1.0x is not the smallest, while it is relatively lightweight and less than 0.6M. Besides, the accuracy of EdgeCRNN is higher than other KWS models from Table 3, which reaches 97.89% with limited computational cost (only 14.54M). This indicates that EdgeCRNN can almost achieve the state of art accuracy in KWS task and is a lightweight model.

We evaluate the performance of EdgeCRNN on edge computing device, which is depicted in Table 4. EdgeCRNN 0.5x can read 11.1 audio data per second on the Raspberry Pi 3B+, which is much faster than Tpool2's 5 per second. It demonstrates that EdgeCRNN reduces latency and computational costs with an accuracy of 97.09%. From the keyword audio length of 1s on Google Speech Commands Dataset, we know the speed of human speech is nearly one keyword per second. It means that EdgeCRNN processing speed can keep up with the speed of human speech in a resource-constrained environment.

Table 3. Accuracy of the related KWS models.

Model	FLOPs	Parameter	Accuracy
Tpool2 [6]	103M	1.09M	91.97%
LSTM [8]	48.4M	0.26M	94.81%
CRNN [9]	19.3M	**0.22M**	97.71%
DS-CNN [14]	56.9M	0.47M	95.38%
DenseNet-BiLSTM [23]	-	0.24M	97.50%
EdgeCRNN 1.0x	**14.54M**	0.59M	**97.89%**

Table 4. Performances of different width Multiplier and platforms. The CPU denotes the test speed on a platform of Intel(R) Core(TM) I3-8100 CPU. The ARM is the Raspberry Pi 3B+.

Model	MFLOPs	Parameters	Accuracy	CPU	ARM
Tpool2 [6]	103	1.09M	91.97%	27.6/s	5.0/s
EdgeCRNN 0.5x	**4.10**	**0.29M**	97.09%	**49.9/s**	**11.1/s**
EdgeCRNN 1.0x	14.54	0.59M	97.89%	25.6/s	5.0/s
EdgeCRNN 1.5x	34.89	1.29M	97.92%	17.3/s	3.1/s
EdgeCRNN 2.0x	57.65	1.72M	**98.05%**	13.5/s	2.3/s

Table 4 compares the effects of different Width Multiplier models, which have four multiples 0.5x, 1.0x, 1.5x, 2x from Table 1. The 2.0x model has the highest accuracy 98.05%, and the 0.5x model processes 11.1 audio per second which is the fastest speed on Raspberry Pi 3B+. In practical applications, we should consider the trade-off between FLOPs and accuracy to choose the most appropriate model.

5 Conclusion

In the paper, we designed a new EdgeCRNN model for edge computing devices applied to KWS. We demonstrated how to improve EdgeCRNN's performance by using feature enhancement methods with repeatedly extracting features. The result shows that EdgeCRNN can process 11.1 audio per second on Raspberry Pi 3B+, and its accuracy rate reaches 98.05%. However, FLOPs are still relatively large on variant EdgeCRNN 1.0x, and there is still room for improvement in accuracy. Moreover, the model test platform is only on ARM. In the future, we will continue to reduce the computational costs, improve the accuracy, and apply the KWS system to different environments.

References

1. Wilpon, J., Miller, L., Modi, P.: Improvements and applications for key word recognition using hidden markov modeling techniques. In: 1991 International Conference on Acoustics, Speech, and Signal Processing, pp. 309–312. IEEE (1991)
2. Silaghi, M.C.: Spotting subsequences matching an hmm using the average observation probability criteria with application to keyword spotting. In: AAAI, pp. 1118–1123 (2005)
3. Chen, G., Parada, C., Heigold, G.: Small-footprint keyword spotting using deep neural networks. In: 2014 IEEE International Conference on Acoustics, Speech and Signal Processing (ICASSP), pp. 4087–4091. IEEE (2014)
4. Benelli, G., Meoni, G., Fanucci, L.: A low power keyword spotting algorithm for memory constrained embedded systems. In: 2018 IFIP/IEEE International Conference on Very Large Scale Integration (VLSI-SoC), pp. 267–272. IEEE (2018)
5. Dinelli, G., Meoni, G., Rapuano, E., Benelli, G., Fanucci, L.: An FPGA-based hardware accelerator for cnns using on-chip memories only: Design and benchmarking with intel movidius neural compute stick. Int. J. Reconfig. Comput. **2019**, 13 p. (2019)
6. Tang, R., Wang, W., Tu, Z., Lin, J.: An experimental analysis of the power consumption of convolutional neural networks for keyword spotting. In: 2018 IEEE International Conference on Acoustics, Speech and Signal Processing (ICASSP), pp. 5479–5483. IEEE (2018)
7. Sainath, T., Parada, C.: Convolutional neural networks for small-footprint keyword spotting (2015)
8. Sun, M., Raju, A., Tucker, G., et al.: Max-pooling loss training of long short-term memory networks for small-footprint keyword spotting. In: 2016 IEEE Spoken Language Technology Workshop (SLT), pp. 474–480. IEEE (2016)
9. Arik, S.O., Kliegl, M., Child, R., et al.: Convolutional recurrent neural networks for small-footprint keyword spotting. arXiv preprint arXiv:1703.05390 (2017)
10. Warden, P.: Speech commands: a dataset for limited-vocabulary speech recognition. arXiv preprint arXiv:1804.03209 (2018)
11. Tucker, G., Wu, M., Sun, M., Panchapagesan, S., Fu, G., Vitaladevuni, S.: Model compression applied to small-footprint keyword spotting. In: INTERSPEECH, pp. 1878–1882 (2016)
12. Zhou, Y., Ebrahimi, S., Arık, S.Ö., et al.: Resource-efficient neural architect. arXiv preprint arXiv:1806.07912 (2018)
13. Anderson, A., Su, J., Dahyot, R., Gregg, D.: Performance-oriented neural architecture search. arXiv preprint arXiv:2001.02976 (2020)
14. Zhang, Y., Suda, N., Lai, L., Chandra, V.: Hello edge: keyword spotting on microcontrollers. arXiv preprint arXiv:1711.07128 (2017)
15. Coucke, A., Chlieh, M., Gisselbrecht, T., Leroy, D., Poumeyrol, M., Lavril, T.: Efficient keyword spotting using dilated convolutions and gating. In: ICASSP 2019–2019 IEEE International Conference on Acoustics, Speech and Signal Processing (ICASSP), pp. 6351–6355. IEEE (2019)
16. McFee, B., et al.: librosa: audio and music signal analysis in python. In: Proceedings of the 14th python in science conference. vol. 8 (2015)
17. Zhang, X., Zhou, X., Lin, M., Sun, J.: Shufflenet: an extremely efficient convolutional neural network for mobile devices. In: Proceedings of the IEEE Conference on Computer Vision and Pattern Recognition, pp. 6848–6856 (2018)

18. Howard, A.G., Zhu, M., Chen, B., et al.: Mobilenets: efficient convolutional neural networks for mobile vision applications. arXiv preprint arXiv:1704.04861 (2017)
19. He, K., Zhang, X., Ren, S., Sun, J.: Deep residual learning for image recognition. In: Proceedings of the IEEE Conference on Computer Vision and Pattern Recognition, pp. 770–778 (2016)
20. Tang, R., Lin, J.: Deep residual learning for small-footprint keyword spotting. In: 2018 IEEE International Conference on Acoustics, Speech and Signal Processing (ICASSP), pp. 5484–5488. IEEE (2018)
21. Hochreiter, S., Schmidhuber, J.: Long short-term memory. Neural Comput. 9(8), 1735–1780 (1997)
22. Cho, K., Van Merriënboer, B., Gulcehre, C., et al.: Learning phrase representations using RNN encoder-decoder for statistical machine translation. arXiv preprint arXiv:1406.1078 (2014)
23. Zeng, M., Xiao, N.: Effective combination of densenet and bilstm for keyword spotting. IEEE Access 7, 10767–10775 (2019)
24. Ma, N., Zhang, X., Zheng, H.T., Sun, J.: Shufflenet v2: practical guidelines for efficient CNN architecture design. In: Proceedings of the European Conference on Computer Vision (ECCV), pp. 116–131 (2018)

Machine Learning Agricultural Application Based on the Secure Edge Computing Platform

Wu Fan[1]📧, Zhuoqun Xu[2]📧, Huanghe Liu[1(✉)]📧, and Zhu Zongwei[1]📧

[1] Suzhou Institute for Advanced Study,
University of Science and Technology of China, Suzhou 215000, China
liuhh@mail.ustc.edu.cn
[2] Graduate School at Shenzhen, Tsinghua University, Shenzhen 518055, China

Abstract. Machine learning (ML) is fast becoming a powerful tool for increasing agricultural production, for instance, ML predicts weather and yield through satellite images. Such approaches, however, most applications are based on expensive cloud servers to handle massive calculations, which will easily lead to important data leakage (e.g. crop cultivation methods, annual output, etc.), and increase the economic burden of farmers. Motivated by the status of agriculture, especially small farms that are underfunded and require data confidentiality. We propose an application for agricultural object detection based on a secure edge computing platform that can be used for agricultural output statistics and automated spraying agriculture. Compared with cloud-based ML agricultural applications, edge-based computing platforms do not require data uploading and downloading, which protects data security and reduces capital costs. We use some techniques in the training model and compression model to solve the problems of model accuracy and real-time, as follows: (1) *Category-based Assisted Excitation model* is proposed to improve the YOLOv3 accuracy. (2) Use layer pruning and channel pruning together to achieve a small-scale structure search and maximize real-time performance. We have evaluated our optimized model based on *NVIDIA Jetson TX2* and *Fruit Dataset*. Its frames per second (FPS) is 11.63, mean average precision (MAP) is 89.6%.

Keywords: Edge computing · Agricultural data protection · Object detector · Model pruning · Assisted learning

1 Introduction

Agriculture is an important industry in the national economy. Since the green revolution in the middle of the 20th century, intelligent technologies such as Machine learning (ML), the Internet of Things (IoT), and cloud computing have promoted industrial agricultural progress, and have also steadily increased the annual output of world grain. Unfortunately, according to United Nations data

© Springer Nature Switzerland AG 2020
X. Chen et al. (Eds.): ML4CS 2020, LNCS 12486, pp. 206–220, 2020.
https://doi.org/10.1007/978-3-030-62223-7_18

[18], the world population will reach 9.8 billion by 2050, which will require 70% increases in global food production. Furthermore, if we consider the food consumed by the livestock industry, this growth rate will reach 103%. At the same time, with the introduction of more and more mechanized and intelligent products in agricultural production, agricultural companies are increasingly demanding the confidentiality of production technical details. Therefore, in the future development of society, compared with other fields, the challenges in the agricultural field (e.g. increasing agricultural output, improving privacy protection) are more important and urgent for humans.

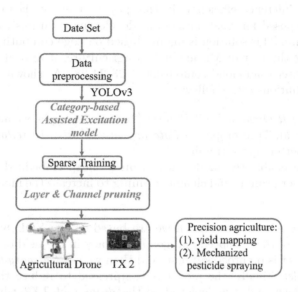

Fig. 1. Low cost precision agricultural solutions for production mapping and mechanized pesticide spraying.

Many researchers have tried to integrate ML, IoT [1, 26, 27] and agriculture to increase crop yields, Generally, the most powerful feature in ML is still image recognition. Regarding the application of CNN object detection technology to agriculture, there are fruit or stem recognition [8, 13] based on Faster R-CNN [20] network structure. Similarly, backbone networks such as VGG [21] and Microsoft ResNet [11] are often used in agriculture. These methods have all improved the accuracy of object detection. Unfortunately, due to the huge computational load of the CNN network, it can only be used on expensive servers, and it must also be equipped with high-speed wireless transmission equipment to facilitate the transfer of pictures collected by the farm back to the cloud. When these solutions are applied in practice, farmers must purchase expensive hardware equipment or build a high-speed wireless base station. However, in developing countries, most farmers cannot purchase expensive equipment due to their small land area and low capital. Besides, because relying on the purchased cloud platform services, farmers must upload a lot of key technical information to the cloud server for processing, and also need to download and analyze the processing results, which will greatly increase the risk of information leakage. In contrast, migrating the ML model to the edge computing platform for processing can effectively enhance the confidentiality of information and reduce costs [14, 22].

Although the ML model is migrated to the edge computing platform, it can effectively reduce costs and protect farmers' private data. The urgent problems need to be solved are the limited energy of the edge computing platform and the low computing power. In order to realize the target detection of agricultural airborne, we need to strengthen the model recognition ability and improve the model forward inference efficiency. In this paper, a set of cheap and efficient solutions is proposed for small farmers in developing countries to achieve precision agriculture. This solution is mainly based on edge computing equipment. While reducing the cost of ML applied to agriculture, it also protects private information better than cloud computing [4, 23, 24, 28]. As shown in Fig. 1. The primary contributions are as follows:

1) Taking *ACFR Orchard Fruit Dataset* [2] as an example, we are encouraged by Saeed et al. [7] to propose a *Category-based Assisted Excitation model* to complete better sparse training.
2) In order to enable the model to run on a cheap embedded platform, we combine layer pruning and channel pruning to increase the model's inference efficiency.

In our proposed scheme (Fig. 1), we are based on the YOLOv3 model [19], which has state-of-the-art speed and good accuracy in the field of object detection. The data set is preprocessed first, and then we use *Category-based Assisted Excitation model*. Finally, the model is compressed to reduce the amount of model calculations, and it is deployed on the *drone* and *TX2*, which can effectively count the number of fruits and finely apply the medicine.

As shown in the experimental results of Fig. 3, we have evaluated our optimized model based on *NVIDIA Jetson TX2* and *Fruit Dataset* [2] (Fig. 2). The mean average precision (MAP) and frames per second (FPS) we trained on the models Faster Rcnn and YOLOv3 are respectively 90, 0.77 and 86.8, 4.61, which does not meet the real-time and accuracy requirements of airborne object detection. In addition, we tested the *Assisted Excitation Model* and improved its shortcomings of poor assist performance for small targets, and proposed a *Category-based Assisted Excitation Model* to increase MAP from 88.1 to 89.8, especially for small target mango AP from 0.875 to 0.911. At the same time, in order to improve the FPS, this article proposes the *Layer and Channel pruning* algorithm to realize the YOLOv3 network structure range search. No matter it is *Assisted Excitation Model* or *Category-based Assisted Excitation Model*, it only helps to improve the accuracy of YOLOv3 during the training process. After the training is completed, it will be removed from the network model of YOLOv3, and will not have any impact on the structure of YOLOv3 model. This is why we are called *AE + YOLOv3* and *CAE + YOLOv3*, so we only need to

Fig. 2. Fruit dataset [2], contains three categories: apple, mango and almond.

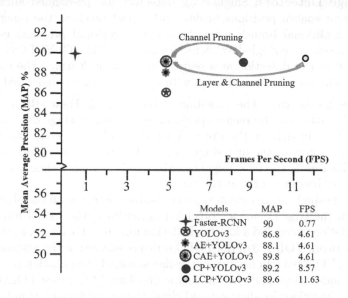

Models	MAP	FPS
Faster-RCNN	90	0.77
YOLOv3	86.8	4.61
AE+YOLOv3	88.1	4.61
CAE+YOLOv3	89.8	4.61
CP+YOLOv3	89.2	8.57
LCP+YOLOv3	89.6	11.63

Fig. 3. Recognition results based on different training methods. *Faster-RCNN* recognition result from literature [2]. *AE + YOLOv3* (Assisted Excitation Model) is the model proposed in literature [7], *CAE + YOLOv3* (Category-based Assisted Excitation Model) is the model proposed in this paper. The *CP + YOLOv3* (Channel pruning) model is based on the *CAE + YOLOv3* model through channel pruning. The *LCP + YOLOv3* (Layer and Channel pruning) model is based on the *CAE + YOLOv3* model through layer pruning and channel pruning. For a more detailed introduction, see Tables 1 and 2.

compress the model with the highest MAP. Finally, the FPS of *Layer and Channel pruning* is increased by nearly 35% compared to *Channel pruning*.

The remaining part of the paper proceeds as follows: Sect. 2 introduces related work in deep learning object detection. Then, the Sect. 3 presents the experimental details, focusing on *Category-based Assisted Excitation model* and *Model compression*. We mainly discuss the experimental results in the last Sect. 4.

2   Related Work

2.1   Object Detector

After Girshick et al. combined selective search and CNN models to propose R-CNN [9] and achieved significant results, object detection has attracted the attention of the academic community. Many state-of-the-art models have been proposed in the past few years. Depending on whether an extra region proposal modules are needed, the object detector can be simply divided into single-stage and two-stage detectors.

Single-Stage Detectors: Single-stage detectors use predefined anchors that frame different spatial positions, scales, and aspect ratios in the image, rather than using additional branch networks (such as regional proposal networks). That is, representative single-level detectors such as SSD [16], YOLOv3 [19], etc. directly treat object detection as a regression problem, learning the class probability and bounding box coordinates with respect to these predefined anchors.

Two-Stage Detectors: The two-stage detectors (e.g. Faster-RCNN [20], R-CNN [9]) algorithm can be seen as performing two single-stage detections. The first stage initially detects the object position, and the second stage further processes the results of the first stage, i.e., each candidate area for single-stage detection. Therefore, the two-stage algorithm will take more time and consume more memory than one-stage at runtime.

Comparing single-stage detectors and two-stage detectors, if the object detection runs on the edge device for precision agriculture, the model must have a faster calculation speed and a lower calculation amount. Therefore, in this paper, the latest network YOLOv3 of the YOLO series is selected as the research object. Regrettably, YOLOv3 still has two major flaws, namely localization problem [19] and foreground-background class imbalance problem [15]. Since YOLOv3 order to speed up detection, localization and classification performed simultaneously, both localization and classification process high-level activation maps behind the network structure (as shown in Fig. 4). These activation maps are suitable for classification, but they are too advanced for localization and will cause more spatial regression errors. Similarly, because YOLOv3 does not need to generate candidate regions, it is necessary to judge each anchor box (about 10^4 to 10^5) on the picture. Most of them are negative examples and can be easily classified. This will cause detector's loss is overwhelmed by negative examples.

2.2   Model Pruning

In order to reduce the cost in actual use, this article uses an embedded computing platform combined with a drone. Its advantages are:

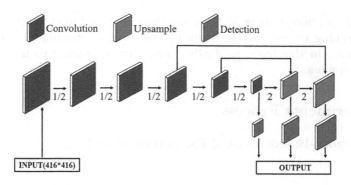

Fig. 4. YOLOv3 network structure diagram. YOLOv3 is composed of many residual modules, each time output three-scale activation tensor at the same time, respectively detect the size of different targets.

1. Avoid using too many expensive physical sensors to collect data. The drone is equipped with *TX2* and a camera to manage the entire orchard.
2. Due to the high real-time requirements of precise spraying of pesticides. In developing countries, if traditional GPU (e.g. NVIDIAGTX 1080) are used, most of them do not have the infrastructure for high-speed image transmission, so high-speed wireless must also be provided on site transmission device. Its deployment cost is extremely high. In this paper, the embedded computing platform is used, and the real-time requirements can be achieved by simply compressing the model and improving the calculation efficiency.

Thus, A highly efficient compression model is very important in this scheme. Extensive research [17] has shown that the main bottlenecks of model deployment on embedded devices are as follows:

1. **Model size:** CNN's powerful recognition capabilities come from millions of tensor parameters, and these tensors will be loaded into memory at runtime. For instance, the size of the YOLOv3 model is about 200 MB, and the Fast-RCNN model exceeds 500 MB. Many embedded platforms do not have such a large amount of memory.
2. **Run-time memory:** During model inference, the middle layer of CNN will generate temporary tensor, which will take up more memory.
3. **Number of computing operations:** Due to the limited energy and computing power of embedded devices, overly complex model calculations will lead to a significant increase in calculation time and extremely fast energy consumption, which cannot meet real-time requirements.

Researchers have proposed many methods to compress CNN. Denton et al. [6] proposes using a low rank matrix to approximate the weight matrix. Similarly, there are also binarization [5], weight pruning [10] for reducing the dimension of the weight matrix. Besides, network quantization [3] and dynamic inference [12] are also good methods. However, most of these methods cannot solve the three bottlenecks mentioned above at the same time. Hence, Liu et al. [17] proposes channel pruning to reduce the model file size while reducing the amount of computation. On this basis, we further adopt layer pruning to maximize the compression model.

3   Experiments Process

3.1   Category-Based Assisted Excitation Model

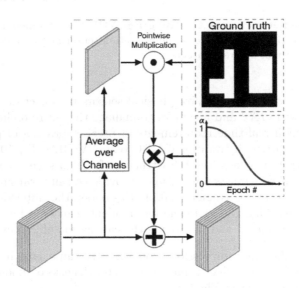

Fig. 5. Assisted excitation layer (AE) [7]. This layer takes an activation tensor as input, and gives the same enhancement activation to all targets.

As shown in Fig. 5, Assisted excitation layer strengthens the effect of target recognition according to ground truth, It increases the MAP of YOLOv3 from 86.8 to 88.1. Not only that, due to the presence of parameter α, when the last training epoch, we can directly delete the Assisted excitation layer. In this way, the yolov3 model will not have any negative impact during deployment.

Although AE [7] has the advantages of enhancing model effects, it also has disadvantages such as the recognition accuracy of small targets has little effect. In response to these shortcomings, we propose a *Category-based Assisted Excitation model* to improve the model recognition ability based on random initialization weights. During training, the first epoch does not have the category loss value of the previous training. We assume that the loss value of each category is the same, that is, the excitation value of each category is the same. As can be seen from the Fig. 6, the excitation level will drop to zero after the last epoch, which means that it no longer works on the YOLOv3 model and can be deleted directly.

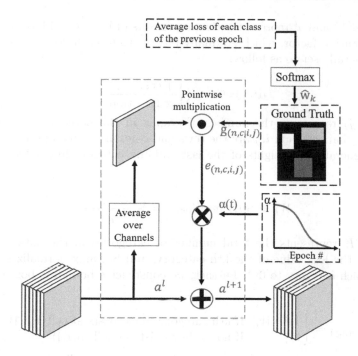

Fig. 6. Category-based assisted excitation layer (CAE). Compared with AE, our CAE model gives different activation intensity according to the performance of different categories of targets for each training. It can effectively solve the defect that AE does not have obvious enhancement effect on small targets.

The *Category-based Assisted excitation layer* can be directly inserted into the YOLOv3 model (As shown in Fig. 7), using the activation tensor as input. Firstly, channel average pooling of the input activation tensor. Secondly, based on the class average loss value output from the last epoch training, the softmax operation is used to convert the loss value of each category into probability values. These probability values will determine the excitation value. Finally, according to the object bounding box locations, the excitation value is multiplied by the Excitation factor α, and the result is added to each input channel pass to the next layer.

Since Category-based assisted excitation can be directly inserted into the model of YOLOv3, we consider it as a layer of network structure, assuming that the input dimension is *[N, C, H, W]*, where N represents batchsize, C is the number of channels, H, W represents the height and width of the activation tensor. The formula of the assisted excitation model is as follows:

$$a^{l+1}_{(n,c,i,j)} = a^l_{(n,c,i,j)} + \alpha(t)e_{(n,c,i,j)} \tag{1}$$

where a^{l+1} and a^l represent activation tensors of layer l and layer $l+1$. $\alpha(t)$ is the excitation factor, which gradually returns to 0 as the training ends, and $\alpha(t)$ is generally set to as follow:

$$\alpha(t) = 0.5 \times \frac{1 + \cos(\pi.t)}{\text{Max\_Iteration}} \qquad (2)$$

(n, c, i, j) represents the number of graphs in the batch, c represents the number of channels, and i, j are the rows and columns. To compute $e(n, c, i, j)$, we first generate the weights of the last training category loss values through Softmax:

$$\hat{W}_k = Softmax(loss_k) = \frac{e^{loss_k}}{\sum_k^K e^{loss_k}} \qquad (3)$$

where K represents the total number of categories in the data set, $loss_k$ represents the loss value of the kth category, and Softmax normalizes the loss value of each category to 0–1. Further, we construct a bounding box map g as follows:

$$g_{(n,i,j)} = \begin{cases} 1.5 * \hat{W}_k & \text{If kth category bbox exists at cell } (n, i, j) \\ 0 & \text{If no \quad bbox exists at cell } (n, i, j) \end{cases} \qquad (4)$$

Finally, we calculate the activation tensor formula as follows:

$$e(n, c, i, j) = \frac{g(n, i, j)}{d} \sum_{c=1}^{d} a_{(n,c,i,j)} \qquad (5)$$

In this article, we insert the Category-based Assisted excitation layer and Assisted excitation layer respectively between the layers of each feature map size change of YOLOv3. As shown in Fig. 7, According to the characteristics of agricultural data sets (the volume of objects in the same category is approximately the same), we uses the category loss value of the previous epoch of training to give different categories different incentive effects, especially for small targets, CAE can effectively enhance their recognition capabilities. Finally, we obtained the best map between the 83–84 layers of the yolov3 model.

3.2   Model Compression

When deploying the model to an embedded platform, it is necessary to meet the real-time requirements. The channel pruning proposed by Zhang et al. [25] is to reduce the model in width, which is very helpful for reducing the size of the model, but for improving the calculation speed, it is not very obvious. Based on our observations, it is proposed that the use of layer pruning (shown in Fig. 8) for YOLOv3 can reduce the model in depth, greatly improve the calculation speed, and meet the real-time requirements. If combined with layer pruning and channel pruning, they can be viewed as a limited range of structural searches.

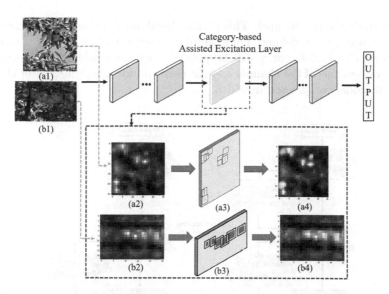

Fig. 7. Category-based Assisted Excitation model (CAE+YOLOv3). (a1) and (b1) are pictures of a batch during model training, (a2) and (b2) are activation tensor maps extracted from the YOLOv3 model, (a3) and (b3) are schematic diagrams of *Category-based Assisted Excitation model* to strengthen different positions, where the shade of blue represents the intensity of different excitations, (a4) and (b4) are the activation tensor after excitation.

Sparsity Training. Those who perform layer pruning and channel pruning must undergo sparse training to make the model weights sufficiently sparse. There is a BN layer behind each convolutional layer in YOLOv3 to accelerate convergence and improve generalization. The BN layer uses mini-batch static correction to normalize the convolution features. The formula is (1):

$$z_{out} = \gamma \times \frac{z_{in} - \mu}{\sqrt{\sigma^2 + \varepsilon}} + \beta \tag{6}$$

where σ^2 and ε are variance and mean of input in a batch. β and γ are bias and scale factor. z_{in} and z_{out} are the input and output of a BN layer. Naturally, we directly use the γ scale factor in the BN layer as an index to measure the importance of this layer. we preform L1 regularization on γ. And the training loss function becomes as follows:

$$L = loss_{yolov3} + \lambda \sum_{\gamma \in \Gamma} g(\gamma) \tag{7}$$

where $loss_{yolov3}$ denotes the original loss function of the YOLOv3 model. $g(\gamma) = |\gamma|$ denotes L1-normalize and λ is a coefficient that balances the two losses.

Channel Pruning. After sparse training, we introduce a factor γ to measure the importance of this channel and layer. We set a global threshold $\hat{T}$ to determine whether to delete the channel. This global threshold $\hat{T}$ refers to the percentage of $|\gamma|$ that needs to be deleted. For example, we set $\hat{T}$ to 75%, which means that the lower 75% of all factor γ will be pruned, including deleting the input and output connections of the channel and the corresponding weights. After that, we can get a model compressed in width.

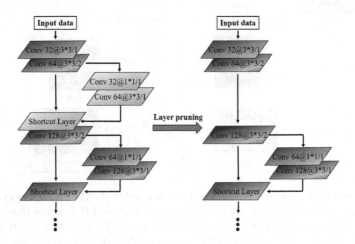

Fig. 8. Schematic diagram of layer pruning algorithm based on YOLOv3 model.

Layer Pruning. In order to further increase the calculation speed and meet the real-time requirements in practical applications, this paper proposes layer pruning. As can be seen in Fig. 8, the traditional channel pruning algorithm is to first sparse the already trained YOLOv3 model. And then delete the channels with weights close to 0 to achieve the purpose of reducing model size. This can reduce the size of the model, reduce the temporary memory of the model operation, and speed up the calculation. But upon closer inspection we found that, in order to ensure the integrity of the model depth, no matter how each channel weight of this layer is close to 0, some channels will be reserved to avoid model disconnection. Because these reserved channels are extensions in the model depth, they will greatly increase the number of calculation steps and slow down the inference speed. Therefore, this paper proposes a layer pruning algorithm for YOLOv3. First, each *shortcut* layer is sorted according to its importance, and the unimportant network layers at the end are deleted. Among them, in order to ensure the integrity of the network structure, each shortcut layer and the above two convolutional layers are deleted.

More specifically, each time a layer is deleted, a shortcut layer and two convolutional layers in front of it will be cut off. Here we only consider the shortcut module in the backbone of the YOLOv3 model. There are a total of 23 shortcuts. Each cut of the shortcut layer means a total of 3 layers are deleted. When performing layer subtraction, first set the layer pruning parameter $\hat{c}$, then collect the γ factor of a convolution layer on each shortcut layer, and sort the collected γ. Finally delete the $\hat{c}$ shortcut layers with the smallest γ value. This also means that $2 * \hat{c}$ convolutional layers have been removed.

4   Results and Discussion

4.1   Category-Based Assisted Excitation Model Results

Table 1. Category-based Assisted excitation model

Brief model	Detailed model	AP			MAP	FPS
		Apples	Mangoes	Almonds		
AE+YOLOv3	Assisted excitation model	0.879	0.889	0.875	0.881	4.61
CAE+YOLOv3	Category-based Assisted excitation model	0.882	0.901	**0.911**	0.898	4.61

In this article, we insert the Category-based Assisted excitation layer and Assisted excitation layer respectively between the layers of each feature map size change of YOLOv3, and the best MAP both between the 83–84 layers of YOLOv3. As can be seen from Table 1, our proposed model has a significant improvement on the smallest target *Almond*. The Category-based Assisted excitation model proposed in this article has the following advantages:

1. Since manually specifying the target effective region of the enhanced activation map, the foreground-background class imbalance problem of the YOLOv3 model can be improved, and the loss of the YOLOv3 detector can be prevented from being overwhelmed by simple negative samples.
2. Because YOLOv3 performs classification and positioning at the same time, localization problems arise. In this paper, the localization problem is solved by enhancing the signal strength of the target area of the activation tensor.

Futhermore, compared with the *Assisted Excitation model* proposed by Saeed et al. [7], the same enhancement strategy is used for each target. Because the objects of large targets occupy more pixels, the intensity of manual activation is greater, which will cause small objects to be ignored due to fewer pixels. The *Category-based Assisted Excitation model* proposed in this paper can evaluate which type of target has the worst training effect according to the category loss value of the last epoch training, and give it the corresponding strength enhancement strategy (in agricultural data sets, the size of the same type of target is generally close).

Table 2. Model compression

Brief model	Detailed model	AP			MAP	FPS
		Apples	Mangoes	Almonds		
CP+YOLOv3	Channel pruning	0.873	0.896	0.908	0.892	**8.57**
LCP+YOLOv3	Layer and channel pruning	0.879	0.898	0.912	0.896	**11.63**

4.2 Model Compression Results

In this article, we compare the methods of channel pruning and mixed channel with layer pruning. In channel pruning, we tested many different channel pruning ratios and fine-tuned them. The best results are shown in Table 2, the channel pruning ratio is 0.85, the MAP is 0.892, and the FPS is 8.57. When mixing channel and layer pruning, the best channel pruning ratio is 0.83, layer pruning parameters are 12, MAP is 0.896, and FPS is 11.63. Although the map is not greatly improved, it greatly speeds up model inference.

5   Conclusion

We propose a cheap precision agriculture solution for farmers in developing countries, using drones and embedded devices to achieve rapid and large-scale inventory production or mechanical spraying. In addition, for each category of agricultural data sets with similar volume sizes, a *Category-based Assisted Excitation model* is proposed to greatly improve the accuracy of the recognition, and a mixed use of layer pruning and channel pruning is proposed to achieve a small-scale optimal structure search. Meet the real-time requirements of actual deployment. Finally, compared to the original YOLOv3, based on the fruit dataset, the *MAP* is increased from 53.6% to 89.6%, and the FPS is increased from 4.05 to 11.63.

References

1. Alreshidi, E.: Smart sustainable agriculture (SSA) solution underpinned by internet of things (IoT) and artificial intelligence (AI). arXiv preprint arXiv:1906.03106 (2019)
2. Bargoti, S., Underwood, J.: Deep fruit detection in orchards. In: 2017 IEEE International Conference on Robotics and Automation (ICRA), pp. 3626–3633. IEEE (2017)
3. Chen, W., Wilson, J., Tyree, S., Weinberger, K., Chen, Y.: Compressing neural networks with the hashing trick. In: International Conference on Machine Learning, pp. 2285–2294 (2015)
4. Ji, C., et al.: Inspection and characterization of app file usage in mobile devices. ACM Trans. Storage (TOS) **16**, 1–25 (2020)
5. Courbariaux, M., Hubara, I., Soudry, D., El-Yaniv, R., Bengio, Y.: Binarized neural networks: training deep neural networks with weights and activations constrained to +1 or −1. arXiv preprint arXiv:1602.02830 (2016)

6. Denton, E.L., Zaremba, W., Bruna, J., LeCun, Y., Fergus, R.: Exploiting linear structure within convolutional networks for efficient evaluation. In: Advances in Neural Information Processing Systems, pp. 1269–1277 (2014)
7. Derakhshani, M.M., et al.: Assisted excitation of activations: a learning technique to improve object detectors. In: Proceedings of the IEEE Conference on Computer Vision and Pattern Recognition, pp. 9201–9210 (2019)
8. Fu, L., et al.: Kiwifruit detection in field images using faster R-CNN with ZFNet. IFAC-PapersOnLine **51**(17), 45–50 (2018)
9. Girshick, R., Donahue, J., Darrell, T., Malik, J.: Rich feature hierarchies for accurate object detection and semantic segmentation. In: Proceedings of the IEEE Conference on Computer Vision and Pattern Recognition, pp. 580–587 (2014)
10. Han, S., Pool, J., Tran, J., Dally, W.: Learning both weights and connections for efficient neural network. In: Advances in Neural Information Processing Systems, pp. 1135–1143 (2015)
11. He, K., Zhang, X., Ren, S., Sun, J.: Deep residual learning for image recognition. In: Proceedings of the IEEE Conference on Computer Vision and Pattern Recognition, pp. 770–778 (2016)
12. Huang, G., Chen, D., Li, T., Wu, F., van der Maaten, L., Weinberger, K.Q.: Multi-scale dense networks for resource efficient image classification. arXiv preprint arXiv:1703.09844 (2017)
13. Jin, S., et al.: Deep learning: individual maize segmentation from terrestrial lidar data using faster R-CNN and regional growth algorithms. Front. Plant Sci. **9**, 866 (2018)
14. Li, J., Kuang, X., Lin, S., Ma, X., Tang, Y.: Privacy preservation for machine learning training and classification based on homomorphic encryption schemes. Inf. Sci. (2020)
15. Lin, T.Y., Goyal, P., Girshick, R., He, K., Dollár, P.: Focal loss for dense object detection. In: Proceedings of the IEEE International Conference on Computer Vision, pp. 2980–2988 (2017)
16. Liu, W., et al.: SSD: single shot multibox detector. In: Leibe, B., Matas, J., Sebe, N., Welling, M. (eds.) ECCV 2016. LNCS, vol. 9905, pp. 21–37. Springer, Cham (2016). https://doi.org/10.1007/978-3-319-46448-0_2
17. Liu, Z., Li, J., Shen, Z., Huang, G., Yan, S., Zhang, C.: Learning efficient convolutional networks through network slimming. In: Proceedings of the IEEE International Conference on Computer Vision, pp. 2736–2744 (2017)
18. United Nations: World population prospects: the 2017 revision, key findings and advance tables. United Nations, New york (2017)
19. Redmon, J., Farhadi, A.: YOLOv3: an incremental improvement. arXiv preprint arXiv:1804.02767 (2018)
20. Ren, S., He, K., Girshick, R., Sun, J.: Faster R-CNN: towards real-time object detection with region proposal networks. In: Advances in Neural Information Processing Systems, pp. 91–99 (2015)
21. Simonyan, K., Zisserman, A.: Very deep convolutional networks for large-scale image recognition. arXiv preprint arXiv:1409.1556 (2014)
22. Wang, X., Kuang, X., Li, J., Li, J., Chen, X., Liu, Z.: Oblivious transfer for privacy-preserving in VANET's feature matching. IEEE Trans. Intell. Transp. Syst. (2020)
23. Wang, X., Li, J., Kuang, X., Tan, Y.A., Li, J.: The security of machine learning in an adversarial setting: a survey. J. Parallel Distrib. Comput. **130**, 12–23 (2019)
24. Wang, X., Li, J., Li, J., Yan, H.: Multilevel similarity model for high-resolution remote sensing image registration. Inf. Sci. **505**, 294–305 (2019)

25. Zhang, P., Zhong, Y., Li, X.: SlimYOLOv3: narrower, faster and better for real-time UAV applications. In: Proceedings of the IEEE International Conference on Computer Vision Workshops (2019)
26. Zhu, Z., Han, G., Jia, G., Shu, L.: Modified densenet for automatic fabric defect detection with edge computing for minimizing latency. IEEE Internet Things J. (2020)
27. Zhu, Z., Tan, L., Li, Y., Ji, C.: PHDFs: optimizing I/O performance of HDFs in deep learning cloud computing platform. J. Syst. Archit. 101810 (2020)
28. Zhu, Z., Wu, F., Cao, J., Li, X., Jia, G.: A thread-oriented memory resource management framework for mobile edge computing. IEEE Access **7**, 45881–45890 (2019)

QoS Investigation for Power Network with Distributed Control Services

Shen Jin[1], Xuesong Liang[1], and Hao Tian[2(✉)]

[1] State Grid Jibei Information and Company, Langfang, China
13488868312@139.com, liang.xuesong@jibei.sgcc.com.cn
[2] School of Computer and Software,
Nanjing University of Information Science and Technology, Nanjing, China
withhaotian@gmail.com

Abstract. In this paper, a distributed control scheme of key technologies is designed, which mainly includes QoS (quality of service) identification module and QoS routing optimization module. At the same time, a new routing method is designed to transform routing tables and optimize QoS multicast routing by using quantum evolutionary algorithm. This paper realizes the traditional centralized control of power network, the comprehensive transformation of service and QoS separation mode, and realizes the distributed QoS control mode according to the power service. The experimental results show that the newly designed scheme can provide different QoS guarantees according to different needs of the service and can effectively improve the QoS performance of the power grid.

Keywords: Distributed control · Power network · QoS

1 Introduction

With the deepening of the reform of the power market and the improvement of the information degree of the power industry, the type and number of power services are increasing rapidly, and the demand for telecommunication indicators tends to be diversified [12]. In order to ensure the quality of service (QoS), routing no longer only takes "reachable" and "shortest path" as the measurement index, but hopes to consider the specific telecommunication requirements of power business and the dynamic characteristics of the network [4,5,13].

At the same time, with the integration of power energy and telecommunication and the rapid development of smart grid, power telecommunication plays a more and more important role in power system [6,20]. The electric power telecommunication network carries all kinds of production and management services in the power system, which directly affects the stability and safe production of the power system, and its reliable operation is more important.

The electric power telecommunication network can alleviate the lack of telecommunication capacity caused by the slow development of the public network and fill the contradiction that the public network is difficult to meet the

© Springer Nature Switzerland AG 2020
X. Chen et al. (Eds.): ML4CS 2020, LNCS 12486, pp. 221–233, 2020.
https://doi.org/10.1007/978-3-030-62223-7_19

special telecommunication needs of some power departments, so as to ensure the normal and efficient production of electric power [8,17]. The service of electric power telecommunication can be divided into two categories: key operation service and transaction management service. The key operation services include telecontrol signal, data acquisition and monitoring control system, energy management system, relay protection signal and dispatching telephone, etc. Business management includes administrative telephone, conference telephone and conference television, management information data and so on. Different electric power telecommunication services have different requirements. There is not much information about the critical operation business. However, there are high requirements for real-time, accuracy and reliability of telecommunication, while transaction management services have many kinds of services, fast change and large telecommunication traffic [14].

In recent years, the global telecommunications system reform, deregulation, breaking monopoly, the introduction of competition mechanism has become an irresistible trend [2]. At the same time, China's reform and opening up is deepening step by step, among which the reform of electric power and telecommunications has been in the forefront [3,10]. In order to meet the high security requirements of the key business of modern electric power telecommunication, it is necessary to establish the technical system of high-speed data network of power system as soon as possible, track and study the technology of transmitting high-speed telecommunication data by power lines, and solve the problems of how to use the new technology to realize the broadband integrated telecommunication platform of key business of electric power telecommunication, such as how to integrate it through IP [15,16].

Therefore, this paper proposes a service classification scheme, a service distributed control scheme and a route optimization scheme to improve the QoS performance of the electric power telecommunication network in Northern Hebei. The traditional centralized control service of the electric power telecommunication network is separated from QoS, and the distributed QoS control mode is implemented according to the electric power telecommunication service. Different QoS guarantees are provided by arranging different routing and resource allocation according to the different requirements of each service. The specific contributions of this paper are as follows:

1) Analyze and diagnose the existing network service situation, evaluate the existing service flow, analyze and monitor the existing service flow status of the electric power telecommunication network, and put forward the classification method and standard of the service in the electric power telecommunication network.
2) Carry out the research on the reliability of electric power telecommunication network, and study the distributed control method of electric power telecommunication network for the purpose of improving network QoS. QoS service identification module and QoS routing optimization module are designed respectively.

3) Design a new routing scheme, which mainly reconstructs the routing table. This routing table is a secondary index routing table containing DSCP values, which includes the definition of the structure, the design of the data structure and the design of the operation function.
4) Use quantum evolutionary algorithm [7] to optimize QoS multicast routing, test it in jibei electric power telecommunication network, and develop a set of distributed QoS control simulation software.

The rest of the paper is organized as follows. In Sect. 2, we review the peer research and work. In Sect. 3, we put forward some models which are helpful to improve the QoS performance of power grid, and describe these models carefully. Analysis of experimental results are included in Sect. 4. Finally, Sect. 5 concludes the paper.

2   Related Work

Recently, the relevant research and business departments have conducted in-depth research and business implementation of the key technologies related to the QoS control algorithm of the electric power telecommunication network.

Li Binglin et al. [1] put forward the QoS guarantee technology of power packet transmission network. In order to meet the requirements of high reliability and low time delay in power production control, the QoS network guarantee architecture of PTN is analyzed, and three planes of transmission plane, management plane and control plane are established by using ASON technology. The QoS guarantee system of PTN is demonstrated from two aspects of traffic control box transmission routing. According to the various stages of traffic from entering the network to leaving the network, flow control mechanisms such as flow classification, traffic management and queue scheduling are implemented. Finally, the cracking-oriented routing control process is demonstrated.

Zhu et al. [11] also studied the load balancing of the network. In order to meet the requirements of both delay and bandwidth of QoS, and take into account the network load balance, a QoS routing algorithm based on traffic engineering is proposed. The algorithm is based on the dynamic weight routing algorithm, and uses the busy degree of the network link as the link weight to make the service distribute evenly in the network, which not only meets the requirement of service bandwidth delay, but also improves the access rate of the service. In view of the fact that the previous methods are not comprehensive enough to consider the delay jitter of the packet network, a set of clock recovery mechanism is proposed, which can ensure the stability of the receiver buffer and the accuracy of clock recovery, and ensure the QoS of TDM services.

Li et al. [19] used fuzzy analytic hierarchy process to comprehensively evaluate the importance of electric power telecommunication business. According to the business classification, the importance index system is established by layer, and then the evaluation matrix is established by pairwise comparison, and the triangular fuzzy number is used to fuzzify the weight vector. Finally, the fuzzy importance index weight of the business is calculated. Based on the degree of service importance, the "top-down" method is adopted to analyze the service reliability of electric power telecommunication network, establish the network reliability evaluation model, and evaluate the reliability of specific examples to verify the feasibility of fuzzy analytic hierarchy process (AHP).

According to the typical structure and telecommunication service characteristics of electric power telecommunication network, Cai et al. [18] propose an optimization algorithm of service route allocation based on the reliability of electric power telecommunication network. The algorithm takes the service average risk degree and service risk balance degree as the network reliability evaluation index, and uses the non-dominated sorting genetic algorithm based on fast classification to optimize the routing allocation of telecommunication services. In the process of genetic coding, the chromosome is encoded by indirect coding based on priority, and a blocking array is added in the decoding process to prevent the occurrence of a dead end. The feasibility and effectiveness of the optimization algorithm applied to power telecommunication network service routing optimization are verified by simulation. This method is suitable for all kinds of service requirements of electric power telecommunication network, such as 1-to-1, 1-to-N, N-to-1 and sequential execution of multiple nodes from the service level, it can provide theoretical reference for the service channel arrangement and network operation mode optimization of the power telecommunication operation department.

In view of the singleness of the traditional risk assessment method of electric power telecommunication network, Jiang Kangming et al. [9] put forward a comprehensive risk evaluation method of electric power telecommunication network based on service. First of all, the evaluation method analyzes the operation risk of the power telecommunication network link based on the service; secondly, it analyzes the importance of each link to the network from the point of view of network topology and obtains the link weight value; using the link weight and link risk value to carry on the comprehensive operation, thus obtains the network risk value and the network risk equilibrium degree these two risk evaluation index values. Taking a basic network composed of 8 nodes and 12 links as an example, the simulation results of the electric power telecommunication network model prove the effectiveness and accuracy of the comprehensive evaluation method, and can provide reference for network risk control. It has practical significance and has a certain application prospect in risk management.

3   System Model

According to the current operation situation of electric power network in Jibei Electric Power Company, the r_i index of service importance is used to reflect the degree of risk caused by a certain service to the safe and reliable operation of electric power network. It refers to the influence degree of service interruption or defect on the safe and stable operation of electric power network, and r_i is proportional to the impact of network risk. Considering the different functions of power system services and their different requirements for transmission channels, when taking the value of r_i, the transmission requirements of service channels and the security requirements of different types of services are combined to evaluate the impact of services on the operation risk of power networks.

After the service identification, the QoS control will perform QoS routing optimization control. The specific method is that when entering the routing phase, the routing is no longer based solely on the destination address, but on the combination of the destination address and the DSCP value. This also reflects the characteristics of QoS business control.

In order to provide different forwarding paths for different services, multiple optional paths to the same destination address need to be maintained in the routing table, which can be achieved by setting the path parameters of each optional path. In the search process, the destination address is taken as the first-level index and the DSCP value of the service as the secondary index, so as to find the corresponding next-hop path for different types of services arriving at the same destination address for forwarding. In this way, we can assign routes according to different power business requirements on the basis of destination routing, so as to improve the service transmission quality of electric power network, and finally realize QoS routing optimization control.

In the aspect of service classification and routing design, the practical application status of the northern Hebei electric power network is fully considered. At the same time, according to the characteristics of the existing Hebei electric power network and the universality of the multicast service, the improved quantum evolutionary algorithm is adopted to optimize the multicast routing of the northern Hebei electric power network, which further improves the QoS performance of the Northern Hebei power grid.

4   Experimental Evaluation

This part shows details of the experiment and the display and analysis of the experiment outcome. According to the practical application test results of the proposed business classification method in the North Hebei electric power network. Figure 1 shows the various service flows measured by Bazhou station on June 28, 2014 from 9:00 am to 11:00 am. Figure 2 shows the time-sharing monitoring chart of the actual flow of Bazhou Station on June 28, 2014, from 9:00 am to 11:00 am. Figure 3 shows the various service flows measured by Wuzhuang station on June 29, 2014, from 9:00 am to 11:00 am. Figure 4 shows the time-sharing monitoring chart of the actual flow of Wuzhuang station on June 29, 2014, from 9:00 am to 11:00 am.

Using the multicast routing optimization scheme proposed in this study, combined with the key technologies mentioned above and the actual situation of the northern Hebei electric power network, the practical application test of the routing optimization scheme was carried out in some areas of northern Hebei electric power in July 2014. This paper mainly verifies the effectiveness and feasibility of the algorithm in QoS multicast routing, and compares the performance with

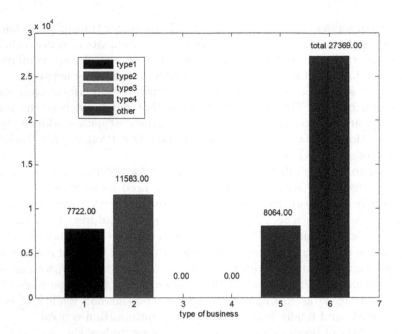

Fig. 1. Traffic monitoring results of Bazhou Station on June 28, 2014

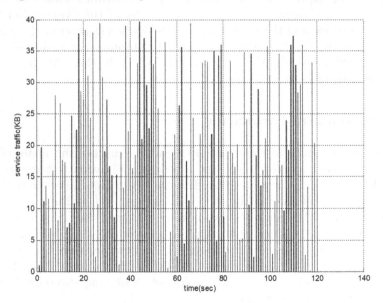

Fig. 2. Real-time operation status of business traffic in Bazhou Station on June 28, 2014

the classical algorithms ACO and QEA. The network topology consists of 30 nodes, which represent 30 actual stations of Hebei electric power network. The

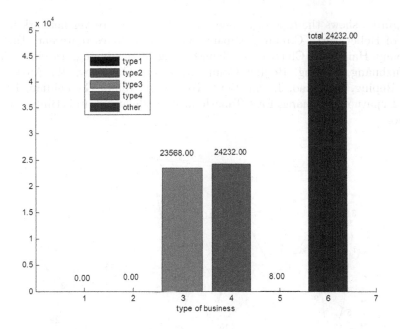

Fig. 3. Traffic Monitoring results of Wuzhuang Station on June 29, 2014

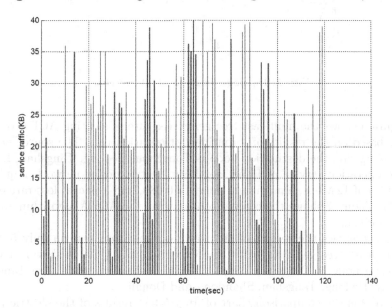

Fig. 4. Real-time Operation status of business flow in Wuzhuang Station on June 29, 2014

bandwidth, delay and packet loss rate of each link are the actual situation of the real-time operation of the network.

Figure 5 shows the topology diagram of the electric power network in some areas of Hebei North Circuit Company. The thirty nodes represent: Tangshan Company, Hancheng, Chaxishan, Changzhuang, JiangJiaying, Taiping, Shunyi, Dingfuzhuang, Xiwang, Beijing Company, Hebei Company, Jia Anzi, Tangshan, Heping, Hongqiao, Jixian, Beisi, Tongzhou, Taihu, Gaobeidian, Hedong, Wali, Lvjiatuo, Leizhuang, East Tangshan, Angezhuang, Lutai, Binhai, Dongli, Beijiao.

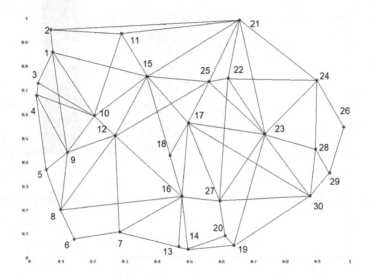

Fig. 5. Topology diagram of 30 test sites

Figure 6 shows the multicast tree generated after executing AQEA on July 2,2014, based on the results of a routing optimization test. The source node is Jiangjiaying site, the destination node is Tongzhou, Hedong, Tangshan, Lutai.

The operation service of Hebei northern electric power network requires a bandwidth of 12 Mbps, a maximum delay of 0.08 s, and a packet loss rate of less than 1%. Figure 7 shows the comparison between the AQEA algorithm and the ACO algorithm.

Figure 8 shows the results of the route optimization test on July 5, 2014. The multicast tree generated after the execution of AQEA is shown in Fig.8. The source node is Tangshan West, and the destination nodes are Tangshan Company, Hedong, Tangshan, Shandong and Dongli.

Figure 9 is the comparison chart of July 5 test results of the electric power network in jibei. As the result of July 2, the optimized route greatly improves the performance of the electric power network's QoS.

In July 2014, we gradually expanded the test scope to 150 stations in the North Hebei electric power network. When the number of nodes increased from 30 to 150 and the number of multicast group members accounted for 15% of the total number of nodes, we compared the cost and convergence time of three

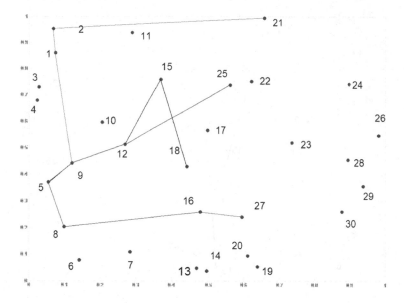

Fig. 6. Routing optimization test results on July 2, 2014

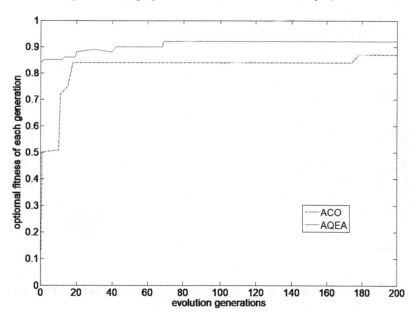

Fig. 7. Comparison of routing optimization test results on July 2, 2014

algorithms: AQEA, QEA and ACO, and obtained the experimental results in Fig. 10 and Fig. 11.

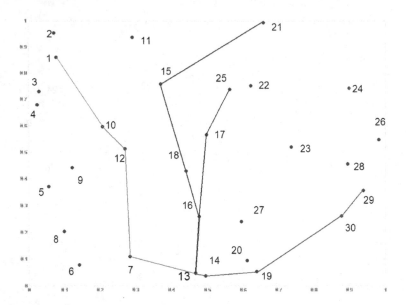

Fig. 8. Routing optimization test results on July 5, 2014

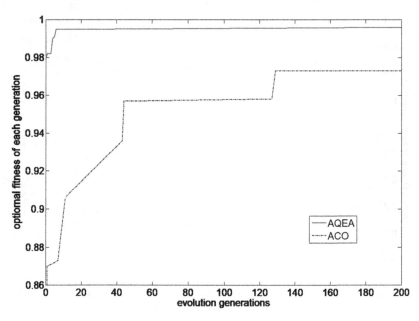

Fig. 9. Comparison of routing optimization test results on July 5, 2014

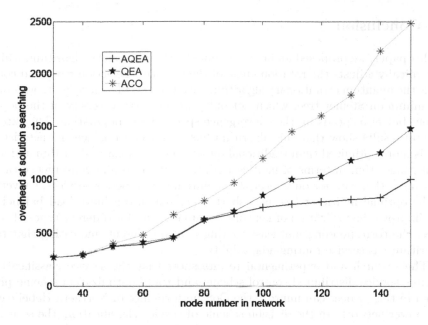

Fig. 10. Comparison of three algorithms for Multicast Tree routing overhead

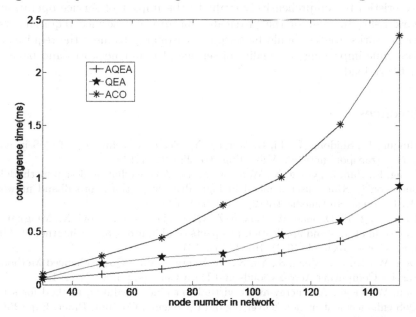

Fig. 11. Comparison of three algorithms for Multicast Tree routing convergence time

5   Conclusion

In this paper, we proposed an improved quantum evolutionary algorithm, which dynamically adjusts the rotation angle of the quantum selection gate, and combines the quantum evolutionary algorithm with the OMST algorithm to generate the minimum Steiner tree, which not only enhances the diversity of the population, but also speeds up the convergence speed of the population. The experimental results show that this algorithm has better convergence characteristics and is more optimized than traditional quantum evolutionary algorithm and ant colony algorithm in terms of multicast routing overhead and convergence time. This algorithm can not only meet the requirements of power services, converge to the optimal multicast tree in a short time, but also achieve load balancing and improve the utilization of network resources. And for different types of services, the corresponding multicast routing is also different, indicating that the algorithm has service routing adaptability.

The research and experimental results show that the service classification scheme, service distributed control scheme and route optimization scheme proposed in this project can improve the QoS performance of Northern Hebei electric power network. In the division scheme of service classification, the security requirements of services are combined with the requirements of transmission characteristics to comprehensively evaluate the impact of service operation on network risks. In view of the physical structure and service requirements of power networks, routes should be selected reasonably to meet the requirements of QoS while improving the quality of service of power networks and balancing the network load.

References

1. Binglin, L., Shidong, L., Li, H., Jiming, Y.: Security technology of QoS in power packet transport network. Value Eng. **16**, 220–223 (2013)
2. Dong, F., Han, H., Gong, X., Wang, J., Li, H.: A constellation design methodology based on QoS and user demand in high-altitude platform broadband networks. IEEE Trans. Multimedia **18**(12), 2384–2397 (2016)
3. Dongsheng, Y., Daohao, W., Bowen, Z., Qiyu Chen, Z.Y., Guoyi, X., Mingjian, C.: Key technologies and application prospects of ubiquitous power internet of things. Pow. Gener. Technol. **40**(2), 107–114 (2019)
4. Dou, W., Xu, X., Meng, S., Yu, S.: An Energy-Aware QoS Enhanced Method for Service Computing Across Clouds and Data Centers, pp. 80–87 (2015)
5. Dou, W., et al.: An energy-aware virtual machine scheduling method for service QoS enhancement in clouds over big data. Concurr. Comput. Pract. Exp. **29**(14), e3909 (2017)
6. Gogoi, S.: A review of the power distribution system in the telecommunications sector. J. Impact Fact. **3**, 143 (2018)

7. Jagatheesan, K., Samanta, S., Choudhury, A., Dey, N., Anand, B., Ashour, A.S.: Quantum inspired evolutionary algorithm in load frequency control of multi-area interconnected thermal power system with non-linearity. In: Hassanien, A.E., Elhoseny, M., Kacprzyk, J. (eds.) Quantum Computing:An Environment for Intelligent Large Scale Real Application. SBD, vol. 33, pp. 389–417. Springer, Cham (2018). https://doi.org/10.1007/978-3-319-63639-9_16
8. Jordehi, A.R.: Optimisation of demand response in electric power systems, a review. Renew. Sustain. Energy Rev. **103**, 308–319 (2019)
9. Kang-ming, J., Ying, Z., Bo-ren, D., Rui Tang, L.: Risk evaluation method of electric power communication network based on services. Pow. Syst. Protect. Control **41**(24), 101–106 (2013)
10. Li, M., Patiño-Echeverri, D., Zhang, J.J.: Policies to promote energy efficiency and air emissions reductions in china's electric power generation sector during the 11th and 12th five-year plan periods: Achievements, remaining challenges, and opportunities. Energy Pol. **125**, 429–444 (2019)
11. Luo, J., Ji, P., Wang, X., Zhu, Y.: A Novel Method of QoS Based Resource Management and Trust Based Task Scheduling, pp. 21–32 (2004)
12. Ning-zhe, X., Hai-feng, Y.: Research on the reliability of electric power telecommunication system. Telecommun. Electr. Pow. Syst. **6**, 26–30 (2007)
13. Qi, L., Chen, Y., Yuan, Y., Fu, S., Zhang, X., Xu, X.: A QoS-aware virtual machine scheduling method for energy conservation in cloud-based cyber-physical systems. In: World Wide Web, pp. 1–23 (2019)
14. Rao, H., Xu, A., Guo, X., Bai, H., et al.: Strategic research on china energy technology revolution system. Strateg. Study Chin. Acad. Eng. **20**(3), 1–8 (2018)
15. Shuai, S., Zhijun, S., Xiaoguang, Y., Yan, Z., Zhongfeng, W.: A Wireless Extended Coverage Scheme for Electric Power Communication Network, pp. 5836–5840 (2019)
16. Tingjun, W., Shangdi, M., Xuebing, L., Shanshan, L., Shuo, Z.: Reliability Evaluation Model of Power Communication Network Considering the Importance of Transmission Service, pp. 355–364 (2020)
17. Villman, G., Lindfors, G., Bergman, S.: Pole for the transmission of electric power and/or telecommunication signals, and use and method (Nov 5 2019), uS Patent 10,465,410
18. Wei, C., et al.: An optimized service routing allocation method for electric power communication network considering reliability. Pow. Syst. Technol. **37**(361)(12), 3541–3545 (2013)
19. Xin, J., Xiaoyuan, W., Si, L.: Evaluation of communication service importance based on fuzzy analytic hierarchy process. Telecommun. Electr. Pow. Syst. **31**(211), 56–61 (2010)
20. Xue, S., Zhang, Y., Xu, X., Xing, G., Xiang, H., Ji, S.: Qet: a qos-basedenergy-aware task scheduling method in cloud environment. Cluster Comput. **20**, 3199–3212 (2017). https://doi.org/10.1007/s10586-017-1047-5

Fog Server Placement for Multimodality Data Fusion in Neuroimaging

Xuan Yan[1], Xiaolong Xu[1,2(✉)], Yu Zheng[1], and Fei Dai[3]

[1] School of Computer and Software,
Nanjing University of Information Science and Technology, Nanjing, China
{xuanyan,yzheng}@nuist.edu.cn, njuxlxu@gmail.com
[2] Engineering Research Center of Digital Forensics, Ministry of Education,
Nanjing, China
[3] School of Big Data and Intelligence Engineering, Southwest Forestry University,
Kunming, Yunnan, China
daifei@swfu.edu.cn

Abstract. Since the findings of the single modality data are unable to provide sufficient sensitivity and specificity for diagnostic measures, multimodality data fusion is adopted in the neuroimaging to detect the important differences between patients and healthy people. Applying fog computing contributes to reducing the redundant modality data transmission and processing brought by the multimodality data fusion. Due to the budget, the scale and the storage space of the fog servers are limited. What's more, the proper location of the fog servers depends on the distribution of the data fusion points and the detailed contents of the data fusion tasks. Therefore, a fog server placement strategy for multimodality data fusion in neuroimaging, named FSPF, is put forward to determine the proper scale and location of the fog servers. Technically, the performance of the fog server location is evaluated by the data fusion time and the hit rate. Then, non-dominated sorting genetic algorithm-III (NSGA-III) is adopted in FSPF to obtain the proper solutions of the next generation and a reference solution is applied to optimize the initial population of the evolution. Finally, adequate experiments have been conducted to testify the efficiency and reliability of our method.

Keywords: Multimodality · Data fusion · Fog computing · NSGA-III

1 Introduction

Neuroimaging, as a relatively new interdisciplinary subject, combines the techniques and methods in medicine, neuroscience, and psychology, providing a novel paradigm for direct and indirect research on the function and structure of the nervous system [12]. Currently, neuroimaging is being applied in various scenarios, including the diagnosis of brain diseases (e.g., brain tumors) and the study of the working mechanism with the brain [17]. Particularly, due to the complex brain structure, utilizing a single imaging technique to image the nerve system

X. Chen et al. (Eds.): ML4CS 2020, LNCS 12486, pp. 234–248, 2020.
https://doi.org/10.1007/978-3-030-62223-7_20

often fails to fully represent the structure of the brain. Therefore, neuroimaging generally exploits multiple imaging techniques (e.g., magnetic resonance imaging and position-emission tomography) meanwhile imaging the brain structure. With these imaging techniques, the brain structures are imaged from different angles, and the data with multiple modalities are generated. Through the multimodal data fusion technology, these multiple datasets about the same brain structure can be integrated into a more unified and global perspective of the brain, which improves people's understanding of the function and the brain structure [10].

Since different imaging equipments are generally distributed in different areas of an institution, or even in different institutions [1,4], the geographical distribution of imaging equipment leads to the traditional resource centralized cloud computing failing to satisfy the bandwidth and storage requirements of multimodal data fusion, which causes network congestion, high service latency, and reduced the quality of service [9]. Fog computing, as a new computing paradigm, extends network, computing and storage resources close to the imaging equipment, providing distributed computing resources for multimodal data fusion. To implement multimodal data fusion, the preprocessed unimodal data stored in fog servers are extracted and fused together, thereby supporting real-time, low-latency multimodal data fusion in neuroimaging [14].

However, due to the limited budget, it is impossible to arrange a fog server for each data fusion point. How to design an applicable fog server placement solution, which reduces the number of placed fog servers while still providing low-latency and high-quality preprocessing services and covering more pieces of image equipment, is still a challenge [7]. Additionally, in view of the limited storage capability of the fog servers, it is difficult to store all the preprocessed data in the fog service [19]. Therefore, when the storage space of the server is full, it is necessary to decide which stored data needs to be discarded when new preprocessed data needs to be stored on the fog server [8]. An unreasonable data discarding scheme will lead to a low hit rate (e.g., the ratio of the required unimodal data being stored in the fog server when multimodal data fusion is conducted), resulting in repeated preprocessing of unimodal data and the waste of computing resources in the fog servers, which consequently elongates the service latency and disrupts the quality of service of the users [3].

To the best of our knowledge, although some researchers studied the placement of edge servers, such as [18,20], all of these previous studies only considers how to balance the workloads of edge severs or enhance execution efficiency of computing services provided by edge severs, without taking the storage of preprocessed data into consideration. Till now, few researchers have studied the fog server placement problem for multimodal data preprocessing in neuroimaging, which aims at optimizing the data preprocess service and improving the hit rate of the data. In this article, a method named FSPF is proposed. In particular, the main contributions of this article are listed as follows.

- Adopt fog computing in multimodality data fusion to avoid the redundant transmission and processing of the modality data.

– Devise the network model, data fusion time model and hit rate model in the fusion process to evaluate the performance of the fog server placement.
– Apply reference solutions to optimize the initial population of the evolution.
– Conduct adequate experiments to verify the effectiveness and reliability of our method.

The remainder of this paper is organized as follows. Section 2 describes the related work of this paper. And then, the system model and problem formulation are presented in Sect. 3. Thereafter, Sect. 4 develops a fog server placement method for multimodal data fusion in neuroimaging. In Sect. 5, sufficient experimental evaluations and analysis are presented to validate the effectiveness of our proposed method. Finally, we conclude the paper and give an outlook of the paper in Sect. 6.

2   Related Work

Neuroimaging is a means to visualize the different nervous systems, which is able to capture neural vulnerability factors, abnormal regions and potential tumors. The neural activity of brain shows three-dimensional dynamic characteristics, so it is not enough to interpret the working mechanism of brain only by recording one-dimensional signals changing with time [2]. It is an important method in the research of brain science to reveal the anatomical structure and function of brain by the imaging method in two-dimensional and three-dimensional space.

Nowadays, the research of brain functional imaging has developed from the functional segregation to the functional integration. Lei et al. [11] studied the data process technique of diseases and they proposed an algorithm based on manifold learning to obtain quick retrieval of neuroimaging data. Shi et al. [16] concentrated on the computer-enabled diagnosis for Parkinson's disease. For the data fusion points are provided with limited computing resources and storage space, fog computing emerges as a potential computing paradigm to execute imaging data.

Fog computing could provide the data fusion points with relatively abundant resources, i.e., computing ability and storage space, which is able to speed up the efficiency of neuroimaging [15]. There are many researches studying the fog computing to optimize computing structure and enable applications. Dong et al. [6] built up a coordinative fog computing to execute offloaded workloads and achieved a joint optimization in terms of QoE and energy. Chiu et al. [5] focused on the latency-driven fog system, and they advocated a model of fog radio access network to promote limited computing resources and realize ultra-low latency. Zhang et al. [21] proposed an energy-aware task offloading method using a fairness scheduling metric, which considers the energy consumption, the historical energy and priority of fog points. Liu et al. [13] studied on how to schedule complex tasks to massive fog points in the proximity and they proposed a dispersive stable key method to minimize service latency in fog environment.

Considering the expensive cost, arranging the fog points near all data fusion points is impossible. Till now, the study of fog points placement for neuroimaging is few. In view of this, we propose a fog server placement strategy for multimodality data fusion in neuroimaging which adopts NSGA-III.

3   System Model and Problem Formulation

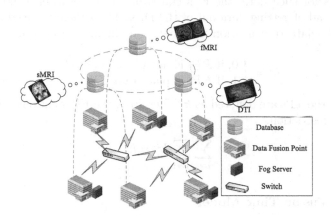

Fig. 1. The framework of the multimodality data fusion system

3.1   Network Model

Although a large number of abnormal areas in patients have been identified in neuroimaging studies, these findings are unable to provide sufficient sensitivity and specificity for diagnostic measures. There is also a lack of consistent findings between studies due to the differences in individual modalities. Therefore, some important differences were detected only in the portion of each modality. In the network shown in Fig. 1, there are N multimodality data fusion points (TPs) where the models are trained. The modality data are stored in the database points (DPs) and different DP stores different types of modality data. The scale of the DPs are denoted as M. Each DP only has one kind of modality data. In short, there is a one-to-one relationship between the DPs and the modalities. The DPs and TPs consist of an undirected graph which is denoted as G. TP_i represents the i-th TP and DP_j represents the j-th DP in the graph. The weight of the edge between TP_i and DP_j is determined according to the time cost of data transmission. It is calculated by

$$w(i,j) = \begin{cases} +\infty, & \text{if } DP_j \text{ can not transfer the modality data to } TP_i, \\ \theta, & \text{if } DP_j \text{ can transfer the modality data to } TP_i, \end{cases} \quad (1)$$

where θ is the time for data transmission between TP_i and DP_j.

Before model training, the data from the DPs needs to go through several pre-processing steps, for example, singular value decomposition. To speed up the model training process and avoid the redundant transmission of modality data, fog computing is adopted in the network. Since the modality data in the DP may be used by several TPs, the processing results of the modality data can be processed and stored in the fog points (FPs). When other TPs send the requirements for such data, the FPs can transfer the processed modality data directly instead of getting data out of the DPs. The FPs are placed on the TPs to reduce the data transmission time between them. The locations of FPs are represented as

$$L_i^j = \begin{cases} 0, \text{ if } FP_j \text{ is not placed on } TP_i, \\ 1, \text{ if } FP_j \text{ is placed on } TP_i. \end{cases} \tag{2}$$

The scale of the TPs are denoted as k. Therefore, the FP locations are supposed to obey the restriction:

$$\sum_{i=1}^{N} \sum_{j=1}^{k} L_i^j = k. \tag{3}$$

3.2   Data Fusion Time Model

The total data fusion time of TP_i, denoted as TT_i, is made up of three parts. The first part is the time for modality data transmission. Define FP_j as the closest FP to TP_i. The DP which stores the a-th data required by TP_i is denoted as DP_a. The transmission time of the a-th data of TP_i is calculated by

$$tr_a = \begin{cases} 2 \cdot dis(TP_i, FP_j), \text{ if } FP_j \text{ has the processed data,} \\ 2 \cdot dis(TP_i, DP_a), \text{ if } FP_j \text{ does not have the processed data,} \end{cases} \tag{4}$$

where $dis(TP_i, FP_j)$ represents the distance between TP_i and FP_j in G.

The second part of the time is the time for data pre-processing. The modality data obtained from the DPs should be pre-processed before the training in the FPs. If the processed modality data are stored in the FPs, the pre-processing time is zero. Therefore, the pre-processing time of the a-th data is calculated by

$$pre_a = \begin{cases} 0, \text{ if } FP_j \text{ has the processed data,} \\ t_a, \text{ if } FP_j \text{ does not have the processed data,} \end{cases} \tag{5}$$

where t_a represents the time needed for pre-processing the a-th data.

The third part is the time for training which depends on the types of the modality data and the models. Define that the time needed for the modality data in DP_h is ω_h and the total scale of the modality data in DP_h is s_h. Therefore, the total training time of TP_i is calculated by

$$te = \sum_{h=1}^{M} \omega_h \cdot s_h. \tag{6}$$

The scale of the modality data used by TP_i is defined as p_i. The total training time of TP_i is the sum of these three parts. Therefore, it is calculated by

$$TT_i = te + \sum_{a=1}^{p_i}(tr_a + pre_a). \tag{7}$$

The final data fusion time, denoted as TT, depends on the last completed FP. It is calculated by

$$TT = \max_{i=1}^{N} TT_i \tag{8}$$

3.3 Hit Rate Model

Due to the budget, the FPs are unable to store all the pre-processed modality data. Therefore, not in all situations can the TPs obtain the required data from the nearest FP. The obtainment situation can be represented as

$$OB_i^j = \begin{cases} 0, \text{ if } TP_j \text{ obtain the modality data from } FP_j, \\ 1, \text{ if } TP_j \text{ does not obtain the modality data from } FP_j. \end{cases} \tag{9}$$

The hit rate is the ratio of the scale of the modality data obtained to the total data scale. High hit rate means that much redundant data transmission is avoided and much time for data pre-processing is saved. The hit rate of FP_i is calculated by

$$HR_i = \frac{1}{p_i} \sum_{i=1}^{p_i} OB_i^j \tag{10}$$

The total hit rate of all the FPs, denoted as HR, is the average of the hit rates of the TPs. It is calculated by

$$HR = \frac{1}{N} \sum_{i=1}^{N} HR_i \tag{11}$$

3.4 Problem Formulation

Our goal is to reduce the training time of the models and increase the hit rate of FPs. The FP placement problem can be defined as a multi-objective optimization problem, which is written as

$$\text{Min}TT, \quad \text{Max}HR. \tag{12}$$

All the FPs should also obey the constraint:

$$2 \cdot dis(TP_i, FP_j) \leq 2 \cdot dis(TP_i, DP_h) + t_h \quad h = 1, 2, 3, \ldots, p_i. \tag{13}$$

where FP_j is the nearest FP to TP_i, DP_h is the DP which stores the h-th modality data and t_h is the pre-processing time for the h-th modality data. The constraint ensure that obtaining the pre-processed modality data from the FPs is superior to obtaining them from the DPs.

4   Fog Server Placement for Multimodality Data Fusion in Neuroimaging

In this part, the problem is simplified as a multi-objective optimization problem. NSGA-III is adopted to obtain the proper solutions. The initial population of the evolution is specially designed to introduce the high-class genes.

4.1   Fitness Functions and Constraints

During the evolution, the fitness functions are used to evaluate the qualities of the solutions obtained. Whether or not these solutions are selected for the new generation depends on their data fusion time and hit rate which are shown in (8) and (11). Both the data fusion time and the hit rate are adopted to comprehensively evaluate the performance of the fog server location.

To ensure that obtaining the modality data from the FPs costs less time than obtaining them from the DPs, the solutions found should obey the constraint shown in (13). Setting more FPs contributes to accelerating the data fusion process. However, due to the limited budget, the scale of the FPs can not be too large in the data fusion system. Define co as the ratio of the scale of FPs to the scale of TPs. co_{max} is preset as the maximum co of the data fusion system.

4.2   Initialization

At this stage, the total scale of the solutions in the population Q, the maximum generation of evolution I and the mutation probability Pm are set in advance. At the beginning of the building of the initial population, Q N-bit binary numbers are generated randomly. An appropriate initial solution will be generated as a reference to optimize these binary numbers. Define v as the maximum scale of the multimodality data that an FP can store. The number of the FPs in the reference solution is $\frac{N}{v}$. Therefore, $\frac{N}{v}$ TPs are chosen from all the TPs to place the fog servers in the reference solution. Define i_{re} as the reference solution for the initial population. a_{re}^m is the m-th bit of i_{re} and b_j^m is the m-th bit of i_j which is the j-th solution in the initial population. The distance between i_{re} and i_j is defined as the hamming distance between them. It is calculated by

$$d(i_{re}, i_j) = \sum_{m=1}^{N} a_{re}^m \oplus b_j^m. \tag{14}$$

If the value of a_{re}^m is the same as the value of b_j^m, the value of b_j^m will not change. Otherwise, b_j^m may be reversed according to the scale of the FPs in i_j.

4.3   Crossover and Mutation

Half of them are the selected solutions from the previous generation, and the other part is the solutions that are restructured and mutated in this stage.

These Q new solutions are generated according to the solutions in the previous generation.

Suppose that solution i_a and solution i_b are paired with each other. The new solutions generated according to i_a and i_b would combine the characteristics of i_a and i_b. i_c is made up of the odd bits in i_a and the even bits in i_b. i_d contains the even bits in i_a and the odd bits in i_b. During the mutation stage, these solutions are partially altered to introduce new genes to maintain the diversity of the population. Since the location of the FPs is represented as a binary number with N bits, each element of the binary number needs to be reversed according to the mutation probability at this stage. This reversion will happen several times according to the probability of the mutation and the length of the binary number.

4.4   Selection

Fitness Selection. Define the population of the evolution as R and the critical layer of the non-dominated sorting result is denoted as the s-th layer. A $1 \times Q$ row vector, denoted as fn, is adopted to represent the value of the solutions in R. $fn[j]$ is the fitness value of the j-th solution in R. In other words, the j-th solution in R is in the $fn[j]$-th layer in the non-dominated sorting result.

$rank[i]$ is defined as the scale of the solutions which control i in R. It is calculated by

$$rank[i] = |\{i'|i' \succ i\}|. \tag{15}$$

The value of $rank[i]$ is zero is equivalent to that the i-th solution is a non-dominated solution in R. All the non-dominated solutions in R are picked out to fill the non-dominated layer. Then, these selected solutions are deleted from R and new non-dominated solutions are chosen to fill the next non-dominated layer. This operation is repeated for several times until the scale of R is 0. The fitness levels of the solution are equal to theri non-dominated sorting levels. Tournament is adopted in the fitness selection. Two individuals are chosen from R randomly and the solution with higher fitness value is selected into the new generation. If they have the same fitness value, both of them will be chosen.

Crowding Degree Selection. After the crossover and mutation process, the scale of individuals rises to $2Q$. We need to pick Q individuals from these $2Q$ individuals to generate the new generation. Obviously, the solution in the lower layer should be selected in this stage. The selection depends on the crowding degree to maintain the population diversity.

The crowding degree selection is based on the positions of the reference points. The reference points are a group of points that are uniformly distributed in the solution space. The horizontal coordinate and vertical coordinate of the solution i are shown in (8) and (11). Define (x_j, y_j) as the position of the reference point P_j and (x_i, y_i) is denoted as the position of solution i. The distance between P_j and i is calculated by

$$dis(P_j, i) = \sqrt{(x_j - x_i)^2 + (y_j - y_i)^2}. \tag{16}$$

If P_j is the closest reference point to i, P_j is associated with i. The solutions whose positions in the non-dominated sorting are lower than the critical layer are placed into R directly as the new individuals. The scale of the solutions in R, which are associated with P_j, is denoted as cn_j. The point with the lowest cn is picked out as the alternative point. If the alternative point is associated with any solution in the critical layer, the closest solution will be put into R as the new individual, and its cn is going to add one. The selected solution is also removed from the critical layer. Otherwise, the alternative point is ignored and a new alternative point will be found. This operation will be repeated until the scale of R is Q.

Final Selection. Since there is more than one solution in the final population, an assessment function is supposed to be determined to choose a proper individual as the final solution. The assessment function, denoted as AF, is adopted to evaluate the performance of the placement solution. It is calculated by

$$AF = \frac{TT}{HR^\omega}, \tag{17}$$

where ω is pre-set as the weight of the hit rate. The solution with a lower value of AF is supposed to have better performance and is more likely to be chosen from the final population. The final solution is the solution with the lowest AF in the last generation.

4.5 Method Overview

Our algorithm is adopted to obtain the placement solution of the FPs to speed up the process of multimodality data fusion. First of all, the pre-determined parameters and the initial population of the evolution are set (Line 3). The initial population is optimized according to the reference solution in the Initialization process. The new individuals of the evolution are selected from the individuals of the previous generation (Line 5). Then, the selected solutions undergo crossover and mutation (Line 7). Crowding degree selection is adopted to obtain the proper solutions and maintain the population diversity (Line 8). A proper individual in the final solution set is figured out and outputted in the last step (Lines 12 and 13).

5   Experimental Evaluation

In this section, the performance of FSPF is evaluated and compared with the performance of niched pareto genetic algorithm II (NPGA-II). In NPGA-II, the diversity of the population is maintained well due to the application of niche count. When selecting the individuals of the next generation in our method, the solution's position in the non-dominant sorting result is given priority. The crowding level which is adopted to maintaining the population diversity is taken into consideration only when the two solutions has the same non-dominant sorting position. The total scale of the modality data for the data fusion process

Algorithm 1. Fog Server Placement for Multimodality Data Fusion in Neuroimaging

---

Input: Q, I, Pm, v
Output: i_{best}
 1: $R \leftarrow \varnothing$
 2: $g \leftarrow 1$
 3: Initialize R
 4: **while** $g \leq I$ **do**
 5:     Conduct fitness selection on R
 6:     Put the result solutions of fitness selection into P
 7:     Conduct crossover and mutation on P
 8:     Conduct crowding degree selection on R
 9:     Put the result solutions of crowding degree selection into R
10:     $g \leftarrow g + 1$
11: **end while**
12: Choose a proper solution in in R as i_0 according to (17)
13: **return** i_0

Table 1. Parameter Settings

Parameter	Description	Value
N	The scale of the TPs	100
M	The scale of the DPs	3
Q	The scale of the population	100
I	The maximum generation of the evolution	200
Pm	The mutation probability	0.1
co_{max}	The maximum co of the data fusion system	0.5

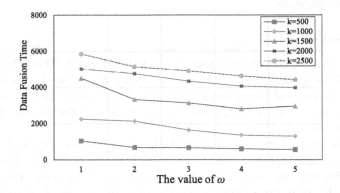

Fig. 2. Impact of ω on data fusion time at different scales of modality data

is denoted as k. The parameter settings of the evaluation part are shown in Table 1. The impact of v and ω on the performance of the final solution are also evaluated in this section.

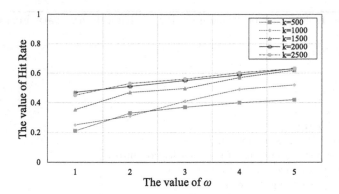

Fig. 3. Impact of ω on hit rate at different scales of modality data

5.1   Impact of ω

The value of v is set as 20 when assessing the impact of ω on the data fusion time and the hit rate. The growth of ω will give the solutions with high hit rates much more advantage in the final selection. They may have higher value of AF and are more likely to be chosen. As shown in Fig. 3, with the increasing of ω, the hit rate of the final solution raises. However, as shown in Fig. 2, the increasing of hit rate does not always cause the decreasing of the data fusion time. Focusing too much attention on the hit rate may decrease the data fusion time. The hit of a modality data with large scale can save much data fusion time while it has the same weight as hitting a small modality data in the hit rate aspect. ω is set to determine the importance of the data fusion time and the hit rate. Its value depends on the practical needs and situations. The value of ω is set as 2 in the following comparisons.

5.2   Impact of v

Due to the budget, the storage space of the FPs is limited. The FPs are unable to store all the modality data which have been pre-processed. v is denoted as the maximum scale of the modality data an FP can store. In this section, the value of v is set as 10, 15, 20, 25 and 30 to evaluate its effect on the data fusion time and the hit rate.

Since the fog servers are empty at the beginning of the data fusion process, as shown in Fig. 5, the hit rate increases with the growth of k. However, the maximum hit rate depends on the details of the modality data. Therefore, the value of the hit rate grows slowly when the value of k is big. As shown in Fig. 4, the data fusion time decreases when v is increasing. The rate of its decreasing is also getting smaller because of the empty fog servers. The fog servers with larger space can store more modality data while the checking of them will also cost more time. Since the value of v depends on the types of the fog servers used, the value of it is determined according to the practical situation. The value of v is set as 20 in the following comparisons.

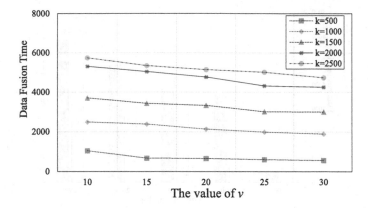

Fig. 4. Impact of v on data fusion time at different scales of modality data

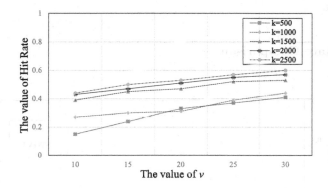

Fig. 5. Impact of v on hit rate at different scales of modality data

5.3 Data Fusion Time Comparison

Since the completion time depends on the last completion point, the data fusion time is defined as the maximum time of all the data fusion point. Compared with NPGA-II, the FSPF prefers the solutions with lower non-dominant sorting order. As a result, the solutions obtained by the FSPF are supposed to have low data fusion time while the population obtained by NPGA-II have high diversity. As shown in Fig. 6, the solutions of FSPF performance better than the solutions of NPGA-II although they have gone through the iterations with the same scale. The data fusion time is made up of the transmission time, the processing time and the training time. Since the training time only depends on the detailed contents of the data fusion tasks, the location of the FPs has little impact on the training time. Therefore, the solutions in FSPF have shorter modality data transmission and processing time than the solutions in NPGA-II. With better fog server locations, the TPs can obtain more modality data from the nearest fog server instead of the remote database and reduce the data transmission time.

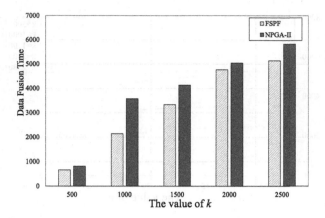

Fig. 6. Comparison on data fusion time by FSPF and NPGA-II at different scales of modality data

5.4   Hit Rate Comparison

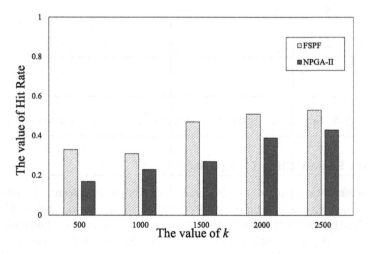

Fig. 7. Comparison on hit rate by FSPF and NPGA-II at different scales of the modality data

Hit rate is defined to measure the performance of fog servers. High rate means that much modality data are obtained from the FPs instead of the DPs. Since FSPF and NPGA-II have different selection strategies in the selection stage, as shown in Fig. 7, the individuals in FSPF have higher hit rates than the individuals in NPGA-II. High hit rate contributes to reduce the workload of the fog servers since the fog servers only need to transfer the pre-processed modality data instead of dealing with them.

6 Conclusion and Future Work

To accelerate the process of multimodality data fusion, fog computing was adopted in our method to avoid the unnecessary modality data processing and transmission. By optimizing the initial population through the reference individual, the high-class genes were introduced into the population at the beginning of the evolution. Since the TPs always access the nearest fog server to get the modality data cached in our method, the hit rate of the TPs may decrease if the target modality data are stored in the next-closest fog server. Therefore, we will focus on optimizing the fog server selection policy of the FPs to improve the hit rate and reduce the time required for multimodality data fusion in the future.

Acknowledgement. This work is supported by the National Key R&D Program of China under Grant 2019YFE0190500, the National Natural Science Foundation of China under grant no. 61702277 and no. 61872219, the Priority Academic Program Development of Jiangsu Higher Education Institutions (PAPD) fund and Jiangsu Collaborative Innovation Center on Atmospheric Environment and Equipment Technology (CICAEET).

References

1. Aine, C.J., et al.: Multimodal neuroimaging in schizophrenia: description and dissemination. Neuroinformatics **15**(4), 343–364 (2017)
2. Cai, H., Qu, Z., Li, Z., Zhang, Y., Hu, X., Hu, B.: Feature-level fusion approaches based on multimodal EEG data for depression recognition. Inf. Fusion **59**, 127–138 (2020)
3. Campos-Taberner, M., et al.: Processing of extremely high-resolution lidar and RGB data: Outcome of the 2015 IEEE GRSS data fusion contest-part a: 2-D contest. IEEE J. Sel. Top. Appl. Earth Obser. Remote Sens. **9**(12), 5547–5559 (2016)
4. Chen, H., Zhang, X., Wang, Q., Bai, Y.: Efficient data fusion using random matrix theory. IEEE Signal Process. Lett. **25**(5), 605–609 (2018)
5. Chiu, T., Pang, A., Chung, W., Zhang, J.: Latency-driven fog cooperation approach in fog radio access networks. IEEE Trans. Serv. Comput. **12**(5), 698–711 (2019)
6. Dong, Y., Guo, S., Liu, J., Yang, Y.: Energy-efficient fair cooperation fog computing in mobile edge networks for smart city. IEEE Internet Things J. **6**(5), 7543–7554 (2019)
7. Farhat, P., Sami, H., Mourad, A.: Reinforcement R-learning model for time scheduling of on-demand fog placement. J. Supercomput. **76**(1), 388–410 (2020)
8. Hu, J., Hong, D., Zhu, X.X.: Mima: mapper-induced manifold alignment for semi-supervised fusion of optical image and polarimetric SAR data. IEEE Trans. Geosci. Remote Sens. **57**(11), 9025–9040 (2019)
9. Jia, B., Hu, H., Zeng, Y., Xu, T., Yang, Y.: Double-matching resource allocation strategy in fog computing networks based on cost efficiency. J. Commun. Netw. **20**(3), 237–246 (2018)
10. Lahat, D., Adali, T., Jutten, C.: Multimodal data fusion: an overview of methods, challenges, and prospects. Proc. IEEE **103**(9), 1449–1477 (2015)

11. Lei, B., et al.: Neuroimaging retrieval via adaptive ensemble manifold learning for brain disease diagnosis. IEEE J. Biomed. Health Inf. **23**(4), 1661–1673 (2019)
12. Li, L., Kang, J., Lockhart, S.N., Adams, J., Jagust, W.J.: Spatially adaptive varying correlation analysis for multimodal neuroimaging data. IEEE Trans. Med. Imaging **38**(1), 113–123 (2019)
13. Liu, Z., Yang, X., Yang, Y., Wang, K., Mao, G.: DATS: dispersive stable task scheduling in heterogeneous fog networks. IEEE Internet Things J. **6**(2), 3423–3436 (2019)
14. Mahmud, R., Kotagiri, R., Buyya, R.: Fog computing: a taxonomy, survey and future directions. In: Di Martino, B., Li, K.-C., Yang, L.T., Esposito, A. (eds.) Internet of Everything. IT, pp. 103–130. Springer, Singapore (2018). https://doi.org/10.1007/978-981-10-5861-5_5
15. Shah-Mansouri, H., Wong, V.W.S.: Hierarchical fog-cloud computing for IoT systems: a computation offloading game. IEEE Internet Things J. **5**(4), 3246–3257 (2018)
16. Shi, J., et al.: Cascaded multi-column RVFL+ classifier for single-modal neuroimaging-based diagnosis of Parkinson's disease. IEEE Trans. Biomed. Eng. **66**(8), 2362–2371 (2019)
17. Uludağ, K., Roebroeck, A.: General overview on the merits of multimodal neuroimaging data fusion. Neuroimage **102**, 3–10 (2014)
18. Wang, S., Zhao, Y., Xu, J., Yuan, J., Hsu, C.-H.: Edge server placement in mobile edge computing. J. Parallel Distrib. Comput. **127**, 160–168 (2019)
19. Xiao, Y., Krunz, M.: Distributed optimization for energy-efficient fog computing in the tactile internet. IEEE J. Sel. Areas Commun. **36**(11), 2390–2400 (2018)
20. Xu, X., et al.: Load-aware edge server placement for mobile edge computing in 5G networks. In: Yangui, S., Bouassida Rodriguez, I., Drira, K., Tari, Z. (eds.) ICSOC 2019. LNCS, vol. 11895, pp. 494–507. Springer, Cham (2019). https://doi.org/10.1007/978-3-030-33702-5_38
21. Zhang, G., Shen, F., Liu, Z., Yang, Y., Wang, K., Zhou, M.: FEMTO: fair and energy-minimized task offloading for fog-enabled IoT networks. IEEE Internet Things J. **6**(3), 4388–4400 (2019)

Event-Triggered Control for Distributed Optimal in Multi-agent Systems with External Disturbance

Yuanshan Liu[1,3], Hongyong Yang[1,3(✉)], Yize Yang[1,2],
and Yuling Li[1,3]

[1] School of Information and Electrical Engineering, Ludong University,
Yantai 264025, China
hyyang@yeah.net
[2] School of Electrical and Electronic Engineering, University of Adelaide,
Adelaide, Australia
[3] Key Laboratory of Cyber-Physical System and Intelligent Control
in Universities of Shandong, Ludong University, Yantai 264025, China

Abstract. In this paper, based on linear quadratic theory, the optimal control problem for multi-agent systems with external disturbances is studied. Firstly, the optimal distributed controller is designed by the performance index function without the disturbances. Then, by using observer to estimate the external disturbances. Next, based on an event-triggered mechanism, the composite control protocol is designed with least sampling interval. The consistency control algorithm is analyzed by means of modern control theory and matrix theory, and distributed event-triggered conditions are obtained. Finally, the proposed algorithm is verified by simulation.

Keywords: Optimal control · Distributed even-triggered mechanism · External disturbance · Multi-agent systems · Least sampling interval

1 Introduction

By communicating and coordinating with each other, multi-agent systems can complete large-scale and complex tasks. With the rapid development of distributed artificial intelligence technology, multi-agent systems have been applied in the social field of intelligent robots coordinated motion, distributed intelligent decision-making, networked computer-aided teaching and medical and so on, which have attracted the attention of a large number of researchers [1–4].

As part of modern control theory, the optimal control theory is to obtain an allowable control signal under certain specific conditions, so that the performance function of the systems has the optimal value. How to obtain the optimal control protocol of the controlled systems is a key problem of optimal control. To obtain the optimal distributed control gain, Cao et al. [5] studied the optimal control problem of the first-order multi-agent systems, and the optimal laplacian matrix is obtained by selecting the appropriate cost function with the linear quadratic regulator theory. In [6],

© Springer Nature Switzerland AG 2020
X. Chen et al. (Eds.): ML4CS 2020, LNCS 12486, pp. 249–261, 2020.
https://doi.org/10.1007/978-3-030-62223-7_21

the performance index function is constructed reasonably, and the distributed optimal control protocol is obtained for continuous time and discrete time systems respectively. The gradient-based optimization method is proposed to solve the optimal parameter selection algorithm, and the finite-time optimal control problem of the second-order multi-agent systems is studied [7]. In the actual application process of the dynamical system, the state is inevitably affected by parameter perturbation or external disturbances. Therefore, based on the above situation, an optimal control protocol was constructed for a class of nonlinear systems with disturbance in [8], where external disturbances were estimated based on the method and the method. In [9], by estimating the disturbance with the disturbance observer, a compound controller with disturbance compensation is designed for DC-DC buck converters. In [10–12], a control protocol based on disturbance observer is designed to achieve consensus stability for multi-agent systems with fixed and switching topology. In [13], disturbance observer based control and related methods are systematically and comprehensively reviewed. Then, the compensation techniques and the process of uncertainty compensation such as integrated disturbance are discussed.

In order to reduce the number of communication between agents and improve the efficiency of hardware resource utilization, an event-triggered mechanism (ETM) is proposed in [14]. Compared with the traditional time-triggered mechanism, this control strategy can save a large amount of energy consumption. In [15], an event-triggered mechanism based on the passive theorem is proposed for dynamic output feedback, and the minimal lower bound of the event trigger interval is obtained. In [16–18], the design method of the trigger condition of Lyapunov function is introduced, and the event-triggered mechanism of nonlinear and linear control systems is studied respectively. A distributed event-triggered mechanism based on minimal sampling time is designed [19, 20], and the average consistency problem of multi-agent systems in fixed and switched topologies is analyzed. Yang et al. [21, 22] studies heterogeneous multi-intelligence, the output convergence problem of the multi-agent systems is designed, and coordinated output control protocol by an event is triggered. If the trigger condition is triggered infinitely in a fixed period of time, it is called as the Zeno behaviour. How to avoid the Zeno behaviour is an urgent problem in the design process of event-triggered conditions. Tabuada et al. [23] proves a lower bound time among two triggering instants by constructing the relationship between multi-agent state and state error.

In this paper, the optimal control problem of the multi-agent systems with matching disturbance is studied. A new design mechanism of event-triggered mechanism is presented. The sufficient conditions for the consensus convergence of multi-agent systems are obtained by using modern control theory and matrix theory. In this paper, the event-triggered strategy avoids the Zeno behaviour in principle.

2 First Section Preliminaries and Problem Formulation

2.1 Algebraic Graph Theory

A multi-agent systems can usually be represented by an undirected graph $G = \{V, E, A\}$, where $V = \{v_1, v_2, \cdots, v_N\} = \{v_1, v_2, \cdots, v_N\}$ represents a non-empty point set associated with N agents., $E \subseteq V \times V$ represents the edge set of the multi-agent systems. $A = (a_{ij})$ is the adjacency matrix, if $(v_i, v_j) \in E$, then $a_{ij} > 0$; otherwise $a_{ij} = 0$. The set of neighbors of the agent i can be defined as E. The degree $\deg(v_i) = d_i = \sum_{j=1}^{N} a_{ij}$ of the agent i indicates the number of neighbor nodes of the agent i, The degree matrix of the graph G can be defined as $D(G) = diag\{d_1, d_2, \cdots, d_N\}$, and the *Laplacian* matrix $L(G) = D(G) - A(G)$. If the graph G is undirected, the L matrix is a symmetric semidefinite matrix.

Assumption 1.1 The graph G is undirected and has at least one global spanning tree.

Definition 1.1 [5]. If $B = [b_{ij}] \in R^{N \times N}$ is a matrix of real matrices, and it can be written as $B = sI_{N \times N} - C$, $s > 0, C \geq 0$, where $C \in R^{N \times N}$, and $\rho(C) \leq s$, $\rho(C)$ is the spectral radius of matrix C, if $\rho(C) \leq s$, matrix B is called a nonsingular M-matrix.

Lemma 1.1. If the function $f(x)$ is continuous on the closed interval $[a, b]$, it can be derived on the open interval (a, b), and $\forall x$, $x + \Delta x \in [a, b]$, there is $\Delta y = f(x + \Delta x) - f(x) = \dot{f}(x + \theta \Delta x) \cdot \Delta x (0 < \theta < 1)$.

Lemma 1.2 [5]. If nonsingular matrix B is a M-matrix, then its square root matrix is also the only M-matrix that exists, that is $C = \sqrt{B}$.

2.2 Problem Formulation

In multi-agent systems, the dynamic equation of the agent i is

$$\begin{cases} \dot{x}_i(t) = ax_i(t) + bu_i(t) + b_{li}d_{li}(t) \\ y_i(t) = cx_i(t) \end{cases}, \quad i = 1, 2, \cdots, N \tag{1}$$

where $x_i(t) \in R^m$, $u_i(t) \in R^m$ and $y_i(t) \in R^m$ represents state, control input and the system output of multi-agent systems respectively. $d_i(t) \in R^m$ represents the disturbance, which includes external disturbance, system uncertainty, parameter uncertainty and other uncertainties in multi-agent systems. Where a and b are scalar parameters known to the systems. Suppose $a > 0$, $b > 0$, $c > 0$ and initial state $x_i(0)$. And the multi-agent systems (1) satisfies the Assumption 1.1.

3 Main Results

3.1 Design of Optimal Controller Based on Linear Quadratic Theory

In order to estimate the disturbance in multi-agent systems (1), the optimal control protocol is designed with two parts. The first part is to obtain the optimal control gain without external disturbance. Then, the disturbance observer is used to estimate the disturbance in the system, and compound controller is constructed with optimal control protocol and the estimated disturbance.

Consider the following performance function

$$J = \sum_{i=1}^{N} J_i = \sum_{i=1}^{N} \int_{t_0}^{\infty} \{ m[\sum_{j \in N_i} a_{ij}(x_i(t) - x_j(t))]^2$$
$$+ n \sum_{j \in N_i} a_{ij}(x_i(t) - x_j(t))^2 + kx_i(t)^2 + ru_i(t)^2 \} dt \tag{2}$$

The performance index function has a definite physical meaning. In time interval $[t_0, \infty)$, the controller consumes the least amount of energy with the least process deviation. The performance function can be written

$$J = \int_{t_0}^{\infty} [x^T(t)Qx(t) + u^T(t)Ru(t)]dt \tag{3}$$

where $Q = mL^2 + nL + kI_N$, $R = rI_N$, L is Laplacian matrix, $m > 0$, $n \geq 0$, $k \geq 0$.

Lemma 2.1. Consider multi-agent systems with a fixed topology and a global spanning tree. For any initial state $x(0)$, there is an optimal distributed controller

$$u^*(t) = -Kx^*(t) \tag{4}$$

If and only if $n^2 - 4m(k + r(ab^{-1})^2) = 0$, where $K = \sqrt{r^{-1}m}L + (ab^{-1} + \frac{\sqrt{r^{-1}n}}{2\sqrt{m}})I_N$ is the optimal feedback control gain, and $x^*(t)$ is the optimal state trajectory.

Proof. It can be obtained from *Riccati* equation $A^T P + PA - PBR^{-1}B^T P + Q = 0_{n \times n}$, where $A = aI_N$, $B = bI_N$, $R = rI_N$ in Eq. (3), one can obtain $b^2 r^{-1}P^2 - 2aP - Q = 0$.

The above formula becomes $(br^{-1}P - ab^{-1}I_N)^2 = r^{-1}Q + (ab^{-1})^2 I_N$. Because of $Q = mL^2 + nL + kI_N$, and $m > 0$, $n \geq 0$, $k \geq 0$, The following equation is established $r^{-1}Q + (ab^{-1})^2 I_N = r^{-1}mL^2 + r^{-1}nL + (r^{-1}k + (ab^{-1})^2)I_N$.   Let $\Delta = r^{-2}n^2 - 4r^{-1}m(r^{-1}k + (ab^{-1})^2)$, when $\Delta = 0$, the above equation is a square expression. By Lemma 1.2 (*M*-matrix), one obtains $\sqrt{r^{-1}Q + (ab^{-1})^2 I_N} = \sqrt{r^{-1}m}(L + \frac{n}{2m}I_N)$. So $K = R^{-1}B^T P = \sqrt{r^{-1}m}L + (ab^{-1} + \frac{\sqrt{r^{-1}n}}{2\sqrt{m}})I_N$. The proof is completed. ∎

3.2   Active Disturbance Rejection Control for Multi-agent Systems

The disturbance $d_i(t)$ in the systems (1) can be estimated by the following time domain disturbance observer

$$\begin{cases} \dot{p}_i(t) = -k_d b_{li}(p_i(t) + k_d x_i(t)) - k_d(ax_i(t) + bu_i(t)) \\ \hat{d}_{li}(t) = p_i(t) + k_d x_i(t) \end{cases} \tag{5}$$

where $\hat{d}_{li}(t) \in R^m$ is the estimated value of the disturbance, $p_i(t) \in R^m$ is the auxiliary intermediate variable, and k_d is the gain of the observer to be designed.

Assumption 3.1. For disturbance $d_{li}(t)$, $\int_{t_0}^{t_f} d_{li}(t)^T d_{li}(t) dt \le \varepsilon$.

Assumption 3.2. $\lim\limits_{t \to \infty} \dot{d}_{li}(t) = 0$.

Theorem 1. If the multi-agent systems (1) satisfies the conditions of Assumption 2.1 and 2.2, the disturbance estimation of *DOBC* can asymptotically track the disturbance in the multi-agent systems (1), by selecting the appropriate disturbance observation gain k_d with $k_d b_{li} > 0$.

Proof. The disturbance estimation error of the disturbance observer (7) is defined as follows $e_{di}(t) = \hat{d}_{li}(t) - d_{li}(t)$, Therefore

$$
\begin{aligned}
\dot{e}_{di}(t) &= \dot{p}(t) + k_d \dot{x}(t) - \dot{d}_{li}(t) \\
&= -k_d b_{li}(p_i(t) + k_d x_i(t)) - k_d(ax_i(t) + bu_i(t)) \\
&\quad + k_d(ax_i(t) + bu_i(t) + b_{li}d_{li}) - \dot{d}_{li}(t) \\
&= -k_d b_{li} e_{di}(t) - \dot{d}_{li}(t)
\end{aligned}
\tag{6}
$$

Since $-k_d b_{li}$ is negative, $\dot{d}_{li}(t)$ is bounded and satisfies $\lim\limits_{t \to \infty} \dot{d}_{li}(t) = 0$, It is easy to prove that the error system (6) is asymptotically stable by ISS theory [25–27]. The proof is completed. ∎

Remark 1. The convergence speed of the error system (6) depends on the value of the disturbance observation gain k_d. The larger k_d is, the faster the error system converges. The solution of the error system (6) is $e_{di}(t) = e^{-k_d b_{li}(t-t_0)} e_{di}(t_0) - \int_{t_0}^{t} e^{-k_d b_{li}(t-s)} \dot{d}_{li}(t) ds$, From the above Eq. (6), it can be seen that the solution of the estimation error depends on the initial state and the $\dot{d}_{li}(t)$. Based on Assumption 2.2, the disturbance estimation can asymptotically tracked to the actual external disturbance in systems.

3.3 Design of Compound Optimal Controller Based on Feedforward Disturbance Compensation

Based on the disturbance observer (5), the composite control protocol can be designed as

$$
u_i^*(t) = -\sqrt{r^{-1}m} \sum_{j \in N_i} a_{ij}(x_i^*(t) - x_i^*(t)) - (ab^{-1} + \frac{n}{2\sqrt{mr}})x_i^*(t) - b^{-1} b_{li} \hat{d}_{li}(t)
\tag{7}
$$

Remark 2. Since the control input of the agent i requires only the state information of its neighbors, the composite control protocol (7) is a distributed controller.

By means of the compound control protocol (7), the system (1) can be rewritten

$$\dot{x}_i^*(t) = ax_i(t) + b[-\sqrt{r^{-1}m} \sum_{j \in N_i} a_{ij}(x_i^*(t) - x_i^*(t))$$

$$- (ab^{-1} + \frac{n}{2\sqrt{mr}})x_i^*(t) - b^{-1}b_{li}\hat{d}_{li}(t)] + b_{li}d_{li}(t) \tag{8}$$

For the convenience of the following formula derivation, let $x^*(t) = [x_1^*(t), \cdots, x_N^*(t)]^T$, $d_l(t) = [d_{l1}(t), \cdots, d_{lN}(t)]^T$, $e_d(t) = [e_{d1}(t), \cdots, e_{dN}(t)]^T$. We have

$$\begin{cases} \dot{x}^*(t) = -b\sqrt{r^{-1}m}Lx^*(t) - (\frac{bn}{2\sqrt{mr}})I_Nx^*(t) - B_le_d(t) \\ \dot{e}_d(t) = -K_dB_le_d(t) - \dot{d}_l(t) \end{cases} \tag{9}$$

Where $K_d = k_dI_N$ is the gain matrix of the disturbance observer, $e_d(t)$ is the disturbance error vector, the matrix $B_l = \text{diag}\{b_{l1}, b_{l2}, \cdots, b_{lN}\}$.

Theorem 2. Consider the system (9) satisfies Assumption 2.1 and 2.2, if there are positive definite matrixes P and E, if

$$\begin{bmatrix} K^TP + PK & PB_l \\ * & -EK_dB_l \end{bmatrix} < 0 \tag{10}$$

then systems (1) is asymptotically stable, and make the disturbance $d_{li}(t)$ can be restrained from the input channel with the *DOBC*.

Proof. Let *Lyapunov* function be $V(t) = x^*(t)^TPx^*(t) + e_d(t)^TEe_d(t)$, then

$$\dot{V}(t) = \dot{x}^*(t)^TPx^*(t) + x^*(t)^TP\dot{x}^*(t) + \dot{e}_d(t)^TEe_d(t) + e_d(t)^TE\dot{e}_d(t)$$

$$= x^*(t)^TP[(-b\sqrt{r^{-1}m}L - (\frac{bn}{2\sqrt{mr}})I_N)x^*(t) + B_l(d_l(t) - \hat{d}_l(t))]$$

$$+ [(-b\sqrt{r^{-1}m}L - (\frac{bn}{2\sqrt{mr}})I_N)x^*(t) + B_l(d_l(t) - \hat{d}_l(t))]^TPx^*(t)$$

$$+ e_d(t)^TE[-K_dB_le_d(t) - \dot{d}_l(t)] + [-K_dB_le_d(t) - \dot{d}_l(t)]^TEe_d(t)$$

Then

$$\dot{V}(t) = x^*(t)^TK^TPx^*(t) + x^*(t)^TPKx^*(t) + e_d(t)^TB_l^TPx^*(t) + x^*(t)^TB_l^TPe_d(t)$$

$$+ e_d(t)^T(-EK_dB_l)e_d(t) - \dot{d}_l(t)^TEe_d(t) + e_d(t)^T(-EK_dB_l)e_d(t) - e_d(t)^TE\dot{d}_l(t)$$

Since $\dot{d}_l(t)$ satisfies Assumption 2.2, it has

$$\dot{V}(t) = x^*(t)^T K^T P x^*(t) + x^*(t)^T PK x^*(t) + e_d(t)^T B_l^T P x^*(t) + x^*(t)^T B_l^T P e_d(t)$$
$$+ e_d(t)^T (-EK_d B_l) e_d(t) + e_d(t)^T (-EK_d B_l) e_d(t)$$
$$= [x^*(t)^T, e_d(t)^T] \begin{bmatrix} K^T P + PK & PB_l \\ * & -EK_d B_l \end{bmatrix} \begin{bmatrix} x^*(t) \\ e_d(t) \end{bmatrix}$$

If the positive matrices P and E make $LMI(10)$ true, that is, the multi-agent systems (1) is asymptotically stable. The proof is completed.∎

3.4   Event-Triggered Mechanism with Least Sampling Interval

In this part, a distributed event-triggered mechanism with least sampling interval will be introduced, which can reduce the frequency of communication between neighbors. So we design event-triggered condition for the consistency control of multi-agents, which uses the state of the agent itself and its neighbors to make decisions. The event-triggered condition of the i agent is defined as

$$\gamma(\|e_i(t_k^i + lh)\|^2) \le \eta_i \alpha(\|x_i(t_k^i + lh)\|^2) \qquad (11)$$

where lh represents the smallest l sampling interval h, $0 < \eta_i < 1$, η_i is the threshold parameter of the event trigger for the i agent to be designed.

The triggering instant for the k-th event of the agent $x_i(t)$ can be expressed as

$$t_k^i = \inf\{t > t_{k-1}^i : \gamma(\|e_i(t_k^i + lh)\|^2) \ge \eta_i \alpha(\|x_i(t_k^i + lh)\|^2)\}(k = 1, 2, \cdots) \qquad (12)$$

For the systems (1), the control protocol (7) with continuous time is given. The control protocol with event-triggered mechanism is designed as follows

$$u_i^*(t) = -\sqrt{r^{-1}m} \sum_{j \in N_i} a_{ij}(x_i^*(t_k^i) - x_i^*(t_k^i)) - (ab^{-1} + \frac{n}{2\sqrt{mr}})x_i^*(t_k^i) - b^{-1}b_{li}\hat{d}_{li}(t) \quad (13)$$

where $x_i(t_k^i)$ represents the sampling state of the agent at time t_k^i. Since the disturbance $d_{li}(t)$ in the input channel is present at all times, $\hat{d}_{li}(t)$ uses the estimated value of the continuous time.

For any agent, let the state error be

$$e_i(t_k^i + lh) = x_i(t_k^i) - x_i(t_k^i + lh) \qquad (14)$$

Therefore

$$
u_i^*(t) = -\sqrt{r^{-1}m} \sum_{j \in N_i} a_{ij}(x_i^*(t_k^i + lh) + e_i(t_k^i + lh) - x_j^*(t_k^i + lh) - e_j(t_k^i + lh))
$$
$$
- (ab^{-1} + \frac{n}{2\sqrt{mr}})(x_i^*(t_k^i + lh) + e_i(t_k^i + lh)) - b^{-1}b_{li}\hat{d}_{li}(t) \tag{15}
$$

Substituting the control protocol (15) into the multi-agent systems (1), one can get

$$
\dot{x}_i^*(t) = ax_i^*(t) + b[-\sqrt{r^{-1}m} \sum_{j \in N_i} a_{ij}(x_i^*(t_k^i + lh) + e_i(t_k^i + lh) - x_j^*(t_k^i + lh) - e_j(t_k^i + lh))
$$
$$
- (ab^{-1} + \frac{n}{2\sqrt{mr}})(x_i^*(t_k^i + lh) + e_i(t_k^i + lh)) - b^{-1}b_{li}\hat{d}_{li}(t)] + b_{li}d_{li}(t) \tag{16}
$$

Let $x^*(t_k^i + lh) = \left[x_1^*(t_k^i + lh), \cdots, x_N^*(t_k^i + lh)\right]^T$, $e(t_k^i + lh) = [e_1(t_k^i + lh), \cdots, e_N$ $(t_k^i + lh)]^T$, $e_d(t) = [e_{d1}(t), \cdots, e_{dN}(t)]^T$. Then, the comprehensive formula of Eq. (6) and Eq. (16) can be written as the following

$$
\begin{cases} \dot{x}^*(t) = -(b\sqrt{r^{-1}mL} + \frac{bn}{2\sqrt{mr}}I_N)(x^*(t_k^i + lh) + e_i(t_k^i + lh)) - B_l e_d(t) \\ \dot{e}_d(t) = -K_d B_l e_d(t) - \dot{d}_l(t) \end{cases} \tag{17}
$$

Theorem 3. Consider that the multi-agent systems (1) satisfies Assumption 1, with the event-triggered condition (11), and the optimal distributed control protocol (15). If

$$
\begin{bmatrix} 2hK^TK + 2K + L^T\eta L & 2*hK^TK + K & -2*hK^TB_l - B_l \\ * & 2hK^TK - I_N & -2*hK^TB_l \\ * & * & 2hB_l^TB_l - 2K_dB_l \end{bmatrix} < 0 \tag{18}
$$

The multi-agent systems (1) can asymptotically convergence. Where K is the optimal feedback control gain, and $B_l = \text{diag}\{b_{l1}, b_{l2}, \cdots, b_{lN}\}$ and K_d are the observer gain matrices of the disturbance observer (5).

Proof. Let *Lyapunov* function be $V(t) = x^*(t)^T I_N x^*(t) + e_d(t)^T I_N e_d(t)$. Since the event-triggered instant t_k^i is a discrete time series, then $\dot{x}^*(t)$ is a piecewise function in this sequence, and therefore, the lagrange mean value theorem of Lemma 2.1 can be obtained

$$
x^*(t) = x^*(t_k^i + lh) + (t - (t_k^i + lh))\dot{x}^*(t_k^i + lh) \tag{19}
$$

when $t \in [t_k^i + lh, t_k^i + (l+1)h)$, it has $t - (t_k^i + lh) < h$. Therefore

$$\dot{V}(t) \leq 2h(K(x^*(t_k^i + lh) + e_i(t_k^i + lh)) - B_l e_d(t))^T(K(x^*(t_k^i + lh) + e_i(t_k^i + lh)) - B_l e_d(t))$$
$$+ (K(x^*(t_k^i + lh) + e_i(t_k^i + lh)) - B_l e_d(t))^T x^*(t_k^i + lh)$$
$$+ x^*(t_k^i + lh)^T(K(x^*(t_k^i + lh) + e_i(t_k^i + lh)) - B_l e_d(t))$$

$$\dot{V}(t) \leq 2x^*(t_k^i + lh)^T K x^*(t_k^i + lh) + x^*(t_k^i + lh)^T Ke(t_k^i + lh) - x^*(t_k^i + lh)^T Be_d(t)$$
$$+ e(t_k^i + lh)^T K x^*(t_k^i + lh) - e_d(t)^T B x^*(t_k^i + lh)$$
$$+ 2h[x^*(t_k^i + lh)^T K^T K x^*(t_k^i + lh) + x^*(t_k^i + lh)^T K^T Ke(t_k^i + lh) \qquad (20)$$
$$+ e(t_k^i + lh)^T K^T K x^*(t_k^i + lh) + e(t_k^i + lh)^T K^T Ke(t_k^i + lh)$$
$$- x^*(t_k^i + lh)^T K^T Ke_d(t) - e(t_k^i + lh)^T K^T Ke_d(t)$$
$$- e_d(t)^T B^T K x^*(t_k^i + lh) - e_d(t)^T K^T Be(t_k^i + lh) - e_d(t)^T B^T Be_d(t)]$$

The distributed event-triggered mechanism is designed to

$$e_i(t_k^i + lh)^T e_i(t_k^i + lh)$$
$$\leq \eta_i(\sum_{j=1}^{N} a_{ij}(x_j(t_k^i + lh) - x_i(t_k^i + lh)))^T(\sum_{j=1}^{N} a_{ij}(x_j(t_k^i + lh) - x_i(t_k^i + lh)))$$

The writing vector form is

$$e(t_k^i + lh)^T e(t_k^i + lh) \leq x(t_k^i + lh)^T L^T \eta L x(t_k^i + lh) \qquad (21)$$

Bring formula (21) to (20) to get

$$\dot{V}(t) \leq \begin{bmatrix} x^*(t_k^i + lh) \\ e(t_k^i + lh) \\ e_d(t) \end{bmatrix}^T \begin{bmatrix} 2hK^T K + 2K + L^T \eta L & 2*hK^T K + K & -2*hK^T B_l - B_l \\ * & 2hK^T K - I_N & -2*hK^T B_l \\ * & * & 2hB_l^T B_l - 2K_d B_l \end{bmatrix} \begin{bmatrix} x^*(t_k^i + lh) \\ e(t_k^i + lh) \\ e_d(t) \end{bmatrix}$$

we can obtain that equation $\dot{V}(t) < 0$ from the condition (18) of Theorem 3. Thus, the asymptotically consensus of multi-agent systems (17) is reached. The proof is completed. ∎

Since the triggered condition for each agent depends on the state of agent itself and the neighbor agent, the event-triggered condition (21) is distributed. If the triggered condition is not satisfied, the controller of the agent will preserve the value of the last triggering time.

4   Numerical Simulation

In this section, we consider a multi-agent systems consisting of 4 agents. Then the topology of the systems is shown in Fig. 1, then the corresponding *Laplacian* matrix is

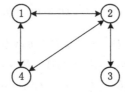

Fig. 1. Communication topology diagram of multi-agent systems.

$$L = \begin{bmatrix} 2 & -1 & 0 & -1 \\ -1 & 3 & -1 & -1 \\ 0 & -1 & 1 & 0 \\ -1 & -1 & 0 & 2 \end{bmatrix}$$

For consistency controller $u_i(t)$, select $\eta_1 = 0.026$, $\eta_2 = 0.024$, $\eta_3 = 0.026$, $\eta_4 = 0.024$. The initial state of the agent is $x_1(0) = 9.64$, $x_2(0) = 1.12$, $x_3(0) = -2.65$, $x_4(0) = 3.72$. According to the controller of the system, the following agents state simulation diagram can be obtained. Assume external disturbance in the input channel is designed as $d_1(t) = 5e^{-2t} * \cos(t)$, $d_2(t) = 2e^{-2t} * \sin(t)$, $d_3(t) = sigmoid(t)$, $d_4(t) = 3 * sigmoid(t)$, and $p_1(t) = 0.20$, $p_2(t) = 0.12$, $p_3(t) = 0.31$, $p_4(t) = 0.02$ is the initial state of the disturbance systems (5).

Figure 2 is the position state of the multi-agent systems with the disturbance observer proposed in this paper. It can be seen from the figure that the algorithm has admirable effect. Figure 3 is the estimation value of the disturbance observer. It can be seen from the figure that it is consistent with the disturbance given in this paper. Figure 4 is the disturbance observation error of each agent's disturbance observer. The disturbance observer can quickly estimate the time-varying disturbance and show good performance. Table 1 shows the multi-agent systems within 20 s of the distributed event-triggered mechanism. It can be seen from the data in the table that the trigger rate of the event-triggered mechanism is 25.36%.

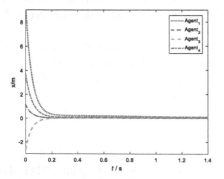

Fig. 2. Position status trajectory of each agent.

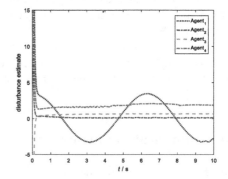

Fig. 3. Disturbance observer estimate of each agent.

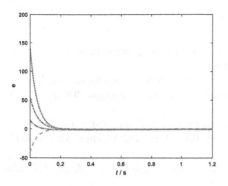 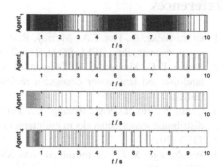

Fig. 4. Disturbance observer estimation error.   **Fig. 5.** Event-triggered instant for each agent.

Table 1.

Agent	1	2	3	4
Number of samples	2020			
Number of triggers	225	80	213	192
Trigger rate	5.25%	1.87%	4.97%	4.48%

It can be seen that the triggering instant of each agent does not occur at the same time in the Fig. (5), which indicates that the triggering strategy designed is indeed distributed in the paper, which is consistent with the expectation.

5 Conclusion

In this paper, the optimal control problem of multi-agent systems with disturbance in fixed topology is considered. Combined with linear quadratic theory and active disturbance rejection control, a composite control protocol based on state feedback and disturbance compensation is designed. Based on the event-triggered mechanism, the control protocol can monitor the error of the sampling state between the current time and the trigger time. The sufficient conditions for the uniform convergence of the systems are obtained by applying theoretical analysis of linear matrix inequality and matrix theory. In the future, the consistency problem of multi-agent systems with unmatched disturbance based on event-triggered mechanism will be studied.

Acknowledgments. The work is supported by the National Natural Science Foundation of China (61673200, 61771231), the Major Basic Research Project of Natural Science Foundation of Shandong Province of China (ZR2018ZC0438) and the Key Research and Development Program of Yantai of China(2019XDHZ085).

References

1. Olfati-Saber, R., Fax, J.A., Murray, R.M.: Consensus and cooperation in networked multi-agent systems. Proc. IEEE **95**(1), 215–233 (2007)
2. Parker, D.C., Manson, S.M., Janssen, M.A., et al.: Multi-agent systems for the simulation of land-use and land-cover change: a review. Ann. Assoc. Am. Geograph. **93**(2), 314–337 (2015)
3. Chen, S., Ho, D.W.C., Huang, C.: Fault reconstruction and state estimator design for distributed sensor networks in multitarget tracking. IEEE Trans. Ind. Electron. **62**(11), 7091–7102 (2015)
4. Wooldridge, M.J.: An Introduction to Multi-Agent Systems, vol. 4, no. 2, pp. 125–128. Wiley (2009)
5. Cao, Y., Ren, W.: Optimal linear-consensus algorithms: an LQR perspective. IEEE Trans. Syst. Man Cybern. Part B Cybern. **40**(3), 819 (2010)
6. Zhang, F., Wang, W., Zhang, H.: Design and analysis of distributed optimal controller for identical multiagent systems. Asian J. Control **17**(1), 263–273 (2015)
7. Li, R., Shi, Y.: Finite-time optimal consensus control for second-order multi-agent systems. J. Ind. Manage. Optim. **10**(3), 929–943 (2017)
8. Liu, R.: Research on Optimal Control Theory and Its Several Applications for Nonlinear Systems. Southeast University (2015)
9. Yang, J., Wu, B., Li, S., et al.: Design and qualitative robustness analysis of an DOBC approach for DC-DC buck converters with unmatched circuit parameter perturbations. IEEE Trans. Circ. Syst. I Reg. Papers **63**(4), 551–560 (2017)
10. Yang, H., Guo, L., Zou, H.L.: Robust consensus of multi-agent systems with time-delays and exogenous disturbances. Int. J. Control Autom. Syst. **10**(4), 797–805 (2012)
11. Yang, H., Guo, L., Han, C.: Robust consensus of multi-agent systems with uncertain exogenous disturbances. Commun. Theor. Phys. **56**(12), 1161–1166 (2011)
12. Yang, H., Zhang, Z., Zhang, S.: Consensus of second-order multi-agent systems with exogenous disturbances. Int. J. Robust Nonlinear Control **21**(9), 945–956 (2011)
13. Chen, W.-H., Yang, J., Guo, L.: Disturbance-observer-based control and related methods— an overview. IEEE Trans. Ind. Electron. **63**(2), 1083–1095 (2016)
14. Dimarogonas, D.V., Frazzoli, E.: Distributed event-triggered control strategies for multi-agent systems. In: Allerton Conference on Communication, Control, and Computing, 2009. Allerton 2009, pp. 906–910. IEEE (2009)
15. Yu, H., Antsaklis, P.J.: Event-triggered output feedback control for networked control systems using passivity: triggering condition and limitations. In: Decision and Control and European Control Conference, pp. 199–204. IEEE (2012)
16. Gao, Y.: Design of Event-triggering Mechanisms for Nonlinear Control Systems. Dalian University of Technology (2017)
17. Abdelrahim, M., Postoyan, R., Daafouz, J., et al.: Stabilization of nonlinear systems using event-triggered output feedback controllers. IEEE Trans. Autom. Control **61**(9), 2682–2687 (2014)
18. Dolk, V.S., Borgers, D.P., Heemels, W.P.M.H.: Output-based and decentralized dynamic event-triggered control with guaranteed lp-gain performance and zeno-freeness. IEEE Trans. Autom. Control **62**(1), 34–49 (2016)
19. Meng, X., Chen, T.: Event based agreement protocols for multi-agent networks. Automatica **49**(7), 2125–2132 (2013)
20. Dimarogonas, D.V., Frazzoli, E., Johansson, K.H.: Distributed event-triggered control for multi-agent systems. IEEE Trans. Autom. Control **57**(5), 1291–1297 (2012)

21. Yang, R., Zhang, H., Yan, H.: Leader-following consensus of multi-agent systems via event-triggered H∞ control with Markovian switching topology. In: Decision and Control, pp. 2671–2676. IEEE (2016)

22. Yang, R., Zhang, H., Hu Yan, H.: Event-triggered cooperative output regulation of heterogeneous multi-agent systems with switching topology. Acta Autom. Sin. **43**(3), 472–477 (2017)

23. Tabuada, P.: Event-triggered real-time scheduling of stabilizing control tasks. IEEE Trans. Autom. Control **52**(9), 1680–1685 (2007)

24. Nair, R.R., Behera, L., Kumar, S.: Event-triggered finite-time integral sliding mode controller for consensus-based formation of multirobot systems with disturbances. IEEE Trans. Control Syst. Technol. **27**(1), 1–9 (2017)

25. Praly, L., Jiang, Z.P.: Stabilization by output feedback for systems with ISS inverse dynamics. Syst. Control Lett. **21**(1), 19–33 (1993)

26. Jiang, Z.-P., Mareels, I., Wang, Y.: A lyapunov formulation of nonlinear small gain theorem for interconnected systems. IFAC Proceedings Volumes **28**(14), 625–630 (1995). https://doi.org/10.1016/s1474-6670(17)46898-4

27. Teel, A.R.: Connections between Razumikhin-type theorems and the ISS nonlinear small gain theorem. IEEE Trans. Autom. Control **43**(7), 960–964 (1998)

Towards Privacy-Preserving Aggregated Prediction from SPDZ

Qi Zhao[1,2], Bo Zhang[1,2], Anli Yan[1,2], Shan Jing[1,2(✉)], and Chuan Zhao[1,2,3]

[1] School of Information Science and Engineering, University of Jinan,
Jinan 250022, China
jingshan@ujn.edu.cn
[2] Shandong Provincial Key Laboratory of Network-Based Intelligent Computing,
University of Jinan, Jinan 250022, China
[3] Shandong Provincial Key Laboratory of Software Engineering, Jinan, China

Abstract. Machine learning models trained on data collected from multiple parties can offer prediction services to clients. However, it raises privacy concerns for both model owners and clients. The models may disclose the details of the training data inadvertently by querying and the clients' private input may be obtained by service providers. In this work, a privacy-preserving aggregated prediction framework is proposed, which combines two privacy-preserving techniques, i.e., Differential Privacy and Secret Sharing, to ensure privacy. Specifically, individual parties first train local models that meet differential privacy. Then two non-colluding servers collect the shares of multi-party trained models and clients' inputs independently and provide online prediction. Finally, the clients reconstruct prediction from servers and aggregate them into the final prediction. It is worth mentioning that during prediction phase, no one can obtain the private information of others. We evaluate the performance of our framework on MNIST dataset. The experimental results show that the framework can strike a balance between utility and privacy.

Keywords: Distributed prediction · Secret sharing · Differential privacy · Secure aggregation

1 Introduction

Machine learning has been widely used in many fields [1–3], related applications are also providing convenience for human life. But machine learning system also faces a variety of security risks [4] during both training and prediction phase.

This work is supported by National Natural Science Foundation of China (No. 61702218, 61672262), China Scholarship Council (No. 201808370046), Shandong Provincial Key Research and Development Project (No. 2019GGX101028, 2018CXGC0706), Shandong Provincial Natural Science Foundation (No. ZR2019LZH015), Shandong Province Higher Educational Science and Technology Program (No. J18KA349), Project of Independent Cultivated Innovation Team of Jinan City (No. 2018GXRC002).

X. Chen et al. (Eds.): ML4CS 2020, LNCS 12486, pp. 262–271, 2020.
https://doi.org/10.1007/978-3-030-62223-7_22

These risks lead to serious privacy leakage particularly in medical, financial, and many other industries.

In the training phase, the performance of the model depends on massive training data collected from various individuals. However, individuals are reluctant to share these data when sensitive information is involved. Although some methods are proposed to solve the above-mentioned problem, such as collaborative learning [5], federated learning [6,7], which sharing model parameters instead of sharing data directly. But recent attacks [8–10] have shown that the shared model parameters can also reveal private information about training data. while in the prediction phase, the trained models are used to receive the inputs from users and provide predictions. The adversary only can obtain limited information, such as the predicted labels. But he still gains potential information about models or training data by analyzing the query output. Fredrikson et al. [11] revealed the original training data by analyzing the probabilities information of the classifier. Shokri et al. [12] proposed the membership inference attack (MIA) which trains multiple shadow models to determine whether a specific record exists in the training set.

To prevent privacy leakage in machine learning, researchers have also designed privacy-preserving frameworks to against malicious attacks. For example, Papernot et al. [4,13] proposed PATE framework, which transfers the knowledge in a semi-supervised way from an ensemble of private classifiers (teachers) to a non-private classifier (student). The adversary can only access the student model. PATE can resist many attacks such as MIA, but it is not suitable for multi-party scenarios. SecureML [14] is a privacy-preserving machine learning framework based on ABY^3 protocol. The data owners can upload the local data to two non-colluding servers and train a global model. The framework guarantees privacy during the training phase, but it can not against the threat from malicious users' queries.

In this paper, we propose an aggregated prediction framework to provide privacy-preserving predictions. To preserve privacy, the participants can train differential private models locally. Two non-colluding servers compute predictions based on the sharing of privacy models and the input from clients. Clients reconstruct the predictions and output the labels with the most votes as the aggregated prediction. Our main contributions are as follows:

- We design a privacy-preserving prediction framework that combines Differential Privacy and Secret Sharing to provide privacy guarantees during prediction stage. The participants who provide the training model and the clients who provide the input can't learn the sensitive information in reverse. The server only learns the shared model and the client's input.
- Our framework further improves the accuracy of the final prediction through aggregation, even if the performance of several training models is not excellent.
- We evaluate our framework on MNIST, and the results show that our framework can guarantee data privacy, model security, and reliable prediction performance at the same time.

The rest of this paper is organized as follows. Section 2 introduces the privacy-preserving technology we used, SPDZ and Differential Privacy.

Section 3 describes the structure and process of the our framework in detail. Section 4 evaluates the performance of the framework, as well as the security and efficiency analysis. Section 5 concludes the paper.

2 Background

2.1 SPDZ

SPDZ is a Multi-Party computation (MPC) protocol based secret sharing proposed by Damgard et al. [15,16], which allows n parties jointly calculate a function without disclosing private inputs even the adversary colludes with $n - 1$ parties. The SPDZ protocol is divided into two phases: online phase and offline phase. To improve the performance of online computation, SPDZ protocol allows a pre-generated of triples independently [17] in the offline phase. And the private inputs and function are neither need to be known. In the online phase, the parties perform interactive computation about actual function.

In this framework, we use Pond [18], a variant of SPDZ. Pond is a vectorized two-party secret sharing protocol with two servers which provides passive security against honest-but-curious adversary. To improve performance, Pond introduces an additional "crypto producer" to generate Beaver triples. Here are some cryptographic preliminaries about Pond:

Shared Values: For a share $\langle x \rangle$ of private tensor x over $\mathbb{Z}_L$, we have $\langle x \rangle_0 + \langle x \rangle_1 \equiv x \ mod \ L$, where $\langle x \rangle_0, \langle x \rangle_1 \in \mathbb{Z}_L$, $\mathbb{Z}_L$ is a ring where L=2^{64} .

Share: Share$_i(x)$: To share a tensor x, we takes randomly $r \in \mathbb{F}_L$, set $\langle x \rangle_i = x - r(\text{mod } L)$, r can be opened to S_{1-i}, where $i \in \{0, 1\}$.

Reconstruction Operation: Rec$_i(x)$: S_{1-i} sends its share $\langle x \rangle_{1-i}$ to S_i who computes $x = \langle x \rangle_0 + \langle x \rangle_1$.

Tensor Addition Operation: To add two shares $\langle a \rangle + \langle b \rangle = \langle c \rangle$, S_i can compute $\langle c \rangle_i = \langle a \rangle_i + \langle b \rangle_i$ locally.

And tensor Multiplication operation is shown in Algorithm 1.

Algorithm 1. Tensor Multiplication operation of Pond protocol.

Input: S_0 holds $\langle x \rangle_0, \langle y \rangle_0$ S_1 holds $\langle x \rangle_1, \langle y \rangle_1$
Output: S_0 gets $\langle x \cdot y \rangle_0$ and S_1 gets $\langle x \cdot y \rangle_1$
1: **for** $i \in \{0, 1\}$ **do**
2:    Crypto provider generates random mask tensors $\langle a_i \rangle, \langle b_i \rangle$, where $\langle ab \rangle_i = \langle a \rangle_i \cdot \langle b \rangle_i$.

3:    Crypto provider sends $\langle a \rangle_i, \langle b \rangle_i , \langle ab \rangle_i$ to S_i
4:    S_i receives $\langle a \rangle_i, \langle b \rangle_i , \langle ab \rangle_i$ from Crypto provider
5: **end for**
6: **for** $i \in \{0, 1\}$ **do**
7:    S_i computes $\langle \alpha \rangle_i = \langle x \rangle_i - \langle a \rangle_i$, $\langle \beta \rangle_i = \langle y \rangle_i - \langle b \rangle_i$
8:    S_i exchange $\langle \alpha \rangle_i, \langle \beta \rangle_i$ with S_{1-i}
9:    S_i computes $Rex_i(\alpha), Rex_i(\beta)$
10:    S_i outputs $-i \cdot \alpha \cdot \beta + \langle x \rangle_i \cdot \beta + \langle y \rangle_i \cdot \alpha + \langle ab \rangle_i$
11: **end for**

2.2 Differential Privacy

Differential Privacy [19,20] is a privacy-preserving technique which provides guarantees the attacks can not infer any sensitive information about the dataset by adding noise to the query responses.

Definition 1 (Differential Privacy). A randomized algorithm $\mathcal{M}$ with domain $\mathcal{D}$ and range $\mathcal{R}$ satisfies (ε, δ)-differential privacy, if for any two adjacent database d and $d' \in \mathcal{D}$ and any set of output $S \subseteq \text{Range}(\mathcal{M})$:

$$\Pr[\mathcal{M}(d) \in S] \leq e^{\varepsilon} \cdot \Pr\left[\mathcal{M}\left(d'\right) \in S\right] + \delta$$

ε and δ is the privacy budget which determines the level of privacy guarantee. In our framework, we train the local models using differentially private SGD algorithm (DPSGD), proposed by Abadi et al. [21], which effectively against the adversary who can access the models' parameters. And we also use the moment accountant [21] to track the privacy loss. Algorithm 2 shows the details of DPSGD.

3 Our Framework

3.1 Overview

In this section, we introduce the details of our framework, and Fig 1 shows the framework architecture. The framework consisting of: multiple participants P_i who provides models, two non-colluding servers S_0, S_1 that performs interactive computation and the client C who receive the users' data. There is also a crypto provider who generates triples. We present the meaning of the relevant symbols in Table 1.

Algorithm 2. Differentially Private SGD. Dataset X, Initial model parameters θ_0, loss function $\mathcal{L}(\theta, x_i)$, minibatch size L, learning rate η, noise scale σ, Clipping norm C ,

---

1: **for** $t \in [T]$ **do**
2:     Take a minibatch with sampling probability L/N
3:     For each $x_i \in L_t$, compute gradient $\mathbf{g}_t(x_i) \leftarrow \nabla_{\theta_t} \mathcal{L}(\theta_t, x_i)$
4:     $\hat{g}_t = \frac{1}{L}\left(\sum_i g_t(x_i) / \max\left(1, \frac{\|g_t(x_i)\|^2}{c}\right) + \mathcal{N}\left(0, \sigma^2 C^2 I\right)\right)$
5:     $\theta_{t+1} \rightarrow \theta_t - \eta_t \hat{g}_t$
6: **end for**
7: **return** θ_t and privacy cost (ε, δ)

Table 1. The meaning of symbol

Symbol	Meaning
P_i	Participants who provide the model
S_0, S_1	Two non-colluding servers
C	Client
D_i, W_i	Local private data and training models of participant P_i
x	The inputs from the client
ε_i, δ_i	Privacy budget of local model w_i
y_i	Prediction labels of each model M_i
y_{ag}	Final prediction
$share_i()$	Secret sharing operation
$\langle a \rangle, \langle b \rangle, \langle ab \rangle$	Multiplication triple

3.2 Threat Model

The goal of our framework is to provide effective prediction while protecting client data and participant models. We assume that the model uploaded by the participants and the data transmitted by the clients are confidential to the server. And the clients cannot deduce any sensitive informations about the training model and data by querying the models. The adversary could be a semi-honest client who can query the servers repeatedly or collude with one of the servers. He wants to analyze limited information to reveal the implicit property of private inputs transmitted by the client or the model uploaded by the participants.

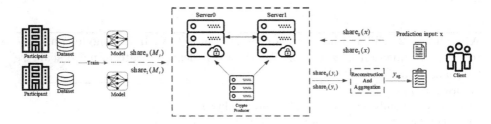

Fig. 1. The architecture of the framework

3.3 Local Model Training and Pre-processing Phase

We assume that the N participant P_i ($i = 1..N$) has its own training dataset D_i locally and trains own model W_i independently. They are reluctant to share these models directly because of privacy concerns. So the models are divided into two shares $share_0(W_i)$ and $share_1(W_i)$ by additive secret sharing scheme.

Algorithm 3. STAGE I – Offline Phase

1: **for** $i \in [1, N]$ **do**
2:     P_i trains local model W_i based on DPSGD
3:     **for** $j \in \{0, 1\}$ **do**
4:         Generate model shares $share_j(W_i)$
5:         Send $share_j(W_i)$ to S_j
6:     **end for**
7: **end for**
8: **for** $i \in \{0, 1\}$ **do**
9:     Crypto provider generates random mask tensors $\langle a_i \rangle, \langle b_i \rangle$, where $\langle ab \rangle_i = \langle a \rangle_i \cdot \langle b \rangle_i$.
10:     Crypto provider sends $\langle a \rangle_i, \langle b \rangle_i, \langle ab \rangle_i$ to S_i
11: **end for**

Each server receives one of the model shares randomly. To ensure the privacy of the model during prediction, the participants can also use privacy-preserving techniques such as differential privacy SGD [21] to train the model. The crypto provider generates the multiplication triple $\langle a \rangle, \langle a \rangle, \langle ab \rangle$ and the shares $\langle a \rangle_i, \langle b \rangle_i, \langle ab \rangle_i$ for two servers that are used in online prediction. The above operations do not need the input data of the client, and can be completed in the offline phase to reduce the calculation cost of the framework. The offline Phase is shown in Algorithm 3.

3.4   Online Prediction and Aggregation

The private inputs are split x into shared values $share_i(x)$, $i \in \{0, 1\}$ in the client before prediction. And the shares are be sent to S_i. Two servers compute the predictions $share_i(y_j), j = 1, 2, ...n$ interactively based the share of models and input. We use a high degree Chebyshev polynomial approximation of the activation function, $f(g) = \sum_{i=0}^{r} k_i g^i$, where r is the degree, k_i is coefficients of the polynomial. Fig 2 shows the approximation of the ReLU activation function. After completing prediction computation, the servers send the prediction shares $share_i(y_j)$ to clients.

Then clients receives the shares from servers and compute prediction results $\text{Rex}(y_j)$: $share_0(y_j) + share_1(y_j) = y_j$ (mod Z_L),where j=1,2,..n. For a given input x and class 1,..,m, where $y_j \in [m]$. And $n_{y_j}(x)$ denotes the number of same prediction results from different model W_j: $n_{y_i}(x) = |\{j : j \in [N], y_i\}|$. Finally, the clients uses prediction results with the larges count $argmax(n_{y_i}(x))$ as final prediction result y_{ag} and output to users.

Algorithm 4. STAGE 2- Online Phase
_____
1: **for** $i \in \{0,1\}$ **do**
2:    Client generates input shares $share_i(x)$
3:    Client send $share_i(x)$ to S_i
4: **end for**
5: **for** $i \in \{0,1\}$ **do**
6:    **for** $j \in (1, N)$ **do**
7:       S_i compute prediction results $share_i(y_j)$
8:       S_i sends $share_i(y_j)$ to client
9:    **end for**
10: **end for**
11: Client run $\text{Rec}(y_j)$ and output y_j
12: Client aggregate y_j into y_{ag}
_____

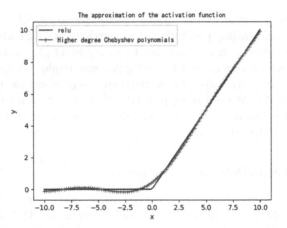

Fig. 2. The approximation of the ReLU function

4 Experiments

4.1 Experimental Setup

We evaluate our framework on MNIST, a dataset of handwritten digits which contains of 60,000 training examples and 10,000 examples. We used TF-Encrypted framework [18] for secure two-party computation (Pond protocol) and TensorFlow Privacy library for DPSGD. To examine the accuracy and training time of our framework, the programs run on a computer with Intel Core i5-8300H CPU, 2.30 GHz, and 16 GB RAM in the local setting. We stack three full connected layers with ReLUs for each model. And the number of participants is set from 10 to 100.

We consider two experimental scenarios: a) the data owned by participants is independent, b) the data owned by participants has intersection. In the first scenario, we partition the training set disjointed and train the models independently. In the second scenario, we sampled randomly a subset from the training set and then train a model on each subset.

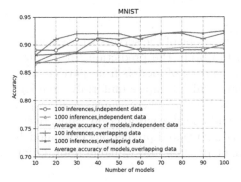

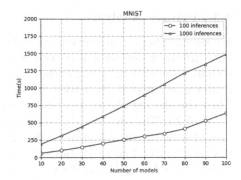

Fig. 3. The accuracy of aggregated prediction

Fig. 4. The computation time of prediction

4.2 Experimental Results

Figure 3 illustrates the accuracy of aggregated prediction without DP guarantee under two scenarios. We train each model on 600 samples from the training set. The final prediction accuracy shows some improvements compared with the average accuracy of the original models. Especially, when the number of models exceeds 50, the prediction accuracy also tends to be stable. And the models trained on overlapping data have a better performance in final aggregated prediction than those trained on independent data. Figure 4 shows that the computation time linearly with the number of models.

In the experiments with DP guarantee, we trained each model on 6000 examples which are randomly sampled from the training set. And the number of models is set to 50 and the average accuracy of models is 83.11%. For DPSGD algorithm, the relevant parameters are as follows: minibatch size $L=50$, learning rate $\eta =0.15$, noise scale $\sigma=1.2$, Clipping norm $C=1.0$. We set $\delta=10^{-4}$ according to the size of the training set, and the corresponding ε is 5.16. Additionally, we introduce some bad models with more than 75% to check the robustness of our framework. Table 2 summarizes the accuracy and runtime averaged over 10000 inferences.

Table 2. Utility and privacy of the framework

Experimental setup	Accuracy	Privacy cost	Runtime average
No bad models	94.75%	Without DP	5364.35 s
20% bad models	93.56%		
50% bad models	93.02%		
No bad models	90.62%	$\varepsilon=5.16$	5511.86
20% bad models	88.67%		
50% bad models	86.74%		

4.3 Privacy Analysis

We assume that the adversary can collude with one of the servers who is honest-but-curious or can be a user who wants to obtain the prediction. In the first scenario, the adversary can obtain the one sharing of models from participants. However, a model W_i is masked by a value r which samples uniformly from $\mathbb{Z}_L$. Then the sharing $share_0 = r$ and $share_1 = W_i - r$, where $share_0 + share_1 \equiv W_i \bmod \mathbb{Z}_L$. The adversary just obtains a random value without any value. In the second scenario, the adversary only can get aggregated predictions from models that meets DP. The predictions also cannot disclose any valuable information about trained models and data.

5 Conclusions

We present a secure distributed aggregation prediction framework that guarantees the privacy of clients' input and training model. We combine with Differential Privacy and Secret Sharing to achieve a balance between privacy and efficiency. The experiments show that the framework can improve the accuracy of the prediction results while maintaining reasonable computational efficiency.

References

1. Zander, S., Nguyen, T., Armitage, G.: Automated traffic classification and application identification using machine learning. In: The IEEE Conference on Local Computer Networks 30th Anniversary (LCN 2005) 1, pp. 250–257. IEEE (2005)
2. Taigman, Y., Yang, M., Ranzato, M.A., Wolf, L.: Deepface: closing the gap to human-level performance in face verification. In: Proceedings of the IEEE Conference on Computer Vision and Pattern Recognition, pages 1701–1708 (2014)
3. Sundermeyer, M., Schlüter, R., Ney, H.: LSTM neural networks for language modeling. In: Thirteenth Annual Conference of the International Speech Communication Association (2012)
4. Papernot, N., McDaniel, P., Sinha, A., Wellman, M.P.: Sok: security and privacy in machine learning. In: 2018 IEEE European Symposium on Security and Privacy (EuroS&P), pp. 399–414. IEEE (2018)
5. Shokri, R., Shmatikov, V.: Privacy-preserving deep learning. In: Proceedings of the 22nd ACM SIGSAC Conference on Computer and Communications Security, pp. 1310–1321. ACM (2015)
6. McMahan, H.B., Moore, E., Ramage, D., Hampson, S., et al.: Communication-efficient learning of deep networks from decentralized data. arXiv preprint arXiv:1602.05629 (2016)
7. McMahan, B., Ramage, D.: Federated learning: collaborative machine learning without centralized training data. Google Research Blog, 3 (2017)
8. Hitaj, B., Ateniese, G., Pérez-Cruz, F.: Deep models under the gan: information leakage from collaborative deep learning. In: Proceedings of the 2017 ACM SIGSAC Conference on Computer and Communications Security, pp. 603–618. ACM (2017)
9. Melis, L., Song, C., De Cristofaro, E., Shmatikov, V.: Exploiting unintended feature leakage in collaborative learning. In 2019 IEEE Symposium on Security and Privacy (SP), pp. 691–706. IEEE (2019)

10. Zhu, L., Liu, Z., Han, S.: Deep leakage from gradients. In: Advances in Neural Information Processing Systems, pp. 14747–14756 (2019)
11. Fredrikson, M., Jha, S., Ristenpart, T.: Model inversion attacks that exploit confidence information and basic countermeasures. In: Proceedings of the 22nd ACM SIGSAC Conference on Computer and Communications Security, pp. 1322–1333. ACM (2015)
12. Shokri, R., Stronati, M., Song, C., Shmatikov, V.: Membership inference attacks against machine learning models. In: 2017 IEEE Symposium on Security and Privacy (SP), pp. 3–18. IEEE (2017)
13. Papernot, N., Abadi, M., Erlingsson, Ú., Goodfellow, I., Talwar, K.: Semi-supervised knowledge transfer for deep learning from private training data (2017)
14. Mohassel, P., Zhang, Y.: Secureml: a system for scalable privacy-preserving machine learning. In: 2017 IEEE Symposium on Security and Privacy (SP), pp. 19–38. IEEE (2017)
15. Damgård, I., Pastro, V., Smart, N., Zakarias, S.: Multiparty computation from somewhat homomorphic encryption. In: Safavi-Naini, R., Canetti, R. (eds.) CRYPTO 2012. LNCS, vol. 7417, pp. 643–662. Springer, Heidelberg (2012). https://doi.org/10.1007/978-3-642-32009-5_38
16. Damgård, I., Keller, M., Larraia, E., Pastro, V., Scholl, P., Smart, N.P.: Practical covertly secure MPC for dishonest majority – or: breaking the SPDZ limits. In: Crampton, J., Jajodia, S., Mayes, K. (eds.) ESORICS 2013. LNCS, vol. 8134, pp. 1–18. Springer, Heidelberg (2013). https://doi.org/10.1007/978-3-642-40203-6_1
17. Beaver, D.: Efficient multiparty protocols using circuit randomization. In: Feigenbaum, J. (ed.) CRYPTO 1991. LNCS, vol. 576, pp. 420–432. Springer, Heidelberg (1992). https://doi.org/10.1007/3-540-46766-1_34
18. Dahl, M., et al.:. Private machine learning in tensorflow using secure computation. arXiv preprint arXiv:1810.08130 (2018)
19. Dwork, C.: Differential privacy: a survey of results. In: Agrawal, M., Du, D., Duan, Z., Li, A. (eds.) TAMC 2008. LNCS, vol. 4978, pp. 1–19. Springer, Heidelberg (2008). https://doi.org/10.1007/978-3-540-79228-4_1
20. Dwork, C.: Differential privacy. In: Bugliesi, M., Preneel, B., Sassone, V., Wegener, I. (eds.) ICALP 2006. LNCS, vol. 4052, pp. 1–12. Springer, Heidelberg (2006). https://doi.org/10.1007/11787006_1
21. Abadi, M., et al.:. Deep learning with differential privacy. In: Proceedings of the 2016 ACM SIGSAC Conference on Computer and Communications Security, pp. 308–318 (2016)

A Secure Neural Network Prediction Model with Multiple Data Providers

Fengtian Kuang, Bo Mi[✉], and Darong Huang[✉]

Chongqingjiaotong University, Chonqing 400074, China
mi_bo@163.com, drhuang@cqjtu.edu.cn

Abstract. With the rapid development of neural network theory, the issue of privacy has attracted much attention, especially for the prediction or classification of some sensitive information, a neural network model that can protect privacy is needed. On the basis of training the model with plaintext data, this article aims to replace the existing model through multiple key homomorphic encryption algorithm combined with bootstrapping and relinearization technology. With the help of real number coding, decoding of the resulting polynomial variant and the approximation of the activation function homomorphic filtering method we implement the prediction of neural network in encryption mode. In our mode, single input or multiple input data can be aggregated and used to complete the data prediction under the premise of the Sematic Secure. Experimental results show that the prediction accuracy of the neural network after encryption comes close to that before encryption, and during the whole process, the server cannot get any real information about the data providers.

Keywords: Homomorphic encryption · Neural network · Encoding

1 Introduction

It is well known that the neural network (NN) training and predicting all need the support of the data, however, the data always inevitably contains sensitive, confidential information, and data reveals that tend to bring losses to the user or institutions, so in all fields, the privacy protection has received wide attention, such as the Internet of things [1, 2], the social network [3–5] the smart grid, cloud computing [6–8] medical diagnosis, etc. How to use neural network without disclosing private information has become an important research field.

Based on the above requirements, many researchers have been working on solving the security and privacy problems in neural networks. One of the important methods is to combine homomorphic encryption with neural network. Homomorphic encryption was originally proposed by Rivest et al. [9] under the scenario of secure database. As a way to encrypt data, it can also be operated without decrypting the ciphertext. Gentry et al. [10] first proposed a full homomorphic encryption scheme based on ideal lattice, which was a breakthrough. Full homomorphism is the scheme that allows any number of operations on the encrypted data. At present, much work is focused on simpler models, for example, Graepel et al. [11] trained two linear dichotomies using a hierarchical homomorphic encryption scheme to preserve the confidentiality of the training

© Springer Nature Switzerland AG 2020
X. Chen et al. (Eds.): ML4CS 2020, LNCS 12486, pp. 272–286, 2020.
https://doi.org/10.1007/978-3-030-62223-7_23

and test data. Kim et al. [12] proposed a logistic regression model training method for encrypted data. The encryption library used was HEAAN developed by the team. The way to handle the Sigmoid function is to use the higher-order. Taylor formula. Dowlin et al. [13] modified a well-trained logistic regression model and introduced personal biological information data encrypted by FV homomorphic encryption scheme into the modified model to obtain the prediction of diabetes. The activation function of the original model is the Sigmoid function, and the modified model processes the Sigmoid function into a 7-order Taylor series expanded near $x = 0$. The support library of the homomorphic encryption scheme is SEAL, and the time conditions of the given encryption parameters are compared. Cheon et al. [14] and Giacomelli et al. [15] also proposed privacy protection logistic regression and privacy protection ridge regression schemes respectively. In terms of neural network under privacy protection, Dowlin et al. [16] trained a convolutional neural network model Crypto Nets using MNIST data set. Their research is divided into two stages: training and prediction. In order to influence the depth of multiplication, the results of ciphertext experiment are not given. Hesamifard et al. [17] introduced a new polynomial approximation excitation function method, combined with batch normalization, and conducted experiments on ciphertext. The homomorphic encryption library was HELib of IBM. In addition, related researches has been focused on solving the problem of privacy protection neural network by combining secure multi-party computing [18, 19], and their solutions include garbled circuits [20–22], secret sharing [23–25] and oblivious transfer [26–28].

However, those previous researches are homomorphic encryption algorithm based on single key, which is difficult to realize the neural network training and prediction with multiple clients participating together. Take the hospital as an example, in order to judge whether the patient is ill or not through the neural network model, it might be needed to input the patient's X-ray results, blood pressure, medical history and other data, but these data need to be input by different departments or patients. In this case, we need a homomorphic encryption algorithm that can satisfy multiple inputs. Lopez-alt et al. [29] proposed a multi-key homomorphic encryption algorithm based on NTRU, which solved this problem for the first time in principle. Soon after, Michael Clear and Ciar'an McGoldrick [30] extended their results to the multi-identity setting and obtained a multi-identity IBFHE scheme that is selectively secure in the random oracle model under the hardness of Learning with Errors (LWE). Based on the scheme put forward by López-Alt et al., Hao Chen et al. presented new relinearization algorithms and bootstrapping techniques and they homomorphically classified an image using a pre-trained Convolutional Neural Networks (CNN), where input data and model are encrypted under different keys.

Our contribution:

1. Based on NN and multi-key homomorphic encryption scheme, we combined with the prediction of privacy neural network with multiple participants.
2. A new polynomial carry and decode method is proposed, which is combined with a parameter adjustment to make the polynomial encoded in binary code decode the correct result after homomorphic calculation.

In this article, using neural network to predict the security requirements of privacy protection data can be briefly described as: multiple participants triple $A_1, A_2, \ldots, A_N$ and B, A_i is data hold party, B is neural network hold party, the model satisfies both $A_1 + A_2 +, \ldots, A_N$ as input data and each A_i as independent data input (i.e. single input and multiple input). A_i wants to obtain prediction results without revealing information about their data. When A_i gets the result, It doesn't know about the parameters of the neural network model of B (Fig. 1).

2   Preliminaries

2.1   Neural Network

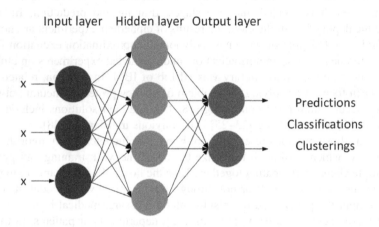

Fig. 1. Neural network model

In Input layer, the Neuron receives a large number of non-linear Input messages. The input message is called the input vector. In Output layer, the message is transmitted, analyzed and weighed in the neuron link to form the Output result. The output message is called the output vector. Hidden layer is a layer composed of numerous neurons and links between the input layer and the output layer. The number of nodes (neurons) in the hidden layer is not fixed, but the bigger the number, the more nonlinear the neural network is, it is customary to select 1.2 to 1.5 times the input node.

2.2   Multi-key Homomorphic Encryption

López-Alt, Tromer and Vaikuntanathan first proposed a multi-key full homomorphic encryption scheme based on NTRU, which realized the homomorphic multiply and added calculation for messages encrypted with different public keys, and finally could be decrypted correctly. But this solution doesn't rely on a standard assumption, after this, Michael Clear and Ciar´an McGoldrick obtained a multi-key fully-homomorphic encryption scheme (FHE) that is secure under LWE in the standard model. Multi-key homomorphic encryption scheme is mainly composed of four parts:

- $(pk, sk, ek) \leftarrow Keygen(1^\kappa)$, for a security parameter κ, output a public key pk, a secret key sk and a (public) evaluation key ek.
- $c \leftarrow Enc(pk, m)$ given a public key pk and message m, outputs a ciphertext c.
- $m' := Dec(sk_1, \ldots, sk_N, c)$ given N secret keys sk_i and a ciphertext c, outputs a message m'.
- $c^* := Eval(C, (c_1, pk_1, ek_1), \ldots, (c_t, pk_t, ek_t))$ given a (description of) a boolean circuit C along with t tuples (c_i, pk_i, ek_i), each comprising of a ciphertext c_i, a public key pk_i, and an evaluation key ek_i, outputs a ciphertext c^*.

3 Our Construction

At first, the user and the server generate their own key string respectively, followed by the user coding and encrypting the initial data that is going to be input later, at the same time, the server codes and encrypts model parameters (here we assume that the model is already trained). Then the user input the encrypted data. After completing homomorphic aggregation of the data, the server will put it into the encrypted model and return the predicted values in ciphertext to the user. Then the user can use its private key to decrypt and decode to get the final forecasting result. The process is as shown in Fig. 2:

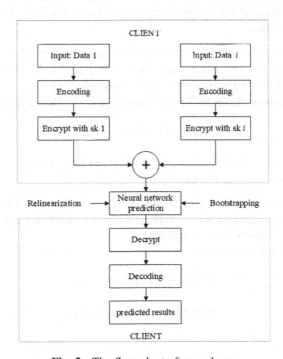

Fig. 2. The flow chart of our scheme

3.1 Encoding

The neural network does not match the elements involved in the calculation in the homomorphic encryption scheme, in which the neural network is a real number involved in the calculation, while the homomorphic encryption is a polynomial calculation. So we need a coding scheme that preserves addition and multiplication. This coding scheme can be constructed in several ways. For example, one way is to use the Chinese Remainder Theorem(CRT) [31] can guarantee the decoding success after the addition and multiplication computation of the encoded data, another method is to use their binary representation. The input data is firstly converted to a binary string and then to a $\{0, 1\}$ polynomial. But this is only for integers, when there are decimal places, this method is obviously not feasible. Based on this problem, [13] gives a method to encode real Numbers into polynomials.

Firstly, the real Numbers are divided into integer and decimal parts. The integer part is still coded as a polynomial according to the previous binary conversion, and the decimal part is coded as a binary and then placed at the end of the integer polynomial. For example, 25.75 is encoded as polynomial:

$$-1x^{N-1} - 1x^{N-2} + 1x^4 + 1x^3 + 1 \tag{1}$$

3.2 Encryption Scheme

After coding, the user and the server use their keys to encrypt the input data and weights respectively, and the server completes the prediction. The specific encryption algorithm is as follows:

- $Keygen(1^\kappa)$: Sample "bounded" polynomials $f', g \leftarrow \chi$ and set $f := pf' + 1$ so that $f \equiv 1 \pmod{p}$. Set the public key $pk := h = pgf^{-1} \in R_q$ and the secret key $sk = f \in R$. (If f is not invertible over R_q, resample f').
- $Enc(pk, m)$: Sample "bounded" polynomials $s, e \leftarrow \chi$. Output the ciphertext:

$$c := hs + pe + m \in R_q \tag{2}$$

- $Dec(sk, c)$: Let $\mu = fc \in R_q$. Output $\mu \pmod{p}$ as the message.
- $Eval(C, (c_1, pk_1, ek_1), \ldots, (c_t, pk_t, ek_t))$

The above is the case where a single key encrypts the message. The following is the case where two keys based on this encryption scheme respectively encrypt the message and complete the homomorphic calculation:

Suppose there are two ciphers

$$c_1 = h_1 s_1 + pe_1 + m_1 \in R_q \tag{3}$$

$$c_2 = h_2 s_2 + pe_2 + m_2 \in R_q \tag{4}$$

Let their sum and product be $c_+ = c_1 + c_2$, $c_\times = c_1 c_2$ respectively, their joint decryption keys are the product of two private keys $f_1 f_2$. The specific decryption process is as follow:

$$f_1 f_2 (c_1 + c_2) = 2(f_1 f_2 (e_1 + e_2)) + f_2 g_1 s_1 + f_1 g_2 s_2) + f_1 f_2 (m_1 + m_2)$$
$$= 2E_{add} + f_1 f_2 (m_1 + m_2) \tag{5}$$

$$f_1 f_2 (c_1 c_2) \pmod 2 = 2(2 g_1 g_2 s_1 s_2 + g_1 s_1 f_2 (2e_2 + m_2) + g_2 s_2 f_1 (2e_1 + m_1)$$
$$+ f_1 f_2 (e_1 m_2 + e_2 m_1 + 2 e_1 e_2)) + f_1 f_2 (m_1 m_2) \pmod 2 \tag{6}$$
$$= m_1 m_2 \pmod 2$$

3.3   Relinearization

In the above multi-key decryption scheme, there exists a problem that will cause leak to the circuit privacy. Circuit privacy is formalized as follow:

Homomorphic encryption scheme ε is circuit private if for any key-pair (sk, pk) output by $Keygen(1^\kappa)$, any circuit C, and any fixed ciphertexts $\psi = <\psi_1, \ldots, \psi_t>$ that are in the image of Enc_λ for plaintexts $x_1, .., x_t$, the following distributions are statistically indistinguishable:

$$Enc_\lambda(pk, C(x_1, \ldots, x_t)) \approx_s Eval_\lambda(pk, C, \psi) \tag{7}$$

In this scheme, it is embodied as there is a ciphertext square case, that is $c = c_1^2 c_2$, decryption c requires $f_1^2 f_2$, so that the decoder can get certain information about the circuit. In order to solve this problem, relinearization technology needs to be introduced so that no matter what the encrypted function is, only a power of each private key is needed in the decryption. The general approach is as follow:

- Generate the pseudo-encrypted ciphertext of the private key f^2:

$$\zeta_\tau = h \cdot s_\tau + p e_\tau + 2^\tau f^2 \in R_q \text{ for } \tau = 0, .., \lfloor \log q \rfloor \tag{8}$$

- Relinearization procedure-split c into its binary representation $\sum_\tau c_\tau 2^\tau$ and compute:

$$\hat{c} = \sum_\tau c_\tau \cdot \zeta_\tau = h \cdot \left(\sum_\tau c_\tau s_\tau \right) + p \cdot \left(\sum_\tau c_\tau e_\tau \right) + f^2 \cdot \left(\sum_\tau c_\tau 2^\tau \right) \tag{9}$$

3.4   Bootstrapping

It is easy to see from the above algorithm, when we decrypt the circuit to a certain depth, the noise will become too large, resulting in the final ciphertext failing to be decrypted correctly. To solve this problem Gentry gave the bootstrapping theorem in [32], the principle of bootstrapping is to use a public evaluation key consists of encryptions of all bits of all secret keys in the process of homomorphism calculation to continuously update the noise of the ciphertext, so as to guarantee the correctness of final result decryption. The specific plan is as follow:

- *Keygen*(1^κ): For every $i \in \{0,\ldots,d_{dec}\}$, sample $g^{(i)}$, $u^{(i)} \leftarrow \chi$ and set $f^{(i)} := pu^{(i)} + 1$ so that $f^{(i)} \equiv 1 \pmod{p}$. If $f^{(i)}$ is not invertible in R_{q_i}, resample $u^{(i)}$. Let

$$h^{(i)} := pg^{(i)}(f^{(i)})^{-1} \in R_{q_{i-1}} \tag{10}$$

And set $pk := h_0 \in R_{q_0}$, $sk := f^{(d_{dec})} \in R_{qd_{dec}}$. For all $i \in [d_{dec}]$ and $\tau \in \{0,\ldots,\lfloor\log q_{i-1}\rfloor\}$, sample $s_\tau^{(i)}, e_\tau^{(i)} \leftarrow \chi$ and compute:

$$\gamma_\tau^{(i)} := h^{(i)}s_\tau^{(i)} + pe_\tau^{(i)} + 2^\tau f^{(i-1)} \in R_{q_{i-1}} \tag{11}$$

$$\zeta_\tau^{(i)} := h^{(i)}s_\tau^{(i)} + pe_\tau^{(i)} + 2^\tau(f^{(i-1)})^2 \in R_{q_{i-1}} \tag{12}$$

Set $ek := \{\gamma_\tau^{(i)}, \zeta_\tau^{(i)}\}_{i\in[d_{dec}],\tau\in\{0,\ldots,\lfloor\log q_i\rfloor\}}$.

- *Enc*(pk,m): Sample $s, e \leftarrow \chi$. Output the ciphertext $c := hs + pe + m \in R_{q_0}$.
- *Dec*$(sk_1,\ldots,sk_N,c)$: Assume w.l.o.g. that $c \in R_{qd_{dec}}$. Parse $sk_i = f_i$ for $i \in [N]$. Let $\mu := f_1 \cdots f_N \cdot c \in R_{qd_{dec}}$. Output $m' := \mu \pmod{p}$.
- *Eval*$(C, (c, pk_1, ek_1), \ldots, (c_t, pk_t, ek_t))$

3.5   Decoding

If the decryption result is decoded directly according to the encoding method, the accuracy will be reduced, so we adjust the initial parameter p, and give a result polynomial carry method. First of all, get the decryption polynomial, start with the smallest non-zero bit of the fractional part, that is x^{N-8}, divide the absolute value of its coefficient by 2, the remainder is the new coefficient of x^{N-8} and the quotient carry to x^{N-7}(The way to carry is absolute value addition), repeat the process until carry to x^{N-1}, x^{N-1} carry to x^0, repeat the calculation until all integer bits are counted. It is important to note that because we normalize the data before we enter it, so, the integer number will not affect the decimal place. For example, The decryption polynomial of $5 \times 5.25 = 26.25$ is $-x^{N-1} + x^4 + 2x^2 + 2$, using the above method, the formula can be $-x^{N-1} + x^4 + x^3 + x$, and $m = 2^{-1} + 2^4 + 2^3 + 2^1 = 26.25$. We give the specific code in the appendix.

3.6   Polynomial Approximation

By using the multiplicative property of homomorphic encryption scheme, all polynomial functions can be replaced. However, activation functions of neural network, such as Sigmoid and tanh, are not in polynomial form, so it is necessary to approximate a polynomial here. In this paper, Sigmoid is used as the activation function of neural network, and it is approximated by Taylor expansion [33]. Specific methods are as follow:

$$
sigmoid = \begin{cases}
\begin{aligned}
& 0.571859 + 0.392773x + 0.108706x^2 \\
& \quad + 0.014222x^3 + 0.000734x^4
\end{aligned} & -\infty < x \le -1.5 \\
\\
1/2 + (1/4) * x - (1/48) * x^3 + (1/480) * x^5 & -1.5 < x \le 1.5 \\
\\
\begin{aligned}
& 0.428141 + 0.3922773x - 0.108706x^2 \\
& \quad + 0.014222x^3 - 0.000734x^4
\end{aligned} & 1.5 \le x < \infty
\end{cases}
\tag{13}
$$

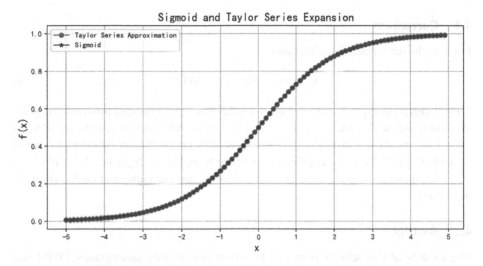

Fig. 3. Sigmoid function and Taylor series approximation

The form of piecewise function enables the Taylor series to better approximate the sigmoid. As shown in Fig. 3, the similarity between them in the interval between −5 and 5 is 0.9999 through the method of $R - square$. After using this method, the activation function is encrypted by homomorphic algorithm, at this point, all model encryption is completed.

3.7 The Encrypted Prediction Process

After the trained model, different from the general neural network prediction method, in order to protect the privacy of users and server models, from the perspective of users, it is necessary to input homomorphic encrypted data to the server. From the view of the server, the weights and activation functions in the trained model are replaced by the multi-key homomorphic encryption algorithm.

3.8   Parameter Selection

The main parameters that define the cryptosystem are the coefficient modulus p,q, the coefficient modulus q and the degree n of the polynomial modulus $(x^n + 1)$, apply $32, 32, 10000002527$ to n,p,q respectively, boundary B is 32. It is easy to calculate that $2np(pB+1)^2 + B < 9np^2B^2 < q/2$ is satisfied by the following correctness proof that will be proved later, the problem of increasing computational noise with increasing depth can be solved by bootstrap technique. As for coding of real numbers, since the data was normalized before the input, it would be generally small. Therefore, the last 8 bits of the encoded code were selected as the decimal place and the first eight bits as the integer bits.

4   Correctness and Security

4.1   Correctness

Look at the decryption function again:

$$fc = pgs + pfe + fm(\bmod\ p) \tag{14}$$

To get correct decryption, we need to ensure there is no wraparound through setting the modulo q and setting the $\phi(x) = x^n + 1$. g, s, f, e in this function are all bounded by $pB + 1$, according to Corollary 3.3 in literature [29], the coefficient boundary of gs and fe is $n(pB+1)^2$. Thus, the coefficients of fc are bounded by $2np(pB+1)^2 + B < 9np^2$ $B^2 < q/2$. therefore, we just need to set $q > 9np^2B^2$, and the ciphertext can be correctly decrypted.

4.2   Security

The security of this scheme is mainly based on two security assumptions, DSPR and RLWE:

$DSPR_{(\phi,q,\chi)}$: $\phi(x) \in \mathbb{Z}[x]$ is a polynomial of degree n, let $q \in Z$ be a prime integer, and let χ denote a distribution over the ring $R \doteq Z[x] < \phi(x) >$. The (decisional) small polynomial ratio problem $DSPR_{(\phi,q,\chi)}$ is to distinguish between the following two distributions: A polynomial $h = g/f$, where f and g are sampled from the distribution χ(conditioned on f being invertible over $R_q \doteq R/qR$), and a polynomial h sampled uniformly at random over R_q.

The RLWE Problem: $a_i(x)$ is a set of random polynomials from $\mathbb{Z}[x]/\langle \varphi(x) \rangle$ with coefficients that are all from R_q. $s_i(x)$ is a small polynomial relative to a bound B in the ring $\mathbb{Z}[x]/\langle \varphi(x) \rangle$. $\eta_i(x)$ is a set of small random polynomials relative to a bound B in the ring $\mathbb{Z}[x]/\langle \varphi(x) \rangle$.

$$b_i(x) = a_i(x) \cdot s_i(x) + \eta_i(x) \tag{15}$$

The decision version of the problem can be stated as follow. Given a list of polynomial pairs $(b_i(x), a_i(x))$, determine whether the $b_i(x)$ polynomials were constructed as $b_i(x) = a_i(x) \cdot s_i(x) + \eta_i(x)$ or were generated randomly from $Z[x]/\langle \varphi(x) \rangle$. The RLWE problem is an algebraic variant of LWE, which is more efficient and is reducible to worst-case problems on ideal lattices. It is also hard for polynomial-time algorithms even on quantum computers [34–36].

We can use the difficulty of DSPR to transform $ph^{-1} \cdot g$ into pH, for a uniformly selected H. After this we can use RLWE to alter the tag cipher $c = pgH + pe + m$ into $c' := \mu + m \in R_q$, where μ is uniformly sampled from R_q. The advantage of the adversary is exactly 1/2 since c' is uniform over R_q, which is independent of the m. So, when cloud server or attacker gets the data they will have no more information except c.

5   Experimental Verification

In order to verify the effectiveness of our method, we adopted the power load data of Chongqing Tongnan Electric Power Co., Ltd. from May 4, 2015 to May 10, 2015, from Monday to Thursday, the short-term electric load is predicted by the electric load data of 96 sampling points from 0:00 to 24 o'clock every day for a total of 24 h.

The experiment is divided into two stages: model training and ciphertext prediction. Model training is mainly to obtain model parameters and provide data for forward propagation of ciphertext prediction. In the model training stage, with the help of scipy and numpy, Python language can be used to efficiently and quickly complete the model training and testing, and save model parameters. In the ciphertext prediction stage, NTRU is selected to provide support for homomorphic encryption operations. The specific environment description is shown in Table 1.

Table 1. Experimental environment.

CPU	OS	RAM	Programming language
i5-10210U 1.60 GHz	Win10 64-bit	16 GB	Python

Firstly, the existing charge data training model was used, and the plaintext data was used for direct prediction. Then the model and the input data are encrypted, where the server encrypts the model, the user encrypts the charge data and then inputs them into the encrypted model to predict the results. In this case we are considering load forecasting for a single area. We also need to take it into account that the power load situation of each region is involved in the prediction. For example, the power load of the whole region of Tong nan is the sum of the power load from each village, and each region does not want to directly upload its own data. Therefore, we apply the method of multi-key homomorphic encryption into NN. Each region generates its private key to encrypt its own data, and then homomorphic aggregation is input to the server to complete the encryption prediction. The specific results are as follow (Fig. 4 and Table 2):

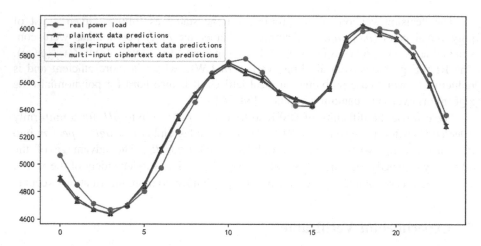

Fig. 4. Single-input and multi-input predicted results

Table 2. Comparison of prediction accuracy and time consumption.

Model	Predicted time	Prediction accuracy
Plaintext model	4 ms	0.9803
Sigel-input model	56.6 s	0.9790
Muti-input model	58.5 s	0.9789

It can be seen from Table 1 that the prediction accuracy of the neural network model with homomorphic encryption is almost the same as the previous model. The impact is mainly on the predicted time. However, considering the privacy protection of people or regions, this meets the acceptable range.

6   Conclusion

To protect privacy within NN, we use multiple key homomorphic filtering algorithm with the help of relinearization and bootstrapping technique for replacement of homomorphism within NN prediction model. Finally, the prediction of multi-input neural network is realized by using appropriate coding and decoding techniques with minimal loss of prediction accuracy. In addition, it should be noted that in the experiment that's been conducted, the data set is relatively small, so A better accuracy is expected with a larger data set.

Acknowledgement. This work was supported by the National Natural Sci-ence Foundation of P.R. China under Grants 61573076, 61663008, 61703063 and 61903053; the Scientifc Re-search Foundation for Returned Overseas Chinese Scholars under Grant 2015-49; the Program for Excel-lent Talents of the Chongqing Higher Schools of P.R. China under Grant 2014-18; the Chongqing Natural Science Foundation of P.R. China under Grant CSTC2017jcyjA1665; the Science and Technology Re-search Project of the Chongqing Municipal Education Commission of P.R. China under Grants KJ1605002, KJ1705121, KJ1705139 and KJZD-K201800701; and the Program of Chongqing innovation and entrepreneur-ship for Returned Overseas Scholars of P.R. China un-der Grant cx2018110.

Appendix

The specific codes of polynomial variants and decoding methods are as follows (Table 3):

Table 3. Codes of polynomial variants and decoding.

```
def decode(ans: list):
ans = [abs(x) for x in ans][::-1]
ans = np.pad(ans, (0, (N - len(ans))), 'constant').tolist()
print(ans)
num = 0
ans_copy = ans[:8]
e_list_copy = ans[16:]
for i, x in enumerate(ans[16:-1]):
    j = e_list_copy[i] // 2
    e_list_copy[i] = e_list_copy[i] % 2
    e_list_copy[i + 1] += j
ans_copy[0] += e_list_copy[-1] // 2
e_list_copy[-1] %= 2
for i, x in enumerate(e_list_copy[-8:][::-1]):
    num += x * 2**(0 - i - 1)
for i, x in enumerate(ans[:7]):
    j = ans_copy[i] // 2
    ans_copy[i] = ans_copy[i] % 2
    ans_copy[i + 1] += j
ans_copy[7] %= 2
for i, x in enumerate(ans_copy):
    num += x * 2 ** i
return num
```

References

1. Stergiou, C., Psannis, K.E., Kim, B.G., et al.: Secure integration of IoT and cloud computing. Future Gener. Comput. Syst. **78**, 964–975 (2018)
2. Alsmirat, M.A., Jararweh, Y., Obaidat, I., et al.: Internet of surveillance: a cloud supported large-scale wireless surveillance system. J. Supercomput. **73**(3), 973–992 (2016). https://doi.org/10.1007/s11227-016-1857-x
3. Gupta, S., Gupta, B.B.: XSS-secure as a service for the platforms of online social network-based multimedia web applications in cloud. Multimed. Tools Appl. **77**(4), 4829–4861 (2016). https://doi.org/10.1007/s11042-016-3735-1
4. Zhang, L., Li, X.Y., Liu, K., et al.: Message in a sealed bottle: privacy preserving friending in mobile social networks. IEEE Trans. Mob. Comput. **14**(9), 1888–1902 (2014)
5. Hamedani, K., Liu, L., Atat, R., et al.: Reservoir computing meets smart grids: attack detection using delayed feedback networks. IEEE Trans. Industr. Inf. **14**(2), 734–743 (2017)
6. Negi, P., Mishra, A., Gupta, B.B.: Enhanced CBF packet filtering method to detect DDoS attack in cloud computing environment. arXiv preprint arXiv:1304.7073 (2013)
7. Li, J., Zhang, Y., Chen, X., et al.: Secure attribute-based data sharing for resource-limited users in cloud computing. Comput. Secur. **72**, 1–12 (2018)
8. Jagadeesh, K.A., Wu, D.J., Birgmeier, J.A., et al.: Deriving genomic diagnoses without revealing patient genomes. Science **357**(6352), 692–695 (2017)
9. Rivest, R.L., Adleman, L., Dertouzos, M.L.: On data banks and privacy homomorphisms. Found. Secure Comput. **4**(11), 169–180 (1978)
10. Gentry, C., Boneh, D.: A fully homomorphic encryption scheme. Stanford University, Stanford (2009)
11. Graepel, T., Lauter, K., Naehrig, M.: ML confidential: machine learning on encrypted data. In: Kwon, T., Lee, M.-K., Kwon, D. (eds.) ICISC 2012. LNCS, vol. 7839, pp. 1–21. Springer, Heidelberg (2013). https://doi.org/10.1007/978-3-642-37682-5_1
12. Kim, M., Song, Y., Wang, S., et al.: Secure logistic regression based on homomorphic encryption: Design and evaluation. JMIR Med. Inf. **6**(2), 1–12 (2018)
13. Dowlin, N., Gilad-Bachrach, R., Laine, K., et al.: Manual for using homomorphic encryption for bioinformatics. Proc. IEEE **105**(3), 552–567 (2017)
14. Cheon, J.H., Jeong, J., Lee, J., Lee, K.: Privacy-preserving computations of predictive medical models with minimax approximation and non-adjacent form. In: Brenner, M., et al. (eds.) FC 2017. LNCS, vol. 10323, pp. 53–74. Springer, Cham (2017). https://doi.org/10.1007/978-3-319-70278-0_4
15. Giacomelli, I., Jha, S., Joye, M., Page, C.D., Yoon, K.: Privacy-preserving ridge regression with only linearly-homomorphic encryption. In: Preneel, B., Vercauteren, F. (eds.) ACNS 2018. LNCS, vol. 10892, pp. 243–261. Springer, Cham (2018). https://doi.org/10.1007/978-3-319-93387-0_13
16. Gilad-Bachrach, R., Dowlin, N., Laine, K., et al.: Cryptonets: Applying neural networks to encrypted data with high throughput and accuracy. In: International Conference on Machine Learning, pp. 201–210. ICML, New York (2016)
17. Hesamifard, E., Takabi, H., Ghasemi, M.: CryptoDL: deep neural networks over encrypted data. arXiv preprint arXiv, 1711.05189 (2017)
18. Mohassel, P., Zhang, Y.: SecureML: a system for scalable privacy-preserving machine learning. In: 2017 IEEE Symposium on Security and Privacy (SP), pp. 19–38. IEEE, San Jose (2017)

19. Rouhani, B.D., Riazi, M.S., Koushanfar, F.: DeepSecure: scalable provably-secure deep learning. In: Proceedings of the 55th Annual Design Automation Conference, pp. 1–6. Association for Computing Machinery, New York (2018)
20. Ball, M., Carmer, B., Malkin, T., et al.: Garbled neural networks are practical. IACR Cryptology ePrint Archive, pp. 1–27 (2019)
21. Chase, M., Gilad-Bachrach, R., Laine, K., et al.: Private collaborative neural network learning. IACR Cryptology ePrint Archive, pp. 1–17 (2017)
22. Wagh, S., Gupta, D., Chandran, N.: Securenn: 3-party secure computation for neural network training. Proc. Priv. Enhanc. Technol. **2019**(3), 26–49 (2019)
23. Chervyakov, N.I., Babenko, M.G., Kucherov, N.N., Garianina, A.I.: The effective neural network implementation of the secret sharing scheme with the use of matrix projections on FPGA. In: Tan, Y., Shi, Y., Buarque, F., Gelbukh, A., Das, S., Engelbrecht, A. (eds.) ICSI 2015. LNCS, vol. 9142, pp. 3–10. Springer, Cham (2015). https://doi.org/10.1007/978-3-319-20469-7_1
24. Narad, S., Chavan, P.: Cascade forward back-propagation neural network based group authentication using (n, n) secret sharing scheme. Proc. Comput. Sci. **78**(C), 185–191 (2016)
25. Kumar, R., Dhiman, M.: Secured image transmission using a novel neural network approach and secret image sharing technique. Int. J. Signal Process. Image Process. Pattern Recogn. **8**(1), 161–192 (2015)
26. Liu, J., Juuti, M., Lu, Y., et al.: Oblivious neural network predictions via minionn transformations. In: Proceedings of the 2017 ACM SIGSAC Conference on Computer and Communications Security, pp. 619–631. Association for Computing Machinery, New York (2017)
27. Riazi, M.S., Samragh, M., Chen, H., et al.: {XONN}: XNOR-based Oblivious Deep Neural Network Inference. In: 28th {USENIX} Security Symposium ({USENIX} Security 19), Santa Clara, CA, pp. 1502–1518 (2019)
28. Agrawal, N., Shahin, Shamsabadi, A., Kusner, M.J., et al.: QUOTIENT: two-party secure neural network training and prediction. In: Proceedings of the 2019 ACM SIGSAC Conference on Computer and Communications Security, pp. 1231–1247. Association for Computing Machinery, New York (2019)
29. López-Alt, A., Tromer, E., Vaikuntanathan, V.: On-the-fly multiparty computation on the cloud via multikey fully homomorphic encryption. In: Proceedings of the Forty-Fourth Annual ACM Symposium on Theory of Computing, pp. 1219–1234. Association for Computing Machinery, New York (2012)
30. Clear, M., McGoldrick, C.: Multi-identity and multi-key leveled FHE from learning with errors. In: Gennaro, R., Robshaw, M. (eds.) CRYPTO 2015. LNCS, vol. 9216, pp. 630–656. Springer, Heidelberg (2015). https://doi.org/10.1007/978-3-662-48000-7_31
31. Gentry, C., Halevi, S., Smart, Nigel P.: Homomorphic evaluation of the AES circuit. In: Safavi-Naini, R., Canetti, R. (eds.) CRYPTO 2012. LNCS, vol. 7417, pp. 850–867. Springer, Heidelberg (2012). https://doi.org/10.1007/978-3-642-32009-5_49
32. Gentry, C., Halevi, S., Smart, N.P.: Better bootstrapping in fully homomorphic encryption. In: Fischlin, M., Buchmann, J., Manulis, M. (eds.) PKC 2012. LNCS, vol. 7293, pp. 1–16. Springer, Heidelberg (2012). https://doi.org/10.1007/978-3-642-30057-8_1
33. Çetin, O., Temurtaş, F., Gülgönül, S.: An application of multilayer neural network on hepatitis disease diagnosis using approximations of sigmoid activation function. Dicle Med. J./Dicle Tip Dergisi **42**(2), 150–157 (2015)
34. Lyubashevsky, V., Peikert, C., Regev, O.: On ideal lattices and learning with errors over rings. In: Gilbert, H. (ed.) EUROCRYPT 2010. LNCS, vol. 6110, pp. 1–23. Springer, Heidelberg (2010). https://doi.org/10.1007/978-3-642-13190-5_1

35. Rathee, D., Schneider, T., Shukla, K.K.: Improved multiplication triple generation over rings via RLWE-based AHE. In: Mu, Y., Deng, R.H., Huang, X. (eds.) CANS 2019. LNCS, vol. 11829, pp. 347–359. Springer, Cham (2019). https://doi.org/10.1007/978-3-030-31578-8_19
36. Yang, Y., Sun, Y., Huang, Q., et al.: RLWE-Based ID-DIA protocols for cloud storage. IEEE Access **7**, 55732–55743 (2019)

GAN-Based Image Privacy Preservation: Balancing Privacy and Utility

Zhenfei Chen[1], Tianqing Zhu[1(✉)] (iD), Chenguang Wang[1], Wei Ren[1], and Ping Xiong[2]

[1] School of Computer Science, China University of Geosciences, Wuhan, China
tianqing.e.zhu@gmail.com
[2] School of Information and Safety Engineering,
Zhongnan University of Economics and Law, Wuhan, China

Abstract. While we enjoy high-quality social network services, image privacy is also under great privacy threats. With the development of deep learning-driven face recognition technologies, traditional protection methods are facing challenges. How to balancing the privacy and the utility of images has been an urgent problem to solve. In this paper, we propose a novel image privacy preservation model using Generative Adversarial Networks(GANs). By generating an fake image that highly matches the key face attributes of the original image, we balance the privacy protection and utility.

1 Introduction

With the development of smartphone and high pixel cameras, people can upload the photos to social platforms at any time to update their network experiences. At the same time, major cloud service providers such as Google, Baidu and Microsoft can provide users with free services based on images. Users can save and manage their photos, and download them on their mobile phones or computers at anytime. However, although the third-party service providers provide free storage services, image privacy is seriously threatened by most advanced deep learning based face recognition algorithms.

To preserve the image privacy, researchers put forward a variety of schemes, such as pixelation, blurring and masking, achieving the purpose of privacy protection by obfuscate the sensitive information in the image [2]. However, with the appearance of faceless recognition technology [12], which can recognize the target from the obfuscated image with human features, the traditional methods are not safe. Although the privacy is effectively protected, the utility for the image may be totally lost. Recently, the image inpainting method based on the Generative Adversarial Network is to generate a highly realistic and natural image that conforms to the original image data distribution through the adversarial training [1]. Although this meets the needs of the usability of the original image to a certain extent, the sensitive information of the original image is not fully protected. Therefore, most of the current methods can not give a good consideration to privacy protection and data usability.

© Springer Nature Switzerland AG 2020
X. Chen et al. (Eds.): ML4CS 2020, LNCS 12486, pp. 287–296, 2020.
https://doi.org/10.1007/978-3-030-62223-7_24

Our aim is to hide the high sensitive information in a image, while maintain the key features of the sensitive information for further processing. Taking a face image as an example, we will preserve the privacy by generating a highly realistic and natural fake face to replace the original face, so that people cannot identify who she is. But at the same time, keep the key attributes of the image, face attributes usually include facial features and expression, to maintain the utility for further processing.

There are several challenges to tackle. How to generate a fake faces to replace the original ones. Second, how to maintain the original face attributes. Third, how to measure the utility of newly generated protected images and the effectiveness of privacy preservation. In order to solve these challenges, we use the technologies of GANs to generate fake faces to replace the original faces. To tackle the second challenge, we propose an attribute transformation method to maintain the key attributes of the face. Finally we measure the utility by calculating the attribute label matching accuracy of image ,and measure the privacy level by estimating the similarity between the fake and the original image.

- We propose a novel image privacy preservation method. The fake image generated by our model can hide the privacy sensitive information of the original image, and maintain the utility of the image.
- We provide new metrics to measure the utility and the privacy of preserved images.

2   Preliminaries

2.1   Image Privacy

Considering the rich sensitive information such as identity, location and event, embedded in images, privacy becomes a critical issue has been widely discussed in recent decades. Currently, the photo hosting platform based on cloud service is in a dilemma, which not only provides reliable photo search service, but also ensures that users' privacy is not violated. Among all the object recognition technologies, face detection is one of the most mature technologies. A typical face recognition system is usually used to verify the identity of an input face image or to determine the identity of an unknown picture by comparing it with the known images in the database. In our paper, identity is the sensitive information that we need to protect, so the anonymous pictures unrecognizable in identity.

2.2   Generative Adversarial Network (GAN)

Generative Adversarial Network (GAN) is an excellent generative algorithm which were proposed by *Goodfellow et al.* in 2014 [6]. GANs is composed of two models, the generator and the discriminator. Both are all implemented by neural network. The generator tries to make the input noise variables $p_z(z)$ learn the real image x, and the generated data distribution p_g approximates the real data distribution $p_{\text{data}}(x)$. Then, GANs represent a mapping from noise space to data space as $G(z, \theta_g)$, where G is a differentiable function represented by a neural network with parameters θ_g. The discriminator output $D(x)$ is a a single scalar, its neural network $D(x, \theta_g)$ is also defined with parameters θ_d, which represents the probability that x came from the data rather than generator G. The objective function of GANs is a minimax optimization problem, for the generator G, the objective function needs to be minimized, while for the discriminator D, the objective function needs to be maximized. Mathematically, it is written as function $V(G, D)$:

$$\min_G \max_D V(D, G) = \mathbb{E}_{x \sim p_{\text{data}}(x)}[\log D(x)] + \mathbb{E}_{z \sim p_z(z)}[\log(1 - D(G(z)))] \quad (1)$$

2.3 Related Work

Obfuscation-Based Privacy Methods. Some traditional approaches were used to obfuscate the identity of images which include human faces. These approaches include blurring, pixelation, and masking. However, there are some apparent defects in these methods. When using pixelation or blurring method, if the block sizes (blur radius) value is set unreasonably, usually it is too small, the protection effect will be worse [9]. Even if these model parameters are set in a normal range, with the rapid development of face recognition technology, the traditional method will still face the dilemma of poor protection effect, [11]. For the masking method, it covers a black space to the sensitive area of human face. Although it has a good effect on privacy protection, it loses the practicability of pictures.

Image Inpainting Methods. Different from suppression some facial attributes to the obfuscation of identities, some researches were carried out with some inpainting methods using deep neural networks for the identity obfuscations. To address the problem of obfuscating identities in social media photos, *Sun et al.* designed a two-stage head inpainting framework which used DCGAN to generate fake landmarks and head images [14], and the obfuscation comes up with a new, unseen identity. What's more, *sun et al.* use the parametric face model, generate the reconstructed face and modify some parameters to generate rendered images [15]. Then, using GAN with the rendered images to generate a realistic image.

Differential Privacy Methods. Differential privacy mechanisms have some attractive properties, such as privacy preservation, security, randomization, composition, and stability, which make them widely used in the field of AI. *Zhu et al.* analyzes the initial idea of some common AI fields, such as multi-agent systems, reinforcement learning, and knowledge transfer, integrating with differential privacy [18]. Besides, at the level of image privacy preservation, *fan et al.* extended the concept of standard difference privacy to image data, they proposed sharing pixelized images with rigorous privacy guarantees [5]. *Yuan et al.* Applied the differential privacy mechanism to the privacy protection of medical images, and prevented the leakage of sensitive information.

Compared with other privacy preservation models, the main difference is that most of the previous methods are based on the original image operation, the methods include image pixelation, masking, blurring and scrambling [4]. This will affect the usability of the original image more or less, and we achieve the purpose of privacy protection by generating as realistic image as possible with the original image, which will not destroy the original distribution in the whole process, thus the needs of image privacy and usability can be met.

3 Image Privacy Preservation Method

3.1 Method Overview

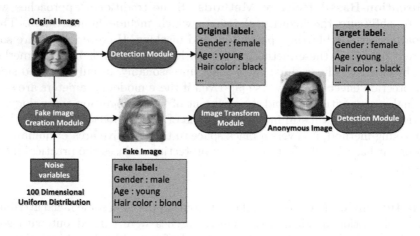

Fig. 1. An overview of the key components of our image privacy preservation method

The purpose of this method is to generate a face that can wipe the identity of the original image while maintain the key attributes of the original image. As show in the Fig. 1, our proposed model consists of three modules: fake image generation module, image transformation module and detection module. The role of detection module is to detect the image attribute label, original image and anonymous image need to detect once respectively. The fake image generation module fed by original image and noise variables used to generate highly realistic fake images. Image transformation module is called multi domain image to image translation, we can generate different face images according to different types of domain labels, its role in our model is to convert the fake image generated by fake image generation module into an image satisfying the domain label of original image.

Based on the above three modules, we formally define the privacy preservation method as: generate a fake face to match the face attributes of the original image as much as possible, and the match means that the attribute label matching accuracy of the two images is higher. The notations are given below:

Let A be the attribute set of face dataset, for each attribute A_i, its value is 1 or -1. Suppose there are m distinct attributes in a dataset, mathematically, it is written as:

$$A = \{A_1, A_2, A_3, \ldots A_m\}$$
$$\text{such that} \quad A_i \in \{1, 0\} \tag{2}$$

Let O be the original face image from dataset and Oc be the original face image attribute label by detection module. Similarly, let P be the protected face image generated by image transform module and Pc be the protected face image attribute label by detection module.

Let Acc be the attribute label matching accuracy, which is defined as follow:

Definition 1 (Attribute Label Matching Accuracy).

$$Acc = \frac{S - (Oc \oplus Pc)}{S}$$
$$\text{such that } S = \sum A_i \tag{3}$$

For example, if A is composed of three attributes, namely $Black\_Hair$, $Male$ and $Young$, then $A = \{Male, Young, Black\_Hair\}$. In attribute $young$, a value of 1 means the age is young, and -1 means old. In attribute $male$, a value of 1 means the gender is male, and -1 means female. In attribute $Black\_Hair$, a value of 1 means the hair color is black, and -1 means other colors, such that blond, brown, and so on. Therefore, for an original image of a old woman with black hair, its attribute label is $\{0, 0, 1\}$, thus, $Oc = \{0, 0, 1\}$.

When we input Oc and fake image into the image transformation module, we will get the P and Pc. Then, we can calculate the attribute label matching accuracy Acc by Eq. 3. The higher the accuracy is, the more face attributes are retained in the original image. Follow the example given above, if $Pc = \{0, 0, 1\}$, the matching accuracy Acc is 100% according to the formula. This is the expected result, which shows that the sensitive information of the original image is effectively protected and the usability is also considered. However, if $Pc = \{0, 1, 1\}$, the matching accuracy Acc is only 66%, because of the error in detecting the attribute young.

In a word, the purpose of the model is to generate an fake image matching the face attributes of the original image. We hope that anonymous image can protect the privacy information of the original image, and maintain image utility.

3.2   Fake Image Generation Module

Our proposed method can generate a highly realistic and natural image which match the original face attributes. Therefore, in this module, we need to generate a number of non-existent fake faces.

DCGAN is a new architecture based on GAN. The network is stable in the training process and can achieve high quality image. Compared with GAN, DCGAN proposes four improvements. Firstly, convolution layer is used to replace pooling layer in traditional convolution neural network. For discriminator, strided convolution is used to replace pooling layer, while fractional-strided convolutions is used in generator, and the purpose is to enable the network to learn its own spatial upsampling and downsampling. Then the full connection layer is removed, which function in the conventional convolution neural network is to output the final vector, but with the deepening of the number of layers, the operation speed will be very slow. Then, batch normalization [7] is used to normalize the input of each layer, which can effectively make each unit obey the zero mean and unit variance, so as to speed up the training process and alleviate the situation of gradient disappearance. The last is to use the appropriate activation function, which can accelerate the learning process.

3.3   Image Transformation Module

In our proposed method, we need to generate a fake image matching the original image attribute label as much as possible, so it is an essential work to transform the attributes of the fake image output by the image generation module.

In the previous method, pip2pip [8] and CycleGAN [17] can complete the image transform of paired data and unpaired data respectively. However, in the task of multi domain label transform, CycleGAN is inefficient and time-consuming. The reason is that the transformation between any two domains needs to be trained separately. If we have three expression domains, namely, *happy*, *sad*, *neutral* and *angry*, to achieve the goal of multi domain transformation, we need to train two generators for each two domains, a total of 12 generators. Therefore, with the increase of the number of fields, the more generators are needed, and the generators with a large number of training are very resource consuming. StarGAN [3], which complete the task of multi domain transformation on the basis of only one generator, meet the needs of our method for image transform task.

3.4   Detection Module

We use the attribute detection algorithm of FaceAttribute [16], which uses *resnet*50 convolutional neural network to extract features of face attributes, and trains a classifier for each attribute.

The function of the module is to detect the facial attributes of the image. The output result is 1 and −1 of based on the two classifications for each label. For example, for the attribute male, if the input image is a female, the detection result is −1, otherwise it is 1. Due to the detection algorithm itself has errors, the accuracy rate is needed to measure the success rate of each attribute detection, the average detect accuracy is about 90%. In our model, this is one of the reasons why the matching degree between the final generated image and the original image label is less than 100%.

4   Experiment and Analysis

In this section, two sets of experiments were conducted to assess the effectiveness of the proposed method. First, the experiment of face attributes label matching is used to evaluate the utility of the proposed method. The more match of the attribute, the higher utility is. Second, similarity performance on challenging face datasets was used to evaluate the privacy preservation of the proposed method. The lower the similarity, the higher privacy preservation capability.

4.1   Experiment Setting

The dataset used in our method is the CelebFace Attributes (CelebA) Dataset [10], which contains 202599 face images, each of which contains 40 boolean attributes. 13 attributes and 21 attributes are selected as the content of face label matching experiment.

4.2   Utility Evaluation

In order to complete the task of image transform in batch, we first use the image generation module to generate a large number of fake images as our fake face datasets. Then 2000 fake images with high quality and rich style were selected as our test set, including 1000 for men and women respectively. In the image transform module, the original image attribute label and fake image are fed in turn to generate the protected image.

Some qualitative experimental results of 13 attributes and 21 attributes shown in the Fig. 5. No anonymization is the result of matching the original image attribte label which marked in the *list_attr_celeba.txt* with the label after detecting the original image in the Fig. 2, which show that the detection module itself has some detection errors, 88.4% in average. In addition, all zero represent the result of matching the original image attribute label with label of all zero, 67.0% in average, which means the worst result of attribute matching accuracy. On average, our method achieves 89.1% accuracy, 73.7% in pixelation, 74.0% in blur and 74.4% in mask. It is not difficult to find that the attribute matching accuracy of 21 attribute is slightly lower than that of 13 attribute in our proposed method. The more attributes to be compared, the greater the error in attribute conversion and detection, the worse the perception integrity of the newly generated anonymous image. Compared with the three traditional anonymization methods, our method greatly improves the usability needs of anonymized images.

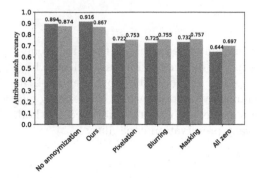 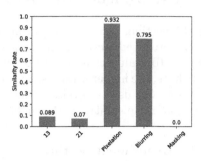

Fig. 2. Comparison of the accuracy of attribute matching between our proposed method and traditional methods.

Fig. 3. Comparison of the similarity between our proposed method and traditional methods such as pixelation, blurring masking

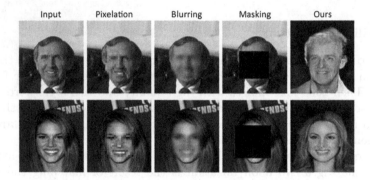

Fig. 4. Comparison of canonical image processing methods for face obfuscation, from left to right are pixelation, blurring, masking and generated by our model.

4.3   Privacy Evaluation

In the experiment of face similarity, we using a pretrained FaceNet model to evaluate the Euclidean distance between a set of real face images and a corresponding set of anonymous images [13]. When the distance is greater than a certain value, which is set to 1.1, two images are considered as different faces. This shows that the greater the distance between two faces, the smaller the similarity, otherwise, the larger the similarity.

We hope that the similarity between the original image and the anonymous image is as small as possible, the more difficult it is for the attacker or face recognition system to violate the identity information of the original image. In general, when the Euclidean distance threshold of our method is set to 1.1, Fig. 3 shows that among all the anonymous methods, the face similarity of our proposed method is less than 10% for both 13 attributes and 21 attributes, only 8.9% and 7.0% respectively. However, the image similarity of pixelation or blurring method

Fig. 5. Some experimental results. In each pair, the input image is the original image, the output1 and output2 are the results of conversion of 13 attributes and 21 attributes respectively. It should be noted that the more attributes in a face are changed, the more obvious the visual artifacts are.

is too high, up to more than 80%, to protect the sensitive information of the original image effectively. It is important to note that, FaceNet can't recognize face after masking anonymization, similarity cannot be calculated, as show in the Fig. 4. Overall, our proposed method has the best performance in protecting the identity privacy of the original image.

5   Conclusions

In order to maximize the utility of the original image and protect its identity privacy. We propose an image privacy protection model, which consists of three parts: detection module, fake image generation module and image transformation module. By generating a highly realistic and natural fake face matching the original image attributes, a qualitative and quantitative method is used to measure the performance of privacy protection and utility of the model. Our method successfully overcomes the shortcomings of the existing methods for utility deficiency, and can balance privacy protection and utility excellently.

References

1. Bertalmio, M., Sapiro, G., Caselles, V., Ballester, C.: Image inpainting. In: Proceedings of the 27th Annual Conference on Computer Graphics and Interactive Techniques, pp. 417–424. ACM Press/Addison-Wesley Publishing Co. (2000)
2. Boyle, M., Edwards, C., Greenberg, S.: The effects of filtered video on awareness and privacy. Environment **11**, 3 (2000)

3. Choi, Y., Choi, M., Kim, M., Ha, J.W., Kim, S., Choo, J.: StarGAN: unified generative adversarial networks for multi-domain image-to-image translation. In: Proceedings of the IEEE Conference on Computer Vision and Pattern Recognition, pp. 8789–8797 (2018)
4. Dufaux, F., Ebrahimi, T.: Video surveillance using JPEG 2000. Proc. SPIE Int. Soc. Opt. Eng. **5588**, 268–275 (2000)
5. Fan, L.: Image pixelization with differential privacy. In: Kerschbaum, F., Para-boschi, S. (eds.) DBSec 2018. LNCS, vol. 10980, pp. 148–162. Springer, Cham (2018). https://doi.org/10.1007/978-3-319-95729-6_10
6. Goodfellow, I.J., et al.: Generative adversarial nets. Stat **1050**, 10 (2014)
7. Ioffe, S., Szegedy, C.: Batch normalization: accelerating deep network training by reducing internal covariate shift. arXiv preprint arXiv:1502.03167 (2015)
8. Isola, P., Zhu, J.Y., Zhou, T., Efros, A.A.: Image-to-image translation with conditional adversarial networks. In: Proceedings of the IEEE Conference on Computer Vision and Pattern Recognition, pp. 1125–1134 (2017)
9. Lander, K., Bruce, V., Hill, H.: Evaluating the effectiveness of pixelation and blurring on masking the identity of familiar faces. Appl. Cogn. Psychol.: Off. J. Soc. Appl. Res. Mem. Cogn. **15**(1), 101–116 (2001)
10. Liu, Z., Luo, P., Wang, X., Tang, X.: Deep learning face attributes in the wild. In: Proceedings of the IEEE International Conference on Computer Vision, pp. 3730–3738 (2015)
11. Mcpherson, R., Shokri, R., Shmatikov, V.: Defeating image obfuscation with deep learning. arXiv: Cryptography and Security (2016)
12. Oh, S.J., Benenson, R., Fritz, M., Schiele, B.: Faceless person recognition: privacy implications in social media. In: Leibe, B., Matas, J., Sebe, N., Welling, M. (eds.) ECCV 2016. LNCS, vol. 9907, pp. 19–35. Springer, Cham (2016). https://doi.org/10.1007/978-3-319-46487-9_2
13. Schroff, F., Kalenichenko, D., Philbin, J.: FaceNet: a unified embedding for face recognition and clustering. In: Proceedings of the IEEE Conference on Computer Vision and Pattern Recognition, pp. 815–823 (2015)
14. Sun, Q., Ma, L., Joon Oh, S., Van Gool, L., Schiele, B., Fritz, M.: Natural and effective obfuscation by head inpainting. In: Proceedings of the IEEE Conference on Computer Vision and Pattern Recognition, pp. 5050–5059 (2018)
15. Sun, Q., Tewari, A., Xu, W., Fritz, M., Theobalt, C., Schiele, B.: A hybrid model for identity obfuscation by face replacement. arXiv Computer Vision and Pattern Recognition, pp. 570–586 (2018)
16. WynMew: Six face attributes predication from a single face image [CP/OL] (2019). https://github.com/WynMew/FaceAttribute
17. Zhu, J.Y., Park, T., Isola, P., Efros, A.A.: Unpaired image-to-image translation using cycle-consistent adversarial networks. In: Proceedings of the IEEE International Conference on Computer Vision, pp. 2223–2232 (2017)
18. Zhu, T., Yu, P.S.: Applying differential privacy mechanism in artificial intelligence. In: 2019 IEEE 39th International Conference on Distributed Computing Systems (ICDCS), pp. 1601–1609 (2019)

A Novel Color Image Encryption Scheme Based on Controlled Alternate Quantum Walks and DNA Sequence Operations

Ting Yan[✉] and Dan Li

College of Computer Science and Technology,
Nanjing University of Aeronautics and Astronautics, Nanjing 211106, China
1776811969401163.com

Abstract. The powerful storage function and convenient service function of cloud computing attract more and more users to save their digit image on the cloud server. However, the insecure data transmission process of cloud computing may lead to the disclosure of user privacy. At the same time, the existing machine learning algorithms do not consider the privacy and security of digit image in the application process. To solve the above problems, a novel color image encryption scheme based on controlled alternate quantum walks (CAQW) and DNA sequence operations is proposed. CAQW is used as a pseudo-random number generator (PRNG) to scramble pixel positions, and DNA encoding rule is used to replace the pixel value, and then the sequence of pseudo-random numbers generated by PRNG and DNA operation rules are used in two rounds of encryption of plaintext images. Our anlaysis and simulation show that this scheme can resist statistical analysis attack, differential attack and other attacks. In conclusion, the color image encryption scheme is robustness and efficient for protection of privacy image security.

Keywords: Cloud computing · Machine learning · Color image encryption · Quantum walks · Pseudo-random number generator · DNA sequence operations

1 Introduction

With the development of informatization, cloud computing has become a trend-leading new technology in the information industry due to its features of data centralization, resource sharing, high interconnection and full openness. However, cloud computing needs to deal with massive data, and the unsecure network transmission may bring severe security problems such as privacy leakage

Supported by NSFC (Grant Nos. 61701229, 6170236761901218), Natural Science Foundation of Jiangsu Province, China (Grant Nos. BK20170802BK20190407), China Postdoctoral Science Foundation funded Project (Grant Nos. 2018M630557, 2018T110499), Jiangsu Planned Projects for Postdoctoral Research Funds (Grant No. 1701139B), the Open Fund of the State Key Laboratory of Cryptology (Grant No. MMKFKT201914).

X. Chen et al. (Eds.): ML4CS 2020, LNCS 12486, pp. 297–306, 2020.
https://doi.org/10.1007/978-3-030-62223-7_25

to users [1]. Processing image data on the cloud is an important part of machine learning. However, the existing machine learning algorithms do not take into account the privacy and security of the data on the cloud. So the image data that is processed in machine learning needs to be encrypted [2].

Digital image has its own unique characteristics, such as large amount of data, high redundancy, strong correlation between pixels, which makes the traditional encryption method in image data processing inefficient and unsatisfactory. Most traditional algorithm, for example AES is not suitable for digital images [3]. Quantum walk is the quantum counterparts of classical random walks [9,10], which is extremely sensitive to initial parameters [11] and can be used as a pseudo-random number generator(PRNG) due to its inherent nonlinear chaotic dynamical behavior [8,12]. Furthermore, the security of controlled alternate quantum walks(CAQW)-based PRNG relies on the infinite possibilities of the initial state rather than the algorithmic complexity of the hard problems.

In order to improve the security of image encryption, many hybird algorithms have been proposed [7,13,14], ?. In recent years, DNA algorithm has attracted more attention because of its advantages, such as large-scale parallel computing, huge storage space and ultra-low power consumption [4–6]. The core of these schemes is DNA encryption and DNA operations, including some biological and algebraic operations on DNA sequences, such as DNA complementarity principle [7], DNA addition [14]. In this paper, DNA rules are used to encrypt image pixel values.

A new CAQW-based image encryption scheme is proposed in this paper to improve the security of encrypted images. This scheme combines permutation with substitution, breaking the relationship among R, G and B components, and designs a two-round encryption operation rule based on DNA algorithm. The paper is structured as follows. In Sect. 2, we introduce the CAQW and DNA rules as the preliminary. In Sect. 3, the image encryption and decryption scheme is described. Analysis results are given in Sect. 4. Finally, a short conclusion is given in Sect. 5.

2　Preliminaries

2.1　Controlled Alternate Quantum Walks

CAQWs [12] take place in the tensor product space $\mathcal{H}_p \bigotimes \mathcal{H}_c$. The evolution of the whole system at each step of the CAQW can be described by the global unitary operator, denoted by U,

$$U = \mathcal{S}_y(\mathcal{I} \bigotimes C)\mathcal{S}_x(\mathcal{I} \bigotimes C). \tag{1}$$

The coin operator C is a 2×2 unitary operator. S_x, S_y, are shift operators.

The final state of CAQWs is

$$|\psi_t\rangle = U(message)\psi_0 = \sum_{x,y} \sum_{\gamma \in \{\uparrow\downarrow\}} \lambda_{x,y,\gamma}|x,y,\gamma\rangle. \tag{2}$$

where $U(message)$ is the global unitary operator controlled by the message.

The probability of finding the walker at position (x, y) after t steps is

$$P(x, y, t) = \sum_{\gamma \in \{\uparrow\downarrow\}} | < x, y, \gamma | U(message) | \psi_0 \rangle |^2. \tag{3}$$

2.2 DNA Encoding and Decoding Rules

DNA sequence consists of four nucleic acid bases A (adenine), G (guanine), T (thymine) and C (cytosine). T and A are complementary, C and G are complementary. For binary signals, 0 and 1 are complementary, so 00 and 11 are complementary and 01 and 10 are complementary. 00, 01, 10 and 11 were coded with four bases A, C, G and T. Because of the complementary relationship between DNA bases, only eight coding combinations conform to the complementation rules, as shown in Table 1. DNA decoding is contrary to DNA coding.

Table 1. DNA encoding rules.

Rule	1	2	3	4	5	6	7	8
00	A	A	T	T	G	G	C	C
01	C	G	C	G	T	A	T	A
10	G	C	G	C	A	T	A	T
11	T	T	A	A	C	C	G	G

2.3 The Addition and Subtraction Operations for DNA Sequence

The addition and subtraction of DNA sequences are based on the traditional addition and subtraction in binary system. Therefore, eight DNA addition and subtraction rules correspond to eight DNA coding schemes. For example, we add [ACGT] and [CTAG] to a sequence [CAGC] using an addition operation shown in Table 2. Similarly, the sequence [CTAG] is obtained by subtracting the sequence [ACGT] from [CAGC].

Table 2. Addtion operation for DNA sequences.

+	A	C	G	T
A	A	C	G	T
C	C	G	T	A
G	G	T	A	C
T	T	A	C	G

3   Color Image Encryption and Decryption Scheme

In this section, we introduce the paremeters for the color image encryption and decryption scheme, which is as follows.

1) N_1, N_2 are the node number of a cycle, notice that, N_1, N_2 are all odd numbers;
2) θ_1, θ_2 are selected to determine the coin operation C_0, C_1 respectively, θ_1, $\theta_2 \in (0, \pi/2)$;
3) a and b are parameters of the initial coin state, $|a|^2 + |b|^2 = 1$, the initial state is $|\psi_0\rangle = |00\rangle(a|0\rangle + b|1\rangle)$;
4) *message* is selected to control every step of the CAQW;
5) k is used to transform the probability distribution obtained by the CAQW into a binary string of length $N_1 \times N_2 \times k$;
6) h is the number of iterations of the CAQW;
7) g is the initial nucleic acid base, $g \in \{A, C, G, T\}$;
8) α is the DNA encoding rule;
9) β is the DNA decoding rule.

So the key format is $(N_1, N_2, (\theta_1, \theta_2), (a, b), message, k, h, g, \alpha, \beta)$.

CAQW-based PRNG is the core of this scheme. Pixel positions are disturbed by circular alignment, and there are two directions (upper and left) to move. The pixel values are replaced with DNA addition rules. The algorithm can be divided into two phases: cyclic by in two directions and DNA sequence operation, as shown belows. The flowchart of encryption scheme is shown in Fig. 1.

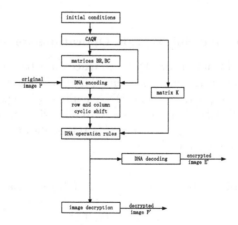

Fig. 1. Flowchart of the proposed encryption scheme.

Step 1. Initial conditions $(N_1, N_2, (\theta_1, \theta_2), (a, b), message, k, h, g, \alpha, \beta)$ is used by CAQW to get enough random numbers for subsequent processes.

1) Set the parameters $(N_1, N_2, (\theta_1, \theta_2), (a, b), message, k, h)$.

2) Run the CAQW under the control of the message. Each direction is a $N_1(N_2)$-length circle. θ_1, θ_2 are the parameters of the two coin operations respectively. The initial state is $|\psi_0\rangle$.

3) Multiply all the values in the obtained probability distribution by 10^8, then modulo 2^k to form a binary string as random numbers. The bit length of the hash value is $N_1 \times N_2 \times k$.

4) Use the last digit of the binary string as *message*, and the final state as the initial state of the next iteration of CAQW. Do this step h times to generate enough random numbers for subsequent image encryption.

Step 2. The pseudo-random sequences $\{x_i\}_{i=1}^L$, $\{y_i\}_{i=1}^L$, $\{z_i\}_{i=1}^L$, $\{w_i\}_{i=1}^L$, $L = 6 \times M \times N$ are obtained to decide the number of cyclic shift steps

$$BR_m = x_m, BC_n = y_n, \tag{4}$$

where BR_m decides the number of moves left or not in m-th row circularly, and BC_n decides whether column moves down in n-column circularly, where $m = 1, 2, \cdots, M$ and $n = 1, 2, \cdots, 12N$.

Step 3. The original RGB image P with the size of $M \times N \times 3$ is decomposed into R, G and B components. Then R, G and B are transformed into binary matrices BR, BG and BB of $M \times 8N$ size. And we combine them into a $M \times 24N$ matrix. Encode the matrix by DNA coding rule α. The DNA sequence matrix T with the size of $M \times 12N$ is obtained.

Step 4. Do rows circular shift and columns circular shift according to BR_m and BC_n. The rows shift result T' is obtained by followings rules. The m-th row of T is moved to left BR_m steps $m = 1, 2, \cdots, M$.

The columns shift S is obtained by following rules. The n-th column of T' is move up BC_n steps , $n = 1, 2, \cdots, 12N$.

Step 5. The pseudo-random number sequences $\{x_i\}_{i=1}^L$, $\{y_i\}_{i=1}^L$, $\{z_i\}_{i=1}^L$, $\{w_i\}_{i=1}^L$ obtained in Step 2 will be used to synthesize a sequence k, it is shown as

$$k(4i - 3) = x_i, \ k(4i - 2) = y_i, \ k(4i - 1) = z_i, \ k(4i) = w_i. \tag{5}$$

Step 6. The sequence k is transformed into matrix k' whose size is $M \times 24N$, and then the matrix k' is encrypted into a matrix K of size $M \times 12N$ by using DNA α encoding rules.

Step 7. DNA operations rules. Transforme the matrix K into sequence KD, the matrix S is transformed into sequence SD, they and known plaintext are used to encrypt the pixel value in two rounds. That is, DNA formulation matrices $E_1 = \{e_{1j}\}_{j=1}^{12MN}$, $E = \{e_j\}_{j=1}^{12MN}$ are calculated by

$$\begin{cases} E_1(1) = SD(1) + KD(1) + g, \\ E_j(1) = SD(j) + KD(j) + E_1(j - 1), \\ E(1) \ = E_1(1) + KD(1) + E_1(12MN), \\ E(j) \ = E_1(j) + KD(j) + E(j - 1), \end{cases} \tag{6}$$

where $j = 1, 2, \cdots, 12MN$, and '+' is the DNA additional operation. g is the initial nucleic acid base.

Step 8. DNA decoding. DNA decoding rules correspond to DNA coding rules, and the matrix E is decrypted by using DNA rule β and then recover RGB image to visualize the encryption image E.

The decryption scheme is contrary to the encryption scheme. The middle decryption result of DNA formulation matrix $F_1 = \{f_{1j}\}_{j=1}^{12MN}$, $F = \{f_j\}_{j=1}^{12MN}$ is recovered by

$$
\begin{cases}
F_1(j) = E(j) - KD(j) - E(j-1), \\
F_1(1) = E(1) - KD(1) - F_1(12MN), \\
F(j) = F_1(j) - KD(j) - F_1(j-1), \\
F(1) = F_1(1) - KD(1) - g,
\end{cases}
\tag{7}
$$

where $j = 1, 2, \cdots, 12MN$, and '$-$' is the DNA subtraction operation. The initial conditions in Step 1 of the encryption algorithm must be used here. And then cyclic step numbers BR_m and BC_n are generated by iterating the same initial conditions as Step 1. Finally, the decrypted image P' is restored by cyclic shift of matrix S. It is noteworthy that the direction of shift is opposite to the encryption process.

4   Analysis Results

Simulation is carried out on MATLAB 2016Ra, and the results are shown in Fig. 2. The color Lena image is used as the plaintext as shown in Fig. 2(a) with the size of 256×256×3. The key is set as $N_1 = N_2 = 49$, $\theta_1 = \pi/3$, $\theta_2 = \pi/5$, $a = b = \sqrt{1/2}, g =' A'$, $h = 41$, $k = 16$, $\alpha = 3$, $\beta = 3$, $message$ is converted from 'HELLOWORLDILOVETHEWORLD' to binary numbers. The encrypted Lena image and corresponding decrypted image are shown in Fig. 2(b) and Fig. 2(c) respectively.

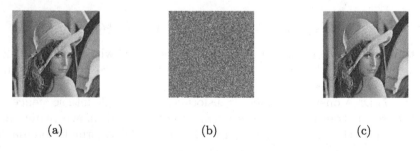

(a)   (b)   (c)

Fig. 2. (Color on line) Encryption and decryption results (a) original Lena image; (b) encrypted Lena image; (c) decrypted Lena image.

4.1   Key Space

The key space is one of the most important measures for image encryption. A good encryption algorithm should have enough key space. The security of CAQW-based PRNG relies on the infinite possibilities of the initial state rather than the algorithmic complexity of the hard problems. And the 2D position dimension of CAQW can be extended to higher dimensions position space, the higher the dimension of is, the larger the key space is, which shows that the key space of our proposed image encryption scheme can be large enough to resist brute force attack.

4.2   Statistical Analysis

Diffusion and confusion in cryptosystems are often used to destroy powerful statistical analysis. The histogram and correlation coefficients of two adjacent pixels are used to evaluate the ability of resistance to statistical attacks.

Histogram Analysis. Image histogram is widely used in image processing, which reflects the pixel gray distribution of image. A good encryption scheme should not display any relationship information between the original image and its encrypted version in the histogram. Histograms of the original Lena image and its encrypted image are shown in Fig. 3. Original image in R, G, B channel are shown in Fig. 3(a), 3(b), 3(c) respectively; encrypted image in R, G, B channel are shown in Fig. 3(d), 3(e), 3(f) respectively. From these configurations, it is clear that the histogram of the encrypted image is the uniform and significantly different from those of the original image.

Correlation Coefficient Analysis. Correlation Coefficient reflects the degree of similarity of two variables. An effective image encryption algorithm should produce an encrypted image with sufficiently low correlation in the horizontal, vertical, and diagonal directions. We use covariance(cov) to measure correlation coefficients between two adjacent pixels x and y, which is defined by the following expressions

$$\begin{cases} r_{xy} & = \frac{cov(x,y)}{\sqrt{D(x)D(y)}}, \\ cov(x,y) = E\{[x - E(x)][y - E(y)]\}, \\ E(x) & = \frac{1}{N}\sum_{i=1}^{N} x_i, \\ D(x) & = \frac{1}{N}\sum_{i=1}^{N}[x_i - E(x)]^2, \end{cases} \tag{8}$$

where N is the total number of pixels, and $E(x)$ and $E(y)$ are the means of x_i and y_i respectively. The correlation coefficients of the horizontal, vertical and diagonal adjacent pixels of the original Lena image and its encrypted image in R, G and B channels are listed in Table 3. This shows that the encryption effect is satisfactory.

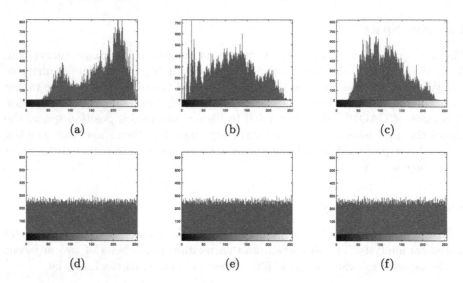

Fig. 3. (Color on line) Histograms of the original Lena image and its encrypted image. (a) Original image in R channel; (c) original image in G channel; (e) original image in B channel; (b) encrypted image in R channel; (d) encrypted image in G channel; (f) encrypted image in B channel.

Table 3. Correlation coefficients of the original and encrypted images in R, G, B channels.

Channels	Directions	Original image	Our algorithm	Ref. [3]	Ref. [13]	Ref. [14]
R channel	Horizontal	0.9447	0.0026	0.0031	−0.0127	0.0054
	Vertical	0.9680	0.0010	−0.0009	0.0067	0.0062
	Diagonal	0.9240	0.0023	0.0027	0.0060	0.0017
G channel	Horizontal	0.9318	0.0019	−0.0018	−0.0075	0.0059
	Vertical	0.9622	0.0025	0.0079	−0.0068	0.0016
	Diagonal	0.9081	0.0021	−0.0002	−0.0078	0.0029
B channel	Horizontal	0.8906	0.0015	0.0033	−0.0007	0.0013
	Vertical	0.9251	0.0028	−0.0049	0.0042	0.0022
	Diagonal	0.8703	0.0017	0.0015	0.0026	0.0004

4.3 Differential Attack

For an encryption algorithm, the ability to resist differential attacks is related to the sensitivity of the original image. By comparing and analyzing plaintext with specific differences, differential attacks attack the cryptographic algorithm by changing the propagation after encryption. It is evaluated by the number of pixels change rate (NPCR) and unified average changeing intensity (UACI). The formula of calculating NPCR and UACI are defined as

$$\begin{cases} NPCR_{R,G,B} = \frac{\sum_{i,j} D_{R,G,B}(i,j)}{L} \times 100\%, \\ UACI_{R,G,B} = \frac{1}{L}\sum_{i,j} \frac{|C_{R,G,B}(i,j) - C'_{R,G,B}|}{255} \times 100\%, \end{cases} \tag{9}$$

where L is the number of pixels in the image. $C_{R,G,B}$ and $C'_{R,G,B}$ are respectively encrypted images before and after one pixel of the original image is changed, and $D_{R,G,B}(i,j)$ is defined by

$$D_{R,G,B}(i,j) = \begin{cases} 1, & if C_{R,G,B}(i,j) \neq C'_{R,G,B}(i,j), \\ 0, & if C_{R,G,B}(i,j) = C'_{R,G,B}(i,j). \end{cases} \tag{10}$$

In the simulation we tried, we only change the lowest bit of one pixel of the plain image randomly. After 100 trials, the mean NPCRs and UACIs of the proposed algorithm are over 99.6 and 33.3 respectively. In other words, the proposed algorithm could resist plaintext attack and differential attack effectively.

5 Conclusion

In this paper, a new color image encryption algorithm based on controlled alternate quantum walks and DNA sequence operations is proposed. The pixel value of the original image is replaced by DNA sequence addition rules, and the position of the pixel is scrambling by two-way cyclic arrangement of pseudo-random sequence generated by CAQW-based PRNG. Analysis results show that the scheme has good encryption effect, which can resist statistical analysis attack and differential attack, etc. The security of CAQW-based PRNG relies on the infinite possibilities of the initial state rather than the algorithmic complexity of the hard problems. Therefore, with the participation of CAQW, the algorithm we proposed can ultimately guarantee the security of private images in the process of cloud computing and machine learning.

References

1. Pope, C.: Biometric data collection in an unprotected world: exploring the need for federal legislation protecting biometric data. JL Pol'y **26**, 769–771 (2018)
2. Li, P., Li, T., Ye, H., et al.: Privacy-preserving machine learning with multiple data providers. Future Gener. Comput. Syst. **87**, 341–350 (2018)
3. Zhang, L., et al.: A novel color image encryption scheme using fractionai-order hyperchaotic system and DNA sequence operations. Chin. Phys. B **26**, 100504 (2017). https://doi.org/10.1088/1674-1056/26/10/100504
4. Wang, X., et al.: Image encryption scheme based on Chaos and DNA plane operations. Multimed. Tools Appl. 9 (2019)
5. Ouyang, X., Luo, Y., Liu, J., et al.: A color image encryption method based on memristive hyperchaotic system and DNA encryption. Int. J. Mod. Phys. B **34**(4), 2050014 (2020)
6. Mohamed, H.G., ElKamchouchi, D.H., Moussa, K.H.: A novel color image encryption algorithm based on hyperchaotic maps and mitochondrial DNA sequences. Entropy **22**(2), 158 (2020)
7. Liu, H., Wang, X.: Image encryption using DNA complementary rule and chaotic maps. Appl. Soft Comput. **12**, 1457 (2012)

8. Abd El-Latif, A.A., Abd-El-Atty, B., Venegas-Andraca, S.E.: Controlled alternate quantum walk-based pseudo-random number generator and its application to quantum color image encryption. Phys. A **547**, 123869 (2019)
9. Childs, A.M., Gosset, D., Webb, Z.: Universal computation by multiparticle quantum walk. Science **339**, 791 (2013)
10. Lovett, N.B., Cooper, S., Everitt, M., Trevers, M., Kendon, V.: Universal quantum computation using the discrete-time quantum walk. Phys. Rev. A **81**, 042330 (2010)
11. Li, D., et al.: Discrete-time interacting quantum walks and quantum hash schemes. Quant. Inf. Proc. **12**, 1501–1513 (2012). https://doi.org/10.1007/s11128-012-0421-8
12. Li, D., et al.: Controlled alternate quantum walks based quantum hash function. Sci. Rep. **8**, 1–7 (2017). https://doi.org/10.1038/s41598-017-18566-6
13. Wang, X., Zhang, H.: A color image encryption with heterogeneous bit-permutation and correlated chaos. Opt. Commun. **342**, 52 (2015)
14. Wei, X., Guo, L.: A novel color image encryption algorithm based on DNA sequence operation and hyper-chaotic system. J. Syst. Softw. **85**, 290 (2012)

Cloud-Assisted Privacy Protection for Data Retrieval Against Keyword Guessing Attacks

Zhenwei Chen[1,2(✉)], Yinghui Zhang[1,2,3], Gang Han[1,2], Jiangyong He[1,2], Rui Guo[1,2,3], and Dong Zheng[1,2,3,4]

[1] School of Cyberspace Security, Xi'an University of Posts and Telecommunications, Xi'an 710121, China
czw0709@163.com, yhzhaang@163.com, hangang668866@163.com,
wrrhjyong@163.com, {guorui,zhengdong}@xupt.edu.cn
[2] National Engineering Laboratory for Wireless Security,
Xi'an University of Posts and Telecommunications, Xi'an 710121, China
[3] Westone Cryptologic Research Center, Beijing 100070, China
[4] Guangxi Cooperative Innovation Center of Cloud Computing and Big Data,
Guilin University of Electronic Technology, Guilin 541004, China

Abstract. Machine learning is more closely linked to data privacy and has obtained rapid development in recent years. As for data privacy, searchable encryption (SE) is widely used as a ciphertext search technology, protecting the privacy of users. However, existing schemes usually support single keyword search, so the remote cloud server (CS) may return some irrelevant results. To address this problem, we propose a server-aided public key encryption scheme with multi-keyword search (SA-PEMKS) scheme. The scheme allows a data user to conduct multiple keyword search in a single search query. Security and performance analysis show that the SA-PEMKS scheme is secure and efficient.

Keywords: Privacy · Public key encryption · Multiple keyword search · Server-aided

1 Introduction

Cloud storage has huge advantages and users can store data in a remote server such that the user's environment is connected to the network, and the data can be easily accessed [1,2]. Of course, cloud storage corresponds to cloud computing which has powerful computing capabilities. Combined with some machine learning algorithms, it can improve the user experience. As the amount of data increases, the optimization and improvement of deep learning algorithms, and significantly increased in computing power, machine learning technology will be the core of network security schemes [4]. Therefore, the combination of machine learning and cloud computing is an inevitable trend [8]. When data is outsourced to a remote cloud server, data owners need to encrypt their data to ensure data

© Springer Nature Switzerland AG 2020
X. Chen et al. (Eds.): ML4CS 2020, LNCS 12486, pp. 307–316, 2020.
https://doi.org/10.1007/978-3-030-62223-7_26

privacy [7,13,16,19,22,23,25,26,29]. So users need to retrieve data in cipher-texts. SE schemes are divided into symmetric encryption and asymmetric encryption. In 2000, Song et al. first put forward a searchable encryption scheme in symmetric form (SSE) [20]. Although the scheme is efficient, there is problem with key distribution. So Boneh et al. first constructed a public key searchable encryption scheme (PEKS) using bilinear mapping in [3], which avoids distribution of keys. Literature [14] proposed a fuzzy keyword query scheme using edit distance and wildcard technology, which overcomes the defect that the traditional schemes only support precise and single keyword query. In 2005, park et al. proposed a public key searchable encryption scheme that supports connection keyword retrieval, but the scheme does not support query of keyword subsets [18]. Many other related results can be found in [21,27,28].

For the above, if a scheme only supports single keyword search, this will undoubtedly return a large amount of irrelevant ciphertext data [5,12], which will consume a lot of computer system resources. According to the conjunctive keyword (that is, the file contains all queried keywords) schemes [10,11,17,24], users can quickly and accurately find files of interest.

Our Contribution. In this paper, we put forward a server-aided public key encryption with multiple keyword search scheme. Specifically, the SA-PEMKS scheme allows the user to issue conjunctive keyword search. This SA-PEMKS scheme is not only efficient in searching, but also brings a good operating experience to users. In terms of storage costs, the SA-PEMKS scheme do not increase the size of trapdoor and ciphertexts search. Next, the analysis of the security and performance of the SA-PEMKS scheme are introduced.

2   Preliminaries

2.1   Bilinear Pairing

We define two multiplicative cyclic groups G_1, G_2. The mapping function e is defined as $G_1 \times G_1 \to G_2$. g_0 is a generator of group G_1. If a mapping function has the following three characteristics, we call it bilinear mapping, the three characteristics are as follows: (1) Bilinear: $e(u^l, v^n) = e(u, v)^{ln}$, $\forall l, n \in_R Z_q^*$, $\forall u, v \in_R G_1$; (2) Non-degenerate: $e(g_0, g_0) \neq 1$. In group G_2, 1 is the identity element; (3) Computable: e can be easily calculated.

2.2   User-KS Protocol

Let's briefly describe this protocol, which consists of two parts. One is the User-KS interaction phase, and the other is the rate limiting phase. The implementation of this protocol requires the use of certificates. This protocol provides an irreplaceable verifiable certificate for KS and each user. In the first phase of the protocol, authentication between the user and the keyword server is performed, this phase runs on HTTP. The second phase of the protocol, the query reply phase, is executed in the UDP phase. Only when the user passes the authentication of the first stage can the execution of the protocol of the second stage be carried out. Specifically, the second stage returns a blind signature of a keyword, its called KS-derived ksd_w. Therefore, the execution of this User-KS interaction phase can ensure that the scheme can resist offline KGA. In the rate limiting phase, the frequency of user access to the system can be reduced, and the protocol is executed online, so the probability of successful online KGA attack can be reduced. The details of the User-KS protocol is in [6,9,31].

3   Construction of SA-PEMKS Scheme

In this section, we describe the detailed construction of the SA-PEMKS scheme. The bottom layer of this SA-PEMKS scheme is PEKS [3]. This SA-PEMKS scheme is more practical than the traditional SE schemes. Because most of the traditional SE schemes support single keyword search, to query multiple keyword, multiple rounds of query must be performed. The SA-PEMKS scheme enables users to search with multiple (conjunctive) keyword. The system model includes four entities, a data sender (DS), a data receiver (DR), a keyword server (KS) and a storage server (SS). During the scheme, the KS is separated from the SS. When a DR (or DS) needs to generate indexes or trapdoor, he first needs to interact with KS to preprocess keyword w as KS-derived ksd_w. Then we define a mapping function, namely: $\rho_1(\cdot)$ maps the keyword location in $ksd_{W'}$ (queried keyword set derived from KS) to the corresponding location in ksd_W (keyword dictionary derived from KS). The specific scheme is as follows:

3.1   Setup

In the system parameters generation stage, k is a security parameter, the system runs the Setup(1^k) algorithm to choose a tuple $<G_1, G_2, e, q, g>$, where the G_1, G_2 own the same primer order q and g is a generator of G_1. Then it chooses four hash functions, $\hat{H}$, H, H_1, H_2, where $\hat{H}$: $\{0,1\}^* \times G_1 \rightarrow \{0,1\}^*$ is a cryptographic collision-resistant hash function, H : $\{0,1\}^* \rightarrow G_1$, H_1 : $\{0,1\}^* \rightarrow Z_q^*$, H_2 : $G_2 \rightarrow \{0,1\}^{log\ q}$. Finally, it publishes the parameters $Para = \{q, e, G_1, g, G_2, \hat{H}, H, H_1, H_2\}$.

3.2   KeyGen

1. $SA\text{-}KeyGen_{KS}$: The algorithm randomly chooses a $\beta \in_R Z_q^*$ as the private key sk_{ks} and computes the $pk_{ks} = g^\beta$ as the public key. It outputs (pk_{ks}, sk_{ks}).
2. $SA\text{-}KeyGen_{DR}$: The algorithm randomly picks a $\alpha \in_R Z_q^*$ as the private key sk_{DR} and computes $pk_{DR} = g^\alpha$ as the public key. It outputs (pk_{DR}, sk_{DR}).

3.3   KS-Derived Keyword

For generating the KS-derived keyword ksd_w, DS (or DR) needs to interact with the KS (run as shown in Sect. 2.2). Then the user can calculate the correct signature σ_w on the keyword w. The KS-derived keyword protocol is as follows:

- Blinding: The user (DS or DR) computes $T = H(ID_{ks}, pk_{ks}, w)$, then randomly picks two elements $u, v \in Z_q^*$ and computes $V = g^v$, $\lambda = VT^u$, then sends the λ to KS.
- Signing: KS computes the $S_1 = \lambda^{sk_{ks}}$, then Then the user can get that value S_1 from KS.
- Unblinding: The user computes $S_2 = S_1(pk_{ks}^{-v})$, $\sigma_w = S_2^{u^{-1}} = T^\beta$. The σ_w is the final signature of w.

Then the user (DS or DR) computes $ksd_w = \hat{H}(w, \sigma_w) = \hat{H}(w, T^\beta)$ and outputs the ksd_w.

3.4   SA-PKES

When DR uploads a file, it needs to extract keywords from the file. Before uploading the SS, you need to encrypt the file and process the keywords to generate an index of its keywords. Our SA-PEMKS scheme allows DR to query multi-keyword (conjunctive) search. The ciphertext generation algorithm (as shown in Algorithm 1) is executed by DS, which will cause a large calculation burden on DS, but this is a one-time encryption.

Algorithm 1: Ciphertexts generation

Input: DR's public key, file set F and KS-derived keywords ksd_W.
Output: File ciphertexts CT, index I.
1 Given $F = \{f_1, \cdots, f_d\}$, $ksd_W = \{ksd_{w_1}, \cdots, ksd_{w_m}\}$;
2 **for** $1 \leq i \leq d$ **do**
3 $\quad$ Encrypt f_i as c_i by using a symmetric encryption algorithm (e.g., AES, DES);
4 $\quad$ Choose an element $x \in_R Z_q^*$;
5 $\quad$ **for** $1 \leq j \leq m$ **do**
6 $\quad\quad$ **if** $ksd_{w_j} \in f_i$ **then**
7 $\quad\quad\quad$ set $\mu_{i,j} = e(g^{H_1(ksd_{w_j})}, pk_{DR}^x)$;
8 $\quad\quad$ **else**
9 $\quad\quad\quad$ set $\mu_{i,j} = 1$;
10 $\quad$ compute $X_i = g^x$;
11 $\quad$ set $I_i = (X_i, \{\mu_{i,j}\})$;
12 return $CT = \{c_1, \cdots, c_d\}$, $I = \{I_1, \cdots, I_d\}$;

3.5 SA-Trapdoor

In this section, the queried keywords are derived from KS. Then DR generates the trapdoor of keyword before sending to the SS. Besides, users can query multiple keyword in one search. If there are more keywords in a file than they are queried, they can also be searched, and the size of the trapdoor generated is constant. The process of trapdoor generation is described in Algorithm 2.

Algorithm 2: Trapdoor generation

Input: DR's private key sk_{DR} and queried keywords $ksd_{W'}$.
Output: Trapdoor $T_{w'}$, the location L.
1 Given $ksd_{W'} = \{ksd_{w'_1}, \cdots, ksd_{w'_l}\}$;
2 **for** $1 \leq \tau \leq l$ **do**
3 $\quad$ compute $A_\tau = H_1(ksdw'_\tau)$;
4 $\quad$ finally, $T_{w'} = g^{(\Sigma^l_{\tau=1} A_\tau)\alpha}$;
5 return $T_{w'}$, $L = \{\rho_1(1), \cdots, \rho_1(l)\}$.

3.6 Search

In Algorithm 3, after receiving the trap door generated by the DR, the SS matches the trap door and the index stored in the SS, and if it matches, returns the related file to the DR, otherwise, stops matching.

Algorithm 3: Ciphertexts retrieval

Input: DR's public key pk_{DR}, trapdoor $T_{w'}$, index I, ciphertext CT and
$\qquad$ queried keyword locations L.
Output: Search result C'.
1 Given $T_{w'}$, $I = \{I_1, \cdots, I_d\}$, $L = \{\rho_1(1), \cdots, \rho_1(l)\}$;
2 **for** $1 \leq i \leq d$ **do**
3 $\quad$ **for** $1 \leq \tau \leq l$ **do**
4 $\quad\quad$ set $Init_0 = 1$;
5 $\quad\quad$ find $\mu_{i,\rho_1(\tau)}$;
6 $\quad\quad$ compute $Init_\tau = Init_{\tau-1} \cdot \mu_{i,\rho_1(\tau)}$;
7 $\quad$ check $H_2(e(T_{w'}, X_i)) = H_2(Init_\tau)$;
8 $\quad$ **if** Equation holds **then**
9 $\quad\quad$ $ksd_{W'} \in f_i$ and picks c_i;
10 $\quad$ **else**
11 $\quad\quad$ $ksd_{W'} \notin f_i$ and abort c_i;
12 return $C' = \{c'_1, \cdots, c'_q\}$, q mains the number of search results;

3.7   Correctness Verification

In this section, we describe the correctness of above scheme in Eq. (1):

$$
\begin{aligned}
e(T_{w'}, X_i) &= e(g^{(\Sigma_{\tau=1}^l A_\tau)\alpha}, g^x) \\
&= e(g^{(\Sigma_{\tau=1}^l A_\tau)}, g^{x\alpha}) \\
&= e(g^{(\Sigma_{\tau=1}^l A_\tau)}, pk_{DR}^x) \\
&= e(g^{A_{\rho_1(1)}}, pk_{DR}^x) \cdots e(g^{A_{\rho_1(l)}}, pk_{DR}^x) \\
&= Init_\tau
\end{aligned}
\tag{1}
$$

If $ksd_{W'} \subseteq ksd_W$, successful search.

Next, we verify the correctness of the signature of the Sect. 3.3, as shown in Eq. (2). If the equation $e(\sigma_w, g) = e(T, pk_{ks})$ holds, the user accepts the signature.

$$
\begin{aligned}
e(\sigma_w, g) &= e(S_2^{u^{-1}}, g) \\
&= e(((S_1(g^{-\beta v}))^{u^{-1}}, g) \\
&= e(((VT^u)^\beta (g^{-\beta v}))^{u^{-1}}, g) \\
&= e(((g^v T^u)^\beta (g^{-\beta v}))^{u^{-1}}, g) \\
&= e(((g^{\beta v} T^{\beta u})(g^{-\beta v}))^{u^{-1}}, g) \\
&= e((T^{\beta u})^{u^{-1}}, g) \\
&= e(T^\beta, g) \\
&= e(T, pk_{ks})
\end{aligned}
\tag{2}
$$

4   Security Analysis

The SA-PEMKS scheme is based on [3], this scheme only can resist CKA. By running the User-KS protocol, our SA-PEMKS scheme can resist the offline KGA. In addition, the security against the online KGA can be obtained by running the rate-limiting mechanism. The details are described in [6].

Here we consider three threat entities, an honest but curious KS, an adversarial SS and an adversarial DR, we assume that two servers can not collude. In SS entity, the goal of the adversarial SS is to break the unforgeability security of the BS scheme. When this scheme is running, because the adversary needs to interact with the KS, we believe that this protocol is run in an online manner. When the SS wants to know the information of a certain keyword, it is impossible to forge a signature. And when a user needs to generate a keyword ciphertext or trapdoor, the user first needs to query the blind signature $\hat{H}$ for the ksd_w, an adversary queried (w_b, σ_b) to the random oracle $\hat{H}$, if above not happens, that is, didn't ever query $\hat{H}$, then the scheme is identical to the original PEKS scheme [3]. So if a adversary wants to break the scheme, he must forgery a signature as (w_b, σ_b). In KS entity, due to the existence of this protocol, only users themselves can know private information. The goal of the adversarial KS is to break the blindness security of the BS scheme. When the adversary chooses two keywords to send to the system, the KS server acts as a malicious signer. The adversary starts the KS-derived keyword. So the adversary wants to know the information about the keyword, he must break the blindness of BS scheme. Next, we introduce the privacy of user, without the participation of the KS server, a user cannot forge a correct KS-derived signature. In the KS-derived keyword stage, an adversarial user wants to query a w to the signing oracle to obtain the signature as $\hat{H}(w, \sigma_w)$ as the KS-derived keyword. If adversary outputs q valid pairs (w_i, σ_i), for each i, the adversary look up w_i in hash query record for the corresponding signature σ_i and outputs as its forgery signatures, otherwise, aborts it. Base on above, if the blind signature scheme [31] is unforgeable and blind, then we say that this SA-PEMKS scheme is secure.

5 Performance Evaluation

In this section, we compare the computational complexity and storage costs between our SA-PEMKS scheme, CLKS scheme [30] and SCF-MCLPEKS scheme [15]. Firstly, we mainly introduce the time-consuming operations, E_1 denotes the exponentiation operation in group G_1, P denotes the pairing operation and T_H denotes the hash-to-point operation. We did not count the hash-to-point operation because it is too small. $|\mathcal{U}|$ denotes the number of data users, l denotes the number of queried keywords, m denotes the number of keywords for each file. Let $|G_1|$, $|G_2|$, $|Z_q|$ express the bit-length of element in groups G_1, G_2, Z_q, respectively. The computational complexity and storage costs are shown in Table 1 and Table 2, respectively.

5.1 Computational Complexity

Table 1. Computational complexity of various schemes

Algorithm	Scheme		
	SA-PEMKS	CLKS	SCF-MCLPEKS
KeyGen	$|\mathcal{U}|E_1$	$2|\mathcal{U}|E_1$	$|\mathcal{U}|E_1 + E_1$
Enc	$(m+2)E_1 + mP$	$(8+m)E_1$	$(3m+1)E_1 + 3mP + T_H$
Trapdoor	E_1	$(9+l)E_1$	lE_1
Search	$P + 2T_H$	$lP + 3P$	$l(2T_H + E_1 + P)$

In Table 1, we show the theoretical computational cost. We can see that in the Enc algorithm, although our scheme calculation cost is higher than the other two schemes, our scheme is practical and supports the connectability of keywords.

In other algorithms, our SA-PEMKS scheme is efficient. For example, the calculated consumption of trapdoor and search in the SA-PEMKS scheme are constant, they are E_1, $P + 2T_H$, but the other two schemes are influence on the number of keywords queried.

5.2 Storage Costs

Table 2. Storage costs of various schemes

Algorithm	Scheme		
	SA-PEMKS	CLKS	SCF-MCLPEKS
KeyGen	$|\mathcal{U}|(|Z_q| + |G_1|)$	$|\mathcal{U}|(2|Z_q| + 2|G_1|)$	$(|\mathcal{U}| + 1)(|G_1| + |Z_q|)$
Trapdoor	$|G_1|$	$l|G_1| + 3|G_1| + |Z_q|$	$l|G_1|$
Search	$2|log\ q|$	$(2 + l)|G_2|$	$l|G_2|$

In Table 2, we compare the storage costs of those three schemes in KeyGen, Trapdoor, Search algorithms. We can see that SA-PEMKS scheme has the smallest storage space in each partial algorithm.

In short, the SA-PEMKS scheme is relatively efficient overall. For example, in the trapdoor generation, the efficiency is higher than the CLKS and SCF-MCLPEKS schemes and its the same in search.

6   Conclusion

About this paper, we propose a SA-PEMKS scheme, which can allow a user to issue multi-keyword in a single query, which can improve user experience for increasing search accuracy. In addition, the scheme has constant trapdoor size and ciphertexts retreval size. The scheme in this paper can resist offline/online KGA under the oracle model, and is feasible in practical application scenarios.

Acknowledgment. This work was supported by National Key R&D Program of China (Grant No. 2017YFB0802000), National Natural Science Foundation of China (Grant No. 61772418, 61802303), Innovation Capability Support Program of Shaanxi (Grant No. 2020KJXX-052), Shaanxi Special Support Program Youth Top-notch Talent Program, Key Research and Development Program of Shaanxi (Grant No. 2019KW-053, 2020ZDLGY08-04), Natural Science Basic Research Plan in Shaanxi Province of China (Grant No. 2019JQ-866), Guangxi Cooperative Innovation Center of Cloud Computing and Big Data (Grant No. YD1903), Basic Research Program of Qinghai Province (Grant No. 2017GZDZX0002) and Sichuan Science and Technology Program (Grant No. 2020-ZJ-701). Yinghui Zhang is supported by New Star Team of Xi'an University of Posts and Telecommunications (Grant No. 2016-02).

References

1. Armbrust, M., et al.: A view of cloud computing. Commun. ACM **53**(4), 50–58 (2010)
2. Berman, D.S., Buczak, A.L., Chavis, J.S., Corbett, C.L.: A survey of deep learning methods for cyber security. Information **10**(4), 122 (2019)
3. Boneh, D., Di Crescenzo, G., Ostrovsky, R., Persiano, G.: Public key encryption with keyword search. In: Cachin, C., Camenisch, J.L. (eds.) EUROCRYPT 2004. LNCS, vol. 3027, pp. 506–522. Springer, Heidelberg (2004). https://doi.org/10.1007/978-3-540-24676-3_30
4. Buczak, A.L., Guven, E.: A survey of data mining and machine learning methods for cyber security intrusion detection. IEEE Commun. Surv. Tutor. **18**(2), 1153–1176 (2015)
5. Chai, Q., Gong, G.: Verifiable symmetric searchable encryption for semi-honest-but-curious cloud servers. In: 2012 IEEE International Conference on Communications (ICC), pp. 917–922. IEEE (2012)
6. Chen, R., et al.: Server-aided public key encryption with keyword search. IEEE Trans. Inf. Forensics Secur. **11**(12), 2833–2842 (2016)
7. Deng, Z., Li, K., Li, K., Zhou, J.: A multi-user searchable encryption scheme with keyword authorization in a cloud storage. Future Gener. Comput. Syst. **72**, 208–218 (2017)
8. Ford, V., Siraj, A.: Applications of machine learning in cyber security. In: Proceedings of the 27th International Conference on Computer Applications in Industry and Engineering (2014)
9. Keelveedhi, S., Bellare, M., Ristenpart, T.: Dupless: server-aided encryption for deduplicated storage. In: Presented as Part of the 22nd {USENIX} Security Symposium ({USENIX} Security 13), pp. 179–194 (2013)
10. Li, H., Liu, D., Dai, Y., Luan, T.H., Shen, X.S.: Enabling efficient multi-keyword ranked search over encrypted mobile cloud data through blind storage. IEEE Trans. Emerg. Top. Comput. **3**(1), 127–138 (2014)
11. Li, H., Yang, Y., Luan, T.H., Liang, X., Zhou, L., Shen, X.S.: Enabling fine-grained multi-keyword search supporting classified sub-dictionaries over encrypted cloud data. IEEE Trans. Dependable Secure Comput. **13**(3), 312–325 (2015)
12. Li, J., Shi, Y., Zhang, Y.: Searchable ciphertext-policy attribute-based encryption with revocation in cloud storage. Int. J. Commun. Syst. **30**(1), e2942 (2017)
13. Li, J., Yao, W., Zhang, Y., Qian, H., Han, J.: Flexible and fine-grained attribute-based data storage in cloud computing. IEEE Trans. Serv. Comput. **10**(5), 785–796 (2016)
14. Li, J., Wang, Q., Wang, C., Cao, N., Ren, K., Lou, W.: Fuzzy keyword search over encrypted data in cloud computing. In: 2010 Proceedings IEEE INFOCOM, pp. 1–5. IEEE (2010)
15. Ma, M., He, D., Kumar, N., Choo, K.K.R., Chen, J.: Certificateless searchable public key encryption scheme for industrial internet of things. IEEE Trans. Industr. Inf. **14**(2), 759–767 (2017)
16. Miao, Y., Ma, J., Liu, X., Weng, J., Li, H., Li, H.: Lightweight fine-grained search over encrypted data in fog computing. IEEE Trans. Serv. Comput. **12**(5), 772–785 (2018)
17. Miao, Y., Ma, J., Wei, F., Liu, Z., Wang, X.A., Lu, C.: VCSE: verifiable conjunctive keywords search over encrypted data without secure-channel. Peer-to-Peer Netw. Appl. **10**(4), 995–1007 (2017)

18. Park, D.J., Kim, K., Lee, P.J.: Public Key encryption with conjunctive field keyword search. In: Lim, C.H., Yung, M. (eds.) WISA 2004. LNCS, vol. 3325, pp. 73–86. Springer, Heidelberg (2005). https://doi.org/10.1007/978-3-540-31815-6_7

19. Shen, J., Liu, D., Liu, Q., Sun, X., Zhang, Y.: Secure authentication in cloud big data with hierarchical attribute authorization structure. IEEE Trans. Big Data (2017)

20. Song, D.X., Wagner, D., Perrig, A.: Practical techniques for searches on encrypted data. In: Proceeding 2000 IEEE Symposium on Security and Privacy, S&P 2000, pp. 44–55. IEEE (2000)

21. Wu, A., Zheng, D., Zhang, Y., Yang, M.: Hidden policy attribute-based data sharing with direct revocation and keyword search in cloud computing. Sensors **18**(7), 2158 (2018)

22. Wu, D., Liu, Q., Wang, H., Wu, D., Wang, R.: Socially aware energy-efficient mobile edge collaboration for video distribution. IEEE Trans. Multimed. **19**(10), 2197–2209 (2017)

23. Wu, D., Si, S., Wu, S., Wang, R.: Dynamic trust relationships aware data privacy protection in mobile crowd-sensing. IEEE Internet Things J. **5**(4), 2958–2970 (2017)

24. Yang, Y., Ma, M.: Conjunctive keyword search with designated tester and timing enabled proxy re-encryption function for e-health clouds. IEEE Trans. Inf. Forensics Secur. **11**(4), 746–759 (2015)

25. Zhang, R., Xue, R., Liu, L., Zheng, L.: Oblivious multi-keyword search for secure cloud storage service. In: 2017 IEEE International Conference on Web Services (ICWS), pp. 269–276. IEEE (2017)

26. Zhang, Y., Chen, X., Li, J., Li, H., Li, F.: Attribute-based data sharing with flexible and direct revocation in cloud computing. KSII Trans. Internet Inf. Syst. **8**(11) (2014)

27. Zhang, Y., Deng, R.H., Shu, J., Yang, K., Zheng, D.: TKSE: trustworthy keyword search over encrypted data with two-side verifiability via blockchain. IEEE Access **6**, 31077–31087 (2018)

28. Zhang, Y., et al.: Privacy-preserving data aggregation against false data injection attacks in fog computing. Sensors **18**(8), 2659 (2018)

29. Zhang, Y., Zheng, D., Deng, R.H.: Security and privacy in smart health: efficient policy-hiding attribute-based access control. IEEE Internet Things J. **5**(3), 2130–2145 (2018)

30. Zheng, Q., Li, X., Azgin, A.: CLKS: certificateless keyword search on encrypted data. NSS 2015. LNCS, vol. 9408, pp. 239–253. Springer, Cham (2015). https://doi.org/10.1007/978-3-319-25645-0_16

31. Zuo, L., Xia, P., Chen, Z.: An efficient short blind signature scheme. Comput. Eng. **45**(6), 1–8 (2019). in Chinese

Deep Learning Algorithms Design and Implementation Based on Differential Privacy

Xuefeng Xu[1] , Yanqing Yao[1,2,3(✉)] , and Lei Cheng[4]

[1] Key Laboratory of Aerospace Network Security,
Ministry of industry and information technology,
School of Cyberspace Science and Technology, Beihang University,
Beijing 100191, China
{xuxf100,yaoyq}@buaa.edu.cn
[2] State Key Laboratory of Software Development Environment, Beihang University,
Beijing 100191, China
[3] Beijing Key Laboratory of Network Technology, Beihang University, Beijing, China
[4] Shenzhen Research Institute of Big Data,
Shenzhen 518000, People's Republic of China
leicheng@sribd.cn

Abstract. Deep learning models bear the risks of privacy leakage. Attackers can obtain sensitive information contained in training data with some techniques. However, existing differentially private methods such as Differential Privacy-Stochastic Gradient Descent (DP-SGD) and Differential Privacy-Generative Adversarial Network (DP-GAN) are not very efficient as they require to perform sampling multiple times. More importantly, DP-GAN algorithm need public data to set gradient clipping threshold. In this paper, we introduce our refined algorithms to tackle these problems. First, we employ random shuffling instead of random sampling to improve training efficiency. We also test Gaussian and Laplace Mechanisms for clipping gradients and injecting noise. Second, we employ zero Concentrated Differential Privacy (zCDP) to compute overall privacy budget. Finally, we adopt dynamical gradient clipping in DP-GAN algorithm. During each iteration, we random sample training examples and set the average gradients norm as the new threshold. This not only makes the algorithm more robust but also doesn't increase the overall privacy budget. We experiment with our algorithms on MNIST data sets and demonstrate the accuracies. In our refined DP-SGD algorithm, we achieve test accuracy of 96.58%. In our refined DP-GAN algorithm, we adopt the synthetic data to train models and reach test accuracy of 91.64%. The results show that our approach ensures model usability and provides the capability of privacy protection.

Keywords: Differential privacy · Deep learning · SGD · GAN

X. Chen et al. (Eds.): ML4CS 2020, LNCS 12486, pp. 317–330, 2020.
https://doi.org/10.1007/978-3-030-62223-7_27

1 Introduction

Nowadays, deep learning has achieved great success in many areas such as computer vision, natural language processing, etc. This mainly thanks to large amounts of data. However, public data typically contain sensitive information. For instance, facial images, incomes, clinical data and so on. Publishing these data is likely to cause privacy leakage. Therefore, how to ensure data privacy is an urgent problem in deep learning. Researchers have proposed some attack models (e.g., Model Inversion [6], Membership Inference [14], and Model Extraction Attack [15]). Attackers can effectively obtain private information by these methods. Therefore, deep learning models should have the ability of privacy protection. In recent years, many researchers have employed differential privacy [4] to protect privacy. Differential privacy, introduced by Dwork in 2006, is a privacy protection standard that does not require specific attack assumptions or care about the background knowledge of attackers. Based on differential privacy, some methods have been proposed (e.g., [1,2,13,16,17]).

In 2015, Shokri et al. [13] designed a differentially private method called Distributed Selective Stochastic Gradient Descent (DSSGD) for distributed collaborative learning. Each participant trains a model on local data and periodically upload gradients to the server. But the overall privacy budget is proportional to the size of the model, which could be about a few millions [9]. In 2016, Abadi et al. [1] proposed state-of-the-art DP-SGD algorithm and adopted Moments accountant (MA) to calculate the overall privacy budget. This algorithm employs random sampling while training neural networks. Subsequently, to improve training efficiency, Yu et al. [16] adopt random shuffling instead of random sampling. More recently, some researchers [2,17] adopted differential privacy in Generative Adversarial Networks (GAN) [7] to synthesize data. These data are very similar to the original and they could be shared with others without concern about privacy issues. In order to achieve training scalability and stability, Zhang et al. [17] assumed that they can access small amounts of public data called D_{pub} to initialize model and set clipping threshold. However, this is not common in practice. If we couldn't get the D_{pub}, we have to split training data and set part of them as the D_{pub}.

In this paper, our motivation is twofold: (1) to improve training efficiency when employing differentially private algorithms, and (2) to perform dynamical gradients clipping only use the training data.

Our techniques and contributions are as follows.

First, we adopt random shuffling instead of random sampling to improve training efficiency (same as in [16]). Recall that the original DP-SGD algorithm [1] adopts random sampling. In each round of iteration, they random sample a fixed number of training data. And then, they perform gradient clipping and noise injecting. However, since sampling is required during every iteration, training efficiency is not guaranteed. Therefore, here we adopt random shuffling instead. At the beginning of each epoch, the training data are randomly shuffled and divided into batches. We make use of these batches to perform gradient clipping and noise injecting. That means we only need to shuffle the training data once in each epoch, instead of sampling many times.

Second, we test injecting Laplace and Gaussian noise in DP-SGD algorithm. To the best of our knowledge, no previous work has tested these two different noise both. So we test them separately. That is, using different gradient clipping methods, then injecting different noise. We adopt zCDP to calculate privacy budgets of these two different mechanisms. We implement our refined DP-SGD algorithm and experiments with MNIST data sets. On the CNN model, the test accuracies achieves 96.58% for injecting Laplace noise and 95.84% for Gaussian noise.

Subsequently, we employ our improved DP-SGD in DP-GAN algorithm [17], and weaken the assumption of dynamic gradient clipping by estimate the clipping threshold only use the training data. The original DP-GAN algorithm assumes that there are a small number of public data sets. They make use of them to initialize model and set clipping threshold. However, we can't always obtain public data in practice. And we can't guarantee that public data and training data are from the same distribution. Therefore, we adopt sampling method to set clipping threshold. During each iteration, we randomly sample some training data and calculate the gradient norm as the new clipping threshold. The refined adaptive gradient clipping can make GAN training more robust and does not increase the overall privacy budget. We also adopt our refined DP-GAN algorithm on MNIST data sets. Using the synthetic data to train models, we achieve test accuracy up tp 91.64%.

In summary, our research contributions are listed below.

- We adopt random shuffling instead of random sampling to improve training efficiency of DP-SGD algorithm.
- We test Laplace and Gaussian Mechanisms separately during gradients clipping and noise injecting.
- We employ zCDP to estimate accumulated privacy budget and present the formulas of the two mechanisms.
- We refine the adaptive gradient clipping procedure by dynamically estimating clipping threshold only using the training data.

The rest of this paper is organized as follows. Section 2 provides some preliminaries. In Sect. 3, we present the detail of differential privacy algorithms and the method for calculating the overall privacy budget. Section 4 reports the experimental results on the MNIST data sets. Finally, we conclude in Sect. 5.

2 Preliminaries

2.1 Some Related Concepts of Deep Learning

Deep learning is a branch of machine learning, which learns features from layers. "Deep" means multiple layers, model usually contains dozens of layers or more in practice. Common neural network structures are Multi-Layer Perceptron

(MLP) [12], Convolutional Neural Network (CNN) [11], and Recurrent Neural Network (RNN) [8].

Gradient descent is adopted to train neural networks: setting initial values for weights W randomly, then in each iteration, calculating gradients ∇_W to update W until convergence. α is learning rate.

$$W \leftarrow W - \alpha \cdot \nabla_W L \tag{1}$$

GAN was proposed by Goodfellow et al. [7], the model has two neural networks called Generator (G) and Discriminator (D) (see Fig. 1). z is the random noise, $x^* = G(z)$ is the fake data generated by G, and x is the true data. We train D to distinguish the data is x or x^*. We train G to learn the distribution of x, then transform noise z to x^*. During training, both G and D gradually increase their abilities. In the end, the fake data x^* generated by G will be very similar to the true data x , even D will not distinguish them well.

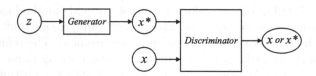

Fig. 1. GAN model

There are two neural networks in GAN called G and D, we need to train them alternately. In other words, G and D play the following two-player minimax game with value function $V(G, D)$:

$$\min_G \max_D V(G, D) = E_{x \sim p(x)}[\log D(x)] + E_{z \sim p(z)}[\log(1 - D(G[z]))] \tag{2}$$

Furthermore, G and D have different loss functions, defined as follows.

$$L_G = \frac{1}{m} \sum_{i=1}^{m} \log(1 - D(G[z_i]))$$
$$L_D = -\frac{1}{m} \sum_{i=1}^{m} [\log D(x_i) + \log(1 - D(G[z_i]))] \tag{3}$$

2.2   Some Related Concepts and Theorems of Differential Privacy

Definition 1 *(see [5]). Algorithm M is (ϵ, δ)-DP if for all neighboring data sets D_1, D_2, and for all output $S \subseteq Range(M)$,*

$$\Pr[M(D_1) \in S] \leq \exp(\epsilon) \cdot \Pr[M(D_2) \in S] + \delta \tag{4}$$

If $\delta = 0$, algorithm M satisfies ϵ-DP.

The definition shows that no matter a single record in the data sets or not, the probability of algorithm M's output doesn't change significantly. The parameter ϵ determines the similarity of output results on neighboring data sets. Smaller ϵ means higher similarity, thus provides a strong ability of privacy protection.

By injecting Laplace or Gaussian noise, we can implement Laplace Mechanism (ϵ-DP) or Gaussian Mechanism ((ϵ, δ)-DP). As for controlling the scale of noise, i.e., consider the trade-off between privacy and usability, the sensitivity is a key parameter. It defines the maximum change between two neighboring data sets.

Definition 2 *(see [5]). For all neighboring data sets D_1 and D_2, the sensitivity of function f is defined as follows (L_1 norm for Laplace Mechanism and L_2 norm for Gaussian Mechanism).*

$$\Delta_1(f) = \max \parallel f(D_1) - f(D_2) \parallel_1$$
$$\Delta_2(f) = \max \parallel f(D_1) - f(D_2) \parallel_2 \tag{5}$$

If adding Laplace noise with scale $\lambda = \Delta_1/\epsilon$, it provides ϵ-DP. If injecting Gaussian noise with scale $N(0, \sigma^2)$, for $\sigma \geq c\Delta_2/\epsilon$ and $c^2 > 2\ln(1.25/\delta)$, it satisfies (ϵ, δ)-DP [5].

One important property of differential privacy is: given an algorithm that satisfies ϵ-DP, no matter what additional processing performs on the output of the algorithm, the post-processing step still satisfies ϵ-DP [5].

In many cases, we need to adopt algorithm on each small subset of data and do iteration. For example, in deep learning, we usually arrange data into batches and use them for training many times. Therefore, here are two useful composition theorems in ϵ-DP, which help us compute the overall privacy budget easily. Composition theorems in (ϵ, δ)-DP is similar to ϵ-DP and they are not given here due to limited space.

Theorem 1 *(see [10]). Each algorithm M_i satisfies ϵ_i-DP and applied on data sets D. The combined algorithm $M = (M_1(D), \ldots, M_n(D))$ satisfies $(\sum_i \epsilon_i)$-DP.*

Theorem 2 *(see [10]). Each algorithm M_i satisfies ϵ_i-DP and applied on disjoint data sets $D_i \subseteq D$. $D_i \cap D_j = \varnothing$, which $i \neq j$. The combined algorithm $M = (M_1(D_1), \ldots, M_n(D_n))$ satisfies $(\max \epsilon_i)$-DP.*

In order to provide tight estimate of overall privacy budget, Bun et al. [3] proposed zCDP. It is a variant of differential privacy which provides improved composition theorems.

Definition 3 *(see rm [3]). Algorithm M is (ξ, ρ)-zCDP if for all neighboring data sets D_1, D_2, and for all $\alpha \in (1, \infty)$,*

$$\mathcal{D}_\alpha(M(D_1) \parallel M(D_1)) \leq \xi + \rho\alpha \tag{6}$$

where $\mathcal{D}_\alpha(M(D_1) \parallel M(D_1))$ is the α-Rényi divergence between the distribution of $M(D_1)$ and $M(D_2)$. They further define $(0, \rho)$-zCDP as ρ-zCDP.

If adding Gaussian noise with scale $N(0, \sigma^2)$, it provides $(\Delta^2/2\sigma^2)$-zCDP.

Bun et al. [3] also give a relationship between DP and zCDP. If M satisfies ϵ-DP, then it also provides $\frac{1}{2}\epsilon^2$-zCDP. Furthermore, if M satisfies ρ-zCDP, it is also $(\rho + 2\sqrt{\rho \ln(1/\delta)}, \delta)$-DP for any $\delta > 0$.

3   Models and Algorithms

3.1   Injecting Noise to Gradients

In this section, we first present the refined DP-SGD algorithm and test two mechanisms (Laplace and Gaussian). We then adopt zCDP to calculating the overall privacy budget and present the formulas.

In the original DP-SGD algorithm proposed by Abadi et al. [1], they randomly sample some training examples then compute the gradients. This provides convenience for MA calculation of overall privacy budget. However, it's not efficient for training. In our refined DP-SGD (see Algorithm 1), we employ random shuffling instead of random sampling. In each training epoch, we split training data into batches and feed each batch of data into the neural network. At the end of the epoch, we shuffle the training data and put them into batches again. The same data batching method was also employed in [16].

Algorithm 1: Differential Privacy SGD (DP-SGD)

Input: Training examples $X = \{x_1, x_2, ..., x_M\}$, lables $Y = \{y_1, y_2, ..., y_M\}$, loss function L, epoch numbers E, batch size m, learning rate α, gradients clipping threshold C, Gaussian noise scale σ and Laplace noise scale λ.

Output: Weights W.

```
 1  Initialize W randomly
 2  for n = 1 to E do
 3  │   for each batch training examples do
 4  │   │   for i = 1 to m do
 5  │   │   │   g_i ← ∇_W L(x_i, y_i, W)
 6  │   │   │   if Choose Gaussian Mechanism then
 7  │   │   │   │   ḡ_i ← g_i/ max(1, ||g_i||_2/C)
 8  │   │   │   else
 9  │   │   │   │   ḡ_i ← g_i/ max(1, ||g_i||_1/C)
10  │   │   │   end
11  │   │   end
12  │   │   if Choose Gaussian Mechanism then
13  │   │   │   g̃ ← (1/m)(Σ_i ḡ_i + N(0, C²σ²I))
14  │   │   else
15  │   │   │   g̃ ← (1/m)(Σ_i ḡ_i + Lap(CλI))
16  │   │   end
17  │   │   W ← W − α · g̃
18  │   end
19  │   shuffle(X)
20  end
21  return W
```

Our refined DP-SGD algorithm contains three procedures. First of all, we divide training data into batches and calculating gradient of every single training example (see step 5). Then, we clip each gradient by L_1 (Laplace Mechanism) or L_2 (Gaussian Mechanism) norm (see step 7 or 9). Finally, we add Laplace or Gaussian noise and average the perturbed gradients to update the weights (see step 13 or 15).

For Gaussian Mechanism, we clip each gradient by L_2 norm to be no greater than C (see step 7 of Algorithm 1). So the sensitivity Δ_2 equals to C. In step 13, we inject Gaussian noise with scale $N(0, C^2\sigma^2)$. Owing to $\Delta_2 = C$, this step provides $\frac{1}{2\sigma^2}$-zCDP. In one epoch, the training data in each batch are disjoint. According to Theorem 2, each epoch satisfies $\frac{1}{2\sigma^2}$-zCDP. Also, the entire training process contains E epochs. During each epoch, we use the same training data. By Theorem 1, the overall Gaussian Mechanism of Algorithm 1 provides $\frac{E}{2\sigma^2}$-zCDP.

The analysis of privacy budget for Laplace Mechanism is similar to Gaussian Mechanism. In step 9 of Algorithm 1, we clip each gradient by L_1 norm. This step sets the sensitivity Δ_1 equal to C. In step 15, we inject Laplace noise with scale $\text{Lap}(C\lambda)$ which provides $\frac{1}{\lambda}$-DP. Therefore, the overall algorithm satisfies $\frac{E}{\lambda}$-DP. Then, in order to unify the two mechanisms, we map ϵ-DP to ρ-zCDP. Thus, Laplace Mechanism of Algorithm 1 satisfies $\frac{E^2}{2\lambda^2}$-zCDP.

3.2 Data Synthesis

In the previous section, we present refined DP-SGD algorithm to train neural networks. However, the model can access sensitive training data which still bear potential risks. In this section, we employ DP-GAN algorithm [17] to generate new data from the original. And model can only access the generated data. These synthetic data can be released and used for model training. The idea depicts in Fig. 2. Due to the post-processing property [5], differential privacy provides theoretically privacy guarantee for the generated data. Another advantage is that we can perform data synthesis beforehand. Thus we can simplifies the training process.

Fig. 2. DP-GAN model

GAN need good training methods. Otherwise, it will not get good results. According to the principles of GAN, we divide the training process into three steps.

Step 1: Using the true data x to train the Discriminator and updating the weights W_D.

Step 2: Producing random noise z and generating the fake data x^*. Then, using x^* to train the Discriminator and updating the weights W_D.

Step 3: Using the fake data x^* to train the Generator and updating the weights W_G (maintain W_D).

More concretely, the above processes are described in Algorithm 2 (see the double slashes). Only in **Step 1**, we can access the training data. So the differential privacy protection only adopted here. We employ our refined DP-SGD in Algorithm 2.

Algorithm 2: Differential Privacy GAN (DP-GAN)

Input: Training examples $X = \{x_1, x_2, ..., x_M\}$, random noise Z, Generator's loss function L_G, Discriminator's loss function L_{D_real} and L_{D_fake}, epoch numbers E, batch size m, sample ratio r, Gaussian noise scale σ and Laplace noise scale λ.

Output: Generator G.

1 Initialize W_G and W_D randomly
2 **for** $n = 1$ *to* E **do**
3   **for** *each batch training examples* **do**
        // Step 1: Train the Discriminator using x
4          $X_s \leftarrow sampling(X, r)$
5          $g_c \leftarrow \nabla_W L(X_s, W)$
6   **if** *choose Gaussian Mechanism* **then**
7             $C \leftarrow \|g_c\|_2$
8   **else**
9             $C \leftarrow \|g_c\|_1$
10   **end**
11   **for** $i = 1$ *to* m **do**
12            $g_i \leftarrow \nabla_W L(x_i, W)$
13   **if** *choose Gaussian Mechanism* **then**
14               $\bar{g}_i \leftarrow g_i / \max(1, \|g_i\|_2 / C)$
15   **else**
16               $\bar{g}_i \leftarrow g_i / \max(1, \|g_i\|_1 / C)$
17   **end**
18   **end**
19   **if** *choose Gaussian Mechanism* **then**
20            $\tilde{g}_{D\_real} \leftarrow \frac{1}{m}(\sum_i \bar{g}_i + N(0, C^2\sigma^2 I))$
21   **else**
22            $\tilde{g}_{D\_real} \leftarrow \frac{1}{m}(\sum_i \bar{g}_i + Lap(C\lambda I))$
23   **end**
24         $W_D \leftarrow W_D - Adam(\tilde{g}_{D\_real})$
        // Step 2: Train the Discriminator using x*
25         $X^* \leftarrow G(Z)$
26         $g_{D\_fake} \leftarrow \nabla_{W_D} L_{D\_fake}(X^*, W_D)$
27         $W_D \leftarrow W_D - Adam(g_{D\_fake})$
        // Step 3: Train the Generator using x*
28         $g_G \leftarrow \nabla_{W_G} L_G(X^*, W_G)$
29         $W_G \leftarrow W_G - Adam(g_G)$
30   **end**
31   shuffle(X)
32 **end**
33 **return** G

During the minimax game between the Generator and Discriminator, the change of gradient values are relatively large. So it is difficult to set a fixed gradient clipping threshold in advance. On the one hand, if we set a small value, we may lose important gradient information which will result in slow convergence. On the other hand, if we set a high threshold, large noise will be injected. Each of the two choices will lead to poor performance of GAN model. Therefore, modifying the algorithm to set a dynamic threshold is a natural choice.

It should be noted that Zhang et al. [17] propose a method to monitor the magnitude of gradients during training. And they set the clipping threshold based on the average gradients. They assume that the GAN can access private data called D_{pri}, and also have access to a small amount of public data called D_{pub}. They use D_{pri} to train the model and D_{pub} to set the clipping threshold. However, we can't always obtain such D_{pub} data in practice. And we can't always guarantee D_{pub} and D_{pri} are from the same distribution.

In our refined algorithm, we adopt the dynamic clipping method and also make some improvements. Instead of using public data D_{pub}, we only use the training data to set the clipping threshold. Before clipping the gradients, we randomly sample a small number of training examples (sampling ratio r, see step 4). Then, we calculate gradients of these samples (see step 5) and set the average as the new clipping threshold (see steps 7 and 9).

Even if we set the threshold dynamically, the privacy budget will not increase due to the sensitivity Δ equals to the clipping threshold C. So Gaussian Mechanism satisfies $\frac{E}{2\sigma^2}$-zCDP and Laplace Mechanism satisfies $\frac{E^2}{2\lambda^2}$-zCDP (using the same formulas as in the previous section).

4   Experimental Results

On MNIST data sets, we conduct experiments of our refined DP-SGD and DP-GAN algorithms. And we adopt TensorFlow framework to build MLP, CNN and GAN models.

4.1   DP-SGD

We evaluate Algorithm 1 on MLP and CNN models. The specific layer settings of models are in Table 1.

The parameters of DP-SGD algorithm are set as follows: batch size $m = 256$, epoch number $E = 30$, gradient clipping threshold $C_{Gau} = 1.0$ and $C_{Lap} = 0.1$, noise scale $\sigma = 1.1$ and $\lambda = 6$. According to the formulas, Gaussian Mechanism satisfies ρ_1-zCDP ($\rho_1 \approx 12.4$) and Laplace Mechanism satisfies ρ_2-zCDP ($\rho_2 = 12.5$). Accuracies after training for 30 epochs are in Table 2.

As we can see the accuracies in Table 2. Due to the noise is injected to gradients, the accuracies of MLP and CNN models trained by DP-SGD algorithm are both lower than trained by SGD algorithm. This is an inherent property of differential privacy: to protect privacy, we have to lose some accuracy.

Table 1. Parameters setting of MLP and CNN models

Model	Layer	Shape	Setting
MLP	Input	(None, 28, 28)	–
	Flatten	(None, 784)	–
	Dense	(None, 128)	a = relu
	Dense	(None, 64)	a = relu
	Softmax	(None, 10)	–
CNN	Input	(None, 28, 28, 1)	–
	Conv2D	(None, 24, 24, 32)	f = 32, k = 5, s = 1, a = relu
	MaxPooling2D	(None, 8, 8, 32)	f = 32, k = 3, s = 3
	Conv2D	(None, 4, 4, 64)	f = 64, k = 5, s = 1, a = relu
	MaxPooling2D	(None, 2, 2, 64)	f = 64, k = 2, s = 2
	Flatten	(None, 256)	–
	Dense	(None, 200)	a = relu
	Softmax	(None, 10)	–

Table 2. Accuracies of MLP and CNN models after training 30 epochs

Algorithm	Train accuracy	Test accuracy
SGD	MLP: 100.0%, CNN: 99.99%	MLP: 97.89%, CNN: 99.19%
Gau-DP-SGD	MLP: 93.08%, CNN: 95.57%	MLP: 92.70%, CNN: 95.84%
Lap-DP-SGD	MLP: 93.05%, CNN: 96.41%	MLP: 93.19%, CNN: 96.58%

4.2 DP-GAN

By DP-GAN algorithm, we can generate new data. However, these data don't contain labels. In supervise learning, data labels are necessary to compute values of loss function. In order to label these data, we first group the original data by their labels. Each group of data is trained by DP-GAN to generate new data. According to the group tags, we can easily label these new data. Then, we put them together to construct the synthetic data sets (see Fig. 3). The specific layer settings of Generator and Discriminator are in Table 3.

We adopt Algorithm 2 to generate new data. The parameters of DP-GAN are set as follows: batch size $m = 256$, epoch number $E = 5$, sampling ratio $r = 0.1$, noise scale $\sigma = 0.224$ and $\lambda = 0.5$. According to the formulas, Gaussian Mechanism satisfies ρ_3-zCDP ($\rho_3 \approx 49.8$), Laplace Mechanism provides ρ_4-zCDP ($\rho_4 = 50$).

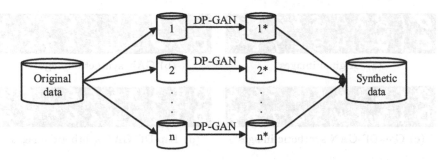

Fig. 3. Data synthesis

We train original GAN and then DP-GAN by Laplace and Gaussian Mechanisms respectively. After that, we employ the corresponding Generator to synthesis new data. The original and synthetic images are demonstrated in Fig. 4. The generated images are very similar to the original. Also, the DP-GAN generated images contain some noise. Using the original and synthetic data, we train MLP and CNN models respectively. Test accuracies after training for 30 epochs are in Table 4.

Table 3. Parameters setting of generator and discriminator

Model	Layer	Shape	Setting
Generator	Input	(None, 100)	–
	Dense	(None, 12544)	–
	Reshape	(None, 7, 7, 256)	–
	Conv2DTranspose	(None, 14, 14, 128)	f = 128, k = 3, s = 2, p = same
	BatchNormalization	(None, 14, 14, 128)	–
	LeakyRelu	(None, 14, 14, 128)	$\alpha = 0.01$
	Conv2DTranspose	(None, 14, 14, 64)	f = 64, k = 3, s = 1, p = same
	BatchNormalization	(None, 14, 14, 64)	–
	LeakyRelu	(None, 14, 14, 64)	$\alpha = 0.01$
	Conv2DTranspose	(None, 28, 28, 1)	f = 1, k = 3, s = 2, p = same, a = tanh
Discriminator	Input	(None, 28, 28, 1)	–
	Conv2D	(None, 14, 14, 32)	f = 32, k = 3, s = 2, p = same
	LeakyRelu	(None, 14, 14, 32)	$\alpha = 0.01$
	Conv2D	(None, 7, 7, 64)	f = 64, k = 3, s = 2, p = same
	BatchNormalization	(None, 7, 7, 64)	–
	LeakyRelu	(None, 7, 7, 64)	$\alpha = 0.01$
	Conv2D	(None, 3, 3, 128)	f = 128, k = 3, s = 2, p = same
	BatchNormalization	(None, 3, 3, 128)	–
	LeakyRelu	(None, 3, 3, 128)	$\alpha = 0.01$
	Flatten	(None, 1152)	–
	Sigmoid	(None, 1)	–

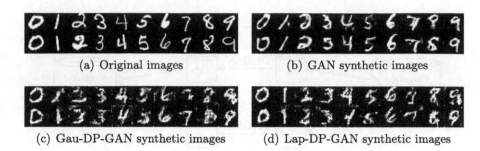

(a) Original images   (b) GAN synthetic images

(c) Gau-DP-GAN synthetic images   (d) Lap-DP-GAN synthetic images

Fig. 4. Original and synthetic images of MNIST

Table 4. Test accuracies of MLP and CNN models after training 30 epochs

Training data	Test accuracy
Original data	MLP: 97.89%, CNN: 99.19%
GAN synthetic data	MLP: 75.88%, CNN: 93.66%
Gau-DP-GAN synthetic data	MLP: 75.15%, CNN: 87.92%
Lap-DP-GAN synthetic data	MLP: 76.14%, CNN: 91.64%

While using the synthetic data to train the MLP model, we didn't get a good result. We think this relate to the layer settings of GAN model. To improve the quality of synthetic data, we employ convolutional layers in the Generator (see Table 3). In other words, the synthetic picture is generated by convolutional layers. However, the MLP model doesn't have these layers. So it may not capture these information to get good accuracy.

5   Conclusion

In this paper, we revisit the privacy leakage in deep learning and adopt differential privacy to tackle this problem. Based on the method of injecting noise to gradients, we simulate the DP-SGD algorithm using Gaussian mechanism and make some improvement. Then we propose an algorithm using Laplace mechanism. Also, we refine the algorithm to improve efficiency: employing random shuffling instead of random sampling. We then adopt zCDP to estimate the overall privacy budget. Moreover, we also employ GAN to synthesize training data. The idea is injecting noise to gradients when using real data to train the Discriminator. We also refined the algorithm to set gradient clipping threshold dynamically. During each iteration, randomly select some training examples, then set the average gradients norm as the new threshold. This not only makes the GAN model more robust, but also doesn't increase the overall privacy budget. We believe that our approaches provide excellent tools for privacy-preserving deep learning. In future research, we plan to adopt Local Differential Privacy (LDP) and study privacy issues in Federated Learning.

Acknowledgment. The above work was supported by Beijing Municipal Natural Science Foundation (Grant No. 4202035), the Fundamental Research Funds for the Central Universities (Grant No. YWF-20-BJ-J-1040), the National Key R & D Program of China (Grant No. 2016QY04W0802), the National Natural Science Foundation of China (Grant No. 61602025, U1636211, and 61170189), and Open Research Fund from Shenzhen Research Institute of Big Data (No. 2019ORF01012).

References

1. Abadi, M., et al.: Deep learning with differential privacy. In: Proceedings of the 2016 ACM SIGSAC Conference on Computer and Communications Security, Vienna, Austria, 24–28 October 2016, pp. 308–318 (2016)
2. Beaulieu-Jones, B.K., et al.: Privacy-preserving generative deep neural networks support clinical data sharing. Circ.: Cardiovas. Qual. Outcomes **12**(7), e005122 (2019)
3. Bun, M., Steinke, T.: Concentrated differential privacy: simplifications, extensions, and lower bounds. In: Hirt, M., Smith, A. (eds.) TCC 2016. LNCS, vol. 9985, pp. 635–658. Springer, Heidelberg (2016). https://doi.org/10.1007/978-3-662-53641-4_24
4. Dwork, C., McSherry, F., Nissim, K., Smith, A.: Calibrating noise to sensitivity in private data analysis. In: Halevi, S., Rabin, T. (eds.) TCC 2006. LNCS, vol. 3876, pp. 265–284. Springer, Heidelberg (2006). https://doi.org/10.1007/11681878_14
5. Dwork, C., Roth, A.: The algorithmic foundations of differential privacy. Found. Trends Theor. Comput. Sci. **9**(3–4), 211–407 (2014)
6. Fredrikson, M., Jha, S., Ristenpart, T.: Model inversion attacks that exploit confidence information and basic countermeasures. In: Proceedings of the 22nd ACM SIGSAC Conference on Computer and Communications Security, Denver, CO, USA, 12–16 October 2015, pp. 1322–1333 (2015)
7. Goodfellow, I.J., et al.: Generative adversarial nets. In: Advances in Neural Information Processing Systems 27: Annual Conference on Neural Information Processing Systems 2014, 8–13 December 2014, Montreal, Quebec, Canada, pp. 2672–2680 (2014)
8. Hochreiter, S., Schmidhuber, J.: Long short-term memory. Neural Comput. **9**(8), 1735–1780 (1997)
9. Jayaraman, B., Evans, D.: Evaluating differentially private machine learning in practice. In: Heninger, N., Traynor, P. (eds.) 28th USENIX Security Symposium, USENIX Security 2019, Santa Clara, CA, USA, 14–16 August 2019, pp. 1895–1912. USENIX Association (2019)
10. Kairouz, P., Oh, S., Viswanath, P.: The composition theorem for differential privacy. IEEE Trans. Inf. Theory **63**(6), 4037–4049 (2017)
11. LeCun, Y., et al.: Backpropagation applied to handwritten zip code recognition. Neural Comput. **1**(4), 541–551 (1989)
12. Minsky, M., Papert, S.A.: Perceptrons: An Introduction to Computational Geometry. MIT Press, Cambridge (1969)
13. Shokri, R., Shmatikov, V.: Privacy-preserving deep learning. In: Proceedings of the 22nd ACM SIGSAC Conference on Computer and Communications Security, Denver, CO, USA, 12–16 October 2015, pp. 1310–1321 (2015)
14. Shokri, R., Stronati, M., Song, C., Shmatikov, V.: Membership inference attacks against machine learning models. In: 2017 IEEE Symposium on Security and Privacy, SP 2017, San Jose, CA, USA, 22–26 May 2017, pp. 3–18 (2017)

15. Tramér, F., Zhang, F., Juels, A., Reiter, M.K., Ristenpart, T.: Stealing machine learning models via prediction APIs. In: 25th USENIX Security Symposium, USENIX Security 16, Austin, TX, USA, 10–12 August 2016, pp. 601–618 (2016)
16. Yu, L., Liu, L., Pu, C., Gursoy, M.E., Truex, S.: Differentially private model publishing for deep learning. In: 2019 IEEE Symposium on Security and Privacy, SP 2019, San Francisco, CA, USA, 19–23 May 2019, pp. 332–349. IEEE (2019)
17. Zhang, X., Ji, S., Wang, T.: Differentially private releasing via deep generative model. arXiv preprint arXiv:1801.01594 (2018), http://arxiv.org/abs/1801.01594

Building Undetectable Covert Channels Over Mobile Networks with Machine Learning

Xiaosong Zhang[1], Ling Pang[2(✉)], Linhong Guo[1], and Yuanzhang Li[3]

[1] Department of Computer Science and Technology, Tangshan University,
Tangshan 063000, China
[2] National Key Laboratory of Science and Technology on Information System
Security, Beijing 100101, China
pangling_nkl@163.com
[3] School of Computer Science and Technology, Beijing Institute of Technology,
Beijing 100081, China

Abstract. Covert channel is an important way to transmit covert message and implement covert communication through the network. However, the existing research on covert channel cannot meet the security requirements of covert communication in the complex mobile networks. There are problems such as low transmission capacity, insufficient adaptability to network complexity, and difficulty in countering the detection of covert channels by adversaries. In this paper, we preprocess video traffics over mobile network, and extract traffic features to build a target model. We analysis traffic data by machine learning method to improve the undetectability of the covert channel. Based on the characteristics of real-time interactive communication, gray code and interval block are employed to improve the robustness of covert communication in the complex network environment. A cover channel over VoLTE video traffic, which is based on video packet reordering supported by machine learning algorithms, is proposed to realize the awareness and confrontation of detection attacks on the network side. The covert channel is built over mobile network to ensure end-to-end reliable covert communication under complex network conditions.

Keywords: Covert channel · Machine learning · Mobile networks · Undetectability

1 Introduction

With the widespread application of high-speed mobile networks and the rise of applications such as remote collaboration of network systems. The mobile network has made great progress in both packet rate and bandwidth. The performance of mobile devices can support device users to make full use of mobile resources. Smart devices enable users to achieve high-quality and high-data-rate

© Springer Nature Switzerland AG 2020
X. Chen et al. (Eds.): ML4CS 2020, LNCS 12486, pp. 331–339, 2020.
https://doi.org/10.1007/978-3-030-62223-7_28

communications. In this case, online voice and video calling through real-time interactive applications over mobile network are increasingly popular.

In the 4G mobile network and the upcoming 5G network, the data transmission rate of real-time interactive communication is much higher than in the past. The network environment and application environment of the mobile network have brought challenges to the construction of efficient covert timing channels. Existing IPD-based covert channel research cannot adapt to the new challenges that the mobile network environment poses to covert channel performance, nor can it give full play to the advantages of mobile network. The complex network environment of real-time voice and video services of the mobile network requires the covert channel to be adaptive, and the high-data-rate communication challenges the undetectability of the traditional covert channels.

Based on covert channel information carrier, the covert channel can be roughly divided into covert storage channel (CSC) and covert timing channel (CTC). The covert storage channel refers to that the sender of the covert channel modifies the channel storage characteristics by pre-constraining rules to embed covert message, and the receiver observes the corresponding changes in the storage characteristics to restore the covert message [1]. The covert timing channel is generally modulated by selecting the time characteristics that can be observed by the receiver, such as system events, performance and behavior in the transmission process of the network channel to transmit covert message [2–10]. In the narrow sense, the covert timing channel specifically refers to a type of covert channel that modulates the inter-packet delay (IPD) during transmission [11–13]. It is also called a IPD-based covert channel. Network transmission noise is an important factor that affects the performance of IPD-based covert channel, mainly including network jitter, packet loss, and packet out of order. When designing the covert channel scheme, the main consideration is how to eliminate or mitigate the impact of the disturbance.

The network covert timing channel detection scheme initially uses a mathematical statistical analysis algorithm to identify covert channels and try to extract covert messages based on changes in channel indicators. With the continuous development of machine learning technology, related theories and statistical knowledge have been continually fused. The field of information security is increasingly utilizing machine learning algorithms to resolve different analysis and detection problems [14]. In recent years, there have been proposed many covert channel detection schemes which are based on statistical schemes and employ various machine learning algorithms. In addition, the covert channel detection schemes are usually highly targeted for detection based on the way the covert message is embedded and the characteristics of the embedded data according to a special scheme. Our solution is inspired by these detection scheme. The machine learning algorithms are applied to the modulation process when constructing the covert timing channel based on real-time interactive applications over mobile network. In order to improve the undetectability of the covert channel to resist the adversary from identifying the covert channel and stealing covert message.

Our contribution is to propose a method that uses machine learning algorithms to assist in the construction of the video traffic covert channel over VoLTE. Since the number of video packets within the interval of voice packets is random, covert message can be modulated into the number of video packets. In order to improve the undetectability of the covert channel, machine learning algorithms are used to detect the autocorrelation of the current video traffic, and the embedding rhythm is adjusted by a trade-off factor to reduce the distribution difference between covert traffic and overt traffic. At the same time, Gray code encoding and interval blocks are used to improve the robustness of the covert channel.

2   Preliminaries

The packet rate of video traffic is much higher than that of general data traffic, which makes the inter-packet delay relatively small, and the randomness is small. It indicates that the inter-packet delay may be seriously affected by network jitter. Although it is possible to overcome this problem by artificially increasing the inter-packet delay, how to bypass the monitoring of the adversary to transmit covert message is a tricky problem.

The selection of the covert channel carrier must ensure the robustness and distribution redundancy of the basic transmission layer corresponding to the traditional channel physical layer. Unlike the inter-packet delay, the number of packets in a small interval of video traffic will not change during the data transmission unless packet loss occurs, and it is completely insensitive to network jitter, thus ensuring that the covert message is extracted losslessly by the covert channel receiver. In order to achieve an effective covert communication, the distribution of the number of interval packets should not be single, and while occupying most of the video traffic, there must be more than two numbers of interval packets that are consistent and continuous. During a video calling, voice signals and video signals need to be transmitted at the same time. Affected by factors such as code rate, content, and number of frames, the numbers of packets carrying the two signals are usually different. Moreover, there is no obvious regularity in the relative distribution of voice packets and video packets. This meets the basic requirements of covert communication.

3   Covert Channel Construction

3.1   System Model

The system model considered in this work consists of senders and receivers who wish to deliver covert message over the LTE network. To this end, we use machine learning methods to optimize the modulation process to establish a robust and undetectable covert channel over VoLTE video traffic. Here, covert communication refers to communication using channels embedded with covert message and overt communication means that the channel used for communication is not

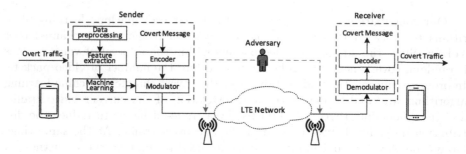

Fig. 1. System model of the proposed covert channel

embedded with covert message. The traffic corresponding to two different channels is called covert traffic and overt traffic. Figure 1 shows the system model of
the covert channel, which shows the traffic from the sender to the receiver.

3.2   Traffic Analysis Based on Machine Learning

Today's network monitoring systems need to cope with increasing data rates and
process large amounts of data in a short time. The analysis method must be fast
and light. Therefore, the proposed method is based on data aggregation, simple
conversion, fast calculation, and inference rules derived from cross-comparison.
In this work, we will use the feature set obtained from such estimations and calculations for the analysis of covert timing channels, which involves aggregation,
basic statistics, autocorrelation and multimodality estimation.

Traffic Preprocessing. After obtaining overt traffic and covert traffic, the
packet information and related traffic time information are preprocessed to pre-
pare for the next steps. In the raw traffic data, there are a lot of messy data that
may even cause deviations in the data mining results. These messy data may
cause deviations in the data mining results. Therefore, it is necessary to use the
knowledge of network security and network protocol to restrain to reduce a lot
of meaningless information. We must preprocess the collected raw traffic data.
First, we extract the attributes and fields related to the mining target, and then
discard the dirty data with problematic or incomplete data. Finally, we obtain
the abnormal traffic attributes with obvious characteristics in the data mining
module to improve the efficiency of later analysis and mining.

Feature Extraction. The feature extraction module is the core of data processing and can find the most effective features from the original features to
represent the overt traffic. On the one hand, feature extraction and optimization
can reduce data storage and data redundancy. On the other hand, the classification of data in low dimensions tends to be higher, which is more conducive

to discovering more meaningful latent variables, helping machine learning algorithms to understand the data in depth and obtain the potential knowledge in the original data for classification [15].

Feature extraction involves various relevant time factors that may be used to build covert channels. Inspired by Iglesias et al. [16], Eq. 1 can be used to express the calculation and estimation performed for each traffic.

$$Traffic\_vec = \{N, P_i, \mu_{S_P}, p_M, \rho_A, n_p, \mu_{\Delta_D}, C\} \tag{1}$$

Where N is the number of unique values, in our case, it represents the number of different n_i. P_i is the number of multimodality distribution peaks obtained by kernel density estimation, that is, the number of prominent peaks that can be observed in the curve fitting the n_i histogram. μ_{S_P} is the mean of the standard deviation of P_i peaks, by which the average distribution width can be calculated. p_M represents the number of packets that matches the Mode. ρ_A is the sum of autocorrelation coefficients, that is, taking the n_i sequence as a time series, and evaluating the autocorrelation to check whether the difference can be detected. n_p is the total number of packets in this traffic. μ_{Δ_D} is the mean of differences of inter-packet delay, where $\Delta_D = time[k] - time[k-1]$, and $time[k]$ represents the capture time of packet k. Finally, assuming that the traffic contains covert channels, C estimates the number of bits of potentially covert message.

If we regard the characteristic data values of communication traffic as a time series, then in terms of autocorrelation, covert traffic is different from overt traffic since the characteristic data value usually follow the autocorrelation pattern, and breaking this pattern implies that there may be covert channels. The autocorrelation coefficient has also been used to detect covert channels previously.

Feature Extraction. The traffic analysis in this paper is a binary classification problem. The traffic analysis model is a description method used to distinguish normal traffic from abnormal traffic. The analysis method is to label the traffic to be analyzed as normal or abnormal based on the analysis model. In machine learning, we can train multiple different models with different algorithms and different parameters, so we will face model selection. We use the cross-validation method for model selection. For models of different complexity, we choose the model with the smallest prediction error for the validation set. Since the validation set has enough data, it is effective to use it to select the model. The training process refers to the process of building a traffic analysis model using machine learning algorithms. After comparing three classification algorithms: decision tree, random forest, and GBDT (Gradient Boost Decision Tree), we decided to adopt GBDT as the deployment algorithm for this work, because its accuracy and recall rate are higher than other classification algorithms.

Generating Trade-Off Parameter. The trade-off parameters of the covert channel are generated under the combined action of predefined rules and machine learning algorithms. We extract statistical information from network traffic capture, and study the difference between overt traffic and covert traffic. The trade-off parameters are given in time to adjust traffic features to resist detection of covert channels.

3.3 Encoding and Modulation

If the trade-off factor f calculated by the machine learning method is 1, the interval block size is a fixed value bs. If there are video packets in the first voice packet interval in the current interval block, the video packet is moved to the next voice interval. That is to say, if there is no video packet in the first voice interval of the interval block, it means that the covert message is not embedded in the current interval block.

If the trade-off factor f is 0, the size of the interval block s_i and the number of embedded bits l_i are determined according to the number n_i of data packets in the voice packet interval, where $s_i = a*n_i$, and a is the adjustment coefficient, which can be changed according to the network environment changes. If there is no video packet in the first voice packet interval in the current interval block, the video packet in the next interval is moved to the first voice interval. In other words, the receiver judges whether covert message is embedded in the current interval block according to whether there are video packets in the first voice interval.

The sender counts the video packets in the current interval block, and the counted video packets vn_i are converted into block values bv_i by performing a modulo operation on 2^{l_i}, and then the block values bv_i and the Gray value gv_i calculated by l_i bits obtained from the secret information using Gray code is compared. If the gv_i is equal to the bv_i, no modulation is required; if the gv_i is greater than the bv_i, the $gv_i - bv_i$ video packets in the next interval block will be moved to the current interval block; If the gv_i is less than the bv_i, the $bv_i - gv_i$ video packets in the current interval block are moved to the next interval block. Reasoning shows that the decoding and demodulation process is the inverse process of encoding and modulation.

4   Experimental Results and Analysis

To analyze the performance of the constructed covert channel, we used VoLTE video traffic between the two phones. Our solution can be implemented on different mobile devices and different versions of android. We chose two Samsung A5108 phones as sender and receiver to test our solution. In the experiment, we have developed a capture program based on the Android kernel to capture traffic packets. According to our solution, covert traffic is generated by encoding and modulating overt traffic.

We use two standard statistical tests, KS (Kolmogorov-Smirnov) test and KLD (Kullback-Leibler Divergence) test, to verify the undetectability of the constructed covert channel. If the proposed covert channel can prevent the two

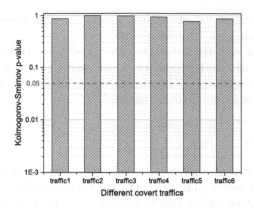

Fig. 2. KS tests for different covert traffics

tests from detecting abnormal traffic, that is to say, it means that the covert channel maintains undetectability.

For the KS test, the p-value is the adjoint probability, which is used to determine whether the two sample distributions are different. When the p-value is greater than 0.05, the two samples are considered to have the same distribution, that is, the assumption can be accepted that the covert channel is undetectable. The results are shown in Fig. 2. All p-values are greater than 0.05, indicating that the covert channel can be regarded as undetectable.

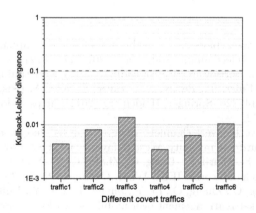

Fig. 3. KLD tests for different covert traffics

KLD is used to measure the distance between two random distributions. When the distribution is the same, the KLD value is zero, and when the distribution difference becomes larger, the KLD value will also become larger. As shown in Fig. 3, the results of KLD detection for covert traffic are as follows. The range of KLD value is (0.00345–0.01367). The KLD value of all covert traffic is less than 0.1, even most values are less than 0.01. This shows that the covert channel can maintain good undetectability.

In summary, through the detection of KS and KLD, the constructed covert channel is verified to be undetectable, which shows that machine learning for traffic analysis during the modulation process significantly improves the undetectability of the constructed covert channel.

5   Conclusion

In this paper, we propose a covert channel with machine learning algorithm for VoLTE video traffic over mobile network. The proposed scheme is an alternative solution of the existing packet reordering covert channels, which modulates the covert message in the relative order of the voice and video packets based on the machine learning of the characteristics of the overt and covert traffics. We discuss encoding and modulation of the covert message to build the robust and safe covert channel. The trade-off factor is employ to adjust the covert traffic feature distribution of the covert traffic to improve the undetectability, and gray code and interval block are adopted to strengthen the robustness of the covert channel. The experimental results show that the proposed covert channel can resist the detection and attacks of adversaries.

Acknowledgment. This work has been supported by the National Natural Science Foundation of China under grant No. U1636213 and No. 61876019.

References

1. Mazurczyk, W., Szczypiorski, K.: Evaluation of steganographic methods for oversized ip packets. Telecommun. Syst. **49**(2), 207–217 (2012)
2. Houmansadr, A., Borisov, N.: CoCo: coding-based covert timing channels for network flows. In: Filler, T., Pevný, T., Craver, S., Ker, A. (eds.) IH 2011. LNCS, vol. 6958, pp. 314–328. Springer, Heidelberg (2011). https://doi.org/10.1007/978-3-642-24178-9_22
3. Cabuk, S.: Network covert channels: design, analysis, detection, and elimination. Ph.D. thesis, Purdue University, West Lafayette, IN, USA (2006)
4. Tan, Y., Zhang, X., Sharif, K., Liang, C., Zhang, Q., Li, Y.: Covert timing channels for iot over mobile networks. IEEE Wirel. Commun. **25**(6), 38–44 (2018)
5. Zhang, X., Liang, C., Zhang, Q., Li, Y., Zheng, J., Tan, Y.: Building covert timing channels by packet rearrangement over mobile networks. Inf. Sci. **445–446**, 66–78 (2018)
6. Tan, Y., Xinting, X., Liang, C., Zhang, X., Zhang, Q., Li, Y.: An end-to-end covert channel via packet dropout for mobile networks. Int. J. Distrib. Sens. Netw. **14**(5), 1–14 (2018)
7. Zhang, X., Zhu, L., Wang, X., Zhang, C., Zhu, H., Tan, Y.: A packet-reordering covert channel over volte voice and video traffics. J. Netw. Comput. Appl. **126**, 29–38 (2019)
8. Zhang, X., Tan, Y., Liang, C., Li, Y., Li, J.: A covert channel over VoLTE via adjusting silence periods. IEEE Access **6**, 9292–9302 (2018)

9. Zhang, Q., Gong, H., Zhang, X., Liang, C., Tan, Y.: A sensitive network jitter measurement for covert timing channels over interactive traffic. Multimed. Tools Appl. **78**(3), 3493–3509 (2018). https://doi.org/10.1007/s11042-018-6281-1
10. Zhang, X., Guo, L., Xue, Y., Zhang, Q.: A two-way volte covert channel with feedback adaptive to mobile network environment. IEEE Access **7**, 122214–122223 (2019)
11. Wu, J., Wang, Y., Ding, L., Liao, X.: Improving performance of network covert timing channel through huffman coding. Math. Comput. Modell. **55**(1C2), 69–79 (2012)
12. Luo, X., Chan, E.W., Chang, R.K.: TCP covert timing channels: design and detection. In 2008 IEEE International Conference on Dependable Systems and Networks with FTCS and DCC (DSN), pp. 420–429, June 2008
13. Ahmadzadeh, S.A., Agnew, G.: Turbo covert channel: an iterative framework for covert communication over data networks. In: 2013 Proceedings IEEE INFOCOM, pp. 2031–2039, April 2013
14. Li, Y., Wang, Y., Wang, Y., Ke, L., Tan, Y.: A feature-vector generative adversarial network for evading PDF malware classifiers. Inf. Sci. **523**, 38–48 (2020)
15. Bhuyan, M.H., Bhattacharyya, D.K., Kalita, J.K.: Network anomaly detection: methods, systems and tools. IEEE Commun. Surv. Tutor. **16**(1), 303–336 (2014)
16. Iglesias, F., Zseby, T.: Are network covert timing channels statistical anomalies? In: Proceedings of the 12th International Conference on Availability, Reliability and Security, ARES 17 (2017)

An Improved Privacy-Preserving Stochastic Gradient Descent Algorithm

Xianfu Cheng[1,3] , Yanqing Yao[1,2(✉)] , and Ao Liu[1,3]

[1] State Key Laboratory of Software Development Environment, Beihang University,
Beijing 100191, China
{buaacxf,yaoyq,liuao}@buaa.edu.cn
[2] Key Laboratory of Aerospace Network Security,
Ministry of Industry and Information Technology,
School of Cyberspace Science and Technology, Beihang University,
Beijing 100191, China
[3] Beijing Key Laboratory of Network Technology, Beihang University,
Beijing 100191, China

Abstract. Deep learning techniques based on neural network have made significant achievements in various fields of Artificial Intelligence. However, model training requires large-scale datasets, these datasets are crowd-sourced and model parameters will contain the encoding of private information, resulting in the risk of privacy leakage. With the trend towards sharing pre-trained models, the risk of stealing training datasets through member inference attack and model inversion attack is further heightened. To tackle this problem, we propose an improved Differential Privacy Stochastic Gradient Descent algorithm, using simulated annealing algorithm and denoising mechanism to optimize the allocation method of privacy loss and improve model accuracy. We also analyze privacy cost under random shuffle data batch processing methods in detail within the framework of Subsampled Rényi Differential Privacy. Compared with existing methods, our experiments show that we can train deep neural networks with non-convex objective function more efficiently with moderate privacy budgets.

Keywords: Differential privacy · Stochastic gradient descent · Deep learning · Non-convex optimization

1 Introduction

In recent years, deep learning techniques based on neural network have made great progress in many artificial intelligence (AI for short) tasks such as image processing and natural language processing, and became a key technology providing convenience for people and promoting social progress.

Privacy Risks in Deep Learning. Recently, studies on member inference attacks [17] and model inversion attacks [7] have disclosed the potential privacy

© Springer Nature Switzerland AG 2020
X. Chen et al. (Eds.): ML4CS 2020, LNCS 12486, pp. 340–354, 2020.
https://doi.org/10.1007/978-3-030-62223-7_29

risks of deep learning models. The deep neural network (DNN for short) has a large number of hidden layers, which enough to encode and remember most characteristics of individuals' data into model parameters [24]. Fredrikson et al. [8] implemented a model inversion attack to recover images from facial recognition systems. The member inference attack experiment proposed by Shokri et al. [16] showed true information of individuals can be extracted from neural networks effectively only in "black box" scenarios.

Moreover, the migration learning method [22] is considered to be next driving force of deep learning. It saves time to train entire neural network from scratch, and will significantly promote the sharing process of pre-trained models. However, the parameters of some well-known shared deep learning models (e.g., LeNet [11], GoogleNet [19], ResNet [9]) are fully exposed, making it easier for adversary to launch inference attacks to infer sensitive data records of individuals in training dataset. Therefore, it is imperative to study privacy-preserving deep learning technologies aiming at protecting secret training data from being stolen by attackers.

Differential Privacy in Deep Learning. In 2006, Dwork et al. [4] proposed the concept of differential privacy (DP for short): it makes the outputs generated by input datasets that differs by only one record cannot be differentially attacked. As an emerging privacy-preserving mechanism, DP not only resist attacks from arbitrary background information, but also provide a method measuring privacy, which can be given rigorous mathematical proof. A deep learning algorithm implemented DP can assure users' privacy hard to be exposed. In addition, true characteristics of original dataset can be obtained by statistical methods, so as to ensure the usefulness of the data.

In the literature [1,13,18], the "gradient add noise" method was mainly used to achieve DP protection during training process of stochastic gradient descent algorithm (SGD for short) in DNNs. We call this method differential privacy stochastic gradient descent (DP-SGD for short). Lee and Kifer [12] implemented a privacy-preserving gradient descent training algorithm with adaptive learning rate under relaxed DP metrics, and achieved good results on binary classification datasets. Lei Yu et al. [23] conducted further research on DP-SGD algorithm. By adaptively allocating DP budget, which is required for each step of gradient descent within a certain total privacy budget, the training accuracy is improved and privacy requirement is guaranteed. In addition, they adopted a DP promotion mechanism called Concentrated Differential Privacy [3], and conducted refined privacy loss analysis on two different data batch processing methods: random shuffle sampling and independent identical distribution (i.i.d. for short) sampling.

In order to obtain a tighter upper bound of cumulative privacy loss in DP-SGD algorithm, Abadi et al. [1] proposed Moments Accountant method (MA for short). Unfortunately, MA is only applicable to privacy analysis in case of i.i.d. sampling, and the study of Abadi et al. does not consider upper security bound of cumulative privacy budget obtained by applying MA. The adaptive algorithm proposed by Lei Yu et al. [23] actually simply adjusts the amount of noise required to apply DP mechanism, and cannot meet requirements of privacy and model convergence under strong privacy guarantee premise. Motivated by the above problems, we propose a new DP-SGD algorithm that can effectively train non-convex objective neural networks.

Our Contributions. The main contributions are as follows:

(1) Based on [23], we add simulated annealing algorithm(SA for short) and post-processing mechanism with denoising effect to solve the problem that deep learning models lose too much accuracy under strong privacy guarantee.
(2) Under random shuffle, we analyze the privacy amplification effect when applying gaussian mechanism according to Rényi Differential Privacy, get a tighter upper bound for privacy.

The remainder of the paper is as follows. We review the background of deep learning and DP in Sect. 2, provide an overview about our approach in Sect. 3, describe our proposed method in Sect. 4, and then give detailed experimental methods and describe the experimental results in Sect. 5. Section 6 does some discussion and Acknowledgments. The necessary proof is provided in the appendix.

2   Background

2.1   Deep Learning

Deep learning generally refers to using a multi-layer neural network to model correlation between data samples and their labels. A standard neural network, the neurons in hidden layer are parameterized by weight matrix $W^{(l)}$ and bias vector $b^{(l)}$. Each layer applies affine transformation to the output of previous layer, and then calculates activation function.

The purpose of training neural networks is to learn parameter $\theta = \{W^{(l)}, b^{(l)} \mid 1 \leq l \leq n\}$ by minimizing loss function L, which represents the degree of misclassified training data. Iteratively calculating gradients of loss L, and update the parameters $W^{(l)}$, $b^{(l)}$ at each step until L converges to local optimum. In practical applications, neural networks' training mostly uses mini-batch SGD algorithm, which can significantly improve learning efficiency of large datasets. During each iteration, the algorithm selects a batch B of $|B|$ samples from training dataset, and calculates gradients of average loss $\frac{1}{|B|} \sum_{x \in B} \nabla_\omega L(\omega, x)$. Then SGD applies the following rules to update parameter ω:

$$\omega = \omega - \eta \frac{1}{|B|} \sum_{x \in B} \nabla_\omega L(\omega, x) \tag{1}$$

Where η is learning rate. The running time of mini-batch SGD algorithm is usually expressed in "epochs". Each epoch consists of all batches of training dataset. In a period of time, a batch of samples used to update parameters through the model is called an iteration.

2.2 Differential Privacy

In this section, we will introduce some definitions and lemmas we need about DP

Definition 1 *(Differential Privacy [4]). Given privacy parameters $\epsilon \geq 0$, $0 \leq \delta \leq 1$, a randomized mechanism $\mathcal{M}$ satisfies (ϵ, δ)-DP if for $\forall S \subset Range(\mathcal{M})$, and for every pair of neighboring datasets $D \sim D'$ (differ by only one record),*

$$Pr[\mathcal{M}(D) \in S] \leq Pr[\mathcal{M}(D') \in S] + \delta \qquad (2)$$

Definition 2 *(Sensitivity [5]). The L_2 sensitivity of a query function $q : \mathcal{D} \to \mathbf{R}^d$ is defined as:*

$$\Delta = \max_{D,D'} \|q(D) - q(D')\|_2 \qquad (3)$$

Remark 1. In this paper, we apply gaussian mechanism with L_2 norm sensitivity to achieve DP, by adding Gaussian noise with zero mean and variance of $\Delta^2 \sigma^2$ to every dimensional of output:

$$q(D) + \mathcal{N}(0, \Delta^2 \sigma^2 \mathbf{I}) \qquad (4)$$

If $\sigma^2 > 2log(\frac{1.25}{\delta})/\epsilon^2$ and $\epsilon \in (0, 1)$, then it satisfies (ϵ, δ)-DP.

2.3 Rényi Differential Privacy

Definition 3 *((α, ϵ)-Rényi Differential Privacy [14]). Given a real number $\alpha \in (1, +\infty)$ and privacy parameter $\epsilon \geq 0$, if for all adjacent datasets pair D and D', a random mechanism $\mathcal{M}$ satisfies:*

$$D_\alpha[\mathcal{M}(D)\|\mathcal{M}(D')] \leq \epsilon, \qquad (5)$$

then we say $\mathcal{M}$ satisfies (α, ϵ)-RDP. Among them, $D_\alpha[\mathcal{M}(D)\|\mathcal{M}(D')] = \frac{1}{\alpha-1} \log \mathbb{E}_{x \sim \mathcal{M}(D')}(\frac{P_{\mathcal{M}(D)}(x)}{P_{\mathcal{M}(D')}(x)})^\alpha$ is called α-Rényi divergence(D_α for short), bounded by ϵ.

Lemma 1. *(Gaussian Mechanism achieve RDP [14]). When the query $q : \mathcal{D}^n \to \mathbb{R}^k$ is applied to the dataset D, the mechanism $\mathcal{M}$ add Gaussian noise $\eta \sim \mathcal{N}(0, \sigma^2 \mathbf{I})$ to the feedback result $q(D)$ and publish the perturbation result $q(D)+\eta$. IF for any adjacent dataset D and D', $\alpha \in (1, +\infty)$, $\mathcal{M}$ satisfies:*

$$D_\alpha[\mathcal{M}(D)\|\mathcal{M}(D')] \leq \alpha \Delta_2^2(q)/2\sigma^2 = \epsilon, \qquad (6)$$

then we say $\mathcal{M}$ satisfies (α, ϵ)-RDP, where $\Delta_2(q)$ is the L_2 norm sensitivity of query q.

Remark 2. The gaussian mechanism makes algorithm $\mathcal{M}$ satisfy (α, ϵ)-RDP for a series of α, so we can use $\epsilon(\alpha)$ to represent privacy level under α moment. In empirical risk minimization algorithm, gaussian mechanism is usually applied to random subsample B of dataset D to make its training process satisfy $(\alpha, \epsilon(\alpha))$-RDP. The mechanism satisfies a privacy amplification theory about the entire dataset D as follows.

Lemma 2 *(RDP for subsampled mechanism [21]). For a random mechanism $\mathcal{M}$ and dataset $D \sim \mathcal{D}^n$, define $\mathcal{M} \circ Subsample$ as*

- *Sample m data points from the dataset without replacement ($q = m/n$ is the sampling probability);*
- *Use $\mathcal{M}$ as the input of the subsampling dataset, if $\mathcal{M}$ satisfies $(\alpha, \epsilon(\alpha))$-RDP for all subsample with integer moments $\alpha > 2$.*

Then $\mathcal{M} \circ Subsample$ satisfies $(\alpha, \epsilon'(\alpha))$-RDP under D. Among them:

$$\epsilon'(\alpha) \leq \frac{1}{\alpha - 1} log(1 + q^2 \binom{\alpha}{2} min\{4(e^{\epsilon(2)} - 1), 2e^{\epsilon(2)}\} + \sum_{j=3}^{\alpha} q^j \binom{\alpha}{j} 2e^{(j-1)\epsilon(j)}) \quad (7)$$

Lemma 3 *(RDP Composition [14]). For the random mechanism $\mathcal{M}_1$ and $\mathcal{M}_2$ acting on the dataset D, if $\mathcal{M}_1$ satisfies (α, ϵ_1)-RDP and $\mathcal{M}_2$ satisfies (α, ϵ_2)-RDP, then their combination $\mathcal{M}_1 \circ \mathcal{M}_2$ satisfies $(\alpha, \epsilon_1 + \epsilon_2)$-RDP.*

RDP provides stronger privacy protection than the same level of (ϵ, δ)-DP, and its conversion relationship with (ϵ, δ)-DP is as follows:

Proposition 1 *(RDP converts to (ϵ, δ)-DP [14]). If $\mathcal{M}$ satisfies (α, ϵ)-RDP, then it also satisfies $(\epsilon(\delta), \delta)$-DP, $\epsilon(\delta) \geq \epsilon + \frac{log(1/\delta)}{\alpha - 1}$.*

Remark 3. When evaluating a series of algorithms in this paper, we unify various improved DP mechanisms into the form of (ϵ, δ)-DP. We propose Algorithm 1 tracks the consumption of (α, ϵ) in the training process by giving the total (ϵ, δ) pairs in advance, and convert the result to (ϵ_i, δ_i) according to Proposition 1.

3   Overview

The problem with DP-SGD is that DNN training often has a large number of iterations, which ultimately leads to a large amount of cumulative privacy loss. Jayaraman et al. [10] verified DP by simulating inference attacks and concluded that the algorithm generates a large amount of cumulative privacy loss, which means that more privacy will be likely to be leaked. Therefore, for allowing lower noise scales or more training iterations, it is crucial to estimate privacy loss strictly. When we fix total privacy budget to a safe value, in order to train model as fully as possible, we should do as follows: (1) each iteration uses a tighter composition privacy analysis method; (2) adopt denoising method to maintain the stability of parameters optimization for disturbance values after

DP processing; (3) avoid loss function falls into local minimum points and use optimization techniques to speed up model convergence.

For tracking DP-SGD's privacy loss, many SGD training models use random shuffle sampling in practice, it divide dataset into batches to improve calculation efficiency, which is different from the i.i.d. random sampling with replacement. When using DP, the privacy costs also different. Therefore, this paper uses the conclusion of Lemma 2 as privacy analysis method in case of random shuffle without replacement.

In our method, the privacy budget required for each iteration is obtained through self-learning. This self-learning method mainly runs SA algorithm at every certain iterations period. The method judges whether to denoise according to parameter's state transition conditions, and then it reallocate privacy budget. While keeping overall privacy budget unchanged, we allocate different privacy budgets to different training periods, and then use denoising techniques to reduce influence on model parameters quality caused by noise, to improve accuracy of test data through model at the same privacy strength.

Algorithm 1 presents our DP-SGD algorithm. In each iteration t, a batch of examples sampled from training dataset, the algorithm computes gradients of loss on every example in batch and then clips them by l_2 norm clipping with a threshold C. The gaussian mechanism adds random noise $\mathcal{N}(0, \sigma_t^2 C^2 \mathbb{I})$ to $\sum_i \hat{g}_t(x_i)$ to perturb gradients in every iteration. After finding a nearly optimal gradients vector by running SA_with_Smooth function, using the result in gradient descent step. In the pseudo code, function $rdpBudgetGet$ is used to obtain privacy budget ϵ_t and noise parameter σ_t for the current training step t.

4   Details of Our Approach

In this section, we will introduce the proposed differential privacy deep learning method in detail. First, we propose our dynamic privacy budget allocation technology and DP-SGD algorithm, and then evaluate privacy loss based on RDP for random shuffle.

4.1   Dynamic Privacy Budget Allocation

Concretely, our dynamic privacy budget allocation follows the idea that, as the model accuracy converges, it is expected to have less noise on the gradients, which allows the learning process to get closer to global optimal spot and achieve better accuracy. Set initial privacy budget to a smaller value, the noise parameters calculated by the smaller budget can accelerate the convergence of loss function in early stage of training. As the number of iterations increases, excessive noise will affect accuracy, so noise needs to be reduced. However, this means will increase privacy budget to the corresponding iteration, not only weakens the security of algorithm, but also accelerate the consumption of total privacy budget. Therefore, our algorithm improves privacy budget consumption and accuracy by using

---

Algorithm 1. Rényi Differentially Private SGD Algorithm

Input: Training samples $x_1, ..., x_N$, learning rate η_t, norm clipping bound C, default total privacy budget ϵ_{tot}, and sampling rate q

1: Initialize ω_0;
2: Initialize cumulative privacy loss $\epsilon_t^{priv} = 0$;
3: **for** $t = 0 \rightarrow T$ **do**
4:     **Dynamic privacy budget allocation:**
5:     $\sigma_t \leftarrow rdpBudgetGet(\epsilon_{tot}, t, T, state)$;
6:     Calculate ϵ_t according to Lemma 1, 2 and Proposition 1;
7:     Cumulative and update ϵ_t^{priv};
8:     **if** $\epsilon_t^{priv} > \epsilon_{tot}$ **then**
9:         break;
10:    **data batching:**
11:    Execute random shuffle to extract batch $\mathbb{B}_t$ of size $|B|$ from training dataset at sampling rate q;
12:    **Compute gradient:**
13:    **for** each $i \in \mathbb{B}_t$ **do**
14:        $g_t(x_i) \leftarrow \nabla_{\omega_t} \mathcal{L}(\omega_t, x_i)$;
15:        **Clip gradient:**
16:        $\hat{g}_t(x_i) \leftarrow g_t(x_i)/max(1, \frac{\|g_t(x_i)\|_2}{C})$;
17:    **Add noise:**
18:    $\bar{g}_t \leftarrow \frac{1}{|B|}(\sum_i \hat{g}_t(x_i) + \mathcal{N}(0, \sigma_t^2 C^2 \mathbb{I}))$;
19:    **Run SA algorithm to get a gradient to find optimal solution:**
20:    $cur\_loss \leftarrow loss\_function(\omega_t - \eta_t \bar{g}_t)$
21:    $\tilde{g}_t, state \leftarrow SA\_with\_Smooth(cur\_loss, pre\_loss, \bar{g}_t)$;
22:    **Descent:**
23:    $\omega_{t+1} \leftarrow \omega_t - \eta_t \tilde{g}_t$
Output: ω_T

Algorithm 2. The details of SA algorithm and denoising method

---

1: **function** $SA\_with\_Smooth(cur\_loss, pre\_loss, g)$
2:     **if** $cur\_loss > pre\_loss$ **then**
3:         $P \leftarrow e^{-\frac{cur\_loss - pre\_loss}{\beta_1 T}}, (\beta_1 > 0)$;
4:         $rand \leftarrow Uniform\_Distribution(0, 1)$;
5:         **if** $rand < P$ **then**
6:             **if** $cur\_loss - pre\_loss > Threshold$ **then**
7:                 //or $cur\_acc - pre\_acc > Threshold$
8:                 $state \leftarrow active$ //Adjust noise scale and privacy budget
9:         **else**
10:            $g = Laplace\_Smooth(g)$
11:    **return** $g, state$

SA algorithm and noise gradients post-processing algorithm (Algorithm 1 line 21, as described in Algorithm 2).

We obtain the noise parameters of iteration t in the rdpBudgetGet function of Algorithm 1 rely on formula 8:

$$\sigma'_n = \begin{cases} Decay\_function(\sigma_n), & \text{if } Loss_n - Loss_{n-1} > \gamma, n > 0 \\ \sigma_n, & else \end{cases} \tag{8}$$

Here, $Loss_n = \frac{1}{m} \sum_{i=(n-1)m+1}^{nm} Loss(i)$ is the average loss of nth iteration period to validation set, we set a threshold $\gamma \in [0,1]$ to determine whether the difference in validation set between average loss of two sets of iterations periods is within an acceptable range. If average loss obtained by the latter set of period cannot be effectively improved than the previous set of period, then run $Decay\_function$ on current noise scale. We will use exponential decay strategy in experiments. Our decay coefficient will be relatively small because we use our decay coefficient will be relatively small because we use SA algorithm and noise gradient post-processing in the training process to reduce the impact of noise on the model performance algorithm and noise gradient post-processing in training process to reduce the impact of noise on model performance, so as to achieve the purpose of enhancing training effect while saving privacy budget.

4.2   Improving DP-SGD

In this subsection, we will introduce SA algorithm, describe the details of post-processing algorithm for noise gradients (Algorithms 2).

Simulated Annealing. The SA algorithm is used to find global optimal solutions in non-convex optimization problems, which can be applied to neural networks to find optimal parameters' solution and improve model accuracy.

In Algorithm 1, we first divide the dataset into a training set, a validation set and a test set. We evaluate the average of loss function obtained by running DP-SGD with sampling validation set in current period during certain number of iterations. As described in Algorithm 2, if the average value of loss function obtained by training during current period less than the value saved in previous period, this shows that current parameters are closer to the minimum point of loss function than the parameters obtained in previous period, then we believe that current noise gradient is better and the algorithm continues to run; otherwise, from the formula 9 we get an annealing probability P. Operating according to this probability, the algorithm will not immediately deny current noise gradient. First, a uniformly distributed random number r is generated in the interval $[0,1]$. If $r < P$, the current result is accepted, then we can choose whether to activate $decay\_function$ according to the size of $cur\_loss - pre\_loss$ or $cur\_acc - pre\_acc$ on validation set. Otherwise the result is not accepted, then use the "denoise value" corresponding to noise gradient in this period to replace original noise gradient, then running gradient descent, reciprocating cycle.

"Denoise" is post-processing strategy of DP mechanism we will introduce in Proposition 2. In formula 9, determine probability P based on the difference of average loss in adjacent periods and the annealing rate $\mathcal{T}$, the value obtained mathod of $\mathcal{T}$ is also a dynamic function.

$$P = \begin{cases} 1, & \text{if } Loss(n+1) < Loss(n) \\ e^{-\frac{Loss(n+1)-Loss(n)}{\beta \mathcal{T}}}, & \beta > 0, \quad else \end{cases} \tag{9}$$

Proposition 2. *(DP Post-processing rm [6]). Let $\mathcal{M} : \mathbb{N}^{|\chi|} \to R$ be a randomized algorithm that is DP. Let $f : R \to R'$ be an arbitrary randomized mapping. Then $f \circ \mathcal{M} : \mathbb{N}^{|\chi|} \to R'$ is DP with same level.*

Post-processing. In this subsection, we consider a specific class of mechanisms that denoise the outputs of gaussian mechanism. Let $\hat{y} \sim \mathcal{N}(f(x), \sigma^2 I)$, we are interested in designing a post-processing function g such that $\tilde{y} = g(\hat{y})$ is closer to f(x) than $\hat{y}$. By Proposition 2 we know $\tilde{y} = g(\hat{y})$ also satisfies DP. This information can be leveraged to design denoising functions.

The denoise methods such as Wavelet Transform [2], Trend filtering [2] and Laplace Smooth [15] are commonly used in practice. In Algorithm 2 line 10, we use Laplace Smooth method to design a post-processing algorithm for denoising noise gradients matrix.

Proposition 3. *(Laplace Smooth [15]). We can use the circulant convolution matrix A_σ to reduce the variance of stochastic gradient vector on-the-fly. The stochastic gradient smoothing can be done by multiplying gradients by the inverse of A_σ.*

$$\omega_{t+1} \leftarrow \omega_t - \eta_t A_\sigma^{-1} \nabla L(\omega_t, x) \tag{10}$$

4.3   RDP Privacy Accountant

Our privacy Accountant method in Algorithm 1 as following theorem:

Theorem 1. *We suppose that a mechanism $\mathcal{M}$ consists of a sequence of k adaptive mechanisms, $\mathcal{M}_1, ..., \mathcal{M}_k$, where each $\mathcal{M}_i : \prod_{j=1}^{i-1} \mathcal{R}_j \times D \to R_i$ and $\mathcal{M}_i$ satisfies (α, ϵ_i)-RDP $(1 \le i \le k)$. Let $\mathbb{D}_1, \mathbb{D}_2, ..., \mathbb{D}_k$ be the result of a randomized partitioning of input domain $\mathbb{D}$. The mechanism $\mathcal{M}(D) = (\mathcal{M}_1(D \cap \mathbb{D}_1), ..., \mathcal{M}_k(D \cap \mathbb{D}_k))$ satisfies*

$$\begin{cases} (\alpha, \epsilon) - RDP, & \text{if } \epsilon_i = \epsilon, \forall i \\ \max_i(\alpha, \epsilon_i) - RDP, & \text{if } \epsilon_i \ne \epsilon_j, \text{for some } i,j \end{cases} \tag{11}$$

The proof of Theorem 1 in this paper can be found in Appendix.

Remark 4. For RDP, Theorem 1 shows that when each disjoint DP mechanism queries disjoint data subsets in parallel and works independently, their composition provides $\max_i \epsilon_i$-RDP instead of $\sum_i \epsilon_i$-RDP. Therefore, the privacy accountant in an epoch in Algorithm 1 satisfies Theorem 1, and the cumulative privacy calculation of multiple epochs satisfies Lemma 3.

5   Experimental Results

In this section, we demonstrate the effectiveness of Algorithm 1 on deep learning tasks, and evaluate the proposed privacy accounting methods. Our implementation is based on the PyTorch implementation [20] of DP-SGD in the paper [1].

5.1   Dataset and Model

MNIST and LeNet5. This is a dataset of handwritten digits consists of 60,000 training examples and 10,000 testing examples [11] formatted as 28X28 size gray-level images. In our experiment, the neural network model for training MNIST is LeNet5 [11]: a Convolutional Neural Network(CNN for short) with two convolutional layers(one of them contains 1 input channel, 6 output channels, and 5*5 convolution filter; the other contains 6 inputs, 16 outputs, and 5*5 convolution filter), two max-pooling layers and a fully connected layer. The activation function we use RELU. The output layer is softmax of 10 classes corresponding to the 10 digits. The loss function computes cross-entropy loss. The non-private training of this model can achieve 0.95–0.97 test accuracy with 1 epoch.

5.2   Results on Datasets

Results on MNIST. In DP model training, we keep batch size at 200, a constant learning rate $lr = 0.5$, RDP moment $\alpha = 5$, parameter $\delta = 1e-5$ ($\delta \ll \sqrt{N}$, N is dataset size) are used by default. We evaluate model accuracy during training under DP budget allocation schedule. We divide training dataset into 58,000 examples for training, 2,000 examples for validation, and 10,000 examples for testing. We sample the validation set use for SA algorithm every certain iterations period and perform testset after training to test availability of our model.

We first do experiments comparing training effect of our dynamic parameters DP-SGD algorithm with the existing fixed parameters DP-SGD algorithm. In DP model training, we use these four settings of parameters in addition to total privacy budget $\epsilon_{tot} = 3$ (Equivalent to RDP $\epsilon = 0.1218$): (1) original model without privacy settings, called non-dp model; (2) DP model with fixed parameters, noise level $\sigma = 1$, l_2 clipping norm 1; (3) DP model with fixed parameters, noise level $\sigma = 2$, l_2 clipping norm 3; (4) our DP model with dynamic parameters, initial noise level $\sigma = 2$, l_2 clipping norm 1. We run these algorithms 1 epoch, 290 iterations, the results shown in Fig. 1.

Figure 1(a), (b) show the training process. Under strong privacy guarantee, the algorithm proposed by us can still ensure model converges more quickly and obtains better training results. After 1 epoch training, the RDP privacy cost ϵ_t^{priv} for our method is 0.1214 ((2.9996, 1e−5)-DP), for parameters setting (2) is 0.000098 ((2.8783, 1e−5)-DP), for parameters setting (3) is 0.000796 ((2.8790, 1e−5)-DP). From left to right, the values of test accuracy in Fig. 3(c) are 0.97, 0.873, 0.8 and 0.91.

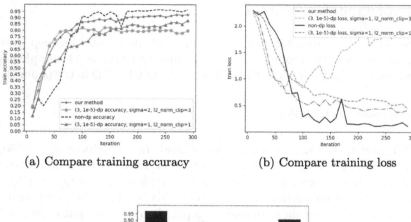

(a) Compare training accuracy

(b) Compare training loss

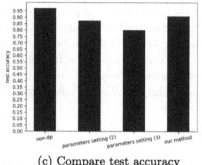

(c) Compare test accuracy

Fig. 1. Comparing our method with fixed parameters DP-SGDs

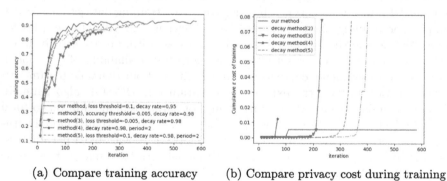

(a) Compare training accuracy

(b) Compare privacy cost during training

Fig. 2. Comparing our method with Dynamic parameters DP-SGDs

The results in Fig. 1 demonstrate the benefit of dynamic privacy parameters as we proposed. Next, We do experiments comparing the training effect of our method with other Dynamic parameters DP-SGD algorithm. In Comparative Experiment, we use these five settings of noise parameters in addition to total privacy budget $\epsilon_{tot} = 3$, initial noise level $\sigma = 2$ and training epochs $num = 2$:

(1) our method with dynamic parameters, keeping l_2 clipping norm 3, the decay condition of noise level σ is $cur\_loss - pre\_loss > 0.1$ and decay rate is 0.95; (2) DP model use SA and denoise with fixed l_2 clipping norm 3, the decay condition of noise level is $cur\_acc - pre\_acc <= -0.005$ and decay rate is 0.98; (3) DP model no use SA and denoise with fixed l_2 clipping norm 3, the decay condition of noise level is $cur\_acc - pre\_acc <= -0.005$, decay rate is 0.98, and we check decay condition every 2 iterations; (4) DP model no use SA, denoise and decay condition, keeping fixed l_2 clipping norm 3 and decay noise level every 2 iterations, decay rate is 0.98; (5) DP model no use SA and denoise with fixed l_2 clipping norm 3, the decay condition of noise level is $cur\_loss - pre\_loss > 0.1$, decay rate is 0.98, and we check decay condition every 2 iterations. We run these algorithms 2 epochs, the results shown in Fig. 2.

Figure 2(a) shows the training accuracy of above five methods in two epochs. Under the premise that privacy cost does not exceed total privacy budget, our method guarantees sufficient training and achieves highest training accuracy. As can be seen from Fig. 2(b), the privacy budget consumption rate of other dynamic parameters DP-SGD algorithms is much faster than our method. From (1) to (5), the values of test accuracy in Fig. 4(a) are 0.922, 0.8876, 0.8782, 0.865 and 0.8688.

Finally, our algorithm trains 10 epochs to achieve 95% test accuracy and $(5, 0.00019)$-RDP (Equivalent to $(2.8784, 1e-5)$-DP) under following parameters settings: dividing training dataset into 50,000 examples for training, 10,000 examples for validation, and 10,000 examples for testing, total privacy budget $\epsilon_{tot} = 3$, initial noise level $\sigma = 2$, RDP moment $\alpha = 5$, using fixed clipping norm 3, the decay condition of noise level σ is $cur\_loss - pre\_loss > 0.1$ and decay rate is 0.96.

6   Conclusion

We present our approach to improve DP-SGD for deep learning model sharing with three original contributions. First, since the training of neural networks involves a large number of iterations, we apply subsample RDP for privacy accounting to achieve tight estimation on privacy loss. Second, We propose a privacy accounting method for random shuffle under RDP. Third, we have implemented a dynamic privacy parameters allocating technique based on SA and denoising algorithm for improving model accuracy over existing budget allocation schemes. Our experiments on large-scale dataset demonstrate the effectiveness of our methods and theorems.

Acknowledgements. The above work was supported by Beijing Municipal Natural Science Foundation (Grant No. 4202035), the Fundamental Research Funds for the Central Universities (Grant No. YWF-20-BJ-J-1040), the National Key R&D Program of China (Grant No. 2016QY04W0802), and the National Natural Science Foundation of China (Grant No. 61602025, U1636211, and 61170189).

Appendix. Proof of Theorem 1

Theorem 1. Suppose that a mechanism $\mathcal{M}$ consists of a sequence of k adaptive mechanisms, $\mathcal{M}_1,...,\mathcal{M}_k$, where each $\mathcal{M}_i : \prod_{j=1}^{i-1} \mathcal{R}_j \times D \to R_i$ and $\mathcal{M}_i$ satisfies (α, ϵ_i)-RDP$(1 \leq i \leq k)$. Let $\mathbb{D}_1, \mathbb{D}_2, ..., \mathbb{D}_k$ be the result of a randomized partitioning of the input domain $\mathbb{D}$. The mechanism $\mathcal{M}(D) = (\mathcal{M}_1(D \cap \mathbb{D}_1), ..., \mathcal{M}_k(D \cap \mathbb{D}_k))$ satisfies

$$\begin{cases} (\alpha, \epsilon) - RDP, & \text{if } \epsilon_i = \epsilon, \forall i \\ \max_i(\alpha, \epsilon_i) - RDP, & \text{if } \epsilon_i \neq \epsilon_j, \text{for some i,j} \end{cases} \tag{12}$$

Proof. Suppose two neighboring datasets D and D'. Without loss of generality, assume that D contains one more element d_e than D'. Let $D_i = D \cap \mathbb{D}_i$ and $D_i' = D' \cap \mathbb{D}_i$. Accordingly, there exists j such that D_j contains one more element than D_j', and for any $i \neq j$, $D_i = D_i'$. Consider any sequence of outcomes $o = (o_1, ..., o_k)$ of $\mathcal{M}_1(D_1), ..., \mathcal{M}_k(D_k)$.

Because only D_j is different from D_j', for any $i \neq j$, we have $Pr[M_i(D_i) = o_i | M_{i-1}(D_{i-1}) = o_{i-1}, ..., M_1(D_1) = o_1]$ equal to $Pr[M_i(D_i') = o_i | M_{i-1}(D_{i-1}') = o_{i-1}, ..., M_1(D_1') = o_1]$

Then, we have
$$Z_j^{(o)} \triangleq \frac{Pr(\mathcal{M}(D)=o)}{Pr(\mathcal{M}(D')=o)}$$
$$= \frac{\prod_{i \in [n]} Pr[\mathcal{M}_i(D_i)=o_i | \mathcal{M}_{i-1}(D_{i-1})=o_{i-1},...,\mathcal{M}_1(D_1)=o_1]}{\prod_{i \in [n]} Pr[\mathcal{M}_i(D_i')=o_i | \mathcal{M}_{i-1}(D_{i-1}')=o_{i-1},...,\mathcal{M}_1(D_1')=o_1]}$$
$$= \frac{Pr[\mathcal{M}_j(D_j)=o_j | \mathcal{M}_{j-1}(D_{j-1})=o_{j-1},...,\mathcal{M}_1(D_1)=o_1]}{Pr[\mathcal{M}_j(D_j')=o_j | \mathcal{M}_{j-1}(D_{j-1}')=o_{j-1},...,\mathcal{M}_1(D_1')=o_1]}$$
$$\triangleq c_j(o_j; o_1, ..., o_{j-1})$$

Once the prefix $(o_1, ..., o_{j-1})$ is fixed, $Z_j \triangleq c_j(o_j; o_1, ..., o_{j-1}) = \frac{Pr(\mathcal{M}_j(D_j)=o_j)}{Pr(\mathcal{M}_j(D_j')=o_j)}$

By the (α, ϵ_j)-RDP property of $\mathcal{M}_j$, $D_\alpha \triangleq \frac{1}{\alpha-1} log\mathbb{E}[Z_j^\alpha] \leq \epsilon$.

Because of randomized partition of the input domain $\mathbb{D}$, the extra element d_e of D is randomly mapped to k partitions. Therefore, j is uniformly distributed over $\{1, ..., k\}$, and thus the random variable $Z^{(o)}$ under random data partition is the mixture of independent random variables $Z_1^{(o)}, ..., Z_k^{(o)}$,

$$f(Z^{(o)}) = \tfrac{1}{k}f(Z_1^{(o)}) + ... + \tfrac{1}{k}f(Z_k^{(o)})$$

where $f(X)$ is the probability distribution function of X.

We have
$$D_\alpha = \tfrac{1}{\alpha-1} log\mathbb{E}[(Z^{(o)})^\alpha] = \tfrac{1}{k} \sum_{j=1}^k \tfrac{1}{\alpha-1} log\mathbb{E}[(Z_j^{(o)})^\alpha]$$

Because $Z_j^{(o)}$ satisfies RDP, by (5) then we have $D_\alpha \leq \tfrac{1}{k} \sum_{j=1}^k \epsilon_j$. If $\forall j \; \epsilon_j = \epsilon$, we have $D_\alpha \leq \epsilon$, and thus the mechanism $\mathcal{M}(D)$ satisfies (α, ϵ)-RDP.

If not all ϵ_j are the same, we replace each ϵ_j with $\max_j \epsilon_j$, we have $D_\alpha = \frac{1}{\alpha-1} log\mathbb{E}[(Z^{(o)})^\alpha] \leq \max_j \epsilon_j$, and the mechanism $\mathcal{M}(D)$ satisfies $(\alpha, \max_j \epsilon_j)$-RDP.

References

1. Abadi, M., et al.: Deep learning with differential privacy. In: Proceedings of the 2016 ACM SIGSAC Conference on Computer and Communications Security, pp. 308–318 (2016)
2. Balle, B., Wang, Y.: Improving the Gaussian mechanism for differential privacy: analytical calibration and optimal denoising. arXiv preprint arXiv:1805.06530 (2018)
3. Bun, M., Steinke, T.: Concentrated differential privacy: simplifications, extensions, and lower bounds. In: Hirt, M., Smith, A. (eds.) TCC 2016. LNCS, vol. 9985, pp. 635–658. Springer, Heidelberg (2016). https://doi.org/10.1007/978-3-662-53641-4_24
4. Dwork, C.: Automata, languages and programming. In: 33rd International Colloquium, ICALP (2006)
5. Dwork, C., McSherry, F., Nissim, K., Smith, A.: Calibrating noise to sensitivity in private data analysis. In: Halevi, S., Rabin, T. (eds.) TCC 2006. LNCS, vol. 3876, pp. 265–284. Springer, Heidelberg (2006). https://doi.org/10.1007/11681878_14
6. Dwork, C., Roth, A., et al.: The algorithmic foundations of differential privacy. Found. Trends® Theor. Comput. Sci. **9**(3–4), 211–407 (2014)
7. Fredrikson, M., Jha, S., Ristenpart, T.: Model inversion attacks that exploit confidence information and basic countermeasures. In: Proceedings of the 22nd ACM SIGSAC Conference on Computer and Communications Security, pp. 1322–1333 (2015)
8. Fredrikson, M., Lantz, E., Jha, S., Lin, S., Page, D., Ristenpart, T.: Privacy in pharmacogenetics: an end-to-end case study of personalized warfarin dosing. In: 23rd {USENIX} Security Symposium ({USENIX} Security 14), pp. 17–32 (2014)
9. He, K., Zhang, X., Ren, S., Sun, J.: Identity mappings in deep residual networks. In: Leibe, B., Matas, J., Sebe, N., Welling, M. (eds.) ECCV 2016. LNCS, vol. 9908, pp. 630–645. Springer, Cham (2016). https://doi.org/10.1007/978-3-319-46493-0_38
10. Jayaraman, B., Evans, D.: Evaluating differentially private machine learning in practice. In: 28th {USENIX} Security Symposium ({USENIX} Security 19), pp. 1895–1912 (2019)
11. LeCun, Y., Bottou, L., Bengio, Y., Haffner, P.: Gradient-based learning applied to document recognition. Proc. IEEE **86**(11), 2278–2324 (1998)
12. Lee, J., Kifer, D.: Concentrated differentially private gradient descent with adaptive per-iteration privacy budget. In: Proceedings of the 24th ACM SIGKDD International Conference on Knowledge Discovery & Data Mining, pp. 1656–1665 (2018)
13. McMahan, H.B., Ramage, D., Talwar, K., Zhang, L.: Learning differentially private recurrent language models. arXiv preprint arXiv:1710.06963 (2017)
14. Mironov, I.: Rényi differential privacy. In: 2017 IEEE 30th Computer Security Foundations Symposium (CSF), pp. 263–275. IEEE (2017)
15. Osher, S., Wang, B., Yin, P., Luo, X., Barekat, F., Pham, M., Lin, A.: Laplacian smoothing gradient descent. arXiv preprint arXiv:1806.06317 (2018)
16. Shokri, R., Shmatikov, V.: Privacy-preserving deep learning. In: Proceedings of the 22nd ACM SIGSAC Conference on Computer and Communications Security, pp. 1310–1321 (2015)
17. Shokri, R., Stronati, M., Song, C., Shmatikov, V.: Membership inference attacks against machine learning models. In: 2017 IEEE Symposium on Security and Privacy (SP), pp. 3–18. IEEE (2017)

18. Song, S., Chaudhuri, K., Sarwate, A.D.: Stochastic gradient descent with differentially private updates. In: 2013 IEEE Global Conference on Signal and Information Processing, pp. 245–248. IEEE (2013)
19. Szegedy, C., et al.: Going deeper with convolutions. In: Proceedings of the IEEE Conference on Computer Vision and Pattern Recognition, pp. 1–9 (2015)
20. Waites, C.: PyVacy: towards practical differential privacy for deep learning (2019)
21. Wang, Y., Balle, B., Kasiviswanathan, S.: Subsampled rényi differential privacy and analytical moments accountant. arXiv preprint arXiv:1808.00087 (2018)
22. Yosinski, J., Clune, J., Bengio, Y., Lipson, H.: How transferable are features in deep neural networks? In: Advances in Neural Information Processing Systems, pp. 3320–3328 (2014)
23. Yu, L., Liu, L., Pu, C., Gursoy, M.E., Truex, S.: Differentially private model publishing for deep learning. In: 2019 IEEE Symposium on Security and Privacy (SP), pp. 332–349. IEEE (2019)
24. Zhang, C., Bengio, S., Hardt, M., Recht, B., Vinyals, O.: Understanding deep learning requires rethinking generalization. arXiv preprint arXiv:1611.03530 (2016)

Recommender Systems with Condensed Local Differential Privacy

Ao Liu[1,3], Yanqing Yao[1,2]([✉]), and Xianfu Cheng[1,3]

[1] State Key Laboratory of Software Development Environment, Beihang University,
Beijing 100191, China
{liuao,yaoyq,buaacxf}@buaa.edu.cn
[2] Key Laboratory of Aerospace Network Security,
Ministry of Industry and Information Technology,
School of Cyberspace Science and Technology, Beihang University,
Beijing 100191, China
[3] Beijing Key Laboratory of Network Technology, Beihang University,
Beijing 100191, China

Abstract. Recommender systems aim at predicting users' future behaviors by learning the users' personal information and historical behaviors. Unfortunately, training by the user's raw data will inevitably cause the user's private information to leak. Moreover, exiting privacy-preserving recommendation methods are based on matrix factorization with Local Differential Privacy (LDP). Because LDP performs poorly in small or multi-dimensional data sets, these methods do not work well with sparse or multi-dimensional features. Motivated by these questions, we propose a privacy-preserving recommendation model based on Deep neural networks and Factorization Machines (DeepFM), which can provide users with recommendations under the promise of protecting users' privacy. In our recommendation model, each user randomly perturbs the calculated gradients to satisfy Condensed Local Differential Privacy (CLDP). The recommender system collects the perturbed gradients to train a recommendation model, which guarantees the safety of users' private information and has excellent accuracy for the recommendation. Experiments on a real-world dataset show that the recommendation accuracy of our algorithm performs better than the existing methods.

Keywords: Privacy-preserving · Recommender system · Condensed local differential privacy · Deep neural network · Factorization machine

1 Introduction

Recommender systems play an increasingly important role in online businesses. An excellent recommender system can recommend suitable products to users, which will reduce users' search time and improve the users' experience. Therefore, we use various recommender system models, such as e-commerce recommendations in Alibaba [2], and video recommendations on YouTube [3].

© Springer Nature Switzerland AG 2020
X. Chen et al. (Eds.): ML4CS 2020, LNCS 12486, pp. 355–365, 2020.
https://doi.org/10.1007/978-3-030-62223-7_30

To train recommendation systems, we need to mine users' history behavior and other information. However, these data include personal private information. Even using an anonymized method, an attacker can reidentify anonymized records by a linkage attack [14]. Differential privacy [6], which ensures high levels of privacy while providing accurate information about users' data, can address this issue. Differential privacy includes centralized differential privacy and local differential privacy [7]. Centralized differential privacy requires a trusted server to collect and perturb users' data for protecting users' privacy. In local differential privacy, each user sends the perturbed data to the server, and the server analyzes the statistical characteristics of the original data by mathematical methods. Therefore, local differential privacy can provide stronger privacy protection than centralized differential privacy.

As one hotspot in privacy-preserving research, local differential privacy (LDP) has achieved great results in various aspects. Duchi et al. [5] proposed a LDP mechanism for continuous values. In the mechanism, there is an incompletely trusted aggregator and some users with private information. For the sake of privacy, each user perturbs his (or her) continuous values to discrete values with the numerical value as the probability parameter. The aggregator can estimate the statistical information of the raw data by collecting the perturbed data. To reduce the estimation error, Wang et al. [18] proposed a locally differentially private protocol for frequency estimation. The protocol is an unbiased estimate with minimum variance for local differential privacy. However, LDP performs poorly in scenarios with sparse data sets or high-dimensional data sets. Gursoy et al. [10] proposed the concept of condensed local differential privacy (CLDP). As a specialization of LDP, CLDP not only has the privacy protection of LDP but also has high utility on small data sets. Recently, LDP has been applied in industry. For example, Google's Chrome browser uses the RAPPOR algorithm [8], and Apple's Safari browser also uses LDP to learn from a user population [1].

There have been several recommender systems that adopt LDP to protect user privacy. Shin et al. [16] proposed a recommender system with LDP. In their model, LDP is used to perturb the gradients of user data and the recommendation model is trained by collecting perturbed gradients. Kim et al. [13] proposed Successive Point-of-Interest Recommendation with LDP (SPIREL) framework. SPIREL not only collects perturbed gradients but also employs perturbed users' check-in history, which can achieve better point-of-interest recommendation quality. Qi et al. [15] proposed a privacy-preserving method for news recommendation model training based on federated learning. This model is also trained by perturbed gradients. There are three problems in above models: (1) these model requires users to continuously calculate and perturb gradient, which has a high communication cost; (2) when the recommender system has too many parameters, perturbed gradients will lead to a decrease in the usefulness of the system [4]; (3) these model do not work well in multi-dimensional data sets.

The goal of this paper is to build a privacy-preserving recommender system that overcomes the limitations of the above models. First, we design a perturbation mechanism that satisfies condensed local differential privacy for training. Compared with gradient descent with LDP [17], our perturbed gradient method is easier to calculate and more useful. Then, we modify the output layer of DeepFM to a linear regression layer. Therefore, DeepFM can be divided into three components: a deep neural network, a factorization machine, and a linear regression layer. When training the model, we train these three parts in sequence through random sampling, which reduces the parameter training for individual users. Thus, it not only improves accuracy but also reduces communication costs.

Compared with existing privacy-preserving recommender systems, our contributions are as follows.

(1) We develop a gradient descent algorithm with CLDP for training recommender systems. Compared with the methods with LDP for training, our gradient descent with CLDP works well on small or multi-dimensional data sets and improves recommendation accuracy under the premise of protecting user privacy.

(2) Existing models [12,13,16] are from matrix factorization, so they only apply users and items information. We propose a recommender system, which consists of a deep neural network, a factorization machine, and a linear regression. Our model supports multi-dimensional features for the recommendation.

(3) In addition to adopting the gradient descent with CLDP, we also use random sampling and partial training. Each time a part of the data is randomly selected to participate in the training of a certain part of the model, which can not only reduce the computational complexity of each user's participation but also save the privacy budget. Therefore, a model with better accuracy can be trained in this way (Fig. 1).

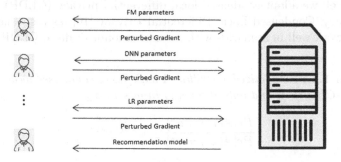

Fig. 1. Overview of our system

2   Related Work

2.1   DeepFM

In this section, we give an overview of DeepFM. DeepFM [9] consists of a factorization machine (FM) and a deep neural network (DNN). FM and DNN components are used to learn the low-order feature interactions and learn high-order feature interactions and nonlinearities, respectively. Suppose the data set consists of X and y, where $X = [x_1, x_2, ..., x_d]$ is d-dimensional feature such as user id and item id, and y is a label such as click or rate. Let $\hat{y}, \hat{y}_{DNN}, \hat{y}_{FM}$ denote the output of DeepFM, DNN, and FM, so we have:

$$\hat{y} = sigmoid(\hat{y}_{DNN} + \hat{y}_{FM})$$

Factorization machine is proposed in [9] to learn feature interactions. The output of FM is the sum of the inner product of latent vector:

$$\hat{y}_{FM} = \langle w, X \rangle + \sum_{i=1}^{d} \sum_{j=1}^{d} \langle v_i, v_j \rangle x_i x_j$$

where $\langle \cdot, \cdot \rangle$ denotes the inner product, and $v_i, v_j \in R^k$ are the latent vector of x_i and v_j.

The compent of DNN is a fully connected neural network, where the input of DNN is the vector $I^{(0)} = [v_1, v_2, ..., v_d]$. The output of l-th layer is also the input of $(l + 1)$-th layer, denoted as:

$$I^{(l+1)} = f(W^{(l)} I^{(l)} + b^{(l)})$$

where f is activation function. $W^{(l)}$ and $b^{(l)}$ is parameters of l-th layer.

2.2   Condensed Local Differential Privacy

In our model, we adopt condensed local differential privacy (CLDP) to protect users' privacy. Condensed Local Differential Privacy [10], as a specialization of LDP, can work well in scenarios with a small amount of data. CLDP is defined as follows.

Definition 1. *A randomized algorithm A satisfies α-condensed local differential privacy (α-CLDP), if and only if for any inputs $x_1, x_2 \in X$:*

$$\frac{Pr[A(x_1) = x^*]}{Pr[A(x_2) = x^*]} \le e^{\alpha \cdot d(x_1, x_2)}$$

where $\alpha > 0$, and $d(x_1, x_2)$ represents the distance between x_1 and x_2. When $d(\cdot, \cdot) \equiv 1$, CLDP will be degraded to LDP.

Similar to LDP, the budget of the privacy α controls the privacy and utility tradeoff. In addition, we need to define a distance function $d(\cdot, \cdot)$, which is also a factor affecting privacy. By definition, we know that CLDP satisfies the indistinguishability property, that an adversary observing x^* will not be able to distinguish whether the raw data is x_1 or x_2.

Besides, we need an algorithm supporting CLDP. Exponential Mechanism (EM) [10] is one of the randomized algorithms satisfying α-CLDP. EM is defined as follows.

Definition 2. *Given a value $x \in X$, A_{EM} represent the Exponential Mechanism. Then, A_{EM} that produces output x^* with the following probability satisfies α-CLDP:*

$$Pr[A_{EM}(x) = x^*] = \frac{e^{-\frac{\alpha \cdot d(x, x^*)}{2}}}{\sum_{x' \in X} e^{-\frac{\alpha \cdot d(x, x')}{2}}}$$

By the definition of EM, we know that when the space of X is larger, the noise is greater and the utility is worse.

3   Privacy-Preserving Recommender Systems

3.1   Gradient Descent with CLDP

Our model protects users' private information by disturbing the gradient. In this section, we first define a gradient perturbation method that satisfies CLDP. Algorithm 1 shows our method for training a privacy-preserving recommender system with parameters W by minimizing the loss function $L(W)$. Each user computes the gradient $\nabla W_{t,i}$, clips the l_2 normal of each gradient, discretizes and perturbs the gradient. And the recommender collects the perturbed gradient and estimates the mean of the gradient for training. Next we describe in more detail of our method.

We use $\nabla W = [v_1, v_2, ..., v_m]$ to denote the gradient vector. In the gradient descent algorithm, the key is the direction of the gradient vector (not the size of the vector). Therefore, we will clip the gradient in advance to make each dimension satisfy $v_i \in [-1, 1]$. In order to randomly perturb the gradient, we first discretize each dimension of the gradient vector. We use 0 and 1 to represent the positive and negative direction of a certain dimension of the gradient, respectively. The discretization method is as follows.

$$Discretize(v_i) = \begin{cases} 1, & with \quad probability \quad \frac{1}{2}v_i + \frac{1}{2} \\ 0, & otherwise. \end{cases}$$

From the above discretization, we can get a binary vector B. We define the distance between two different binary vectors as $l1$ distance:

$$d(B, B') = \sum_{i=1}^{m} |B[i] - B'[i]|$$

Algorithm 1: Gradient Descent with CLDP

Input: Data set $\{(X_1, y_1), (X_2, y_2), ..., (X_n, y_n)\}$, Loss function
　　　$L(W) = \frac{1}{n} \sum_{i=1} nL(W, X_i, y_i)$, and Privacy budget α
Output: Model parameter W_T
Initialize W_0 randomly
for $t \leftarrow 1$ *to* T **do**
　　Randomly select C users
　　for $i \leftarrow 1$ *to* C **do**
　　　　Compute gradient: $\nabla W_{t,i} = \nabla_{W_{t,i}} L(W, X_i)$
　　　　Clip gradinet: $W_{t,i} = W_{t,i} * \frac{1}{\max(1, \|W_{t,i}\|_2)}$
　　　　Discretize gradinet: $B_{t,i} = Discretize(W_{t,i})$
　　　　Perturb gradinet: $B_{t,i}^* = Perturb(B_{t,i})$
　　　　Send $B_{t,i}^*$ to the aggregator
　　Estimate gradinet by the aggregator: $\hat{B}_t^* = Estimate(\{B_{t,1}^*, B_{t,2}^*, ..., B_{t,C}^*\})$
　　Send gradinet to all users: $W_{t+1} \leftarrow W_t - \eta \hat{B}_t^*$
return W_T

---

where $B[i]$ is i-th bit of the vector B. For each binary vector B, we use a perturbation function to generate a new value B^*.

Theorem 1. *Let's use Perturb($\cdot$) represent the perturbation function. If Perturb($\cdot$) is to perturb each bit of the input vector with the following probability, then Perturb($\cdot$) satisfies α-CLDP, where $\alpha = ln(\frac{p}{q})$, $p + q = 1$.*

$$Pr[B^*[k] = 1] = \begin{cases} p, & if \quad B[k] = 1 \\ q, & if \quad B[k] = 0 \end{cases}$$

Proof. For any input vector B_i and B_j, we have that

$$\frac{Pr[Perturb(B_i) = B^*]}{Pr[Perturb(B_j) = B^*]} = \frac{p^{n_i} q^{m-n_i}}{p^{n_j} q^{m-n_j}} = \frac{(\frac{p}{q})^{n_i}}{(\frac{p}{q})^{n_j}} = (\frac{p}{q})^{n_i - n_j}$$

where n_i (or n_j) is the number of different dimensions between B_i (or B_j) and B^*. According to the definition of distance, we have $n_i = d(B_i, B^*)$. By the inequality of distance, we get that

$$\frac{Pr[Perturb(B_i) = B^*]}{Pr[Perturb(B_j) = B^*]} = (\frac{p}{q})^{d(B_i, B^*) - d(B_j, B^*)} \leq (\frac{p}{q})^{d(B_i, B_j)} = e^{\alpha \cdot d(B_i, B_j)}$$

In a recommender system, each user calculates the vector B^* and sends it to the recommender. The recommender can estimate the frequency of the positive and negative directions of each dimension of all the users' gradient vectors.

Theorem 2. *For the perturbation function Perturb($\cdot$), the estimation $\hat{f}_i$ is unbiased.*

$$\hat{f}_i = \frac{k_i - qC}{p - q}$$

where C is the total number of users. k_i represents the number of 1 in i-th dimension in perturbed gradients.

Proof. Let's use f_i represent the number of 1 i-th dimension in discretized gradients, we have that

$$E[\hat{f}_i] = E[\frac{k_i - qC}{p - q}] = \frac{E[k_i] - qC}{p - q} = \frac{f_i * p + (C - f_i) * q - qC}{p - q} = f_i$$

3.2 Recommender System

The architecture of our model is similar to the DeepFM, which consists of a deep neural network (DNN) and a factorization machine (FM). The difference is that we modify the output layer and embedding layer of DeepFM. Our model is shown in Fig. 2. The embedding layer of our model consists of DNN embeddings and FM embeddings. The output layer is a linear regression (LR). The purpose of this modification is that we expect to divide the model into three parts: DNN, FM, and LR, and we train the parameters of each part separately.

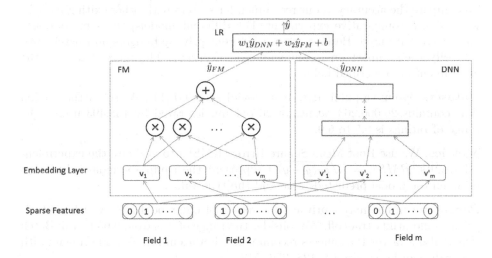

Fig. 2. The architecture of our model

Correspondingly, all users would be randomly divided into three parts to train the three parts of the model, which brings two benefits: (a) the training parameters of user participation will be reduced, which reduces the computational complexity and communication cost; (b) the perturbation will change small, which increases the utility of gradients. The detailed steps of our model training are as follows.

(1) Randomly divide all users into three parts: Part 1, Part 2, and Part 3;
(2) Use Algorithm 1 and Part 1 to train the FM component;
(3) Use Algorithm 1 and Part 2 to train the DNN component;
(4) Send parameters of FM and DNN to the user of Part3, and each user calculates the output of two components;
(5) Use Algorithm 1 and Part 3 to train the LR component.

Through the above steps, the recommender can get all the parameters of the model. The recommender sends the final parameters to all users. Then, users can obtain recommendations on the local. Throughout the process, the users' raw data will not be disclosed to the recommender. Considering a special case, we trained two weak models (FM and DNN) when α is small. Then, we will obtain a strong recommender system by training the LR component. There are only three parameters in the LR component. If the amount of data is enough, we can always get a good LR component even if α. Thus, the models we obtain are better than FM model, DNN model, and DeepFM model.

4   Evaluation

4.1   Experimental Setup

To compare the accuracy of our recommender system with other exiting models, we design a comparative experiment. For different models, the same datasets and metrics are used. Besides, we use different privacy budgets and batch sizes to verify their impact on recommendation accuracy. The more details of the experiment are described below.

Datasets. We use a public datasets: MovieLens-20M [11]. We select the version that contains 20,000,263 ratings of 26,744 movies rated by 138,493 users. The range of ratings is 0.5 to 5.0.

Metrics. We use Root Mean Square Error (RMSE) to evaluate the experimental results. $RMSE = \sqrt{E[(\hat{y} - y)^2]}$ represent the sample standard deviation between the model predicted value and the true value.

Parameters. The major privacy parameter of our model is α, which controls privacy and utility tradeoff. We consider the range of α is from 0.05 to 1.5. Batch size is also a factor that affects recommendation accuracy. We experiment with four values of batch size 64, 128, 256, 512.

Comparisons. We chose DeepFM without privacy protection as the baseline. Existing methods are based on matrix factorization and LDP [12,16], which are different from the model and privacy-preserving technology. Thus, we only compare them with their optimal case to show the better accuracy of our model.

Environment. We implement our model in Python 3.6.9 and Pytorch 1.5.0+cu101. Since the clipping gradient and perturbing gradient are time-consuming, all experiments need to be trained on GPU.

4.2   Experimental Results

We implement a recommender system using the model shown in Fig. 2, DeepFM [9] and MF [16]. For the data, we randomly select 20% of data as the test set, and the remaining data as the training set. We train the DeepFM by gradient descent as a baseline (Non-Private DeepFM). Besides, we train our model and DeepFM by the gradient descent with CLDP. The results are shown in Table 1.

Table 1. RMSE on MovieLens-20M

α	0.05	0.1	0.2	0.5	1.0	1.5
Our model with CLDP	1.4358	1.3488	1.1689	1.21111	1.0818	1.0741
DeepFM with CLDP	3.2836	1.4759	1.3585	1.2319	1.2034	1.1603
Non-Private DeepFM	0.9430					
Non-Private MF	1.1729					

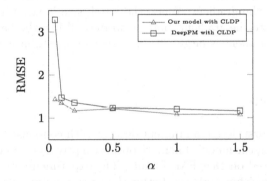

Fig. 3. RMSE with α

Prediction Accuracy over Various Models. Compared with other models, our model is only weaker than the baseline (Non-Private DeepFM) without privacy protection. When $\alpha > 0.2$, our model is better than the best case (Non-Private MF) of the existing privacy protection model [12,16]. Using the same gradient perturbation algorithm, our model outperforms the DeepFM model at any privacy budget.

Prediction Accuracy over Various Privacy Budgets. As shown in Fig. 3, when the privacy budget is small, the performance of the model is worse, and when the privacy budget is larger, the performance of the model is better. Besides, our model has fewer performance fluctuations over various privacy budgets. When the α is relatively small, our model still maintains good performance.

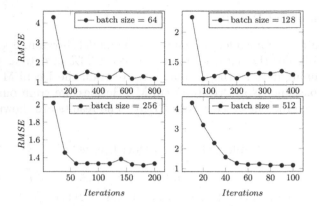

Fig. 4. RMSE with batch sizes ($\alpha = 1.0$)

Prediction Accuracy over Various Batch Sizes. As shown in Fig. 4, when the batch size is small, RMSE is not convergent; when the batch size is large, RMSE is convergent. The reason is that the batch size affects the accuracy of the estimation of the gradient. When the batch size is large, there are enough samples to estimate the gradient more accurately. When the batch size is small, the noise of the gradient is large, which leads to the estimation of the gradient is not accurate.

5   Conclusion

In this paper, we first design a gradient descent with condensed local differential privacy for training the model. Then, we propose a privacy-preserving recommendation system based on DeepFM. Finally, The experiments on MovieLens-20M show that our algorithm performs better than the existing methods. Therefore, our model can recommend suitable products for users under the premise of ensuring privacy.

Acknowledgements. The above work was supported by Beijing Municipal Natural Science Foundation (Grant No. 4202035), the Fundamental Research Funds for the Central Universities (Grant No. YWF-20-BJ-J-1040), the National Key R&D Program of China (Grant No. 2016QY04W0802), and the National Natural Science Foundation of China (Grant No. 61602025, U1636211, and 61170189).

References

1. Learning with Privacy at Scale (2017). https://machinelearning.apple.com/2017/12/06/learning-with-privacy-at-scale.html
2. Chen, Q., Zhao, H., Li, W., Huang, P., Ou, W.: Behavior sequence transformer for e-commerce recommendation in alibaba. arXiv Information Retrieval (2019)

3. Covington, P., Adams, J., Sargin, E.: Deep neural networks for YouTube recommendations. In: Proceedings of the 10th ACM Conference on Recommender Systems, pp. 191–198 (2016)
4. Duchi, J., Rogers, R.: Lower bounds for locally private estimation via communication complexity. In: Proceedings of 32nd Annual Conference on Learning Theory, vol. 99, pp. 1–31 (2019)
5. Duchi, J.C., Jordan, M.I., Wainwright, M.J.: Local privacy and statistical minimax rates. In: Foundations of Computer Science, pp. 429–438 (2013)
6. Dwork, C.: Differential privacy. In: Proceedings of the 33rd International Conference on Automata, Languages and Programming, vol. 2, pp. 1–12 (2006)
7. Dwork, C., Roth, A.: The algorithmic foundations of differential privacy. Found. Trends Theor. Comput. Sci. **9**, 211–407 (2014)
8. Úlfar Erlingsson, Pihur, V., Korolova, A.: RAPPOR: randomized aggregatable privacy-preserving ordinal response, pp. 1054–1067 (2014)
9. Guo, H., Tang, R., Ye, Y., Li, Z., He, X.: DeepFM: a factorization-machine based neural network for CTR prediction. In: International Joint Conference on Artificial Intelligence, pp. 1725–1731 (2017)
10. Gursoy, M.E., Tamersoy, A., Truex, S., Wei, W., Liu, L.: Secure and utility-aware data collection with condensed local differential privacy. IEEE Trans. Dependable Secure Comput. 1 (2019)
11. Harper, F.M., Konstan, J.A.: The movielens datasets: history and context. Ksii Trans. Internet Inf. Syst. **5**(4), 19 (2016)
12. Hua, J., Xia, C., Zhong, S.: Differentially private matrix factorization. In: Proceedings of 24th International Joint Conference on Artificial Interlligence, pp. 1763–1770 (2015)
13. Kim, J.S., Kim, J.W., Chung, Y.D.: Successive point-of-interest recommendation with local differential privacy. arXiv Information Retrieval (2019)
14. Merener, M.M.: Theoretical results on de-anonymization via linkage attacks. Trans. Data Priv. **5**(2), 377–402 (2012)
15. Qi, T., Wu, F., Wu, C., Huang, Y., Xie, X.: Privacy-preserving news recommendation model training via federated learning. arXiv Information Retrieval (2020)
16. Shin, H., Kim, S., Shin, J., Xiao, X.: Privacy enhanced matrix factorization for recommendation with local differential privacy. IEEE Trans. Knowl. Data Eng. **30**(9), 1770–1782 (2018)
17. Wang, N., et al.: Collecting and analyzing multidimensional data with local differential privacy. In: Proceedings of the 35th Annual International Conference on Data Engineering, pp. 638–649 (2019)
18. Wang, T., Blocki, J., Li, N., Jha, S.: Differentially private protocols for frequency estimation. In: Proceedings of the 26th USENIX Security Symposium, pp. 729–745 (2017)

Exploiting Bluetooth to Enquire Close Contacts Without Privacy Leakage

Suhang Wang[1], Chen Wang[2], and Jian Xu[2(✉)]

[1] College of Medicine and Biological Information Engineering,
Northeastern University, Shenyang, China
[2] Software College, Northeastern University, Shenyang, China
xuj@mail.neu.edu.cn

Abstract. An outbreak of infectious diseases does as much harm to human society as a war, and which is even more difficult to prevent. The prevention of infectious diseases needs to start from the source, meanwhile, to identify anyone in close contact. Finding the close contacts via Bluetooth search signals to better identify potential patients can help to reduce the impact on human society caused by droplet transmission of infectious diseases. In this study, we use Bluetooth search record and machine learning to identify close contacts on the premise of protecting patients' privacy. We proposed a classification method based on privacy protection, which can store and calculate user's private information without revealing it on an untrusted server, and without knowing the user's plain text message of the saved information. This method can be carried out with acceptable computational overhead and achieve a higher accuracy.

Keywords: Privacy preservation · Machine learning · Contact analysis

1 Introduce

Various acute respiratory infectious diseases can spread rapidly in a short time, such as SARS, H1N1, COVID-19, etc. In 2009, H1N1 flu broke out in the United States and spread to 214 countries and regions. Within three months, more than 70,000 people were diagnosed with H1N1 virus. In 2019, pneumonia caused by the new coronavirus has infected more than two million people. These diseases are usually spread by the droplets generated when the patient sneezes, coughs and speaks. To some extent, people who have been in close contact with patients are more likely to be infected. In order to prevent the outbreak of infection early, after each patient is diagnosed, his close contacts should be found and isolated early.

Through traditional epidemiological investigation, it will consume a lot of manpower, material and financial resources, and will miss many strangers who pass by the patient, and will cause panic to other unrelated persons. In order to find as many people as possible in contact with the patient and save public re-sources as much as possible, we can use the short-range communication technology of mobile phones to record people who have been in contact with the patient.

© Springer Nature Switzerland AG 2020
X. Chen et al. (Eds.): ML4CS 2020, LNCS 12486, pp. 366–375, 2020.
https://doi.org/10.1007/978-3-030-62223-7_31

With the rapid development of the mobile phone industry, everybody has one or more mobile phones. Regardless of whether it is a smart phone with a few thousand dollars or an elderly machine with a few hundred dollars, there is a short-distance communication technology that has been used for many years-Bluetooth technology. Since Bluetooth technology is a short-distance communication technology, only when the two users are close to each other, their Blue-tooth signals can be searched by other's devices. After that, through the strength of the Bluetooth signal, we can roughly estimate the distance between the users. In order to determine whether it is a close contact.

Assuming that user A meets user B at this moment, their mobile phone will search for the other's Bluetooth signal and record it and upload it to the cloud server. When user A is diagnosed as a patient, we can calculate the Bluetooth search record, and then, estimate the approximate distance between the user who has been in contact with A. Since the Bluetooth signal is a short-distance communication technology, only when two users are within a certain range can they search for the other party's signal. We can also classify them and divide the contacts into different levels, such as ordinary contacts (such as weak Bluetooth signal strength and a long distance between two users), and close contacts (close distance between users, there is a greater risk of being infected). Unlike GPS, which can record the user's detailed location information, the Bluetooth signal only saves the relative position between users. That is, the two users have encountered each other, and cannot know where they met. Compared with GPS, it can protect the privacy of users to a certain extent.

In this article, we propose a close contact query scheme based on privacy protection. This scheme takes into account the privacy of the user and enables the close contact of the patient to be found without being informed of the user's plaintext information. The main contributions of this article are as follows:

1. The query scheme we proposed can protect user's privacy. In the entire system, CDC can only learn user's private information if authorized. In addition, all information in the system is encrypted, and no entity can know its specific meaning without authorization.
2. We propose a classification scheme to protect user privacy. This scheme is based on homomorphic encryption, which can directly calculate ciphertext with-out decryption, and divide patient contacts into close contacts and ordinary contacts.
3. The privacy information uploaded by the user only represents the relative position between the users, and close contacts can be found without the user's precise location information.

The arrangement of the other chapters in this article is as follows: The second section introduces the system model and design goals. Section 3 conducts infection analysis, and Section 4 introduces privacy-preserving query schemes and encryption schemes. Section 5 summarizes this paper.

2 Related Work

Today, academia has proposed a series of encryption-based machine learning algorithms, such as Naive Bayes [1–3], decision trees [4, 5], linear discriminant classifiers [6], and more general kernel methods [7]. These algorithms have been widely used in practice [8]. [9] proposed a k-nearest neighbor classification algorithm based on the Paillier cryptosystem [10], which can operate on the ciphertext of the medical system. Due to the rarity, unpredictability and correlation of abnormal events, [11] proposed a Bayesian adaptive semi-supervised adaptive hidden Markov model to adjust abnormal events. In literature [12], a privacy-preserving clinical decision support system based on naive Bayes classification is proposed. It first gathers ground data for training, and then enables untrusted cloud servers to perform secure classification algorithms on encrypted data. Users can also retrieve top-k diagnosis results based on their interests and requests. These schemes need to use the labeled training data set to obtain the learning/classification model.

Secure two-party computation protocols for generic functions exist in theory [13–17] and in practice [18–20]. In order to operate the encrypted data flexibly, [15] introduces a "double homomorphic" encryption scheme to perform secure multi-party calculations. With the help of advanced and effective homomorphic encryption technology [16], Graepel et al. proposed a privacy-preserving machine learning solution to hand over heavy computing tasks to powerful cloud servers. This privacy-preserving machine learning solution mainly solves the privacy problem in the data training stage.

3 System Model and Design Goals

In this section we present the model and design goals of the system.

3.1 System Model

The entire system consists of three entities: CDC, user (patient), computing cloud server and database, as shown in the Fig. 1.

User searches for nearby Bluetooth signal through the short-distance communication technology of the smartphone, records the Bluetooth signal. Then, the user encrypts the searched data and sends it to database for storage. When CDC obtains the user's authorization, it can get the data saved by the user in the database. Then, CDC and the server classify the user's data while protecting the user's privacy, and obtain the final classification result.

The cloud server has computing function. After receiving the query request sent by the CDC, the Bluetooth signal uploaded by the user is calculated. Finally, CDC gets the result.

CDC is the entity that issues the calculation request. After a user is diagnosed with an infectious disease, the user authorizes CDC to query his data. CDC queries the data stored by the user in the database. By calculating these data, CDC finds close contacts of the patient.

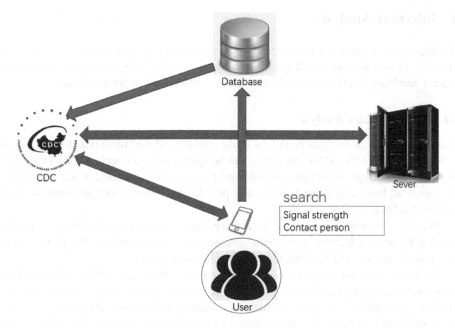

Fig. 1. System model

Database is an entity used to store user data. It can re-encrypt the user's data and send the re-encrypted data to the CDC.

3.2 Privacy Requirements and Design Goals

In this system, the user's various privacy information should be kept secret from all entities except authorized entities. The specific privacy requirements are as follows:

1. The user's precise Bluetooth search record should be kept secret from all unauthorized entities, such as the server, CDC, etc. The database only saves the encrypted information;
2. The results of close contacts enquiry. The result can get the user's health status, which is the most important information in the whole system. Except for the CDC, no entity can know the health status of the cloud server returned, so as to avoid leakage of user health information;
3. The patient's identity information should be protected. After the CDC sends a query request to the database, the database cannot infer whether the queried patient is infected by the queried user.

4 Infection Analysis

Whether to be a close contact depends on various factors such as contact time and distance. In this section, we discuss the analysis model of close contacts, and use K-nearest neighbor to divide contacts into close contacts and ordinary contacts.

4.1 Close Contact Analysis

We first propose an analysis model for close contacts. Many infectious diseases, such as SARS, COVID-19, H1N1 virus, etc., can be spread among people through sneezing or coughing through the droplets of infected persons. For example, in the classroom, the patient u_a^* has many contacts with other people, and these people are more likely to be infected by u_a^*.

Whether the normal person u_b is a close contact with the patient u_a^* is mainly affected by several factors, such as the distance between u_a^* and u_b, the contact time between u_a^* and u_b, and the infectivity of infectious diseases.

Different infectious diseases have different infectivity, such as Class A infectious diseases, namely plague, cholera, Class B infectious diseases, namely viral hepatitis, measles, etc., and Class C infectious diseases, namely tuberculosis, dysentery, etc. Due to the different infectiousness, the judgment of their close contacts is also different. As the level increases, the infectivity increases in turn.

Another important factor is the distance between u_a^* and u_b. The longer the distance, the lower the risk of being infected and the less likely it is to be in close contact.

The last important influencing factor is the contact time between u_a^* and u_b. The longer the contact time between the two users, the higher the risk of being infected.

4.2 Contact Analysis

We use KNN (k-NearestNeighbor) to analyze close contacts. KNN classifies by measuring the distance between different feature values. If most of the k nearest samples in the feature space of a sample belong to a certain category, the sample is also divided into this category. In the KNN algorithm, the selected neighbors are all objects that have been correctly classified. This method determines the category to which the samples to be classified belong based on the category of the nearest sample or samples in the decision of classification.

First, we calculate the distance between the test data and each training data. Second, sorting by increasing distance. Third, picking K points with the smallest distance. Fourth, counting the number of occurrences of the category of the first K points. Finally, returning the most frequent category of the first K points as the predicted classification of test data.

5 Privacy-Preserving Infection Analysis Approach

In this section, we use the user's encrypted Bluetooth search signal to analyze close contacts.

5.1   Bluetooth Signal Collection

When two users are in close contact, their smartphones can be searched by Bluetooth. Through the searched device information, we can judge that the two users are close to each other. From the searched Bluetooth name and signal strength, we can know its identity information and the approximate distance between the two users. User upload information format as shown in Fig. 2.

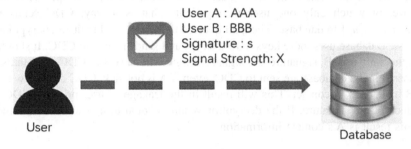

User A : AAA
User B : BBB
Signature : s
Signal Strength: X

User   Database

Fig. 2. User upload information

Because the signal strength can infer the distance between two users, it is very sensitive information. In order to prevent user privacy from leaking, any entity other than authorized entities cannot obtain information in plain text. So, the data needs to be encrypted. Finally, save the encrypted data in the server.

Here, we use Elgamal cryptosystem to encrypt the user's Bluetooth signal strength. Let $\mathbb{G}$ be a cyclic group of p with generator $g \in \mathbb{Z}_p^*$ [21]. User A randomly selects his secret key $SK = x \in \mathbb{Z}_p$. Then, A computers $h = g^x$. User A's public key $PK = (\mathbb{G}, g, p, h)$. During the encryption, A randomly selects $r \in \mathbb{Z}_p$. Then, A computes as Eq. (1).

$$
\begin{aligned}
E(M) &= (c_1, c_2) \\
&= (g^r \bmod p, M \cdot h^r \bmod p) \\
&= (g^r \bmod p, M \cdot (g^x)^r \bmod p)
\end{aligned}
\tag{1}
$$

When decrypting, the decryptor only computes $M = c_2/c_1^x$.

5.2   Data Query Scheme with Privacy-Preserving

If u_a^* is diagnosed with an infectious disease, CDC needs his authorization to query his data. But the user cannot directly give his secret key to CDC. Otherwise, CDC can query his privacy data without the user's authorization. Here, we use a re-encryption scheme to re-encrypt the user's data.

User selects a random number $x_1 \in (0, x)$, x is secret key. Then, let $x_2 = x - x_1$. The user sends x_1 to the database as the re-encryption key, and x_2 to the CDC as the decryption key. First, database uses x_1 to decrypt user's data. The result $c_2' = c_2/c_1^{x_1} = g^{xr}/g^{rx_1} = g^{r(x-x_1)}$. Then, database sends $E'(M) = (c_1, c_2')$ to CDC. Finally, CDC use x_2 decrypts $E'(M)$.

In addition, the database can infer that the user being queried has been diagnosed with a disease. So, we should do something to interfere with the database to speculate on the user's health. Each time CDC queries user data, it sends multiple users to the database, of which only one user is a patient. That is to say, CDC sends $Q = \{u_a^*, u_b, u_c, \ldots, u_n\}$ to database. Then, all queried users will send their re-encrypt key to database. Database uses these keys to re-encrypt and sends results to CDC. It should be noted that only user B, signature and signal strength will be sent to CDC. If both user A and user B in the database are sent to CDC, even if A is not sick, CDC can know that A and B have been in contact. This will result in the leakage of user privacy. CDC will first decrypt the signature. If the decryption result is equal to u_a^*'s signature, it means that this result is A's contact information.

5.3   Privacy-Protected Data Classification

Today, classifiers have many applications in various industries, such as medical or genomics prediction, spam detection, facial recognition, and finance. Many applications handle sensitive private data [22–24], so it is important that the data and the classifier remain private [25].

In this paper, we use an encrypted KNN classifier. It is possible to classify without revealing private data and get the final result. Next, we will introduce several important components of the classifier.

Dot Product Protocol
The dot product protocol calculates the dot product of two vectors encrypted by FHE. The return result is the Euclidean distance square of the test data to be encrypted and the encrypted training data.

C enter the unencrypted data to be tested. S input encrypted training data. C has the public key and S has the private key. The specific process is shown as Algorithm 1.

Minimum Protocol
The minimum protocol is used to obtain the index of minimum value in the ciphertext encrypted by Paillier. First compare the values in the array two by two, then, assign the smaller value of the two to the array with the lower index, and assign 0 to the array with the larger index. Second, record the index of the original smaller side, and the end of one cycle. Finally, all smaller squares form a new array, and then continue to compare the new array until the number of arrays is 1. The last one is the minimum value. The specific process is shown in the Fig. 3.

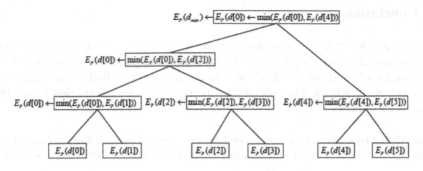

Fig. 3. The process of obtaining the minimum value

The above is the dot product protocol and minimum protocol in the encryption KNN classification. Through the above protocol, combined with the KNN classifier, the data can be classified in the case of encryption. The encrypted KNN classifier can classify patient data and find close contacts without revealing patient privacy.

Algorithm 1. Dot product protocol

1. Input:
   C: $X = (x_1, ..., x_d) \in \mathbb{Z}^d$, pk_f
   S: $Y = (y_1, ..., y_d) \in \mathbb{Z}^d$, sk_f
2. S: for $1 \leq i \leq d$:
3. S: $E_f(y_i) \leftarrow Enc(y_i, pk_f)$
4. S: send $E_f(y_i)$ to C
5. C: $E_f(s) \leftarrow E_f(0)$
6. C: for $1 \leq i \leq d$:
7. $E_f(x_i) \leftarrow Enc(x_i, pk_f)$
8. $E_f(z_i) \leftarrow ((E_f(x_i) - E_f(y_i)) \cdot (E_f(x_i) - E_f(y_i)))$
9. $Ef(s) \leftarrow E_f(s) + E_f(z_i)$
10. Return $E_f(s)$

---

6 Conclusion

In this paper, we propose a new approach to finding close contacts. And, this method does not reveal the user's privacy. First, we analyzed the influencing factors of close contacts. In addition, we use KNN to classify contacts and find close contacts. We propose a query scheme that only obtains the user's private information when authorized by the user.

Acknowledgments. This work is supported by the National Natural Science Foundation of China (61872069), the Fundamental Research Funds for the Central Universities (N2017012).

References

1. Vaidya, J., Kantarcıoğlu, M., Clifton, C.: Privacy-preserving naive bayes classification. VLDB J. **17**(4), 879–898 (2008)
2. Wright, R., Yang, Z.: Privacy-preserving Bayesian network structure computation on distributed heterogeneous data. In: Proceedings of the Tenth ACM SIGKDD International Conference on Knowledge Discovery and Data Mining, pp. 713–718 (2004)
3. Yang, Z., Zhong, S., Wright, R.N.: Privacy-preserving classification of customer data without loss of accuracy. In: Proceedings of the 2005 SIAM International Conference on Data Mining. Society for Industrial and Applied Mathematics, pp. 92–102 (2005)
4. Blum, A., Dwork, C., McSherry, F., Nissim, K.: Practical privacy: the SuLQ framework. In: Proceedings of the Twenty-Fourth ACM SIGMOD-SIGACT-SIGART Symposium on Principles of Database Systems, pp. 128–138 (2005)
5. Lindell, Y., Pinkas, B.: Privacy preserving data mining. In: Proceedings of the 2000 ACM SIGMOD International Conference on Management of Data, pp. 439–450 (2000)
6. Du, W., Han, Y.S., Chen, S.: Privacy-preserving multivariate statistical analysis: linear regression and classification. In: Proceedings of the 4th SIAM International Conference on Data Mining, vol. 233 (2004)
7. Laur, S., Lipmaa, H., Mielikäinen, T.: Cryptographically private support vector machines. In: Proceedings of the 12th ACM SIGKDDACM, pp. 18–624 (2006)
8. Bost, R., Popa, R., Tu, S., Goldwasser, S.: Machine learning classification over encrypted data. In: Proceedings of National Academy Science Armenia, pp. 1–14 (2015)
9. Samanthula, B.K., Elmehdwi, Y., Jiang, W.: k-nearest neighbor classification over semantically secure encrypted relational data. IEEE Trans. Knowl. Data Eng. **27**(5), 1261–1273 (2015)
10. Paillier, P., Pointcheval, D.: Efficient public-key cryptosystems provably secure against active adversaries. In: Lam, K.-Y., Okamoto, E., Xing, C. (eds.) ASIACRYPT 1999. LNCS, vol. 1716, pp. 165–179. Springer, Heidelberg (1999). https://doi.org/10.1007/978-3-540-48000-6_14
11. Zhang, D., Gatica-Perez, D., Bengio, S., McCowan, I.: Semi-supervised adapted HMMs for unusual event detection. In: Proceedings of IEEE Computer Society Conference on Computer Vision and Pattern Recognition, pp. 611–618 (2005)
12. Liu, X., Lu, R., Ma, J., Chen, L., Qin, B.: Privacy-preserving patient-centric clinical decision support system on naive Bayesian classification. IEEE J. Biomed. Health Informat. **2**(20), 1261–1273 (2016)
13. Yao, A.C.: Protocols for secure computations. In: FOCS, pp. 160–164 (1982)

14. Goldreich, O., Micali, S., Wigderson, A.: How to play any mental game. In: STOC, pp. 218–229 (1987)
15. Lindell, Y., Pinkas, B.: An efficient protocol for secure two-party computation in the presence of malicious adversaries. In: Naor, M. (ed.) EUROCRYPT 2007. LNCS, vol. 4515, pp. 52–78. Springer, Heidelberg (2007). https://doi.org/10.1007/978-3-540-72540-4_4
16. Ishai, Y., Prabhakaran, M., Sahai, A.: Founding cryptography on oblivious transfer – efficiently. In: Wagner, D. (ed.) CRYPTO 2008. LNCS, vol. 5157, pp. 572–591. Springer, Heidelberg (2008). https://doi.org/10.1007/978-3-540-85174-5_32
17. Lindell, Y., Pinkas, B.: A proof of security of Yao's protocol fortwo-party computation. J. Cryptol 22, 161–188 (2009)
18. Henecka, W., Kögl, S., Sadeghi, A.-R., Schneider, T., Wehrenberg, I.: TASTY: tool for automating secure two-party computations. In: CCS, pp. 451–462 (2010)
19. Malkhi, D., Nisan, N., Pinkas, B., Sella, Y.: Fairplay-secure two-party computation system. In: USENIX Security Symposium, pp. 287–302 (2004)
20. Ben-David, A., Nisan, N., Pinkas, B.: FairplayMP: a system for secure multi-party computation. In: CCS, pp. 17–21 (2008)
21. Exploiting Social Network to Enhance Human-to-Human Infection Analysis without Privacy Leakage
22. Wiens, J., Guttag, J., Horvitz, E.: Learning evolving patient risk processes for C. diff colonization. In: ICML (2012)
23. Singh, A., Guttag, J.: Cardiovascular risk stratification using non-symmetric entropy-based classification trees. In: NIPS Workshop on Personalized Medicine (2011)
24. Singh, A., Guttag, J.: Leveraging hierarchical structure in diagnostic codes for predicting incident heart failure. In: ICML Workshop on Role of Machine Learning in Transforming Healthcare (2013)
25. Bost, R., Popa, R.A., Tu, S., Goldwasser, S.: Machine learning classification over encrypted data. In: NDSS, vol. 4324, p. 4325 (2015)

A Differentially Private Random Decision Tree Classifier with High Utility

Datong Wu[1], Taotao Wu[2], and Xiaotong Wu[3(✉)]

[1] Changzhou University, Changzhou, China
[2] Huawei Company, Shenzhen, China
[3] School of Computer Science and Technology, Nanjing Normal University, Nanjing, China
wuxiaotong@njnu.edu.cn

Abstract. Random decision tree-based classifiers are one of the most efficient approaches in data mining to implement classification prediction. However, the structure of decision trees possibly causes the privacy leakage of data. It is necessary to design novel random decision trees to satisfy some privacy requirement. In this paper, we propose a differentially private random decision tree classifier with high utility. We first construct a private random decision tree classifier satisfying differential privacy, which is a strong privacy metric with rigorously mathematical definition. Then, we analyze the privacy and utility of the basic random decision tree classifier. Next, we propose two improved approaches to reduce the number of the non-leaf and leaf nodes so as to increase the count of class labels in the leaf nodes. Extensive experiments are used to evaluate our proposed algorithm and the results show its high utility.

Keywords: Random decision tree · Differential privacy · Privacy protection · Classification prediction

1 Introduction

With the explosive development of machine learning and artificial intelligence, a huge number of intelligent service and applications have been widely applied to various scenes. It greatly brings the convenience and high efficiency of the daily life of people. In the algorithms of machine learning, decision tree-based classification is one of the most common measurements to accurately predict users' preference. There have been a lot of decision tree classification algorithms, including ID3, C4.5, CART and random decision trees (RDT) [4]. Although these algorithms provide a certain amount of prediction accuracy, it is possible for the structure of decision trees to cause the privacy leakage of data. The attacker takes advantage of the leaf nodes to recognize the record. As a result, the focus of *privacy-preserving data mining* (PPDM) [1] is on how to preserve the structure of different data mining algorithms from the possible privacy leakage of data.

In recent years, there have been a series of works to research various mechanisms for different decision tree classifiers with privacy preservation. In the

© Springer Nature Switzerland AG 2020
X. Chen et al. (Eds.): ML4CS 2020, LNCS 12486, pp. 376–385, 2020.
https://doi.org/10.1007/978-3-030-62223-7_32

existing privacy metrics, differential privacy (DP) is a strong privacy guarantee with rigorously mathematical definition [2]. Therefore, the previous works funnel into combine decision tree models with differential privacy. For different decision tree models, the works can be classified into two parts, including greedy decision trees and random decision trees [4]. The part of works is to modify greedy decision trees by the mechanisms satisfying differential privacy [5,8,10]. For example, Friedman et al. [5] utilized exponential mechanism to select the proper feature of each non-leaf node and Laplace mechanism to perturb the number of class labels of each leaf node in a greedy decision tree. The others utilized Laplace mechanism to just modify leaf nodes in a random decision tree [3,6,9]. Compared to greedy decision trees, the advantage of random decision trees is to not allocate privacy budget to non-leaf nodes so as to reduce the utility loss.

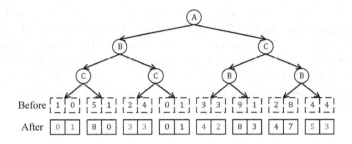

Fig. 1. A simple example for a random decision tree with differential privacy.

In order to make random decision trees satisfy differential privacy, there are two main steps. The first one is to select a certain number of attributes and then construct non-leaf nodes. The second one is to add instances and use Laplace mechanism to perturb the count of class labels of each leaf node. However, for some leaf nodes, it may cause the huge error when the number of class labels is relatively small. Here, we take Fig. 1 as an example to illustrate the disadvantage. In Fig. 1, the first leaf layer consists of leaf nodes before perturbation, where the second layer consists of leaf nodes after perturbation by Laplace mechanism. Each rectangle represents the number of training instances, which has the corresponding class label. It is obvious to find that for some leaf nodes (i.e., red number), they seriously change the correct prediction and make wrong prediction. The reason is that some leaf nodes have the few number of training instances. In particular, for random decision trees, some works suggest to divide training dataset to multiple small ones, which each is allocated to a random decision tree [3].

In order to address the above challenge, the paper attempts to modify the structure of private random decision tree to improve the number of instances in leaf nodes. We adopt the top-down approach to decrease the number of subnodes by aggregating multiple values of an attribute. We also adopt bottom-up approach to prune and merge the leaf nodes.

Algorithm 1. Basic RDT for Differential Privacy Basic-RDT
___
Input: dataset D, the number of candidate attribute h, privacy budget ϵ
Output: RDT with differential privacy R
1: generate h candidates $\mathcal{C}$ from attributes
2: $R \leftarrow$ None
3: $R \leftarrow$ BuildTree(None, $\mathcal{C}$)
4: UpdateTree(R, D)
5: PrivacyProcess(R, ϵ)
6: **return** R
___

2   Related Work

For greedy decision trees, it needn't allocate privacy budget for the non-leaf nodes so as to reduce the noisy. Jagannathan et al. [6] proposed a simple random decision tree with differential privacy. For each leaf node, it utilized Laplace mechanism to add the noisy for the count of class labels. Rana et al. [9] designed differentially private random forest to get the high utility. In the above approaches, both of them use global sensitivity to compute the privacy. Instead, Fletcher et al. [3] designed smooth sensitivity-based differentially private random decision forests to improve the accuracy.

3   Preliminaries and Motivation

Assume that there is a training dataset $\mathcal{D}$, which consists of n records. The dataset has m attributes and a class attribute. Meanwhile, private random decision trees are used to predict the class label of the test instance and satisfy some privacy metric.

3.1   Random Decision Trees and Differential Privacy

Random decision tree (RDT) is one of the most "random" approaches in the existing random decision algorithms. In general, it generates k decision trees (k is typically 10 to 30). Each decision tree is constructed by Algorithm 1.

Once all the decision trees are constructed, it can predict the probability of the new instance x according to the following equation:

$$\Pr[t|x] = \sum_{i=1}^{k} \alpha_i[t] / \left(\sum_{\tau} \sum_{i=1}^{k} \alpha_i[\tau] \right), \tag{1}$$

in which t is the class label and α_i represents the count for label t in the leaf node reached by x.

Differential privacy is a strong privacy metric with rigorously mathematical definition. If some randomized algorithm satisfies ϵ-differential privacy, it should achieve the following requirements:

Algorithm 2. Build the Structure of RDT BuildTree

Input: parent node p, candidate attribute $\mathcal{C}$
Output: RDT with differential privacy $\mathcal{N}$
1: **if** $\mathcal{C}$ is not null **then**
2:     generate leaf node ℓ with parent node p
3:     **return** ℓ
4: **end if**
5: randomly select an attribute c from candidates $\mathcal{C}$
6: create a non-leaf node $\mathcal{N}$ with attribute c and parent node p
7: $\mathcal{C} \leftarrow \mathcal{C} - c$
8: **for** $v \in \mathcal{V}(c)$ **do**
9:     sub-node $s = \mathsf{BuildTree}(\mathcal{N}, \mathcal{C})$
10:    add s as a child of $\mathcal{N}$
11: **end for**
12: **return** $\mathcal{N}$

Definition 1 (Differential Privacy). *A randomized algorithm $\mathcal{M}$ satisfies ϵ-differential privacy if and only if for any two datasets D_i and D_j that differ at most one record and for any output $y \in Range(\mathcal{M})$, we have*

$$\Pr[\mathcal{M}(D_i) = y] \leq \exp(\epsilon) \cdot \Pr[\mathcal{M}(D_j) = y], \tag{2}$$

in which $Range(\mathcal{M})$ demotes the set of all possible outputs of the algorithm $\mathcal{M}$ and ϵ is privacy budget.

In general, a mechanism giving ϵ-Differential Privacy is related to the sensitivity of a query function, which is defined as follows.

Definition 2 (Global Sensitivity). *For any query $q : \mathcal{D} \rightarrow \mathcal{R}^d$, the global sensitivity of q is*

$$\Delta q = \max_{D_i, D_j} ||q(D_i) - q(D_j)||_1, \tag{3}$$

in which D_i and D_j differ in at most one record.

The Laplace mechanism is one of the efficient mechanisms that satisfy differential privacy.

Definition 3 (Laplace Mechanism). *For any query $q : \mathcal{D} \rightarrow \mathcal{R}^d$, it satisfies ϵ-differential privacy by the following mechanism*

$$\mathcal{M}(D) = q(D) + Laplace(\Delta q/\epsilon). \tag{4}$$

Meanwhile, differential privacy also satisfies the following composition properties.

Lemma 1 (Sequential Composition [7]). *Assume that there are a group of mechanisms satisfying ϵ_i-differential privacy. When the mechanisms are applied to some dataset D, the combination providers $\sum_i \epsilon_i$-differential privacy.*

Algorithm 3. Update the leaf nodes of RDT UpdateTree

Input: dataset D, random decision tree R

1: $n \leftarrow$ the number of records in dataset D
2: $r \leftarrow$ root node of R
3: **for** $i \in [n]$ **do**
4:      AddInstance($r, D[i]$)
5: **end for**

Lemma 2 (Parallel Composition [7]**).** *Assume that there are a group of mechanisms satisfying ϵ_i-differential privacy. When the mechanisms are applied to a set of disjoint datasets D_i, the combination providers $\max_i \epsilon_i$-differential privacy.*

3.2   Basic RDT with Differential Privacy

Since the structure of a random decision tree possibly leaks the instance, which is derived by an attack. For example, when two datasets that differ at most one record are applied to the same random decision tree, there is only a leaf node that has different class labels. Therefore, the random decision tree doesn't satisfy differential privacy. In order to design random decision tree with differential privacy, the common solution is to utilize Laplace mechanism to perturb the leaf nodes.

Algorithm 1, 2, 3, 4, 5, 6 and 7 show the operations to construct a random decision tree that satisfies differential privacy. Algorithm 1 presents the construction of private random decision tree that consists of three important components, including constructing the nodes, adding instances, privacy processing (i.e., Algorithm 2, 3, 4, 5, 6 and 7). In detail, Algorithm 2 mainly constructs the nodes of a random decision tree. At first, it randomly selects an attribute as a feature at a non-leaf node. Then, it splits the node and generates sub-nodes according to the attributes' value. Algorithm 3 updates the leaf nodes by the training dataset. Algorithm 4 shows how an instance is added to the leaf node. It attempts to reach the leaf node by each non-leaf nodes with the same

---

Algorithm 4. Add an instance of RDT AddInstance

Input: node r, instance d

1: **if** r is non-leaf node **then**
2:      get attribute γ of node r
3:      get sub-node s of node r that has value $d[\gamma]$
4:      AddInstance(s, d)
5: **else**
6:      get class label t of instance d
7:      $\alpha[t]$ is of t-labeled rows at node r
8:      $\alpha[t] = \alpha[t] + 1$
9: **end if**

Algorithm 5. Build the structure of Private-RDT BuildPrivateTree

---

Input: parent node p, candidate attribute $\mathcal{C}$, the number of sub-nodes ζ
Output: RDT with differential privacy $\mathcal{N}$

1: **if** $\mathcal{C}$ is not null **then**
2:     generate leaf node ℓ with parent node p
3:     **return** ℓ
4: **end if**
5: randomly select an attribute c from candidates $\mathcal{C}$
6: create a non-leaf node $\mathcal{N}$ with attribute c and parent node p
7: $\mathcal{C} \leftarrow \mathcal{C} - c$
8: $\mathcal{V} \leftarrow$ the values of attribute c
9: **if** $\zeta > |\mathcal{V}|$ **then**
10:    $\gamma \leftarrow 1$
11: **else**
12:    $\gamma \leftarrow |\mathcal{V}|/\zeta$
13: **end if**
14: **for** $v \in \zeta$ **do**
15:    sub-node $s \leftarrow$ BuildTree$(\mathcal{N}, \mathcal{C})$
16:    randomly generate γ values θ from $\mathcal{V}$
17:    add s as a child of $\mathcal{N}$ with index θ
18:    $\mathcal{V} \leftarrow \mathcal{V} - \theta$
19: **end for**
20: **return** $\mathcal{N}$

---

value. When reaching the leaf node, the corresponding class label will increase. Algorithm 7 shows simple privacy operations for the random decision tree. For each leaf node, it will utilize Laplace mechanism to add the noisy for the count of each label.

Theorem 1. *The private random decision tree by Algorithm* Basic-RDT *satisfies ϵ-differential privacy.*

Proof. The structure of a private random decision tree by Algorithm Basic-RDT can be divided into two parts. The first part consists of the non-leaf nodes, while the second part contains the leaf nodes. Since the non-leaf node doesn't use the instance in the dataset, it won't cause the leakage of privacy. Instead, the attack gets the instance by comparing two random decision trees that differ in leaf nodes with only one instance. By Laplace mechanism, each leaf node guarantee the privacy requirement, i.e., differential privacy. Assume that the privacy budget is ϵ. Since each instance reaches only one leaf node, the parallel composition of differential privacy (i.e., Lemma 2) implies that each leaf node satisfies ϵ-differential privacy. As a result, the private random decision tree satisfies ϵ-differential privacy.

Algorithm 6. Prune and Merge Private-RDT PrunePrivateTree

Input: private random decision tree R, threshold τ

1: $\mathcal{N} \leftarrow$ leaf nodes of R
2: **for** $\ell \in \mathcal{N}$ **do**
3:     get $\alpha'[t]$ for label t of ℓ
4:     **if** $\forall\, \alpha'[t] == 0$ **then**
5:         prune the leaf node ℓ
6:         check the parent node of ℓ and prune
7:     **else if** $\forall\, \alpha'[t] < \tau$ **then**
8:         merge the leaf node ℓ with its neighbor
9:     **end if**
10: **end for**

---

4   Improved Private-RDT

4.1   Privacy Analysis

When predicting class label for an instance by Eq. (1), the key factor is the count of t-labeled rows at the leaf node in the i-th private random decision tree, i.e., $\alpha'_i[t]$. After the perturbation by Laplace mechanism, $\alpha'_i[t] = \alpha_i[t] + Lap(\Delta/\epsilon)$. Assume that there are two different class labels, i.e., t and t', and only one private random decision tree. In a leaf node reached by a test instance x, the probability to predict label t is

$$\Pr[t|x] = \frac{\alpha'[t]}{\alpha'[t] + \alpha'[t']} = \frac{\alpha[t] + Lap(\Delta/\epsilon)}{\alpha[t] + \alpha[t'] + 2Lap(\Delta/\epsilon)}. \tag{5}$$

By the above equation, it is easy to find that the probability $\Pr[t|x]$ depends on not only the real count of the training instances, but also the error due to Laplace mechanism. When $\alpha[t]$ and $\alpha[t']$ are relatively small or their difference is nearly equal, $\Pr[t|x]$ is totally decided by $Lap(\Delta/\epsilon)$. This implies that the prediction value is not fully meaning for the real prediction of the label.

Therefore, there are two following directions for the private random decision tree to improve the prediction accuracy as follows:

- Adding the count of instances in the leaf node.
- Increasing the difference of the count between different labels in the leaf node.

4.2   Implementation

In order to improve the prediction accuracy, we attempt to transform the structure of the private random decision tree based on the discussion in Sect. 4.1. We will consider the problem from two aspects. The first one is to reduce the branches of each non-leaf nodes, while the second one is to prune and merge the leaf nodes.

At first, we adopt the top-down approach to construct the private random decision tree based on Algorithm 2. In detail, after an attribute is chosen,

Algorithm 7. Privacy Process of RDT PrivacyProcess

Input: private random decision tree R, global sensitivity Δ, privacy budget ϵ

```
1: leaf nodes N of R
2: for ℓ ∈ N  do
3:     T ← labels of ℓ
4:     for t ∈ T  do
5:         α[t] = α[t] + Lap(Δ/ε)
6:         if α[t] < 0 then
7:             α[t] = 0
8:         end if
9:     end for
10: end for
```

---

we don't generate the sub-nodes according to its values. Instead, we just generate the specified number of sub-nodes. Algorithm 5 shows the concrete process of constructing private random decision tree. In detail, we first get all the values for the selected attribute and then choose one or multiple values as a set appended to a node (line 7–18). By the approach, we reduce the number of branches of a node so as to aggregate more data.

We adopt the bottom-up approach to prune and merge the leaf nodes in a private random decision tree. At first, we prune those leaf nodes to decrease the number of nodes, which are not reached by training instances. Meanwhile, when all the counts of the class labels of a leaf node don't exceed a given threshold, the leaf node will be merged with its neighbor node util the new leaf node satisfies the requirement. Algorithm 6 represents the detailed operations.

5   Experimental Evaluation

Datasets. In the experiment, we select two real datasets from UCI Machine Learning Repository[1], i.e., adult and nursery.

Comparison Algorithm. We compare our algorithm **Improved-PRDT** with the basic random decision tree classifier **RDT** and its private version **Basic-PRDT**. Meanwhile, we also compare different data allocation approaches in terms of accuracy.

5.1   Impact of Parameters and Comparison

The Number of Training Instances. We first investigate the impact of the number of training instances. We set the key parameters as follows: (i) the number of random decision trees is 20; (ii) privacy budget is 1; and (iii) the depth of a random decision tree is 5. The concrete results are shown in Fig. 2. It is obvious

---

[1] http://archive.ics.uci.edu/ml/datasets.php.

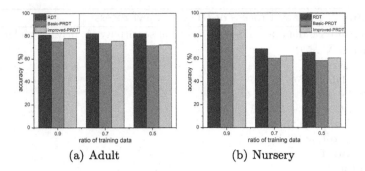

Fig. 2. The impact of the training instances

to find that there is a certain amount of the influence. For dataset nursery, the accuracy is greatly decreasing as the number of instances decreases. Meanwhile, in both of two datasets, our proposed algorithm Improved-PRDT is better than RDT in terms of accuracy.

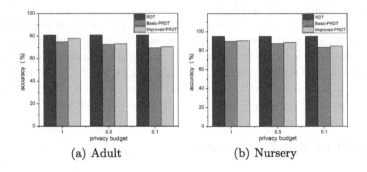

Fig. 3. The impact of privacy budget

Privacy Budget. In Fig. 3, privacy budget has a little of influence on the accuracy. It is easy to find that the accuracy is decreasing as privacy budget decreases. Meanwhile, Fig. 2 and 3 show that our proposed approach Improved-PRDT is better than PRDT in terms of accuracy.

6   Conclusion

This paper proposes an improved differentially private random decision tree classifier. In order to reduce the influence of the noisy by Laplace mechanism, we design the up-down and bottom-up approaches to reduce the number of nodes in a random decision tree. Extensive experiments show our approach has the higher utility than the basic private random decision tree classifier. In the future, we plan to add more performance metrics to further analyze our approach.

References

1. Aggarwal, C.C., Yu, P.S.: Privacy-preserving data mining: a survey. In: Gertz, M., Jajodia, S. (eds.) Handbook of Database Security - Applications and Trends, pp. 431–460. Springer, Boston (2008). https://doi.org/10.1007/978-0-387-48533-1_18
2. Dwork, C.: Differential privacy: a survey of results. In: Agrawal, M., Du, D., Duan, Z., Li, A. (eds.) TAMC 2008. LNCS, vol. 4978, pp. 1–19. Springer, Heidelberg (2008). https://doi.org/10.1007/978-3-540-79228-4_1
3. Fletcher, S., Islam, M.Z.: Differentially private random decision forests using smooth sensitivity. Expert Syst. Appl. **78**, 16–31 (2017)
4. Fletcher, S., Islam, M.Z.: Decision tree classification with differential privacy: a survey. ACM Comput. Surv. **52**(4), 83:1–83:33 (2019)
5. Friedman, A., Schuster, A.: Data mining with differential privacy. In: Proceedings of the 16th ACM SIGKDD International Conference on Knowledge Discovery and Data Mining, pp. 493–502. ACM (2010)
6. Jagannathan, G., Pillaipakkamnatt, K., Wright, R.N.: A practical differentially private random decision tree classifier. Trans. Data Priv. **5**(1), 273–295 (2012)
7. McSherry, F.: Privacy integrated queries: an extensible platform for privacy-preserving data analysis. In: Proceedings of the ACM SIGMOD International Conference on Management of Data, SIGMOD, pp. 19–30. ACM (2009)
8. Mohammed, N., Chen, R., Fung, B.C.M., Yu, P.S.: Differentially private data release for data mining. In: Proceedings of the 17th ACM SIGKDD International Conference on Knowledge Discovery and Data Mining, pp. 493–501. ACM (2011)
9. Rana, S., Gupta, S.K., Venkatesh, S.: Differentially private random forest with high utility. In: 2015 IEEE International Conference on Data Mining, ICDM, pp. 955–960. IEEE Computer Society (2015)
10. Zhao, L., et al.: Inprivate digging: Enabling tree-based distributed data mining with differential privacy. In: 2018 IEEE Conference on Computer Communications, INFOCOM. pp. 2087–2095. IEEE (2018)

Research on Blind Signature Based Anonymous Electronic Cash Scheme

Ying Wang, Haojia Zhu, and Fengyin Li[✉]

School of Information Science and Engineering, Qufu Normal University,
Rizhao 276826, China
Lfyin318@126.com

Abstract. With the development of network economy, as a new transaction method, electronic cash makes online transactions become more convenient. However, online transactions also bring the risk of user privacy disclosure, which has attracted wide attention. To solve this problem, this paper proposes a new blind signature scheme based on RSA and applies it to electronic cash system. The electronic cash scheme increases the difficulty of analyzing the relationship between electronic currency addresses by confusing the relationship between the user's public address and the actual address, which improves the privacy protection level of the proposed electronic cash scheme. The proposed anonymous electronic cash system can be used to protect the privacy of user identity and complete user anonymous transactions and meet the security and efficiency requirements. Finally, the performance analysis shows that the communication cost of anonymous electronic cash system in this paper is low, which significantly improves the security of electronic cash anonymous transactions and has a good application prospect.

Keywords: Blind signature · RSA algorithm · Anonymity electronic cash · Electronic cash system · Privacy disclosure.

1 Introduction

As the form of the Internet is becoming more and more mature, online transactions are becoming more and more popular with low-cost, wide-field, and easy-to-use advantages, and they are becoming more and more widely used. They are becoming the center of research and application [15]. Electronic cash exists in the Internet in the form of digital information. Through the Internet, our ideal electronic cash is independent, secure (non-reusable, unforgeable), transferable, separable, anonymous, convenience, robustness and atomicity etc. [6,9].

Compared with traditional currencies, the most significant advantage of electronic cash is that it can realize the anonymity of user payments. D.Chaum [4] first implemented an anonymous electronic cash system by using blind signatures. However, the calculation amount of this system is relatively large, and the efficiency of payment is limited.

© Springer Nature Switzerland AG 2020
X. Chen et al. (Eds.): ML4CS 2020, LNCS 12486, pp. 386–392, 2020.
https://doi.org/10.1007/978-3-030-62223-7_33

Most of the existing electronic cash systems either focus on the security of payment instructions and order information as well as the integrity and non-repudiation of transactions, reducing anonymity and the protection of users' personal privacy; or due to the limitations of payment systems, Intentionally or unintentionally leaked the user's personal privacy [14]. The main reason is when the electronic payment system designed, the issue of personal privacy on the Internet did not receive attention from everyone, but now this problem cannot be avoided and must be resolved as soon as possible [2].

The work to be done in this paper is to realize an anonymous electronic cash system [7,13] that can meet the security and efficiency requirements based on the existing electronic cash system research and according to people's consumer psychology and online transaction requirements for electronic cash. By obfuscating the relationship between the user's public address and the actual address, and increasing the difficulty of analyzing the relationship between electronic money addresses, this paper designs and implements an anonymous electronic cash system, which significantly improves the anonymous security and efficiency of electronic cash.

2 Preliminary

2.1 RSA Algorithm

The RSA public key cryptographic algorithm is one of the most effective security algorithms for secure communication and digital signatures on the network. The reliability of the RSA algorithm is based on the factorization of large numbers [5].

The algorithm flow of RSA is as follows:

Firstly, calculate the public key (n, e) and private key d

(1) Pick two large prime numbers independently p and q, calculate $n = p * q$.
(2) Calculate the Euler function value $\varphi(n) = (p - 1)(q - 1)$ of n, randomly choose an integer e, make $1 \leq e \leq \varphi(n)$ and $\gcd(\varphi(n), e) = 1$ hold, get user public key $PK = (n, e)$.
(3) Calculate multiplicative inverse d of $\varphi(n)$, satisfy $ed \equiv 1 \bmod \varphi(n)$, get user private key $SK = d$.

When encrypting, the plaintext M is encrypted by the public key to obtain the ciphertext C: $C = M^e \bmod n$; When decrypting, the ciphertext C is decrypted by the private key to obtain the plaintext M:

$$C^d \bmod n = (M^e \bmod n)^d \bmod n = M^{ed} \bmod n = M.$$

2.2 RSA Signature Algorithm

It is assumed that the public key cryptosystem of RSA has been established, and the public and private key pair of user A is assumed to be $<PK_A, SK_A> = <(n, e), d>$. If user A wants to digitally sign a message M and send it to signer B. The digital signature algorithm is as follows:

(1) Implementation of the signature

User A uses his own private key SK_A to sign message M and gets the signature:

$$S_A = D(M, SK_A) = (M^d) \bmod n.$$

The message M is then sent to the signer with the signature.

(2) Signature verification

After message B and signature received by signer B, using the public key of sender A to verify the signature using the following equation:

$$(S_A)^e \bmod n == M.$$

If the equation holds, the signature is verified and the signature is valid; otherwise, the signature is invalid.

2.3   Blind Signature

Blind signature: Allow the messager to blind the message firstly, and then let the signer sign the blinded message. Finally, the message owner removes the blind factor from the signature to get the signer's signature on the original message. Blind signature [3] is a special digital signature technology adopted by the receiver without allowing the signer to obtain the specific content of the signed message.

The specific process of blind signature is as follows:

(1) Blindness: The sender uses his public key to encrypt the message M to be signed to obtain the ciphertext C;
(2) Blind signature: After the signer receives C from the sender, he performs blind signing with his private key, obtains the signed message S, and sends S to the sender;
(3) Unblinding: The messager uses his private key to unblind, and obtains the signer's signature on M; The use of blind signature technology in the electronic cash system can well protect the privacy of users and achieve anonymity.

3   Blind Signature Based Anonymous Electronic Cash Scheme

This section proposes a blind signature scheme based on RSA, which is applied to the electronic cash system and implements an anonymous electronic cash system.

3.1 Design of Blind Signature Scheme Based on RSA

The blind signature scheme of electronic cash based on RSA designed in this paper is as follows:

(1) Set up:
- Signer B randomly selects two large prime numbers p and q, calculate $n = p * q$, $\varphi(n) = (p - 1) * (q - 1)$;
- Signer B randomly selects a large integer e to make it satisfy $\gcd(e, \varphi(n)) = 1$;
- Calculate according to Euclidean algorithm to make it satisfy $ed = 1$ mod $(\varphi(n))$;
  Get the public and private key pair of signer B $< PK_B, SK_B >=< (n, e), d >$.
(2) Sign:
- User A selects the message M to be signed;
- User A encrypts the message M to be signed with the public key PK_A: $C_i = M^{PK_A}$ mod n;
- User A sends the ciphertext C_i to signer B.
(3) BlindSign:
- After receiving C_i, Signer B uses its private key SK_B to blindly sign it and obtains: $\{C_i\}_{Bpriv} = C_i^{SK_B}$ mod n;
- Signer B sends S_i to messager A.
(4) Unblind:
  Messager A receives S_i from signer B, and uses his private key SK_A to unblind it: $\{C_i\}_{Bpriv}^{SK_A}$ mod $n = \left[(M^{PK_A})^{SK_B}\right]^{SK_A}$ mod $n = M^{SK_B} = \{M\}_{Bpriv}$ get the signature $\{M\}_{Bpriv}$ of signer B for message M.
(5) Verify:
  Messager A verifies whether M after literacy is equal to the original M: $\{C_i\}_{Bpriv}^{SK_A}$ mod $n \underset{=}{?} M^{SK_B}$. The interactive flowchart of blind signature based on RSA is shown in Fig. 1:

3.2 Anonymous Electronic Cash Scheme

Anonymous electronic cash system [1] consists of two main bodies: user and bank, and three protocols: deposit, withdrawal and payment. Users need to register and log in to the electronic cash system in order to perform the functions of the system. The user's consumption in the bank can be viewed through the function of recording transaction information in the electronic cash system. At the same time, the bank can also view it, but it will not reveal the user's private information [8]. The deposit and withdrawal process of the electronic cash system is a transaction between the user and the bank, and the payment process is a transaction between the merchant and the user.

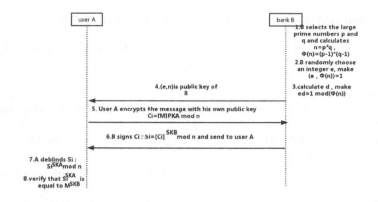

Fig. 1. RSA blind signature interaction diagram.

(1) Deposit process

The user's deposit activity is after submitting a deposit application. When saving money, the user provides idU (user ID), account number, electronic cash, denomination, etc. to the bank. The bank verifies that the electronic cash is valid and has not been used, then verify the idU, transfer the corresponding amount in the account, and add the cash to the database that has used electronic cash. The specific process is as follows:

- At time t_1, user A transfers electronic cash from his account K_{in} to an escrow address K_{esc}.
- Bank B detects whether user A has transferred cash to K_{esc}. If the cash arrives, bank B will post $\{C_i\}_{Bpriv}$ to the public log.
- User A checks whether bank B posted $\{C_i\}_{Bpriv}$ to the public log. If B has been published, use the anonymous identity of A' (to prevent disclosure of the real address of user A) to post "Bank B has been published $\{C_i\}_{Bpriv}$" to the public log. User A unblinds at time t_3: $\{C_i\}_{Bpriv}{}^{SK_A} \bmod n = \left\{\{M^{PKA}\}^{SK_B}\right\}^{SK_A} \bmod n = M^{SK_B} = \{M\}_{Bpriv}$, and then get signed message $\{M\}_{Bpriv}$ and post to public log; If bank B does not publish to the public log, user A publishes evidence, to the public log. User A can then proceed with the normal procedure (see steps after publication).
- Calculate Beacon $x = Beacon(t_3, \omega, \rho)$ (It is all electronic cash when the transaction is completed at time t, which is used to compare with the bank's given fee ρ). If $x \leq \rho$, bank B keeps the deposit (handling fee) and informs user A. If $x > \rho$, bank B deducts a cash handling fee of ρ. At time t_4, the remaining electronic cash is transferred from the escrow address K_{esc} to the output address K_{out} of user A.

(2) Withdrawal process

The user applies for electronic cash from the bank, the bank checks the relevant legality, and transfers the electronic cash from K_{esc} to the user's output address K_{out}. The specific process is as follows:

- User A proves to the bank that he is the holder of his account firstly, then express the withdrawal request with mixed parameters as $D = (v, t_1, t_2, t_3, t_4, \omega, \rho)$.
  User A uses his public key PK_A to encrypt the output address K_{out} to obtain the ciphertext $C_i = [M = (K_{out}, n)]^{PK_A} \bmod n$, which is send to bank with withdrawal request.
- Bank B checks the legitimacy of the withdrawal application D by checking whether the time point is reasonable and whether the cash withdrawal exceeds the number of bank accounts. If it is legal, blindly sign C_i, K_{esc}, D respectively $\{C_i\}_{Bpriv} = C_i{}^{SK_B} \bmod n$, $\{K_{esc}\}_{Bpriv} = K_{esc}{}^{SK_B} \bmod n$, $\{D\}_{Bpriv} = D^{SK_B} \bmod n$, which will be send to user A; If it is illegal, B refuses to sign, and A destroys the output address to prevent the leakage of privacy.
- At time t_4, bank B transfers the electronic cash from the escrow address K_{esc} to the output address K_{out} of user.
- User A unblinds the message $\{C_i\}_{Bpriv}$, $\{K_{esc}\}_{Bpriv}$, $\{D\}_{Bpriv}$ signed by bank B to see if the amount is consistent with the amount of withdrawal cash requested. And then user A will check if their output account K_{out} has received electronic cash. If not, user A detects the cash theft by bank B, and A issues evidence $\{M\}_{Bpriv}$, records transactions v before t_1, K_{in} and K_{esc} to the public log to prove that the user has completed the above normal steps and waits to receive money, and urges bank B to transfer funds. If successful, user A withdraws the cash and completes the withdrawal process.

(3) Payment process

Users can use the electronic cash that has been anonymous, and transactions with merchants require verification of electronic cash [10]. The merchant verifies the signature of the electronic cash through the bank to confirm whether the electronic cash is legal. Where PK_B is the public key of bank B, M is the message that needs to be encrypted, $\{M\}_{Bpriv}$ is the unblindness message signed by bank B, and M' is the message that needs to be verified.

- The user sends a consumption request $\left(PK_B, M, \{M\}_{Bpriv}\right)$ to the merchant and provides sufficient electronic cash.
- The merchant requests the bank to verify the validity of the electronic cash through the consumption request $\left(PK_B, M, \{M\}_{Bpriv}\right)$ sent to the bank by the user.
- Banks use their public key PK_B to verify the validity of electronic cash:
  $M' = \{M\}_{Bpriv} = \left(M^{SK_B}\right)^{PK_B} \bmod n \overset{?}{=} M$

If $M' = M$, it proves that the electronic cash is indeed a legal electronic cash signed by the bank, and informs the merchant and the user that the consumption is successful; otherwise, it indicates that the electronic cash is invalid, the consumption behavior is not allowed and the merchant is informed to end the transaction with the user.

4   Conclusion

In view of the problems that the anonymity, efficiency and security of the current e-cash system [11,12] can not meet the actual application requirements, this paper proposes a new RSA blind signature scheme, and applies this blind signature scheme to the anonymous e-cash system, which realizes the anonymity of the user's identity, ensures the security and efficiency of the anonymous e-cash system, and protects the user Identity privacy. Compared with other blind signature schemes, the results show that the RSA blind signature scheme and the anonymous e-cash system in this paper are better in security and efficiency. The next step of this paper is to apply RSA blind signature scheme and anonymous e-cash system to more scenarios and protect the privacy of users.

References

1. Canard, S., Pointcheval, D., Sanders, O., Traoré, J.: Divisible e-cash made practical. Digit. Technol. Appl. (2015)
2. Kang, C.: Efficient divisible e-cash system based on group signature. Digit. Technol. Appl. 221–223 (2017)
3. Wei, C.: Design of RSA blind signature scheme based on hash algorithm. China Comput. Commun. 109–114 (2015)
4. Chaum, D.: Blind signatures for untraceable payments. In: Chaum, D., Rivest, R.L., Sherman, A.T. (eds.) Advances in Cryptology, pp. 199–203. Springer, Boston (1982). https://doi.org/10.1007/978-1-4757-0602-4_18
5. Wang, F.: A blind signature scheme based on RSA algorithm. Comput. Knowl. Technol. **15**(02), 277–278 (2019)
6. Wang, F., Chang, C.-C., Chang, S.-C.: Robust off-line e-cash scheme with recoverability and anonymity revocation. Secur. Commun. Netw. **9**, 2412–2421 (2016)
7. Islam, S.K.H., Amin, R., Biswas, G.P., Obaidat, M.S., Khan, M.K.: Provably secure pairing-free identity-based partially blind signature scheme and its application in online e-cash system. Arab. J. Sci. Eng. **41**(8), 3163–3176 (2016)
8. Islam, S.K.H., Biswas, G.P.: A pairing-free identity-based authenticated group key agreement protocol for imbalanced mobile networks. Ann. Telecommun. **67**(11–12), 547–558 (2012)
9. Zhang, J., Feng, C., Ma, J., Zhang, B., Xu, C., Li, Z.: Transferable electronic cash system at any cost. J. Beijing Inst. Technol. **39**(03), 67–73 (2019)
10. Feng, J.: Research on the security of e-cash payment system in the new era of e-commerce. Digit. World 295–295 (2018)
11. Xu, L.: Lightweight password and its application in e-cash payment. Ph.D. thesis, Jilin University (2016)
12. Xin, L., Bo, Z.: Improved endorsed e-cash system with DAA-A. J. Comput. Res. Dev. **53**(10), 2412–2429 (2016)
13. Liu, P.: Design and implementation of bank online payment system based on. Ph.D. thesis, Jilin University (2018)
14. Scheir, M., Balasch, J., Rial, A., Preneel, B., Verbauwhede, I.: Anonymous split e-cash toward mobile anonymous payments. ACM Trans. Embed. Comput. Systems. **14**, 1–25 (2015)
15. Zhang, J., Li, Z., Gao, Y., Feng, C., Guo, H.: Transferable e-cash system of equal length with optimal anonymity based on spending chain. Acta Electron. Sinica **43**, 1805–1809 (2015)

A Verifiable E-Lottery Scheme

Yin Zhang, Fanglin An, Kejie Zhao, and Jun Ye$^{(\boxtimes)}$

School of Computer Science and Cyberspace Security, Hainan University,
Haikou, China
yejun@hainanu.edu.cn

Abstract. With the development of Internet and computer technology, e-lottery gradually becomes the main form of lottery tickets purchased buy people. The e-lottery existing at present only realizes the function that the traditional lottery tickets can be purchased online, and the generation of winning numbers is still making use of the traditional way, did not consider the situation where the lottery issuers or lottery buyer interfered with the final lottery result. Based on the discussion of the history and development of lottery and some e-lottery schemes, this article presents a new scheme of electronic lottery which references the linear equations combined with Hash function based on the verifiable random number to generate the winning numbers. While generating lottery numbers, we will provide a set of numbers for purchasers to verify. It's worth noting that this scheme achieves that the players can purchase lottery anonymously and participate in the generation of winning number, and that they are able to verify whether they definitely take part in the generation. And to emphasize one point, this scheme is aimed at the two-color ball lottery with a wide range of popularity.

Keywords: Electronic lottery · Verifiable random number · Linear equations

1 Introduction

With the globalization of the Internet and the rapid development of e-commerce, the proportion of electronic lottery tickets is increasing. Electronic lottery is a form of electronic lottery scheme in real life. The whole lottery scheme only needs to be operated on the network. With the continuous development of communication, network and computer technology, cryptography is playing an increasingly important role in the field of electronic lottery. Cryptography has changed the way people live and work. Information technology in society has become the trend and core of today's world development. Whether for the state, enterprises, scientific research institutions and other organizations, or individuals engaged in all walks of life, whether or not they can obtain and safely enjoy the required information is the decisive key.

Our scheme analyzes the two-color ball electronic lottery game process. Players can place bets at any lottery issuers authorized e-lottery distributors to purchase lottery tickets. Players save the redemption voucher themselves. This voucher is the two-color ball lottery ticket. Players can randomly choose the number in the number pool, or they can choose the number to bet. The lottery issuers is responsible for generating the final winning numbers, and finally determines whether the player wins according to certain

© Springer Nature Switzerland AG 2020
X. Chen et al. (Eds.): ML4CS 2020, LNCS 12486, pp. 393–401, 2020.
https://doi.org/10.1007/978-3-030-62223-7_34

rules, and the player's winning level. The two-color ball set bonus is 50% of the total sales, of which the current bonus is 49% of the total sales, and the adjustment fund is 1% of the total sales. The flow of the two-color ball lottery game is shown in Fig. 1.

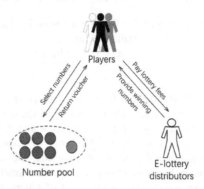

Fig. 1. Two-color ball lottery game flow.

Compared with traditional lottery, electronic lottery has better performance in anonymity and privacy [1]. However, e-lottery has limitations in online processing and scalability [2]. In the operation of electronic lottery, a major concern of lottery players is whether lottery issuers have cheated when generating lottery numbers and final winning numbers. In the design of the electronic lottery protocol, the key is how to generate random numbers that are not controlled by human factors. This is no longer a problem, but to convince lottery buyers(players) that the winning numbers are random, a trusted third party is required. Although in some electronic lottery schemes, electronic lottery buyers are allowed to verify whether they have participated in the generation of random numbers, but this process needs to publish a large amount of data, which affects the security and efficiency of the protocol. In the current electronic lottery draw system, the number of winnings is generated by the issuer, and the lottery buyers of the lottery cannot participate. If the lottery issuer falsifies or the lottery system is artificially destroyed, the winning numbers generated will not be fair.

In order to solve the various problems faced by the electronic lottery, we have proposed the scheme of this article. Our scheme has the following contributions:

1. This article proposes a two-color ball lottery scheme based on linear equations and verifiable random numbers, which can meet the requirements of electronic lottery and does not require the participation of a trusted third party;
2. Players can participate in the generation of winning numbers and players can easily verify whether the number they selected participates in the generation of the final winning number, which has fairness, impartiality and trustworthiness and the calculation efficiency is greatly improved.

Subsequent structural arrangements of this article: Sect. 2 introduces the research status of verifiable random numbers and electronic lottery solutions, Sect. 3 introduces the knowledge required before understanding this scheme, Sect. 4 carefully analyzes the details of this scheme, and finally One section is a summary of this article.

2 Related Work

The lottery results generated by electronic lottery often make people feel untrustworthy, so the industry needs to improve the previous random number generation scheme to make the generation of random numbers more secure and verifiable.

Zhang Y et al. [3] proposed the method of generating numbers by using the DNA storage function in chromosomes to generate and transport key, which is an emerging technology in the field of information security. However, the economic cost is too high and it is not suitable for general projects. Christodoulou K et al. [4] proposed a process based on one-dimensional cellular automata (CA), whose evolution is con-sistent with that of blockchain. The generated random numbers can validate and trace (but not predict) the outcome of the process. Liu et al. [5] proposed a both parties verifiable random number generation and verification scheme using one-way function. This scheme does not require a third party, and both parties participate equally in the generation of random numbers and can verify the results, which not only reduces the computational burden of both parties, but also ensures the security and fairness of data transaction. Yu et al. [6] proposed a novel verifiable data trading scheme is pro-posed based on the technology of forgetting transfer and block chain, which guaran-tees unfair risk to users under the IND-CCA hypothesis. Pasqualini L et al. [7] used rein-forcement learning to generate random number generators, but reinforcement learning required upfront learning costs, and the generated random Numbers could not be verified. The method of Lee E C et al. [8] is to observe the entropy of inorganic reactions in chemistry with microscopic machines, and then generate random Numbers. Although the randomness of the generated random numbers is high enough, it is difficult to collect data for the chemical reactions used. Qu Wen et al. [9] proposed a new method for generating multivariate non-normal data with given multivariate skewness and kurtosis. The data produced by this method is regular and unsafe to some extent.

Many fair electronic lottery schemes are very well constructed, but there are also some disadvantages in certain aspects.

Chin-ling Chen et al. [10] continued their research on e-lottery, and proposed that users could fairly participate in lottery contests on mobile devices by using elliptic curve cryptography and public key infrastructure. Yi-ning Liu et al. [11] made use of the forgetting transfer mechanism based on elliptic curve cryptography (ECC) to improve the lottery protocol, which can resist the risk of unfair lottery results caused by the collusion of lottery players. Grumbach et al. [12] overcome the unfairness of traditional online lottery and proposed a novel distributed online lottery scheme. The scheme can verify the random process and results without relying on a third party, but the scheme requires a large amount of computation. The unpredictable performance of the blockchain property contributes well to the generation of public random numbers. A fair e-lottery scheme has been constructed by using the entropy from the Bitcoin blockchain. Pierrot et al. [13] analyzed such a method and found that its security could not meet the standards. Xia Z et al. [14] proposed a new electronic lottery scheme using symmetric binomial in order to prevent the attacker from having a strong attack computing power and improve the security performance of the existing electronic lottery scheme. In this case, security and fairness are guaranteed, and no trusted third party or delay function is involved. Medeleanu et al. [15] used the unique advantages of electronic signatures to propose an electronic lottery system based on anonymous signatures, but each user consumes a lot of computer resources. Jung-San Lee et al. [16] also proposed a mobile lottery mechanism called Penny M-lottery based on the mobile environment, and better protected user privacy under the premise of fair participation of users. Oblivious signature has been applied in many fields (including electronic lottery and electronic auction), and has proved to play a huge role. Tso et al. [17] optimized two forgotten signature methods and combined them into one scheme, combined with electronic lottery. After that, the user's personal privacy can be protected and the verifiable function can be realized, but the solution cannot guarantee the successful construction of the solution when it emphasizes perfect security. In order to solve various challenges faced by electronic lottery, Chen et al. [18] proposed a fair electronic lottery scheme with the help of verifiable random function and digital signature algorithm (DSA), but the computational complexity of the scheme can be optimized. Kunal et al. [19] proposed a verifiable lottery system solution with random functions. This solution is based on the randomness of the underlying algorithm of the Ethereum platform, and realizes the fairness of online lottery. The probability of users winning is the same.

3   Basic Knowledge

3.1   The Double Chromosphere Lottery Game Rules

Two-color ball lottery bets are divided into red ball number area and blue ball number area, and combined game rules are adopted. Each bet number consists of 6 red ball numbers and 1 blue ball number. Red ball numbers are selected from 1–33; blue ball numbers are selected from 1–16.

Winning Results are Randomly Generated. Every random possible number combination is equally likely to be the winning numbers. No player can predict the outcome of the winning.

Winning Results are Publicly Verifiable. Every player can verify the winning results, and even the lottery issuers can't cheat during the generation process.

Total Lottery Sales and Number of Winning Tickets are Publicly Verifiable. The winning amount is usually related to the total sales of the lottery, so the number of lotteries sold should be publicly verifiable. In some lottery schemes, the prize amount of each winning player is not fixed, it depends on the total number of winning lotteries, so the number of winning lotteries should also be publicly verifiable.

Winning Lottery Tickets Cannot be Forged. Neither the player nor the lottery issuers can falsify the lottery. Players cannot counterfeit lottery tickets that they did not purchase, nor can the same lottery issuers counterfeit a lottery ticket with the same winning lottery number as the result of the winning.

Player Anonymity. Anonymity of players is very important, especially for winning players. If the information of a winning player is leaked, he is likely to be seriously threatened by extortion.

Confidentiality of Lottery Content. In some lottery schemes, players bet on a single number or select a combination of numbers from a pre-defined field. In the case of more than one winning player, the prize money will be evenly distributed to everyone. In this case, we need to ensure the confidentiality of the lottery content, otherwise various attacks may occur.

Fairness in Buying Lottery Tickets and Receiving Bonuses. Buying lottery tickets and receiving prizes are based on the principles of fair trade. In other words, either party (the lottery issuer and the player) gets each other's items, or neither party ends up with each other's items.

3.2 The Pseudo-Randomness of the Double Chromosphere Lottery Tickets

If the generation of the winning lottery ticket is a completely random process, the possibility of cheating in the two-color lottery is very small, but this is not the case, because the absolute random number must be affected and restricted by the level and technology of people making random numbers. Absolute random number is just an ideal random number. It is a kind of theoretical data. This situation is very difficult to reach. It is a theoretical assumption. It is very difficult to really generate random numbers. Practice has shown that the generation of true random numbers is extremely difficult. Although computer technology is very advanced now, it is impossible to produce absolute random numbers, but only relatively random numbers (i.e., pseudo-random numbers). Pseudo-random numbers can be close to absolute random numbers and can continue to trend toward absolute random numbers, but pseudo-random numbers cannot be equal to absolute random numbers.

The so-called pseudo-random numbers are numbers that sometimes obey and sometimes do not obey certain rules. The higher the degree of compliance, the higher the "pseudo" component of its pseudo-randomness, and the more opportunities for deciphering, the easier it is; conversely, the higher the randomness, the less chance of deciphering, and deciphering The harder it becomes, the more difficult it is to decipher. No matter what kind of lottery is pseudo-random-relatively random numbers or combinations.

4   Electronic Lottery Scheme

4.1   The Double Chromosphere Lottery Algorithm Model

First, a system of linear equations $AX = Y$ mod p is constructed, A as a full rank matrix of 6×6. All numbers in a matrix exist in a finite field p.

$$
A = \begin{pmatrix}
a_{11} & a_{12} & a_{13} & a_{14} & a_{15} & a_{16} \\
a_{21} & a_{22} & a_{23} & a_{24} & a_{25} & a_{26} \\
a_{31} & a_{32} & a_{33} & a_{34} & a_{35} & a_{36} \\
a_{41} & a_{42} & a_{43} & a_{44} & a_{45} & a_{46} \\
a_{51} & a_{52} & a_{53} & a_{54} & a_{55} & a_{56} \\
a_{61} & a_{62} & a_{63} & a_{64} & a_{65} & a_{66}
\end{pmatrix}
\tag{1}
$$

And

$$
X = \begin{pmatrix}
x_1 \\
x_2 \\
x_3 \\
x_4 \\
x_5 \\
x_6
\end{pmatrix}
\tag{2}
$$

is an unknown vector.

$$
Y = \begin{pmatrix}
y_1 \\
y_2 \\
y_3 \\
y_4 \\
y_5 \\
y_6
\end{pmatrix}
\tag{3}
$$

is a known vector, then there exists a X in a finite field, such that $AX = Y \bmod p$. Then use Clem's rule to calculate the value of each number in.

$$
x_i = \frac{d_i}{d} = \frac{\begin{vmatrix}
a_{11} & a_{12} & \cdots & a_{1(i-1)} & y_1 & a_{1(i+1)} & \cdots & a_{16} \\
a_{21} & a_{22} & \cdots & a_{2(i-1)} & y_2 & a_{2(i+1)} & \cdots & a_{26} \\
a_{31} & \cdots & \cdots & \cdots & y_3 & \cdots & \cdots & a_{36} \\
a_{41} & \cdots & \cdots & \cdots & y_4 & \cdots & \cdots & a_{46} \\
a_{51} & \cdots & \cdots & \cdots & y_5 & \cdots & \cdots & a_{56} \\
a_{61} & a_{62} & \cdots & a_{6(i-1)} & y_6 & a_{6(i+1)} & \cdots & a_{66}
\end{vmatrix}}{\begin{vmatrix}
a_{11} & a_{12} & a_{13} & a_{14} & a_{15} & a_{16} \\
a_{21} & a_{22} & a_{23} & a_{24} & a_{25} & a_{26} \\
a_{31} & a_{32} & a_{33} & a_{34} & a_{35} & a_{36} \\
a_{41} & a_{42} & a_{43} & a_{44} & a_{45} & a_{46} \\
a_{51} & a_{52} & a_{53} & a_{54} & a_{55} & a_{56} \\
a_{61} & a_{62} & a_{63} & a_{64} & a_{65} & a_{66}
\end{vmatrix}} \bmod p
\tag{4}
$$

In this way, you can get X, and the output verifiable random number is $r = x_1 || x_2 || x_3 || x_4 || x_5 || x_6$.

Here, we briefly introduce the modulo operation, which is the *mod* operation above.

The modulo operation is the remainder operation. "mod" is the abbreviation of "Module". Modular operations are mostly used in programming. The meaning of mod is to find the remainder. Modular operations are widely used in number theory and program design, from the discrimination of odd and even numbers to the discrimination of prime numbers, from the calculation of modular powers to the calculation of the greatest common divisor, from the problem of grandchildren to the problem of Caesar ciphers, all are filled with modulo operations. Although many number theory textbooks have a certain introduction to modulo operation, most of them are based on pure theory, and there is not much involved in the application of modulo operation in program design.

In the above formula, $d_i = M \bmod p$, $d = N \bmod p$, then $x_i = \frac{M}{N} \bmod p$, among them, $\frac{M}{N}$ has a high probability that it is not an integer. Here we use the method of calculating the inverse of N in the finite field p. Let the inverse of N in the finite field p be N^{-1}, and then the formula for calculating x_i can be written as $x_i = M \cdot N^{-1} \bmod p$. All x_i are integers in the finite field p.

4.2 Algorithm Implementation of the Double Chromosphere Lottery System

Combining the verifiable random numbers based on the linear equations and the hash function, an electronic lottery scheme is constructed, which makes the scheme meet the requirements previously proposed. The scheme is divided into 5 stages: Setup, Ticket purchase, Winning result generation, Prize claiming, and Purchaser verification.

Setup. The lottery issuer constructs a system of linear equations $AX = Y \bmod p$, A is a 6×6 full rank matrix, X is an unknown vector, Y is a known vector, since p is a prime number, and our red ball number range is 1–33, we take the smallest prime number 37 that greater than 33, as the value of p. Here we put the number of the double chromosphere lottery ticket purchased by the user (6 red ball Numbers and 1 blue ball Numbers) to the first row of the A matrix, $(a_{11}, a_{12}, a_{13}, a_{14}, a_{15}, a_{16})$, and the first y_1 of the Y vectors, respectively. At the same time, when the player buys a lottery ticket is going to get a serial number T, the other Numbers in the matrix are expressed as $a_{ij} = \left(H\left(a_{(i-1)j}\right) + H(T) \right) mod33 + 1$, among them $2 \leq i \leq 6$, $1 \leq j \leq 6$; $y_i = \left(H(y_{i-1}) + H(T) \right) mod16 + 1$, among them $2 \leq i \leq 6$. $H(\cdot)$ is operation for hash function. In this way, when the user enters a 7-digit number, a set of X can be generated, and the generated set of numbers is a verifiable random number for the user to verify.

Ticket Purchase. When the player selects a set of numbers $a_1, a_2, a_3, a_4, a_5, a_6, a_7$, a random serial number T will be sent by the lottery issuer, and each set of numbers corresponds to a serial number T.

Winning Result Generation.

- The lottery issuer divided the verifiable random number $ticket_k$ (k is the number of players) of all the tickets into 7 groups on average. If not equal grouping, the last group is the group with missing or redundant data: the size of $\{ticket_1, \cdots, ticket_K\}$, $\{ticket_{K+1}, \cdots, ticket_{2K}\}, \cdots, \{ticket_{6K+1}, \cdots, ticket_k\}$ and K can be adjusted according to the size of k.

- Lottery issuer firstly multiply the verifiable random numbers of each lottery by two and add the results, then to get the hash value of data obtained by last operation, finally let the hash values obtained from the first six groups be mod 33 and add 1, and add 1 to the hash value mod16 of the last group. This can get 6 numbers between 1–33 and a number between 1–16. Since it is a mod operation, the data obtained in the first 6 may be repeated. For the repeated numbers, repeat the hash operation and mod operation plus 1, until the numbers is no longer repeated. The 7 numbers obtained in this way are used as winning numbers and announced to all players.

Prize Claiming. If a player buys the same number as the winning ticket, that player wins. The lottery issuer checks whether the number, sequence and random number he bought are the same as the number, sequence and random number he generated when he bought the ticket in the first place to determine the authenticity of the winner.

Purchaser Verification. Players can verify that they are involved in the generation of winning Numbers simply by checking that their verifiable random numbers are involved in the generation of winning numbers. If players participate, the winning numbers are not controlled by others. Since the scheme adopts the method of constructing linear equations, when verifying that the random number can be verified, players only need to matrix multiply the red ball numbers of their lottery numbers with the verifiable random numbers obtained, and let the result mod p, verify

$$(a_1 \quad a_2 \quad a_3 \quad a_4 \quad a_5 \quad a_6) \begin{pmatrix} x_1 \\ x_2 \\ x_3 \\ x_4 \\ x_5 \\ x_6 \end{pmatrix} \mod p = a_7,$$ if the number is the same as the

number of basketball, so the above formula is established, and the players can verify that their lottery ticket has participated in the generation of winning numbers.

5 Conclusion

Verifiable random numbers have played an important role in the design of electronic lottery in recent years. When designing the double chromosphere lottery system, this article proposes a verifiable random number based on the system of linear equations and a hash function to generate solutions, do not need most of the past need to rely on the existence of the trusted third party, of computing center only to take the functions of calculation, don't need validation of responsibility, reduce the security hidden danger.

References

1. Sun, X.: Study of a secure e-lottery scheme based on e-cash. In: 2009 IEEE International Conference on Intelligent Computing and Intelligent Systems, vol. 3, pp. 195–197. IEEE (2009)
2. Hämäläinen, P., Hännikäinen, M., Hämäläinen, T.D., et al.: Design and implementation of real-time betting system with offline terminals. Electron. Commer. Res. Appl. 5(2), 170–188 (2006)
3. Zhang, Y., Liu, X., Sun, M.: DNA based random key generation and management for OTP encryption. Biosystems 159, 51–63 (2017)
4. Christodoulou, K., Chatzichristofis, S.A., Sirakoulis, G.C., et al.: RandomBlocks: a transparent, verifiable blockchain-based system for random numbers. J. Cell. Autom. 14(5–6), 335–349 (2019)
5. Jianxiang, Liu, Yining, Liu: Random number generation and verification scheme participated by both parties. Comput. Eng. Appl. 54(18), 121–124 (2018)
6. Yu, H., et al.: A novel fair and verifiable data trading scheme. In: International Conference on Frontiers in Cyber Security, pp. 308–326. Springer, Singapore (2019). https://doi.org/10.1007/978-981-15-0818-9_20
7. Pasqualini, L., Parton, M.: Pseudo Random Number Generation: a Reinforcement Learning approach. Procedia Comput. Sci. 170, 1122–1127 (2020)
8. Lee, E.C., Parrilla-Gutierrez, J.M., Henson, A., et al.: A crystallization robot for generating true random numbers based on stochastic chemical processes. Matter 2(3), 649–657 (2020)
9. Qu, W., Liu, H., Zhang, Z.: A method of generating multivariate non-normal random numbers with desired multivariate skewness and kurtosis. Behav. Res. Methods 52(3), 939 (2020). https://doi.org/10.3758/s13428-019-01291-5
10. Chen, C.-L., Chiang, M.-L., Lin, W.-C., Li, D.-K.: A novel lottery protocol for mobile environments. Comput. Electr. Eng. 49, 146–160 (2016)
11. Liu, Yining., Liu, Gao, Chang, Chin-Chen: Lottery protocol using oblivious transfer based on ECC. J. Internet Technol. 18(2), 279–285 (2017)
12. Grumbach, S., Riemann, R.: Distributed random process for a large-scale peer-to-peer lottery. In: Chen, L.Y., Reiser, H.P. (eds.) DAIS 2017. LNCS, vol. 10320, pp. 34–48. Springer, Cham (2017). https://doi.org/10.1007/978-3-319-59665-5_3
13. Pierrot, C., Wesolowski, B.: Malleability of the blockchain's entropy. Crypt. Commun. 10 (1), 211–233 (2018)
14. Xia, Z., Liu, Y., Hsu, C.-F., Chang, C.-C.: An information theoretically secure e-lottery scheme based on symmetric bivariate polynomials. Symmetry 11, 88 (2019)
15. Răcuciu, M., Nen, M., Liepe, Z., Antonie, N.F.: Fair e-lottery system proposal based on anonymous signatures. Appl. Econ. 51(27), 2921 (2019)
16. Lee, Jung-San., Chen, Ying-Chin., Kang, Ya-Han, Yang, Ren-Kai: Preserving privacy and fairness for an innovative e-commerce model: penny M-lottery. J. Internet Technol. 20(5), 1387–1400 (2019)
17. Tso, R.: Two-in-one oblivious signatures. Future Gener. Comput. Syst. 101, 467–475 (2019)
18. Chen, C.L., Liao, Y.H., Leu, F.Y., et al.: An E-lottery system with a fair purchasing environment and an arbitration mechanism. J. Internet Technol. 21(3), 655–671 (2020)
19. Sahitya, K., Borisaniya, B.: D-Lotto: the lottery dapp with verifiable randomness. In: Kotecha K., Piuri V., Shah H., Patel R. (eds.) Data Science and Intelligent Applications. Lecture Notes on Data Engineering and Communications Technologies, vol 52. Springer, Singapore (2021). https://doi.org/10.1007/978-981-15-4474-3_4

Re-Training and Parameter Sharing with the Hash Trick for Compressing Convolutional Neural Networks

Xu Gou[1]($\boxtimes$), Linbo Qing[1], Yi Wang[2], and Mulin Xin[2]

[1] College of Electronic Information Engineering, Sichuan University,
Chengdu 610065, China
gouxu@scu.edu.cn
[2] College of Computer Science, Chongqing University,
Chongqing 400044, China

Abstract. As an ubiquitous technology for improving machine intelligence, deep learning has largely taken the dominant position among nowadays most advanced computer vision systems. To achieve superior performance on large-scale data sets, convolutional neural networks (CNNs) are often designed as complex models with millions of parameters. This limits the deployment of CNNs in embedded intelligent computer vision systems, such as intelligent robots that are resource-constrained with real-time computing requirement. This paper proposes a simple and effective model compression scheme to improve the real-time sensing of the surrounding objects. In the proposed framework, the Hash trick is first applied to a modified convolutional layer, and the compression of the convolutional layer is realized via weight sharing. Subsequently, the Hash index matrix is introduced to represent the Hash function, and its relaxation regularization is introduced into the fine-tuned loss function. Through the dynamic retraining of the index matrix, the Hash function can be updated. We evaluate our method using several state-of-the-art CNNs. Experimental results showed that the proposed method can reduce the number of parameters in AlexNet by 24 × with no accuracy loss. In addition, the compressed VGG16 and ResNet50 can achieve a more than 60 × increased speed, which is significant.

Keywords: Model compression · Machine learning · Parameter learning and tuning · Computational and artificial intelligence

1 Introduction

In recent years, convolutional neural networks (CNNs) have produced great changes in the field of computer vision [1]. CNN-based models have been applied in image classification [2–4], multi-target detection [5, 6], semantic segmentation [7–9], and behavior recognition tasks [10, 11], achieving the most advanced results. These applications also promote the intellectualization of robot control, allowing robots to understand the scene and automatically complete specific tasks through computer vision algorithms. The success of CNNs is attributed to its own complex structure and

© Springer Nature Switzerland AG 2020
X. Chen et al. (Eds.): ML4CS 2020, LNCS 12486, pp. 402–416, 2020.
https://doi.org/10.1007/978-3-030-62223-7_35

millions of parameters which allow the network to model complex high-level patterns, giving the network more discriminatory power.

When mapping and running a network on a computer platform, a large number of parameters will result in high memory requirements. Taking classification networks as an example, the size of the trained AlexNet [2] is approximately 230 M, and that of the VGG16 [3] is approximately 527 M. Therefore, convolutional neural networks require large amounts of hardware resources, hindering their deployment on embedded computing devices with limited memory. Especially in robots and intelligent image sensors, the computing power and memory of the equipped hardware are small, which leads to the inefficient use of existing models and poor real-time performance.

This dilemma has led to some compression of neural networks. The work of Denil et al. shows that there is much redundancy among the weights of a neural network and proves that a small number of weights are enough to reconstruct a whole network [12]. In this paper, we proposed a new network architecture that aimed to reduce and limit the memory overhead of convolutional neural networks. We focus on convolutional layer compression by extending HashedNet [13] to the convolutional layer and grouping the weighting matrix of the convolutional layer with the Hash function, this makes the weights of the same group share the same value. Furthermore, a Hash index matrix is proposed to represent the hash function that reflects the shared state of the weight matrix. Then, a relaxation regularization of is introduced into the fine-tuned loss function. Through alternate optimization, the best sharing weight in the optimal sharing state is obtained as desired.

The proposed method is verified on two real-world deep learning benchmark datasets. The image classification experiments on three network models, including AlexNet, VGG16 and ResNet50 [38], showed that the proposed method could greatly reduce the size of the neural network model, while having little effect on the prediction accuracy. The experiments also showed that the method had a good effect on the acceleration of the convolution network. The compressed networks can be deployed on the embedded systems of the robots, and improve the speed of the robot's perception for surrounding objects.

2   Related Work

Network shaping has become the most common solution for compressing deep neural networks. It aims to eliminate the redundancy in the original network and generate networks that take up less memory. The study of neural network compression can be traced back to the 1990s. Le Cun et al. introduced the Optimal Brain Damage method, which prunes weights via theoretically reasonable saliency measurements [14]. Subsequently, Hassib et al. presented the Optimal Brain Surgeon method to eliminate the unimportant weights, which were determined by the second derivative information [15]. In recent years, Han et al. proposed a network pruning pattern for pruning unimportant weights by learning the connections in neural networks [16]. The work of Srinivas et al. was no longer focused on the weights in the network but on removing the neurons, thus ensuring that the overall structure of the network remains the same [17]. Wen et al. [18] and Huang et al. [19] studied selecting the structure of CNNs (i.e., the filter, channel, filter shape, and layer depth) via structured sparsity to obtain a compact structure. In addition, Denton et al. attached the weight of the fully connected layer to the low rank matrix and decomposed it using the singular value decomposition method [20]. Lebedev et al. followed this direction and proposed Canonical Polyadic decomposition for convolutional layer tensors in [21].

When constructing a neural network, the float point accuracy was usually 32 bits. In the large network model, it consumed more memory resources. Weight sharing is also a popular model compression method that allows multiple weights to share a single parameter value to reduce storage requirements. HashedNet [13] used a low-cost hash function to randomly group connection weights into hash buckets and allowed all connections within the same hash bucket to share a single parameter value. Remarkably, Courbariaux et al. believed that floating-point weights may be replaced with 1-bit binary weights in a CNN's forward and reverse training, which may enable the hardware to simplify the multiplication operations into simple accumulation operations and reduce the storage space by a large amount [22]. The author then further changed the activation value to 1 bit, reducing the memory consumption [23]. XNOR-Net turned both the filter and convolutional input into binary code [24]. Recently, Wess et al. introduced Weighted Quantization Regularity (WQR) to reduce the precision degradation due to quantization [25].

In addition, some researchers have found that the number of weights and the number of operations in a CNN cannot directly reflect the actual energy consumption of the network, so the energy-aware CNN compression method was proposed. Yang et al. defined the concept of energy-aware pruning (EAP), which directly uses a CNN's energy consumption to guide model compression [26]. The SCNN [27] and TIE [28] specifically implemented a processor to improve efficiency. Knowledge distillation [29–31], as another popular model compression method, counts on the knowledge of both transfer learning and the teacher model to guide the training of a simple model. Finally, it was found that the student model is close to or better than the teacher model with less complexity while achieving similar predictions.

3   Methodology

3.1   Random Weight Sharing

In a standard fully connected network, there are $(n^l + 1) \times n^{l+1}$ weight connections between layer l and layer $l + 1$, and each weight connection corresponds to an element in the weight matrix W^l, where n^l is the number of neurons in the l-th layer. Assuming that layer l only allows for $K^l \ll (n^l + 1) \times n^{l+1}$ different weights, the immediate solution is calculated as follows:

- Reduce the number of neurons in layer l and layer $l + 1$ [17];
- Reduce the bit accuracy of weights [20].

Nevertheless, when the allowed K^l is small enough, both methods can significantly reduce the generalization capabilities of the network.

Weight sharing is proposed to compress the network model, which keeps a constant weight matrix W^l but reduces its effective memory footprint using weight partitioning. The basic idea of weight sharing is that only K^l different weights are allowed in the weight matrix W^l, and they are stored in a weight vector w^l. Here, the weights in W^l are randomly shared via multiple weights. Figure 1 shows a simple example of random weight sharing.

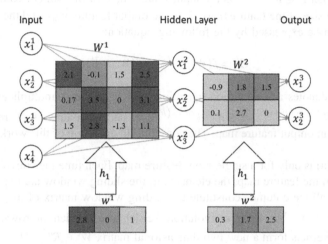

Fig. 1. Example of random weight sharing for a fully connected network

3.2 Hashing Trick for Convolutional Kernels

Chen et al. introduced Hash functions into fully connected layers and achieved weight random sharing [13]. In this method, the shared weight of each connection was determined using a Hash function. Specifically, in the l-th fully connected layer, $W_{i,j}^l$ is assigned an element in w^l indexed by the hash function $h^l(i,j)$:

$$W_{i,j}^l = w_{h^l(i,j)}^l \tag{1}$$

Here, the hash function $h^l(i,j)$ maps the subscript (i,j) to a natural number in $\{1, 2, \cdots, K^l\}$, indicating the weight sharing status. For example, in Fig. 1, $h^1(3,2) = 1$; therefore, $W_{3,2}^1 = w_{h^1(3,2)}^1 = w_1^1 = 2.8$. In summary, the entire network in Fig. 1 is compressed to 1/3 of the original size, i.e., the 18 weights stored in the virtual matrices W^1 and W^2 are compressed to 6 real values in w^1 and w^2.

This Hash technique greatly reduces the storage requirements of the neural network while mostly retaining the performance of the network, and the Hash process does not introduce additional memory overhead. However, the above work focuses on a fully connected neural network, and the convolutional layer plays a crucial role in the popular neural network model. This paper extends the hash function to the convolutional layer.

The weight of a convolutional neural network (CNN) can be regarded as a 4-D matrix, $W^l \in R^{n^l \times n^{(l+1)} \times s \times s}$, where n^l and $n^{(l+1)}$ respectively denote the number of input and output channels of the l $(1 \le l \le L)$-th convolutional layer, and $S \times S$ represents the size of the convolution kernel. To implement the hashing technique in the convolutional layer, this work converts the convolution operation into a fully connected operation.

Assume that $I^l \in R^{h^l \times w^l \times n^l}$ is the input feature map of the l-th convolutional layer, $h^l \times w^l$ is the size of the feature map, O^l is the output feature map, and the convolution operation can be expressed by the following equation:

$$O^l = f\left(W^l \odot I^l\right) = f\left(\bar{W}^l \times \bar{I}^l\right) \tag{2}$$

Here, $\odot$ denotes a convolution operation, and $\times$ is matrix multiplication. At this time, $\bar{W}^l \in R^{n^{(l+1)} \times (s \times s \times n^l)}$, $\bar{I} \in R^{(s \times s \times n^l) \times (h^l \times w^l)}$, and each line of O^l represents an extrusion of an output feature map. The convolution operation of this work is shown in Fig. 2(a).

Figure 2(a) is only for a single input feature map. Each time the convolution kernel is slid once in the feature map, the elements in the sliding window are expanded into a column, and all the columns constitute the sliding window matrix of the input feature map $\bar{I}^l \in R^{(s \times s) \times (h^l \times w^l)}$. Each convolution kernel is expanded in rows, and $n^{(l+1)}$ convolution kernels form a new two-dimensional matrix $\bar{W}^l \in R^{n^{(l+1)} \times (s \times s)}$. The kernel matrix $\bar{W}^l$ is multiplied by the sliding window matrix $\bar{I}^l$, and each obtained row is an output feature map. $n^{(l+1)}$ convolutions are available to form $n^{(l+1)}$ feature maps. Similarly, the convolution calculation was extended to n^l input feature maps, as shown in Fig. 2 (b). At this time, the sliding window matrix is $\bar{I}^l \in R^{(s \times s \times n^l) \times (h^l \times w^l)}$, and each of its columns is composed of elements in the sliding window connected by columns. Each row of the kernel matrix $\bar{W}^l \in R^{n^{(l+1)} \times (s \times s \times n^l)}$ is obtained by connecting each convolution kernel by rows.

Following the above transformation, the convolution operation can be completed via matrix multiplication and thus taking the convolutional layer as a fully connected layer. At this point, the parameter sharing at the fully connected layer can be extended to the convolution layer. Similar to the fully connected layer, the elements in w^l are assigned to the new convolution matrix $\overline{W}^l$ by the Hash function $h^l(i,j)$:

$$\bar{W}^l_{i,j} = \bar{w}^l_{h^l(i,j)} \tag{3}$$

where the Hash function $h^l(i,j)$ mapped the subscript (i,j) to a natural number in $\{1, 2, \cdots, K^l\}$.

After introducing the Hash function into the convolution operation of the above transformation, the forward propagation of the convolutional layer becomes the following:

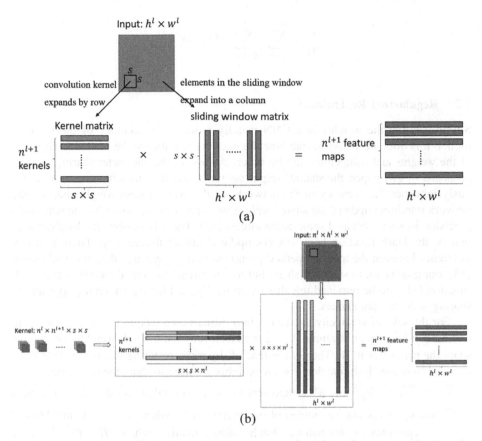

Fig. 2. (a) How the convolution kernel matrix changed a single input feature map; (b) How the convolution kernel matrix changed multiple input feature maps

$$O^l(i,:) = f\left(\sum_{j=1}^{s \times s \times n^l} \bar{W}^l_{i,j} \bar{I}^l(j,:)\right) = f\left(\sum_{j=1}^{s \times s \times n^l} \bar{w}^l_{h^l(i,j)} \bar{I}^l(j,:)\right) \quad (4)$$

At this time, in the back propagation, $\delta^l_j = \left(\sum_{i=1}^{n^{(l+1)}} w^l_{h^l(i,j)} \delta^{(l+1)}_i\right) f'$

$\left(\sum_{j=1}^{s \times s \times n^l} \bar{w}^l_{h^l(i,j)} \bar{I}^l(j,:)\right)$ represents the gradient of loss function L on activation j, which is

also called the error term. Then, the gradient of the shared weight value $\bar{w}^l_k$ in loss function L is as follows:

$$\frac{\partial L}{\partial \overline{w}_k^l} = \sum_{i=1}^{n^{(l+1)}} \sum_{j:h^l(i,j)=k} \overline{I}^l(j,:) \delta_i^{(l+1)} \tag{5}$$

3.3   Regularized Re-Training

Simply sharing the weights in a CNN usually reduces the accuracy of the network model. It is often necessary to fine-tune the network to enhance the favorable structure of the weights and compensate for the accuracy loss. In the parameter sharing method proposed in this paper, the shared weight vector w and the Hash function $h(\bullet)$ obviously influence the accuracy of the network. In the original hash weight sharing, the network retraining updated the shared weight vector w to compensate for the network's precision loss and obtained some better effects [13]. There is an obvious disadvantage, that is, the Hash function $h(\bullet)$ was not updated during the training. There is a key difference between the training method proposed in this paper and that in Chen's work [13]: our goal is not to statically share, but to encourage the shared weight w and Hash function $h(i,j)$ to be retrained together dynamically, and finally obtain the appropriate sharing state and parameters.

For the sake of simplicity, we take a two-dimensional weight matrix $W \in R^{m \times n}$ in one hidden layer as an example. Using the Hash function $h(\bullet)$, K weights are used to share the parameter in W. Then, we extend W by rows, resulting in a row vector $\overline{W}$ of $m \times n$. Using the Hash function $h(\bullet)$, K weights are used to share the $m \times n$ parameter in $\overline{W}$. Let $\overline{W}_k = \left[\overline{w}_1^{(k)}, \cdots, \overline{w}_{n_k}^{(k)}\right]$ represent the k-th group that contains the parameters in $\overline{W}$, and n_k represents the number of parameters in W, where $h(i,j) = k$. In addition, $H \in \mathcal{H}$ represents a normalized Hash index matrix, where $H \in R^{(m \times n) \times K}$. If $h(i,j) = k \in (1, 2, \cdots, K)$, then $H((i-1) \times n + j, k) = \frac{1}{\sqrt{n_k}}$, and the other elements in H are set to 0. Obviously, matrix H reflects the Hash function $h(\bullet)$, and the Hash matrix may be derived according to the weight vector w. H reflects the sharing structure of the elements in W.

In this work, we introduced the Hash index matrix H into the loss function and used the following equation to regularize H:

$$\min_{\overline{W}, H \in \mathbb{H}} Tr\left(\overline{W}^T \overline{W}\right) - Tr\left(H^T \overline{W}^T \overline{W} H\right) \tag{6}$$

where Tr is the trace of the matrix. Then, Eq. (6) can be rewritten as follows:

$$\min_{\overline{W}, H \in H} Tr\left(\overline{W}^T \overline{W}\right) - Tr\left(H^T \overline{W}^T \overline{W} H\right)$$

$$= \min \left(Tr\left(\overline{W}_k^T \overline{W}_k\right) - \left(\frac{e^T}{\sqrt{n_k}}\right) \overline{W}_k^T \overline{W}_k \left(\frac{e}{\sqrt{n_k}}\right) \right)$$

$$= \min \sum_{k=1}^{K} Tr\left(\left(I - \frac{ee^T}{n_k}\right) \overline{W}_k^T \overline{W}_k\right) = \min \sum_{k=1}^{K} \left(\overline{W}_k \left(I - \frac{ee^T}{n_k}\right) \overline{W}_k^T\right) \quad (7)$$

$$= \min \sum_{k=1}^{K} \left\| \overline{W}_k \left(I - \frac{ee^T}{n_k}\right) \right\|_F^2 = \min \sum_{k=1}^{K} \left\| \overline{W}_k - m_k e^T \right\|_F^2$$

$$= \min \sum_{k=1}^{K} \sum_{i=1}^{n_k} \left\| \overline{w}_i^{(k)} - m_k \right\|^2$$

This shows that Eq. (6) makes the parameters in the Hash buckets come together. Following the work of Zha et al. [32], we further ignore the special structure of H and relax it into an arbitrary orthogonal matrix. Then, Eq. (6) can be relaxed as the trace maximization problem on a Stiefel manifold:

$$\min_{w, H \in \mathcal{H}} Tr\left(\bar{W}^T \bar{W}\right) - Tr\left(H^T \bar{W}^T \bar{W} H\right)$$
$$s.t. H^T H = I \quad (8)$$

When W is given, Eq. (8) is simplified to the following:

$$\max_{H \in \mathcal{H}} Tr\left(H^T \bar{W}^T \bar{W} H\right) = \max_{H \in \mathcal{H}} Tr\left[(\bar{W} H)^T (\bar{W} H)\right] = \max_{H \in \mathcal{H}} \|\bar{W} H\|_2^2$$
$$s.t. H^T H = I \quad (9)$$

This is an optimization problem of orthogonal constraints, which is solved using the projection method proposed in [33]. Thus, during fine tuning, the relaxation regular loss function proposed can be expressed as follows (where λ is a scalar):

$$\min_{V, H \in H} L + \frac{\lambda}{2} \left[Tr\left(W^T W\right) - Tr\left(H^T W^T W H\right)\right],$$
$$s.t. H^T H = 1 \quad (10)$$

L is the loss function for training a neural network, such as a cross entropy or a quadratic loss function.

In the fine tuning process, the problem of Eq. (10) was solved by alternating iterations of w and H. When H is fixed, Eq. (10) is expressed as a function of the shared weight vector w. We updated w using the stochastic gradient descent method (SGD), and its gradient is as follows:

$$\nabla L + \lambda w (I - HH^T) \tag{11}$$

∇L is obtained via Eq. (5). Further, when w is given, the same solution as in Eq. (9) was used to update H. In view of the interaction between H and w in the iteration process, H was used as the index of the Hash function. In the training process, the optimization of the weight sharing state was promoted, and finally, the sharing weight vector rose to its primary level in the optimal sharing state. Both w and H are updated in each iteration.

The additional complexity caused by applying the relaxation regularization term consists of two parts.

- Update H. The projection method proposed in document [33] was used to update the solution of H in Eq. (9), and its computational complexity was $\mathcal{O}(2(m \times n)K^2 + 2(m \times n)K)$.
- Update w. w was updated using the stochastic gradient descent method (SGD), and the only additional burden was $\mathcal{O}((m \times n)K^2)$.
- Therefore, the total additional complexity was $\mathcal{O}(3(m \times n)K^2 + 2(m \times n)K)$.

4 Experiments

In the experiments, we evaluate the method proposed in this paper by analyzing the accuracy and efficiency of the network. To measure the accuracy of the model, we performed image classification using the CIFAR dataset [36] and ImageNet [37]. In addition, the efficiency of the network is measured by computing the acceleration of the network model test. The experiments in this paper evaluated AlexNet [2] and two deeper common network architectures: VGG16 [3] and ResNet50 [38]. The proposed method is implemented on TensorFlow. In the fine-tuning process, the initial learning rate was 0.001, and the learning rate became 1/10 of the original after 5,000 iterations. The top-1 and top-5 accuracy are used to verify the classification performance.

4.1 CIFAR Classification

We start by using the CIFAR dataset to evaluate our approach. The CIFAR-10 dataset consists of 60 K 32 × 32 color images in 10 classes, and each class has 6 K images. These images are divided into 50000 training pictures and 10000 test pictures. CIFAR-100 is similar to CIFAR-10 except that it has 100 classes, each containing 600 images. There are 500 training images and 100 testing images per class. AlexNet was used to classify the CIFAR datasets. In the experiment, the images are resized to 224 × 224 and the model is trained for 240 epochs total on a single GPU with batch size of 32.

Table 1 shows the classification accuracy of AlexNet on the CIFAR-10 and CIFAR-100 datasets after being compressed 24 times by our method, and the results are compared with those of HashedNet [13], XNOR-Net [24] and DeepCompression (DC) [16]. AlexNet-QurNRe means that there is no regular term in the retraining loss function, and only the cross entropy is used to train the convolution neural network after weight sharing. Some exact values are not reported in some papers and cannot be calculated, so $\approx$ is used to represent approximate values.

It can be seen that the accuracies of AlexNet-Qur and AlexNet-QurNRe outperform all the other methods. Compared with the original baseline, the accuracy of AlexNet-Qur on the CIFAR-100 dataset is only slightly reduced (by 1.5%), and the accuracy on the CIFAR-10 dataset is even better than the baseline. Moreover, the network retrained using relaxation regularization achieved higher classification accuracy than the networks that were generally retrained. This initially illustrated the effectiveness of the proposed method. Compared with XNORNet and DeepCompression, the proposed method displayed an effect of the general compression on the network. We will continue to discuss the classification accuracy under different compression ratios in Sect. 4.3.

Table 1. Results of classification tasks using CIFAR 10 and CIFAR 100

Model	CIFAR-10			CIFAR-100		
	Top-1 Acc.	Top-5 Acc.	#Param. $\downarrow$	Top-1 Acc.	Top-5 Acc.	#Param. $\downarrow$
AlexNet	56.6	80.2		41.8	76.9	
AlexNet-XNORNet	44.2	69.2	54×	36.5	65.8	52×
AlexNet-HashedNet	≈ 41.8	≈ 67.3	$\approx 8\times$	≈ 33.7	≈ 61.3	$\approx 8\times$
AlexNet-DC	57.2	80.3	35 ×	**39.1**	73.6	30 ×
AlexNet-Our$_{NRe}$	56.3	81.1	24×	38.3	75.1	24×
AlexNet- Our	**58.9**	**82.1**	24×	38.5	**75.4**	24×

4.2   ImageNet Classification

To further demonstrate the effectiveness of our approach, VGG16 and ResNet50 were subjected to more experiments using the ImageNet LSVRC 2012 classification task. The ImageNet LSVRC 2012 dataset consists of 1.2 million training examples and 50 K validation examples from 1000 categories. Using the standard pipeline, we pre-process the images to 224 × 224 for training and perform left-right flips for data augmentation. The mini-batch size is 64 on one GPU for VGG16 and ResNet50. We train the models for 100 epochs.

All the results for ImageNet classification are summarized in Table 2. VGG16 and ResNet50 are compressed 50 and 20 times, respectively, using our proposed method. The results obtained on ImageNet are similar to those on CIFAR. Both the VGG16 and ResNet50 that were compressed using the proposed approach obtain the best classification results. In addition, compared to AlexNet, the compression effect of large-scale networks was greatly improved. The compression of VGG16 using this method exceeds that of DeepCompression while maintaining the network accuracy.

Table 2. Results of classification tasks using ImageNet.

Model	Top-1 Acc.	Top-5 Acc.	#Param. ↓
VGG16	71.9	90.7	
VGG16-XNORNet	≈ 50.3	≈ 71.4	≈ 54×
VGG16-HashedNet	≈ 49.7	≈ 71.0	≈ 12 ×
VGG16-DC	68.8	89.1	49 ×
VGG16-Our$_{NRe}$	**68.8**	90.2	50 ×
VGG16- Our	66.7	**93.2**	50 ×
ResNet50	77.2	93.3	
ResNet50-XNORNet	51.2	73.2	57×
ResNet50-HashedNet	≈ 48.7	≈ 73.0	≈ 14 ×
ResNet50-DC	75.9	92.8	17×
ResNet50-Our$_{NRe}$	71.6	91.8	20 ×
ResNet50- Our	**76.0**	**93.1**	20 ×

4.3 Results with Varying Compression Factors

In the above experiment, the proposed method obtained the best classification accuracy, but the compressed network hasn't reached to the minimum level. For completeness, in this section, we compress AlexNet, VGG16, and ResNet50 to different sizes and verify their performance under different compression ratios. Figure 3 shows the performance of each neural network under different compression factors using different methods. It can be observed that the proposed method was superior to all other baseline methods, especially when the compression factor is very small (i.e., a very small model). HashedNet and XNOR-Net failed to provide better results compared to standard neural networks (black lines). Regularization could be used to improve the performance of this method. Among all the methods, only the method proposed in this paper maintains the performance under small compression factors regardless of whether or not it was regularized.

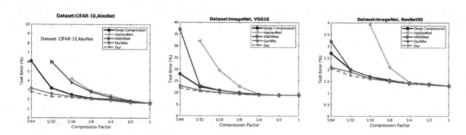

Fig. 3. Error rates under different compression factors

4.4   Regularization Effect

From the classification experiments using the CIFAR dataset and ImageNet, it was found that the relaxation regularization conducted in this work effectively improved the accuracy of the compressed network. In this experiment, we further analyzed the effect of regularization on the convergence after fine-tuning.

First, VGG16 was compressed using the weight sharing method, and then the conventional cross entropy loss without the regularization term and the relaxation regular retraining proposed in this paper were observed. Next, the Weighted Quantization-Regularization (WQR) [25] proposed by Wess et al. was used to train VGG16, and the process is the same as that in the original paper. Figure 4 compares the effect of regularization on the convergence rate. It was found that regularization, regardless of WQR or slack regularization, was able to speed up the convergence during retraining. Moreover, when using targeted relaxation regularization, the network achieved the same accuracy with a minimum number of iterations. This faster convergence was consistent with the experimental observations below as far as test speed was concerned.

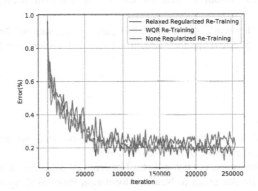

Fig. 4. Convergence rate: Comparison with or without regularization

We evaluated the absolute model acceleration performance when using the GPU by specifically testing the forward run time of each compressed model. The compressed models in Table 1 and Table 2 are involved in this test. This evaluation work was done using a GeForce GTX TITAN X in a TensorFlow environment with a batch size of 32, and it was accelerated using CUDA9.0. AlexNet is tested on the CIFAR-10 dataset, and VGG16 and ResNet50 are tested on ImageNet. Table 3 shows the acceleration relative to the original network. The compressed models have some acceleration and our method achieves the best acceleration when using VGG16 and ResNet50. Combined with Table 1 and Table 2, it can be said that the promotion of our method on the GPU leads to better results than the other methods.

Table 3. The absolute model acceleration performance (GPU speed up).

Model Method	AlexNet	VGG16	ResNet50
HashedNet	27×	39 ×	49×
XNOR-Net	46×	53×	62×
DC	3.5×	4×	5×
Our	45×	60×	**69** ×

5 Conclusion

In this work, we proposed a simple and effective compressed convolution scheme in order to reduce and limit the memory overhead of convolutional neural networks. We extend HashedNet to the convolutional layer and introduced the relaxation regularization of a Hash index matrix into the loss function. The experiments showed that the proposed method was capable of greatly reducing the size of the neural network model with little effect on the prediction accuracy. Our future work will incorporate energy-aware regularizations into our method for direct minimization of energy consumptions.

Acknowledgments. This work was supported in part by the National Natural Science Foundation of China (no.61672120) and the Sichuan Science and Technology Program under Grant 2018HH0143.

References

1. LeCun, Y., Bottou, L., Bengio, Y.: Gradient-based learning applied to document recognition. Proc. IEEE **86**(11), 2278–2324 (1998)
2. Krizhevsky, A., Sutskever, I., Hinton, G.E.: Imagenet classification with deep convolutional neural networks. In: Advances in Neural Information Processing Systems, pp. 1097–1105 (2012)
3. Simonyan, K., Zisserman, A.: Very deep convolutional networks for large-scale image recognition. In: International Conference on Learning Representations (2015)
4. He, K., Zhang, X., Ren, S. (eds.): Deep residual learning for image recognition. In: The IEEE Conference on Computer Vision and Pattern Recognition, pp. 770–778 (2016)
5. Ren, S.Q., He, K., Girshick, R.: Faster R-CNN: towards real-time object detection with region proposal networks. Trans. Pattern Anal. Mach. Intell. **39**, 1137–1149 (2017)
6. Redmon, J., Farhadi, A.: YOLOv3: An incremental improvement. arXiv:1804.02767 (2018)
7. Long, J., Shelhamer, E., Darrell, T.: Fully convolutional networks for semantic segmentation. In: The IEEE Conference on Computer Vision and Pattern Recognition, pp. 3431–3440 (2015)
8. Ronneberger, O., Fischer, P., Brox, T.: U-Net: Convolutional networks for biomedical image segmentation. In: Navab, N., Hornegger, J., Wells, W.M., Frangi, A.F. (eds.) MICCAI 2015. LNCS, vol. 9351, pp. 234–241. Springer, Cham (2015). https://doi.org/10.1007/978-3-319-24574-4_28

9. Chen, L.C., Papandreou, G., Kokkinos, I.: DeepLab: semantic image segmentation with deep convolutional nets, atrous convolution, and fully connected CRFs. IEEE Trans. Pattern Anal. Mach. Intell. **40**(4), 834–848 (2018)

10. Wang, L., et al.: Temporal Segment Networks: Towards Good Practices for Deep Action Recognition. In: Leibe, B., Matas, J., Sebe, N., Welling, M. (eds.) ECCV 2016. LNCS, vol. 9912, pp. 20–36. Springer, Cham (2016). https://doi.org/10.1007/978-3-319-46484-8_2

11. Diba, A., Sharma, V., Gool, L.V.: Deep temporal linear encoding networks. In: IEEE Conference on Computer Vision and Pattern Recognition, pp. 1541–1550 (2017)

12. Denil, M., et al.: Predicting parameters in deep learning. In: Advances in Neural Information Processing Systems, pp. 2148–2156 (2013)

13. Chen, W., et al.: Compressing neural networks with the hashing trick. In: International Conference on Machine Learning, pp. 2285–2294 (2015)

14. LeCun, Y., Denker, J., Solla, S.A.: Optimal brain damage. In: Advances in Neural Information Processing Systems, pp. 598–605 (1990)

15. Hassibi, B., Stork, D.G.: Second order derivatives for network pruning: optimal brain surgeon. In: Advances in Neural Information Processing Systems, pp. 164–171 (1993)

16. Han, S., Mao, H., Dally, W.J.: Deep compression: compressing deep neural networks with pruning, trained quantization and huffman coding. In: International Conference on Learning Representations (2016)

17. Srinivas, S., Babu, R.V.: Data-free Parameter Pruning for Deep Neural Networks. The British Machine Vision Association (2015)

18. Wen, W., et al.: Learning structured sparsity in deep neural networks. In: Advances in Neural Information Processing Systems, pp. 2074–2082 (2016)

19. Huang, Z., Wang, N.: Data-driven sparse structure selection for deep neural networks. In: Proceedings of the European Conference on Computer Vision (ECCV), pp. 304–320 (2018)

20. Denton, E.L., Zaremba, W., Bruna, J., LeCun, Y., Fergus, R.: Exploiting linear structure within convolutional networks for efficient evaluation. In: Advances in Neural Information Processing Systems, pp. 1269–1277 (2014)

21. Lebedev, V., Ganin, Y., Rakhuba, M., Oseledets, I.V., Lempitsky, V.S.: Speeding-up convolutional neural networks using fine-tuned cpdecomposition. arXiv:1412.6553

22. Courbariaux, M., Bengio, Y., David, J.P.: Binaryconnect: training deep neural networks with binary weights during propagations. In: Advances in Neural Information Processing Systems, pp. 3123–3131 (2015)

23. Hubara, I., et al.: Binarized neural networks: Training neural networks with weights and activations constrained to +1 or −1. arXiv:1602.02830

24. Rastegari, M., Ordonez, V., Redmon, J., Farhadi, A.: XNOR-Net: ImageNet classification using binary convolutional neural networks. In: Leibe, B., Matas, J., Sebe, N., Welling, M. (eds.) ECCV 2016. LNCS, vol. 9908, pp. 525–542. Springer, Cham (2016). https://doi.org/10.1007/978-3-319-46493-0_32

25. Wess, M., Dinakarrao, S.M.P., Jantsch, A.: Weighted quantization-regularization in DNNs for weight memory minimization toward HW implementation. IEEE Trans. Comput. Aided Des. Integr. Circuits Syst. **37**(11), 2929–2939 (2018)

26. Yang, T.J., Chen, Y.H., Sze, V.: Designing energy-efficient convolutional neural networks using energy-aware pruning. In: Proceedings of the IEEE Conference on Computer Vision and Pattern Recognition, pp. 5687–5695 (2017)

27. Parashar, A., et al.: SCNN: an accelerator for compressed-sparse convolutional neural networks. In: ACM/IEEE 44th Annual International Symposium on Computer Architecture (ISCA), pp. 27–40 (2017)

28. Deng, C., et al.: TIE: energy-efficient tensor train-based inference engine for deep neural network. In: Proceedings of the 46th International Symposium on Computer Architecture, pp. 264–278 (2019)
29. Hinton, G., Vinyals, O., Dean, J.: Distilling the knowledge in a neural network. arXiv preprint arXiv:1503.02531 (2015)
30. Romero, A., et al.: Fitnets: Hints for thin deep nets. arXiv preprint arXiv:1412.6550 (2014)
31. Zagoruyko, S., Komodakis, N.: Paying more attention to attention: improving the performance of convolutional neural networks via attention transfer. In: International Conference on Learning Representations (2017)
32. Zha, H., et.al.: Spectral relaxation for k-means clustering. In: Advances in Neural Information Processing Systems, pp. 1057–1064 (2002)
33. Absil, P.A., Mahony, R., Sepulchre, R.: Optimization Algorithms on Matrix Manifolds. Princeton University Press, Jersey (2019)
34. Sabour, S., Frosst, N., Hinton, G.E.: Dynamic routing between capsules. In: Advances in Neural Information Processing Systems, pp. 3856–3866 (2017)
35. Cheng, Y., et al.: A survey of model compression and acceleration for deep neural networks. arXiv preprint arXiv:1710.09282
36. Krizhevsky, A., Hinton, G.: Learning multiple layers of features from tiny images. Master's thesis, Department of Computer Science, University of Toronto (2009)
37. Russakovsky, O., Deng, J., Su, H., et al.: Imagenet large scale visual recognition challenge. Int. J. Comput. Vis. **115**(3), 211–252 (2015)
38. He, K., Zhang, X., Ren, S., Sun, J.: Deep residual learning for image recognition. In: The IEEE Conference on Computer Vision and Pattern Recognition, pp. 770–778 (2016)
39. Li, R., Wang, S., Zhu, F., Huang, J.: Adaptive graph convolutional neural networks. In: Advances in AAAI Conference on Artificial Intelligence, pp. 3546–3553 (2018)

Survey on Privacy-Preserving Machine Learning Protocols

Ruidi Yang[✉] [iD]

School of Management and Engineering, Capital University of Economics
and Business, Beijing 100070, China
yangruidi_1201@163.com

Abstract. Machine learning, especially deep learning, is a hot research field in
academia, and it is revolutionizing industry. However, the privacy-preserving
problems are not solved. In this paper, we investigate the privacy-preserving
technology in machine learning application. We first introduce the models in
privacy-preserving machine learning protocols, and then we give an overview of
the main privacy-preserving machine learning technologies. At last, we analyze
the existing problems.

Keywords: Privacy-preserving · Machine learning · Secure multi-party
computation · Homomorphic encryption

1 Introduction

Machine learning, especially deep learning, is currently a hot research area in academia
and has set off a revolution in industry. From the perspective of application fields,
image recognition, voice recognition, machine translation, personalized recommendation, etc. are all direct application fields of machine/deep learning; in addition,
machine/deep learning has also been quickly applied to the video industry, medical
industry, financial industry In unmanned driving, the application of artificial intelligence based on deep learning has become the current hot field. In addition, Amazon,
Google, Microsoft, Baidu, Meituan, Tencent and other top technology companies have
also begun to provide Machine Learning as a Service (MLaaS) services.

The rapid development of machine learning has brought new opportunities for
information security research. With the rapid development of cloud computing, Internet
of Things, big data and other technologies, the massive application data has increased,
which has brought huge challenges to information security. Traditional information
security technologies have low efficiency when solving massive data problems. It has
been more than 30 years of using machine learning to solve problems in the field of
information security. In recent years, the use of machine learning, especially deep
learning algorithms, to solve information security problems under massive data has
received extensive attention from academia and industry. Zhang Lei et al. [1] summarized machine learning in chip and system hardware security, system software
security, network infrastructure security, network security detection, application software security, social network security from three levels of system security, network

security and application security And other solutions in the field of information security. Zhang Yuqing et al. [2] summarized the ten problems and opportunities faced by deep learning in cyberspace security.

While using machine learning algorithms to solve information security problems, the privacy protection problems inherent in machine learning applications are increasingly prominent. Taking the MLaaS service for image recognition as an example, the customer provides the image to the service provider, and the service provider uses the trained model to predict the objects in the image, and returns the prediction result to the customer. For the purpose of protecting privacy, customers often do not want to disclose their image content and prediction results; for the purpose of protecting commercial profits, service providers do not want to disclose the parameter information of their models. In addition to the privacy exposure in the prediction phase, the training phase of the machine learning algorithm also has the risk of leaking privacy. For example, many hospitals hope to jointly train a treatment effect model for predicting the clinical performance of patients based on their respective information. Each hospital's database records the clinical performance, treatment methods, and treatment effect data of different patients. For the purpose of protecting patient privacy information, the hospital does not want to directly provide data information in the database when cooperatively training models. In recent years, research on privacy protection problems in machine learning applications has gradually attracted the attention of scholars at home and abroad, and will be a hot research field for a long time in the future.

This article takes the theme of privacy-preserving machine learning protocols as the theme. It first discusses the privacy protection model in machine learning applications, then reviews the research progress of privacy-preserving machine learning protocols, analyzes research trends, and finally summarizes the current problems.

2   Privacy Protection Model for Machine Learning Applications

Machine learning algorithms usually include two stages, model training and prediction. Correspondingly, the privacy protection machine learning protocol faces two problems: one is how to achieve privacy protection during the model training phase, that is, how to protect the training sample data during the construction of the optimal prediction function; the second is how to achieve privacy during the prediction phase Protection, that is, how to protect prediction data, optimal function parameters, and prediction results during the use of the optimal prediction function. According to the distribution of privacy data, the number of participants and the communication methods between participants, we summarize several different models of privacy protection machine learning protocols.

Definition1: Privacy-Preserving Machine Learning training protocol
Multiple participants separately hold part of the sample data, and they want to jointly obtain the required model parameters based on the sample data of all participants without revealing their respective sample data.

The distribution of private data is divided into horizontal and vertical divisions. Horizontal split data refers to all the attribute information of one or more samples for each participant. Vertical segmentation means that each participant holds part of the attribute information in all samples. In Fig. 1, the sample data of all participants is abstracted into a table in a two-dimensional space. Each column in the table corresponds to an attribute of the sample, and each row corresponds to a piece of sample information. At this time, horizontal segmentation means that each participant has one or more lines of information in the table. For example, participant P1 owns the data in row 1, P2 owns the data in rows 2 and 3. Vertical segmentation means that each participant has one or more columns of information in the table. For example, participant P1 has data in column 1 and P2 has data in columns 2 and 3. In recent years, image recognition applications based on machine learning have developed rapidly. In this type of application, horizontal segmentation means that each participant has one or more pictures. If color channels are used as the basis for attribute division of each picture, vertical division means that each participant has information on one or more color channels in all pictures.

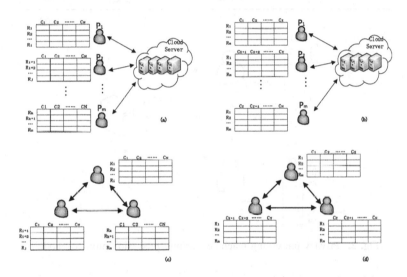

Fig. 1. Privacy-preserving machine learning training protocol model

The number of participants is generally divided into two cases and two participants. The communication modes between participants are generally divided into two types. One is a model based on cloud services, and the other is a model where participants communicate with each other. In the cloud service model, participants do not communicate directly, and each participant communicates with the cloud server. The mode of communication between participants means that there is no third party, and there is a communication channel between every two participants to communicate directly.

420   R. Yang

Definition2: Privacy-Preserving Machine Learning Prediction Protocol
The client holds the data to be predicted, and the server holds the prediction model. The client and the server hope to use the prediction model to predict the client's data without revealing their respective data.

There are two models of privacy-preserving machine learning prediction protocols, as shown in Fig. 2. Figure 2-(a) is a two-party model, the client holds a complete data to be predicted, the server holds all the parameters of the prediction model, and the two participants complete the calculation purpose through information interaction. Figure 2-(b) is a multi-party model, the client is composed of multiple participants, and each client has some attribute information of the data to be predicted. Each client uses a communication channel with the server to complete the calculation purpose.

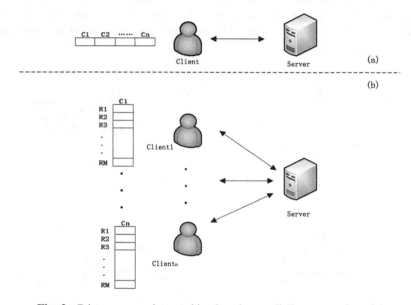

Fig. 2. Privacy-preserving machine learning prediction protocol model

3   Research Status and Development Trends of Privacy-Protected Machine Learning Protocols

There are many algorithms in the field of machine learning, such as Convolutional Neural Networks (CNN), Deep Neural Networks (DNN), Support Vector Machines (SupportCX Vector Machine, SVM), Fisher Linear Discriminant (Fisher's Linear Discriminant Classification, FLD) Linear Regression (LiR), Logistic Regression (LoR), Decision Tree (DT), Bayes (Bayes), Random Forests (RF), etc. With the development of deep learning and the popularization of applications, research on privacy protection technologies for neural networks (mainly referring to CNN and DNN) is a current research hotspot.

The concept of deep learning originated from the research of artificial neural networks. In the era of big data, the massive data that deep learning needs to collect has triggered a great demand for privacy protection. Whether it can store and protect this massive information affects the ability of deep learning. An important factor for good development. Shokri and Shmatikov [3] based on the privacy issues reflected in the application of deep learning and neural networks, using the optimization algorithms used in modern times, designed an accurate neural network model that can jointly learn a given target, thereby solving the protection Deep learning for privacy. Chase et al. [4] also proposed private collaborative neural network learning. M. Dahl [5] uses CNN deep learning mode to enable encrypted data to complete training and prediction, thereby downgrading the risk of personal privacy exposure and greatly increasing the enthusiasm of participation. P. Mohassel and Y. Zhang. [6] developed a new type of privacy-protected deep learning protocol for three machine learning algorithms: linear regression, logistic regression, and neural network. Under the premise of ensuring security, it has a very good speed. Great promotion. Gilad-Bachrach [7] proposed a CryptoNets method, which can be transformed from the learned neural network and can also be applied to encrypted data. Barni [8] proposed a privacy protection protocol that can be used for neural network computing, so that the neural network can also perform secure data processing. On this basis, C. Orlandi, A. Piva, and M. Barni. [9] made improvements from the perspective of the degree of interaction, so that multi-party computing agreements are no longer indispensable and information disclosure is avoided.

In order to improve the applicability of deep learning privacy protection and lower the application threshold, many experts have proposed a deep learning framework that can protect privacy. In 2017, Rouhani [10] and others proposed DeepSecure, a novel framework for large-scale habituation of the latest deep learning modules in a privacy-protected environment. The biggest feature of this module is that it can accurately analyze the data produced by distributed clients under the premise of ensuring security and efficiency. In the same year, Riazi et al. [11] also proposed Chameleon, a hybrid protocol framework that can be used to evaluate security functions without the need to disclose any private information. Subsequently, Juvekar et al. [12] conducted research from the aspect of running time, combined with homomorphic encryption and traditional two-party computing technology, and proposed a framework that can effectively reduce the delay GAZELLE. Liu et al. [13] introduced MiniONN, a training method that does not require model changes. This method can also effectively predict the forgotten neural network, and has advantages in response delay and message size. Bourse et al. [14] perfected the FHE structure proposed by Chillotti et al. On the basis of it, they added symbolic functions that can be used to activate neurons in the network, and proposed a new neural network homomorphism evaluation framework FHE-DiNN, Improve the evaluation efficiency.

SVM is a linear classifier with the largest interval defined in the feature space and a binary classification model, so it can often be applied to the field of cryptography as a means of protecting data privacy. Since 2006, Laur et al. [15] designed a support vector machine classifier that can be used exclusively in the field of cryptography. Many experts and scholars have conducted research on SVM. Rahulamathayan [16] uses the known client-server data classification protocol of support vector machines to propose a safe and efficient data classification technology for privacy protection. Subsequently, in order to solve the privacy leakage problem that image classification may cause, Makri [17] also proposed a special image classification system using support vector machines, which can solve image classification problems safely and efficiently. Barnett et al. [18] also expanded the SVM technology used in image processing and enabled SVM with polynomial kernels, exemplifying the practical application of nonlinear support vector machines with high applicability and high accuracy in image classification. In view of the increasingly widely used outsourcing technology, Lin [19] proposed a more applicable privacy protection outsourcing support vector machine, so that SVM is no longer limited by technology or computing resources, and can better provide services when outsourcing. In order to solve the inherent privacy leakage problem of SVM classifiers, Lin [20] et al. Proposed a post-processing method for the SVM classifier. This post-processing SVM classifier, which can effectively resist attacks, does not disclose the private content of the training data. Known as "Privacy Protection SVM Classifier" (PPSVC). Vaidya et al. [21] constructed a global SVM classification model PP-SVM from data distributed in multiple parties, which can safely and efficiently protect privacy, ensuring the confidentiality of data and the effectiveness of the obtained results. Subsequently, from the perspective of reducing the computational load, Teo et al. [22] proposed the Teo-Han-Lee algorithm with various matrix operations, which is more effective than Vaidya et al.'S SVM algorithm, and can reduce the password by reducing operations. Cost, the applicability in big data mining is more extensive.

Artificial intelligence is the hottest scientific research field, and machine learning is an important branch of artificial intelligence. Machine learning aims to study how to enable computers to acquire new knowledge and skills through learning, and continuously improve their performance. With the rapid development and wide application of various technologies such as big data, cloud computing, and outsourcing, many questions about privacy protection have emerged in the process of machine learning, threatening the security of data and affecting people's Application of learning. In this regard, many experts and scholars have proposed solutions that can effectively protect privacy. Graepel et al. [23], on the premise of ensuring data privacy, combined with a hierarchical homomorphic encryption scheme, defined a new machine learning algorithm. In order to learn fully homomorphic encrypted data, Aslett et al. [24] proposed a new machine learning method capable of learning and predicting encrypted data from random forests and naive Bayes. Bost [25] proposed a machine learning scheme for encrypted data based on the new building block library, which can effectively perform classification on various data sets under the premise of protecting privacy.

4   Problems

In recent years, neural networks have made breakthroughs in image recognition, speech recognition and other fields, making it one of the most successful models in the field of deep learning. As mentioned above, although the research on privacy-preserving machine learning protocols based on neural networks is developing rapidly, there are still some issues that have not received attention and attention.

(1) The research of multi-party privacy protection neural network prediction protocol is relatively inadequate.

The current privacy protection neural network prediction protocol has achieved many research results. For example, CryptoNets designed by Microsoft in 2016 was the first privacy protection framework for convolutional neural networks. Subsequently, SecureML, DeepSecure, Chameleon, MiniONN and FHE-DiNN were successively released in 2017. The problems solved by these protocols can be described by the following models:

The client holds the privacy data to be predicted $X = (X_1, X_2, \cdots X_n)$, where X is a matrix and X_i is the i-dimensional feature vector. The server holds the model P based on the convolutional neural network training. Both parties to the agreement hope to use the server's model P to predict the client's data X to obtain the classification label L of X; at the same time, after the agreement is executed, the client cannot know the parameters in the server's model P, nor can the server know the input data X and prediction result L of the client.

This model describes a two-party calculation problem. The data to be predicted is completely held by a client. However, in real life, many data are distributed in different institutions. Consider the following application issues:

A bank has a predictive model that can predict the risk of lending to lenders based on the lender's credit history, house holdings and mortgages, and criminal records. Credit information records, house holdings and mortgages, and criminal record information are in the database of the credit information center, the public security system, and the real estate registration agency. As citizens'private information, these institutions are often reluctant to disclose the information in their databases to other institutions or individuals. Of course, banks are also reluctant to disclose the parameters in their prediction models. At this time, how to use the model to evaluate the lender's loan risk?

The above problem is a typical secure multi-party computing problem. Banks can be regarded as servers that hold prediction models, and credit information centers, public security systems, and real estate registration agencies can be regarded as clients that separately hold some feature data. The problem at this time is that three clients and one server use prediction The feature data distributed in three places is used for prediction, and the input information of each participant is required to be protected.

From another perspective, the existing privacy-preserving neural network prediction protocol mainly solves the privacy protection problem when predicting between a client and a cloud server in MLaaS applications. Essentially, this is a secure two-party computing problem. It is a research hotspot in secure multi-party computing to extend the secure two-party computing protocol to the secure multi-party computing protocol. Therefore, it is very necessary to study the neural network prediction protocol for multi-party privacy protection.

(2) Research on privacy-protected neural network training protocols based on feature segmentation is relatively weak.

In the privacy-protecting neural network training protocol, each participant holds some sample data. They hope to use the neural network-based machine learning algorithm to train all participants' samples to obtain the training model without revealing their respective sample information. In 2017, Dahl designed a privacy-preserving neural network training protocol using secure two-party computing [5], but they only gave a theoretical solution without code implementation. In the same year, Mohassel et al. [6] designed a privacy-preserving neural network training protocol based on secure two-party computing and additive homomorphic encryption technology, and the corresponding experimental model was implemented in the SecureML application framework they designed. Researcher Chase et al. [3] of Microsoft Research used secure multi-party computing and differential privacy technology to design a privacy-preserving neural network training protocol and gave experimental models and experimental comparisons. In the existing research results, the samples held by each participant have the same structure, and it can be understood that all samples are distributed to each participant in a "horizontal split" manner. Corresponding to "horizontal segmentation" is "vertical segmentation", which is our proposed feature-based segmentation, which means that each participant has some feature information of the sample. Chase et al. [3] pointed out that the privacy-preserving neural network training based on feature segmentation is one of the key problems in the field that needs to be solved urgently.

5 Conclusion

With the rapid development of information technology, machine learning is playing an increasingly important role in various fields. However, the issue of privacy protection in machine learning applications is still not well resolved. Based on the summary of the privacy protection machine learning protocol model, this paper introduces and analyzes the privacy protection machine learning protocol research progress and trends and existing problems, hoping to provide useful help to researchers and engineering technicians in related fields.

References

1. Zhang, L., Cui, Y., Liu, J.: Application of machine learning in cyberspace security research. Chinese J. Comput. **41**, 1–34 (2018)
2. Zhang, Y., Dong, Y., Liu, C.: Status, trends and prospects of deep learning applied to cyberspace security. Comput. Res. Dev. **55**, 1117 (2018)
3. Shokri, R., Shmatikov, V.: Privacy-preserving deep learning. In: Proceedings of the 22nd ACM SIGSAC Conference on Computer and Communications Security, pp. 1310–1321. ACM (2015)
4. Chase, M., Gilad-Bachrach, R., Laine, K., Lauter, K., Rindal, P.: Private Collaborative Neural Network Learning. IACR Crypt. ePrint Archive **2017**, 762 (2017)
5. Dahl, M.: Private image analysis with MPC: training CNNs on sensitive data using SPDZ (2017).https://mortendahl.github.io/2017/09/19/private-image-analysis-with-mpc/
6. Mohassel, P., Zhang, Y.: SecureML: A System for Scalable Privacy-Preserving Machine Learning. IACR Crypt. ePrint Archive **2017**, 396 (2017)
7. Gilad-Bachrach, R., Dowlin, N., Laine, K., Lauter, K., Naehrig, M., Wernsing, J.: CryptoNets: applying neural networks to encrypted data with high throughput and accuracy. In: International Conference on Machine Learning, pp. 201–210 (2016)

8. Barni, M., Orlandi, C., Piva, A.: A privacy-preserving protocol for neural-network-based computation. In: Proceedings of the 8th Workshop on Multimedia and Security, pp. 146–151. ACM (2006)
9. Orlandi, C., Piva, A., Barni, M.: Oblivious neural network computing via homomorphic encryption. EURASIP J. Inf. Secur. **2007**(1), 1–11 (2007). https://doi.org/10.1155/2007/37343
10. Rouhani, B.D., Riazi, M.S., Koushanfar, F.: Deepsecure: Scalable provably-secure deep learning. CoRR.abs/1705.08963 (2017)
11. Riazi, M.S., et. al.: Chameleon: A hybrid secure computation framework for machine learning applications. Cryptology ePrint Archive, Report 2017/1164 (2017). https://eprint.iacr.org/2017/1164
12. Juvekar, C., Vaikuntanathan, V., Chandrakasan, A.: GAZELLE: A Low Latency Framework for Secure Neural Network Inference. Cryptology ePrint Archive, Report 2018/073 (2018). https://eprint.iacr.org/2018/073
13. Liu, J., Juuti, M., Lu, Y., Asokan, N.: Oblivious neural network predictions via minionn transformations. In: Proceedings of the 2017 ACM SIGSAC Conference on Computer and Communications Security, CCS 2017, Dallas, TX, USA, October 30 – November 03, pp. 619–631 (2017)
14. Bourse, F., Minelli, M., Minihold, M., Paillier, P.: Fast homomorphic evaluation of deep discretized neural network. IACR Cryptology ePrint Archive, 2017:1114 (2017). https://eprint.iacr.org/2017/1114
15. Laur, S., Lipmaa, H., Mielik¨ainen, T.: Cryptographically private support vector machines. In: Proceedings of the 12th ACM SIGKDD International Conference on Knowledge Discovery and Data Mining, pp. 618–624. ACM (2006)
16. Rahulamathavan, Y., Phan, R.C.-W., Veluru, S., Cumanan, K., Rajarajan, M.: Privacy-preserving multi-class support vector machine for outsourcing the data classification in cloud. IEEE Trans. Dependable Secure Comput. **11**(5), 467–479 (2014)
17. Makri, E., Rotaru, D., Smart, N.P., Vercauteren, F.: PICS: Private Image Classification with SVM. IACR Cryptology ePrint Archive 2017/1190 (2017)
18. Barnett, A., Santokhi, J., Simpson, M., Smart, N.P., Stainton-Bygrave, C., Vivek, S., Waller, A.: Image classification using non-linear support vector machines on encrypted data. IACR Crypt. ePrint Archive **2017**, 857 (2017)
19. Lin, K.-P., Chen, M.-S.: Privacy-preserving outsourcing support vector machines with random transformation. In: Proceedings of the 16th ACM SIGKDD international conference on Knowledge discovery and data mining, pp. 363–372. ACM (2010)
20. Lin, K.-P., Chen, M.-S.: On the design and analysis of the privacy-preserving SVM classifier. IEEE Trans. Knowl. Data Eng. **23**(11), 1704–1717 (2011)
21. Vaidya, J., Yu, H., Jiang, X.: Privacy-preserving SVM classification. Knowl. Inf. Syst. **14**(2), 161–178 (2008)
22. Teo, S.G., Han, S., Lee, V.C.: Privacy preserving support vector machine using non-linear kernels on hadoop mahout. In: 2013 IEEE 16th International Conference on Computational Science and Engineering (CSE), pp. 941–948. IEEE (2013)
23. Graepel, T., Lauter, K., Naehrig, M.: ML Confidential: Machine learning on encrypted data. In: Kwon, T., Lee, M.-K., Kwon, D. (eds.) ICISC 2012. LNCS, vol. 7839, pp. 1–21. Springer, Heidelberg (2013). https://doi.org/10.1007/978-3-642-37682-5_1
24. Aslett, L.J., Esperanca, P.M., Holmes, C.C.: Encrypted Statistical Machine Learning: New Privacy Preserving Methods. arXiv preprint arXiv:1508.06845 (2015)
25. Bost, R., Popa, R.A., Tu, S., Goldwasser, S.: Machine learning classification over encrypted data. In: NDSS (2015)

Efficient Privacy-Preserving Binary Tree Search

Ruidi Yang[1] and Maohua Sun[1,2]

[1] School of Management and Engineering, Capital University of Economics and Business, Beijing 100070, China
sunmaohua@cueb.edu.cn
[2] Project of High-Level Teachers in Beijing Municipal Universities in the Period of 13th Five-Year Plan (CN), Grant Numbers: CIT&TCD201904097; CUEB Supporting Plan for the Youth Backbone Teachers, Beijing, China

Abstract. Binary search tree is a common structure in computer programming and is currently widely used in many scenarios, such as routing search engine in routers, massive data concurrent query, set/multiset, map in C++ STL, and Linux Such technology is applied to memory management and the like. However, with the development of network technology, people's demand for privacy protection has gradually increased. The leakage of many key information will cause serious consequences, and also restrict the application and development of network technology. In the process of binary tree search, it is easy to have such a problem: the searched party may only want to provide the location of the searched data without exposing all the data in the entire binary search tree; at the same time, the searcher does not want to expose itself The information you need to find. This leads to issues related to the privacy protection of binary search trees. In response to the above problems, we have proposed a binary tree search solution that can protect privacy, which is used to solve the data leakage problem that may exist during the search process of the binary tree. The feature of the scheme proposed in the text is that it integrates two technologies of binary search tree and obfuscation circuit, so as to effectively protect the binary search tree and perform the search without leaking data. And the security analysis shows that the protocol we proposed is very safe and efficient, which can protect the data beneficially.

Keywords: Binary search tree; privacy-preserving · Oblivious transfer · Garbled circuit · CMP · GMW

1 Introduction

With the advent of the era of big data, while data brings great value, data leakage is also threatening people's lives. How to protect personal privacy and prevent sensitive information from leaking has become a new challenge in the security field. More and more scholars are devoted to the research on privacy protection, and have proposed various measures for privacy protection in terms of differential privacy, homomorphic encryption, and secure multi-party computing.

© Springer Nature Switzerland AG 2020
X. Chen et al. (Eds.): ML4CS 2020, LNCS 12486, pp. 426–436, 2020.
https://doi.org/10.1007/978-3-030-62223-7_37

In order to achieve fast search, a binary search tree came into being. As a common type derived from the binary tree, it not only supports fast data search, but also can quickly insert and delete a piece of data. Binary search trees not only have the advantages of fast insertion and deletion of linked lists, but also the function of fast search in arrays, so they are widely used in file systems or databases that require efficient sorting and retrieval.

In the era of big data, the binary search tree has brought us convenience, while the hidden danger of privacy leakage is also hindering the application and development of the binary search tree. In order to make better use of the advantages of the binary search tree, and to avoid these security risks while conducting efficient data queries, privacy-preserving binary tree search came into being.

1.1 Related Work

Early research on the binary search tree algorithm mainly focused on solving the problem of BST tree balance. Soviet mathematicians Adelson-Velskii and Landis proposed the concept of self-balancing binary search tree (AVL tree) [1], which limited the height difference between the left and right subtrees to 1, greatly improving the search efficiency of the BST tree. Subsequently, many scholars also devoted themselves to the study of balanced trees. Shi-Kuo Chang [2] describes a method for balancing a binary search tree on a highly parallel computer, so that the search in BST can be smoothly performed on a multiprocessor computer system. E. Haq [3] developed an effective parallel algorithm from the iterative algorithm using the shared memory model, which is used to balance any binary search tree in linear time.

Rudolf Bayer further proposed the concept of balanced binary B-tree [4] on the basis of balanced binary tree. Then Leo J. Guibas and Robert Sedgewick [5] perfected this algorithm, and officially named it "red-black tree". The red-black tree performs specific operations when inserting and deleting to maintain the balance of the binary search tree, thereby improving the performance of the search.

In recent years, many scholars have proposed more novel and improved schemes for binary search trees. For example, Vadym Borovskiy proposed a visualization algorithm for binary search trees [6], which simplifies the operation when using a large binary search tree, thereby improving efficiency. Rajesh Ramachandran added the concept of caching on the basis of the binary search tree, and proposed the Kakkot tree with cache [7], which is used to accelerate the search process on the binary search tree, reducing the time complexity and improving the Search tree efficiency. Dr. R. Chinnaiyan [8] put forward new insights into the construction of binary search tree. By looking for the insertion order of key elements, the problem of imbalance in the BST tree is solved more deeply. For the parallel algorithm of the binary tree [9] improved the previously proposed parallelization method, and studied a new method for constructing a cost-effective IP search scheme using a parallel binary search tree on the graphics processing unit.

However, these existing methods mainly focus on the improvement of the binary tree itself, and do not solve the problem of privacy protection that may occur during the binary tree search process.

In this paper, based on the perfect binary search tree and combining obfuscation circuits, a novel and efficient privacy-preserving binary tree search scheme is proposed. The obfuscation circuits we use are MUP and GMW, which play a role in protecting privacy by performing XOR gate operations on the data, and GMW can minimize consumption, so the communication volume and consumption are very low. The security analysis shows that the algorithm proposed in this paper has certain security, and can effectively search and protect privacy when faced with high-dimensional data.

1.2   Our Contribution

The main innovations of our work are:

1. Propose a privacy protection scheme for binary search tree, which can perform efficient binary tree search without revealing its data.
2. The search algorithm in the binary tree is combined with the obfuscation circuit, thereby protecting the privacy of the data in the binary search tree.
3. The novel obfuscation circuit we use has the advantages of low consumption and low communication overhead, so it is full of advantages when facing high-dimensional data sets.

1.3   Article Structure

Based on above analysis, this paper proposes a privacy-preserving binary search tree protocol. Section 1 of this article introduces the current development process of the binary search tree and explains the main contributions of this article. Section 2 introduces the cryptographic tools, binary search tree and circuit used in the scheme. Section 3 focuses on the composition of the binary search tree we proposed to protect privacy. Section 4 introduces the security proof and theoretical analysis of our protocol. The last section of the paper draws conclusions.

2   Preliminary

2.1   Oblivious Transfer

Oblivious Transfer is a basic cryptographic primitive. It was first proposed by Michael O. Rabin [10] in 1981 and is currently widely used in secure multi-party computing and other fields. In the OT protocol based on the RSA encryption system structure proposed by Rabin, when the sender S sends a message m to the receiver R, the receiver R accepts the message m with a probability of 1/2. At the end of the protocol interaction, S does not know whether R accepted the message, thereby protecting the privacy of receiver R. Subsequently, S. Even, O. Goldreich, and A. Lempel [11] improved the OT protocol in 1985, and further proposed 1-out-2 OT as shown in Fig. 1. In this new scheme, the sender S enters two lengths For a 1-bit character string (m_0, m_1), the receiver R enters a selection bit r. When the sender S and the receiver R jointly execute the dazed transmission protocol, the receiver can get m_r, but cannot know m_{1-r}; the sender cannot know the receiver's choice r, so the sender S and The privacy of the receiver R is guaranteed in this interaction.

Fig. 1. Oblivious transfer

2.2 Binary Search Tree

Binary search tree is a data structure that can quickly query whether it contains a certain value. It is either an empty tree, or any node on the tree, satisfying the following properties:

- If its left subtree is not empty, the values of all nodes on the left subtree are less than the value of its root node;
- If its right subtree is not empty, the values of all nodes on the right subtree are greater than the values of its root nodes;
- Its left and right subtrees are also binary search trees.

Binary search tree is a classic data structure. It not only has the advantage of fast insertion and deletion of linked lists, but also has the function of fast search in arrays. Therefore, it needs efficient sorting and retrieval in file systems or databases. It has been widely used. Search is an important operation in computer information management, and the search efficiency of the binary search tree is related to the depth of the tree. When the depth difference between the left and right subtrees of the binary search tree is low, there will be a higher search efficiency, so we must try to keep the depth of the left and right subtrees of the binary search tree balanced.

In this article, we are using the perfect binary search tree (perfect binary tree) as shown in Fig. 2. Except for the last layer without any sub-nodes, there are two sub-nodes under each node. That is, when the depth is $k(k \geq -1)$, the tree has $2^{k+1} - 1$ nodes.

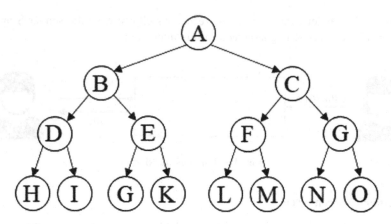

Fig. 2. Perfect binary tree

Algorithm1 algorithm for searching by binary sorting tree
Require: Binary search tree T, query point Q
Ensure: Output query finds the node key equal to Q
(△ Means to explain the meaning of the algorithm)
1.current ← root; △ Find from the root node, curr is the record currently visiting
2.while current ≠ null & Q ≠ current.value △ If the current node is not empty and is not equal to the query point Q, then compare the size of Q and the current node
3.if Q <current.value
        current ← current.left; △ If Q is less than the current node, enter its left subtree to search
    else
        current ← current.right; △ If Q is greater than the current node, insert its right subtree to search
4. △ Repeat step 3 according to the judgment of step 2
    end while
    key ← current; △ until finding an equal node or the current node is empty, find the interruption and get the result
    Output key

2.3   Garbled Circuit

The obfuscation circuit is a safe computing concept applied to Boolean circuits proposed by the Turing Award winner Yao [12] in the 1980s. The obfuscation circuit presents the calculation as a Boolean circuit, allowing both parties to perform a confidential operation on the plaintext without encrypting the plaintext. It enables participants to calculate the answer to a certain data without revealing the specific numbers they entered during the calculation process, thus achieving the purpose of protecting private data.

Based on the obfuscation circuit, Kolesnikov et al. [13] designed a circuit for comparing two numbers: a data comparison circuit. The data comparison circuit is composed of a composite multiplexer MUX and a comparator CMP. When the control signal $C = 0$, the output $outputx, y = min(x, y)$; and when the control signal $C = 1$, the output $outputx, y = max(x, y)$. The comparator CMP circuit designed by Kolesnikov et al. 13 is shown in Fig. 3. When comparing two data of n bits, the comparator CMP needs to use 3n XOR gates and n AND gates.

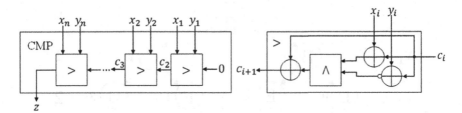

Fig. 3. Comparison circuit (CMP)

Since the obfuscation circuit was proposed, many other multi-party security computing frameworks have also been proposed, such as GMW [14], SPDZ [15], KS [13], etc. These security frameworks are still being gradually optimized and improved, and have been obtained More widely used. Among them, the GMW circuit is a novel idea used by GoldReich [14] and others to design a confusion circuit evaluation scheme. The GMW confusion circuit evaluation scheme uses a Boolean circuit composed of XOR and AND gates to represent the function function f to be calculated, and then secret sharing and daze transmission technology based on XOR operation finally realizes the Boolean circuit. Safe valuation. Its essence means that when evaluating the XOR gate, it only needs to perform the XOR operation on the obfuscated input data, and does not need to obfuscate the truth table, so there is no hash operation or symmetric encryption brought by the confusion truth table. operating. The biggest advantage of the GMW scheme is that it can perform cost-free evaluation operations on XOR gates, thereby greatly reducing the amount of calculation and complexity, and improving the calculation efficiency.

3   Our Construction for Privacy-Preserving Binary Search Tree Protocol

Taking the interaction between the client and the server as an example, the conventional binary search tree often does not include protection of privacy, which may easily cause privacy leakage. The biggest feature of our solution is the integration of obfuscation circuit and binary search tree. The main function is to ensure that the client and server do not expose too much privacy under the premise of high efficiency, so as to achieve the application of binary search tree privacy protection. The text combines the CMP circuit and the GMW scheme to perform XOR gate and AND gate operations on the numbers to be compared to complete the realization of the obfuscation circuit.

In addition, our demonstration assumes the structure of a binary tree as shown in Fig. 4. The binary tree has a total of 4 layers. Except for the leaf nodes, each node has two branches, and the leaf nodes are at the lowest level. The label on the left indicates the result of the comparison, and the label on the right indicates the depth of the current tree.

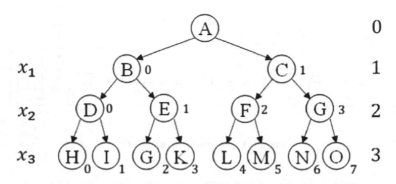

Fig. 4. Perfect binary tree

We combine the CMP circuit with the GMW scheme. We assume that this tree is in the hands of the server, we first use the CMP comparison circuit to compare it with the client, assuming that the CMP comparison circuit contains the data x_i held by the server and the data y_i held by the client, and compares the results of each layer This is indicated by the label on the left. For example, the data obtained in the first comparison is x_1, then the result obtained by comparing with a number above the first layer is represented by x_2, and so on. For a schematic diagram of our structure, see Fig. 5.

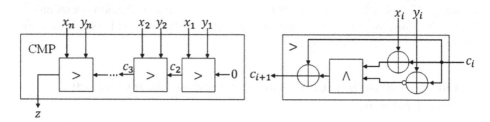

Fig. 5. Comparison circuit (CMP)

Then use the GMW scheme to evaluate the obtained results, split the input share of the AND gate into x_1 and x_2, and finally distribute it to the client and server.

The specific algorithm is as follows:

Protocol1 privacy-preserving binary search tree protocol
Require:
server: Binary tree T
client: data to be queried a
Ensure: Output query finds the node key equal to a

1. Compare a with the data on layer 0 first using the GMW scheme, and through an exclusive OR operation, split the data on a and layer 0 into two parts, namely a_1, a_2, t_1, t_2.

$$a_1 \oplus a_2 \leftarrow a$$
$$t_1 \oplus t_2 \leftarrow t$$

2. The client and server send a number in the hand to each other, and then the two use the CMP circuit in combination with the GMW program to conduct a security assessment. The result of the evaluation is the output control signal C of the CMP circuit. Control signal C is a 1-bit data $(C = 0, 1)$.

$$C \leftarrow CMP(a, t)$$

3. Perform an XOR operation on C, and send c_1 to the client, and c_2 to the server, and c_1 and c_2 in the hands of both parties can form a control signal C together.

$$c_1 \oplus c_2 \leftarrow C$$

4. The server sends the obtained component c_2 to the client, and the client calculates $c_1 \oplus c_2 = C$. According to the c_1 in his hand, XOR or c_2 sent from the server gets the real C, so that the size of a and t Comparing results.

$$C \leftarrow c_1 \oplus c_2$$
$$x_1 \leftarrow C$$

5. The server generates a random number r at each layer, (assuming that the input of the fourth layer is m_0 to m_7 at this time) and performs the operation of $m_i = m_i' \oplus r$ on each input data, and calculates The value of m_i'. In the process of executing OT,

the input of the server is m_i', and the input of the client is $x_1x_2x_3 = D$ (x_1,x_2,x_3 represent the control signal C output by each previous level. From this layer, determine which number is compared with the next comparison. That is, x_1 is the highest bit of the binary, x_2 is the next bit, and x_3 is the next bit. The position of the number in the binary search.

(If the result of the first comparison x_1 is 0, then enter the left branch of the first layer. Assuming $x_1 = 1, x_2 = 0$, $x_3 = 1$, then it can be extrapolated, at this time the client's The input is 101, which is 5. Actually, what we want to input at this time is the number of the client's eight numbers whose index is 5. That is his sixth number.)

6. After performing the OT operation, the client gets the m_i' of the data at the position it entered. (When the client executes OT every time, the input is the output data on all the CMP circuits obtained as a certain bit in the binary number, and then get a number, and then execute the OT protocol with the server. At this time, the client gets A share in the data he wants, because the input of the server is to give him the XOR of each data in this layer.)

7. We then use CMP circuits for this layer. First, suppose that the data output by the client is $x_1x_2x_3 = D$, and the data D input by it needs to be split into two data again through the exclusive OR operation $D = D_1 \oplus D_2$. This is done because the client input is the same at each layer, so if the client input is simply split into two parts, the server can easily guess the value of the client input through multiple operations, resulting in privacy Give way. Therefore, when performing the share operation in each layer, the client needs to split his input data again into the XOR of the two data, and then choose one of them to keep, and then send the other to the server.

$$D_1 \oplus D_2 \leftarrow D$$

8. At this time, the input of the server is the random number r it generates on this layer. The server's component on the first line of the CMP circuit is the share that the client sent to him, and the second circuit is r.
9. The client's input on the first line is the XOR of one of the two numbers it generates (the other is sent to the server). The input on the second circuit is the data sent by the server that it obtained by executing OT.
10. By this method of sequential comparison, you can gradually determine the subtree to be entered in the next layer. When the bottom layer is calculated, the server directly uses all the data as the input of the OT without the need of XOR on the random number r, so that the client can directly obtain the value of the leaf node Key at this time.

4 Efficiency and Security Analysis

(1) Efficiency analysis

Compared with other options, our protocol has the advantage of low consumption. Since there are only two types of AND gates and XOR gates in the CMP circuit, and because GMW does not need to communicate when evaluating the XOR gate, no traffic is generated, and only the AND gate will generate traffic And consumption. Therefore, when there is only one AND gate and three XOR gate circuits in the circuit, when using the CMP circuit to compare the binary search tree, only one AND gate calculation and one oblivious transfer are required for each layer, only very low consumption will be generated.

(2) Security analysis

The GMW scheme requires two participants to share information on each line. Suppose the input of a certain circuit is x and y, x is controlled by the client, and y is controlled by the server. The client splits x into x_1 or x_2, and sends x_2 to the server; the server splits y into y_1 or y_2, and sends y_1 to the client. At this time, on the x line, client has x_1 and server has x_2; on the y line, the client has y_1 and the server has y_2. Therefore, each participant can have a shared value on each line. This setting also ensures that the value on each line is shared between the client and server, and the security of the GMW circuit under the semi-honest model.

In oblivious, the sender S enters two lengths For a 1-bit character string (m_0, m_1), the receiver R enters a selection bit r. When the sender S and the receiver R jointly execute the dazed transmission protocol, the receiver can get m_r, but cannot know $m_{1\ r}$; the sender cannot know the receiver's choice r, so the sender S and The privacy of the receiver R is guaranteed in this interaction, So it is safe under the semi-honest model.

By using the GMW and the OT protocol, the security of the privacy-preserving binary search tree protocol could be guaranteed.

5 Conclusion

At present, the privacy leakage problem that may exist in the operation process of the binary search tree has not been well resolved. Aiming at this situation, the text proposes a new and effective scheme, which combines the obfuscation circuit with it to construct a binary tree search that can protect privacy. After the calculation is completed, the searcher only obtains the data of the location to be searched, and cannot know the data of any other location; the searched party cannot know the data obtained by the searcher, thereby protecting the privacy of both parties. The algorithm uses CMP and GMW circuits and OT. Compared with the existing binary search tree scheme, the scheme proposed in the text adds the function of protecting privacy, and under the premise of high efficiency, the security can also be guaranteed.

In future work, we will continue to improve the privacy protection method of binary tree search. We will mainly focus on the further improvement of algorithm efficiency, and the design of algorithms that can resist more malicious attackers. At the same time, it will also improve the applicability of the algorithm, so that the protection scheme of the binary search tree combined with the obfuscation circuit can be applied in a wider range.

References

1. Adelson-velskii, G.M., Landis, E.Nl.: Doklady akademia nauk sssr (1962)
2. Chang, S.K.: Parallel balancing of binary search trees. IEEE Trans. Comput. **23**, 441–445 (1974)
3. Haq, E., Cheng, Y., Iyengar, S.S.: New algorithms for balancing binary search trees. In: IEEE Conference Proceedings, pp. 378–382 (1988)
4. Bayer, R.: Symmetric binary B-trees: data structure and maintenance algorithms. Acfa Inf. **1**(4), 290–306 (1972)
5. Guibas, L.J., Sedgewick, R.: A dichromatic framework for balanced trees. In: Proceedings of the 19th Symposium on the Foundations of Computer Science (1978)
6. Borovskiy, V., Müller, J., Schapranow, M.P., Zeier, A.: Binary search tree visualization algorithm. IEEE (2009)
7. Ramachandran, R.: Kakkot Tree — A Binary Search Tree with caching. IEEE (2012)
8. Chinnaiyan, R., Kumar, A.: Construction of estimated level based balanced binary search tree. In: ICECA (2017)
9. Shekhar, A., Goyal, J.: Parallel binary search trees for rapid IP lookup using graphic processors. In: Proceedings of IMKE, pp. 176–179 (2013)
10. Rabin, M.O.: How to exchange secrets by oblivious transfer, Aiken Computation Lab, University Harvard, USA, Technical Report TR-81 (1981)
11. Even, S., Goldreich, O., Lempel, A.: A randomized protocol for signing contracts. Commun. ACM **28**, 637–647 (1985)
12. Yao, A.: Protocols for secure computation. In: Proceedings 23rd Annual Symposium on Foundations of Computer Science (FOCS), pp. 160–164 (1982)
13. Kolesnikov, V., Sadeghi, A., Schneider, T.T.: Improved garbled circuit building blocks and applications to auctions and computing minima. Crypt. Network Secur. (2009)
14. Goldreich, O., Micali, S., Wigderson, A.: How to Solve any Protocol Problem. In: Proceedings of STOC (1987)
15. Damgård, I., Pastro, V., Smart, N., Zakarias, S.: Multiparty computation from somewhat homomorphic encryption. In: Safavi-Naini, R., Canetti, R. (eds.) CRYPTO 2012. LNCS, vol. 7417, pp. 643–662. Springer, Heidelberg (2012). https://doi.org/10.1007/978-3-642-32009-5_38

Privacy-Preserving Classification of Personal Data with Fully Homomorphic Encryption: An Application to High-Quality Ionospheric Data Prediction

Zheng Li$^{(\boxtimes)}$ (ID) and Maohua Sun (ID)

School of Management and Engineering, Capital University of Economics and Business, Beijing 100070, China
LizhengCueb@163.com, sunmaohua@cueb.edu.cn

Abstract. In recent years, the problem of data leakage is really common, so designing a safe and efficient privacy-preserving machine learning protocol has become an urgent demand to many researchers. The fully homomorphic encryption algorithm has attracted the interest of many researchers. This algorithm can directly operate on the ciphertext without decryption, and the decrypting result is the same as that obtained by performing the same processing on the plaintext. At present, many scholars have designed privacy-preserving machine learning protocols, and have achieved good results. However, as one of the most frequent used algorithms, there are relatively few studies concentrating on the privacy-preserving protocols for logistic regression and fewer focusing on the prediction process. Therefore, we propose a privacy-preserving protocol to solve the data leakage problem during the logistic regression process. Based on the semi-honest assumption and BGV fully homomorphic encryption algorithm, our protocol is mainly focused on the prediction process of logistic regression. In this protocol, there are two parties (client and server), the client holds the test set data and label data, the server holds the model coefficients obtained from the training process. The two parties execute the protocol to finish the logistic regression prediction process in ciphertext. Finally, the client side obtains the prediction category of the dependent variable and calculates the accuracy of the prediction result. During this process, the server will not learn anything about the test set, nor will the client know any information about the model used by the server.

Keywords: Full homomorphic encryption · Privacy-Preserving machine learning protocol · Logistic regression prediction process · Two parties

M. Sun—Project of High-level Teachers in Beijing Municipal Universities in the Period of 13th Five-year Plan (CN), Grant Numbers: CIT&TCD201904097; Funding Program for Youth Backbone Teachers of Capital University of Economics and Business.

X. Chen et al. (Eds.): ML4CS 2020, LNCS 12486, pp. 437–446, 2020.
https://doi.org/10.1007/978-3-030-62223-7_38

1 Introduction

The ability to extract information by scanning personal data has significant economic and social value. Machine learning [1] models can analyze personal data to extract valuable information. Although it can benefit the data manipulator, it seriously violates the privacy of the user.

In recent years, there have been numerous privacy leak accidents: 87 million users' information was leaked by Facebook. In this accident, Facebook sold some internal data to third parties. The video conferencing software Zoom has also caused lots sensations because of the privacy leak. The software sent user data to Facebook when users download it, and allows the meeting initiators to record videos without the permission of everyone. This also led to the disclosure of about 15,000 conference videos involving privacy information. It is said that the total number of privacy information in eight large-scale breaches of over 100 million data has exceeded 6 billion last year, mainly personal information. Therefore, the concern of data security is increasing rapidly.

In this article, we propose a privacy-preserving logistic regression solution that is provably secure. In our solution, there are two groups, nicknamed Alice and Bob (see Fig. 1). Alice has a group of trained logistic regression model coefficients that can classify test set data. Bob has test set data. Our solution relies on a privacy-preserving protocol to finish the logistic regression prediction process in ciphertext. This protocol can prevent Alice from learning information about Bob's personal data, and Bob does not know anything about Alice model.

The main contribution of this article is designation and implementation of the privacy-preserving logistic regression protocol based on fully homomorphic encryption.

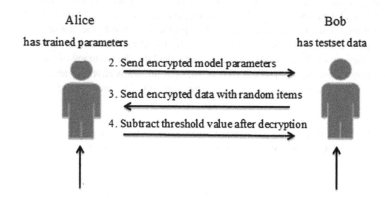

Fig. 1. Roles of Alice and Bob in FHE based logistic regression prediction process

2 Preliminaries

2.1 Logistic Regression

In logistic regression, a value x is input to determine whether it belongs to category 0 or 1. The general form of the binary logistic regression model is to use the sigmoid function as the activation function [2]:

$$\sigma(z) = h_\theta(x) = \frac{1}{1+e^{-\theta x}} = \frac{1}{1+e^{-z}} \tag{1}$$

x is the input of the model and $h_\theta(x)$ is the output of the model. θ is the model parameter. The corresponding relationship between $h_\theta(x)$ and the binary classification outputs 0 and 1 is that, if $h_\theta(x) > 0.5$, that is $\theta_x > 0$, y is 1, and if $h_\theta(x) < 0.5$, that is $\theta_x < 0$, y is 0.

We use the maximum likelihood function to derive the loss function, and the result is the maximum probability that all samples are predicted to be correct. We take the logarithm of the likelihood function for easy calculation. By maximizing the log-likelihood function and inverting the log-likelihood function, the expression of the loss function $J(\theta)$ is [3]:

$$J(\theta) = -\frac{1}{m}\sum_{i=1}^{m}\left(y^{(i)}\log\left(h_\theta\left(x^{(i)}\right)\right) + \left(1 - y^{(i)}\right)\log\left(1 - h_\theta\left(x^{(i)}\right)\right)\right) \tag{2}$$

Below we explain the more commonly used gradient descent method for optimizing the loss function. The calculation process is to find the minimum value of $J(\theta)$ in the direction of gradient descent (the maximum value can also be found in the direction of gradient's ascent [4]). We need to set the learning rate α to represent the negative gradient direction, indicating the search step in the gradient direction. The gradient direction can be derived by derivation of the function. The determination of the step size is more troublesome. If it is too large, it may diverge without finding the extreme point. If it is too small, it may cost more iterations and time. The iteration formula is:

$$\theta_j = \theta_j - \alpha\sum_{i=1}^{m}\left(h_\theta\left(x^{(i)}\right) - y^{(i)}\right)x_j^{(i)} \tag{3}$$

Constantly update the value of θ_j until $J(\theta)$ converges to a smaller value and stop iterating, and the training parameters can be used to predict in the sigmoid function.

2.2 Full Homomorphic Encryption Algorithm

Homomorphic encryption algorithm [5] is a kind of encryption algorithm, which was proposed by Rivest et al. in the 1980 s. This structure allows users to directly perform calculations on encrypted data without decryption. The result of decryption is the same as the result in plaintext calculation process. An encryption scheme with homomorphic properties means that two plaintexts a and b satisfy the encryption function:

$$Dec(En(a) \odot En(b)) = a \oplus b \qquad (4)$$

En is the encryption operation and *Dec* is the decryption operation. $\odot$ and $\oplus$ correspond to the operations on the plaintext and ciphertext fields respectively. When $\oplus$ represents addition, the encryption is called addition homomorphic encryption (such as Paillier homomorphic encryption scheme): when $\oplus$ represents multiplication, the encryption is called multiplicative homomorphic encryption (such as El Gamal homomorphic encryption scheme), The specific process is shown in Fig. 2.

The fully homomorphic encryption algorithm refers to an encryption function that satisfies both addition homomorphism and multiplication homomorphic encryption. The algorithm supports homomorphic encryption schemes of any depth, but the fully homomorphic encryption scheme has a large computational overhead and is likely to increase noise. The most commonly used fully homomorphic encryption schemes are the Brakerski-Gentry-Vaikuntanathan (BGV) and Brakerski-Fan-Vercauteren (BFV) schemes, both of which allow cryptographic calculations of finite field elements.

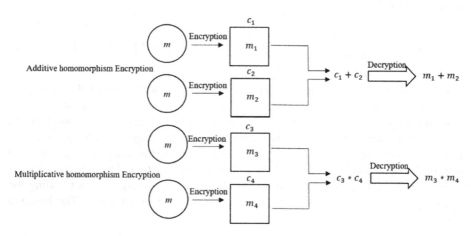

Fig. 2. Schematic diagram of addition and multiplication homomorphism encryption

2.3   BGV Encryption Scheme

In 2009, Craig Gentry first proposed Gentry09, which is the first fully homomorphic encryption scheme. In 2010, Smart et al. proposed the BGV encryption scheme, which simplifies Gentry09. The implementation process mainly uses modulus changing technology and private key exchange technology instead of bootstrap technology. The BGV solution can be implemented in the Helib library of IBM Research and the PALISADE library/framework of the New Jersey Institute of Technology. It supports homomorphic encryption operations of data addition and multiplication, subtraction and shift, which can make the operation results of plaintext data as same as the decrypted ciphertext data. The specific process is shown in Fig. 3.

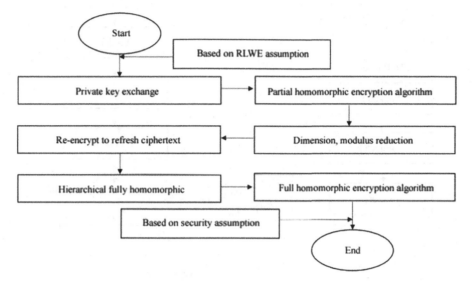

Fig. 3. Schematic diagram of BGV fully homomorphic encryption algorithm

2.4 Socket Transmission Protocol

Socket is an intermediate software abstraction layer for communication between the application layer and the TCP/IP protocol family. It is a set of interfaces. In the design mode, Socket is actually a facade mode, which hides the complex TCP/IP protocol family behind the Socket interface. For users, a simple set of interfaces is all. Let Socket organize data to conform to the specified protocol. The basic mode is open-write/read-close mode. One side opens the file and writes it for transmission, and the other side receives the data and reads it into the local area. The triplet (ip, address, protocol, port) indicates the progress of the network. The specific process is shown in Fig. 4.

3 Secure Protocol

3.1 Problem Description

In the classification process, the data is distributed between the server Alice and the client Bob. We assume that the protocol is conducted under a semi-honest model and both parties are "honest but curious." Alice have a set of parameters θ^A which were got during logistic regression training process in plaintext, $\theta^A = \theta_1, \theta_2, \ldots, \theta_{d+1}, \ \theta \in R^{d+1}$. Bob has test dataset and its sample categories, $\{x_i^B, y_i\}_{i=1}^N$, $x_i^B = (1, x_{i1}, x_{i2}, \ldots, x_{id})$, $x \in R^{d+1}$ is $d + 1$ dimensional feature, vector $y \in \{0, 1\}$ is the actual category label. Alice

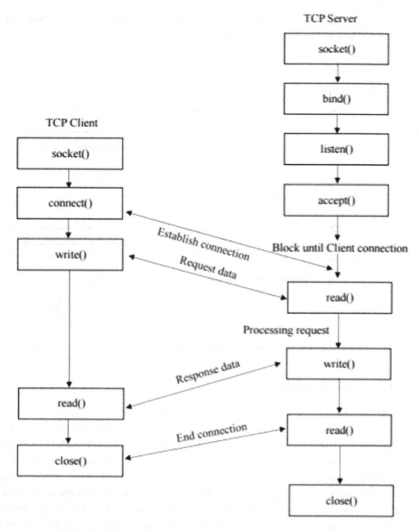

Fig. 4. Schematic diagram of socket communication process

and Bob predict the label based on the parameter θ^A and the test data x_i^B in a joint and collaborative manner under the ciphertext. They bring the parameter into the sigmoid function, and then divide the categories $\{0,1\}$ according to the independent variable threshold. In the prediction process, the data of Alice and Bob are both local, and no information about parameters, test data, and tags can be detected.

3.2   Security Definition

We suppose that Alice and Bob are non-complicit and semi-honest participants. Under the semi-honest model, although Alice and Bob follow the training protocol during the collaboration and perform the steps in accordance with the requirements, they are curious about each other's private data. During the collaboration, they will retain all the collected information of the other party for reasoning. If during the prediction process, neither A nor B can obtain additional sensitive information from each other, such as test set data and model parameters, the prediction process is safe.

3.3   Protocol Design

Protocol π_{LRP}:

Step1. Alice (server side) generates a pair of public and private keys and sends the public key to Bob (client side).

Step2. Alice encrypts the trained model parameter θ^A with the public key, and puts $\left[\theta^A\right]_A$ in the specified directory.

Step3. Bob obtains $\left[\theta^A\right]_A$ in the specified directory, encrypts the test set data x_i^B with the public key to obtain $\left[x_i^B\right]_A$, generates a random number c_i, and encrypts $[c_i]_A$, calculate $\left[r_i^B\right]_A = \left[\theta^A\right]_A \left[x_i^B\right]_A + [c_i]_A$, send $\left[r_i^B\right]_A$ to Alice.

Step4. Alice decrypts the received information $\left[r_i^B\right]_A$ from Bob. Then uses the private key to obtain r_i^B, and gets d_i through r_i^B subtracting the threshold of x(the independent variable value when the function's dependent variable is 0.5), sends d_i directly to Bob.

Step5. Bob receives d_i, calculates $e_i = d_i - c_i$, compares e_i with 0, if e_i is greater than 0, it will be recorded as the first category(1), if e_i is less than 0, it will be recorded as the second category(0), equal to 0 is the same as the label category.

In this protocol, we generate the public and private keys from the server side, which can avoid the client's reasoning about the server-side model parameters under the semi-honest model. The server firstly encrypts the model coefficients and sends them to the client. The client encrypts the test set data and multiplies the two ciphertexts. At the same time, because the server side holds the public and private keys, in order to avoid the server side's guessing of the test data under the semi-honest model, we set a random item, then encrypt it and add it to the multiplied ciphertext to calculate a result. After that, we send the result to the server. After decrypting the data, the server subtracts the threshold value and sends it directly to the client. The client classifies the data after subtracting random items. In this protocol, the introduction of random items prevents the server from predicting the client's data. At the same time, because the client does not have the public and private keys, client cannot speculate the server-side model coefficients.

We find that the model is theoretically safe. Therefore, the above protocol is selected for experiment in this paper.

3.4   Truncate

In the formal prediction process, the test set data and weight data are all in the form of decimals. However, fully homomorphic encryption schemes usually only support integer operations. Therefore, we use integers to represent the two parts of the data.

Because any real number can be scaled to an integer of arbitrary precision, we can determine the required precision, then multiply it by a fixed integer and round to the nearest integer.

For plaintext, we directly used logistic regression for classification, and found that the accuracy of the data is set to 1, 2, 3 digits after the decimal point, and the accuracy is the same. For the ciphertext, the calculation accuracy is set to 10,100,1000 multiply 1, 2 or 3 digits after the decimal point. We found that the accuracy is the same when the accuracy is set to 2 and 3 digits. However, when the accuracy is set to 1 digit, the accuracy is sharply declination, therefore, the 2-digit accuracy setting is the best classification accuracy and calculation cost.

4 Experimental Result

We use the Johns Hopkins Ionospheric [6] dataset as our experimental data set. We firstly divide the dataset (351 samples, 34 features variables and a binary category variable) into a training set and a test set according to the ratio of 7: 3. Then we preprocess the training set data. We use the sigmoid function as the prediction function, the log-likelihood function as the loss function and set the learning rate to 0.01. After that, we iterate the model parameters with the gradient descent algorithm until the loss value becomes stable (less than 1e-10), then we stop the iteration and save the parameters. Finally, we obtained the model parameters at the 25971th iteration.

Then, we implement π_{LRP} protocol from Sect. 3 on Alibaba Cloud's servers. The server's RAM is 2 GB, and the experimental environment is Ubuntu16.04.3. Under the Linux operating system, we firstly generate the public and private key through BGV encryption scheme, then we start the server side and client-side programs (first start server side, then start client side). The two programs respectively play the roles of server (Alice) and client (Bob) to simulate the protocol process.

In our experiment, we used C++ for program programming, Helib homomorphic encryption library(BGV encryption scheme) is used to generate the public and private key and execute encryption and decryption operations. Socket is used to transmit data to the other side through different port numbers. The security level of the ciphertext is set to 99.8391 to ensure actual security. For the possible plaintext space, we specify p = 999007 (plaintext prime modulus), m = 32767 (ring number), phi (m) = 27000 (Eulerian function), r = 1 (Hensel lifting), bits = 590 (module The number of digits in the number chain), c = 2 (number of columns in the key switch matrix), nslots = 180. Test set data has 106 samples, 34 features variables and a binary category variable (Table 1).

Table 1. Run time for running one-time protocol

Protocol	Time (run one-time)			
	Generate key	Preprocessing	Server	Client
	82.8985 s	89.4002 s	324.056 s	324.112 s

Due to the limited memory space of the Linux system (2 GB), we cannot achieve a privacy-preserving logistic regression prediction process for 106 samples with 34 feature value data in the test set at one time. We chose to encrypt and transmit 2 samples at one time, transmitting 53 times. It takes about 82.8985 s to generate the key, about 89.4002 s for data preprocessing, about 324.112 s for the client to run, and 324.056 s for the server. The communication cost of running a program is about 32.7 MB, the total cost is about 1733.9 MB, and the overall running time is about 5.2 h (Table 2).

Table 2. Test set accuracy rate table

Plaintext accuracy	Ciphertext accuracy
89.623%	88.680%

5 Related Work

The interest in privacy-preserving machine learning (PPML) [7] has grown substantially over the last decade. Privacy-preserving logistic regression algorithm [8] is proposed by Wu et al. [9]. They propose to approximate the logistic function using polynomials, and train the model using LHE [10]. However, the complexity is exponential in the degree of the approximation polynomial, and as we will show in experiments, the accuracy of the model is degraded compared to using the logistic function. Aono et al. considered a different security model where an untrusted server collects and combines the encrypted data from multiple clients and transfers it to a trusted client to train the model on the plaintext. By carefully approximating the cost function of logistic regression with a degree 2 polynomial, the optimal model can be calculated by solving a linear system. However, in this setting, the plaintext of the aggregated data is leaked to the client who trains the model.

Our protocol can obtain a higher accuracy and avoid data leakage under the semi-honest model and transmission process.

6 Conclusion

This paper mainly studies the designation and implementation of the fully homomorphic encryption protocol in the privacy protection prediction process. We designed the two parties to participate in the protocol (client and server) under the semi-honest assumption and started two programs to play the above two roles. In the prediction process, the server cannot guess the data information of the client, and the client cannot guess the model parameters of the server. We successfully implemented the above operations through the BGV encryption scheme and the socket transmission protocol, but there are also some aspects that can be optimized. In the subsequent research, further improvement work is needed. The deficiencies in the previous work are mainly reflected in two aspects:

(1) The run time: In the process of this article, due to the lack of memory space, the data was operated many times to achieve the overall prediction process. This process generated a large amount of data repeated transmission time, which also led to the low effectiveness of the algorithm. At the same time, there are 180 slots in the plaintext space. However, we only use a few of them. The waste of this slot also increases the cost of information transmitted and affects the running time. Therefore, in future experiments, it is necessary to increase the memory space of the virtual machine and adjust the parameters to reduce the waste of slots.

(2) The accuracy rate: The accuracy rate of our experiment is currently ideal, but there is still a little loss in the accuracy. This is partly due to the truncation of the weight and test data during the preprocessing process and r the decimal converted to an integer. As a result of the above-mentioned losses, we can improve the BGV scheme in subsequent experiments to support decimal encryption operations, or further study to come up with other methods to reduce precision loss, or generate a new homomorphic encryption scheme that supports decimal calculations. Further improve our prediction accuracy.

References

1. Mohassel, P., Zhang, Y.: Secureml: a system for scalable privacy-preserving machine learning. In: Proceedings of the 2017 ACM SIGSAC Conf on Computer and Communications Security. pp. 18–21 (2017)
2. Aono, Y., Hayashi, L.T., Wang, L.: Privacy-preserving logistic regression with distributed data sources via homomorphic encryption. IEICE Trans. Inf. Syst. **99**(8), 2079–2089 (2016)
3. De Cock, M., Dowsley, R., Nascimento, A.C., Railsback, D., Shen, J., Todoki, A.:. High performance logistic regression for privacy-preserving genome analysis. *arXiv preprint* arXiv:2002.05377 (2020)
4. Nardi, Y., Fienberg, S.E., Hall, R.J.: Achieving both valid and secure logistic regression analysis on aggregated data from different private sources. J. Priv. Conf. **4**, 1–10 (2012)
5. Zhou, H., Wornell, G.: Effiient homomorphic encryption on integer vectors and its applications. pp. 1–9 (2014)
6. Sigillito, V.G., Wing, S.P., Hutton, L.V., Baker, K.B.: Classification of radar returns from the ionosphere using neural networks. J. Hopkins Apl Tech. D. **10**, 262–266 (1989)
7. Chaudhuri, K., Monteleoni, C.: Privacy-preserving logistic regression. In: Advances in Neural Information Processing Systems. pp. 289–296 (2009)
8. Slavkovic, A.B., Nardi, Y., Tibbits, M.M.: "Secure" logistic regression of horizontally and vertically partitioned distributed databases. In: Seventh IEEE International Conference on Data Mining Workshops (ICDMW 2007). pp. 723–728, IEEE (2007)
9. Wu, S., Teruya, T., Kawamoto, J., Sakuma, J., Kikuchi, H.: Privacy-preservation for stochastic gradient descent application to secure logistic regression. In: The 27th Annual Conference of the Japanese Society for Artificial Intelligence. vol. 27, pp. 1–4 (2013)
10. Aono, Y., Hayashi, T., Trieu Phong, L., Wang, L.: Scalable and secure logistic regression via homomorphic encryption. In: Proceedings of the Sixth ACM Conference on Data and Application Security and Privacy. pp. 142–144, ACM (2016)

An Improved Method for Data Storage Based on Blockchain Smart Contract

Dongxiang Song(✉)📧 and Mingju Yuan📧

Dehong Teachers' College, Yunnan 678400, China
562868736@qq.com

Abstract. With the development of blockchain technology, more and more blockchain systems have emerged. Traditional applications based on Ethereum smart contracts have the problem of requiring the off-chain database to assist in data operations and smart contract execution, which consumes a large amount of gas and causes waste of resources. This paper proposes an improved method for storage of smart contract data based on blockchain to optimize the data upload format of off-chain systems. Use solidity language to design smart contract storage variables and implement the function of adding, deleting, checking and modifying data on the chain. This method is a combination of general frameworks and gives detailed algorithm design and implementation methods. In this paper, the functional and performance tests of the proposed method are carried out through experiments to verify the integrity and feasibility of the system functions. The experimental results show that the improved system implements the function of adding, deleting, and modifying data on the chain. Compared with the traditional system, the improved system reduces the gas consumption. The more obvious with the increase of uploading data to reduce gas consumption.

Keywords: Blockchain · Ethereum · Smart contract · Gas

1 Introduction

With the rapid development of information technology, there are more and more applications of blockchain technology [1]. The mainstream is based on Ethereum [2] DApp (Decentralized Application) decentralized application [3]. DApp uses blockchain as its decentralized data layer [4] backend, but the storage layer and frontend are hosted on traditional centralized servers [5, 6]. Because the data structure mapping of smart contracts [7] is similar to the key-value storage of non-relational databases, the disadvantage is that it is only suitable for storing some simpler data, and the storage of more complex data requires the assistance of a local relational database. When a traditional DApp stores a relational two-dimensional table model, the smart contract needs to perform a total number of tuple operations. According to the Ethereum protocol [8], malicious attacks and abuse on the Ethereum network are prevented. Each calculation step performed in a contract or transaction requires a charge of gas [9], which costs a lot of gas consumption.

X. Chen et al. (Eds.): ML4CS 2020, LNCS 12486, pp. 447–460, 2020.
https://doi.org/10.1007/978-3-030-62223-7_39

In view of the current gas consumption problems of DApps, it is inspired by the advantages of storing data in relational databases that are more complicated and easy to maintain. This paper proposes an improved method of data storage based on block-chain smart contracts. The main contributions of this article are as follows:

(1) Optimize the system architecture and off-chain upload data format, intelligently design the upload data JSON format and optimization algorithm, and the optimized local database only provides basic data. When the system stores a two-dimensional table model, the smart contract only needs one operation, which reduces the number of operations and gas consumption performed before optimization;

(2) Optimize smart contracts that perform data operations, and design addition, modification, reading, and deletion algorithms. The optimized algorithm enables data to be executed on smart contracts. It does not require the assistance of off-chain databases, and reduces gas consumption on the basis of providing normal services.

(3) Build an experimental platform, the test system uses web3.js as the interface layer, nodeJS and electron build the server, and Ganache builds a simulated Ethereum network. Through experiments, the improved system realizes the functions of adding, modifying, reading and deleting data. Compared with the traditional system, the improved system has lower gas consumption.

2 Relate Work

In recent years, researchers have proposed many solutions for data storage in the blockchain. The domestic scholar Han Juru [11] and others proposed the blockchain trusted log storage and verification system, which implements the integrity verification of local data and blockchain storage data. Because there is too much data in the log, there is a large gas consumption. Ji Lusheng [12] and others proposed an off-chain personal data protection scheme based on blockchain. The system designs smart contract data structure, reduces gas consumption, and realizes on-chain storage of personal data. Data security is guaranteed, and most of the operation of system architecture design data is done off-chain. Cao Didi [13] 's research and implementation of a trusted certificate storage system based on blockchain smart contracts realized the basic operation of on-chain data and low gas consumption. Because of the complexity of storing data, the design uses data fingerprinting to extract the hash value generated by the complex storage data and store it on the blockchain, and part of the data is stored on the blockchain. Foreign scholar EthernityDB [14] uses smart contracts to write simulation databases. Because of the limitations of the smart contract language, it is possible to implement part of the data query function on the chain. In order to realize the query, each query needs to execute a complex smart contract function, which increases the gas consumption of contract execution. In summary, the improvement method proposed in this paper. On the basis of reducing gas consumption, the system's operations on data are completed on the chain. The blockchain stores all data, and the complexity of the smart contract execution algorithm is not high.

3   Method

3.1   Ethereum Related Technology

Ethereum is a blockchain implementation. As shown in Fig. 1, in the Ethereum network, many nodes [15, 16] are connected to each other to form the Ethereum network. Ethereum node software provides two core functions: data storage and contract code execution [16]. In each Ethereum full node, complete blockchain data is stored. Ethereum not only saves transaction data on the chain, but also compiles the contract code after [17] on the chain. Ethereum Virtual Machine [10] (EVM: Ethereum Virtual Machine) can achieve Turing [18] completeness, mainly to execute smart contracts. Smart contract [19] is a concept proposed by Nick Szabo in the 1990 s and is a series of commitments specified in digital form. A smart contract represents a generation written in a high-level language [20] (Solidity) and stored as bytecode in the blockchain. Web3.js [21] is the official Javascript API of Ethereum to help smart contract developers use HTTP or IPC to interact with local or remote Ethereum nodes.

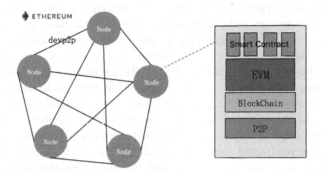

Fig. 1. Ethereum node architecture diagram

3.2   System Architecture Optimization

Data Storage Method Design. The traditional DApp architecture based on Ethereum is shown in Fig. 2. The front-end website, NodeJS server [22], and electron framework [23] form the off-chain system. NodeJS is a JavaScript [24] running environment based on Chrome V8 engine, allowing JavaScript to run on the server-side development platform [25]. electron framework [28] is a framework that uses JavaScript, HTML and CSS to create native programs. Traditional systems only store some important data in the blockchain through smart contracts. The local database assists in the maintenance of all data, with the purpose of reducing complex data for smart contract operations. With the improved architecture, the local database only provides basic data to upload to the blockchain, and the blockchain manages all data on the blockchain through smart contract functions.

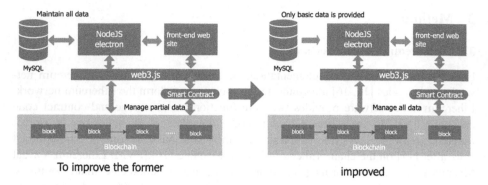

Fig. 2. Improve the decentralized blockchain back-end architecture diagram with centralized front-end and storage

Upload Data Format Optimization. On Ethereum, each smart contract has its own storage space. Although smart contracts do not have query language (such as SQL) or database component support, smart contracts can provide data initialization, reading, or storage functions through code. The web3.js interface can only pass data in JSON format. JSON [26] is a lightweight data storage format that has nothing to do with the development language [27]. The traditional system stores the relational two-dimensional table model, as shown in Fig. 3. There are only two parameters in the uploaded format. TableArray stores the main data of the two-dimensional table, and tableName stores the table name. As can be seen in the data of tableArray, only one piece of data can be uploaded at a time, increasing the number of smart contract executions. The improved upload format has four main parameters, namely: table-Array: stores the field names and corresponding data of the two-dimensional table; tableFieldCount: stores the number of fields of the two-dimensional table; table-DataCount: stores the two-dimensional table The number of data records corresponding to the field; tableDataCount: stores the name of the two-dimensional table. The tableArray contains all the data needed to upload the relational two-dimensional table model, including fields and records.

The optimized data acquisition method is: assuming that the uploaded two-dimensional data table is S, the field Field is 4, and the number of records is 3. The data stored in the tableArray array is to traverse the stored data from left to right in each row of S, until the entire two-dimensional table is traversed. The tableArray is: "["Field1", "Field2", "Field3","Field4", "Record11", "Record12", "Record13", "Record14", "Record21", "Record22", "Record23", "Record24", "Record31", "Record32", "Record33", "Record34"]"; the fields in the two-dimensional table are Field 1, Field 2, Field 3, Field 4, tableFieldCount is 4; The records in the two-dimensional table are 3. tableDataCount is 2; tableName is a two-dimensional table.

Algorithm 3-1 describes the upload data format optimization algorithm. Enter the parameters result and sendTableName. Result is the received query array of the corresponding data table, which contains all the information of the data table. sendTableName is a custom system table name, the specific optimization algorithm is as follows:

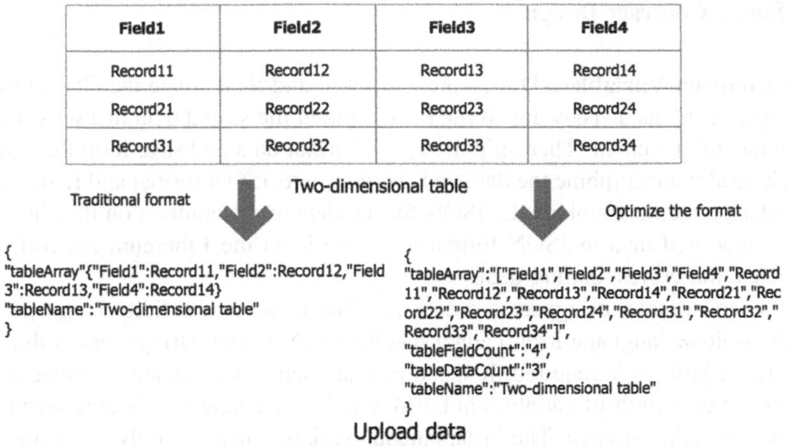

Field1	Field2	Field3	Field4
Record11	Record12	Record13	Record14
Record21	Record22	Record23	Record24
Record31	Record32	Record33	Record34

Two-dimensional table

Traditional format

Optimize the format

```
{
"tableArray"{"Field1":Record11,"Field2":Record12,"Field
3":Record13,"Field4":Record14}
"tableName":"Two-dimensional table"
}
```

```
{
"tableArray":["Field1","Field2","Field3","Field4","Record
11","Record12","Record13","Record14","Record21","Rec
ord22","Record23","Record24","Record31","Record32","
Record33","Record34"]",
"tableFieldCount":"4",
"tableDataCount":"3",
"tableName":"Two-dimensional table"
}
```

Upload data

Fig. 3. Improve system upload blockchain data format

Algorithm 3-1: Upload data format optimization algorithm OptimizeFormat(result, sendTableName)

Input:
result: two-dimensional table data;
sendTableName: two-dimensional table name
1. Initialize optimizeArr [], optimizeData {}, colNum ← 0
2. optimizeData.tableName Stores the data table name
3. for i [1, result [0] .length] do // Traverse the array of data table fields
4. optimizeArr.push (result [0] [i]) // Get the field name of the data table
5. colNum ++
6. end for
7. for j [1, result.length] do // Traverse the number of rows in the data table
8. for k ← result [j] .length // Traverse the data corresponding to the number of rows in the data table
9. optimizeArr.push (result [j] [k]) // Get data table data
10. end for
11. end for
12. optimizeData.tableData ← Convert optimizeArr array to json format // Get the data of the entire two-dimensional table of variables
13. optimizeData.tableDataCount ← colNum // Get the number of two-dimensional table fields
14. optimizeData.tableDataCount ← result.length // Get the number of rows of two-dimensional table data
15. return optimizeData // Return optimized data

3.3 Smart Contract Design

Smart Contract Variables. Design the variables, and then create the CURD function to manipulate the data. They are: Write data: Upload the stored data in JSON format to the contract on the client. Then split the JSON format data and save it on the Ethereum network; read data: combine the data on Ethereum into JSON format and return it to the client; change the data: upload the JSON format data to the contract on the client. Then split the modified data in JSON format and save it on the Ethereum network; delete data: delete the corresponding data.

The smart contract designed to access the data table uses solidity language. However, the solidity language itself cannot handle JSON format strings, and a third-party library (JsmnSolLib) is required. It specifies that each array element is called a token.

There are two kinds of variables in EVM, one is instantaneous variable memory and permanent variable storage. The instantaneous variable memory only consumes 3 gas. Permanent variable storage consumes different gas according to different data structures, but it is much higher than 3gas. In order to reduce gas consumption, in the design of smart contract variables. Store important user information, two-dimensional data table content information, two-dimensional data table field name information, and two-dimensional data table name information in storage, using array mapping storage. The main storage variables in the smart contract are shown in Table 1.

Contract Function. The complexity of the algorithm will also cause gas consumption, so in order to operate the optimized upload data above. This article designs smart contract operation functions as shown in Table 2. They are: add data saveData (), read data getData (), update data updataData (), delete deleteData () and getNames (). The sending user's Ethereum address is added to the parameters to distinguish different users' operations on the data. The user's real information is not stored in the system. Every time the smart contract function state variable changes and executes, the blockchain creates a transaction. There is a hash value as a verification mark in the transaction, which ensures the anonymity and non-tampering of the blockchain system. Because the processing algorithm for uploading data is mainly to add data and obtain data, the two algorithms are introduced in detail below.

Adding Data. In the add data saveData () algorithm, enter five parameters. Respectively, the sending user's Ethereum address sendAddress, data table name tableName, data table record tableArray, data table field number tableFieldCount, data table row record number tableDataCount. There is no return value, the permanent variables tableData, tablelFildName, tableName are updated during the algorithm. The specific process is as follows: the first step: use the third-party smart contract JsmnSolLib library to analyze the JSON format data uploaded by the off-chain system; the second step: save the field names in order to the tableData of the two-dimensional table field; After the corresponding data of the two-dimensional table field is split, it is saved in the tableData array. The detailed algorithm flow chart is shown in Fig. 4:

Read Data. In the read data getData algorithm, enter five parameters. These are the sending user's Ethereum address sendAddress, the data table name tableName, and the number of returned data rows topNum. Returns the length of the data table, fieldnames.

Table 1. Main storage data structure table in smart energy contract

Variable name	Type of data	Description

tablePerson	struct player {
	string name;//User name
	unit id;//ID
	address Paddress//Ethereum
	address}
	mapping (address => player)
	private tablePerson//Storage user
		player is user information,
		including user name, ID, and
		Ethereum address.
		players is an array of stored users.

tableData	mapping(address =>mapping (string =>mapping (uint =>mapping (string =>string)))) private tableData	tableData is an array of stored data table contents, from left to right, the key values are: user Ethereum address, two-dimensional table name, table content row record, and field name.
tablelFildName	mapping(address =>mapping (string => string[])) private tableFieldName	tableFieldName is an array of field names for storing two-dimensional data tables. From left to right, the key values are: user Ethereum address and table field name
tableName	mapping(address =>mapping (string => string[])) private tableName	tableName is an array for storing two-dimensional data table names, from left to right, the key values are: user Ethereum address and table name

length, and the result of all records in the data table. The specific process is as follows: the first step: now the two-dimensional data table content information stored in the blockchain tableData is an array format, and the array content needs to be converted into the string format of the tableArray parameter in Fig. 4; the second step: imitate the array format Need to combine data table field names first;The third step is to combine the corresponding records in the data table fields. The detailed algorithm flow chart is shown in Fig. 5:

4 Experiment and Result

Lab Environment. The experiment in this article is based on Ethereum and developed using JavaScript. The NodeJS server, Web3.js interface, and Electron framework are used. Ganache is used to simulate an Ethereum operating environment, where the remix [28] editor is used to debug and deploy smart contracts. The detailed experimental environment is shown in the following Table 3:

Table 2. Contract core function description

Function name	Parameter	Output	Explanation
saveData()	sendAddress//Send user Ethereum address tableName//Data table name tableArray//Data table record tableFieldCount//Number of data table fields tableDataCount//Number of data table row records	No return value	Adding data
getData()	sendAddress//Send user Ethereum address tableName//data table name topNum//Return the number of data rows	fieldnames.length//Data table field length result//Data table record	Retrieve data
updataData()	sendAddress//Send user Ethereum address tableName//data table name tableContentId//Update data record id	seccess	Change the data
deleteData()	sendAddress//Send user Ethereum address tableName//data table name tableContentId//Delete data record id	seccess	Delete data
getNames()	sendAddress//Send user Ethereum address	tableName//table name	Get a collection of data table names

Function Test. Use Ganache to create a simulated Ethereum environment called SAFE-ALARM. As shown in Fig. 6, deploy the smart contract DataSaveContract to the address $0 \times 3735158082f63c209F45F8e6CEDd072F39815aD8$.

Use the remix compiler to view the smart contract method. Use the data storage saveData () function to obtain Fig. 6. The data is uploaded to the blockchain in the json format in the decoded input field, and the upload format is the same as the optimized format type in 3.3 of this article. As shown in Fig. 7, the off-chain system clicks to view the data in the name of the data table to trigger the smart contract getData () function to get the content of Fig. 8. The content completely displays the information of the data and improves the system to realize the data reading function. Clicking the modify and delete buttons in Fig. 8 triggers the smart contract data update updateData () and data delete deleteData () functions. The results show that the operations were successfully executed, and the system was improved to implement data update and delete functions. Through the experimental function test, the improved system can complete the function of adding, deleting, checking and modifying the blockchain data.

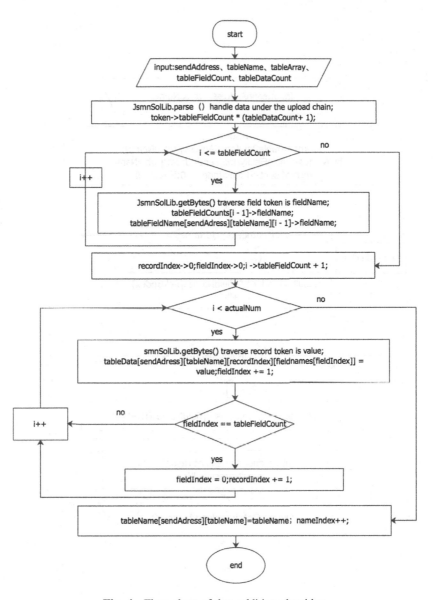

Fig. 4. Flow chart of data addition algorithm

System Performance Test. The experiment uses the same system environment, the system uses the system before and after optimization. Including: the data upload format of the off-chain system before optimization and the data upload format of the optimized off-chain system; the smart contract before optimization and the smart contract after optimization. The system performs data addition function operations separately, and records the gas consumed successfully for each operation.

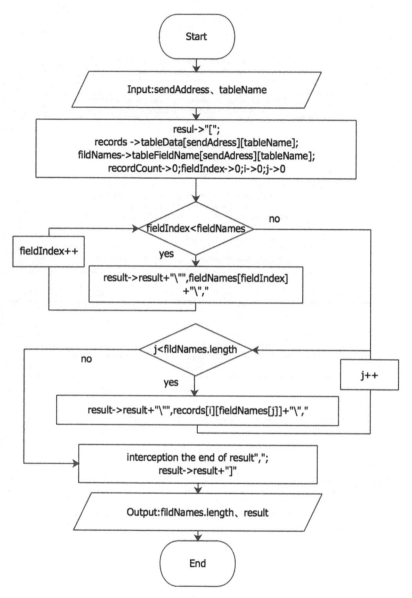

Fig. 5. Flow chart of data reading algorithm

Gas consumption is a measure of how much a smart contract needs to pay for the operation of a smart contract. It is an important indicator of the system's resource consumption. In this article, we use Tx to represent the transaction fee gas, the fee required to execute a smart contract. See formula (1):

Table 3. Stand-alone information table environment

Software/hardware	Version/Model
Operating system	MacOS 10.11.6
Memory	8 GB
CPU	Intel Core i5 2.7 GHz
Node.js	10.18.0
Web3	0.20.6
Electron	7.1.11
ganache	2.0.1

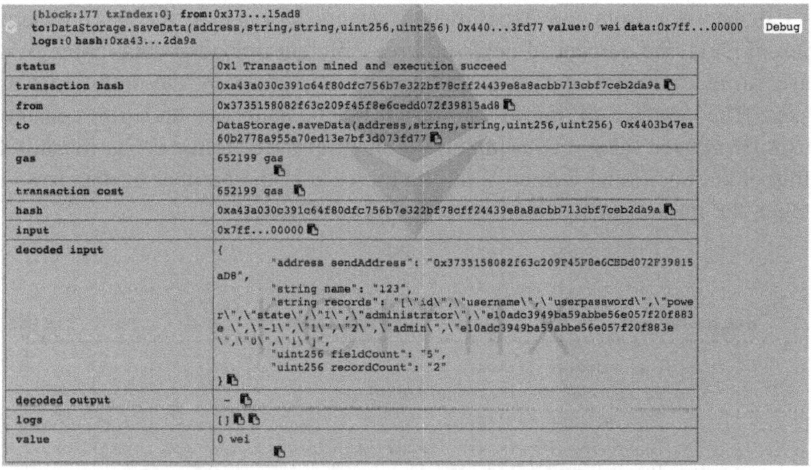

Fig. 6. Execute smart contract saveData() function transaction information graph

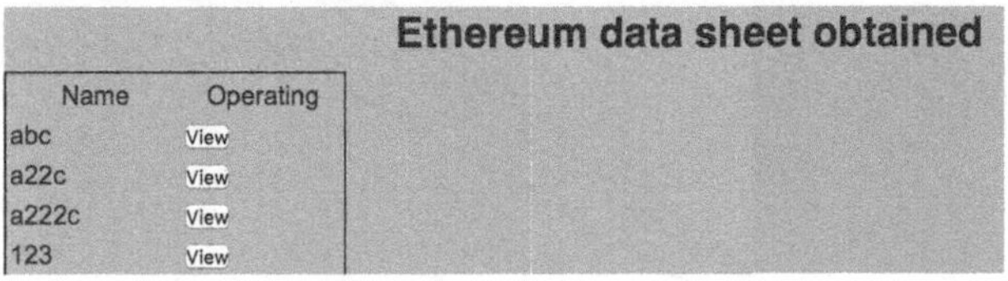

Fig. 7. The off-chain system obtains the name map of the Ethereum storage data table

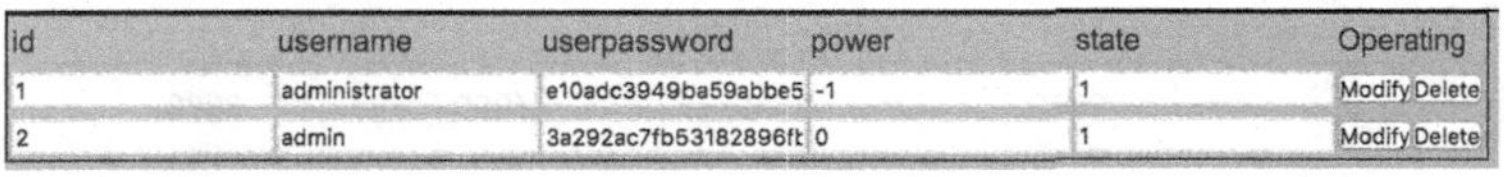

Fig. 8. Read the data table map of the corresponding data table name of Ethereum

$$Tx = \text{Actual Gas Used} * \text{Gas Price} \qquad (1)$$

Actual Gas Used is the gas consumed by smart contract execution, and Gas Price is the gas unit price for executing smart contracts.

In the experiment, the gas consumption test of the off-chain upload data is tested, and the smart contract is used to obtain the gas consumption required to obtain the off-chain upload data and add it to the blockchain. In the experiment, the number of fields in the uploaded two-dimensional data table is Fields = 9, 12, 15, and the number of bytes in each field is the same. The number of data records in the data table Records = 1000, 2000, 3000, 4000, 5000, 6000, 7000, 8000, 9000, each row of data is the same. The average value is taken through 6 sets of experiments, and the gas consumption of the two data upload formats is counted. As shown below:

As can be seen from the experimental results in Fig. 9, the gas consumption diagram of Field, the number of fields in three different uploaded data tables. With the increase of the number of fields, the gas consumption in the traditional format increases. The number of improved format fields increases and gas consumption increases. Moreover, the gas consumption of the improved format is significantly lower than that of the traditional format. With the increase of the number of data rows in the data table, the improvement effect becomes more obvious.

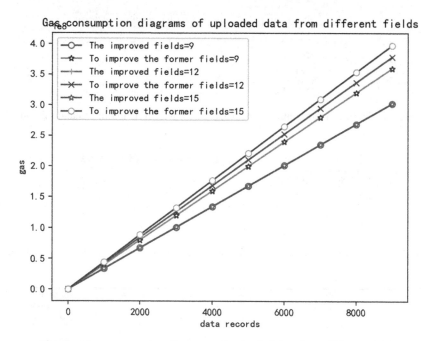

Fig. 9. Gas consumption diagrams of uploaded data from different fields

5 Conclusion

This paper proposes a method for optimizing the data upload format of off-chain systems for the gas consumption of data storage in traditional blockchain applications. Design smart contract storage variables and low-complexity smart contract addition, modification, reading, and deletion algorithms based on the data structure characteristics of the Ethereum virtual machine. It is proved through experiments that the improved system realizes the functions of adding, modifying, reading and deleting data on the chain. Compared with the traditional system, when the system performs data upload operations, the gas consumption is significantly reduced with the increase of the number of data records, which avoids the waste of system resource costs and greatly improves the system resource utilization rate. In the future work, the work that needs to be studied is to optimize the system efficiency and increase the speed of block production.

Acknowledgment. This work is funded by the Science Research Fund of Yunnan Provincial Department of Education (2020J0835), Dr. Gan Jianhou workstation, Computer Science and Technology discipline innovation team building for intelligent education in ethnic areas (2020xhxtd07).

References

1. Yong, Y., Feiyue, W.: Current status and prospects of blockchain technology development. J. Autom. **42**(4), 481–494 (2016)
2. Atzei, N., Bartoletti, M., Cimoli, T.: A survey of attacks on ethereum smart contracts (SoK). In: Maffei, M., Ryan, M. (eds.) POST 2017. LNCS, vol. 10204, pp. 164–186. Springer, Heidelberg (2017). https://doi.org/10.1007/978-3-662-54455-6_8
3. He, P., Yu, G., Zhang, Y., et al.: Prospective overview of blockchain technology and applications. Comput. Sci
4. Azahari, A., Alsaqour, R., Uddin, M., et al.: Review of error detection of data link layer in computer network. Middle East J. Sci. Res. **18**(8), 1105–1110 (2014)
5. Skoutas, D., Sacharidis, D., Kantere, V., Sellis, T.: Efficient semantic web service discovery in centralized and p2p environments. In: Sheth, A., et al. (eds.) ISWC 2008. LNCS, vol. 5318, pp. 583–598. Springer, Heidelberg (2008). https://doi.org/10.1007/978-3-540-88564-1_37
6. Das, P., Das, A.: Centralized authorization service (CAuthS) or authorization as a service (AuthaaS) a conceptual architecture. Int. J. Comput. Appl. **113**(18), 1–9 (2015)
7. Chen, T., et al.: An adaptive gas cost mechanism for ethereum to defend against underpriced dos attacks. In: Liu, J.K., Samarati, P. (eds.) ISPEC 2017. LNCS, vol. 10701, pp. 3–24. Springer, Cham (2017). https://doi.org/10.1007/978-3-319-72359-4_1
8. Albert, E., Gordillo, P., Livshits, B., Rubio, A., Sergey, I.: EthIR: A Framework for High-Level Analysis of Ethereum Bytecode. In: Lahiri, S.K., Wang, C. (eds.) ATVA 2018. LNCS, vol. 11138, pp. 513–520. Springer, Cham (2018). https://doi.org/10.1007/978-3-030-01090-4_30
9. Yang, R., Murray, T., Rimba, P., Parampalli, U.: Empirically analyzing ethereum's gas mechanism. In: 2019 IEEE European Symposium on Security and Privacy Workshops (EuroS&PW). pp. 310–319, IEEE (2019)

10. Yoichi, H.: Defining the ethereum virtual machine for interactive theorem provers. In: International Conference on Financial Cryptography & Data Security (2017)
11. Han, J., Ji, Z., Li, Y., et al.: Trusted log storage and verification system based on blockchain. Comput. Eng. **45**, 13–17 (2005)
12. Ji, L., Zhang, G., Yang, J.: Blockchain-based off-chain personal data protection scheme. Comput. Eng. pp. 1–10 (2020)https://doi.org/10.19678/j.issn.1000-3428.00.EC0057024
13. Cao, D.: Research and Implementation of Trusted Credential Deposit System Based on Blockchain Smart Contract. (2019)
14. Helmer, S., Roggia, M., Ioini, N., Pahl, C.: EthernityDB – integrating database functionality into a blockchain. In: Benczúr, A., et al. (eds.) ADBIS 2018. CCIS, vol. 909, pp. 37–44. Springer, Cham (2018). https://doi.org/10.1007/978-3-030-00063-9_5
15. Pustisek, M., Kos, A., Sedlar, U.: Blockchain Based Autonomous Selection of Electric Vehicle Charging Station (2018)
16. Sidney, A., Myriam, B., Maksym, B.: Towards verifying ethereum smart contract bytecode in Isabelle/ HOL. In: the 7th ACM SIGPLAN International Conference. ACM (2018)
17. Ahmed, K., Andrew, M., Elaine, S.: Hawk: the blockchain model of cryptography and privacy-preserving smart contracts. In: IEEE Symposium on Security & Privacy. IEEE (2016)
18. Hodges, A.: Alan Turing: The enigma. Random House, New York (2000)
19. Nick, S.: Formalizing and securing relationships on public networks. First Monday, 2 (9) (1997)
20. Yang, Z., Lei, H.: Lolisa: Formal syntax and semantics for a subset of the solidity programming language. *arXiv preprint* arXiv:1803.09885 (2018)
21. Yan, C.: Research and design of secure voting system based on blockchain. Hangzhou Dianzi University
22. Leeuw, J.R.: jsPsych: A JavaScript library for creating behavioral experiments in a Web browser. Behav. Res. Methods **47**(1), 1–12 (2014). https://doi.org/10.3758/s13428-014-0458-y
23. Pope, T., Hofer, W.: Exact orbital-free kinetic energy functional for general many-electron systems. Front. Phys. **15**(2), 1–6 (2020). https://doi.org/10.1007/s11467-019-0948-6
24. Nikola, B., Guy, P., Stefano, S.: A tutorial on blockchain and applications to secure network control-planes. In: Smart Cloud Networks & Systems. IEEE (2016)
25. Flanagan, D.: JavaScript: the definitive guide. Oreilly Assoc. Inc **215**(1), 1–4 (2006)
26. Jones, M., Tarjan, P., Goland, Y., et al.: JSON Web Token (JWT) (2015)
27. Mee, C.D, Daniel, E.D.: Computer data storage. Bob Miner (1988)
28. Savelyev, A.: Contract law 2.0: 'Smart' contracts as the beginning of the end of classic contract law. Inf. Communic. Technol. Law **26**(2), 1–19 (2017)

Security Problems and Countermeasures of Network Accounting Information System

Yanling Hu[✉]

Jilin Engineering Normal University, Changchun Jilin, China
hyl0306@jlenu.edu.cn

Abstract. With the rapid development of network technology, the network environment has brought unprecedented opportunities to the development of network accounting information system, as well as the Problems of accounting information system security. Because of the openness of the network, the network accounting information system may be attacked from any corner of the world. This paper introduces the existing problems of network accounting information system security. Then, the countermeasures to solve the problems are put forward from two aspects of technical methods and design methods.

Keywords: Network accounting information system(NAIS) · Security problem · Technical methods · Design method

1 The Security Problems in NAIS

In the network accounting information system, the most core and key problem is the security of accounting data transmission and storage. Generally speaking, the following security risks exist in network accounting information system.

1.1 Security Hidden Attacks

Accounting information system under the network environment is facing an open environment. Accounting information is transmitted through network lines, which is vulnerable to illegal interception, tampering with information, hacker attacks and virus threats.

For example, stealing information means that the data information is transmitted in plaintext on the network. If the enterprise does not adopt any encryption measures, the intruder can intercept the transmitted information on the gateway or router through which the data packet passes.

Tampering information means that the attacker tampers the information and data transmitted on the network in the middle through various technical means and methods,

---

Network accounting information system (NAIS) is integrated with computer technology, communication technology and network technology. Network accounting information system based on the Internet platform, because of the universality and openness of the Internet, attacks may come from any corner of the world. Therefore, the security of network accounting information system is the main problem facing accounting information system.

© Springer Nature Switzerland AG 2020
X. Chen et al. (Eds.): ML4CS 2020, LNCS 12486, pp. 461–469, 2020.
https://doi.org/10.1007/978-3-030-62223-7_40

and then sends them to the destination. Attackers can destroy the integrity of information in three ways. (1) Tampering with information - changing the order of information flow, changing the content of information, such as the delivery address of goods purchased; (2) Deleting information - deleting some parts of a message; and (3) Inserting information - inserting some information into the message so that the recipient can not understand or receive the wrong information

Hacker attack means can be divided into non-destructive attack and destructive attack. Non-destructive attack is usually to disrupt the operation of the system, not to steal system data, usually using denial of service attacks or information bombs; destructive attack is to intrude into other people's computer systems, steal confidential information of the system, and destroy the data of the target system [1].

Network viruses threats refer to computer viruses transmitted through network channels. Distinguish from network virus function. It can be divided into Trojan horse virus and worm virus. Trojan Horse Virus is a backdoor program, it will lurk in the operating system, steal user information such as QQ, online bank password, account number, game account password, etc. Worm viruses are relatively advanced. They spread widely and can initiate attacks by exploiting vulnerabilities in operating systems and programs. Each worm has a module that can scan vulnerabilities in computers. Once it is found, it spreads out immediately. Because of the characteristics of worms, it is more harmful. It can infect all computers in this network through the network after infecting a computer. After being infected, the worm will send a large number of data packets, so the infected network speed will be slower, and it will also be caused by the high CPU and memory occupancy or near the deadlock state.

Distinguishing from the route of network virus transmission. It can be divided into vulnerability virus and mail virus. Comparatively speaking, email viruses are easier to remove. They are transmitted by e-mail. Viruses are hidden in attachments. False information deceives users to open or download the attachment. Some email viruses can also be spread through browser vulnerabilities, so that users can only browse the contents of the email. Without looking at the attachments, viruses can also enter. The most widely used vulnerability virus is the Windows operating system, and Windows operating system operating vulnerabilities are many, Microsoft will issue security patches regularly, even if you do not run illegal software, or unsafe connections, vulnerability virus will use operating system or software vulnerabilities to attack your computer, for example. For example, the popular shock wave and shock wave viruses in 2004 are one kind of vulnerable viruses, which cause the paralysis of network computers all over the world and cause huge economic losses [2].

1.2 Security Risks Due to Data Sharing

Data sharing is to enable users who use different computers and software in different places to read other people's data and perform various operations and analysis. Data sharing brings convenience for enterprises to use information, but at the same time, there is also the risk of information leakage.

The realization of data sharing will enable more people to make full use of existing data resources, reduce duplicate work and corresponding costs of data collection and data collection, and focus on developing new applications and system integration.

As more departments and personnel have access to financial data, the risk of data leakage increases.

Because the data provided by different users may come from different ways, their data content, data format and data quality are very different, which brings great difficulties to data sharing. Sometimes they even encounter the thorny problem that data format can not be converted or lost information after data conversion format, which seriously hinders the data from being transformed. Flow and share among departments and software systems [3].

2   Security Characteristics of NAIS

The network accounting information system has four security characteristics: first, information confidentiality: the information transmitted on the network has confidentiality requirements. For example, the account and user name of the settlement fund can not be known to others, so there are generally encryption requirements in information transmission. Second, the certainty of the identity of both sides of the transaction: the two sides of the online transaction are often strangers, thousands of miles apart. In order to make the transaction successful, the first thing is to confirm the identity of the other side. Enterprises should consider that customers are not cheaters, and customers will worry that the online store will not be a cheater, so confirming the identity of the other side is the premise of facilitating the transaction. Thirdly, the non-repudiation of transactions: because of the ever-changing business situation, once a transaction is concluded, it can not be denied, otherwise it will certainly damage the interests of one party. Therefore, all aspects of the electronic transaction communication process must be undeniable. Fourthly, it should not be tampered with: the transaction documents should not be tampered with, otherwise the commercial interests of one party will inevitably be damaged. Therefore, electronic transaction documents should also be tampered with to ensure the seriousness and fairness of commercial transactions [4].

There are now solutions for the above security problems, as shown in Table 1.

Table 1. Solutions to the security problems of network accounting information system

Problem	Solution	Functional	Techniques
Data interception and modification	Encryption	Transform data to prevent leaks Data is encoded to prevent tampering	Symmetric/asymmetric encryption
Camouflage	Certification	Verify the identity of the sender and receiver	A digital signature
Hacker(unauthorized access to a network)	A firewall	Filtering information into the network	Firewall virtual private network VPN

3 Technical Methods to the Security Problem of NAIS

By strengthening the safety management of the network accounting information system and improving the protection ability of the network accounting information system, the system can resist various threats, effectively protect the assets of enterprises and provide complete accounting information. In the process of constructing the network accounting information system, we must overcome the idea of "reconstructing and setting up the information system with less emphasis on safety, technology and management, and use and maintenance". Safety management and technical system based on "inspection and management, confidentiality and protection, detection and prevention, evaluation and service" should be established step by step. By means of management and technology, the technical risk prevention ability of accounting information system has been improved to a new level. In order to make better use of the advantages brought by network accounting and ensure the quality and safety of information and data, we should start from the following aspects, take network technology as the basis, and combine accounting needs to ensure the safe and effective transmission of information on the network [5].

(1) System Encryption Management

In order to protect the data from being eavesdropped or modified during transmission, it is necessary to encrypt the data (encrypted data is called ciphertext). In this way, even if someone steals the data (ciphertext), it can not be restored to plaintext (unencrypted data) without a key, thus ensuring the security of the data. Because the receiver has the correct key, the ciphertext can be restored to the correct plaintext. The process of information encryption is implemented by various encryption algorithms, which provide a great deal of security protection at a very small cost. In most cases, information encryption is the only way to ensure the confidentiality of the message.

In the accounting information system, for some links that need to be strictly controlled, a "double password" is set up. Only when the "double password" is in place at the same time can the operation be carried out. "Double password" shall be set up by two persons in charge of the authority in accordance with the regulations and shall not be notified to others. Only when the "dual password" is processed by "union key", can the corresponding operation be performed. This not only strengthens the control management, guarantees the data security, but also protects the relevant personnel, and facilitates the separation of their respective responsibilities [6].

(2) Establishing Strict Data Storage Measures

In order to improve the security of accounting system data and the ability of self-rescue under unexpected circumstances, double backups should be established. After backup, two data should be held by different personnel with corresponding passwords, one for encrypted storage and the other for non-encrypted use by specific operators. Distributed storage can be used for some important data [7]. The so-called distributed storage refers to the use of a certain algorithm for data files, which divides data into two or more new strings to form two or more new files, and exists in different physical storage devices, even in remote devices.

(3) Prevention of Computer Viruses

Computer viruses are always concerned about computers and ready to attack them. But computer viruses are not uncontrollable. We can reduce the damage caused by computer viruses through the following aspects:

- Install the latest anti-virus software, upgrade the virus library of anti-virus software every day, regularly check and kill the virus on the computer, and turn on all monitoring of anti-virus software when surfing the Internet. Develop good Internet habits, such as opening unknown emails and attachments carefully, trying not to use viral websites, using more complex passwords as far as possible, guessing simple passwords is a new way for many network viruses to attack systems [9].
- Do not execute software that has not been antivirus processed after downloading from the network; do not browse or log on unfamiliar websites casually; strengthen self-protection now there are many illegal websites, and be infiltrated into malicious code, once opened by users, will be implanted Trojan horse or other viruses.
- To cultivate self-conscious information security awareness, when using mobile storage devices, as far as possible do not share these devices, because mobile storage is also the main way of computer transmission, but also the main target of computer virus attack. In places where the information security requirements are high, the USB interface on the computer should be sealed. At the same time, special aircraft should be used when conditions permit [8].
- Patch the whole system with Windows Update function, and upgrade the application software to the latest version, such as: player software, communication tools, etc., to avoid virus intrusion into the system by way of web Trojan horse or spread virus through other application software vulnerabilities; computer that will be attacked by virus will carry out virus transmission. Isolation as soon as possible, in the process of using the computer, if there is a virus or computer abnormality on the computer, the network should be interrupted in time; when the computer network has been interrupted or network abnormality is found, the network should be interrupted immediately so as to prevent the virus from spreading in the network.

(4) Authentication Technology

E-commerce authentication is one of the necessary measures to ensure the security of e-commerce. The so-called certification, is through the certification center to identify the digital certificate. Authentication is divided into entity authentication and information authentication. Here, entity refers to the entities that participate in communication, such as individuals, customer programs or service programs, and entity authentication refers to the identity authentication of these entities that participate in communication. Passwords are the most common way to authenticate a user's identity, but often fail because many users use passwords that can be easily broken. Other methods include identification of physical characteristics such as fingerprints, smart CARDS and tokens. A token is a credit card-sized, portable device. When the user logs into the network, the server will ask for a password. The user simply enters the password into the token and enters it into the server along with the response that appears [11]. Smart CARDS work similarly to tokens, except that a card reader is required to automate the process of entering a password and sending a reply. Information authentication occurs when the recipient of the information receives the information and USES relevant technologies to authenticate the information to confirm who is the sender of the information and whether the information has been tampered with or replaced in the transmission process.

(5)   Virtual Private Network (VPN)

VPN(Virtual Private Network) is the Virtual Private Network, that is, with the help of the public Network to form enterprise Private Network. In a VPN, use local connections to isps instead of dial-up or frame relay connections to remote users and leased lines. VPNS allow private enterprise intranets to expand securely over the Internet or other network services, making it easier and more reliable for e-commerce networks and extranets to connect with business partners, suppliers, and customers. VPNS are designed to provide reliability, security, and performance in traditional WAN environments at a lower cost and with more flexible connections to isps [9].

4   Design Method to the Security Probiems of NAIS

On the basis of the above analysis and the actual situation of accounting information and network security technology, this paper puts forward a life cycle model of accounting information system security from the desin point of view (see Fig. 1). In the life cycle of accounting information system security, security strategy is the core of the life cycle of accounting information security. In the life cycle model of accounting information security, security strategy is at the core. A good and reasonable security strategy can help users evaluate network security, formulate security objectives, determine feasible security levels, and select and implement security solutions. The life cycle of network accounting information security includes four stages and six aspects.

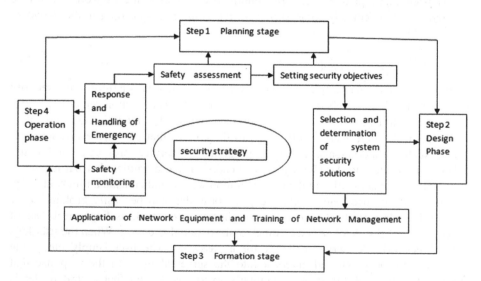

Fig. 1. Life cycle model of network accounting information system security

4.1 Network Accounting Information System Security Planning Stage

At this stage, according to the needs of users, the security strategy of network accounting information is formulated, and under the guidance of security strategy, the content of network accounting information security is formulated. At this stage, the content of network accounting information security is involved. The first one is security assessment: make necessary security assessment of existing networks and systems, and clarify the current status of network accounting security, existing problems and current security level. The second is to formulate security objectives: on the basis of security assessment, fully considering the security, feasibility and reliability requirements of the network system, to formulate security objectives suitable for network accounting information.

4.2 Design Stage of Network Accounting Information System Security

According to the clear security goal of network accounting information in the planning stage, the security design of network accounting information is carried out. This stage involves the third item of the security content of network accounting information, which is to select and determine the system security solution. In this stage, according to the security strategy of network accounting information and the security goal of the previous stage, the overall design of network accounting information security should be carried out [10]. Two points should be paid attention to in the design: one is that the network security technology is not complete; the other is that the protection of network accounting information should be focused [11]. On this basis, system security solutions are selected and determined.

4.3 The Stage of NAIS Security Establishment

On the basis of choosing and defining the system security solution in the previous stage, the network accounting security system is specifically set up, including the fourth application of network equipment and the training of network management personnel. The performance provided by the equipment is closely related to the running environment. Most of the performance indicators obtained from the outside are optimized and suitable for testing in the network environment of the equipment. Even if the equipment is tested in the benchmark mode or the maximum load mode, its performance indicators can not be fully trusted, because our running network is definitely different from the testing network, we must do a good job of network equipment testing [12]. The operation of equipment can not be separated from the operation of human beings, so the training of network administrators'network accounting security system should be done well.

4.4 The Stage of Safe Operation of NAIS

At this stage, two security contents of network accounting information are involved. The fifth item of safety monitoring and the sixth item of emergency response and handling. The fifth security monitoring is mainly to check whether there are security vulnerabilities; check the security log to see whether there are successful violations; performance testing, mainly for internal network equipment, to check whether the network has bottlenecks and the use of network bandwidth due to changes in business. The sixth emergency response and handling mainly refers to how to deal with system security vulnerabilities once they are found. Pay attention to collecting and sorting out the latest network security vulnerability information, and pay special attention to vulnerability reports related to their own systems. Network information security can not be achieved by one's own efforts, nor can we wait until they suffer losses to make up for it. We should learn more from others experience and learn from others' failures. There are absolutely no loopholes in the system. The most important thing to achieve security is to find and remedy loopholes as soon as possible. Therefore, it is very important to collect the latest information on security loopholes. We should pay attention to the upgrading of the network information security maintenance system itself [13].

With the development of network accounting information system, the security of information system has become the core problem that restricts the development of network accounting. Computer security technology should keep pace with The Times and keep innovating. Only by establishing a security system can the security of accounting information system be guaranteed. But at present network accounting information system in the market role is not fully shown. The main reason is that users do not fully trust the security measures of the network accounting information system. This paper probes into the security problems of the network accounting information system, and puts forward the countermeasures from the technical method and the life cycle design method of the accounting information system, hoping to contribute to the popularization and application of the network accounting information system.

References

1. Zhang Xiaomin is in line with the current situation to promote the construction of accounting information. Financ. Econ. Circles, (17), 23–25. (2015)
2. Research on the Security of Accounting Information System under Liu Runlong's Network Environment, China Business, (8) (2015)
3. Ma, Y.: Analysis of computer network information security related technologies. Electron. Test. (18) (2018)
4. Zhang, G.: Analysis and countermeasure research on computer network information system security. Electron. Prod. (16) (2016)
5. Zhengbing.: Research on computer network information security in big data era. Sci. Technol. Innov. Appl. (14) (2019)
6. Li, M.: Analysis of computer network information security and countermeasure in big data era. China's Strategic Emerging Industries. (04) (2018)
7. Song, W.: Computer network information security management and protection. Electron. Technol. Software Engineering. (06) (2017)
8. Pengchi .: Analysis of security problems and solutions of computer network information. Inf. Communication. (07) (2014)
9. Zhou, Y., Pan, Z.: Data integrity and data security in network environment topic research. Library Inf. Work. (4), 48–50 (2001)

10. Seanconvery, Network Security Architectures. Cisco Sys-terms (2004)
11. Yu, XS.: Research on security problems and countermeasure of information system under network environment. Inf. Sci. (12), 1314–1316 (2003)
12. Zhao, Q.: Network information security life cycle. Netwk. Secur. Technol. Appl. (12), 56–57 (2002)
13. Wenjun, W.: Web Application Security Threats and Prevention. Electronic Industry Press, Beijing (2013)

Analysis on Industrial Internet Traffic Characteristics

Shiyu Chen[1(✉)], Qianmu Li[1], Huaqiu Long[2], and Jian Jiang[3]

[1] School of Cyber Science and Engineering, Nanjing University of Science
and Technology, Nanjing 210094, China
13809028951@139.com
[2] Intelligent Manufacturing Department, Wuyi University,
Jiangmen 529020, China
[3] Jiangsu Zhongtian Internet Technology Co., Ltd., Nantong 226009, China

Abstract. Digital economy is an important engine to promote high-quality growth of China's economy. In the future, Chinese enterprises will face the inevitable requirement to transform from traditional economy to digital economy. Industrial Internet is an important support for digital economy transformation of enterprises. Analysis on network traffic characteristics is the premise to guarantee the service quality and improve the performance of industrial Internet. These services include refined operation and maintenance management, traffic control, network protocol design and network performance analysis. Moreover, analysis on network traffic characteristics is also helpful for industrial Internet platform to build a more effective network model, configure network node resources efficiently and maintain industrial Internet security. Data that conform to norms of feature analysis are acquired by preprocessing datasets of industrial Internet traffic provided by ZTE. Then, industrial Internet traffic characteristics, such as self-similarity, periodicity and burstiness, are analyzed and verified. The research results of this paper are helpful to predict industrial Internet traffic and analyze its performance.

Keywords: Digital economy · Network security · Industrial internet traffic

1 Introduction

Industrial Internet is the digital, informationalized and intelligent transformation of the whole industry. First, elements and resources are connected in the whole process of industrial production by using connection (communication) technology. Then through the computing technology, data are stored and calculated, data value are mined, production processes are optimized, and weaknesses are resolved. These bring efficiency and productivity improvement, cost reduction and profit growth. Technically, industrial Internet is the combination of industrial technologies revolution and information and communication technologies (ICT) revolution, rather than that of industry and Internet. Industry is empowered by industrial Internet, which achieves digital, networked and intelligent development of industrial economy through the comprehensive connection of all elements, all industrial chains and all value chains. Cloud computing and edge

© Springer Nature Switzerland AG 2020
X. Chen et al. (Eds.): ML4CS 2020, LNCS 12486, pp. 470–483, 2020.
https://doi.org/10.1007/978-3-030-62223-7_41

computing are empowered by data center, which makes it possible for industrial Internet to realize the interconnection of all things.

In the field of performance analysis on industrial Internet, traffic is the main carrier to describe and reflect the state of industrial Internet, and it is the main parameter to evaluate the operation load and the state of industrial Internet. Traffic behavior is the main component of industrial Internet behavior. Therefore, the description of traffic characteristics is the basis of performance analysis on industrial Internet.

2   Preprocessing of Industrial Internet Traffic

With the increase of industrial Internet bandwidth and the emergence of industrial Internet applications, tremendous amounts of data generated by operating industrial Internet is a severe challenge when collecting, storing, searching and online analyzing. Furthermore, dirty data in raw data may affect efficiency and experimental results of algorithms. Data preprocessing techniques can speed up and improve efficiency of the subsequent mining process. These techniques mainly include data cleaning, data integration, data reduction, and data transformation.

2.1   Data Cleaning

Data cleaning is mainly used to ensure data consistency and improve data quality. Raw data are generally dirty. They tend to be noisy, inaccurate, missing, redundant, etc. There are many reasons for causing inconsistencies in industrial Internet datasets. For example, packet loss, which is caused by asymmetric routes and transmission link congestion, may lead to incomplete flow data in the process of transmission. Incomplete data read or written, which is caused by congestion of network card and storage device, may lead to abnormal flow data. Abnormal packets, which are designed to attack industrial Internet, are difficult to distinguish from dirty data.

Data cleaning routines attempt to delete redundant data, correct outliers, and fill in missing values (e.g., fill in average values or fixed values) manually or automatically. Data cleaning generally focuses on labeled (training) data sets, because it is impossible to manually analyze large scale of data sets.

2.2   Data Integration

Data integration merges data from multiple sources into a coherent data store and a unified format. These sources may include multiple databases, data cubes, or files. The unified format is the data format specified for analyzing and processing according to actual situation. The coherent data store refers to a fixed store form.

There are a number of issues to consider during data integration, such as entity identification, redundancy, and conflict detection. Entity identification is to match up equivalent real-world entities from multiple data sources. Redundancy refers that an attribute may be redundant if it can be derived from another attribute or set of attributes. These redundancies can be detected by correlation analysis. Conflict detection is that attribute values from different sources may differ for the same real-world entity.

2.3 Data Reduction

Data reduction techniques are to obtain a reduced representation of the data set that is much smaller in volume, yet closely maintains the integrity of the original data. These strategies include data cube, feature selection, dimensionality reduction, numerosity reduction, and data compression, concept hierarchy and discretization. Next, a closer look at individual techniques are as follows.

1. **Data cube** displays any n-dimensional data as a series of $(n - 1)$-dimensional cubes.
2. **Feature selection and dimensionality reduction** can reduce data size by, for instance, aggregating, eliminating redundant features, or clustering.
3. **Numerosity reduction** refers that the data are replaced by alternative, smaller representations. Common numerosity reduction techniques include clusters, sampling, and histograms.
4. **Data compression** refers that transformations are applied so as to obtain a compressed representation of the original data. Common techniques include principal component analysis and wavelet transform.
5. **Discretization** and **concept hierarchy generation** replace raw data values by ranges or higher-level concepts. Discretization is to discretize the continuous values by binning (e.g., discretize each bin value by the bin mean).

2.4 Data Transformation

In data transformation, the data are transformed into forms appropriate for mining. Strategies for data transformation include normalization and binning for numerical data, concept hierarchy generation for nominal data, and discretization for continuous numerical data.

Normalization (or standardization), where data are scaled to fall within a smaller or common range such as [−1.0, 1.0] or [0.0, 1.0]. The purpose is not only to facilitate data processing but also to speed up the algorithm's convergence. Common methods for data normalization are min-max normalization and z-score normalization.

Discretization, where the raw values of a numeric attribute are replaced by interval labels or conceptual labels. This simplifies the original data, reduces the data scale, and improves operation speed of algorithms. Discretization techniques include binning, clustering, ChiMerge, and information gain.

3 Self-similarity of Industrial Internet Traffic

Traffic self-similarity means that the local and global structure of traffic packet sequence are similar to some extent. In addition, traffic has long-range dependence, which corresponds to short-range dependent models such as Poisson distribution. From the point of view of physics, long-range dependence is the continuous phenomenon in the process of self-similarity. Burst characteristic is reflected in multiple time scales, so it is also called multi-scale behavior characteristic. Therefore, traffic self-similarity can be interpreted that traffic packet sequence shows self-similar and burst characteristic in multiple time scales.

3.1   Definition and Properties of Self-similarity

Definition 1. Let random process $\{X(t)\}$. For any $\lambda > 0$, if $X(t) \overset{d}{=} \lambda^{-H} X(\lambda t)$ holds, $\{X(t)\}$ is self-similar. In the formula, $H \in (0.5, 1)$ is Hurst parameter or self-similar parameter, $\overset{d}{=}$ denotes $\{X(t)\}$ and $X(\lambda t)$ are equal in finite dimensions.

From Definition 1, if $\{X(t)\}$ is self-similar, it has the following properties:

Property 1. The traffic packet sequence $\{X(t)\}$ has invariance of time scale, which can also be described that the shape of $X(\lambda t)$ is consistent with that of $\{X(t)\}$ after being normalized by λ^{-H}.

Property 2. $E\{X(t)\} = 0$.

Property 3. $E\{|X(t)|^q\} = E\{|X(1)|^q\} t^{qH}$.

3.2   Hurst Parameter Estimation

Hurst is an important parameter to determine whether traffic data is self-similar or not. The value of Hurst represents the degree of self-similarity. If the value of Hurst $H = 0.5$, the random time sequence conforms to Poisson process. It means that traffic data has no self-similarity. If $H \in (0.5, 1)$, the random time sequence is positive correlation. It means that traffic data has self-similarity, the degree of which strengthens with the increase of H value. If $H \in (0, 0.5)$, the random time sequence is negative correlation. It means that traffic data has no self-similarity. The commonly used estimation methods includes variance-time plot, R/S (Rescaled Adjusted Range) plot, periodogram, Whittle estimation, and wavelet analysis Estimation.

This paper compares the characteristics of the above five estimation methods, as shown in Table 1:

Table 1. Comparison of Hurst parameter estimation methods

Method	Evaluation index				
	Self-similarity	Visualization	Real-time	Complexity	Others
Variance-time plot	Yes	Yes	No	$O(n)$	A mass of data need to be obtained in advance
R/S plot	Yes	Yes	No	$O(n^2)$	Independent of edge distribution
Periodogram	Yes	Yes	No	$O(n \log n)$	Appropriate cut-off frequency needs to be determined
Whittle estimation	Yes	No	No	$O(n^2)$	A quantification method with high complexity
Wavelet analysis	Yes	No	No	$O(n \log n)$	A method with accurate estimation

As can be seen from Table 1, the first three methods are visualization methods. By drawing random process on the logarithm axis and using the linear fitting, these approaches perform statistical analysis on traffic data and sample points respectively. Then the slope is calculated to get the estimation of Hurst parameter according to the drawn straight line. Variance-time plot has the poor robustness. Periodogram needs to determine the appropriate cut-off frequency. Whittle estimation can only estimate the short-range correlation of traffic packet sequence but not long-range correlation of it, and this approach has a high complexity. Wavelet Analysis can accurately estimate Hurst parameter, but cannot obtain the confidence interval of parameter. The calculation of this method is also complex. In summary, R/S plot is used in this paper to calculate the value of Hurst parameter.

R/S plot is a common estimation method, which is also used in this paper. The process of calculation is as follows:

a. Divide observation process N into K segments. Then calculate $R(k_i, n)/S(k_i, n)$ for each segment, where k_i denotes starting with the i-th traffic data, and $k_i = iN/k, i = 1, 2, \ldots, k_i + n \leq N$;
b. Take logarithm on both sides of the formula and get $\log[R(k_i, n)/S(k_i, n)] - \log n$. Draw the figure, and carry out linear fitting. The slope of the straight line is the value of Hurst parameter.

3.3   Periodicity of Traffic Data

Periodicity refers to the regular fluctuation of traffic data when time changes. The periodicity of industrial Internet traffic packet sequence includes year, month, week, day, hour, minute, second, etc. According to the periodicity, in the industrial Internet management, resource allocation strategies with different cycles and the same time can be adjusted for adjusting and controlling the resource allocation in the next cycle in advance, so as to improve the management efficiency.

3.4   Burstiness of Traffic Data

The burstiness of industrial Internet traffic is caused by the following two reasons:

First, the heavy-tailed distribution of variables in the industrial Internet, such as bytes of files, causes the burstiness of traffic. Willinger et al., [1] propose that the traffic generated by the superposition of many heavy-tailed ON/OFF information sources is similar to the traffic generated by industrial Ethernet. Some scholars describe each web browser as an ON/OFF information source that obeys the Pareto distribution, and find that files whose size obeys the Pareto distribution in the web server mainly determine the self-similarity of Web traffic. [9] shows that TCP traffic, TELNET traffic and FTP data connection have burst arrival rate. Moreover, the distribution of bytes in each burst obeys the heavy-tailed distribution.

Second, the interaction among protocols in industrial Internet results in the burstiness of network traffic. [10] shows that in the network with many TCP protocol interactions between remote source and destination, used protocols determine the dynamic behavior of data traffic, resulting in self-similarity. [11] shows that retransmission mechanism is the cause of self-similarity.

The burstiness of large amounts of traffic will cause congestion of industrial Internet, increase the queuing delay and the packet loss rate, etc. These make industrial Internet unstable and reduce the service quality. In addition, many behaviors threaten the security of industrial Internet such as denial of service attack, worm virus, information stealing, etc. These behaviors make the system unable to operate.

4 Experiments and Results Analysis

4.1 Dataset Preprocessing

This paper analyzes the dataset provided by ZTE. The dataset contains traffic data information on key nodes of A, B, C large-scale industrial clusters, where the size of traffic in area A is 9.22 GB, that in area B is 19.5 GB, and that in area C is 50.7 GB. Due to large amounts of data, the regular of data files must first be analyzed, and then the data suitable for traffic characteristics analysis and prediction are acquired by preprocessing techniques.

1. **Data File Analysis**

Traffic data are stored in CSV files. The way of data storage is that traffic data collected according to minute, hour, day, week, and month are stored in the corresponding CSV files respectively, and the date is marked. For example, to store traffic collected from March 1 to March 31 of a certain year. First, the number of bytes of traffic at 100 fixed time points on several nodes is collected every day. Then, the number of bytes of traffic are stored in 31 files respectively according to a day.

All files in this paper are stored according to the above format. The fields and their meanings are shown in Table 2:

Table 2. Description of fields in files

Field name	Description
noid	Node number
Name	Node name
time	Time
kb	The number of bytes
avgSpeed	Average speed rate
maxSpeed	Maximum speed rate
port_type	Port type
service_type	Service type
city	City
area1	Sub-area 1
area2	Sub-area 2

As can be seen from Table 2, this paper only focuses on the fields of *noid*, *time* and *kb*. So the data related to these three fields are needed to be extracted, and then preprocess them.

2. Preprocessing

As mentioned above, traffic information of all nodes are stored according to the different time scales. Therefore, a complete traffic information of a node can only be obtained by extracting the continuous traffic information of each node in all dates under the corresponding time scales. For example, for traffic information collected from March 1 to March 31 of a certain year, daily files contain the number of bytes of traffic at fixed time points on several nodes. Hence, it is necessary to extract all of the number of bytes of a node in 31 files for the complete analysis.

As a result, the first step is to obtain the dataset that only contains the fields of *noid*, *time* and *kb* by datasets reduction. Then, traffic data of the same node are integrated from different files. The regular of traffic data is as follows:

The following time scales of data are collected for a single node in area A:

a. **Minute-level traffic data.** Traffic data at 96 fixed time points per day are collected from March 23, 2017 to April 27, 2017. The total number of collected traffic information is 96 * 36 = 3456;

b. **Hour-level traffic data.** Traffic data within 24 h per day are collected from April 17, 2017 to April 27. The total number of collected traffic information is 24 * 11 = 264;

c. **Day-level traffic data.** Traffic data of all days per month are collected from December 2016 to April 2017. The total number of collected traffic information is 142;

d. **Week-level traffic data.** Traffic data for 20 weeks are continuously collected from 2016 to 2017. The total number of collected traffic information is 20;

e. **Month-level traffic data**. Traffic data for 4 months are continuously collected from December 2016 to March 2017. The total number of collected traffic information is 4.

The following time scales of data are collected for a single node in area B:

a. **Minute-level traffic data.** Traffic data at 96 fixed time points per day are collected from March 2, 2017 to April 6, 2017. The total number of collected traffic information is 96 * 36 = 3456;

b. **Hour-level traffic data.** Traffic data within 24 h per day are collected from March 3, 2017 to April 6, 2017. The total number of collected traffic information is 24 * 35 = 840;

c. **Day-level traffic data.** Traffic data of all days per month are collected from July 2015 to April 2017. The total number of collected traffic information is 632;

d. **Week-level traffic data.** Traffic data for 50 weeks are continuously collected from 2016 to 2017. The total number of collected traffic information is 50;

e. **Month-level traffic data**. Traffic data for 21 months are continuously collected from July 2015 to March 2017. The total number of collected traffic information is 21.

The following time scales of data are collected for a single node in area C:

a. **Minute-level traffic data.** Traffic data at 96 fixed time points per day are collected from May 22, 2017 to June 26, 2017. The total number of collected traffic information is 96 * 36 = 3456;

b. **Hour-level traffic data.** Traffic data within 24 h per day are collected from May 24, 2017 to June 26, 2017. The total number of collected traffic information is 24 * 34 = 816;

c. **Day-level traffic data.** Traffic data of all days per month are collected from May 2015 to June 2017. The total number of collected traffic information is 784;

d. **Week-level traffic data.** Traffic data for 83 weeks are continuously collected from 2015 to 2017. The total number of collected traffic information is 83;

e. **Month-level traffic data**. Traffic data for 22 months are continuously collected from August 2015 to May 2017. The total number of collected traffic information is 22.

The outliers of field kb are − 9999999 and 450000. If the ratio of outliers to missing values is over 15%, the node will be removed. If the ratio is below 15%, outliers and missing values will be replaced by average value.

In addition, datasets normalization is applied to improve the speed of training due to the value of field kb in traffic data files is large. In this paper, min-max normalization method mentioned before is used to transform the data to fall within the range $[-1.0, 1.0]$.

4.2   Self-similar Analysis of Traffic

1. Self-similar verification of traffic in area A

Because of space limitations, this paper only selects minute-level traffic of a node in area A. The historical traffic data are shown in Fig. 1.

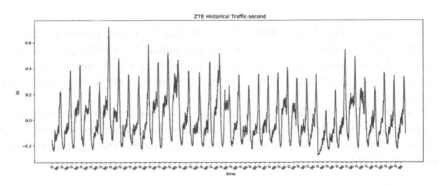

Fig. 1. Minute-level traffic packet sequence in area A

It can be observed from Fig. 1 that traffic have significant periodicity, i.e., approximately 96 intervals per periodicity. Moreover, the values of traffic at some time points are much greater than before and after values. The large difference between the highest and lowest values of traffic shows that minute-level traffic of this node is an unstable time series, and it has burstiness. From the shape of traffic packet sequence, the traffic packet sequence has self-similarity because its local fluctuation trend is consistent with overall's.

Next, Hurst parameter is calculated to further verify self-similarity of this traffic packet sequence. The R/S plot mentioned before is used to estimate Hurst parameter. The experimental results are shown in Fig. 2.

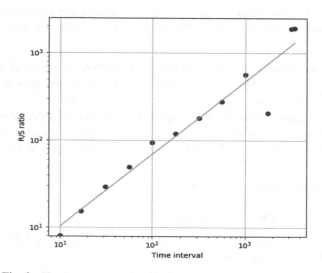

Fig. 2. Hurst parameter of traffic in area A estimated by R/S plot

As shown in Fig. 2, the slope of drawn line is Hurst parameter. Its value $H = 0.8274$ that satisfies $0.5 < H < 1$. Therefore, minute-level traffic packet sequence in area A has self-similarity. Moreover, this traffic packet sequence is predicted by nonlinear time series models. (Notice that the original data are directly used without normalization).

When the length of traffic packet sequence is less than 100, Hurst value obtained is not convincing. Therefore, this paper just calculates Hurst parameter of a node in area A under minute-level, hour-level and day-level time scales. The experimental results are shown in Table 3.

Table 3. Hurst values of a node in area A under different time scales

Time scale	The number of traffic	Hurst value
Minute-level	3456	0.8274
Hour-level	840	0.8335
Day-level	142	0.8430

It can be observed from Table 3 that Hurst values of hour-level and day-level traffic data are also in the range [0.5, 1]. Therefore, it also has self-similarity can be predicted by nonlinear time series model.

2. Self-similar verification of traffic in area B

In order to verify the effectiveness of prediction model for abnormal traffic data in the next subsection, the nodes with strong burstiness are specially selected while selecting the node traffic of this province. The historical traffic data are shown in Fig. 3.

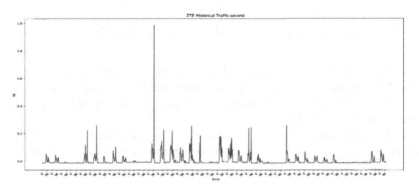

Fig. 3. Minute-level traffic packet sequence in area B

It can be observed from the figure above that part of the traffic are relatively stable and the number of bytes is small. Part of the traffic increase abruptly and the duration also accounts for a certain proportion. Overall, however, the traffic data are still periodic, which is approximately 96 intervals. The traffic seem to be relatively stable in some time periods, which also means that the time periods of collecting traffic in area A and area B are the same. The peak and valley values of minutely traffic in this province are relatively larger, which indicates that the minutely traffic in this province are unstable time series showing strong burst. On the other hand, some traffic may be abnormal. From the shape of traffic packet sequence, the traffic packet sequence has self-similarity because its local fluctuation trend is consistent with overall's.

Next, Hurst parameter is calculated to further verify self-similarity of this traffic packet sequence. The R/S plot mentioned before is used to estimate Hurst parameter. The experimental results are shown in Fig. 4.

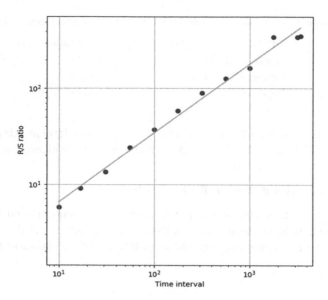

Fig. 4. Hurst parameter of traffic in area B estimated by R/S plot

As shown in Fig. 4, the slope of drawn line is Hurst parameter. Its value $H = 0.7189$ that satisfies $0.5 < H < 1$. Therefore, minute-level traffic packet sequence in area B has self-similarity. Moreover, this traffic packet sequence is predicted by nonlinear time series models.

The Hurst parameter of a node in area A is calculated under minute-level, hour-level and day-level time scales. The experimental results are shown in Table 4.

Table 4. Hurst values of a node in area B under different time scales

Time scale	The number of traffic	Hurst value
Minute-level	3456	0.7189
Hour-level	840	0.7370
Day-level	632	0.7511

It can be observed from Table 4 that Hurst values of hour-level and day-level traffic data are also in the range [0.5, 1]. Therefore, it also has self-similarity can be predicted by nonlinear time series model.

3. Self-similar verification of traffic in area C

The traffic data of a node selected in area C, with more frequent and intensive volatility than the traffic in area A, and more abnormal traffic than the traffic in area B. The historical traffic data are shown in Fig. 5.

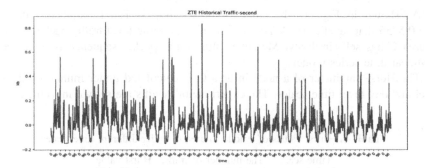

Fig. 5. Minute-level traffic packet sequence in area C

It can be observed from the figure above that the traffic fluctuation in area A is more unstable. However, it also has obvious periodicity, which is approximately 96 intervals. It can be seen that the time period of the collecting traffic data in area A, area B and area C are the same. Traffic is very prominent at many time points, much greater than the front and rear time value. Moreover, the differences between highest and lowest value of traffic are relatively large. These mean the minute level traffic of this node is an unstable time series with a strong burst. Moreover, the numbers and differences of traffic at the prominent time points are larger than the nodes selected in area A. From the shape of traffic packet sequence, the traffic packet sequence has self-similarity because its local fluctuation trend is consistent with overall's.

Next, Hurst parameter is calculated to further verify self-similarity of this traffic packet sequence. The R/S plot mentioned before is used to estimate Hurst parameter. The experimental results are shown in Fig. 6.

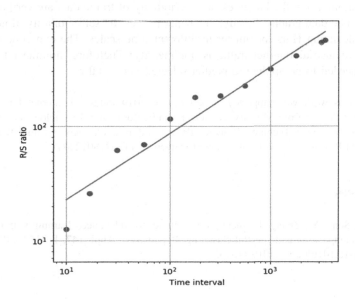

Fig. 6. Hurst parameter of traffic in area C estimated by R/S plot

As shown in Fig. 6, the slope of drawn line is Hurst parameter. Its value $H = 0.5755$ that satisfies $0.5 < H < 1$. Therefore, minute-level traffic packet sequence in area C has self-similarity. Moreover, this traffic packet sequence is predicted by nonlinear time series models.

The Hurst parameter of a node in area C is calculated under minute-level, hour-level and day-level time scales. The experimental results are shown in Table 5.

Table 5. Hurst values of a node in area C under different time scales

Time scale	The number of traffic	Hurst value
Minute-level	3456	0.5755
Hour-level	816	0.6090
Day-level	784	0.7016

It can be observed from Table 5 that Hurst values of hour-level and day-level traffic data are also in the range [0.5, 1]. Therefore, it also has self-similarity can be predicted by nonlinear time series model.

5   Conclusions

This paper introduces industrial Internet traffic characteristics, and then adopts a number of node traffic information for experiments based on traffic datasets provided by ZTE. Characteristics of the datasets are firstly observed and analyzed so as to figure out the regular of data store. Second, traffic data of each node in different time scales are acquired by preprocessing techniques such as cleaning, integration, reduction, and transformation. Then, the burstiness and periodicity of traffic data are verified through drawing traffic data graphs. Finally, this paper proves the self-similarity of node traffic data by calculating Hurst parameter in different time scales. The experimental results show that industrial Internet traffic is nonlinearity. Therefore, nonlinear time series model is needed to be applied to predict selected node traffic.

Funding. This work was supported in part by the 2019 Industrial Internet Innovation and Development Project from Ministry of Industry and Information Technology of China, 2018 Jiangsu Province Major Technical Research Project "Information Security Simulation System", Fundamental Research Funds for the Central Universities (30918012204).

References

1. Li, Q., Song, Y., Zhang, J., Sheng, V.S.: Multiclass imbalanced learning with one-versus-one decomposition and spectral clustering. Expert Syst. Appl. **147**, 113152 (2020). https://doi.org/10.1016/j.eswa.2019.113152

2. Hou, J., Li, Q., Tan, R., Meng, S., Zhang, H., Zhang, S.: An intrusion tracking watermarking scheme. IEEE Access **7**, 141438–141455 (2019). https://doi.org/10.1109/ACCESS.2019. 2943493

3. Hou, J., et al.: Low-cohesion differential privacy protection for industrial Internet. J. Supercomput. **76**(11), 8450–8472 (2020). https://doi.org/10.1007/s11227-019-03122-y

4. Li, Q., Tian, Y., Wu, Q., Cao, Q., Shen, H., Long, H.: A cloud-fog-edge closed-loop feedback security risk prediction method. IEEE Access **8**(1), 29004–29020 (2020)

5. Li, Q., et al.: Safety risk monitoring of cyber-physical power systems based on ensemble learning algorithm. IEEE Access **7**, 24788–24805 (2019)

6. Li, Q., Meng, S., Wang, S., Zhang, J., Hou, J.: CAD: command-level anomaly detection for vehicle-road collaborative charging network. IEEE Access **7**, 34910–34924 (2019)

7. Li, Q., Meng, S., Zhang, S., Hou, J., Qi, L.: Complex attack linkage decision-making in edge computing networks. IEEE Access **7**, 12058–12072 (2019)

8. Li, Q., Wang, Y., Ziyuan, P., Wang, S., Zhang, W.: A time series association state analysis method in smart internet of electric vehicle charging network attack. Transp. Res. Record **2673**, 217–228 (2019)

9. Shicheng, C., et al.: DISL: deep isomorphic substructure learning for network representations. Knowl.-Based Syst. **189**, 105086 (2019). https://doi.org/10.1016/j.knosys.2019. 105086

10. Li, Q., Yin, X., Meng, S., Liu, Y., Ying, Z.: A security event description of intelligent applications in edge-cloud environment. J. Cloud Comput. **9**(1), 1–13 (2020). https://doi.org/ 10.1186/s13677-020-00171-0

11. Meng, S., Li, Q., Zhang, J., Lin, W., Dou, W.: Temporal-aware and sparsity-tolerant hybrid collaborative recommendation method with privacy preservation. Concurr. Comput.-Pract. Exp. **32**(2), 5447 (2020). https://doi.org/10.1002/cpe.5447

12. Li, Q., Hou, J., Meng, S., Long, H., Dou, W.: GLIDE: a game theory and data-driven mimicking linkage intrusion detection for edge computing networks. Complexity **2020**, 18 (2020). https://doi.org/10.1155/2020/7136160. Article Id 7136160

13. Hou, J., Li, Q., Meng, S., Ni, Z., Chen, Y., Liu, Y.: DPRF: a differential privacy protection random forest. IEEE Access **7**, 130707–130720 (2019). https://doi.org/10.1109/ACCESS. 2019.2939891

User Personalized Location k Anonymity Privacy Protection Scheme with Controllable Service Quality

Ting Liu[1], Guanghui Yan[1(✉)], Gang Cai[1], Qiong Wang[2], and Mingjie Yang[2]

[1] School of Electronic and Information Engineering,
Lanzhou Jiaotong University, Lanzhou, China
648979805@qq.com
[2] State Grid Gansu Information and Telecommunication Company,
Lanzhou, China

Abstract. The existing location privacy protection methods only provide the privacy protection parameter k for users to choose to achieve their personalized privacy protection requirements, but users can not control the quality of service. To this end, this thesis proposes a user personalized location k anonymity privacy protection scheme with controllable service quality. The quality of service is quantified according to service similarity, and both it and the degree of privacy protection are used as user-controllable parameters, which meets the user's more personalized privacy protection needs. At the same time, the background knowledge of historical query probability is quantified. The greedy strategy combined with the position entropy measurement mechanism is used to generate a k-anonymity set that can resist the attacker's background knowledge inference attack, and a perturbation location is selected to complete the anonymity. The performance comparison experiment results show that this method can obtain very good privacy protection performance and efficiency.

Keywords: Service similarity · Background knowledge · Location entropy

1 Introduction

The growing popularity of various location-based services (LBS) greatly facilitates users' travel and social activities, but also poses serious privacy threats to users, because untrusted LBS service providers or malicious attackers may illegally use or disclosure the location privacy of users [1, 2].

Scholars have proposed many methods to solve the problem of location privacy disclosure, such as policy control technology [3, 4], anonymous protection technology [5, 10–16] and encryption protection technology [6–8]. Among them, the location k anonymity technology is favored by researchers because of its convenient and efficient characteristics. There are numerous research results that use this type of technology as the basis for implementing LBS privacy protection methods [9].

Existing methods fail to achieve a good trade-off between the service quality of user's location service and the degree of location privacy protection. In addition, in the

© Springer Nature Switzerland AG 2020
X. Chen et al. (Eds.): ML4CS 2020, LNCS 12486, pp. 484–499, 2020.
https://doi.org/10.1007/978-3-030-62223-7_42

existing methods for realizing personalized privacy protection of users, users can only control the degree of privacy protection, but cannot control the required service quality, that is, they cannot meet the more personalized privacy protection requirements of users, and the resource overhead is large.

In response to the above problems, we present a user personalized location k anonymity privacy protection scheme with controllable service quality. Different from the existing methods, this method quantifies the quality of service, and both it and the degree of privacy protection are used as user-controllable parameters to achieve a more personalized location privacy protection for users. At the same time, the background knowledge of historical query probability is quantified. The greedy strategy combined with the location entropy measurement mechanism is used to generate a k anonymous set that can resist the attacker's background knowledge inference attack, and the use of perturbation location reduces the communication overhead. Compared with the existing methods, the experimental results show that the method can obtain very good performance and efficiency of privacy protection.

2 Related Work

Gruteser [10] proposed the location k anonymity technology, and used the quadtree search algorithm to realize the location k anonymity, completed the spatial generalization of the user's location, and quickly realized the protection of location privacy. However, the excessive anonymous area reduces the quality of service and increases the cost of resources, and the fixed privacy parameter k cannot provide users with personalized privacy protection. In order to solve the problems in reference [10], Mokbel et al. [11] proposed an improved k anonymity algorithm Casper. This method preferentially merges he sibling nodes when generating the anonymous region, reduces excess anonymous region, and adds the controllability of the privacy parameter k which can realize personalized privacy protection requirements of users.

Due to the complexity of spatial query calculation in anonymous region, researchers have proposed a fuzzy method to generate dummy locations to protect the location privacy. Kido et al. [12] used random strategy to generate dummy locations on map to achieve k anonymity. Rinku et al. [13] put forward the concept of service similarity, which improved the quality of service.

Most of the existing methods assume that the attacker does not have relevant background knowledge, so they cannot well resist inference attacks by attackers with background knowledge. In order to make the location privacy protection method have stronger ability to resist attacks, researchers have proposed location privacy protection methods that take into account certain background knowledge.

For example, the EPLA algorithm proposed by Zhao et al. [14] considers that the background knowledge of the user's query content is different in different locations. Zhang et al. [15] proposed the Cor-k algorithm to resist association matching attacks. Niu et al. [16] searched the location points close to the historical query probability of the user's location in the global scope of the map to generate an anonymity set to resist background knowledge attacks.

The location privacy protection method that incorporates a certain background knowledge shows a stronger degree of privacy protection, but the measurement standard of the degree of privacy protection is relatively single. Therefore, researchers have proposed the location entropy measurement mechanism [17] and applied it as a reference measurement index in the design process of location privacy protection methods to improve the degree of privacy protection [18, 19]. Among these methods, users can only obtain more personalized privacy protection by controlling the degree of privacy protection, and cannot control the required service quality.

3   Preliminaries

3.1   Service Similarity

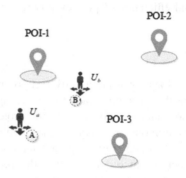

Fig. 1. Service similarity diagram

When users obtain LBS services at close locations, the query results obtained have a certain similarity. And the closer the distance, the greater the similarity of the query results, or even the same, that is, the service similarity [13]. As shown in Fig. 1, when users located at locations A and B and querying the points of interest (POI) closest to them respectively, they will get the same query result, namely POI-1, which shows high service similarity.

The service similarity between two locations can be measured according to the similarity of query results, the formula is

$$
\begin{aligned}
S_d &= S(A, B) \\
&= S((x_A, y_A), (x_B, y_B)), \quad 0 \le S_d \le 1 \\
&= \frac{F_r(x_A, y_A) \cap F_r(x_B, y_B)}{r}
\end{aligned}
\tag{1}
$$

$S(\cdot)$ is the service similarity calculation function; $F(x, y)$ is the query function; $F_r(x, y)$ is the first r query result sets at the location (x, y); r is the number of query results.

The query function and sorting rules are defined by the LBS server. By default, this thesis uses Euclidean distance sorting.

3.2 Quantitative Background Knowledge

This thesis only considers historical query probability background knowledge and quantifies it: for ease of processing, the map is divided into a $n \times n$ grid map. Each grid represents a location unit of equal size. Each location unit has a corresponding historical query probability, the calculation formula is:

$$P_{hi} = \frac{N_{qi}}{N_q}, \ i = 1, 2, 3, \cdots, n^2 \tag{2}$$

N_{qi} is the number of historical queries of location unit i; N_q is the total number of historical queries of all location units; and the ratio P_{hi} between N_{qi} and N_q is the historical query probability of location unit i.

3.3 Location Entropy Measurement Mechanism

Using location entropy to measure the strength of privacy protection. The greater the entropy, the greater the uncertainty of the attacker's identification of the user's location from the anonymous set. Therefore, the method in this thesis selects the k anonymous set with the largest entropy in the anonymous candidate region to improve privacy protection. The location entropy is defined as:

$$H = -\sum_{j=1}^{k} p_j log_2 p_j \tag{3}$$

H is the location entropy. When the recognition probabilities of the user in the anonymity set are all equal, the maximum entropy H_{max} can be obtained, $H_{max} = log_2 k$; p_j is the normalized historical query probability of the location in the anonymity set:

$$p_j = \frac{P_{hj}}{\sum_{j=1}^{k} P_{hj}} \tag{4}$$

3.4 Generate Label Similar Map

The original map is divided into a $n \times n$ grid map Map, each grid corresponds to a location unit m_{ij}, $Map = \{m_{ij} | i, j = 1, 2, 3, \cdots, n\}$. The LBS server divides the Map into label similar map (Lsm) based on service similarity, $Lsm = \{z_1, z_2, z_3, \cdots, z_q\}$, $1 \leq q \leq n^2$. Attach the N_{qi} of each location unit to Lsm to generate Lsm containing the number of historical queries.

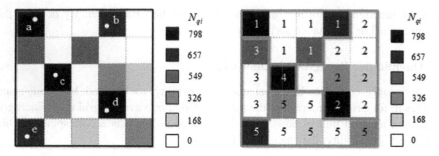

Fig. 2. 5×5 grid map *Map*   **Fig. 3.** *Lsm* containing N_{qi}

Figure 2 is a 5×5 grid map containing 5 POI. The generation steps of *Lsm* containing N_{qi} are as follows:

1. Generate query result table. Set $r = 3$, calculate the query results of each location unit according to the function $F_r(x, y)$, and get the query results table corresponding to the location unit one by one, as shown in Table 1.
2. Calculate service similarity S_d. According to the query results in Table 1 and Eq. 1 calculate the S_d between every two location units.

Table 1. Query results table

i	Query results				
	$j = 1$	$j = 2$	$j = 3$	$j = 4$	$j = 5$
1	$\{a,c,b\}$	$\{a,b,c\}$	$\{b,a,c\}$	$\{b,c,a\}$	$\{b,d,c\}$
2	$\{a,c,e\}$	$\{c,a,b\}$	$\{b,c,a\}$	$\{b,d,c\}$	$\{b,d,c\}$
3	$\{c,a,e\}$	$\{c,a,d\}$	$\{c,d,b\}$	$\{d,b,c\}$	$\{d,b,c\}$
4	$\{e,c,a\}$	$\{c,e,d\}$	$\{d,c,e\}$	$\{d,c,b\}$	$\{d,b,c\}$
5	$\{e,c,d\}$	$\{e,c,d\}$	$\{d,e,c\}$	$\{d,c,e\}$	$\{d,c,e\}$

3. Generate *Lsm*. Put the same label on the location unit of $S_d = 1$ and merge into the same partition to get *Lsm* containing different partitions.
4. Generate *Lsm* containing N_{qi}. The LBS server counts N_{qi} of each location unit and attaches it to *Lsm* to generate *Lsm* containing N_{qi}, as shown in Fig. 3.
5. Generate partition similarity table T. Calculate the S_d between each partition according to the query results in Table 1 and Eq. 1, and generate a service similarity table T for different partition, as shown in Table 2.

Table 2. Service similarity between different partitions

Partition	S_d				
	z_1	z_2	z_3	z_4	z_5
z_1	1.00	0.67	0.67	0.67	0.33
z_2	0.67	1.00	0.33	0.67	0.67
z_3	0.67	0.33	1.00	0.67	0.67
z_4	0.67	0.67	0.67	1.00	0.67
z_5	0.33	0.67	0.67	0.67	1.00

4 Location Privacy Protection Method

4.1 Anonymous Candidate Region Generation Conditions

To realize the user's more personalized privacy protection needs is to allow user to choose and control the location privacy protection degree and service quality by themselves. The privacy protection degree can be controlled by the privacy protection degree measurement parameter k. The service quality is the matching degree between the query results after anonymity and the query results before anonymity. The matching degree can be directly quantified by S_d, so S_d is taken as the control parameter of service quality.

In order to generate a location k anonymity set that meets the user's required quality of service and can effectively resist attackers' background knowledge inference attacks. Firstly, generate an Acr based on the value of the service quality measurement parameter input by the user, and then combined with the attacker's background knowledge, the k anonymity set with the largest entropy value is selected in the Acr. In order to ensure that the k anonymity set with the largest entropy value can be selected from the generated Acr, we conducted relevant experiments to verify and select the alternative generation conditions of the Acr. The experimental conditions are as follows: the number of location units in Acr should be greater than k; the number of location units in Acr should be as small as possible to ensure that the k anonymity set with the largest entropy value is generated. The experimental results are shown in Fig. 4.

The experimental results show that when the number of location contained in Acr is greater than or equal to $2k - 2$, a k anonymity set with entropy close to the optimal entropy can be generated, and the maximum entropy of the k anonymity set generated in each case is only 0.02–0.05 different from that of the optimal k anonymity set. Although increasing the number of location in Acr on the basis of $2k - 2$ will generate k anonymity set with entropy closer to or even equal to optimal entropy, it will also increase the computational overhead and the entropy increase space is small. In order to better guarantee the performance of all aspects of the location privacy protection method, another generation condition of Acr is set to the number of location in Acr is greater than or equal to $2k + 1$.

The *Acr* generation condition is: the number of location in *Acr* is greater than or equal to $2k + 1$; the service quality of each location in *Acr* is greater than or equal to the S_d value given by the user.

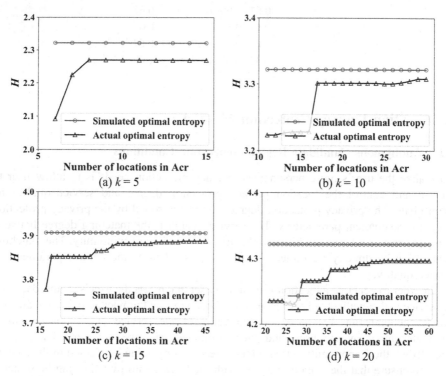

Fig. 4. The max H of k anonymity set vs. the number of location units in *Acr*

The experimental results show that when the number of location contained in *Acr* is greater than or equal to $2k - 2$, a k anonymity set with entropy close to the optimal entropy can be generated, and the maximum entropy of the k anonymity set generated in each case is only 0.02–0.05 different from that of the optimal k anonymity set. Although increasing the number of location in *Acr* on the basis of $2k - 2$ will generate k anonymity set with entropy closer to or even equal to optimal entropy, it will also increase the computational overhead and the entropy increase space is small. In order to better guarantee the performance of all aspects of the location privacy protection method, another generation condition of *Acr* is set to the number of location in *Acr* is greater than or equal to $2k + 1$.

The *Acr* generation condition is: the number of location in *Acr* is greater than or equal to $2k + 1$; the service quality of each location in *Acr* is greater than or equal to the S_d value given by the user.

4.2   User Personalized Location Privacy Protection Parameter Selection Comparison Table

This thesis studies the relationship between the privacy protection measurement parameter k, the service quality measurement parameter sd and the anonymity success rate through experiments, and a privacy protection parameter selection comparison table containing the value relationship among them is given to guide users to use location privacy protection method.

K takes a positive integer greater than or equal to 2; the value of S_d is related to the size of r. Therefore, examine the relationship between k, S_d, and anonymity success rate at different r values. In the experiment, $k = 5, 10, 15, 20, 30, r = 8, 10, 14, 20$. The experimental results are shown in Fig. 5.

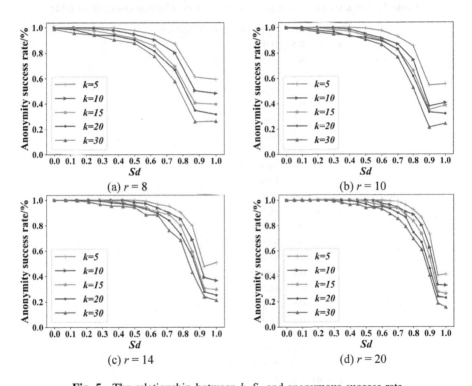

Fig. 5. The relationship between k, S_d and anonymous success rate

When r is larger, the search range of the POI query is larger, and the division of S_d is more detailed, so the partition on Lsm is also more detailed. Therefore, with the increase of r, the anonymity success rate corresponding to the location privacy protection method under the same k and S_d values is also greater, which is consistent with the experimental results.

It can be seen from Fig. 5. that under the same r value, when the k value is constant, as the S_d value continues to increase, the anonymity success rate continues to decrease.

Similarly, when the S_d value is constant, the anonymity success rate decreases with the increase of k value.

According to further research and analysis, under different r and k values, when $S_d < 0.5$, the anonymity success rate can reach an average of 99.09%. And when $r = 20$, the anonymity success rate under the same k and S_d values is higher than when r is other values. The query result when $r = 20$ is enough to meet the POI query service that users need daily. At this time, when the k value is different and $S_d < 0.5$, the service quality is low, but the anonymity success rate can reach an average level of 99.76%. Therefore, only a comparison table of the relationship between the partial k and S_d values and the anonymity success rate when $r = 20$, $S_d \geq 0.5$, and k takes different values is shown in Table 3.

Table 3. Location privacy protection parameters selection comparison table

k	S_d	Anonymity success rate (%)
$k = 10$	0.5	100
	0.55	99.5
	0.6	97.4
	0.65	96.4
	0.7	94.2
	0.75	90.8
	0.8	88.6
	0.85	80.3
	0.9	62.4
	0.95	33.0
	1.0	32.6
$k = 20$	0.5	96.9
	0.55	95.0
	0.6	94.6
	0.65	93.2
	0.7	89.9
	0.75	86.3
	0.8	74.4
	0.85	66.7
	0.9	46.0
	0.95	23.8
	1.0	22.8
$k = 30$	0.5	95.6
	0.55	94.4
	0.6	93.0
	0.65	89.2
	0.7	85.3
	0.75	79.0
	0.8	69.4
	0.85	60.8
	0.9	40.6
	0.95	18.5
	1.0	15.3

Combining this table, users can clearly choose the value of privacy protection parameters that meet their privacy protection needs according to the relationship between k, S_d and anonymity success rate. Realize more personalized location privacy protection with controllable service quality.

4.3 Anonymous Candidate Region Generation Algorithm

User personalized location k anonymity privacy protection scheme with controllable service quality allows users to choose degree of privacy protection and service quality according to their privacy protection needs.

In order to implement this method, an anonymous candidate region must first be generated based on the parameter values entered by the user, and then anonymity should be achieved on this basis.

Algorithm 1. Anonymous Candidate Region Generation Algorithm

---

1 Input: Lsm, T, k, S_d , user location L_u

2 Output: Acr

3 Determine the user's partition z_u on Lsm according to L_u ;

4 Combine T to sort other partitions in descending order according to the service similarity of z_u ;

5 $Acr \leftarrow z_u$

6 **while** $L_{count}(Acr) < 2k + 1$ **do**

7   Take out the partition z_i according to the partition order sorted in step 4;

8   **if** $T(z_u, z_i) \geq S_d$ **then**

9         $Acr \leftarrow z_i$

10 Return Acr

4.4 Perturbation Location Generation Algorithm

The greedy strategy can solve the optimal solution of the one-dimensional problem well, and the time complexity is low. Therefore, the greedy strategy is used to select the k anonymous set with the largest entropy in the Acr. Since all the location points in the k anonymous set can meet the service quality required by the user, a perturbation location is randomly selected in the anonymous set to request the LBS service query to reduce communication overhead.

Algorithm 1. Perturbation Location Generation Algorithm

---

1 Input: Lsm containing N_{qi}, Acr, k, L_u

2 Output: perturbation location L_p

3 On the Lsm containing N_{qi}, use Eq.2 to calculate the P_{hi} of each location unit on
   the Lsm;

4 $Acr \leftarrow Acr / L_u$

5 anonymous set $\leftarrow L_u$

6 **for** $(i=1; i \leq k-1; i++)$ **do**

7     $v \leftarrow 0$

8     $H_{max} \leftarrow 0.0$

9   **for** $(j=1; j \leq \text{sizeof}(Acr); j++)$ **do**

10   k anonymous set $\leftarrow Acr[j] \cup k$ anonymous set

11   Use Eq.4 and P_{hi} to calculate the p_j of the location in k anonymous set;

12   Calculate $H(k$ anonymous set$)$ using Eq.3 and p_j;

13   **if** $H(k$ anonymous set$) > H_{max}$ **then**

14             $H_{max} \leftarrow H(k$ anonymous set$)$

15             $v \leftarrow j$

16   k anonymous set $\leftarrow k$ anonymous set $/ Acr[j]$

17   k anonymous set $\leftarrow Acr[v]$

18     $Acr \leftarrow Acr / Acr[j]$

19 $\forall L_p \in k$ anonymous set

20 Return L_p

4.5 Security Analysis

The attacker can be divided into a passive attacker and an active attacker according to the means of execution. Due to PKI can effectively resist passive attacks, this thesis only considers inference attacks performed by active attackers attacking LBS servers.

Inference attack refers to an attack method where the attacker uses the background knowledge obtained by himself to infer the sensitive privacy information of the user at the k anonymous set.

An attacker who captures the LBS server can obtain all data information in the server. After receiving the perturbation location, the attacker tries to infer the user's true location based on the mastered background knowledge P_{hi} combined with the location privacy protection mechanism.

However, our method also considers P_{hi} when anonymizing, and in the k anonymous set with the largest entropy, the P_{hi} of each location is very similar, or even the same. Therefore, even if the attacker has background knowledge P_{hi}, he cannot infer the user's real location. In other words, our method can well resist the inference attacks of attackers with background knowledge P_{hi}.

5 Performance Evaluation

5.1 Experimental Environment and Performance Metrics

All experiments in this thesis are implemented using Python programming language coding, and use NA dataset [20] to verify the performance of the proposed method. The software and hardware environment is: Windows 10 64-bit professional operating system, Inter i7 processor, 64 GB memory.

Performance metrics:

1. Degree of location privacy protection: using H measurement.
2. Quality of service: using degree of query accuracy Q measurement. The calculation formula of Q is shown in Eq. 5.

$$
\begin{aligned}
Q &= \frac{|R(L_u) \cap R(A_S)|}{|R(A_S)|} \\
&= \frac{|R(L_u) \cap (R(L_1) \cap R(L_2) \cap R(L_3) \cap \cdots \cap R(L_k))|}{|R(L_1) \cap R(L_2) \cap R(L_3) \cap \cdots \cap R(L_k)|}
\end{aligned}
\tag{5}
$$

In Eq. 5, $R(A_S)$ is the query result set of A_s; $R(L_u)$ is the query result of the user's location; Q is the proportion of $R(A_S)$ that contains $R(L_u)$. The larger the Q, the higher the service quality.

3. Time overhead: based on the time measurement taken to complete anonymity.
4. Communication overhead: use k anonymous set or perturbation location query result metric.

5.2   Analysis of Experimental Results

The P_{hi} of the k anonymous set centralized locations generated by the optimal selection method are all equal, and the optimal entropy can be obtained, which is used as a benchmark to measure the degree of privacy protection of other methods.

DLS and Random methods can also provide users with personalized privacy protection, but users can only control the degree of privacy protection. Our method provides users with parameter control of degree of privacy protection and quality of service quality. The experimental conditions are $2 \leq k \leq 30$, $r = 20$, and $S_d = 0.5$. At this time, our method achieved achieves a better trade-off between privacy protection and service quality.

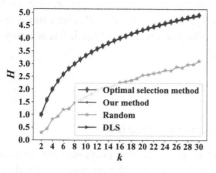

Fig. 7. H vs. k

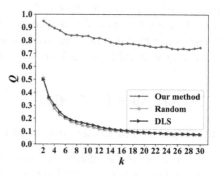

Fig. 8. Q vs. k

H vs. k. As Fig. 7 depicts, as k increases, the entropy of each method is also increasing. Among them, the entropy of the optimal selection method is the largest, and the entropy of the DLS is closest to the optimal selection method. The entropy of our method is only 0.5% lower than that of the optimal selection method on average, indicating that our method can provide a high degree of privacy protection. This is because our method also considers the attacker background knowledge. The Random method without considering the background knowledge of the attacker has the lowest privacy protection.

Q vs. k. Figure 8 shows that our method Q is very high, which is much higher than the DLS and Random methods which select k anonymous set in the global scope of the map. In other words, our method can provide users with a high quality of service. In the experiment, $S_d = 0.5$, therefore, the service similarity between each location unit in the Acr and the user's location is at least 0.5, so the generated perturbation location can obtain a high quality of service.

t vs. k. Figure 9 shows the time cost of each method. The Random method which using only the random selection strategy has the lowest time cost. According to the analysis, the time complexity of our anonymous algorithm is $O(k^2)$, the time complexity of the DLS method is $O(Nk^2)$, because DLS uses an exhaustive strategy to generate anonymous set. In general, $N \gg k$, so the time cost of our method is smaller than DLS. According to statistical analysis, the time cost of our method is 88.6% lower than the DLS on average.

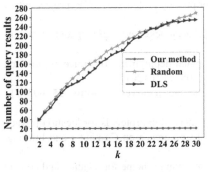

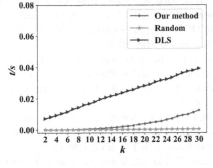

Fig. 9. t vs. k Fig. 10. Number of query results vs k

Number of query results vs. k. As can be seen from Fig. 10, our method has the lowest communication overhead and remains the same, because our method ultimately generates a perturbation location request query. However, the communication cost of DLS and Random methods that generate k anonymous set in the global scope of the map is much higher than our method. When $k = 30$, the number of query results reaches about 275, and the huge communication overhead seriously reduces the performance of the DLS and Random.

6 Conclusion

Our propose a new user personalized location k anonymity privacy protection scheme with controllable service quality.

Firstly, it quantifies quality of service and background knowledge, and provides users with controllable degree of privacy protection and quality of service control parameters. Then, using the greedy strategy combined with the location entropy measurement mechanism to generate k anonymous set that can resist the attacker's background knowledge inference attack. And choose to a perturbation location in the anonymous set to complete anonymity. This method can not only provide users with more personalized privacy protection, but the experimental results show that this method achieves a better trade-off between privacy protection and service quality, which can effectively resist attackers' background knowledge inference attacks, and has low time overhead and communication overhead.

References

1. Zhang, X.J., Gui, X.L., Wu, Z.D.: Privacy preservation for location-based services: a survey. J. Softw. **26**, 2373–2395 (2015)
2. Sheng, W., Fenghua, L., Ben, N., et al.: Research progress on location privacy-preserving techniques. J. Commun. **37**, 124–141 (2016)
3. World Wide Web Consortium (W3C). Platform for privacy preferences (P3P) project. http://www.w3.org/P3P. Accessed 6 May 2020
4. IETF. Geographic location/privacy (GeoPriv). http://datatracker.ietf.org/wg/geopriv/charter/. Accessed 6 May 2020
5. Sun, Y., Zhang, B., Zhao, B., et al.: Mix-zones optinal deployment for protecting location privacy in VANET. Peer-to-Peer Netw. Appl. **8**, 1108–1121 (2015)
6. Wang, L., Meng, X.F.: Location privacy in big data era: a survey. J. Softw. **25**, 693–712 (2014)
7. Di, C., Hao, L., Shilei, Z.: CSEP: circular shifting encryption protocols for location privacy protection. In: 2017 IEEE/ACIS 16th International Conference on Computer and Information Science (ICIS). IEEE (2017)
8. Peng, T., Liu, Q., Wang, G., Xiang, Y.: Privacy preserving scheme for location and content protection in location-based services. In: Wang, G., Ray, I., Alcaraz Calero, J.M., Thampi, S.M. (eds.) SpaCCS 2016. LNCS, vol. 10066, pp. 26–38. Springer, Cham (2016). https://doi.org/10.1007/978-3-319-49148-6_3
9. He, W.: Research on LBS privacy protection technology in mobile social networks. In: Advanced Information Technology, Electronic and Automation Control Conference, pp. 73–76. IEEE (2017)
10. Gruteser, M., Grunwald, D.: Anonymous usage of location-based services through spatial and temporal cloaking. In: Proceedings of the 1st International Conference on Mobile Systems, Applications and Services, pp. 31–42. ACM Press, New York (2003)
11. Mokbel, M.F., Chow, C.Y., Aref, W.G.: Casper*: query processing for location services without compromising privacy. ACM Trans. Database Syst. **34**, 1–48 (2009)
12. Kido, H., Yanagisawa, Y., Satoh, T.: An anonymous communication technique using dummies for location-based services. In: Proceedings of the International Conference on Pervasive Services, pp. 88–97. IEEE, Piscataway (2005)
13. Rinku, D., Ramakrisha, T.: Exploiting service similarity for privacy in location based search queries. IEEE Trans. Parallel Distributer Syst. **25**, 374–383 (2013)
14. Zhao, D., Zhang, K., Jin, Y., Wang, X., Hung, P.C.K., Ji, W.: EPLA: efficient personal location anonymity. In: Li, F., Shim, K., Zheng, K., Liu, G. (eds.) APWeb 2016. LNCS, vol. 9932, pp. 263–275. Springer, Cham (2016). https://doi.org/10.1007/978-3-319-45817-5_21
15. Lei, Z., Lili, Y., Jing, L., et al.: Location privacy protection algorithm based on correlation coefficient. In: Proceedings of the 4th International Conference on Control, Automation and Robotics (ICCAR), pp. 332–335. IEEE, Piscataway (2018)
16. Ben, N., Qinghua, L., Xiaoyan, Z., et al.: Achieving k-anonymity in privacy-aware location-based services. In: Proceedings of the 33th IEEE Conference on Computer Communications, pp. 754–762. IEEE, Piscataway (2014)
17. Jiang, T., Wang, H.J., Hu, Y.C.: Preserving location privacy in wireless LANs. In: Proceedings of the 5th International Conference on Mobile Systems, Applications and Services, pp. 246–257. ACM, New York (2007)
18. Xia, F., Yawei, L.: Dynamic Mix-zone scheme with joint-entropy based metric for privacy-perserving in IoV. J. Commun. **39**, 76–85 (2018)

19. Ni, L., Tian, F., Ni, Q., Yan, Y., Zhang, J.: An anonymous entropy-based location privacy protection scheme in mobile social networks. EURASIP J. Wirel. Commun. Netw. **2019**(1), 1–19 (2019). https://doi.org/10.1186/s13638-019-1406-4
20. Zhang, X.J., Gui, X.L., Jiang, J.H.: A user-centric location privacy-preserving method with differential perturbation for location-based services. J. Xi'an Jiaotong Univ. **50**, 79–86 (2016)

Attack and Repair Strategies for Computer Network About Viruses

Sheng Hong$^{(\boxtimes)}$ and Yue Wang

School of Cyber Science and Technology,
Beihang University, No. 37, Xue Yuan Road, Beijing 100191, China
shenghong@buaa.edu.cn

Abstract. The threat of computer viruses has become an increasingly important issue, so it is necessary to improve the protection of computer networks against computer viruses. This article puts forward the idea of using the curve area method to calculate the resilience of computer networks. In addition, three factors affecting computer networks in terms of computer viruses and four repair strategies for computer networks are studied. The results show that the increased infection rate and the increase in the number of initial infected nodes will not cause the network to crash; the medial-based attacks have the greatest impact on the network; the medial-based repair strategy is better than the balanced repair strategy and has the best repair effect on the network.

Keywords: Computer network · Network resilience · Scale-free network

1 Introduction

The globalization of computer networks has made more and more computers, portable phones, laptops, mp3 players and many electronic products that depend on computers in our daily lives. In this case, computer network viruses and their destructiveness pose a great threat to companies and individuals. With the increasing use of information technology (IT), the threat of computer viruses has become an increasingly important concern [1–3].

There are many ways to attack computers with the help of viruses. Some viruses only attack the core devices of a complex network. The Stuxnet virus in 2010 was the first virus to specifically attack real-world infrastructure, by infecting industrial control procedures at Iran's nuclear facilities and then gaining control of a key device called a centrifuge [4]. And Emotional Simian is the virus that specifically targets gatekeeper devices. Some viruses attack any host in a network. For example, the Brutal Kangaroo is a tool suite for attacking Microsoft windows, which breaks into closed computer networks through USB drives. When multiple computers in a closed network are invaded, they form a hidden network for data exchange and task collaboration.

With the help of computer virus propagation model, the propagation characteristics of computer virus are studied, and matrix theory and Lyapunov's first theorem are usually used to study the stability of computer networks [1–3, 5–9]. However, in the field of complex network, resilience not only emphasizes the ability to buffer the external impact factors, but also emphasizes the ability to recover the system function

© Springer Nature Switzerland AG 2020
X. Chen et al. (Eds.): ML4CS 2020, LNCS 12486, pp. 500–510, 2020.
https://doi.org/10.1007/978-3-030-62223-7_43

after the failure [10, 11]. Therefore, in this paper, we propose that resilience can be used to determine the stability and balance of the network. and on this basis, this paper also studies the three factors affecting computer network in terms of computer viruses and the advantages and disadvantages of four restoration strategies.

The remainder of this paper is organized as follows. Section II provides the method background of the research, recalling the definition of system resilience. Section III studies three factors that affect the stability of the network and four rescue strategies. Three factors that affect system stability are: optimization of parameters, initial number of infected nodes, and different attack methods. The four restoration strategies are random restoration, restoration based on degree, restoration based on betweenness and balanced restoration. Section IV is the conclusion of this paper.

2 Background of Method

2.1 Definition of System Resilience

As shown in Fig. 2, we define a quantifiable and time-dependent system performance function $F(t)$ that is the basis for the assessment of system resilience [13–15]. Under rated operating conditions, it is rated at $F(t_0)$. The system runs at this level until it suffers a disruptive event at the time te. Interrupt events usually reduce system performance to a certain level $F(t_d)$ at a moment in time t_d. Then, recovery action is started, improving system performance until it achieves the target level of target performance $F(t_r)$ at time tr. This target level $F(t_r)$ can be the same as, close to, or better than the original system performance $F(t_0)$. This paper considers the recovery to be complete at this point. The dotted curve in Fig. 2 represents the target system performance $\hat{F}(t)$ if not affected by disruption, which typically evolves due to the dynamic nature of service requirements and system upgrades. In this study, to simplify the explanation, it is assumed that it is equal to $F(t_0)$ and remains constant. In addition, we should note that there are various policies for recovery activities, and system performance ultimately depends on the recovery policy. We believe that this period $td \leq t \leq tr$ is generally considered to be the recovery time [14].

We define $R(t)$ as the resilience of the system at the time $t(t \geq t_d)$. The cumulative system function $R(t)$ that has been restored at time t is described in its basic form and is normalized by the expected cumulative system function, which, assuming that the system has not been affected by interference during that time period, is expressed as

$$R(t) = \frac{\int_{td}^{t}[F(\tau) - F(t_d)]d\tau}{\int_{td}^{t}[\hat{F}(\tau) - F(t_d)]d\tau}, t \geq t_d \tag{1}$$

As shown in Fig. 1, $R(t)$ is quantized by the ratio of the area having the oblique fringe S1 to the area of the shaded portion S2 [12].

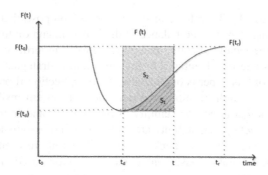

Fig. 1. Conceptual illustration of the proposed resilience measurement [12].

Note that Eq. (2) focuses primarily on the resiliency dimension, and $R(t)$ is in the range of $[0, 1]$. $R(t) = 0$ when $F(t) = F(t_d)$, which means that the system has not yet recovered from its interrupted state (that is, there has been no "resilience" action); $R(t) = 1$ when $F(t) = \hat{F}(t)$, which corresponds to the ideal situation where the system to return to its target state immediately after the disruption. This resilience quantification is consistent with the original meaning of the resilience concept and can simultaneously measure the size and speed of the system recovery operation. More importantly, this definition of system resilience is different from the cumulative consideration of restored system functions, which is not memoryless.

2.2   System Performance Representation

In the network composed of computers, each computer is equivalent to a node. With the help of SIR infectious disease model, nodes are divided into three types: nodes that have no protection ability and are susceptible to virus infection (S), nodes that are infected with virus (I), and nodes that have protection ability and will never be infected with such virus (R). The probability of the computer infected with the virus is referred to as infection rate, which is denoted as β; the probability that an infected computer can eliminate the virus is called the recovery rate, which is denoted as μ.

In this paper, network performance is defined as the sum of all the nodes on the network. Therefore, this paper also analyzes the operation ability of the three types of nodes.

In the article [14], it is pointed out that "after a computer is infected by a virus, its running speed will slow down obviously, the computer will crash frequently, the files will be deleted, the partition table of the hard disk will be damaged, and even the hard disk will be formatted illegally. What's more, it will cause damage to the computer hardware and it is difficult to repair it."

Ordinary users usually prevent the virus by installing the latest anti-virus software. But the security software itself needs to constantly monitor the file system, processes, user behavior, etc. to know the existence of harmful files, which take up CPU processing time and memory. So the security software will certainly slow down the system, especially some on some low-configuration computers.

In the process of computer operation, the system keeps reading and writing files and memory. This action can be imagined as pulling goods with trucks. System protection software is the equivalent of a checkpoint. Originally, the truck was going all the way from departure to arrival. Now all of a sudden there are checkpoints in the middle of the road, and every truck has to stop at the checkpoint to pass the inspection before it can continue on its way.

Through the above analysis, we can conclude that the ability of computer operation after virus infection decreases dramatically, even to 0. After installing anti-virus software, the running ability of the computer decreases slightly. Therefore, we define that computers in the state S have a running ability of a; computers in the state I have a running ability of b; computers in the state R have a running ability of c. Formally, the system performance function is defined as:

$$F(t) = S(N) * a + I(N) * b + R(N) * c \qquad (2)$$

where formula 2 satisfies $a, b, c \in [0, 1]$ and $a \geq c > b$.

In this study, time is discrete. Thus, the discrete time period $t = 1$ T is considered below instead of the continuous time period in the elastic definition of Eq. 2. Discretization of Eq. 2 yields Eq. 3:

$$R(T) = \frac{\sum_{t=1}^{t=T} [F(t) - F_{min}]}{T \cdot (F_{max} - F_{min})} \qquad (3)$$

wherein, $F(t)$ represents the performance of the entire network at any time, F_{min} represents the lowest network performance value during the [0, T] period, and F_{max} represents the maximum system performance value during the [0, T] period.

At the same time, in order to facilitate the calculation and analysis of the system performance, the parameters in formula 2 are taken as fixed values, that is, a = 1, b = 0, c = 0.95. Due to the scale-free nature of the computer network, the simulation is carried out on the BA scale-free network with 1000 nodes.

3 Simulation

3.1 Parameter Optimization on Resilience

The influence of parameters such as restoration rate μ and infection rate β on resilience was studied. The results are shown in Fig. 2 and Fig. 3. Each node in the graph is averaged over 200 iterations.

From Fig. 2, we can see that the trend of the curves is basically the same. Under the computer network, the parameter μ increases rapidly at first and then decreases slowly, and the peak value is around 0.1. In Fig. 3, it can be seen that the infection rate β is increasing under the BA scale-free network, with a large increase in (0, 0.1) and a slow increase in (0.1, 1).

Through the analysis, we can draw a conclusion that by improving the restoration rate within (0, 0.1), we can improve the network resilience, and continue to improve the restoration rate, it may cause the decline of network resilience. And an increase in infection rates does not cause the network to crash.

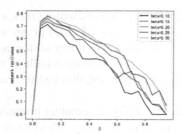

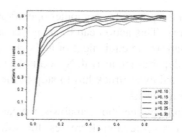

Fig. 2. The influence of parameter infection rate optimization on network resilience

Fig. 3. The influence of parameter restoration rate optimization on network resilience

3.2 The Influence of the Number of Infection Nodes on Network

Attacks on networks vary in scale. Sometimes it attacks just one computer. Sometimes it attacks a large number of computers simultaneously, such as botnets.

Botnet is defined as "a general computing platform constructed by invading a number of non-cooperative user terminals in cyberspace, which can be remotely controlled by attackers".

Notable attacks include the 2008 outbreak of the conficker botnet [17], which was so pervasive that it infected more than 10 million computers in a short period of time.

Therefore, in view of the above actual situation, this paper explores whether the increase of the number of initial fault nodes, that is, I nodes, will affect the size of network resilience, and whether it will cause network paralysis.

Within the scope of the value, the initial fault node value step size is 10, and the value of resilience is the result of 1000 iterations. The simulation results are shown in Fig. 4 below.

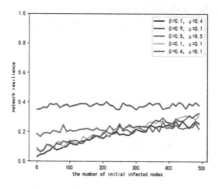

Fig. 4. Network resilience under different number of initial infected nodes

According to Fig. 4, we conclude that there is no network crash. At the same time, there was no significant relationship between resilience and the number of initial infected nodes.

Further, we compute the correlation coefficient between the initial number of infected nodes and the resiliency, as shown in Table 1 below:

Table 1. Correlation coefficient of initial infection node and resilience

Correl method of correlation coefficient	0.272
Pearson method of correlation coefficient	0.272

The correlation coefficient between the initial number of nodes and resilience is less than 0.3, so we assume that the initial number of nodes is independent of resilience.

3.3   The Effect of Different Attack Methods on Network

3.3.1   One-Time Deliberate Mass Attack

The attack to the general network can be divided into random attack and selective attack. Selective attack uses two different methods. The first method is based on degree, that is to say, the nodes with high degree in the network are infected in order. The second method is based on the betweenness, that is to say, the nodes with high betweenness in the network are infected first.

Each attack can be iterated 1000 times to obtain the average value of resilience. The simulation results are shown in Fig. 5. We can intuitively see that computer network has strong fault tolerance to random attacks of viruses, but it is vulnerable to selective attacks of viruses. What's more, the attacks based on betweenness are more harmful to the network than the attacks based on degree.

3.3.2   Persistent Attack

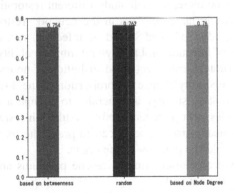

Fig. 5. Average resilience under three attacks

In addition to one-time mass attack, there are persistent attacks on a network in real life. This section selects the attack method based on the degree of nodes. Every time the network evolves, it attacks the network once, and it attacks 10, 50, 100, or 150 nodes each time. The results are shown in Figs. 6 and 7.

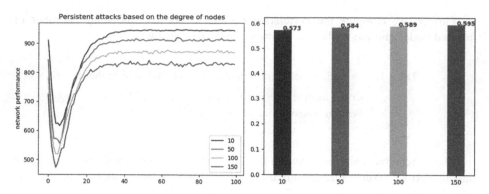

Fig. 6. Network performance with 10, 50, 100, and 150 attack nodes

Fig. 7. The average network resilience under the number of 10, 50, 100 and 150 attack nodes

Figure 6 shows that as the number of attacking nodes increases, the maximum proportion of infection increases but the duration of infection does not change much. Figure 7 shows that the network resilience does not change much, which is less than the resilience of a one-time mass attack. This shows that the damage of persistent attacks to the network is greater than that of one-time mass attacks. In Fig. 7, since the determination condition of the network stability does not change with the increase of the attack intensity, the network resilience gradually increases, but the impact is not great.

3.4   Comparison of Restoration Strategy

In the previous section, we only study the impact of different attack methods on complex networks. Furthermore, we will study different restoration strategies.

When viruses spread in large numbers in the network, restoration is often inevitable. In fact, in the process of rapid spread of infection, recovery operations often cannot change the risk of infection probability and immune ability in a short time [20]. However, restoration strategy can affect the distribution of nodes in different states in the network, that is, temporarily change the proportion of the three types of nodes S, I and R. In reality, restoration strategy is generally to change a certain proportion of infected nodes into nodes with protection ability. Although restoration behavior does not improve the final steady-state value, it can improve the maximum proportion of infections in the crisis and the duration of the crisis.

In addition, the choice of rescue timing, rescue programs and rescue efforts may affect the resilience of the network.

3.4.1   Selection of the Restoration Strategies

First of all, assuming that the restoration effort is 20%, it is to take 20% of the total infected nodes. This paper considers a total of four restoration strategies, and then in each strategy, the restoration was carried out when the proportion of infection was the largest. Finally, the advantages and disadvantages of each strategy were evaluated according to the value of network resilience. The four strategies are as follows:

- Strategy I: random restoration: randomly select the node to restore;
- Strategy II: restoration based on the degree of the node: the node with the larger node degree is recovered only after the node with the smaller node degree is recovered.
- Strategy III: restoration based on betweenness: after the node with the large betweenness is completely recovered, it will start to recover the node with the small betweenness.
- Strategy IV balanced restoration: the same proportion of recovery in all degrees

Figures 8 are simulation results. From Fig. 8, we can clearly see that the value of resilience obtained under the betweenness-based restoration strategy is 0.783, which is significantly higher than the value of resilience under other restoration strategies, which further shows that the importance of network nodes in the repair process is better measured by its betweenness rather than node degree.

In addition to resilience, the duration of infection is also a major indicator of our concern. As shown in Table 2 below, it shows the duration of infection under four restoration strategies. When the repair capability is limited, given the repair sequence based on the intervening method, the network can be restored to the normal state most quickly. The random restoration strategy is even lower than the balanced restoration strategy.

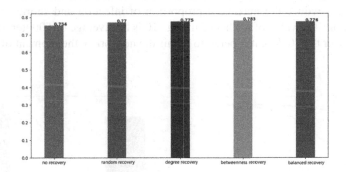

Fig. 8. Average resilience under four restoration strategies

Table 2. Infection duration under four restoration strategies

Restoration strategy	The moment when the maximum infection rate is reached	The moment of reaching steady state	Infection duration
Random restoration	6	78	71
Restoration based on the degree	6	64	58
Restoration based on betweenness	6	41	35
Balanced restoration	6	73	67

3.4.2 The Choice of Rescue Timing

In the article "Contagion and Bailout Strategy in Complex Financial Network" [18–20], it is pointed out that there are two critical restoration moments: the moment of maximum slope and the moment of maximum infection rate. The moment when the slope is maximum corresponds to the moment when the infected node increases fastest. The moment of maximum infection rate is the first moment that satisfies the nature that the infection rate will no longer exceed that moment after the rescue is carried out.

Figure 9 shows that the network performance curves after rescue at different times. From the figure, we can clearly see that rescue under the moment of maximum slope can effectively reduce the maximum proportion of infection and shorten the time of crisis infection. The value of resilience in Fig. 10 is the average of 500 iterations. Since 0.898 is greater than 0.806, it is better to repair the network at the moment of maximum slope.

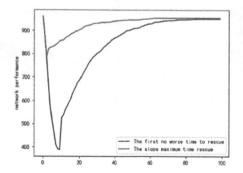

Fig. 9. Network performance curve at different repair moments

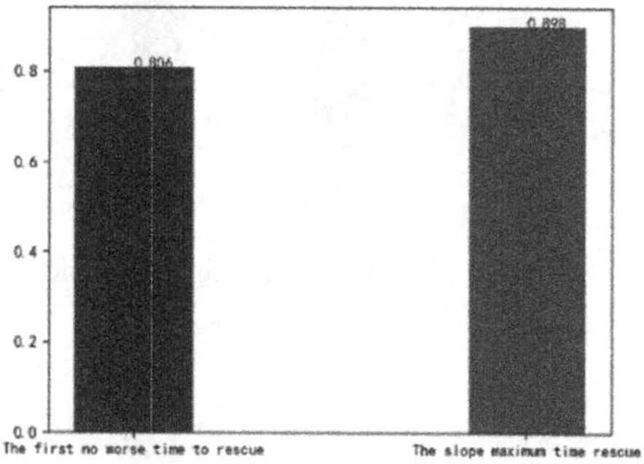

Fig. 10. Resilience at different repair moments

4 Conclusion

This paper uses the curve area method to calculate the resilience of the computer network, on this basis, three factors affecting the computer network and four restoration strategies in terms of computer viruses are studied. We conclude that:

1. The resilience calculated by the curve area method can be a good measure of computer networks.
2. The increase in the number of infected nodes and the infection rate will not cause a network crash.
3. Attacks based on betweenness have the greatest impact on the network. And the damage of persistent attacks to the network is greater than that of one-time mass attacks.
4. The restoration strategy based on the betweenness is superior to the balanced recovery strategy and the restoration effect is the best. What's more, it is better to repair the network at the moment of maximum slope.

Acknowledgments. The authors are highly thankful for National Key Research Program (2019YFB1706001), Industrial Internet Innovation Development Project (TC190H46B), National Natural Science Foundation of China (61773001).

References

1. Mishra, B.K., Jha, N.: SEIQRS model for the transmission of malicious objects in computer network. Appl. Math. Model. **34**(3), 710–715 (2010)
2. Mishra, B.K., Pandey, S.K.: Dynamic model of worms with vertical transmission in computer network. Appl. Math. Comput. **217**(21), 8438–8446 (2011)
3. Mishra, B.K., Saini, D.K.: SEIRS epidemic model with delay for transmission of malicious objects in computer network. Appl. Math. Comput. **188**(2), 1476–1482 (2007)
4. Donohue, I., et al.: Navigating the complexity of ecological stability. Ecol. Lett. **19**(9), 1172–1185 (2016)
5. Jung, E., Lenhart, S., Feng, Z.: Optimal control of treatments in a two-strain tuberculosis model. Discrete Continuous Dyn. Syst. Ser. B **4**, 473–482 (2002)
6. Zaman, G., Kang, Y.-H., Jung, I.-H.: Optimal treatment of an SIR epidemic model with time delay. Biosystems **1**, 43–50 (2009)
7. Ren, J.G., Yang, X.F., Zhu, Q.Y., et al.: A novel computer virus model and its dynamics. Nonlinear Anal. Real World Appl. **1**, 376–384 (2012)
8. Fei, S.-U., Lin, Z.-W., Yan, M.-A.: Modeling and analysis of Internet worm propagation. J. China Univ. Posts Telecommun. **17**(4), 63–68 (2010)
9. Yuan, J.L., Yang, Z.D.: Global dynamics of an SEI model with acute and chronic stages. J. Comput. Appl. Math. **2**, 465–476 (2008)
10. Gao, J., Baruch, B., Albert-László, B.: Author Correction: Universal resilience patterns in complex networks. Nature **568**(7751), 5–6 (2019)
11. Holling, C.-S.: Resilience and stability of ecological systems. Ann. Rev. Ecol. Syst. **4**(1), 1–23 (1973)
12. Fang, Y., Pedroni, N., Zio, E.: Resilience-based component importance measures for critical infrastructure network systems. IEEE Trans. Reliab. **65**(2), 502–512 (2016)

13. Barker, K., Ramirez-Marquez, J.E., Rocco, C.M.: Resilience-based network component importance measures. Reliab. Eng. Syst. Saf. **117**, 89–97 (2013)
14. Cimellaro, G.P., Reinhorn, A.M., Bruneau, M.: Framework for analytical quantification of disaster resilience. Eng. Struct. **32**(11), 3639–3649 (2010)
15. Baroud, H., et al.: Importance measures for inland waterway network resilience. Transp. Res. Part E Logist. Transp. Rev. **62**, 55–67 (2014)
16. Wang, X.: Harm and prevention of computer virus. Private Sci. Technol. **11**, 91 (2015)
17. Fang, B., Cui, X., Wang, W.: Overview of botnets. Comput. Res. Dev. **48**(08), 1315–1331 (2011)
18. Hu, Z., Li, X.: Contagion and bailout strategy in complex financial network. Finan. Trade Econ. **38**(04), 101–114 (2017)
19. Daron, A., Asuman, O., Alireza, T.-S.: Systemic risk and stability in financial networks. Am. Econ. Rev. **105**(2), 564–608 (2015)
20. Huser, A.-C.: Too interconnected to fail: a survey of the interbank networks literature. J. Netw. Theor. Finan. **1**(3), 1–50 (2015)

Vulnerability Variants and Matching in Networks

Meihui Lan[1](✉) and Wei Gao[2]

[1] School of Information Engineering, Qujing Normal University,
Qujing 655011, China
lanmeihui123@163.com
[2] Department of Mathematics and Science Education,
Faculty of Education, Harran University, Sanliurfa, Turkey
gaowei@ynnu.edu.cn

Abstract. In the network security research, the vulnerability of the network is always considered in the network designing stage, and there are some variables defined to measure the vulnerability from the perspective of graph theory. The most famous parameters are toughness and isolated toughness, which are also related to the existence of factional factor and path factor. In this article, we mainly study the relationship between the existence of matching extendable and some variants which connect with vulnerability of network. By means of graph theory tricks, several results are given from a theoretical perspective.

Keywords: Network · Vulnerability · Toughness · Matching

1 Introduction

The vulnerability of computer network is a hot topic in network security and computer design. From the point of view of network structure, the denser the network site is, the stronger it is; on the contrary, the network with sparse sites is vulnerable to attack. The network is modeled by graph. Let graph model $G = (V(G), E(G))$ represent a specific network, where $V(G)$ is a vertex set, each element of which corresponds to site, $E(G)$ is an edge set, and its element corresponds to channels between sites. From the perspective of graph theory, the larger the vertex cut or edge cut is, the stronger the graph is, and the stronger the ability to resist attacks is.

We only discuss simple graphs in this paper, i.e., undirected and finite graphs without multiple edges and loops. Let $G[S]$ be the subgraph deduced by $S \subseteq V(G)$, and write $G - S = G[V(G) \setminus S]$. For any $x \in V(G)$, let $N_G(x)$ and $d_G(x) = |N_G(x)|$ be the neighbourhood and the degree of x in G. A matching is a edge set in which no two edges have the common vertex, and a matching with

Supported by Design of equipment access system based on 3D printing cloud service platform (No. 2019530101000686).

X. Chen et al. (Eds.): ML4CS 2020, LNCS 12486, pp. 511–518, 2020.
https://doi.org/10.1007/978-3-030-62223-7_44

k edges is called a k-matching. Given a matching M, $V(M)$ is used to express the set of the vertices of the edges in M and $|M|$ is used to denote the edge number in M. A matching is called a perfect matching if $V(M) = V(G)$. The number of odd components and the number of components of G are denoted by $\omega_0(G)$ and $\omega(G)$, respectively.

Set M and M' as two different matchings of G, and we say that M is an extension of M or M can be extended to M if $M \subset M$. Assume G is a connected graph with perfect matchings. Graph G is called k-extendable if any k-matching can be extended to a perfect matching in G. We always require that $|V(G)| \geq 2k + 2$ for k-extendable graphs. Yu [17] introduced a concept of n-factor-critical graph, that is, after deleting any n vertices the resulting subgraph has a perfect matching.

Let G be a graph and n, k be non-negative integers with $|V(G)| \geq n + 2k + 2$ and $|V(G)| \equiv n \pmod 2$. Liu and Yu [18] extended the concepts of k-extendability and n-factor-criticality to (n, k)-extendable graph: if removing any n vertices from G the remaining subgraph contains a k-matching and further, each k-matching in this subgraph can be extended to a perfect matching. It is obvious that $(0, k)$-extendable graph is k-extendable graph and $(n, 0)$-extendable graph is exactly an n-factor-critical graph. A graph is called $E(m, n)$-extendable if removing edges of any n-matching, then the resulting subgraph is m-extendable. Specially, $E(m, 0)$-extendability is called m-extendability. Clearly, both (n, k)-extendability and $E(m, n)$-extendability are considered as general matching extensions. All notations and symbols used in this paper are standard in graph theory. If there are other special symbols, we will make a special explanation.

In the graph setting, the researchers use some variants to measure the vulnerability of networks, where toughness and isolated toughness are two classic parameters. Chvátal [1] first introduced the notation of toughness to test the vulnerable of networks: $t(G) = +\infty$ if G is a complete graph; otherwise

$$t(G) = \min\{\frac{|S|}{\omega(G - S)} : \omega(G - S) \geq 2\}$$

in which $\omega(G - S)$ is the number of connected elements of $G - S$. Yang et al. [2] borrowed the definition of isolated toughness which was stated below: if G is complete, then $I(G) = +\infty$; else wise,

$$I(G) = \min\{\frac{|S|}{i(G - S)}\Big| S \subset V(G), i(G - S) \geq 2\},$$

where $i(G - S)$ is the number of isolated vertices of $G - S$.

Enomoto et al. [3] introduced a variant of toughness, remarked as $\tau(G)$. If G is completed, then $\tau(G) = +\infty$; else wise,

$$\tau(G) = \min\{\frac{|S|}{\omega(G - S) - 1} : \omega(G - S) \geq 2\}.$$

For this variant, Enomoto [4] showed that $\tau(G) \leq \kappa(G)$ if G is not completed, where $\kappa(G)$ is a connectivity of graph G. Combining with the well-known fact that $\kappa(G) \leq \lambda(G) \leq \delta(G)$ for every graph G, we get

$$\tau(G) \leq \kappa(G) \leq \lambda(G) \leq \delta(G)$$

for a non-completed graph G, where $\lambda(G)$ and $\delta(G)$ are edge-connectivity and minimum degree of G, respectively.

Zhang and Liu [5] introduced a variant of isolated toughness, denoted by $I'(G)$. If G is completed, then $I'(G) = +\infty$; else wise,

$$I'(G) = \min\{\frac{|S|}{i(G-S)-1} \Big| S \subset V(G), i(G-S) \geq 2\}.$$

In computer science, many problems on network design, e.g., file transfer, building blocks, coding design, scheduling problems and so on, are connected to the factors and factorizations of graphs [6]. Specifically, the problem of file transfer can be transformed as factorizations of graphs. Meanwhile, the problem of telephone network design can be transformed into path factors of graphs. In recent years, the researchers found that there is strong relationship between vulnerability variants and the existence of path factor (see Zhou et al. [7–11] for more details). More related results on factor and fractional factor can be referred to Gao et al. [12–16].

The aim of our paper is to determine some sufficient conditions for the existence of matching in different settings from vulnerability variant point of view.

2   Matching Extendability in Networks

There are some well-known results on the existence of perfect matching and matching extend graphs. Tutte [19] pointed out that for graph G with even vertex number. Then G contains a perfect matching iff $\omega_0(G-S) \leq |S|$ holds for any $S \subseteq V(G)$. Let $f_c(G-S)$ be the number of factor-critical components of $G - S$. Lovász and Plummer [20] determined that for graph G with even vertex number. Then G contains no perfect matchings iff there exists a set $S \subset V(G)$ with $f_c(G-S) \geq |S| + 2$.

Our main result in this section is presented as follows which reveals the relationship between $\tau(G)$ and n-factor-critical graph.

Theorem 1. $n \in \mathbb{N}$. $\varepsilon > 0$ is a small constant and G is a graph with $\tau(G) \geq \varepsilon+1$ and $|V(G)| \equiv n\,(mod2)$. Then G is n-factor-critical if $\kappa(G) > \frac{(n-1)(1+\varepsilon)}{\varepsilon}$.

Proof. The tricks to prove this result mainly follow from Lu and Yu [21]. Assume that G is not a n-factor-critical graph, and thus there exists a subset S with $|S| = n$ satisfying that $G - S$ has no perfect matching. In light of Tutte's theory, there exists $T \subseteq V(G) - S$ satisfying $\omega_0(G - S - T) \geq |T| + 2$. Hence, we have

$$1 + \varepsilon \leq \tau(G) \leq \frac{|S| + |T|}{|T| + 1} \leq \frac{\kappa(G)}{\kappa(G) - n + 1}$$

which reveals

$$\kappa(G) \leq \frac{(n-1)(1+\varepsilon)}{\varepsilon}$$

a confliction.

Using the example presented in Lu and Yu [21], we can see that the connectivity condition in the theorem is tight. Moreover, we have the following corollaries.

Corollary 1. $n, k \in \mathbb{N}$. $\varepsilon > 0$ is a constant and G is a graph with $\tau(G) \geq \varepsilon + 1$. Then G is k-extendable if $\kappa(G) > \frac{(2k-1)(1+\varepsilon)}{\varepsilon}$.

Corollary 2. $n, m \in \mathbb{N}$. $\varepsilon > 0$ is a constant and G is a graph with $\tau(G) \geq \varepsilon + 1$. Then G is $E(m, n)$-extendable if $\kappa(G) > \frac{(2m+2n-1)(1+\varepsilon)}{\varepsilon}$.

3   Fractional k-Extendable Graph in Networks

Set $g(x) \leq f(x)$ as two integral valued functions defined on the vertex set of graph G, and $h(e) \in [0, 1]$ as a function defined on the edge set of G. Set

$$d_G^h(x) = \sum_{e \sim x} h(e),$$

where $e \sim x$ implies vertex x is associated with edge e. h is called a indicator function if for any $x \in V(G)$, we have $g(x) \leq d_G^h(x) \leq f(x)$. The spanning subgraph of G containing all edges with $h(e) > 0$ is called a fractional (g, f)-factor of G. A fractional (g, f)-factor is called a fractional k-factor if $g(x) = f(x) = k$ for any $x \in V(G)$.

Let G be a graph with order at least $2k + 2$ having a k-matching. Then G is called a fractional k-extendable if every k-matching M of G is contained in a fractional 1-factor such that $h(e) = 1$ for all $e \in M$. We also say that M can be extended to a fractional 1-factor of G. Obviously, G is fractional k-extendable iff for every k-matching M of G, $G - V(M)$ has a fractional 1-factor. If a graph has a fractional 1-factor, then we say that G is a fractional 0-extendable. A graph G is said to be a maximally fractional k-extendable if G is fractional k-extendable and for each $e \in E(\bar{G})$, $G + e$ is not fractional k-extendable, where $\bar{G}$ is the complement of G.

There are some known results on fractional k-extendable graphs (we always assume $k \in \mathbb{N}$):
• (Ma and Liu [22]) Let G be a graph with a k-matching and $k > 0$. Then G is fractional k-extendable iff

$$i(G - S) \leq |S| - 2k$$

established for any $S \subseteq V(G)$ such that $G[S]$ contains a k-matching.
• (Ma and Liu [22]) If G is a fractional k-extendable graph with $k \geq 1$, then G is also fractional $(k - i)$-extendable for any $i \in \{1, \cdots, k\}$.

- (Ma and Liu [22]) Graph G is fractional k-extendable iff for any i-matching M of G, $i \in \{1, \cdots, k\}$, $G - V(M)$ is fractional $(k - i)$-extendable.
- (Ma and Liu [22]) Let G be a graph with $|V(G)| \geq 2k + 4$ and F be any fixed 1-factor of G. If $G - V(e)$ is fractional k-extendable for each $e \in F$, then G is fractional k-extendable.
- (Ma and Liu [22]) Let G be a graph has a fractional 1-factor. Then G is maximal fractional k-extendable iff both of the following two conditions hold.
(1) $i(G - S) \leq |S| - 2k$ for all $S \subset V(G)$ where $G[S]$ has a k-matching.
(2) For any $e \in E(G)$, there exists a $T \subseteq V(G) - V(e)$ with $(k - 1)$-matching in $G[T]$ such that $i(G - V(e) - T) = |T| - 2k + 4$ or $i(G - V(e) - T) = |T| - 2k + 3$.
- (Ma and Liu [22]) Let G be a graph with a fractional 1-factor. If $i(G - S) \leq |S| - 2k$ for all $S \subseteq V(G)$ with $|S| \geq 2k$, then both of the following (1) and (2) hold.
(1) G is fractional k-extendable.
(2) $G + e$ is also k-extendable for any $e \in E(\overline{(G)})$.
- (Li and Yan [23]) $k \in \mathbb{N} \cup \{0\}$. Let G be a graph with $\kappa(G) \geq 2k + 2$, $I'(G) > k + 1$ and $|V(G)| \geq 2k + 2$. Then G is fractional k-extendable.
- (Li and Yan [23]) $k \geq 1$. Let G be a graph with $\kappa(G) \geq 2k + 1$, $I(G) > k + \frac{1}{2}$ and $|V(G)| \geq 2k + 2$. Then G is fractional k-extendable.
- (Li and Yan [23]) $k \geq 2$. Let G be a graph with $\kappa(G) \geq 2k + 2$, $I(G) > k$ and $|V(G)| \geq 2k + 2$. Then G is fractional k-extendable.
- (Li and Yan [23]) $k \geq 3$. Let G be a graph with $\kappa(G) \geq 2k + 2$, $I(G) > 1 + \frac{2k}{3}$ and $|V(G)| \geq 2k + 2$. Then G is fractional k-extendable.
- (Li and Yan [23]) $k \in \mathbb{N}$. Let G be a graph with $\kappa(G) \geq 2k + 1$, $I(G) > 1 + \frac{2k}{\kappa(G) - 2k + 1}$ and $|V(G)| \geq 2k + 2$. Then G is fractional k-extendable.

The necessary and sufficient condition for a graph with fractional 1-factor is given as follows which will be used later.

Lemma 1. (Liu and Zhang [24]) *A graph G has a fractional 1-factor if and only if $i(G - S) \leq |S|$ for any $S \subseteq V(G)$.*

The main result in this section is manifested as follows which studies the relationship between $I'(G)$ and fractional k-extendable graph.

Theorem 2. *Let $k \in \mathbb{N}$, G be a graph with $\kappa(G) \geq 2k + 1$, $I'(G) > 1 + \frac{2k+1}{\kappa(G) - 2k}$ and $|V(G)| \geq 2k + 2$. Then G is fractional k-extendable.*

Proof. Clearly, the result holds for complete graphs. In what follows, we assume G is not a complete graph. Let M be a k-matching of G, and thus $|V(M)| = 2k$. Set $G' = G - V(M)$. In terms of Lemma 1, we only need to check that $i(G' - S) \leq |S|$ for any $S \subseteq V(G')$. By means of $\kappa(G) \geq 2k + 1$, we acquire G' is connected.

If $S = \emptyset$, then $i(G' - S) = |S| = 0$. If $S \neq \emptyset$, we consider the following cases.

Case 1. $i(G' - S) \leq \kappa(G) - 2k$.
In this case, we have $\kappa(G') \geq \kappa(G) - 2k \geq 1$. If $G' - S$ is connected, then $i(G' - S) \leq 1 \leq |S|$. If G'-S is not connected, then $|S| \geq \kappa(G) - 2k$, we also have $i(G' - S) \leq |S|$.

Case 2. $i(G' - S) \geq \kappa(G) - 2k + 1$.

Since $i(G' - S) = i(G - V(M) - S) = i(G - (V(M) \cup S)) \geq \kappa(G) - 2k + 1 \geq 2$, we get

$$1 + \frac{2k+1}{\kappa(G) - 2k} \leq I'(G) \leq \frac{|S \cup V(M)|}{i(G - (V(M) \cup S)) - 1}$$

$$= \frac{|S| + |V(M)|}{i(G - V(M) - S) - 1} = \frac{|S| + 2k}{i(G' - S) - 1}.$$

It implies that

$$|S| + 2k \geq (1 + \frac{2k+1}{\kappa(G) - 2k})(i(G' - S) - 1)$$

$$= i(G' - S) + \frac{2k+1}{\kappa(G) - 2k} i(G' - S) - 1 - \frac{2k+1}{\kappa(G) - 2k},$$

and

$$|S| - i(G' - S) \geq \frac{2k+1}{\kappa(G) - 2k} i(G' - S) - 1 - \frac{2k+1}{\kappa(G) - 2k} - 2k$$

$$\geq \frac{2k+1}{\kappa(G) - 2k}(\kappa(G) - 2k + 1) - 1 - \frac{2k+1}{\kappa(G) - 2k} - 2k$$

$$= 0.$$

That is to say, in any case, we have $i(G' - S) \leq |S|$. Using Lemma 1, G' has fractional 1-factor. Therefore, G is fractional k-extendable.

4   Discussion

Toughness, isolated toughness and related parameters measure the ruggedness of a network, which is an important parameter to be considered in the network design stage, and is also the key research content of network security graph model calculation.

In this paper, the method of modern graph theory is used to study the correlation between matching extension and variables $I'(G)$ and $\tau(G)$ in the network, and two related conclusions are given. However, we didn't know how good the Theorem 2 is. Thus, we raise the following open problem as the end of paper.

Problem 1. What is the tight $I'(G)$ bound related to $\kappa(G)$ for a graph G to be fractional k-extendable.

Acknowledgments. We thank the reviewers for their constructive comments in improving the quality of this paper.

References

1. Chvátal, V.: Tough graphs and Hamiltonian circuits. Discr. Math. **5**, 215–228 (1973)
2. Yang, J., Ma, Y., Liu, G.: Fractional (g, f)-factors in graphs. Appl. Math. J. Chin. Univ. Ser. A **16**, 385–390 (2001)
3. Enomoto, H., Jackson, B., Katerinis, P., Saito, A.: Toughness and the existence of k-factors. J. Graph Theor. **9**, 87–95 (1985)
4. Enomoto, H.: Toughness and the existence of k-factors. II. Discr. Math. **189**, 277–282 (1998)
5. Zhang, L., Liu, G.: Fractional k-factor of graphs. J. Syst. Sci. Math. Sci. **21**(1), 88–92 (2001)
6. Alspach, B., Heinrich, K., Liu, G.: Orthogonal factorizations of graphs. In: Diuctz, J.H., Stinson, D.R. (eds.) Contemporary DesignTheory: A Collection of Surveys, pp. 13–37. Wiley, New York (1992)
7. Zhou, S.: Remarks on path factors in graphs. RAIRO Oper. Res. https://doi.org/10.1051/ro/2019111
8. Zhou, S.: Some results about component factors in graphs. RAIRO Oper. Res. **53**(3), 723–730 (2019)
9. Zhou, S., Wu, J., Zhang, T.: The existence of $P_{\geq 3}$-factor covered graphs. Discussiones Mathematicae Graph Theor. **37**(4), 1055–1065 (2017)
10. Zhou, S., Yang, F., Xu, L.: Two sufficient conditions for the existence of path factors in graphs. Sci. Iranica (2019). https://doi.org/10.24200/SCI.2018.5151.1122
11. Zhou, S.Z., Sun, Z.R.: Some existence theorems on path factors with given properties in graphs. Acta Math. Sinica Eng. Ser. **36**(8), 917–928 (2020). https://doi.org/10.1007/s10114-020-9224-5
12. Gao, W., Wang, W., Dimitrov, D.: Toughness condition for a graph to be all fractional (g, f, n)-critical deleted. Filomat **33**(9), 2735–2746 (2019)
13. Gao, W., Guirao, J.L.G., Chen, Y.: A toughness condition for fractional (k, m)-deleted graphs revisited. Acta Math. Sinica Eng. Ser. **35**(7), 1227–1237 (2019)
14. Gao, W., Guirao, J.L.G.: Parameters and fractional factors in different settings. J. Inequal. Appl. **2019**(1), 1–16 (2019). https://doi.org/10.1186/s13660-019-2106-7
15. Gao, W., Guirao, J.L.G., Abdel-Aty, M., Xi, W.: An independent set degree condition for fractional critical deleted graphs. Discrete Contin. Dyn. Syst. Ser. S **12**(4–5), 877–886 (2019)
16. Gao, W., Guirao, J.L.G., Wu, H.: Two tight independent set conditions for fractional (g, f, m)-deleted graphs systems. Qual. Theor. Dyn. Syst. **17**(1), 231–243 (2018)
17. Yu, Q.: Characterizations of various matching extensions in graphs. Austr. J. Combinator. **7**, 55–64 (1993)
18. Liu, G., Yu, Q.: Generalization of matching extensions in graphs. Discr. Math. **231**, 311–320 (2001)
19. Tutte, W.T.: The factorization of linear graphs. J. London Math. Soc. **22**, 107–111 (1947)
20. Lovász, L., Plummer, M.D.: Matching theory. Ann. Discr. Math. **29** (1986)
21. Lu, H., Yu, Q.: Binding Number, toughness and general matching extendability in graphs. Discr. Math. Theor. Comput. Sci. **21**(3), 1–8 (2019)
22. Ma, Y., Liu, G.: Some results on fractional k-extendable graphs. Chin. J. Eng. Math. **21**(4), 567–573 (2004)

23. Li, Z., Yan, G.: Some result on the graphic isolated toughness and the existence of fractional factor. Acta Math. Appl. Sin. **27**(2), 324–333 (2004)
24. Liu, G., Zhang, L.: Maximum fractional $(0, f)$-factors of graphs. Math. Appl. **13**(1), 31–35 (2000)

A File-Level Continuous Data Protection Scheme for Enforcing Security Baseline

Xiangxiang Jiang[1,2], Yuxi Ma[1], Gang Zhao[3], Xiaohui Kuang[3],
Yuanzhang Li[1], and Ruyun Zhang[4(✉)]

[1] School of Computer Science and Technology, Beijing Institute of Technology,
Beijing, China
jxxiang1996@163.com, mayucc@126.com,
popular@bit.edu.cn
[2] Artificial Intelligence and Blockchain, Guangzhou University,
Guangzhou, China
[3] National Key Laboratory of Science and Technology on Information
System Security, Beijing, China
zhao-gang20@126.com, xiaohui_kuang@163.com
[4] Zhejiang Lab, Hangzhou, Zhejiang, China
zhangry@zhejianglab.com

Abstract. Massive data is the basis of machine learning, and continuous data protection is an effective means to ensure data integrity and availability. At present, continuous data protection adopts the same backup strategy in different host security environments, ignoring the potential relationship between host security state and data destruction, resulting in a low utilization rate of backup storage space. To make better use of backup storage space and improve data recovery speed, this paper proposes a file-level continuous data protection scheme for enforcing security baseline (SB-CDP). SB-CDP combines a security baseline with continuous data protection to dynamically adjust the backup strategy based on the host security status provided by the security baseline. The experimental results show that, on the one hand, SB-CDP can effectively utilize the backup storage space, on the other hand, it can effectively improve the data recovery speed and reduce the impact on the system performance.

Keywords: Security baseline · File level continuous data protection · Full backup · Incremental backup · Quantitative analysis

1 Introduction

Machine learning is an important way to achieve artificial intelligence, and machine learning can not do without a lot of data support [1]. The completeness and availability of the data set will have a direct impact on the results of machine learning. The data will be threatened by natural disasters, human errors, malicious attacks, etc. and cause damage and loss [2]. Therefore, the protection of data to ensure the availability and integrity of data has attracted more and more attention. But a large number of data backups inevitably take up a large amount of storage space and result in long recovery time.

© Springer Nature Switzerland AG 2020
X. Chen et al. (Eds.): ML4CS 2020, LNCS 12486, pp. 519–529, 2020.
https://doi.org/10.1007/978-3-030-62223-7_45

In order to improve the effective utilization of backup storage space and improve the speed of data recovery, this paper proposes a file-level continuous data protection scheme for enforcing security baseline. The security baseline is the minimum safety guarantee of a system and can be considered as the shortest board of a safety barrel [3, 4]. Due to differences in equipment, applications, and security configuration strategies in different systems, there is no standard template for the construction of security baselines. However, the security baseline management system generally includes three parts: establishment and optimization of the security baseline, detection and control of the security baseline, and risk measurement and output [5]. The architecture diagram of the security baseline is shown in Fig. 1.

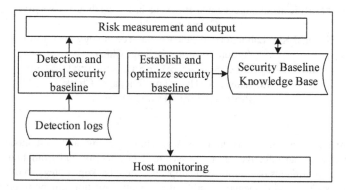

Fig. 1. The architecture diagram of the security baseline.

The rest of the paper is organized as follows: Sect. 2 introduces the research background and related work of file-level continuous data protection. Section 3 introduces the design and implementation of SB-CDP and then focuses on data backup and restoration. Section 4 introduces the process of using the quantitative analysis model to determine the full backup frequency. Section 5 gives the experimental results and analyzes storage overhead and restoration overhead. Section 6 summarizes the methods proposed in this paper.

2 Background and Related Works

File-level continuous data protection acts on the file system and achieves the purpose of continuous data protection by intercepting and recording changes in file data and metadata [6–8]. File-level continuous data protection can protect important files, but its backup and recovery performance will be worse than block-level continuous data protection. It is often used in scenarios where specific important files or data are protected.

The interception of file operations can be achieved by intercepting system calls or through FUSE [9–11] to implement a user-mode file system. For example, Wang et al. modified the kernel system call table through the loadable kernel module to monitor the

Linux file system in 2004 [12]. In 2015, a file-level continuous data protection cCDP based on cloud object storage proposed by Nagapramod et al. uses the user space file system FUSE to intercept file operations [13].

File-level continuous data protection mostly uses file operation logs or incremental backup to protect data. For example, in 2008, Huang et al. proposed a method for tracking and intercepting file operations by loading file filter drivers and recording the intercepted content in a log file in the form of reverse manipulation to achieve continuous file-level data protection [14]. In 2009, Sheng et al. proposed a centralized file-level continuous data protection method for differential storage, which uses a combination of mirroring and differential to record file changes on storage, thereby saving storage resources [15]. The file-level continuous data protection based on differential backup proposed by Ding et al. in 2010 not only realizes differential backup, reduces storage overhead, but also realizes file recovery from both directions, effectively shortening the recovery time [16].

3   System Architecture of SB-CDP

A file-level continuous data protection scheme for enforcing security baseline includes four modules: file configuration module, file operation interception and backup module, security baseline module, and file restoration module. The overall structure of SB-CDP is shown in Fig. 2.

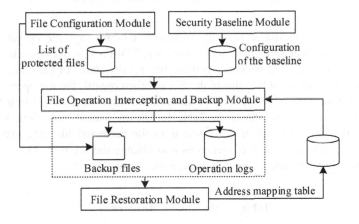

Fig. 2. The overall structure of SB-CDP.

The file configuration module is used to configure the files to be protected and perform a full backup of the initial files. The file operation interception and backup module is used to continuously capture and record changes to file data and metadata. The security baseline module is used to provide real-time host security status and backup strategies under different security conditions for the file operation interception and backup module. The file restoration module is used to perform file restoration according to the provided file path and restoration point in time.

3.1   Interception and Backup of File Operations

The file operation interception and backup module of SB-CDP is a user-mode file system CDPFS based on the userspace file system FUSE. CDPFS has the function of continuously capturing and recording file data and metadata changes. It determines whether the current file is a file that needs to be protected according to the file path, and if so, records the file operation. CDPFS's working principle is shown in Fig. 3.

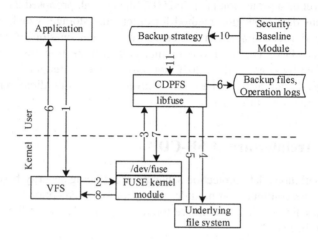

Fig. 3. The architecture diagram of CDPFS.

For file operations that change file metadata, CDPFS logs file operations to the database. For file operations that change file data, CDPFS first decides whether to use incremental backup or full backup based on the security status of the current host and the number of incremental backups of the file and then records the file operations to the database. The file operation types and additional information recorded in the database and restore operation are shown in Table 1. The truncation operation, the rename operation (the new file path after rename is in the protected file list), and the write operation are considered as file operations that change the file data. Other operations are considered as file operations that change file metadata.

Table 1. The table of file operations.

File operation	Additional Information	Restore operation
write	backup file path	ridff or rsync
rename	backup file path	ridff or rsync
truncate	backup file path	ridff or rsync
chown	uid, gid	lchown(path,uid,gid)
chmod	mode	chmod(path,mode)
mknod	mode, rdev	mknod(path,mode,rdev)
utimens	lastAccess, lastModify	utimensat(0,path,timespec,0)
unlink	null	unlink(path)

3.2   Data Restoration

The SB-CDP file restoration module, for a given restoration object and restoration point in time, combines file operation logs and full/incremental backup files to restore files to a specified point in time. The specific steps are as follows:

(1) Find a full backup in the database table that records the full backup of the file before the restoration time point and closest to the restoration time point;
(2) Copy this backup file to a temporary directory on the backup disk;
(3) Filter out the file operation log of the file between the full backup time point and the restoration time point in the database table recording the file operation log;
(4) The full backup file in the temporary directory combined with the file operation log filtered in (3) to reconstruct the file operation to form a restored file copy;
(5) Establish a mapping relationship between the protected file and the file copy in the backup disk;
(6) Copy the file in the backup disk to the protection disk;
(7) After the copy is completed, remove the mapping relationship and delete the file copy in the temporary directory.

Algorithm: restoration algorithm	
1:	**Input:** file path P, restoration point time T
2:	**Output:** restored file F
3:	R←GetReferenceFile(P,T)
4:	Copy file with file path R.path to temp file f
5:	L←GetOperationLog(P,T,R.time)
6:	**for** L_i **in** L
7:	redo(f, L_i)
8:	**end for**
9:	Establish a mapping relationship between p and f
10:	Copy temp file f to restored file F
11:	Remove the mapping relationship between p and f
12:	**return** F

4   Quantitative Analysis Model

4.1   Theoretical Analysis

To make more effective use of backup storage space and improve data restoration speed, the backup strategy is dynamically adjusted according to the security baseline. The frequency of full backup determines the storage overhead and restoration performance. Therefore, the frequency of full backup, that is, the number of incremental backups, is an important parameter in SB-CDP, which needs to be quantified to determine the appropriate value. For ease of description, the following symbols are defined, as shown in Table 2.

Table 2. Symbol description table.

Symbol	Symbol description
H_{t_1}	Host status at the time t_1
R	The host is in data restoration state
H_{t_2}	Host status at the time t_2
p_r	Probability of host data restoration
p_f	Probability of full backup stability
p_i	Probability of incremental backup stability
p_s	The probability that the host is in a safe state at the time t_2
N	Number of incremental backups in a backup cycle

In order to facilitate quantification, the following definitions are made and analyzed with the help of Bayesian network diagrams. Bayesian network is a kind of directed acyclic graph, which is used to describe the conditional dependencies between random variables [17, 18]. Random variables are represented by circles, conditional dependencies are represented by arrows, and the degree of dependency is represented by weights [19, 20].

Definition 1: The security status of the host is given by the security baseline. The security status of the host is divided into 0 to n levels. The higher the level, the more dangerous the host is, and the greater the probability p_r that data restoration is required.

Definition 2: The longer the restoration chain, that is, the greater the number of incremental backups N, the worse the reliability of the restoration. Note that the probability of stable existence of incremental backup is p_i, and the probability of full backup stability is p_f, then the probability of correct data restoration is $p_f \cdot (p_i)^{\frac{N}{2}}$.

Definition 3: The probability p_s that the host data is available at the moment t_2 is the sum of the probability that the host lost data at the previous moment and restored correctly at this time and the probability that the data did not lose data, ie: $p_s = (1 - p_r) + p_r \cdot p_f \cdot (p_i)^{\frac{N}{2}}$.

From the above definition, a Bayesian network diagram is shown in Fig. 4 and the following formula can be obtained.

$$N = 2 \cdot \log_{p_i} \frac{p_s + p_r - 1}{p_r \cdot p_f} \tag{1}$$

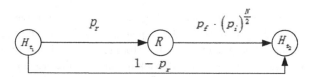

Fig. 4. Bayesian network diagram for quantitative analysis.

4.2   Quantitative Solution

The backup strategy is dynamically adjusted according to the results of real-time monitoring and analysis of the host by the security baseline, thereby improving the effective utilization of backup storage space and increasing the speed of data restoration. In order to determine the backup strategy of the host under different security states, the values of p_i, p_f and p_s, are shown in Table 3.

Table 3. Table of probability values.

Symbol	Value
p_i	0.99
p_f	0.98
p_s	0.95

Besides, the security status of the host is divided into 0 to 4 levels. The higher the level, the more dangerous the host is, and the greater the probability that data restoration is required. Table 4 shows the probability that the host needs to restore data in different security states.

Table 4. Host security status and the probability of data restoration required.

Host security status	Data restoration probability
0	0.15
1	0.35
2	0.55
3	0.75
4	0.95

According to the functional relationship of N and p_r in formula (1), the number of incremental backups N in one cycle can be calculated as shown in Table 5. This article will conduct experiments based on Table 5 to test and analyze the backup storage overhead and restoration time overhead of the host under different security states.

Table 5. Backup strategy for enforcing security baseline.

Host security status	Incremental backup times
0	76
1	26
2	14
3	9
4	6

5   Experimental Results

The experiment and analysis of SB-CDP are mainly divided into the following two parts: The first part is a comparative analysis of the backup storage overhead of the host under different security states. The other part is a comparative analysis of the restoration time overhead of the host under different security states. SB-CDP runs on Linux 4.4.58 system with 4G memory and 20G hard disk size. The database uses SQLite.

5.1   Storage Space Overhead

The starting file size is 10 MB. Under different backup strategies, an additional write operation is performed on the file, each 8 KB of data is added, and the number of additions is 50, 100, 150, 200 times. Figure 5 shows the backup storage space cost under different backup strategies.

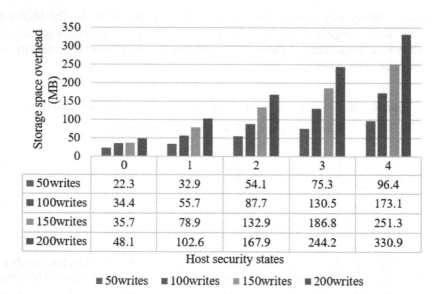

Fig. 5. Backup storage overhead for enforcing security baseline.

It can be seen from Fig. 5 that the more dangerous the host is, the more backup storage space is occupied. When the host is in a safe state, the probability of data corruption and loss is low, the full backup frequency is low, and the backup storage space is relatively small. When the host is in a dangerous state, the probability of data corruption and loss is high, the frequency of full backups is high, and more backup storage space is used.

5.2   Restoration Time Overhead

Under different backup strategies, perform five restoration operations on the files and calculate the average restoration time. The average restoration time under different backup strategies is shown in the broken line in Fig. 6.

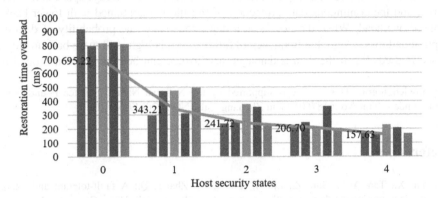

Fig. 6.   Restoration time overhead for enforcing security baseline.

It can be seen from Fig. 6 that the more dangerous the host state is, the shorter the restoration time is. When the host is in a safe state, the probability of data corruption and loss is low, so the frequency of full backup is low, and the restoration time will be longer. When the host is in a dangerous state, the probability of data corruption and loss is high, and the frequency of full backup is high. If data corruption and loss occurs, data restoration can be realized in a short time.

Dynamically adjusting the backup strategy according to the security status of the host provided by the security baseline can improve the effective utilization of backup storage space and increase the speed of data restoration after a disaster. When the host is in a more secure state, full backups are performed less frequently, and continuous protection of files is maintained with lower backup storage overhead. When the host is in a more dangerous state, the full backup frequency is higher, ensuring that data restoration can be completed in a short time after data is damaged or lost.

6   Conclusion

This paper proposes a file-level continuous data protection scheme for enforcing security baseline. Its main innovation lies in the combination of security baseline and continuous data protection and the real-time adjustment of backup strategy according to the host security state provided by security baseline, thus improving the effective utilization rate of backup storage space and the speed of baseline recovery.

At the time of backup, a combination of the full backup and incremental backup is used to back up file operations that change file data, and the frequency of full backup is dynamically adjusted according to the security status of the host given by the security baseline. The full backup frequency is determined through quantitative analysis by the Bayesian network. When the host is in a safe state, the probability of data corruption and loss is low, the full backup frequency is low, the backup storage space is relatively small, and the continuous data protection of the file is maintained with lower backup storage overhead. When the host is in a dangerous state, the probability of data corruption and loss is high, the frequency of full backups is high, and more backup storage space is used. But if the data is damaged and lost, it can be restored in a short time.

Acknowledgment. This work was supported by the National Natural Science Foundation of China under Grant No. 61876019 and Zhejiang Lab (NO.2020LE0AB02).

References

1. Yu, X., Tan, Y.A., Sun, Z., Liu, J., Liang, C., Zhang, Q.: A fault-tolerant and energy-efficient continuous data protection system. J. Ambient Intell. Hum. Comput. **10**(8), 2945–2954 (2019)
2. Yu, X., Zhang, C., Liang, C., Khaled, A., Zheng, J., Zhang, Q., et al.: A high performance hierarchical snapshot scheme for hybrid storage systems. Chin. J. Electron. **27**(1), 76–85 (2018)
3. Chen, Y., Wang, Q., Sun, M., Chen, P., Qiao, Z., Chen, Z.: Automatic security baseline verification method based on SCAP and cloud scanning. In: Liu, Q., Mısır, M., Wang, X., Liu, W. (eds.) CENet2018 2018. AISC, vol. 905, pp. 944–954. Springer, Cham (2020). https://doi.org/10.1007/978-3-030-14680-1_102
4. Jun, C., Jie, R., Hong, C., Yaping, W.: Automated security baseline verification based on SCAP. Comput. Era **4**, 9 (2016)
5. Yong-Hong, G.: Study and applications of operation system security baseline. Comput. Secur. **10** (2011)
6. Laden, G., Ta-Shma, P., Yaffe, E., Factor, M., Fienblit, S.: Architectures for controller based CDP. In: FAST, vol. 7, pp. 21–36 (2007)
7. Yang, Q., Xiao, W., Ren, J.: Trap-array: a disk array architecture providing timely restoration to any point-in-time. ACM SIGARCH Comput. Arch. News **34**(2), 289–301 (2006)
8. Chatterjee, P., Enoch, S.S., Narayanan, A.: Continuous data protection of files stored on a remote storage device (Apr 22 2014), US Patent 8,706,694
9. Vangoor, B.K.R., Tarasov, V., Zadok, E.: To FUSE or not to FUSE: performance of user-space file systems. In: 15th USENIX Conference on File and Storage Technologies (FAST 17), pp. 59–72 (2017)
10. Bent, J.M., Faibish, S., Gupta, U., Pedone, J.: Cluster file system with a fuse file system interface (Jan 2 2018), US Patent 9,858,290
11. Burihabwa, D., Felber, P., Mercier, H., Schiavoni, V.: SGX-FS: hardening a file system in user-space with Intel SGX. In: 2018 IEEE International Conference on Cloud Computing Technology and Science (CloudCom), pp. 67–72. IEEE (2018)
12. Wang, Y., Yu, S.J.: LINUX file system real-time monitoring method. J. Beijing Univ. Technol. 108–113 (2004)

13. Mandagere, N., Routray, R., Song, Y., Du, D.: Cloud object storage based continuous data protection (cCDP). In: 2015 IEEE International Conference on Networking, Architecture and Storage (NAS), pp. 244–254. IEEE (2015)
14. Huang, Z.G., Guo, Y.D., Yang, Z.B.: Design and implementation of file-level CDP. Comput. Appl. **28**, 277–279 (2008)
15. Sheng, Y.H., Liu, C.Y., Ju, D.P., Wang, D.S.: A centralized differential archiving method for file level continuous data protection. J. Front. Comput. Sci. Technol. **3**(4), 413–422 (2009)
16. Ding, H., Guo, Y.D., Dong, W.Y., Wang, L.X.: File-level continuous data protection based on differential backup. J. Inf. Eng. Univ. **11**(6), 692–695 (2010)
17. Li, X., Chen, G., Zhu, H.: Quantitative risk analysis on leakage failure of submarine oil and gas pipelines using Bayesian network. Process Saf. Environ. Protect. **103**, 163–173 (2016)
18. Hosseini, S., Barker, K.: A Bayesian network model for resilience-based supplier selection. Int. J. Prod. Econ. **180**, 68–87 (2016)
19. Wu, J., Zhou, R., Xu, S., Wu, Z.: Probabilistic analysis of natural gas pipeline network accident based on Bayesian network. J. Loss Prevent. Process Ind. **46**, 126–136 (2017)
20. Ojha, R., Ghadge, A., Tiwari, M.K., Bititci, U.S.: Bayesian network modelling for supply chain risk propagation. Int. J. Prod. Res. **56**(17), 5795–5819 (2018)

A Novel Method of Network Security Situation Assessment Based on Evidential Network

Xiang Li[1], Xinyang Deng[1(✉)], and Wen Jiang[1,2]

[1] School of Electronics and Information,
Northwestern Polytechnical University, Xi'an, China
xinyang.deng@nwpu.edu.cn
[2] Peng Cheng Laboratory, Shenzhen, China

Abstract. Network security situation awareness is a new type of network security technology. It evaluates the network security situation in real time from a macro perspective. Also it can predict the trend of the development of the network security situation, providing a basis for the decision analysis of administrators. It is difficult to obtain complete and accurate information in network security situation assessment by using evidential network. So we introduce an evidential network based on Bayesian network to solve that problem. Firstly, transform the parent node information and inference rules into plausibility function so as to be compatible with imperfect and inaccurate information. Secondly, we use the full probability formula of Bayesian network as reference to make similar reasoning under the framework of evidence theory. Then transform the inference result to BPA form by using the minimum specificity algorithm, and obtain the final result by projection. Finally, an example of network security situation assessment is given to illustrate the rationality and effectiveness of the method.

Keywords: Network security situation assessment · Evidence theory · Bayesian network · Evidential network

1 Introduction

In recent years, the rapid development of the Internet makes the use of computer systems more and more common and people have become more and more inseparable from the network. Network security has become a key issue related to all areas of the network. How to perceive the situation of network security in time and effectively has aroused enough attention from relevant researchers.

Network security situational awareness refers to that in the large-scale network environment, Network security situation awareness refers to the acquisition, understanding, display and prediction of future development trends of security elements that can cause changes in network security situation in a large-scale network environment [1, 2], which can provide direct and effective global information, real-time response capability "afterwards" and timely early warning capability "in advance" to realize dynamic security protection for security managers. Situation assessment is the core part of the network, which reflects the overall security status of the network by

© Springer Nature Switzerland AG 2020
X. Chen et al. (Eds.): ML4CS 2020, LNCS 12486, pp. 530–539, 2020.
https://doi.org/10.1007/978-3-030-62223-7_46

comprehensively analyzing the security factors of all aspects of the network. Tim Bass [3] introduced situational awareness into the field of network security for the first time. He believes that the fusion of multi-sensor data to form network situational awareness is the key breakthrough of the next generation intrusion detection system. Since then, research teams from different countries have proposed a variety of data models and platforms based on different knowledge systems.

Wen et al. [4] applied Bayesian network to evaluate network security situation. Ye et al. [5] used deep learning to extract the characteristics of large-scale network data, and analyzed and evaluated the network security situation. Vinayakumar [6] proposed a network security situation prediction method based on domain name systems data analysis. Chen et al. [7] proposed a hierarchical evaluation method, and obtained the three-level security threat situation by using the host, service and system for hierarchical calculation. Liu et al. [8] applied cloud models and Markov chain to carry out network security situation assessment.

None of the above methods fully consider the uncertainty and randomness of network security situation assessment. And each method has its own disadvantages, firstly the prior probability of Bayesian network is difficult to obtain. Then, for a deep learning model, it requires a lot of data and a lot of time to train the model and it is difficult to evaluate in real time. Finally, the hierarchical structure model and paired comparison matrix of AHP are mostly determined based on experience, with strong subjectivity.

Based on the comprehensive comparison of various methods, this paper chooses to use evidential network based on Bayesian network for evaluation. The existing evaluation methods mainly analyze the security events caused by attacks, and the threats caused by the peak of normal behavior are not investigated enough. Therefore, this paper comprehensively analyzes the normal behavior and attack behavior in the network environment to evaluate the network security situation.

The rest of the paper is arranged as follows. Section 2 briefly introduces D-S evidence theory and Bayesian network. In Sect. 3, the method proposed in this paper are introduced. An example of network security assessment is given in Sect. 4 to illustrate the effectiveness of the method in this paper. Finally, the conclusion is given in Sect. 5.

2 Preliminaries

2.1 Evidence Theory

Evidence theory [9, 10] is an imprecise reasoning theory first proposed by Dempster and further developed by Shafer, also known as The Dempster-Shafer Theory of Evidence. The subjective Bayes method must give the prior probability, while the evidence theory can deal with the uncertainty caused by ignorance. When the probability value is known, the evidence theory becomes the probability theory.

Assuming that Θ is the exhaustive set of all possible values variables X, and the elements are mutually exclusive. We call Θ frame of discernment (FOD). Assuming that there are N elements in Θ, $\Theta = \{A_1, A_2, \ldots, A_N\}$, so the number of the elements of the power set of Θ is 2^N, $2^\Theta = \{\{\emptyset\}, \{A_1\}, \ldots, \{A_N\}, \{A_1, A_2\}, \ldots, \{A_1, A_N\}, \ldots, \{\Theta\}\}$ and each member of the set corresponds to a subset of the values of X.

Definition 2.1. A basic probability assignment (BPA) is a function $m : 2^\Theta \rightarrow [0, 1]$, which satisfies:

$$\begin{cases} m(\emptyset) = 0 \\ \sum_{A \in 2^\Theta} m(A) = 1 \end{cases} \tag{1}$$

where A is any subset of Θ. The function $m(A)$ represents the evidence's support degree for A. A is called the focal element of m when $m(A) > 0$.

Definition 2.2. Given a BPA, the believe function Bel and the plausibility function Pl represent the lower and upper limits of the degree of trust for each proposition, respectively. The definition is as follows:

$$Bel(A) = \sum_{B \subseteq A} m(B) \qquad \forall A \subseteq \Theta \tag{2}$$

$$Pl(A) = 1 - Bel(\bar{A}) = \sum_{B \cap A \neq \emptyset} m(B) \qquad \forall A \subseteq \Theta \tag{3}$$

Definition 2.3. For a BPA, its specificity was measured by Sp function. The definition is as follows:

$$Sp = \sum \frac{m(A)}{|A|} \qquad \forall A \subseteq \Theta \tag{4}$$

Definition 2.4. If m is a BPA on a FOD Θ, a PPT function $BetP_m$ P: $\Theta \rightarrow [0, 1]$ associated with m is defined by

$$BetP_m(x) = \sum_{x \in A, A \in \Theta} \frac{1}{|A|} \frac{m(A)}{1 - m(\emptyset)} \tag{5}$$

where $m(\emptyset) \neq 1$ and $|A|$ is the cardinality of proposition A.

2.2   Bayesian Network

A Bayesian network [11] is a directed acyclic graph (DAG), which is composed of variable nodes and directed edges. The nodes represent random variables, and the directed edges between nodes represent the relations between nodes (from the parent node to the child node). The relationship strength is expressed by conditional probability, and the information is expressed by prior probability for a node without parents. It is suitable for expressing and analyzing uncertain and probabilistic events, and for making decisions that depend on various control factors conditionally. It can make inferences from incomplete, inaccurate or uncertain knowledge or information [12].

Definition 2.5. Assuming that $G = (I, E)$ represents a DAG, where I represents the set of all nodes in the graph, and E represents the set of directed connection edges. $X = X_i i \in I$ is the random variable represented by a node i in the DAG. The conditional probability distribution of node X can be expressed as:

$$p(x) = \prod_{i \in I} p\left(x|x_{pa(i)}\right) \tag{6}$$

where $x_{pa(i)}$ represents the cause of a node i.

For any random variable, its joint distribution can be obtained by multiplying their local conditional probability distributions:

$$P(X_1 = x_1, \ldots, X_n = x_n) = \prod_{i=1}^{n} P(X_i = x_i | X_{i+1} = x_{i+1}, \ldots, X_n = x_n) \tag{7}$$

Bayesian network is probabilistic reasoning, and it can be extended to evidential network reasoning within the framework of evidence theory [13].

3   The Proposed Method

In this section, an evidential network model is introduced to network security assessment based on approaches in evidence theory [14]. There are two problems when reasoning by traditional evidential network [15]: Firstly, the information of the parent node is difficult to express completely and accurately, and it is difficult to obtain the information of the root node when the number of focal elements in the parent nodes is large. Then, for a non-parent node, the size of its conditional belief mass table increases exponentially with the rise of the cardinalities of its parents' FODs. On one hand, the size of such table is huge; On the other hand, it is a big challenge to generate such a huge conditional belief mass table.

Aiming at the two problems, the solution of this paper is proposed as follows: Firstly, Transform the parent node information from the expression of BPA to the expression of plausibility function Pl. Then, transform the reasoning rules from the conditional belief mass table to conditional plausibility function table. This makes the network still able to reason in the case of incomplete inference rules. As shown in Fig. 1 shows the process of this method.

Step 1. Construct an evidential network. An evidential network is defined as a directed acyclic graph (DAG). For example, there are three nodes, including two parent nodes X with FOD $\Theta_X = \{X_1, X_2\}$, Y with FOD $\Theta_Y = \{Y_1, Y_2\}$, and a child

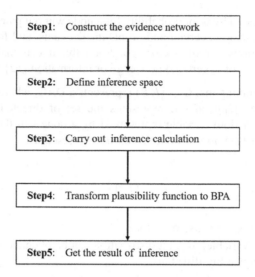

Fig. 1. A flowchart of the introduced evidential network.

node of X and Y called Z with FOD $\Theta_Z = \{Z_1, Z_2\}$. We can construct an evidential network show in Fig. 2. The parent node represents the network parameters obtained, and the child node represents the network security situation evaluation results. The evidence network may have more than one layer.

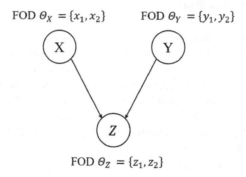

Fig. 2. An example of evidential network.

Step 2. By simplifying an extension operator given in [14], we use it to do the evidential network reasoning. As modelled in [14], the space composed of the parent node FOD called E_e, the space composed of the child node FOD called E_s. For example, in the evidential network shows in Fig. 2, $E_e = \{\Theta_X, \Theta_Y\}$ and $E_s = \{\Theta_Z\}$. $Pl_e(\cdot)$ is the plausibility function on E_e, which may be incomplete; $Pl_s(\cdot|B \subseteq E_e)$ is the plausibility function on E_s, which may be incomplete, and is valid when the subset B of E_e is definitely true. If the information we obtain on parent nodes is BPA and the rules we obtain is conditional belief mass table, we can use the formula (3) to transform to the plausibility function $Pl_e(\cdot)$ and the conditional plausibility function table $Pl_s(\cdot|B\subseteq E_e)$. If the information on parent nodes and rules are plausibility function and conditional plausibility function table respectively, we can skip this step.

Step 3. Determination of the $Pl_{sr}(A \times B)$ values on $E_s \times E_r$, for all available data, using the formula from [14]:

$$Pl_{sr}(A \times B) = Pl_s(A|B\subseteq E_r)Pl_e(B) \tag{8}$$

where $Pl_{sr}(\cdot)$ represents a joint distribution plausibility function.

Step 4. There are many such $m(\cdot)$ functions, rather than just one, will satisfy an incompletely defined plausibility function. In order to obtain the $m(\cdot)$ on space E and keep as much information as we can and don't impose information, we use the minimum specificity algorithm proposed by Appriou [14] to transform plausibility function to BPA. Thus, out of all the possible functions, we look for the function that has least specificity $Sp(m)$.

Step5. Determination of the mass function $m_s(\cdot)$ on Es on the basis of $m_{sr}(\cdot)$, using the formula:

$$m_s(A) = \sum_{B\subseteq E_r} m_{sr}(A \times B) \tag{9}$$

So far, we have obtained the inference result of the child node, and we can proceed to the next inference or evaluate the situation of the child node according to this result.

4 Case Study

In this section, an example mentioned in paper [16] will be used to confirm the effectiveness of the proposed method. Because the security of network will be affected by the peak of normal behavior and attack behavior, this paper divides the network security into normal behavior and attack behavior to consider the network security situation. The change of network resources will reflect the change of network security situation. CPU resources and memory resources are important resources in the network. Improper use of the network or when the network is attacked, the two resources may be exhausted, resulting in network performance degradation or even crash. Therefore, this paper selects CPU utilization and memory consumption as security factors to evaluate the network security situations.

Step 1. According to the above analysis, an evidential network is constructed as follows (Fig. 3):

In the evidential network MC, CPU, NB, AB and NS represent memory consumption, CPU utilization, normal behavior, attack behavior and network security respectively. And the FOD of MC, CPU, NB, AB have two elements $\Theta = \{G_1, G_2\}$, G_1 and G_2 represent the good and bad for assessment of the FOD.

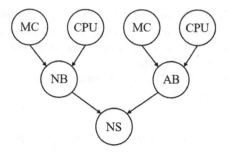

Fig. 3. The evidential network we construct for network security situation assessment [16].

The FOD of NS have four elements $\Theta = \{G_1, G_2, G_3, G_4\}$. Elements from G_1 to G_4 means excellent, good, ordinary and bad.

Step 2. Network security has a greater impact on CPU utilization. Compared with normal behavior, the harm caused by attack behavior to network environment is much more serious. In order to simplify the calculation, we assume that the conditional plausibility function table between memory consumption, CPU utilization and normal behavior and attack behavior is same. For the evidential network, suppose we have the following conditional plausibility function Tables 1 and 2.

Table 1. The conditional plausibility function table between {CPU, MC} and {NB}/{AB}.

CPU \ MC	$\{G_1^1\}$	$\{G_2^1\}$	$\{G_1^1, G_2^1\}$
$\{G_1^2\}$	$Pl(G_1) = 1$ $Pl(G_2) = 0.1$ $Pl(G_1, G_2) = 1$	$Pl(G_1, G_2) = 1$	
$\{G_2^2\}$	$Pl(G_1) = 0.8$ $Pl(G_2) = 0.3$ $Pl(G_1, G_2) = 1$	$Pl(G_1) = 1$ $Pl(G_2) = 0.8$ $Pl(G_1, G_2) = 1$	
$\{G_1^2, G_2^2\}$			

From the conditional plausibility function table, we can see that the inference rules are incomplete and imprecise. For example, we do not have the information when CPU is G_1, G_2 while MC is G_1. And the description of child node is fuzzy when CPU is G_1 while MC is G_1.

Table 2. The conditional plausibility function table between {AB, NB} and {NS}.

AB \ NB	$\{G_1^3\}$	$\{G_2^3\}$	$\{G_1^3, G_2^3\}$
$\{G_1^4\}$	$Pl(G_1, G_2) = 1$ $Pl(G_3, G_4) = 0.2$	$Pl(G_1, G_2) = 0.8$ $Pl(G_3, G_4) = 0.3$	
$\{G_2^4\}$	$Pl(G_1) = 0.8$ $Pl(G_2) = 0.6$ $Pl(G_3, G_4) = 0.4$	$Pl(G_1, G_2) = 0.3$ $Pl(G_3) = 0.6$ $Pl(G_4) = 0.5$	
$\{G_1^4, G_2^4\}$			

Then for the evidential network, assume we have the information of the parent node as follows:

$$m_{MC1}(\{G_1\}, \{G_2\}, \{G_1, G_2\}) = (0.6, 0.3, 0.1)$$
$$m_{CPU1}(\{G_1\}, \{G_2\}, \{G_1, G_2\}) = (0.8, 0.1, 0.1)$$
$$m_{MC2}(\{G_1\}, \{G_2\}, \{G_1, G_2\}) = (0.7, 0, 0.3)$$
$$m_{MCPU2}(\{G_1\}, \{G_2\}, \{G_1, G_2\}) = (0.9, 0.05, 0.05)$$

When reasoning from MC and CPU to NB, we can find that $E_r = \{MC, CPU\}$, $E_s = \{NB\}$. Other reasoning processes are similar as above.

Step 3. Compute the $Pl_{sr}(A \times B)$ values on $E_s \times E_r$ with formal (8). When reasoning from MC and CPU to NB, the result of $Pl_{sr}(A \times B)$ as follow:

$$Pl_{sr}\big(\{G_1, G_2\} \times \{G_1^1, G_1^2\}\big) = 0.63 \qquad Pl_{sr}\big(\{G_1, G_2\} \times \{G_2^1, G_1^2\}\big) = 0.36$$
$$Pl_{sr}\big(\{G_1, G_2\} \times \{G_2^1, G_2^2\}\big) = 0.08 \qquad Pl_{sr}\big(\{G_1, G_2\} \times \{G_1^1, G_2^2\}\big) = 0.14$$
$$Pl_{sr}\big(\{G_2\} \times \{G_1^1, G_1^2\}\big) = 0.063 \qquad Pl_{sr}\big(\{G_1\} \times \{G_2^1, G_1^2\}\big) = 0.288$$
$$Pl_{sr}\big(\{G_2\} \times \big(G_2^1, G_1^2\big)\big) = 0.108 \qquad Pl_{sr}(\{G_1\} \times \{G_2^1, G_2^2\}) = 0.08$$
$$Pl_{sr}\big(\{G_2\} \times \{G_2^1, G_2^2\}\big) = 0.064$$

By the same way, we can obtain $Pl_{sr}(A \times B)$ between {MC, CPU} and {AB}.
Step 4. Transform $Pl_{sr}(A \times B)$ to $m_{sr}(A \times B)$ by minimum specificity algorithm in Sect. 3. The result are as follows:

$$m_{sr}(\{G_1, G_2\} \times \{G_2^1, G_1^2\}) = 0.108 \qquad m_{sr}(\{G_1, G_2\} \times \{G_1^1, G_1^2\}) = 0.063$$
$$m_{sr}(\{G_1\} \times \{G_2^1, G_1^2\}) = 0.497 \qquad m_{sr}(\{G_1, G_2\} \times \{G_1^1, G_2^2\}) = 0.072$$
$$m_{sr}(\{G_1\} \times \{G_1^1, G_1^2\} \cap \{G_1, G_2\} \times \{G_1^1, G_2^2\}) = 0.064$$
$$m_{sr}(\{G_1, G_2\} \times \{G_1^1, G_2^2\} \cap \{G_1\} \times \{G_2^1, G_1^2\}) = 0.058$$
$$m_{sr}(\{G_1, G_2\} \times \{G_1^1, G_2^2\} \cap \{G_1\} \times \{G_2^1, G_2^2\}) = 0.01$$
$$m_{sr}(\{G_1\} \times \{G_2^1, G_1^2\}) = 0.122$$

Step 5. Compute the mass function $m_s(\cdot)$ on Es on the basis of $m_{sr}(\cdot)$ by formal (9). The result are as follows:

$$m_{NB}(\{G_1\}, \{G_1, G_2\}) = (0.625, 0.375)$$
$$m_{AB}(\{G_1\}, \{G_1, G_2\}) = (0.7455, 0.2545)$$

So far, we obtain the information on nodes NB and AB. In order to obtain the information on node NS, we just need to regard the NB and AB as parent nodes and repeat the above procedures. Finally, the BPA on node NS as follows:

$$m_{NS}(\{G1, G2\}, \{G1, G2, G3\}, \{G1, G2, G4\}, \{G1, G2, G3, G4\})$$
$$= (0.4687, 0.0573, 0.0477, 0.4265)$$

We can assess the network security situation according to the result. For example, we transform the BPA to probability by PPT function to make the assessment more intuitive.

The result computed by the formal (5) is as follows:

$$P(G_1) = 0.3759 \qquad P(G_2) = 0.3759$$
$$P(G_3) = 0.1257 \qquad P(G_4) = 0.1225$$

We can conclude that the current network security situation is at a good level.

5   Conclusion

This paper has mainly studied the evaluation of network security situation based on evidential network and evaluate the network security situation by evidential network based on Bayesian network. Firstly, D-S evidence theory and Bayesian network are introduced, and then an evidential network based on Bayesian network is proposed to evaluate network security situation. Finally, an example is given to verify the feasibility of the method.

Acknowledgment. The work is partially supported by National Natural Science Foundation of China (61703338, 61671384), Equipment Pre-Research Fund (61400010109).

References

1. Li, Z., Goyal, A., Chen, Y., et al.: Towards situational awareness of large-scale botnet probing events. IEEE Trans. Inf. Foren. Secur. **6**(1), 175–188 (2011)
2. Gong, Z., Zhuo, Y.: Research on network situational awareness. J. Softw. **7**, 131–145 (2010)
3. Bass, T.: Intrusion detection systems and multisensor data fusion: creating cyberspace situational awareness. Commun. ACM **43**(4), 99–105 (2000)
4. Wen, Z., Cao, C., Zhou, H.: Network security situation assessment method based on naive Bayesian classifier. Comput. Appl. **35**(8), 2164–2168 (2015)
5. Ye, L., Tan, Z.: A network security situation assessment method based on deep learning. Intell. Comput. Appl. **9**(06), 73–75+82 (2019)
6. Vinayakumar, R., Poornachandran, P., Soman, K.P.: Scalable framework for cyber threat situational awareness based on domain name systems data analysis. In: Roy, S.S., Samui, P., Deo, R., Ntalampiras, S. (eds.) Big Data in Engineering Applications. SBD, vol. 44, pp. 113–142. Springer, Singapore (2018). https://doi.org/10.1007/978-981-10-8476-8_6
7. Chen, X., Zheng, Q., Guan, X., et al.: Quantitative hierarchy threat evaluation model for network security. J. Softw. **17**(4), 885–897 (2006)
8. Liu, H., Liu, J., Hui, X.: Network security situation assessment based on cloud model and Markov Chain. Comput. Dig. Eng. **47**(6), 1432–1436 (2019)
9. Dempster, A.P.: Upper and lower probabilities induced by a multivalued mapping. Ann. Math. Stat. **38**(2), 325–339 (1967)
10. Shafer, G.: A Mathematical Theory of Evidence. Princeton University Press, Princeton (1976)
11. Yakowitz, J.: An introduction to Bayesian Networks. Technometrics **39**(3), 336–337 (1997)
12. Terent'Yev, A.N., Bidyuk, P.I.: method of probabilistic inference from learning data in Bayesian networks. Cybern. Syst. Anal. **43**(3), 391–396 (2007)
13. Simon, C., Weber, P., Evsukoff, A.: Bayesian networks inference algorithm to implement Dempster Shafer theory in reliability analysis. Reliab. Eng. Syst. Saf. **93**(7), 950–963 (2008)
14. Appriou, A.: Uncertainty theories and multisensor data fusion. In: ISTE (2014)
15. Deng, X., Jiang, W.: Dependence assessment in human reliability analysis using an evidential network approach extended by belief rules and uncertainty measures. Ann. Nucl. Energy **117**, 183–193 (2018)
16. Cheng, S., Niu, Y., Li, J., Tong, K., et al.: A method of network security situation assessment based on evidential reasoning rules. Comput. Dig. Eng. **46**(8), 1603–1607 (2018)

Research and Application of Digital Signature Technology

Yanli Wang[1,2], Ying Zheng[1], and Fengyin Li[1(✉)]

[1] School of Information Science and Engineering, Qufu Normal University,
Rizhao 276826, China
Lfyin318@126.com
[2] School of Computer Science, Nankai University, Tianjin 300071, China

Abstract. With the development of science and technology, the spread of images on the Internet is getting faster and faster, which also reduces the cost of infringement and brings immeasurable losses to image creators. In order to solve the problem of digital image infringement, this paper uses encryption algorithm and signature algorithm to design a verifiable message delivery scheme based on timestamp, and applies it to the copyright protection of digital image, designs and implements a copyright protection system based on digital signature and timestamp. Our system provides a new reference solution for the copyright registration protection of digital images, realizes the protection of digital image copyright through a small amount of encryption and decryption operations and a small amount of information transmission. After analysis, our copyright protection system has high computing efficiency and security, the calculation efficiency and advantages are more prominent when transmitting large data information, and it has good application prospects.

Keywords: Digital signature · Timestamp · RSA · Hybrid encryption

1 Introduction

Digital and Internet make it very convenient and efficient to copy and spread information. Digital images can also be copied and spread at a very low cost, which makes digital images easy to be stolen and infringed. In the fields of news, design, photography, e-commerce, the phenomenon of image theft is particularly prominent. Rampant phenomenon of image theft has brought incalculable losses to the image creators. However, due to the difficulties of identification of image theft and the high cost of litigation, the infringed often choose to swallow the image infringement, which also contributes to the proliferation of the phenomenon of image theft. Therefore, the research of copyright protection technology has become one of the key problems to be solved.

The ultimate purpose of copyright protection is not "how to prevent use", but "how to control use". The key of Internet copyright protection [15] is to find a balance between promoting the development of Internet and protecting the interests of copyright owners.

© Springer Nature Switzerland AG 2020
X. Chen et al. (Eds.): ML4CS 2020, LNCS 12486, pp. 540–546, 2020.
https://doi.org/10.1007/978-3-030-62223-7_47

This paper uses the advantages of symmetric encryption algorithm and asymmetric encryption algorithm [7], combined with timestamp [1,13], to propose a new verifiable message delivery algorithm based on timestamp. The algorithm not only reduces the number of encryption and decryption, but also transmits less encrypted information. The computing efficiency and advantages of the algorithm are more prominent when transmitting large data information.

First, according to the message digest algorithm [2,14,16] to calculate the hash value of the picture. The sender adds a timestamp to the message digest and authenticates the time when the picture is generated, so as to verify whether the picture has been edited or not. Then perform mixed encryption, and the receiver decrypts the ciphertext through the mixed decryption algorithm. In this process, the sender and receiver deliver a timestamp message instead of a message digest, which further reduces the amount of information transmitted and improves the communication efficiency.

2   Proposed RSA Digital Signature Scheme

RSA cryptosystem was proposed by Rivest, Shamir and adlem in 1978 [3]. It can be used for both encryption and digital signature [4,12]. The security of RSA [5] is based on the difficulty of large prime number decomposition. Because RSA's public key and key are a pair of prime numbers. For example, the information to be transmitted is added to prime number A and B when encoding, and then transmitted to the receiver after encoding. Even if the data is intercepted, if there is no private key of the receiver, decryption is actually the process of decomposing the two prime numbers. From this point of view, RSA algorithm process is relatively simple, the key is to find a large enough prime number (the larger the prime number, the more complex the decryption process).

Digital signature [6] is an authentication mechanism that allows message senders to attach code as a digital signature. Public key cryptosystem is suitable for encryption model and authentication model [8]. Digital signature is a process in which the signer signs a message with his private key, and then the verifier verifies the signature with the public key of the signer. Nowadays, with the development of cryptography, digital signature has become an important branch, especially in identity authentication, data integrity, non repudiation and anonymity.

The specific steps of RSA digital signature [9–11] are as follows:

(1) Key generation:

- Two different prime numbers p and q are selected.
- Calculate product $n = p \times q$, $\Phi(n) = (p - 1) \times (q - 1)$.
- Select a random integer e greater than 1 and less than $\Phi(n)$, so that gcd $(e, \Phi(n)) = 1$; Note: gcd is the maximum common divisor.
- Calculate d to make $d \times e = 1 \bmod \Phi(n)$; Note: $(d \times e) \bmod \Phi(n) = 1$.
- Finally, RSA key generation algorithm takes (e, n) as the public key and d as the private key.

(2) Signature:

$$S = M^d \bmod n$$

Where s is the signature and M is the message digest. The sender sends the message and signature (m, s) to the receiver.

(3) Verify:

The receiver decrypts s using the sender's public key (e, n) to get M'

$$M' = S^e \bmod n$$

Compare the two message digest. If $M = M'$, the verification succeeds; otherwise, the verification fails.

The digital signature process is as follows (see Fig. 1):

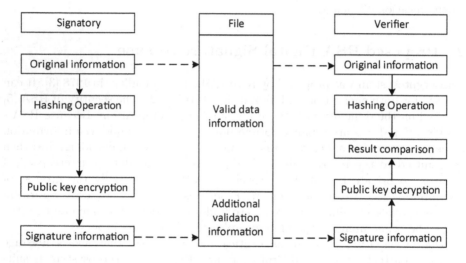

Fig. 1. Digital signature

3 Verifiable Message Delivery Scheme Based on Timestamp

3.1 Verifiable Message Delivery Scheme

This paper combines symmetric encryption and asymmetric encryption algorithms to cover the message digests to be transmitted with timestamp information, and proposes a verifiable message delivery scheme based on timestamps. The specific process of the scheme is as follows (see Fig. 2):

(1) The sender first performs a hash operation on the information to generate a message digest M, and adds a timestamp TS (timestamp TS is generated by the sender's system) to M, and saves it in the system.

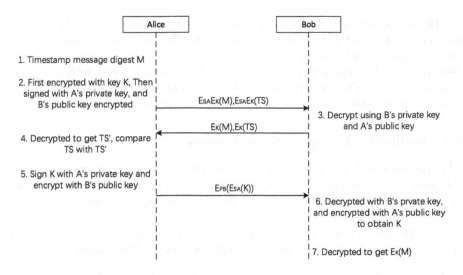

Fig. 2. Verifiable message delivery scheme based on timestamp

(2) The sender uses the symmetric key K to encrypt the time-stamped message digest M to obtain $E_K(M)$ and $E_K(TS)$. The sender uses the symmetric key K to encrypt the time-stamped message digest M to obtain $E_K(M)$ and $E_K(TS)$. Then use own private key for digital signature to get $E_{SA}(E_K(M))$ and $E_{SA}(E_K(TS))$. Finally, it is encrypted with the receiver's public key and sent to the receiver.

(3) After receiving the encrypted message, the receiver first decrypts it with its private key to get $E_{SA}(E_K(M))$ and $E_{SA}(E_K(TS))$. Then use the public key of the sender to decrypt it to get $E_K(M)$ and $E_K(TS)$. This verifies the legitimacy of the sender.

(4) Because the sender does not know the symmetric key K, it cannot decrypt the message $E_K(M)$. Therefore, the receiver directly transmits the encrypted timestamp message $E_K(TS)$ to the sender.

(5) After receiving the encrypted timestamp message $E_K(TS)$, the sender decrypts it with the symmetric key K to obtain a timestamp TS', and then compares it with the timestamp TS stored in the system. If $TS' = TS$, the receiver has received the encrypted message.

(6) The sender uses his own private key to sign the symmetric key K, and then uses the receiver's public key to encrypt the signed key message, and then sends it to the receiver.

(7) After receiving the encrypted key message, the receiver decrypts it with its own private key, and then decrypts it with the sender's public key to obtain the symmetric key K.

(8) The receiver then uses the symmetric key K to decrypt the received encrypted message $E_K(M)$ to obtain the message digest M'.

(9) If the message digest $M = M'$, the data is complete, the plaintext has not been changed, and the digital signature is valid; otherwise, it is invalid.

The innovation of this scheme is to introduce timestamp, reduce the times of data encryption and decryption, and also reduce the time of confirming information encryption and decryption, and improve the efficiency of data encryption, decryption and transmission while ensuring the reliability and security of data transmission and the non-repudiation of sender and receiver, which is more suitable for the occasion with high data transmission requirements.

3.2 Verifiable Message Delivery Process

This process combines RSA algorithm and digital signature algorithm, so that the message sent is not only encrypted, but also with digital signature, which can greatly increase its security. The following is the specific process:

(1) Key generation

The key generation is to obtain the public and private keys. In this method, there is a symmetric key K, two public keys and two private keys.

- Random selection of prime numbers p and q. Prime numbers p and q are public.
- Calculate $g = h^{(p-1)/q} \bmod p$, where $1 < h < p - 1$ and the parameter g is public.
- Generate temporary symmetric key K
- Generate the first private key x, $x < q$
- Generate the first public key y, where $y = g^x \bmod p$
- Calculate $n = pq$
- Calculate $\varphi(n) = (p-1)(q-1)$
- Generate the second public key e, where e is prime with respect to $\varphi(n)$
- Generate the second private key d, where $d = e^1 \bmod \varphi(n)$

After generating the keys, two public and two private keys are obtained. The first public and first private keys are created digitally, and the other public and private keys are used for encryption and decryption.

(2) Encryption and signature

This process is to transform the message digest into encrypted message (ciphertext) and add a digital signature to the message. C, for ciphertext, M_1 for timestamp message digest, r and s for its digital signature.

- Get the ciphertext. Symmetric encryption results in $C_1 = E_k(M_1)$, asymmetric encryption results in $C_2 = M_1^e \bmod n$, $C = C_1 + C_2$
- Randomly select the integer k, where $0 < k < q$
- Calculate $r = (g^k \bmod p) \bmod q$
- Digital signature $s = k^{-1}[M_1 + xr] \bmod q$

(3) Decryption and verification

The process is to convert the ciphertext into a message digest and verify the digital signature.

- Get a message digest. $M_1 = C^d \bmod n$

- Calculate $w = s^{-1} \bmod q$
- Calculate $u_1 = M_1 w \bmod q$
- Calculate $u_2 = rw \bmod q$
- Calculate $v = ((g^{u1} y^{u2}) \bmod p) \bmod q$

If $v = r$, the received digital signature is valid; otherwise, the received digital signature is invalid.

4 Concluding Remarks

In this paper, a new verifiable message delivery algorithm based on timestamp is proposed by using the advantages of symmetric encryption algorithm and asymmetric encryption algorithm. The algorithm not only reduces the number of encryption and decryption, but also transmits only a small timestamp information, not a large amount of encrypted information. The calculation efficiency and advantages of the algorithm are more prominent when transmitting large data information. Based on the verifiable message delivery algorithm proposed in this paper, this paper implements a digital image copyright protection system, which solves the problems of tedious registration of copyright, difficulty in image identification, and long litigation time by legal means. With stable low service cost, real-time registration processing and tamper proof registration information, it provides a new reference solution for the copyright registration protection of digital images, and provides a convenient platform for creators to register, simplify the confirmation of rights and safeguard rights.

References

1. Making Timestamps a New Tool for Copyright Protection (2016)
2. Baohu Duan, J.W.: New discussion on digital signature technology. Comput. Eng. Sci. (2009)
3. Barrett, P.: Implementing the Rivest Shamir and Adleman public key encryption algorithm on a standard digital signal processor. In: Odlyzko, A.M. (ed.) CRYPTO 1986. LNCS, vol. 263, pp. 311–323. Springer, Heidelberg (1987). https://doi.org/10.1007/3-540-47721-7_24
4. Gao, L.: Research on digital signature technology based on public key algorithm. Master's thesis, Southwest University of Science and Technology (2018)
5. Hu, J.: Research and implementation of RSA encryption algorithm. Ph.D. thesis, Anhui University of Technology (2011)
6. Huang, S.: Application of RSA digital signature algorithm in software encryption. Appl. Netw. Secur. Technol. 04, 84–86 (2018)
7. Jiang, C.: Asymmetric encryption algorithm. Neijiang Sci. Technol. 8–148 (2012)
8. Lu, K.: Computer Cryptography. Tsinghua University Press, Beijing (2003)
9. Sun, W.: Improvement and implementation of public key RSA encryption algorithm. Ph.D. thesis, Anhui University (2014)
10. Wang, X.: Design of two digital signature schemes. Ph.D. thesis, Guizhou Normal University (2017)

11. Chen, Y., Peiqiang Cong, Z.C.: An improved scheme of elliptic curve digital signature. Res. Inf. Secur. **005**(003), 217–222 (2019)
12. Zhang, R.: Research and application of digital signature. Ph.D. thesis, Shaanxi Normal University (2015)
13. Zhang, S.: Research on a trusted timestamp service system based on identity authentication. Master's thesis, Graduate School of Chinese Academy of Sciences (National Time Service Center) (2016)
14. Zhang, X.: Principle and Technology of Digital Signature. Mechanical Industry Press, Beijing (2004)
15. Zhang, X.: Legal protection of network copyright. Ph.D. thesis, Shandong University (2012)
16. Zhu, L.: High speed implementation of hash function encryption algorithm. Ph.D. thesis, Shanghai Jiaotong University (2007)

A Low Energy-Consuming Security Data Aggregation Protocol

Hui Dou[1,2], Yuling Chen[1(✉)], Yangyang Long[1], and Yuanchao Tu[1]

[1] State Key Laboratory of Public Big Date, College of Computer Science
and Technology, Guizhou University, Guiyang, China
ylchen3@gzu.edu.cn
[2] School of Computer Science, Nankai University, Tianjin, China

Abstract. With the popularization of wireless sensor network (WSN), its security problem has attracted more and more attention and research. In the process of node transmission, a mass of redundant information will be generated in the whole network, the transmission of such information will consume a quantity of energy. Data aggregation technology is an important technology of WSN. It is a challenging research problem to provide efficient data aggregation while ensuring data privacy. CPDA protocol can effectively protect the privacy of data as a classic data aggregation privacy protection protocol, but the communication overhead is expensive and the calculation is complicated. Through the analysis of CPDA protocol, we propose a low energy-consuming security data aggregation protocol (LECPDA). The protocol ameliorates the CPDA protocol by splitting private data into two pieces and mixing them with shared seeds. Finally, Simulations show that LECPDA protocol has lower communication overhead and computation cost than CPDA protocol while satisfying the general privacy protection requirements.

Keywords: Internet of things · Wireless sensor network · Security · Data aggregation

1 Introduction

Wireless sensor network (WSN) [1] is an emerging product of network revolution. As an crucial component of the internet of things [2], WSN has attracted worldwide attention since its birth. As a variety of information acquisition and processing technology, it has quickly become a research hotspot in plenty related domains and has high application value and extensive application scenarios in such fields as medical [3–5], home automation [6] and national defense. In a representative WSN, the sensor nodes are usually resource and power constrained. In order to save resources and energy, avoid large scale communication in the network, the concept of data aggregation [7] is proposed. The fundamental purpose of data aggregation is to achieve bandwidth and energy efficiency. For resource-limited sensors, it has been proved to be highly effective. Many scholars have done abundant research in data aggregation [8–10]. Madden et al. [11] proposed the TAG algorithm, which is a tree-based topology structure. It enormously lowers the communication overhead in network transmission

© Springer Nature Switzerland AG 2020
X. Chen et al. (Eds.): ML4CS 2020, LNCS 12486, pp. 547–557, 2020.
https://doi.org/10.1007/978-3-030-62223-7_48

through data aggregation in the sensor network, but TAG algorithm does not provide privacy protection for data. In practical applications, sensor networks are often faced with serious security problems [12], these threats will restrict the application and development of sensor networks.

Literature [13] proposed CPDA protocol based on clustering structure with perturbation data and the SMART protocol based on tree topology structure to slice and recombine private data. Both protocols exploit the random key pre-distribution scheme [14] for encryption. Zeng et al. [15] proposed PAPF scheme, which constructed a set of p-functions using the algebraic nature of modular operation. Nodes did not need to perturb their private data through data exchange, and cluster heads could recover aggregated results from the perturbation data. Sen [16] studied and described CPDA protocol at a deeper level, analyzed and proposed the vulnerability of CPDA in security, established two effective attack models and proposed countermeasures. One is to deal with the attack initiated by the malicious cluster head node, the other is to deal with the attack initiated by the malicious cluster-member node, both of which are internal attacks. This solution makes CPDA protocol more secure. In the past few years, many literatures have proposed successively the scheme for privacy protection data aggregation in WSN [17–21]. In the future, secret sharing technology [22] and knowledge related to artificial intelligence [23] can also be used for research.

In conclusion, the problems of high communication overhead and heavy computation are common in the existing data aggregation protocols of privacy protection. we propose a low energy-consuming security data aggregation protocol, LECPDA, which mainly divides and merges private data, reduces communication consumption and calculation, guarantees the privacy of data in the aggregation process.

The rest is organized as follows: Sect. 2 introduces data aggregation model and CPDA protocol. Section 3 shows the three phases of our new protocol named LECPDA, cluster stage, within the cluster aggregation and aggregation between clusters. Section 4 analyzes the experimental results of computing, communication overhead and privacy protection. Section 5 concludes the paper.

2 Relevant Knowledge

2.1 Data Aggregation Model

Suppose there are N nodes in a cluster, one of which is the cluster head node. The data aggregation function is shown in Eq. (1):

$$y(t) = f(d_1(t), d_2(t), \ldots, d_N(t)) \tag{1}$$

Where, $d_i(t)$ represents the information gathered by sensor node i at time t. Data aggregate functions contain *sum*, *mean*, *min*, *max* and *count*. The aggregation function that we use is the *SUM* function.

The LECPDA protocol adopts a hop-by-hop data aggregation mode and a node-to-node encryption and decryption mode. Its key allocation and management strategy is the same as CPDA protocol, which adopts the random key pre-distribution scheme [14].

2.2   CPDA Protocol

CPDA protocol is a data aggregation protocol based on cluster structure with pertur-bation data, which effectively reduces the risk of private data being eavesdropped by neighbor nodes. The protocol mainly includes three steps:

> Step 1: Cluster stage, through the node send HELLO and JION messages repeatedly built into the cluster group.
> Step 2: Aggregation within cluster stage, each node in the cluster will have a private data known only to this node. Nodes in the cluster will broadcast their seeds in the cluster. Each node in the cluster has a private data known only to the local node. Nodes in the cluster broadcast their seeds in the cluster, all nodes within the cluster share each other's seed values. The nodes in the cluster will stochastically generate two random numbers, which are known only by this node. The node in the cluster combine their seed values, private data and two random numbers into polynomials. Then the perturbation data of the nodes in the cluster are obtained. Before sending the perturbation data, it is encrypted and then sent to the neighbor nodes in the cluster. After receiving the encrypted perturbation data sent by its neighbor node, the node in the cluster aggregates it with its own perturbation data. Besides the cluster head, other nodes in the cluster send the result of aggregation to the cluster head node. After the cluster head node gets all the aggregate values, it uses matrix knowledge to get the aggregate values of all the private data of the nodes in the cluster without knowing each other's private data.
> Step 3: Aggregation between clusters stage, the cluster head node uses the TAG tree to upload the aggregate result to the base station.

3   Low Energy-Consuming Security Data Aggregation Protocol LECPDA

3.1   LECPDA Protocol Cluster Stage

LECPDA protocol adopts the clustering method of CPDA protocol. The node send HELLO and JION messages repeatedly built into the cluster group. The formation of the cluster mainly includes the following four aspects: a, b, c and d, as exhibited in Fig. 1. Part a: Query server Q sends hello messages to other sensor nodes, Part b: Nodes A and B send JOIN messages to join Q, nodes C and D become cluster heads broadcasting HELLO messages. Part c: Node F obtains two HELLO messages and stochastically chooses one to add. Part d: Multiple clusters are built.

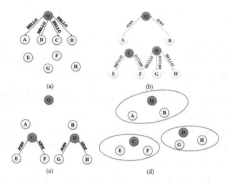

Fig. 1. Clustering process

3.2 Aggregation Within Cluster Stage

Assume one cluster with nodes A, B and C, where A represents the cluster head. a, b, c are the private data of each node separately. Here we will divide a into a_1 and a_2, that is $a = a_1 + a_2$. Similarly, b will be divided into b_1 and b_2, that is $b = b_1 + b_2$, c will be divided into c_1 and c_2, that is $c = c_1 + c_2$. Where, nodes A, B, C will broadcast their seeds in the cluster, they are not the same. They are X, Y, Z separately. So nodes A, B, C share the information of X, Y and Z. Then, the nodes can obtain the perturbation data through polynomial calculation, as exhibited in Eq. (2):

$$\begin{cases} V_{AB} = X + a_1 \\ V_{AC} = X + a_2 \end{cases} \tag{2}$$

The node A encrypts the perturbation data V_{AB} with the shared key and transmits it to the node B. The node A encrypts the perturbation data V_{AC} using the shared key and transmits it to the node C.

$$Enc(V_{AB}, K_{AB}), Enc(V_{AC}, K_{AC})$$

The perturbation data obtained by node B calculation is exhibited in Eq. (3):

$$\begin{cases} V_{BA} = Y + b_1 \\ V_{BC} = Y + b_2 \end{cases} \tag{3}$$

The node B encrypts the perturbation data V_{BA} with the shared key and transmits it to the node A. The node B encrypts the perturbation data V_{BC} using the shared key and transmits it to the node C.

$$Enc(V_{BA}, K_{BA}), Enc(V_{BC}, K_{BC})$$

The perturbation data obtained by node C calculation is exhibited in Eq. (4):

$$\begin{cases} V_{CA} = Z + c_1 \\ V_{CB} = Z + c_2 \end{cases} \tag{4}$$

The node C encrypts the perturbation data V_{CA} with the shared key and transmits it to the node A. The node C encrypts the perturbation data V_{CB} using the shared key and transmits it to the node B.

$$Enc(V_{CA}, K_{CA}), Enc(V_{CB}, K_{CB})$$

After the node A receives the perturbation data V_{BA} and V_{CA}, F_A can be calculated as Eq. (5):

$$F_A = V_{BA} + V_{CA} = Y + Z + b_1 + c_1 \tag{5}$$

The node B receives perturbation data and get F_B as Eq. (6):

$$F_B = V_{AB} + V_{CB} = X + Z + a_1 + c_2 \tag{6}$$

The node C receives perturbation data and get F_C as Eq. (7):

$$F_C = V_{AC} + V_{BC} = X + Y + a_2 + b_2 \tag{7}$$

The node B and node C transmit aggregation data F_B and F_C to the cluster head node separately. Now the cluster head node A knows F_A, F_B, F_C, X, Y, Z. So $a + b + c$ can be obtained without knowing b and c. Figure 2 exhibit the specific process of data aggregation within the cluster.

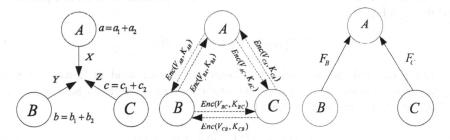

Fig. 2. Aggregation within cluster

3.3   Aggregation Between Clusters Stage

The process of aggregation between clusters of the LECPDA protocol is the same as the CPDA protocol, which is based on the TAG tree, the cluster head nodes uses the TAG tree to upload the aggregation value to the base station.

4   Experiment and Results

In this paper, the proposed LECPDA protocol and CPDA protocol were simulated by MATLAB software. The two protocols were compared and analyzed from the aspects of calculation, communication overhead and privacy protection.

4.1   Calculation

In the CPDA protocol and LECPDA protocol, the computing overhead mainly includes the computing overhead of cluster head node and the computing overhead of cluster node. Here, an arithmetic operation, data encryption, data decryption and cluster head aggregation are defined as $y1$, $y2$, $y3$ and $y4$.

(1) CPDA protocol

After the node in the cluster receives the data sent by the neighbor node, the sensor node will perform data calculation. Suppose a cluster contains three sensor nodes. Take the node A as an example, the nodes in the cluster are mainly operated as Eq. (8):

$$\begin{cases} v_A^A = a + r_1^A x + r_2^A x^2 \\ v_B^A = a + r_1^A y + r_2^A y^2 \\ v_C^A = a + r_1^A z + r_2^A z^2 \end{cases} \qquad (8)$$

Where, a stands for privacy information. x, y and z stands for the seeds. r_1^A and r_2^A stands for the stochastic numbers. v_B^A and v_C^A stands for the perturbation data. In the process of data aggregation, 15 arithmetic operations $y1$ were performed on the nodes in the cluster. Then node A encrypts the perturbed data and sends it, while node A also decrypts the received data, involving 2 data encryption $y2$ and 2 data decryption $y3$. Finally, the node A computes the sum of v_A^A, v_B^A and v_C^A, including two arithmetic operations $y1$. Therefore, the calculation cost of cluster members in CPDA protocol is exhibited in Eq. (9):

$$C_{CPDA} = 17y1 + 2y2 + 2y3 \qquad (9)$$

Compared with the nodes in the cluster, the cluster head node has one more aggregation operation $y4$, so the computational overhead of the cluster head node in the CPDA protocol is exhibited in Eq. (10):

$$C_{CPDA1} = 17y1 + 2y2 + 2y3 + y4 \qquad (10)$$

(2) LECPDA protocol

After the node in the cluster receives the data sent by the neighbor node, the node will perform data operation. Suppose there are three sensor nodes in a cluster. Take the nodes A as an example, the main operations of the nodes in the cluster are as exhibited in Eq. (11):

$$\begin{cases} V_{AB} = X + a_1 \\ V_{AC} = X + a_2 \end{cases} \tag{11}$$

Where, X is the random seed of the node, a_1 and a_2 is the two data slices by the private data of the node A, V_{AB} and V_{AC} respectively represents the perturbation data sent by the node A to node B and node C. During the node segmentation of private data, $y1$ arithmetic was performed once. In the process of data aggregation in the cluster, 2 arithmetic operations $y1$ were performed on the nodes in the cluster. Then, the node A will encrypt the perturbation data V_{AB} and V_{AC}, then send them to the node B and C, at the same time, the node A will receive and decrypt the perturbation data V_{BA} and V_{CA} sent by B and C, involving 2 data encryption and 2 data decryption. Finally, the node A calculates the sum of the perturbation data V_{AB} and V_{AC}. The node performs an arithmetic operation $y1$. Therefore, the computing overhead of cluster members in LECPDA protocol is exhibited in Eq. (12):

$$C_{LECPDA} = 4y1 + 2y2 + 2y3 \tag{12}$$

Compared with the nodes in the cluster, the cluster-head node has one more aggregation operation $y4$, so the computational overhead of the cluster head node in the LECPDA protocol is exhibited in Eq. (13):

$$C_{LECPDA1} = 4y1 + 2y2 + 2y3 + y4 \tag{13}$$

Through the above comparison and analysis, the calculation amount of LECPDA protocol is lower than that of CPDA protocol.

4.2 Communication Overhead

In the LECPDA protocol, the sensor nodes in the cluster need to broadcast their seeds in the cluster. If there are m sensor nodes in a cluster, there are m sensor nodes broadcasting the seed. Among them, each sensor node stochastically selects two sensor nodes to send its two privacy shard information, then m sensor nodes will send $2m$ data, and the last $m-1$ sensor nodes will send the obtained aggregation data to the cluster head node. As a consequence, the communication overhead of nodes within the cluster in LECPDA protocol is exhibited in Eq. (14):

$$S_{LECPDA} = m + 2m + m - 1 = 4m - 1 \tag{14}$$

In the CPDA protocol, the communication overhead of nodes in the cluster is exhibited in Eq. (15):

$$S_{CPDA} = m + m \times (m - 1) + m - 1 = m^2 + m - 1 \tag{15}$$

As can be seen from Fig. 3, as the amount of node within the cluster adds, the communication overhead of LECPDA protocol is much smaller than CPDA protocol.

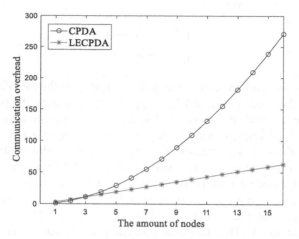

Fig. 3. Communication overhead comparison

4.3 Privacy Protection

In the LECPDA protocol, assume there are m sensor nodes in a cluster, each sensor node in the cluster stochastically selects two neighbor nodes, then sends the encrypted information to the selected neighbor node. In this process, each sensor node only sends two encrypted messages, and each sensor node only gets two encrypted messages. When the attacker obtains the encryption key of communicate with the two sensor nodes, the sensor node will be cracked and the private data will be exposed. The probability of node information being exposed is exhibited in Eq. (16):

$$P_1(q) = \sum_{k=m_c}^{d_{\max}} P(m = k)\left(1 - \left(1 - \frac{2}{k}q^2\right)^k\right) \qquad (16)$$

Where, m_c stands for the least value of cluster, $d_{\max}$ stands for the maximum of cluster, q stands for the percentage that links between nodes is broken.

The probability of node information being exposed in CPDA protocol is exhibited in Eq. (17):

$$P_2(q) = \sum_{k=m_c}^{d_{\max}} P(m = k)\left(1 - \left(1 - q^{k-1}\right)^k\right) \qquad (17)$$

Figure 4 exhibits the probability of obtaining the privacy data of CPDA and LECPDA protocol for different q. As can be seen from Fig. 4, LECPDA protocol can meet the general privacy protection requirements. The probability of private data being cracked is related to the probability p_c of a node becoming a cluster-head node, so the appropriate p_c should be selected. Under different p_c, the probability of privacy data being cracked is exhibited in Fig. 5:

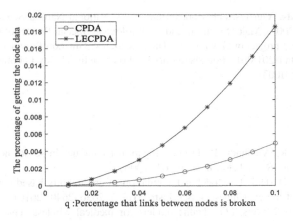

Fig. 4. Privacy protection comparison

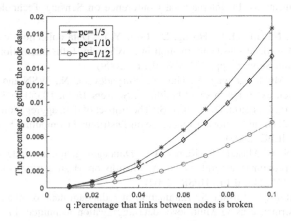

Fig. 5. Privacy comparison under different p_c

As can be seen from Fig. 5, under different p_c, the probability of privacy data being cracked is different. With the p_c decrease, the probability of privacy data being cracked will also decrease.

5 Conclusion

Privacy protection is an important research topic in WSN node communication. Through the improvement of CPDA protocol, we propose a low energy-consuming security data aggregation protocol LECPDA. LECPDA protocol can effectively lower the communication consumption of sensor nodes and simplify the calculation steps compared with CPDA protocol. This paper only carries on the theoretical analysis. In addition, how to further protect privacy while reducing communication consumption, further research is needed in these areas.

Acknowledgments. Our research work is funded by National Natural Science Foundation of China (No. 61962009), Major Scientific and Technological Special Project of Guizhou Province (20183001), Talent project of Guizhou Big Data Academy. Guizhou Provincial Key Laboratory of Public Big Data ([2018]01), Foundation of Guizhou Provincial Key Laboratory of Public Big Data (2019BDKFJJ003).

References

1. Rajagopalan, R., Varshney, P.: Data-aggregation techniques in sensor networks: a survey. IEEE Commun. Surv. Tutor. **8**(4), 48–63 (2006)
2. Hu, X., Wei, Q., Hui, T.: Model and simulation of creditability-based data aggregation for the internet of things. Chinese J. Sci. Instr. **31**(11), 2636–2640 (2010)
3. Messier, G.G., Finvers, I.G.: Traffic models for medical wireless sensor networks. IEEE Commun. Lett. **11**(1), 13–15 (2007)
4. Mathur, A., Newe, T.: Comparison and overview of Wireless sensor network systems for Medical Applications. In: International Conference on Sensing Technology, pp. 272–277 (2014)
5. Lawrence, E., Navarro, K.F., Hoang, D., Lim, Y.Y.: Data collection, correlation and dissemination of medical sensor information in a WSN. In: Fifth International Conference on Networking and Services, pp. 402–408. IEEE (2009)
6. Ghavat, H., Mukhopadhyay, S., Gui, X., Suryadevara, N.: WSN-and IOT-based smart homes and their extension to smart buildings. Sensors **15**(5), 10350–10379 (2015)
7. Krishnamachari, L., Estrin, D., Wicker, S.: The impact of data aggregation in wireless sensor networks. In: 22nd International Conference on Distributed Computing Systems Workshops, pp. 575–578. IEEE (2002)
8. Al-Karaki, J.N., Ul-Mustafa, R., Kamal, A.E.: Data aggregation in wireless sensor networks-exact and approximate algorithms. In: Workshop on High Performance Switching and Routing, pp. 241–245. IEEE, HPSR (2004)
9. Nagesh, R., Raga, S., Mishra, S.: Elimination of redundant data to enhance wireless sensor network performance using Multi level data aggregation technique. In: 10th International Conference on Computing, Communication and Networking Technologies (ICCCNT), pp. 1–5. IEEE (2019)
10. Vinodha, D., Anita, E.M.: Secure data aggregation techniques for wireless sensor networks: a review. Arch. Comput. Methods Eng. **26**(4), 1007–1027 (2019)
11. Madden, S., Franklin, M.J., Hellerstein, J.M, Hong, W.: TAG: a tiny aggregation service for ad-hoc sensor networks. ACM SIGOPS Oper. Syst. Rev. **36**(SI), 131–146 (2002)
12. Ozdemir, S., Yang, X.: Secure data aggregation in wireless sensor networks: a comprehensive overview. Comput. Netw. **53**(12), 2022–2037 (2009)
13. Wenbo, H., Xue, L., Hoang, N., Klara, N., Tarek, A.: PDA: privacy-preserving data aggregation in wireless sensor networks. In: 26th IEEE International Conference on Computer Communications, Barcelona, Spain, pp. 2045–2053. IEEE Press (2007)
14. Laurent, E., Virgil, D.G.: A key-management scheme for distributed sensor networks. In: 9th ACM conference on Computer and Communications Security, Washington, MD, pp. 41–47. ACM Press (2002)
15. Zeng, W., Lin, Y., Wang, L.: Privacy-preserving data aggregation based on the p-function set in wireless sensor networks. In: 2010 10th IEEE International Conference on Computer and Information Technology, pp. 2831–2836. IEEE (2010)

16. Sen, J.: Secure and energy-efficient data aggregation in wireless sensor networks. In: 2012 2nd IEEE National Conference on Computational Intelligence and Signal Processing (CISP), pp. 23–26. IEEE (2012)
17. Shen, X., Zhu, L., Xu, C.: A privacy-preserving data aggregation scheme for dynamic groups in fog computing. Inf. Sci. **514**, 118–130 (2020)
18. Hu, P., et al.: A secure and lightweight privacy-preserving data aggregation scheme for internet of vehicles. Peer-to-Peer Netw. Appl. **13**(3), 1002–1013 (2020). https://doi.org/10.1007/s12083-019-00849-6
19. Yasuda, S.: Verifiable privacy-preserving data aggregation protocols. IEICE Trans. Fund. Electron. Commun. Comput. Sci. **103**(1), 183–194 (2020)
20. Liu, Y.N.: A practical privacy-preserving data aggregation (3PDA) scheme for smart grid. IEEE Trans. Industr. Inf. **15**(3), 1767–1774 (2019)
21. Guo, Z.W., Ding, X.J.: Low energy-consuming cluster-based algorithm to enforce integrity and preserve privacy in data aggregation. In: 13th International Symposium on Distributed Computing and Applications to Business, pp. 152–156 (2014)
22. Li, P., Li, S.J., Yan, H.Y., Ke, L.S., Huang, T., Hassan, A.: A group identification protocol with leakage resilience of secret sharing scheme. Complexity, 1–13 (2020)
23. Hassan, Saeed-Ul., Waheed, H., Aljohani, N.R., Ali, M., Ventura, S., Herrera, F.: Virtual learning environment to predict withdrawal by leveraging deep learning. Int. J. Intell. Syst. **34**(8), 1935–1952 (2019)

Research on Blockchain-Based Identity Authentication Scheme in Social Networks

Xinying Yu[1,2], Rui Ge[1], and Fengyin Li[1(✉)]

[1] School of Information Science and Engineering, Qufu Normal University,
Rizhao 276826, China
Lfyin318@126.com
[2] School of Computer Science, Nankai University, Tianjin 300071, China

Abstract. In service-oriented social network, aiming at the unreliability problems of reviews submitted by users to the service vendors, this paper puts forword a blockchain-based identity authentication scheme. By considering the features of openness and immutability of blockchain, the proposed scheme constructs an identity registration process and an authentication process based on a blockchain network. In the proposed scheme, the identity authentication function is implemented by combining the cryptography confidentiality and the non-modifiability of the blockchain network. Therefore, only the users who have successfully been authenticated as the legitimate users can submit reviews to the service vendors. Besides, the registration and authentication records of the users' identity are all stored in the blockchain network, as well as the reviews submitted by the users to the service vendors. As a result, this scheme can ensure the authenticity and credibility of users' reviews of service vendors so that other users can obtain the credible reviews of the service vendors.

Keywords: Social network · Blockchain · Identity authentication · Cryptography confidentiality

1 Introduction

With the rapid development of Internet technology, the relationship between people and the Internet has become increasingly close. In service-oriented social networks, the authenticity of reviews is important to both users and service vendors. Based on other users' real reviews, users can select reliable service vendors, and service vendors can make targeted improvements to their services to attract more potential users for greater benefits [7].

In the social network, if service vendors can reject or delete negative reviews and insert fake positive reviews, or malicious users can leave false negative reviews at will, then the reputation of service vendors will be unreliable. This will

X. Chen et al. (Eds.): ML4CS 2020, LNCS 12486, pp. 558–565, 2020.
https://doi.org/10.1007/978-3-030-62223-7_49

mislead users to make wrong service choices and will seriously hinder the development of social networks. Therefore, the research on blockchain-based identity authentication scheme in social networks has become one of the most urgent issues.

The current reviews of service vendors are usually maintained by trusted third-party organizations, and the trusted third parties are responsible for the selecting of real reviews. Trusted third-party organizations are generally implemented through public key infrastructure (PKI), which provides identity authentication services by issuing keys and digital certificates [11,13]. By ensuring the authenticity of the user's identity, the credibility of the evaluation of the service provider is guaranteed. However, the security and transparency of the trusted third-party is the bottleneck of the entire system [8].

With the key characteristics of decentralisation, persistency, anonymity and auditability, blockchain has become a solution to overcome the over-reliance and insufficiency of trust on third-party institutions in traditional PKI [9,12]. Therefore, this paper proposes a blockchain-based decentralized identity authentication scheme, in which the identity authentication function is implemented by combining the cryptography confidentiality and non-modifiability of the blockchain netowork. The cryptography public keys and identity authentication records are stored in the blockchain to form a continuous contextual data record structure.

The identity authentication scheme greatly reduces the dependence on the original authentication center, and realizes the open, transparent and auditable characteristics of the identity authentication process, enhancing the credibility of identity authentication. Only users who have successfully passed the authentication can submit their reviews. The user's identity registration and authentication records are stored in the blockchain, as well as their reviews on the service vendors, ensuring that the service vendors receive real and objective reviews.

2 Preliminary

The following briefly introduces the blockchain and identity authentication technologies used in this paper.

2.1 Blockchain

Blockchain is not only a new technology, but a fusion of existing public-key cryptography, P2P networks, consensus mechanisms, and other technologies. These technologies are cleverly combined with databases to form an open distributed "ledger" that is not controlled by a single organization, which can effectively record, transfer, store, and display new data.

The blockchain is mainly composed of a peer-to-peer network, a ledger structure, and a consensus mechanism. The distributed ledger is open throughout the network and is managed in a decentralized manner. User nodes on the entire network reach consensus through a consensus mechanism. The blockchain network is jointly controlled by all nodes, and only the majority of users agree to the change to take effect. Each node stores a copy of the distributed ledger locally, which copies all legal transactions and consensus transactions in the peer-to-peer network. Any node can find the user's transaction information through the local ledger. The transaction records stored in the blockchain are the corresponding data in the blockchain ledger. The blockchain transaction data structure is shown as follows (see Fig. 1).

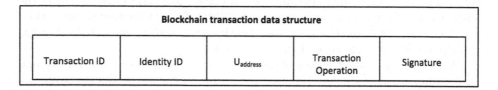

Fig. 1. Blockchain transaction data structure.

Tx_id represents the transaction ID. ID_i represents the user's identity ID, which is used to identify the user. $U_{address}$ represents the user's blockchain address, also known as the hash public key. The identity ID corresponds to the user's blockchain address, and is the credential that uniquely identifies the user information. Operation means the identity authentication process, including registration operation (RE) and identity authentication operation. Signature indicates that the user signs the identity authentication information group through the private key, and authenticates the signature stored in the blockchain node through the user's public key during the authentication phase [3].

The blockchain structure is divided into two parts, the header and the body. The block header is linked to the previous block, which can provide tamper resistance and integrity protection for the blockchain database. The block header mainly includes the version number, the previous block hash value (Prev-Hash), the Merkle tree, the time stamp, and relevant data (Nonce, etc.) participating in the consensus mechanism. The block body mainly stores related transaction records (Tx) and all data records that have been verified during the block creation process. The blocks verified by the nodes will be added to the original blockchain in chronological order, and the blocks are connected by a hash value, which is the unique identifier of the original blockchain. The new block can find the block connected to the original blockchain through the Prev-Hash value recorded in the block header. There are constantly new blocks to find the previous block in this way, thereby forming a chain structure. The chain is called the blockchain [4].

2.2   Identity Authentication Technology

Before the advent of blockchain-based identity authentication technology, traditional identity authentication technology was mainly based on public key infrastructure (PKI). PKI is a technology of identity certification and privacy protection. It binds identity and public key by means of digital certificates issued by trusted institutions. Using a private key signature can prove user identity, and using public key encryption can protect data privacy. PKI issues digital certificates to public keys and related user identity information to achieve the integrity, non-repudiation and confidentiality of identity authentication of entities in communication.

However, there are some problems with the identity authentication mechanism of PKI: Data is landing exists between modules, and data cannot be shared and communicated; The centralized management system model has a high risk of data leakage, inconsistent data authentication formats, and security levels. With the continuous improvement and development of the blockchain, the advantages of the blockchain in the field of identity authentication gradually appear. There were many shortcomings in the early blockchain-based identity authentication schemes, most of which used the Bitcoin blockchain. These solutions separate sensitive identity data from the blockchain storage (usually stored at the client terminal), so that the blockchain only serves as a verification function. The Bitcoin platform is open to everyone, and security issues are not fully guaranteed. Each write requires verification of all nodes to synchronize the blockchain database, and time is expensive.

With the continuous deepening of the research on the application of blockchain to identity authentication technology, according to the technical characteristics of blockchain decentralization, detrust, traceability, and non-tampering, blockchain-based identity authentication technology has gradually gained recognition. Reference [1] proposed a biometric and password-based two-factor authentication scheme based on blockchain. The biometrics were authenticated using the hash algorithm and elliptic curve algorithm, reducing the number of public key algorithm signatures and verifications. Conner et al. [2,14] proposed a distributed PKI authentication system based on blockchain to associate user identities with certificates to solve the decentralization problem faced by traditional PKI systems. Raju et al. [6] proposed the use of Ethereum's anonymous account wallet to implement network user identity management through public key addresses. Reference [5] proposed a method of constructing a PKI digital certificate system based on blockchain technology. This method can be applied to multiple fields as a security infrastructure, such as 4G small base station device authentication, network slice authentication, multi-CA mutual trust, etc. Reference [10] proposed a privacy-enhancing user identity management system using blockchain technology which places due importance on both anonymity and attribution, and supports end-to-end management from user assertion to usage billing. However, the existing blockchain-based authentication schemes still have the common problems of large calculation amount and low authentication efficiency.

3   Blockchain-Based Identity Authentication Scheme

3.1   Blockchain-Based Identity Authentication Scheme

The blockchain-based identity authentication scheme authenticates the identity of the user who submitted the review. Only after the identity authentication is successful can the user submit a review to the service vendor and store it in the blockchain. The identity authentication scheme consists of an identity registration, authentication center and blockchain network. When the user performs identity registration and authentication, the identity registration certification center is linked through the identity authentication interface layer. The identity authentication interface layer is linked with the blockchain network through the blockchain SDK to implement data transmission and interaction.

The Identity Registration Certification Center (IRC) is responsible for generating a private key for the user during the registration phase, calculating the corresponding public key, and using the user's private key to sign his identity information group M. In the authentication phase, a public key is used to verify the identity information group M stored in the blockchain distributed storage system. The blockchain network consists of the blockchain server and a distributed storage system. Blockchain servers mainly include node management, consensus mechanism management, and distributed storage functions. The Blockchain server (BS) is responsible for verifying the validity of the user's blockchain address $U_{address}$, and is responsible for data interaction with each node in the blockchain network.

In the registration module, users enter registration identity information, and use cryptography and consensus mechanisms to make registration information stored on each node of the blockchain network. In the authentication module, the user enters the identity information for successful registration and performs identity authentication on the BS. If a user's identity authentication is successful, all the user's identity authentication records will be stored in the blockchain node corresponding to the user, thereby broadcasting consensus to the entire blockchain network. The structure of the blockchain-based identity authentication scheme is shown as follows (see Fig. 2).

3.2   Identity Registration Module

In the user's identity registration phase, an aggregatable digital signature scheme is used to generate keys and sign. The IRC generates a private key for the user applying for registration, calculates the corresponding public key from the private key, and calculates the corresponding blockchain address of the user based on the public key. If the blockchain address is verified to be valid, the user's private key is used to sign the identity information group, and the identity information and related operation records of the successfully registered user are stored in the blockchain network.

The specific process of the user during the identity registration module is as follows (see Fig. 3).

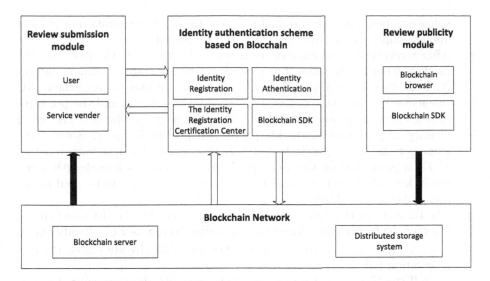

Fig. 2. Structure of the blockchain-based identity authentication scheme.

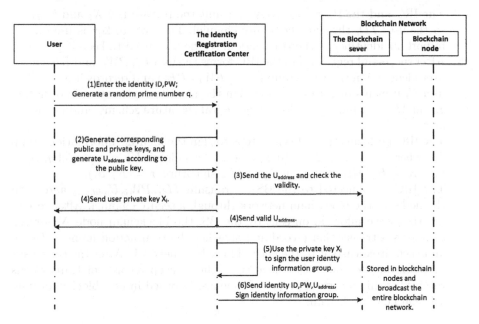

Fig. 3. The workflow of the Identity registration module.

(1) The user makes a preliminary registration request on his mobile terminal. User U_i enters his identity ID_i, password PW_i, identity registration information RE_i and a random prime number q (when the user performs a registration operation, the mobile terminal automatically allocates and selects the

prime numbers q and the original root α of the q) for registration operation, and transmits to the IRC through a secure channel.

(2) After receiving the information transmitted by the user, the IRC uses the random integer generation function $Gen()$ to generate a random integer $X_i(1<X_i<q-1)$, and uses X_i as the private key of user U_i. And then, IRC calculates $Y_i = a^{X_i} \bmod q$, based on the random prime q and the primitive root α assigned by user U_i, and uses Y_i as the user's public key. The user's identity ID_i corresponds to his public and private key pair. Because the length of the user's public key at this time is not fixed, a hash function $H(Y_i)$ is performed on the user's public key to obtain a fixed-length user's public key, which is denoted as H_{pk}. At this point, H_{pk} can be used as the user's blockchain address $U_{address}$.

(3) The BS receives the user's $ID_i, PW_i, U_{address}$ sent by the IRC, and checks whether the blockchain address corresponding to the user U_i already exists:

① If the $U_{address}$ corresponding to the user ID_i already exists, the registration fails.

② If the $U_{address}$ corresponding to the user ID_i does not exist, the registration is successful.

(4) The IRC and the BS respectively transmit the private key X_i and $U_{address}$ to the user ID_i through the secure channel. The private key is used as an important identifier of the transaction, so the user need to keep it properly.

(5) After successful registration, the IRC forms the user U_i, PW_i, and RE_i into a user identity information group $(ID_i \mid PW_i \mid RE_i)$ and records it as M. The user U_i uses his private key X_i to sign the identity registration information group M according to the following digital signature scheme, and records it as σ_i.

The IRC performs the following steps to sign the identity information group M, where: $\forall k_i \in Z_q^*, H_1 : \{0,1\}^* \rightarrow Z_q^*$, calculates $K_i = \alpha^{k_i} \bmod q$, $S_i = k_i + X_i + H_1(M_i) \bmod q$, and gets M's signature $\sigma = (K_i, S_i)$.

(6) The IRC is connected to the BS to transmit $ID_i, PW_i, U_{address}$ and σ_i to the nodes of the blockchain network through a secure channel. After receiving the above information sent by the BS, the blockchain node $N1$ or $N2$ composes a transaction record and attaches the transaction number Tx_id, and then broadcasts it to the entire blockchain network. After the consensus mechanism, the nodes that have the right to keep records of transactions received within a certain period of time are recorded in new blocks, forming a brand new blockchain.

4   Conclusions

This paper proposes an identity authentication scheme based on blockchain, which is composed of an identity registration, authentication center and blockchain network. The user's identity registration and authentication records are stored in an immutable and decentralized blockchain network, as well as the reviews submitted by the users to the service vendors. The blockchain maintains the received reviews to ensure the authenticity of the reviews. Potential users can check other uses' reviews on the service vendors and make their own reasonable choices. Security analysis shows that the identity authentication scheme based on blockchain can effectively guarantee the authenticity of the users' identity, and further ensure the authenticity and credibility of users' reviews of service vendors.

References

1. Chen, Y., Du, Y., Yang, G.: Efficient attribute-based authenticated key agreement protocol. Comput. Sci. **41**(4), 150–154 (2014)
2. Fan, J., Chen, J., Du, Y., Wang, P., Sun, Y.: DelQue: a socially aware delegation query scheme in delay-tolerant networks. IEEE Trans. Veh. Technol. **60**(5), 2181–2193 (2011)
3. Fromknecht, C., Velicanu, D.: Certcoin : A namecoin based decentralized authentication system 6.857 class project (2014)
4. Fromknecht, C., Velicanu, D., Yakoubov, S.: A decentralized public key infrastructure with identity retention. IACR Cryptology ePrint Archive 2014, 803 (2014)
5. Liang, X., Li, X., Lu, R., Lin, X., Shen, X.: SEER: a secure and efficient service review system for service-oriented mobile social networks, pp. 647–656 (2012)
6. Liang, X., Lin, X., Shen, X.S.: Enabling trustworthy service evaluation in service-oriented mobile social networks. IEEE Trans. Parallel Distrib. Syst. **25**(2), 310–320 (2014)
7. Matsumoto, S., Reischuk, R.M.: IKP: Turning a PKI around with blockchains. IACR Cryptology ePrint Archive 2016, 1018 (2016)
8. Nash, A., Duane, W., Joseph, C.: PKI: Implementing and Managing E-security. McGraw-Hill Inc., London (2001)
9. Pu, H.E., Ge, Y.U., Zhang, Y.F., Bao, Y.B.: Survey on blockchain technology and its application prospect. Computer Science (2017)
10. Raju, S., Boddepalli, S., Gampa, S., Yan, Q., Deogun, J.S.: Identity management using blockchain for cognitive cellular networks. In: 2017 IEEE International Conference on Communications (ICC), pp. 1–6. IEEE (2017)
11. Shunmuganathan, S., Saravanan, R.D., Palanichamy, Y.: Secure and efficient smart-card-based remote user authentication scheme for multiserver environment. Can. J. Electr. Comput. Eng. **38**(1), 20–30 (2015)
12. Wei, W.: Overview of the development of PKI technology. Reliability and Environmental Testing for Electronic Products 2002
13. Hu, Z., Ding, W., Gao, Z., Zhu, X., Wang, J.: A multi-stage cascaded wireless security authentication scheme based on blockchain technology. Comput. Sci. **46**(12), 180–185 (2019)
14. Zhou, Z.C., Li, L., Guo, S., Hui, Z.: A biometrics and password two-factor cross domain authentication scheme based on blockchain technology. J. Comput. Appl. **38**(6), 100–107 (2018)

A Secure Multi-party Computational Adversary Selection Model Based on Time-Varying of Entropy

Xinyu Zhang[1,2], YuJun Liu[3], Yuling Chen[1(✉)], and Zhan Wang[1]

[1] State Key Laboratory of Public Big Date, College of Computer Science and Technology, Guizhou University, Guiyang, China
ylchen3@gzu.edu.cn
[2] School of Computer Science, Nankai University, Tianjin, China
[3] Technical Center of Beijing Customs, Beijing, China

Abstract. In cryptography, secure multi-party computation involves multi-party participant entities, each of them has its own secret input and wants to jointly compute a function through some interaction protocol. In this process, cheating by any of the parties will cause errors in the final result. In order to prevent parties from cheating, many experts have proposed protocols with semi-honest security, malicious security and covert security. However, existing protocols can only detect and deal with malicious attackers after being attacked. This passive approach will not only consume more resources, but also cause excessive losses for participants. To solve the above problems, this paper proposes an optimal participant selection model based on the time-varying entropy. Over time, we evaluate the safety entropy of the secure multi-party computation model. Once the entropy value exceeds the expectation, we will reselect the adversary through the reputation mechanism, thus always ensuring the safe state of the model. Our model can better predict the unsafe state of the system, and the security of the model can be guaranteed by the choice of the adversary. At this same time, it has better efficiency in the design of password protocol.

Keywords: Secure multi-party computation · Time-varying entropy · Optimal participant selection model · Reputation mechanism

1 Introduction

Secure multi-party computation is the combination of cryptology and distributed computation. It is a new research area in information security. Secure multi-party computing (SMC) refers to the calculation of a function by multiple participants in a distributed environment, the input information of the function is provided by these participants, and the input information of each participant is confidential; After the calculation is completed, each participant obtains the correct calculation result, but cannot obtain the input information of other participants. Recently, many exports devote themselves to search about the definition, model, security proof theory, fairness, basic modules, application protocols, methodology and feasibility study in secure multi-party computation.

© Springer Nature Switzerland AG 2020
X. Chen et al. (Eds.): ML4CS 2020, LNCS 12486, pp. 566–577, 2020.
https://doi.org/10.1007/978-3-030-62223-7_50

In cryptography, secure multi-party computation [2, 3] involves multi-party participant entities, each of them has its own secret input and wants to jointly compute a function through some interaction protocol. Yao [2] proposed the problem of millionaires, which introduced the pioneering theory for secure two-party computing (STPC). Goldriech et al. [3] extended STPC to SMPC. The main task of SMPC is to guarantee security of the computation in the presence of various external attacks. [6, 7, 23] expose the notion of covert adversaries, which may deviate arbitrarily from the protocol specification in an attempt to cheat, but do not wish to be "caught" doing so. Wang et al. [19] simulated the corruption of both parties in two-party protocols at the first time and proposed an incentive-driven attacking model where the attacker leverages corruption costs, benefits and possible consequences. [9] consider a two-party game between a protocol designer and an external attacker. The goal of the attacker is to break security properties such as correctness or privacy, possibly by corrupting protocol participants, the goal of the protocol designer is to prevent the attacker from succeeding. [21] propose a secure computation protocol under asymmetric information scenario in the presence of rational parties to guarantee the computation security in enterprise information system. [8, 10] change the direction by bridging cryptography, game theory and reputation systems, and that propose a "social model" for repeated rational secret sharing. Asharov et al. [4] utilized reputation systems for carrying out secure multiparty computation. On this basis, they provide formal definitions of secure computation and carry out a theoretical study of feasibility. Wang et al. [5] introduced the reputation from mobile social networks into the definition of utility, giving rational parties an incentive to achieve more efficient applications. Nathan et al. [11] responded and predicted through trust and reputation, and proposed the RaPTaR model, which is a way to extend existing trust and reputation models to give agents the ability to monitor the output of interactions with a group of agents over time to identify any likely changes in behavior and adapt accordingly. Bellini et al. [20] provided a comprehensive survey designed to analyze and evaluate the use of blockchain in distributed trust and Reputation Management systems (DTRMS) environments. Kang et al. [22] took reputation as a standard to measure the reliability and credibility of mobile devices, and designed an employee selection scheme based on reputation by using multi-weight subjective logic model for reliable joint learning. Moreover, we propose an effective incentive mechanism combining reputation with contract theory to motivate high-reputation mobile devices with high-quality data to participate in model learning. Recently, the application of information theory to solve the equilibrium problem of rational secure multi-party computing model has become a hot topic for many scholars. Entropy is introduced to measure the quality of cryptographic processes from different angles in [14]. Through the equilibrium solutions, the stable region, complexity entropy, and efficiency of the multichannel supply chain system, [15] ensure that manufacturers even retailers take the maximization of channel profit as the business objective and play the channel service game under the optimal pricing. [16] constructs a set of unified basic theoretical system of network space security, and reveals some basic laws of hacker attack and defense and security evolution. Equally it puts forward the idea of information theory, game theory and security general theory to realize the quantitative law of network space security's ecological development. [12, 13, 17, 18] et al. studied the system insecurity from shannon's information entropy [1] to the security entropy of the network system from the perspective of dynamic development.

Since we cannot guarantee that adversaries always follow the protocol rules in secure multi-party calculations, we judge the current model's safety by recording changes in the model's entropy value. However, the change in the model's entropy value will continue to change with time and the number of collaborations. In order to ensure the safety of the model at all times. In this paper, we propose a secure multi-Party computational adversary selection model based on time-varying of entropy. Specifically, our contribution is as follows:

1. We studied the time-varying entropy in secure multi-party computations. We found that the security of the model and the state of the adversary are changing over time.
2. We propose a reputation evaluation mechanism to ensure that all adversaries in the mechanism have a reputation value. And it is used to update the reputation value of the adversary while it is in a secure multi-party computation.
3. we propose a secure multi-Party computational adversary selection model based on time-varying of entropy, which used to better predict the unsafe state of the system, and through the selection and replacement of adversaries, we can always ensure the safety of the model.

The main structure of this article: Sect. 2 presents some preliminaries such as security entropy, time-varying entropy, secure multi-party computation. In Sect. 3, we describe the application of time-varying entropy in secure two-party computing and secure multi-party computing, and infer the behavior of the adversary. In Sect. 4, we propose a reputation evaluation mechanism and describe our adversary selection rules in detail. Finally, we summarized and prospected in Sect. 5.

2 Preliminaries

Definition 1 (security entropy): Is a physical quantity used to evaluate the degree of security in a system. Security entropy is used to solve security measurement problems. The computation method is similar to information entropy and heat entropy, which is expressed as:

$$H(p_1, p_2, \ldots p_n) = -\sum_{i=1}^{n} p_i \log p_i \qquad (1)$$

n is the number of all the independent unsafe factors in the system. p_i is the probability of an unsafe event caused by the ith unsafe factor. In this case, the factors of insecurity are independent of each other, which means that the change of one factor is completely independent of the change of another factor.

Definition 2 (Time-varying entropy): Let all unsafe factors of the system be $q_1, q_2, \ldots, q_n$, (the unsafe factors here may be interrelated and influence each other). We record the security entropy of the system at time t as $Q(t, q_1, q_2, \ldots, q_n)$, Or abbreviated as $Q(t)$. When $Q(t) = 0$, the security entropy of the system reaches the maximum value, and the safety of the system reaches the minimum value at this time. If $Q(t)$ increases with time, the differential $\frac{\mathrm{d}Q(t)}{\mathrm{d}t} > 0$, Conversely, if $Q(t)$ decreases with time, that is, differentiate $\frac{\mathrm{d}Q(t)}{\mathrm{d}t} < 0$, then the system will become more and more secure.

Definition 3 (Reputation mechanism): In secure multi-party computing, trust is considered a necessary condition for interactions between adversaries. Therefore, we construct a reputation mechanism for parties in secure multi-party computing. We set the initial reputation value θ for participants, where $\theta = \frac{1}{n}$, n is the number of participants. When the adversary complies with the protocol rules, the system executes $\theta_i = \theta_i + \sigma$; In contrast, the system executes $\theta_i = \theta_i - \sigma$ when the adversary violates the rules, σ is the reward value or penalty value.

Definition 4 (Real adversary): It is a kind of adversary between honest adversaries and malicious adversaries. The real adversary has a reputation value, which represents the probability that the real adversary will follow the protocol. And the reputation value will continue to change with the number of participations in the model and the status of cooperation.

3 Time-Varying Entropy in a Secure Multi-party Computing Model

In this section we will discuss the behavior of honest and malicious adversaries in secure multi-party computing. We consider a secure multi-party computing model, which consists of the honest adversary, the malicious adversary, a network, the service and environment, etc. It is obviously a limited system, that is, the limited adversary and the limited insecurity factor, etc. As mentioned in the previous section of this article, the second law of thermodynamics shows that the safety entropy of this model will automatically increase automatically as time passes. This means that the insecurity of the model is also increasing. Especially, the existence of malicious adversaries is the main factor leading to an increase in security entropy. Because the essence of malicious adversaries is to engage in sabotage, take any action to deviate from the agreement, and thus mess up the established order of the model; On the contrary, the goal of honest parties is to work together to obtain honest results. Our goal is to ensure that participants can provide and receive services in the model in the established order. Since honest adversaries and malicious adversaries continue to act as participants in the secure multi-party computing model, the security entropy of the model is continuously increased and decreased, that is, the security entropy of the model is always time-varying. Below we will introduce the time-varying security entropy in secure multi-party computation step by step.

3.1   Two-Party Computation

In this section, we introduce the time-varying entropy in secure two-party computation. We are temporarily divided into two categories (1) Only one party is a real adversary. (2) Both parties are real adversaries.

One Party is a Real Adversary: We consider the situation where there is only one real adversary (There is an insecure factor). For $n = 1$ mentioned in Definition 5, this is the simplest case. At this time, there is only one insecurity factor in the model (the uncertainty of the real adversary's behavior), so we get:

$$\frac{\mathrm{d}Q(t)}{\mathrm{d}t} = f(\mathbf{Q})$$

If $f(\mathbf{Q})$ is expanded into a Taylor series, the following equation is obtained:

$$\frac{\mathrm{d}Q(t)}{\mathrm{d}t} = a_1 Q + a_{11} Q^2 + \ldots$$

The constant term is not included in this formula, because we can assume that unsafe factors will not occur naturally, that is, the moment the participant has just performed the calculation, the model will not have safety problems.

If only the first item in the Taylor series is kept, then there is:

$$\frac{\mathrm{d}Q(t)}{\mathrm{d}t} = a_1 Q$$

This shows that the security posture of the model will depend entirely on whether the constant a_1 is positive or negative. If a_1 is negative, then the security entropy as a whole is decreasing, that is, the security of the model is getting better and better. Explain that the real adversary in the model is in a state of honest calculation, and the parties could cooperate safely, which is beneficial to parties; If a_1 is positive, then the overall security entropy is developing in an increasing direction, that is, the security of the model is getting worse. It means that the real adversary in the model deviates from the agreement, and the parties cannot safely perform cooperative calculations, which is harmful to the parties. Moreover, this increasingly safe (or increasingly unsafe) situation of the model follows the exponential law.

$$Q = Q_0 e^{a(1)t}$$

Where Q_0 represents the safety entropy of the model at the initial time $(t = 0)$ (Fig. 1).

We can see from the picture that the law of the index shows that if both parties remain honest, the security posture of the model is developing in a good direction, and the speed of getting better will become faster and faster. On the contrary, if the party arbitrarily deviate from the agreement, the security situation of the model is developing in the direction of bad, and the rate of deterioration will become faster and faster, or

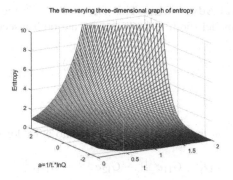

Fig. 1. The time-varying three-dimensional graph of entropy.

even collapse in an instant. If a bit more detailed, that is to keep the first two of the above Taylor series, then there is

$$\frac{dQ(t)}{dt} = a_1 Q + a_{11} Q^2$$

The solution to this equation is:

$$Q = \frac{a_1 c e^{a(1)t}}{1 - a_{11} c e^{a(1)t}}$$

Note that with the extension of time, the curve we draw is a logarithmic curve. Obviously, when a_1 is negative, the model is in a safe state. When a_1 is positive, the model will lose its balance and gradually change in the direction of increasing entropy (Fig. 2).

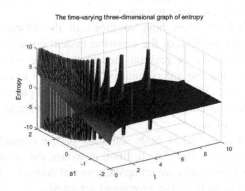

Fig. 2. The time-varying three-dimensional graph of entropy.

Both Parties are Real Adversaries: That is, when $n = 2$, there are two main insecurity factors in the model (both real adversaries are both insecurity factors).

$$\begin{cases} \dfrac{dQ_1}{dt} = f_1(Q_1, Q_2) \\ \dfrac{dQ_2}{dt} = f_2(Q_1, Q_2) \end{cases}$$

Under the assumption that it can be expanded into a Taylor series, its solution is:

$$\begin{cases} Q_1 = Q_1^* - G_{11}e^{\lambda(1)t} - G_{12}e^{\lambda(2)t} - G_{111}e^{2\lambda(1)t} - \cdots \\ Q_2 = Q_2^* - G_{21}e^{\lambda(1)t} - G_{22}e^{\lambda(2)t} - G_{211}e^{2\lambda(1)t} - \cdots \end{cases}$$

Where Q_1^* and Q_2^* are the static solutions of Q_1 and Q_2 obtained by $f_1 = f_2 = 0$, G is the integral constant; and $\lambda(1)$ and $\lambda(2)$ are the characteristic equation $(a_{11} - \lambda)(a_{22} - \lambda) - a_{12}a_{21} = 0$, the root of the quadratic equation is

$$\lambda = \frac{C}{2} \pm \sqrt{-D + \frac{C^2}{4}}$$

Among them $C = a_{11} + a_{12}$, $D = a_{11}a_{22} - a_{12}a_{21}$
So, we know:

(1) If $C < 0, D > 0, E = C^2 - 4D > 0$, then both roots of the characteristic equation are negative, the model will stretch over time and tend to be stable at rest. At this time, the model will be in a completely safe state, indicating that the participants are honest Participate in calculations.
(2) If $C < 0, D > 0, E = C^2 - 4D < 0$, then both roots of the characteristic equation are complex solutions with negative real parts. At this time, with the development of time, the safety entropy (Q_1, Q_2) of the model will approach a static state (Q_1^*, Q_2^*) along a spiral curve trajectory.
(3) If $C = 0, D > 0, E < 0$, then both solutions of the characteristic equation are imaginary, and the solution of the equation system contains periodic terms, and there will be oscillation or rotation around the static state. That is, the point (Q_1, Q_2) representing the safety entropy will draw a closed curve around the stationary state (Q_1^*, Q_2^*). At this time, the safe multi-party computing model is unstable, and the probability of being honest and deviating from the agreement seems to be a tug of war.
(4) If $C > 0, D > 0, E > 0$, then both solutions of the characteristic equation are positive, and there is no static at all. In other words, the model is more confusing at this time, the participants are completely out of control, and the real adversary betrayed and deviated from the agreement arbitrarily.

3.2 Multi-party Computation

In this section we will discuss the changes of entropy in secure multiparty computations. For each $i(i = 1, 2, \ldots, n)$. Then, the time-varying situation of each $Q_i(t)$ can be described by the following n Eqs. (2):

$$
\begin{cases}
\frac{dQ_1}{dt} = f_1(Q_1, Q_2, \ldots, Q_n) \\
\frac{dQ_2}{dt} = f_2(Q_1, Q_2, \ldots, Q_n) \\
\cdots \cdots \\
\frac{dQ_n}{dt} = f_n(Q_1, Q_2, \ldots, Q_n)
\end{cases}
\tag{2}
$$

Here, any change of Q_i is a function of all other $Q_j(j \neq i)$; conversely, any change of Q_i will also affect the change of the entire equation. Below we discuss the equations carefully for some special cases.

If each Q_i does not change with time, that is:

$$
\frac{dQ_j}{dt} = 0, i = 1, 2, \ldots, n
$$

Or $f_1(Q_1, Q_2, \ldots, Q_n) = f_2(Q_1, Q_2, \ldots, Q_n) = \ldots = f_n(Q_1, Q_2, \ldots, Q_n) = 0$; Then the security entropy of the model is at a static state, that is, both parties honestly follow the agreement to cooperate and calculate, and the integrity of the model is neither bad nor good. If the model has just been put into operation ($t = 0$), the honest probabilities of the real adversary can maintain the normal operation of the model and make its unsafe entropy always stand still, then the protocol is successful.

Let $(Q_1^*, Q_2^*, \ldots, Q_n^*)$ be a set of solutions at rest. For each $i = 1, 2, \ldots, n$, we introduce a new variable $Q_i' = Q_i^* - Q_i$, then the system of equations is transformed into the following form (3):

$$
\begin{cases}
\frac{dQ_1'}{dt} = f_1(Q_1', Q_2', \ldots, Q_n') \\
\frac{dQ_2'}{dt} = f_2(Q_1', Q_2', \ldots, Q_n') \\
\cdots \cdots \\
\frac{dQ_n'}{dt} = f_n(Q_1', Q_2', \ldots, Q_n')
\end{cases}
\tag{3}
$$

If this system of equations can be expanded into a Taylor series, we can get the system of Eqs. (4):

$$
\begin{cases}
\frac{dQ_1'}{dt} = a_{11}Q_1' + a_{12}Q_2' + \ldots + a_{1n}Q_n' + a_{111}Q_1'^2 + a_{112}Q_1'Q_2' + a_{122}Q_2'^2 + \cdots \\
\frac{dQ_2'}{dt} = a_{21}Q_1' + a_{22}Q_2' + \ldots + a_{2n}Q_n' + a_{211}Q_1'^2 + a_{212}Q_1'Q_2' + a_{222}Q_2'^2 + \cdots \\
\cdots \cdots \\
\frac{dQ_n'}{dt} = a_{n1}Q_1' + a_{n2}Q_2' + \ldots + a_{nn}Q_n' + a_{n11}Q_1'^2 + a_{n12}Q_1'Q_2' + a_{n22}Q_2'^2 + \cdots
\end{cases}
\tag{4}
$$

Then the general solution of this system of equations is:

$$\begin{cases} Q'_1 = G_{11}e^{\lambda(1)t} + G_{12}e^{\lambda(2)t} + \ldots + G_{1n}e^{\lambda(n)t} + G_{111}e^{2\lambda(1)t} + \ldots \\ Q'_2 = G_{21}e^{\lambda(1)t} + G_{22}e^{\lambda(2)t} + \ldots + G_{2n}e^{\lambda(n)t} + G_{211}e^{2\lambda(1)t} + \ldots \\ \ldots\ldots \\ Q'_n = G_{n1}e^{\lambda(1)t} + G_{n2}e^{\lambda(2)t} + \ldots + G_{nn}e^{\lambda(n)t} + G_{n11}e^{2\lambda(1)t} + \ldots \end{cases}$$

Here, each G is a constant, $\lambda(i), i = 1, 2, \ldots, n$ is the characteristic root of the determinant of the following $n \times n$ order matrix $B = (b_{ij})$ with respect to λ, the root of equation $\det(B) = 0$. When $B = (b_{ij})$, $b_{ii} = a_{ii} - \lambda$, $i, j = 1, 2, \ldots, n$, $b_{ij} = a_{ij}, i \neq j$ The root $\lambda(i)$ of the above equation may be either real or imaginary. Below we consider several special cases.

Case 1: If all the characteristic roots $\lambda(i)$ are real and negative, then according to the general solution, Each Q'_i will approach 0 with time (because $e^{-\infty} = 0$), This shows that the real adversaries in secure multi-party computing are reliable. Because the change rate of safety entropy tends to 0, it means that various unsafe factors are being gradually controlled, and the order of the model is also being restored.

Case 2: Similarly, if all the characteristic roots $\lambda(i)$ are complex numbers and the negative numbers are in the real part, then according to the general solution, it can be seen that each Q'_i also approaches 0 with time. At this time, participants are also ensuring safe and honest calculations.

$$Q_i = Q_i^* - Q'_i, i = 1, 2, \ldots, n$$

Therefore, according to the system of Eqs. (3), in case 1 and case 2, A approaches the static value B. At this time, the safe equilibrium state of the model is stable, because in a long enough time, the model is more and more close to the static, and the rate of change of the unsafe entropy of the model is always close to 0, that is, the order of the model is long-term stable.

Case 3: If there is a characteristic root $\lambda(i)$ is positive or 0, then the balance of the model is unstable, that is, the security of the model is also unstable. At this time, the real adversary arbitrarily deviated from the agreement, and the model is now in an extremely unstable state.

Case 4: If there are some characteristic roots $\lambda(i)$ that are positive and complex, then the model contains periodic terms, because the exponential function with an exponential complex number has the following form:

$$e^{(a-ib)t} = e^{at}[cos(bt) - sin(bt)i]$$

Here i is an imaginary unit. At this time, the security state of the model will periodically vibrate, that is, a repeated tug of war between the honest calculation of multiple real adversaries and the probability of deviation from the agreement. The overall trend of the model is toward the unsafe direction with increased security entropy.

4 Adversary Selection Model

We present the adversary selection model in Fig. 4. In order to ensure the security of the multi-party computing model, our proposed model follows the strictest pattern in the time-varying entropy. We design adversary selection models suitable for secure multi-party computing and a reputation evaluation mechanism in Fig. 3.

Reputation Evaluation Mechanism

Here we evaluate and record the reputation value θ of the participants. Each time the participant performs a cooperative calculation, the reputation value is updated.

The initial reputation value of the participant entering the model is $\theta = \dfrac{1}{n}$

n is the number of participants. σ is the reward value.
- If the participants cooperate honestly, the reputation value increases $\theta_i = \theta_i + \sigma$.
- If the participant deviates from the agreement, the reputation value decreases $\theta_i = \theta_i - \sigma$.
- The updated reputation value is re-recorded in the reputation evaluation center.

Fig. 3. The time-varying three-dimensional graph of entropy.

Adversary selection model

Step1: First, we randomly selected n participants for cooperative computing.

Step2: We calculate the entropy of the model H_1 based on the credibility θ of the participants.

$$H(\theta_1, \theta_2, ...\theta_n) = -\sum_{i=1}^{n} \theta_i \log \theta_i$$

Step3: The credit value of participants is updated through the credit evaluation mechanism.

Step4: Continue to randomly select n participants for cooperative calculation and get the entropy value H_2.

Step5: Compare H_1 with H_2.

If $H_1 \geq H_2$, it means that the multi-party computing model is in a safe state.

If $H_1 < H_2$, we will re-select the adversary. We will select participants with high reputation values to replace until the condition $H \geq H$ is met

---

Fig. 4. The time-varying three-dimensional graph of entropy.

Since the entropy value of the model will change continuously with time. Therefore, we strictly control the adversary of each cooperative calculation to ensure that its entropy value is less than or equal to the previous entropy value. At the same time, if the result of the cooperative calculation is correct, all participants get an increase in the reputation value in the reputation evaluation system, and if the result of the cooperative calculation is wrong, the reputation value of the participants decreases. Since the smaller the change of entropy value with time, the higher the security of the model. Real adversaries will also obey the agreement in order to increase their reputation value, so our model will be in an increasingly safe state.

5 Conclusion and Future Work

Secure multi-party computing is one of the most common cryptographic protocols, among which the most important is how to ensure the security of the computing process. In this paper, we add a reputation evaluation mechanism to record the reputation value of participants and update it in the computation. The entropy value of the model is calculated by the reputation value and used to regulate the security of the model. We propose a strict adversary selection model based on the time-varying principle of entropy. Our model predicts the state of secure multi-party computation, and also guarantees the optimal choice of participants in the model. In the future, we will look for more effective methods in the evaluation of reputation values, and study the storage of reputation values.

Acknowledgments. Our research work is funded by National Natural Science Foun-dation of China (No. 61962009), Major Scientific and Technological Special Project of Guizhou Province (20183001), Talent project of Guizhou Big Data Academy. Guizhou Provincial Key Laboratory of Public Big Data ([2018]01), Foundation of Guizhou Provincial Key Laboratory of Public Big Data (2018BDKFJJ009).

References

1. Shannon, C.E.: A mathematical theory of communication. Bell Syst. Tech. J. **27**(379–423), 623–656 (1948)
2. Yao, A.C.: Protocols for secure computation. In: 2013 IEEE 54th Annual Symposium on Foundations of Computer Science, pp. 160–164. IEEE (1982)
3. Goldreich, O., Micali, S., Wigderson, A.: How to play any mental game. In: Proceedings of the Nineteenth Annual ACM Symposium on Theory of Computing, pp. 218–229. ACM (1987)
4. Asharov, G., Lindell, Y., Zarosim, H.: Fair and Efficient Secure Multiparty Computation with Reputation Systems. In: Sako, K., Sarkar, P. (eds.) ASIACRYPT 2013. LNCS, vol. 8270, pp. 201–220. Springer, Heidelberg (2013). https://doi.org/10.1007/978-3-642-42045-0_11
5. Wang, Y., Zhao, C., Xu, Q., et al.: Fair secure computation with reputation assumptions in the mobile social networks. Mobile Inf. Syst. 1–8 (2015)

6. Aumann, Y., Lindell, Y.: Security against covert adversaries: efficient protocols for realistic adversaries. In: Vadhan, S.P. (ed.) TCC 2007. LNCS, vol. 4392, pp. 137–156. Springer, Heidelberg (2007). https://doi.org/10.1007/978-3-540-70936-7_8
7. Asharov, G., Orlandi, C.: Calling out cheaters: covert security with public verifiability. In: Wang, X., Sako, K. (eds.) ASIACRYPT 2012. LNCS, vol. 7658, pp. 681–698. Springer, Heidelberg (2012). https://doi.org/10.1007/978-3-642-34961-4_41
8. Nojoumian, M., Stinson, D.R.: Socio-rational secret sharing as a new direction in rational cryptography. In: Grossklags, J., Walrand, J. (eds.) GameSec 2012. LNCS, vol. 7638, pp. 18–37. Springer, Heidelberg (2012). https://doi.org/10.1007/978-3-642-34266-0_2
9. Garay, J., Katz, J., et al.: Rational protocol design: cryptography against incentive-driven adversaries. In: IEEE Symposium on Foundations of Computer Science. IEEE (2013)
10. Wang, Y., Liu, Z., et al.: Social rational secure multi-party computationx. Concurr. Comput. Pract. Exp. **26**(5), 1067–1083 (2014)
11. Caroline, P., Nathan, G.: Improving trust and reputation assessment with dynamic behaviour. Knowl. Eng. Rev. **35**, e29 (2020)
12. Yang, Y., Peng, H., et al.: General theory of security and a StudyCase in internet of things. IEEE Internet of Things J. **4**(2), 592–600 (2017)
13. Yang, Y., Niu, X., et al.: Games based study of nonblind confrontation. Math. Prob. Eng. (2017)
14. Stefan, R., Sandra, K.: Password security as a game of entropies. Entropy **20**(5), 312 (2018)
15. Yimin, H., Xingli, C., et al.: The complexity and entropy analysis for service game model based on different expectations and optimal pricing. Entropy **20**(11), 858 (2018)
16. Yang, Y., Niu, X.: The General Theory of Information Security. Publishing House of Electronics Industry, Beijing (2018)
17. Yang, Y., Niu, X., et al.: A secure and efficient transmission method in connected vehicular cloud computing. IEEE Network
18. Yang, Y., Niu, X., Li, L., Peng, H., Ren, J., Qi, H.: General theory of security and a study of hacker's behavior in big data era. Peer-to-Peer Netw. Appl. **11**(2), 210–219 (2016). https://doi.org/10.1007/s12083-016-0517-5
19. Wang, Y., Metere, R., Zhou, H., et al.: Incentive-driven attacker for corrupting two-party protocols. Soft Comput. Fus. Found. Methodol. Appl. **22**(23), 7733–7740 (2018)
20. Bellini, E., Iraqi, Y., Damiani, E., et al.: Blockchain-based distributed trust and reputation management systems: a survey. IEEE Access **8**, 21127–21151 (2020)
21. Wang, Y., et al.: Secure computation protocols under asymmetric scenarios in enterprise information system. Enterpr. Inf. Syst. 1–21 (2019)
22. Kang, J., Xiong, Z., Niyato, D., et al.: Incentive mechanism for reliable federated learning: a joint optimization approach to combining reputation and contract theory. IEEE Internet of Things J. **6**(6), 10700–10714 (2019)
23. Hong, C., Katz, J., Kolesnikov, V., Lu, W., Wang, X.: Covert security with public verifiability: faster, leaner, and simpler. In: Ishai, Y., Rijmen, V. (eds.) EUROCRYPT 2019. LNCS, vol. 11478, pp. 97–121. Springer, Cham (2019). https://doi.org/10.1007/978-3-030-17659-4_4

An Efficient Public Batch Auditing Scheme for Data Integrity in Standard Model

Haining Yang[1] , Ye Su[1] , Jing Qin[1,2(✉)] , Jinhua Ma[3] ,
and Huaxiong Wang[4]

[1] School of Mathematics, Shandong University, Jinan 250100, China
hainingcode@163.com, sy0422@163.com, qinjing@sdu.edu.cn
[2] State Key Laboratory of Information Security, Institute of Information
Engineering, Chinese Academy of Sciences, Beijing 100093, China
[3] Fujian Provincial Key Laboratory of Network Security and Cryptology, College
of Mathematics and Informatics, Fujian Normal University, Fuzhou 350117, China
jinhuama55@hotmail.com
[4] Division of Mathematical Sciences, School of Physical and Mathematical Sciences,
Nanyang Technological University, Singapore, Singapore
hxwang@ntu.edu.sg

Abstract. The cloud storage auditing constructions derived from the primitives of homomorphic linear authenticator and polynomial-based authentication tag outperform other types of constructions in terms of the efficiency in verifier's side. However, the batch auditing overheads regarding the storage and the computation in known constructions can be further reduced. And these constructions are improper for the standard batch auditing model. In this paper, we propose an efficient cloud storage auditing scheme supporting the batch auditing in standard model. To this end, the only nonce in the existing constructions is replaced with multiple nonces that are corresponding to each involved data owner. And the extended Euclidean algorithm is employed to generate the aggregated proof for batch auditing. In the proposed scheme, the overheads regarding storage and computation are both reduced to be as approximately large as the number of the involved data owners. The security analysis and the performance evaluation show that the proposed scheme is secure and efficient as expected.

Keywords: Cloud storage auditing · Batch auditing · Cloud computing

1 Introduction

Cloud computing as a prevalent technology has been gaining great popularity recently. An increasing number of individuals and organizations prefer to utilize the cloud services in a pay-per-use manner. It is universally known that cloud storage is a major branch of the cloud computing services. A common practice

X. Chen et al. (Eds.): ML4CS 2020, LNCS 12486, pp. 578–592, 2020.
https://doi.org/10.1007/978-3-030-62223-7_51

in cloud storage is the data owner purchases the service to store huge volumes of data in the cloud server. The cloud storage is low-cost, location independent and scale [2,3] compared with the traditional local storage [4]. In other words, a data owner can utilize the cloud storage service to store the data in a cost-efficient manner, and later access these data and process them virtually anywhere and anytime. Despite these significant advantages, the cloud storage raises a series of security concerns regarding the data security and privacy. For example, the cloud server may discard the data that is rarely accessed or has never been accessed [21]. Moreover, the cloud server may even attempt to hide the event of data loss to maintain a good reputation [19]. These potential threats can actually breach the data integrity, which will in turn cause the unexpected negative effects on the subsequent data usage. How to determine whether the data is intact or not becomes a crucial security issue to be addressed [5,7,17,20,23].

Trivially, the data owner can first download the whole database from cloud server, and then check the integrity of these data with the locally stored authentication information. In this solution, the number of the authentication information is identical to the size of the database. However, the goal of achieving economies of scale in cloud storage is actually defeated in this solution where the data owner needs to afford large overheads regarding the communication and storage. In order to check the data integrity without retrieving the data from cloud server and without accessing the whole database, the novel technique of cloud storage auditing is proposed. Ateniese et al. [1] in 2007 first introduced the model of Provable Data Possession (PDP) for public auditing. In this model, not only the data owner but also an authorized third party auditor can check the data integrity without sacrificing the private information. Another model for cloud storage auditing is the private auditing called Proof of Retrievability (PoR) [11,12,15]. In contrast to the public auditing, the private auditing only allows the data owner to check the data integrity. We can observe that the public auditing is sufficient for more realistic cases than private auditing, and many works have devoted to this topic, such as [8,10,22,24,25].

In practical deployments, the data owner can employ the public auditing to securely delegate auditing tasks to a professional company. This company works as the third party auditor to check the data integrity on behalf of the data owner. This can help the data owner get rid of the computational burden resulting from the frequent auditing operations. As a professional organization, the specific company may usually execute multiple auditing tasks delegated by different data owners concurrently. The batch auditing can efficiently fulfill these public batch auditing tasks instead of repeatedly one by one [6,13,20,29]. In the standard model of batch auditing [21,23], the third party auditor collects the auditing delegations (issued by challenge tokens) from multiple data owners, and then check the data integrity for these data owners. The computational overhead is reduced and the probability of detecting the corrupted data is increased in the batch auditing. Thanks to the data owner's knowledge of the challenge tokens, the data owner is able to conduct a spot check on the third party auditor's operations by performing the auditing procedures. The third party auditor's misbehaviours can be detected in the case when the spot check is conducted, which would drive the third party auditor to behave strictly following the given procedures. A conclusion is reached that the investigation into public batch auditing in standard model is meaningful.

The cloud storage auditing is widely applied in verifiable database [9], electronic medical system [14] and fog computing [18]. In these practical cases, mobile devices such as smartphone are usually used to access the outsourced data. Unfortunately, these devices just have constrained bandwidth and computational resources, which would impose restrictions on accessing the outsourced data. When the mobile devices are used in the cloud storage auditing, the high auditing efficiency in the verifier's side becomes an important aspect. The works [26–28,30] proposed the constructions for public auditing based on the primitives of homomorphic linear authenticator and polynomial-based authentication tag. The overheads regarding communication and computation in these constructions are both constant in these solutions. However, the overheads that the verifier spends in performing batch auditing are the times of the number of involved data owners. Ideally, these overheads should approximately equal to the number of involved data owners.

Apart from the efficiency concern, the solutions of batch auditing in works [26–28,30] are unqualified for the standard model. These solutions just use one nonce to issue the batch auditing request to the cloud server, rather than collect the corresponding nonces from each data owner, respectively. They are invalidate for the auditing tasks delegated by multiple data owners in the standard model where many nonces are involved in. The ineffectiveness of the spot check on the third party auditor's operations is another weakness of these solutions. This follows the fact that the only nonce is chosen by the third party auditor so that the data owners are unable to effectively detect the third party auditor's misbehaviours. In particular, the third party auditor can deceive the data owner with a previous proof related to the correct operations but the current operations are incorrect. In order to remedy these limitations of the constructions based on homomorphic linear authenticator and polynomial-based authentication tag, a strengthened construction in the standard batch auditing model needs to be considered.

1.1   Our Contributions

The public batch auditing for data integrity in standard model is investigated in this work. A strengthened scheme based on the primitives of homomorphic linear authenticator and polynomial-based authentication tag is proposed. In contrast to the same type of known works, the proposed scheme is more efficient and qualified for the standard batch auditing model. The details of the contributions are described as follows.

1) The public batch auditing construction based on the primitives of homomorphic linear authenticator and polynomial-based authentication tag is

strengthened in the standard model. Thanks to the multiple nonces in standard model, the proposed scheme is equivalent to the parallel implements of known construction underlying the same primitives. It is challenging to realize this functionality in a subtle way that avoids directly combining the parallel operations of the known construction. We solve this problem by employing extended Euclidean algorithm to generate the aggregated proof. This is a generic approach to transform the construction qualified for one nonce into the construction for multiple nonces.

2) The third party auditor's potential malicious behaviours can be discouraged. In addition to satisfying the practical case of multiple nonces, the proposed scheme allows the data owners to conduct a spot check on the auditing process. The third party auditor's misbehaviours can be detected with a specific probability that increases with the number of the spot check growing.

3) The storage and computation in the verifier's side is as large as the number of the involved data owners. It is noted that the proposed scheme is strengthened in the standard model at an affordable price. This requirement becomes significant for the overheads of storage and computation in the verifier's side, because the verifier usually process a huge amount of auditing tasks. These overheads in the proposed scheme is approximately as large as the number of involved data owners. The proposed scheme is more efficient than the same type of existing solutions that are however unqualified for the standard model.

1.2   Related Works

Cloud storage auditing is a promising approach to check the data integrity in cloud computing. The signature-based constructions are mainly investigated in the research community. However, the efficiency of the storage and computation for the verifier is not so satisfactory, which is related to the number of data blocks. This would cause heavy storage and computation burden for the resource-constrained verifier, if the data is divided into many blocks. For this limitation, Yuan et al. [27] in 2013 first put forward the novel idea to construct cloud storage auditing scheme based on the homomorphic linear authenticator and polynomial-based authentication tag. The overheads of communication and computation in this scheme are constant. Subsequently, Yuan et al. [28] in 2015 further proposed a public auditing scheme that is proper for dynamic data sharing with multiuser modification. This scheme allows the authorized data users to modify the data, and outperforms the scheme [27] in the functionality. Yu et al. [26] in 2016 pointed out that the scheme [28] fails to achieve auditing soundness when the cloud server colludes with a general data user. Zhang et al. [30] in 2019 also showed an attack that is different from the attack in [26]. They propose a solution to remedy this drawback in [26]. These mentioned schemes are all derived from the primitives of homomorphic linear authenticator and polynomial-based authentication tag, which achieves good performance in the efficiency for verifier. Lots of subsequent works attempted to improve in the aspects of functionality and security. However, the efficiency of storage and computation can be further improved in these schemes. In addition, these constructions cannot implement the public batch auditing in standard model.

1.3 Paper Organization

The remaining parts are organized as follows. In Sect. 2, we give the background and preliminaries related to our work. In Sect. 3, we propose our construction for the efficient public batch auditing. In Sect. 4, we give the security analysis for our construction. In Sect. 5, we give the performance analysis for our construction. In Sect. 6, we conclude our work.

2 Background and Preliminaries

In this section, we give the background and the preliminaries. We first explain the notations used in this paper. And then we describe the problem statement about our work, which includes the system model, threat model and design goals. Finally, we present the necessary cryptographic knowledge used in our work.

2.1 Notations

In this paper, we use $a \xleftarrow{\$} \mathbb{Z}_p$ to denote the process of randomly choosing a value a from $\mathbb{Z}_p$. We use $[1,n]$ to denote the set $\{1,2,\cdots,n\}$. We use $\{a_i\}_{i=1}^n$ to denote the set where the subscripts of the element range from 1 to n. We use $w\backslash\{a\}$ to denote the set excluding element a. We use $Sign()$ to denote a secure digital signature scheme.

2.2 Problem Statement

As shown in Fig. 1, three kinds of entities are involved in the system for efficient public batch auditing. That is, the data owners, the cloud server and the third party auditor. More details are presented as follows.

1) The data owners have huge amounts of data, respectively. Every data owner processes the data by dividing them into blocks, and generates the file tag and authentication tag. Then the data owner stores the data blocks and authentication information in a cloud server to reduce local storage overhead (See process (I) in Fig. 1). In order to check the data integrity, it usually chooses to delegate the auditing task to public auditor (See process (II) in Fig. 1).

2) The third party auditor is also called public auditor. It is authorized to check the integrity of the outsourced data on behalf of data owners (See process (II) and (III) in Fig. 1). Ideally, it provides the credible auditing result for data owners (See process (V) in Fig. 1). However, it may convince the data owner that the outsourced data is intact without proceeding the auditing operations.

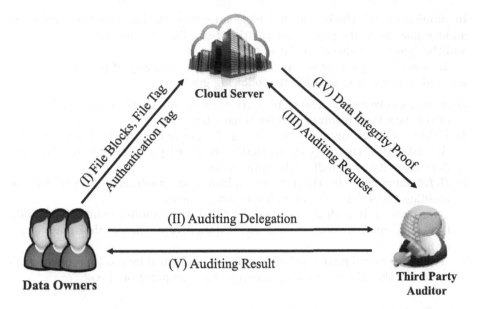

Fig. 1. System model for public batch cloud storage auditing.

3) The cloud server owns almost unlimited storage and computation resources. It can provide the storage service for the resource-constrained data owners. It also needs to provide a proof about the data integrity to the third party auditor (See process (IV) in Fig. 1).

Among these three kinds of entities, the data owners are considered to be honest who will strictly obey the prescribed procedures. The third party auditor should ideally be credible but curious [16] who honestly checks the data integrity and provides the trustworthy auditing result for data owner but is curious about private information of the outsourced data. However, it may covert to be malicious to deceive the data owner in order to save the resources. The cloud server is considered to be semi-honest. In usual case, the cloud server can provide the on-demand and scalable cloud services for data owners, but it will try to conceal the fact of data corruption incidents for its reputation. The cloud server may hide this negative fact by lunching below attacks to the third party auditor.

1) *Forgery attack*: the cloud server may forge the data, the authentication information and the proof corresponding to corrupted data to pass the verification.
2) *Substitution attack*: the cloud server may replace the corrupted data and its authentication information with another new data and the corresponding authentication information to pass the verification.
3) *Replay attack*: the cloud server may deceive the third party auditor by the previous proofs.

In addition to the attacks launched by cloud server, the fact that the third party auditor may learn the private information regarding the underlying data in the auditing process is also a crucial security concern.

In order to implement secure and efficient functionality of public cloud storage auditing, we need to fulfill the following goals.

1) *Auditing correctness*: The third party auditor can always verify the integrity of the data if all involved entities behave honestly.
2) *Public auditing*: Any party besides the data owner can verify the integrity of the data. It is the property to enable the third party auditor to check the data integrity on behalf of the data owners.
3) *Batch auditing*: The third party auditor can simultaneously perform the auditing tasks delegated by multiple data owners.
4) *Data privacy*: In auditing process, the third party auditor cannot learn additional information about the underlying data except whether the data is intact or not.
5) *High efficiency*: The public batch auditing performed by the third party auditor needs the minimum communication and computational cost.

2.3   Basic Cryptographic Knowledge

Definition 1 (Symmetric Bilinear Pairing). *Let $\mathbb{G}$ and $\mathbb{G}_T$ be cyclic multiplicative groups whose order are the prime p, and g be the generator of group $\mathbb{G}$. A bilinear pairing is a map $e: \mathbb{G} \times \mathbb{G} \to \mathbb{G}_T$, which satisfies the following properties:*

1) *Bilinearity: $e(a^u, b^v) = e(a, b)^{uv}$ holds for all u, $v \in \mathbb{Z}_p$ and a, $b \in \mathbb{G}$.*
2) *Non-degeneracy: There exist a and $b \in \mathbb{G}$ such that $e(a, b) \neq 1$.*
3) *Computability: There exists an efficient algorithm to compute $e(a, b)$ for all a, $b \in \mathbb{G}$.*

Definition 2 (Discrete Logarithm (DL) Assumption). *Given the value $g^a \in \mathbb{G}$ where g is the generator of the p-order group $\mathbb{G}$ and $a \in \mathbb{Z}_p$ (p is a prime), the probability of determining a from g^a in polynomial time is negligible.*

3   Our Construction

– **Setup:** Given the security parameter λ, the trust authority first generates a tuple $(e, g, p, \mathbb{G}, \mathbb{G}_T)$ with the bilinear mapping $e : \mathbb{G} \times \mathbb{G} \to \mathbb{G}_T$, where g is a generator of the cyclic group $\mathbb{G}$, the prime p is the order of group $\mathbb{G}$. It also chooses a secure hash function $H : \{0,1\}^* \to \mathbb{G}$. It chooses a value $a \xleftarrow{\$} \mathbb{Z}_p$ to generate the system public key g^{a^j} for $j \in [1, n]$. a is the system master secret key that is only known to the trust authority. The master secret key and the master public key are

$$MSK = a, MPK = \left((e, g, p, \mathbb{G}, \mathbb{G}_T), H, \left\{ g^{a^j} \right\}_{j=1}^{n} \right).$$

The trust authority can go offline after publishing the public key.

- **KeyGen:** The data owner $t \in [1,T]$ generates a signature key-pair $(sk_t, pk_t) \xleftarrow{\$} Sign()$. This data owner also chooses a random value $\delta_t \xleftarrow{\$} \mathbb{Z}_p^*$ to compute $\varphi_t = g^{\delta_t^{-1}}$, where t can be regarded as the identity information. The secret key and the public key are respectively

$$SK_t = (\delta_t, sk_t), PK_t = (\varphi_t, pk_t).$$

- **FileProcess:** Suppose the data owner $t \in [1,T]$ wants to store the file F_t in cloud server, this data owner first processes F_t by using erasure code to obtain the file F_t'. F_t' consists of m blocks $\{F_{t,i}'\}_{i=1}^m$, each block $F_{t,i}'$ has n elements, i.e., $F_{t,i}' = \{F_{t,i,j}'\}$ where $i \in [1,m]$ and $j \in [1,n]$. The data owner then chooses a file name $name_t \xleftarrow{\$} \mathbb{Z}_p^*$ to generate the file tag θ_t with the secret key sk_t

$$\theta_t = name_t \| m \| Sign(sk_t, name_t \| m).$$

It also generates authentication tag $\sigma_t = \{\sigma_{t,i}\}_{i=1}^m$ for file block $F_{t,i}'$ as

$$\sigma_{t,i} = \left(H(name_t\|t\|i) \cdot \prod_{j=1}^n \left(g^{a^j}\right)^{F_{t,i,j}'} \right)^{\delta_t} = \left(H(name_t\|t\|i) \cdot g^{f_{\vec{\alpha}}(a)} \right)^{\delta_t},$$

where $\vec{\alpha} = (F_{t,i,1}', \cdots, F_{t,i,n}')$.
The data owner stores the processed file F_t', the file tag θ_t and the authentication tag σ_t on the cloud server.

- **Challenge:** On receiving the auditing requests regarding data owner $t \in w$ where w is a subset of $[1,T]$, in order to verify the integrity of files $\{F_t'\}_{t\in w}$ on behalf of these data owners, the third party auditor first receives the file tags $\{\theta_t\}_{t\in w}$ and verifies these signatures with the public keys $\{pk_t\}_{t\in w}$, respectively. If the signatures cannot pass verification, the third party auditor will reject and stop. Otherwise, it recovers the file names $\{name_t\}_{t\in w}$ and m. Then, it randomly chooses a d-element subset D of $[1,m]$ and the random values $\{r_t\}_{t\in w}$ from $\mathbb{Z}_p^*$. It sends the challenge message $Challenge = (D, \{r_t\}_{t\in w})$ to the cloud server.

- **ProofGen:** On receiving the challenge message $Challenge = (D, \{r_t\}_{t\in w})$, the cloud server first computes $\mu_t = \{\mu_{t,i}\}_{i\in D} = \{r_t^i \bmod p\}_{i\in D}$. The cloud server generates the polynomial $f_{\vec{\beta}}(x) \in \mathbb{Z}_p[x]$, where

$$\vec{\beta} = \left(\sum_{t\in w}\sum_{i\in D} \mu_{t,i} F_{t,i,1}', \cdots, \sum_{t\in w}\sum_{i\in D} \mu_{t,i} F_{t,i,n}' \right).$$

Then, it computes $\psi(x) = \dfrac{f_{\vec{\beta}}(x) - R(x)}{\sum_{t\in w}(x - r_t)}$ where $R(x)$ is the remainder of polynomial division $\dfrac{f_{\vec{\beta}}(x)}{\sum_{t\in w}(x - r_t)}$, i.e., $f_{\vec{\beta}}(x) = \psi(x)\sum_{t\in w}(x - r_t) + R(x)$.

Suppose the coefficient vector of $\psi(x)$ is $(\psi_0, \cdots, \psi_n)$ and the coefficient vector of $R(x)$ is $(R_0, \cdots, R_n)$. The cloud server computes for $t \in w$

$$\phi_t = \prod_{i \in D} \sigma_{t,i}^{\mu_{t,i}}, \eta = \prod_{j=0}^{n} \left(g^{a^j} \right)^{\psi_j} = g^{\psi(a)}, \gamma = \prod_{j=0}^{n} \left(g^{a^j} \right)^{R_j} = g^{R(a)}.$$

It sends the proof $P = \left(\{\phi_t\}_{t \in w}, \eta, \gamma \right)$ to the third party auditor.

- **Verify:** After receiving the proof $P = \left(\{\phi_t\}_{t \in w}, \eta, \gamma \right)$, the third party auditor first computes

$$v = \prod_{t \in w} \prod_{i \in D} H\left(name_t \| t \| i\right)^{\mu_{t,i}}.$$

Then, the third party auditor verifies the data integrity by checking whether the following equation holds

$$\prod_{t \in w} e\left(\phi_t, \varphi_t\right) \overset{?}{=} e\left(\eta, g^{|w|a - \sum_{t \in w} r_t}\right) e\left(g, \gamma \cdot v\right).$$

4 Security Analysis

The proposed scheme is correct and secure. In this section, we will prove the correctness and the security of this scheme.

4.1 Correctness

A valid auditing scheme for cloud data storage must satisfy the requirement of correctness. This requirement states that if every entity participating in this scheme strictly follows prescribed procedures, the proof resulted by cloud server can always pass the third party auditor's checking.

Theorem 1. *The proposed auditing scheme for cloud data storage is correct.*

Proof. We denote $H\left(name_t \| t \| i\right)$ as $g^{s_{t,i}}$. So we have

$$e\left(\eta, \phi \cdot g^{-\sum_{t \in w} r_t}\right) e\left(g, \gamma \cdot v\right)$$

$$= e\left(g^{\frac{f_{\vec{\beta}}(a) - R(a)}{\sum_{t \in w}(a - r_t)}}, g^{|w|a - \sum_{t \in w} r_t}\right) e\left(g, g^{R(a)} \cdot \prod_{t \in w} \prod_{i \in D} g^{s_{t,i} r_t^i}\right)$$

$$= e\left(g^{\frac{f_{\vec{\beta}}(a) - R(a)}{\sum_{t \in w}(a - r_t)}}, g^{\sum_{t \in w}(a - r_t)}\right) e\left(g, g^{R(a) + \sum_{t \in w} \sum_{i \in D} s_{t,i} r_t^i}\right)$$

$$= e(g,g)^{f_{\vec{\beta}}(a) - R(a) + R(a) + \sum_{t \in w} \sum_{i \in D} s_{t,i} r_t^i}$$

$$= e(g,g)^{f_{\vec{\beta}}(a) + \sum_{t \in w} \sum_{i \in D} s_{t,i} r_t^i}$$

$$= e(g,g)^{\sum_{t \in w} \sum_{i \in D} \mu_{t,i} F'_{t,i,1} a + \cdots + \sum_{t \in w} \sum_{i \in D} \mu_{t,i} F'_{t,i,n} a^n + \sum_{t \in w} \sum_{i \in D} s_{t,i} r_t^i}$$

$$= e(g,g)^{\sum_{t \in w} \sum_{i \in D} \sum_{j=1}^{n} r_t^i F'_{t,i,j} a^j + \sum_{t \in w} \sum_{i \in D} s_{t,i} r_t^i}, \tag{1}$$

$$\prod_{t \in w} e\left(\phi_t, \varphi_t\right) = \prod_{t \in w} e\left(\prod_{i \in D} \sigma_{t,i}^{\mu_{t,i}}, \varphi_t\right)$$

$$= \prod_{t \in w} e\left(\prod_{i \in D} \left(H\left(name_t \| t \| i\right) \cdot g^{f_{\vec{\alpha}}(a)}\right)^{\delta_t \mu_{t,i}}, g^{\delta_t^{-1}}\right)$$

$$= e\left(g, g\right)^{\sum_{t \in w} \sum_{i \in D} st_{,i} r_t^i + \sum_{t \in w} \sum_{i \in D} r_t^i f_{\vec{\alpha}}(a)}$$

$$= e\left(g, g\right)^{\sum_{t \in w} \sum_{i \in D} st_{,i} r_t^i + \sum_{t \in w} \sum_{i \in D} r_t^i \sum_{j=1}^n F'_{t,i,1} a^j}$$

$$= e\left(g, g\right)^{\sum_{t \in w} \sum_{i \in D} st_{,i} r_t^i + \sum_{t \in w} \sum_{i \in D} \sum_{j=1}^n r_t^i F'_{t,i,j} a^j}. \tag{2}$$

From Eq. (1) and Eq. (2), we can observe that these two equations are equal. So, the proposed auditing scheme for cloud data storage is correct.

4.2 Auditing Soundness

Auditing soundness is an important security requirement in one auditing scheme. It can prevent the proof from passing the verification if the integrity of the data stored in cloud server is compromised.

Theorem 2. *The proposed scheme for cloud storage achieves auditing soundness.*

Proof. Suppose the forged proof corresponding to challenge $\left(D, \{r_t\}_{t \in w}\right)$ is $P' = \left(\{\phi'_t\}_{t \in w}, \eta', \gamma'\right)$ and $P' \neq P$, where P is the correct proof. In other words, P is honestly generated by cloud server corresponding to the challenge $\left(D, \{r_t\}_{t \in w}\right)$. In order to prove this theorem, we assume that the forged proof P' can pass the verification. So we have

$$\prod_{t \in w} e\left(\phi'_t, \varphi_t\right) = e\left(\eta', g^{|w|a - \sum_{t \in w} r_t}\right) e\left(g, \gamma' \cdot v\right), \tag{3}$$

$$\prod_{t \in w} e\left(\phi_t, \varphi_t\right) = e\left(\eta, g^{|w|a - \sum_{t \in w} r_t}\right) e\left(g, \gamma \cdot v\right). \tag{4}$$

From Eq. (3) and Eq. (4), we can obtain

$$\prod_{t \in w} e\left(\phi_t \phi_t'^{-1}, \varphi_t\right) = e\left(\eta \eta'^{-1}, g^{|w|a - \sum_{t \in w} r_t}\right) e\left(g, \gamma \gamma'^{-1}\right), \tag{5}$$

This implies that

$$\prod_{t \in w} e\left(\phi_t'^{-1}, \varphi_t\right) e\left(\eta', g^{|w|a - \sum_{t \in w} r_t}\right)\left(g, \gamma'\right)$$

$$= \prod_{t \in w} e\left(\phi_t^{-1}, \varphi_t\right) e\left(\eta, g^{|w|a - \sum_{t \in w} r_t}\right) e\left(g, \gamma\right)$$

$$= e\left(g, g\right)^{-\sum_{t \in w} \sum_{i \in D} r_t^i st_{,i}}. \tag{6}$$

We denote ϕ_t', η' and γ' as g^{b_t}, g^c and g^d respectively, where b_t, c and $d \in \mathbb{Z}_p$. So we can derive below equation from Eq. (6),

$$e\left(g,g\right)^{\sum_{t \in w} b_t \delta_t^{-1} + c\left(\sum_{t \in w} r_t - |w|a\right) - d} = e\left(g,g\right)^{\sum_{t \in w} \sum_{i \in D} r_t^i s_{t,i}}. \tag{7}$$

Apparently, it is equivalent to following equation hold,

$$g^{\sum_{t \in w} b_t \delta_t^{-1} + c\left(\sum_{t \in w} r_t - |w|a\right) - d} = g^{\sum_{t \in w} \sum_{i \in D} r_t^i s_{t,i}}. \tag{8}$$

In Eq. (8), the items of $c\left(\sum_{t \in w} r_t - |w|a\right) - d$ and $\sum_{t \in w} \sum_{i \in D} r_t^i s_{t,i}$ can be computed by the cloud server itself.

Given the public values $\{\varphi_t\} = \left\{g^{\delta_t^{-1}}\right\}_{t \in w}$ and the known value g^h where $h = \sum_{t \in w} \sum_{i \in D} r_t^i s_{t,i} - c\left(\sum_{t \in w} r_t - |w|a\right) + d$, we can show how the cloud server to determine the corresponding values $\{b_t\}_{t \in w}$. In order to make Eq. (8) holds, for any $t \in w \backslash \{t_0\}$, cloud server can first choose the random values $k_t \in \mathbb{Z}_p$ as b_t to compute

$$\varphi_t^{k_t} = \left(g^{\delta_t^{-1}}\right)^{k_t}, \tag{9}$$

and then determine the value $b_{t_0} = k_{t_0} \in \mathbb{Z}_p$ such that $\varphi_{t_0}^{k_{t_0}} = g^{h - \sum_{t \in w \backslash \{t_0\}} k_t \delta_t^{-1}}$. So $g^{b_{t_0}} = g^{k_{t_0}} = \left(g^{h - \sum_{t \in w \backslash \{t_0\}} k_t \delta_t^{-1}}\right)^{\delta_{t_0}}$, where δ_{t_0} is crucial to determine the value of b_{t_0}. This implies that if cloud server successfully forges the proof, it needs to recover $\delta_{t_0}^{-1}$ from $\varphi_{t_0} = g^{\delta_{t_0}^{-1}}$ and then compute δ_{t_0}. This suggests that cloud server can solve the discrete logarithm problem regarding the instance $g^{\delta_{t_0}^{-1}}$, which contradicts the cryptographic assumption that the discrete logarithm problem is hard. Therefore, we can conclude that the proposed scheme for cloud storage achieves auditing soundness.

5   Performance Evaluation

5.1   Theoretical Analysis

In Table 1, we give the overhead comparisons among the communication, storage and computation in the verifier's side. For simplicity, $\mathbb{Z}_p$ is used to denote the element in $\mathbb{Z}_p$ or $\mathbb{Z}_p^*$, G is used to denote the element in $\mathbb{G}$, G_T is used to denote the element in $\mathbb{G}_T$, Tag is used to denote the file tag, A_1 and S_1 are respectively used to denote the operations of addition and subtraction in $\mathbb{Z}_p$ or $\mathbb{Z}_p^*$, M_2 and E_2 are respectively used to denote the operations of multiplication and exponent in $\mathbb{G}$, $Pair$ is used to denote the operation of pairing computation, M_3 is used to denote the operation of multiplication in $\mathbb{G}_T$. The communication overhead is referred to the size of the challenge that the verifier sends to the cloud server. The storage overhead is referred to the size of the response from the cloud server. And the computation overhead is referred to the number of operations involved in

Table 1. The overhead comparisons in verifier's side with some existing works.

Works	Standard model	Communication overhead	Storage overhead	Computation overhead
[21]	Yes	$(d + |w|) Z_p$	$2 |w| Z_p + G_T$	$(2 |w| - 1) M_2 + 3 |w| E_2$ $+ (|w| + 1) Pair + |w| M_3$
[27]	No	$(d + 1) Z_p$	$2 |w| G + |w| Tag$	$(|w| + 1) S_1 + |w| M_2 + 2 |w| E_2$ $+ 3 |w| Pair + (3 |w| - 1) M_3$
[30]	No	$(d + 1) Z_p$	$2 |w| G + |w| Tag$	$(|w| + 1) S_1 + |w| M_2 + 2 |w| E_2$ $+ 3 |w| Pair + (3 |w| - 1) M_3$
Ours	Yes	$(d + |w|) Z_p$	$|w + 2| G + |w| Tag$	$|w| A_1 + S_1 + M_1 + M_2 + E_2$ $+ (|w| + 2) Pair + |w| M_3$

the verification equations. It is noted the hash operations on the data identifier information in **Verify** algorithm can be pre-processed in offline mode, which implies that these operations cannot impose an effect on the online verification time. For this reason, the time in processing the data identifier information is not considered in the computation overhead.

In order to support the validity of our scheme, we give the overheads of the scheme in [21] that is an outstanding work in the cloud storage auditing field. The subsequent works have rich functionalities but the mentioned overheads in Table 1 are not significantly changed. In the proposed scheme, we employ the extended Euclidean algorithm in such a way that most of the operations corresponding to the involved data owners can be securely delegated to the cloud server. Through the computations by cloud server, many values that should be sent to the verifier in [27,30] are aggregated. So we can observe from Table 1 that our scheme has less overheads regarding storage and computation compared with the schemes in the works [27,30]. In order to propose a scheme based on the homomorphic linear authenticator and polynomial-based authentication tag for the standard batch auditing model, it is unavoidable to replace the only one nonce in the schemes of [27,30] with multiple nonces. So the communication overhead in our scheme is more than that of the schemes in [27,30]. However, this overhead is the same to that of the scheme in [21]. This indicates that our scheme is proper for the standard batch auditing model at reasonable cost. From above, our scheme is an efficient public cloud storage auditing scheme in the standard batch auditing model.

5.2   Experiment Result

We give the time comparisons in the verification in Fig. 2. The computation overhead in verifier's side is measured by the time cost in the experiment. To obtain these experiment results, we use C programming language based on Pairing-Based Cryptography Library-0.5.14 (PBC-0.5.14), GNU Multiple Precision Arithmetic Library-6.1.2 (GMP-6.1.2). All of the results are obtained on the same computer with Intel(R) Core (TM) i7-8550U CPU @ 2.00 GHz and 512 MB RAM running Ubuntu 18.04. We set the base field size to be 512 bits and the size of an element in group Z_p to be $|p| = 160$ bits.

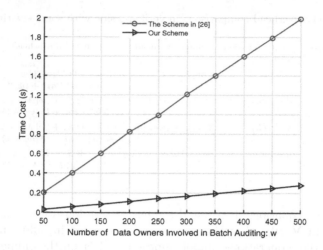

Fig. 2. The comparisons for computation overhead.

In our scheme, the number of the involved data owners in batch auditing can be regarded as the number of auditing tasks. We can easily see from Fig. 2 that the time cost in the verification grows with the increase of the number of auditing tasks. The time cost in our scheme is lower than that of the scheme in work [27]. In order to show the superiority of our scheme, we choose to change the number of auditing tasks from 50 to 500. Both the time cost of our scheme and the scheme in work [27] grows with the increase of the number of auditing tasks. And the difference regarding time cost between our scheme and the scheme in work [27] becomes more and more significant. These facts indicate that our scheme is efficient in verification, and is practical in the cloud environment where the number of auditing tasks is usually very large.

6   Conclusion

In this work, we comprehensively investigate the public batch auditing that employs the primitives of homomorphic linear authenticator and polynomial-based authentication tag as the building blocks. We analyze the weaknesses in existing constructions and propose a strengthened construction. The proposed scheme inherits the merits of the same type of existing constructions, meanwhile additionally improves the efficiency in the verifier's side and meets the condition of standard model. The proposed scheme is proved to be secure under the auditing soundness requirement that can prevent the cloud server from forging proof to deceive the verifier. The performance analysis is given to show that the proposed scheme is more efficient and practical than the existing constructions.

Acknowledgments. This work is supported by National Natural Science Foundation of China under Grant (No. 61772311) and China Scholarship Council (No. 201906220077).

References

1. Ateniese, G., et al.: Provable data possession at untrusted stores. In: Proceedings of the 14th ACM Conference on Computer and Communications Security, pp. 598–609 (2007)
2. Chen, X., Li, J., Huang, X., Ma, J., Lou, W.: New publicly verifiable databases with efficient updates. IEEE Trans. Dependable Secure Comput. **12**(5), 546–556 (2014)
3. Chen, X., Li, J., Weng, J., Ma, J., Lou, W.: Verifiable computation over large database with incremental updates. IEEE Trans. Comput. **65**(10), 3184–3195 (2015)
4. Dewan, H., Hansdah, R.: A survey of cloud storage facilities. In: 2011 IEEE World Congress on Services, pp. 224–231. IEEE (2011)
5. Kolhar, M., Abu-Alhaj, M.M., Abd El-atty, S.M.: Cloud data auditing techniques with a focus on privacy and security. IEEE Secur. Privacy **15**(1), 42–51 (2017)
6. Li, J., Zhang, L., Liu, J.K., Qian, H., Dong, Z.: Privacy-preserving public auditing protocol for low-performance end devices in cloud. IEEE Trans. Inf. Forensics Secur. **11**(11), 2572–2583 (2016)
7. Li, Y., Yu, Y., Min, G., Susilo, W., Ni, J., Choo, K.K.R.: Fuzzy identity-based data integrity auditing for reliable cloud storage systems. IEEE Trans. Dependable Secure Comput. **16**(1), 72–83 (2017)
8. Li, Y., Yu, Y., Yang, B., Min, G., Wu, H.: Privacy preserving cloud data auditing with efficient key update. Future Gener. Comput. Syst. **78**, 789–798 (2018)
9. Miao, M., Wang, J., Wen, S., Ma, J.: Publicly verifiable database scheme with efficient keyword search. Inf. Sci. **475**, 18–28 (2019)
10. Oqaily, M., et al.: SegGuard: segmentation-based anonymization of network data in clouds for privacy-preserving security auditing. IEEE Trans. Dependable Secure Comput. (2019). https://doi.org/10.1109/TDSC.2019.2957488
11. Sebé, F., Domingo-Ferrer, J., Martinez-Balleste, A., Deswarte, Y., Quisquater, J.J.: Efficient remote data possession checking in critical information infrastructures. IEEE Trans. Knowl. Data Eng. **20**(8), 1034–1038 (2008)
12. Shacham, H., Waters, B.: Compact proofs of retrievability. In: Pieprzyk, J. (ed.) ASIACRYPT 2008. LNCS, vol. 5350, pp. 90–107. Springer, Heidelberg (2008). https://doi.org/10.1007/978-3-540-89255-7_7
13. Shen, J., Shen, J., Chen, X., Huang, X., Susilo, W.: An efficient public auditing protocol with novel dynamic structure for cloud data. IEEE Trans. Inf. Forensics Secur. **12**(10), 2402–2415 (2017)
14. Shen, W., Qin, J., Yu, J., Hao, R., Hu, J.: Enabling identity-based integrity auditing and data sharing with sensitive information hiding for secure cloud storage. IEEE Trans. Inf. Forensics Secur. **14**(2), 331–346 (2018)
15. Shen, W., Su, Y., Hao, R.: Lightweight cloud storage auditing with deduplication supporting strong privacy protection. IEEE Access **8**, 44359–44372 (2020)
16. Sookhak, M., et al.: Remote data auditing in cloud computing environments: a survey, taxonomy, and open issues. ACM Comput. Surv. (CSUR) **47**(4), 1–34 (2015)
17. Tian, H., et al.: Dynamic-hash-table based public auditing for secure cloud storage. IEEE Trans. Serv. Comput. **10**(5), 701–714 (2015)
18. Tian, H., Nan, F., Chang, C.C., Huang, Y., Lu, J., Du, Y.: Privacy-preserving public auditing for secure data storage in fog-to-cloud computing. J. Netw. Comput. Appl. **127**, 59–69 (2019)

19. Tian, H., Nan, F., Jiang, H., Chang, C.C., Ning, J., Huang, Y.: Public auditing for shared cloud data with efficient and secure group management. Inf. Sci. **472**, 107–125 (2019)

20. Wang, B., Li, B., Li, H.: Panda: public auditing for shared data with efficient user revocation in the cloud. IEEE Trans. Serv. Comput. **8**(1), 92–106 (2013)

21. Wang, C., Wang, Q., Ren, K., Lou, W.: Privacy-preserving public auditing for data storage security in cloud computing. In: 2010 Proceedings IEEE Infocom, pp. 1–9. IEEE (2010)

22. Wang, H., He, D., Yu, J., Wang, Z.: Incentive and unconditionally anonymous identity-based public provable data possession. IEEE Trans. Serv. Comput. **12**(5), 824–835 (2019)

23. Wang, Q., Wang, C., Ren, K., Lou, W., Li, J.: Enabling public auditability and data dynamics for storage security in cloud computing. IEEE Trans. Parallel Distrib. Syst. **22**(5), 847–859 (2010)

24. Wang, Y., Tao, X., Ni, J., Yu, Y.: Data integrity checking with reliable data transfer for secure cloud storage. Int. J. Web Grid Serv. **14**(1), 106–121 (2018)

25. Yu, Y., et al.: Identity-based remote data integrity checking with perfect data privacy preserving for cloud storage. IEEE Trans. Inf. Forensics Secur. **12**(4), 767–778 (2016)

26. Yu, Y., Li, Y., Ni, J., Yang, G., Mu, Y., Susilo, W.: Comments on public integrity auditing for dynamic data sharing with multiuser modification. IEEE Trans. Inf. Forensics Secur. **11**(3), 658–659 (2015)

27. Yuan, J., Yu, S.: Secure and constant cost public cloud storage auditing with deduplication. In: 2013 IEEE Conference on Communications and Network Security (CNS), pp. 145–153. IEEE (2013)

28. Yuan, J., Yu, S.: Public integrity auditing for dynamic data sharing with multiuser modification. IEEE Trans. Inf. Forensics Secur. **10**(8), 1717–1726 (2015)

29. Zhang, J., Dong, Q.: Efficient ID-based public auditing for the outsourced data in cloud storage. Inf. Sci. **343**, 1–14 (2016)

30. Zhang, J., Wang, B., He, D., Wang, X.A.: Improved secure fuzzy auditing protocol for cloud data storage. Soft. Comput. **23**(10), 3411–3422 (2019)

A Block Chain Dynamic Key Sharing and Updating Scheme Based on the (t, n) Threshold

Wei Tang[1,2,3], Yu-Ling Chen[2(✉)], and Yun Yang[4]

[1] College of Mathematics and Statistics, Guizhou University, Guiyang, China
Tangwei@gztvu.com, 923320372@qq.com
[2] State Key Laboratory of Public Big Date, Guizhou University, Guiyang, China
ylchen3@gzu.edu.cn, 61997525@qq.com
[3] College of Information Engineering, Guizhou Radio and Television
University, Guiyang, China
[4] Ministry of Foundation, Guizhou Electronic Commerce Vocational College,
Guiyang, China

Abstract. Key sharing and updating is the core problem in key management. In order to solve the centralization, security and secret share loss in the process of key management, we propose a decentralized (t, n) threshold dynamic key sharing and updating scheme in the Blockchain system, which makes full use of the advantages of Blockchain decentralization and traceability for key sharing and updating. Firstly, we generated and stored the key based on Diffie-Hellman key exchange protocol to complete the formation of the node Shared key. Secondly, a threshold scheme (t, n) of key sharing is designed based on Lagrange polynomial interpolation function, and the sub-key of each block node is stored in different places to realize key sharing of block chain. Finally, the chameleon hash function is used to update and modify the historical content for node loss in block chain sharing. The analysis shows that this scheme can realize the secure sharing and updating of the key in the Blockchain system.

Keywords: Block chain · Key exchange · (t, n) threshold · Key sharing and updating · Chameleon hash function

1 Introduction

1.1 Related Works

Key management is a key issue in network security issues, specifically addressing issues related to the entire process from key generation to final destruction, including the initialization of the system, key generation, storage, distribution, update, revocation, control, destruction, and other processes [1–5]. As we all know, the security of information depends on the protection and management of keys. Different cryptographic algorithms determine different key management mechanisms and have different effects on key management, so how to generate, distribute, share and update keys becomes the core issue of key management [6–8]. The idea of Threshold secret sharing

© Springer Nature Switzerland AG 2020
X. Chen et al. (Eds.): ML4CS 2020, LNCS 12486, pp. 593–606, 2020.
https://doi.org/10.1007/978-3-030-62223-7_52

for key decentralization was first proposed in 1979 by Shamir and Blakley, which provides new ways for secure use and sharing of keys. As far as key integrity is concerned, key hosting can be divided into full key hosting and decentralized key hosting, which is significantly better than full key hosting in terms of security [9–11]. As a result, decentralized key hosting has been studied in a bit more depth. Most of the currently proposed schemes use threshold segmentation for decentralized key management. Among the various proposed key management schemes, the polynomial-based key sharing scheme proposed by Shamir is easy to understand and implement, so it has attracted many scholars to study it in depth, and a large number of new schemes have also emerged.

The key management process is mainly about key sharing and updating, especially how to achieve safe key sharing and timely updating has become an important research hotspot. The basic idea of key management is that the key management center divides the key into n sub-keys and distributes the sub-keys to each key shareholder, and in the key synthesis stage the original key can be synthesized as long as the t sub-keys of n sub-keys cooperate. However, there is a key generation and distribution center in such a process, and it is easy for the key to be tampered with and lost during the key sharing process, which makes the security of the key to be threatened.

The concept of Blockchain was introduced by Satoshi Nakamoto in 2008 [1, 2], and Blockchain technology has been rapidly developing since then. As a novel technology, Blockchain is widely used in cryptocurrencies and Internet finance. It is a decentralized system architecture with stronger computing power, lower cost, higher reliability and self-growth ability, and Blockchain technology has characteristics such as "decentralized", "traceable" and "tamper-proof", and can establish a peer-to-peer trusted account between unfamiliar nodes, which is ideal for key management without the participation of trusted third parties. But how to generate and store keys between the nodes of the Blockchain, and at the same time design a reasonable scheme to enable secret sharing and updating of each node of the Blockchain [11–15]. In response to this problem, Wang Ruijin and Tang Chunming have proposed key management ideas in the Blockchain context in the Blockchain key fragmentation storage and multiparty negotiation scheme respectively. There are some interesting applications for decentralized peer-to-peer networking systems in areas such as file sharing, content distribution, privacy protection, etc. And one simple yet powerful application is the simultaneous transformation of the user of the network into the builder of the network [15–17].

1.2   Motivations and Contributions

Using the advantages of block chain to design a key management system has become one of the important ways to realize secure key sharing and updating. Firstly, in the generation stage of the key, based on the decentralized point-to-point system, each node is both the generator and the user of the key. Secondly, in the whole life cycle of key management, with the help of decentralized point-to-point system, the interaction time and information processing time between nodes become shorter and the transaction cost is lower. Finally, in terms of security, in a decentralized point-to-point system, each node jointly maintains the security of the system, and the block chain has the characteristics of traceability.

If the key sharing mode in the Blockchain is equated with the transaction process of cryptocurrency, how to broadcast the transaction record in the transaction process to the whole system and obtain the consensus of all members is the key to realize the key sharing. In terms of resisting attacks, considering witch attacks and malicious node attacks, this paper proposes a block chain technology that can be modified based on multi-party cooperation, which can be used to remove malicious nodes and guarantee the entry and exit mechanism of nodes.

Through the above analysis, this paper proposes a key sharing and updating scheme based on block chain and threshold scheme. The main contributions are as follows:

1) The diffie-Hellman key exchange protocol is used to generate and store the key, and the Shared key is formed and exchanged between block nodes, which has a good advantage in secret security sharing.
2) The key of each block node is decomposed into sub-keys and stored in other block nodes. Meanwhile, a threshold scheme (t, n) of key sharing is designed based on Lagrange polynomial interpolation function to realize key sharing in block chain.
3) In combination with the voting mechanism, a consensus node is selected from the block chain network node, and the consensus node uses chameleon hash function to change the block chain data. This solution to the Blockchain node loss and malicious attacks and other issues to provide a feasible solution, effectively prevent Blockchain can not work properly and other problems.

1.3 Organization

This paper is organized as follows: In Sect. 2, we outline some of the preliminary knowledge needed for this paper. In the Sect. 3, We study the algorithms of Blockchain key generation and distribution. In Sect. 4, We construct and analyze a block chain key sharing scheme based on (t, n) threshold. In Sect. 5, Block chain change algorithm based on Hash trap function. In Sect. 6 and 7, we analyze the security of the proposed scheme and conclude the results and discussing future work.

2 Preliminaries

2.1 Blockchain Key Technologies

The core idea of Blockchain is to allow each participating node in the system to generate a block of data by solving the value of some Hash function, each block of data contains all the exchange information data of the system at a certain time. The validation node uses the Hash function to generate information features to verify the validity of the transaction data in the block of data, and links to the next block of data, thus forming a Blockchain. Recorded information is verified for authenticity by all nodes in the system.

Broadly speaking, Blockchain technology is a new distributed infrastructure and computing paradigm that uses Blockchain-style data structures to verify and store data, uses distributed node consensus algorithms to generate and update data, uses cryptography to ensure the security of data transmission and access, and uses automated scripting code composed of smart contracts to program and operate data. According to the different application scenarios and participants, it can be divided into alliance chain, public chain and private chain.

The Blockchain system consists of two main types of actors: users and miners, with users trading data and miners competing to mine for bookkeeping rights to generate blocks. Each block consists of two parts, a block header and a block body, where the block header includes the block header hash value, random number, timestamp, etc. The block body is a collection of specific transactions, mainly a Merkle tree storing data information, which stores information and data obtained from the block chain system over a period of time. Mining is to find a random number that satisfies the requirement so that the block head hash is less than a predetermined target hash value (Fig. 1).

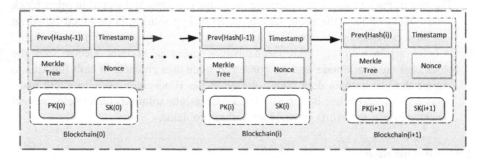

Fig. 1. Block chain structure diagram

The diagram above is a schematic of the block chain. Starting from the original block, the newly generated block header needs to reference the hash value of the previous block, and the block information of each peer node is jointly maintained by all the nodes. Nodes in the Blockchain generate new block by completing block certificates and broadcasting them to the entire network, currently the main Blockchain certificates include POW, POS, DPOS, etc.

Hash algorithms are used in Blockchain to generate blocks and form consensus, where Merkle tree is to generate the hash value of the root node by computing the hash value of the information stored by the leaf node. Its role is to quickly generalize and verify the existence and integrity of block data. In addition, the Blockchain uses a signature algorithm to process the transaction process of information, in general, we can equate the address and the public key, the public key is used to receive foreign data for storage, the private key is used to pass data information. A private key is a unique credential for ownership of data information, and the generation, storage, use and updating of a private key requires extreme caution (Fig. 2).

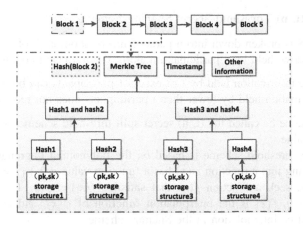

Fig. 2. The structure of block

2.2 Discrete Logarithm Problem

(1) Discrete logarithmic problems on finite domains

Set $GF(q)$ is a finite domain, where q is a large prime number and g is the generating element of z_p^*. Selecting the secret key x of user A, $x \leftarrow_R Z_p^*$, while using the public key y of selected user A makes $y \equiv g^x (\bmod p)$. The difficult problem with discrete logarithms is that values in the known public key y for the secret key x are known to be computationally difficult.

(2) The Diffie-Hellman Secret Key Negotiation Agreement

Based on the discrete logarithm problem of finite domains, there are two existing users A, B for secret key negotiation.

Step 1, A picks a random number $a(0 \leq a \leq q - 1)$, calculates $K_A = g^a (\bmod q)$ and sends K_A to B.

Step 2, B picks a random number $b(0 \leq b \leq q - 1)$, calculates $K_B = g^b (\bmod q)$ and sends K_B to A.

Step 3, A calculates $K = K_A = \left(g^b\right)^a (\bmod q)$, B calculates $K = K_B = \left(g^a\right)^b (\bmod q)$, In this case K is the shared key.

The basic security attributes of key negotiation are as follows:

1) Known key security. Each session key is temporary and unique, so it is not vulnerable to attack.
2) Perfect forward confidentiality. if one or more participants are compromised even over a long period of time, the pre-generated session key will not be affected.
3) The key is uncontrollable, and since the key is generated by negotiation between the participants, including random numbers, etc., none of the parties have any prior control over the generation of the key.
4) Key sharing agnostic, every participant is aware of the key negotiation protocol.

2.3   Shamir (t, n) Threshold Secret Sharing Scheme

The set secret S is broken down into n parts of information, each of which is called a sub-key or shadow, held by a participant, making the following condition valid.

1) Some of the information held by t or excess t participants can be reconstructed s.
2) Partial information held by fewer than t participants does not reconstruct s.

Let this scheme be called the (t, n) secret split threshold scheme, where t is called the threshold value.

The Shamir threshold scheme is based on the polynomial Lagrange interpolation formula. Knowing that a function $\varphi(x)$ has a function value $\varphi(x_i)$ $(i = 1, 2 \cdots, t)$ at t different points, seek a function $f(x)$ that satisfies $f(x_i) = \varphi(x_i)$ $(i = 1, 2 \cdots, t)$ to approximate $\varphi(x)$. $f(x)$ is the interpolation function of $\varphi(x)$, and $f(x)$ is taken as Lagrange algebraic interpolation in the Shamir scheme.

It is known that the value of the function $\varphi(x)$ at different points of t is $\varphi(x_i)$ $(i = 1, 2 \cdots, t)$, and we can construct the interpolation polynomial of order t − 1

$$f(x) = \sum_{j=1}^{t} \varphi(x_j) \prod_{\substack{l=1 \\ l \neq j}}^{t} \frac{(x - x_l)}{x_j - x_l} \tag{1}$$

The above formula constructs $f(x)$ by using t different values of functions of the polynomial of order t − 1. If the key S is viewed as $f(0)$ and the n sub-keys as $f(x_i)$ $(i = 1, 2 \cdots, n)$. Using any t sub-keys, $f(x)$ can be reconstructed so that the secret key S can be derived, which is the Shamir threshold scheme.

It is constructed along the following ways:

Let $GF(q)$ be a finite domain, where q is a large prime number, satisfying $q \geq n + 1$. Let secret S be a random number selected at random on the finite domain $GF(q) \backslash \{0\}$, denoted as $s \leftarrow_R GF(q) \backslash \{0\}$, where the selection of t − 1 coefficient also satisfies $a_i \leftarrow_R GF(q) \backslash \{0\}(i = 1, 2, \cdots, t - 1)$. Construct a t − 1 sub-polynomial on $GF(q)$.

$$f(x) = a_0 + a_1 x + a_2 x^2 + \cdots + a_{t-1} x^{t-1}$$

The n participants of that secret division are noted as $P_1, P_2, \cdots, P_n$, where p_i is assigned to the sub-key $f(i)$. If any t participants $P_{i_1}, \cdots, P_{i_t} (1 \leq i_1 < i_2 < \cdots < i_t \leq n)$ want to get the secret S, a linear set of equations can be constructed using $\{(i_j, f(i_j)) | j = 1, 2, \cdots, t\}$ as follows.

$$\begin{cases} a_0 + a_1(i_1) + \cdots + a_{t-1}(i_1)^{t-1} = f(i_1) \\ a_0 + a_1(i_2) + \cdots + a_{t-1}(i_2)^{t-1} = f(i_2) \\ \qquad\qquad \vdots \\ a_0 + a_1(i_t) + \cdots + a_{t-1}(i_t)^{t-1} = f(i_t) \end{cases} \tag{2}$$

Since all are not the same, the Lagrange interpolation formula constructs the following polynomial.

$$f(x) = \sum_{j=1}^{t} f(i_j) \prod_{\substack{l=1 \\ l \neq j}}^{t} \frac{(x - x_l)}{x_j - x_l} \pmod{q} \tag{3}$$

From this can be obtained the secret $S = f(0)$.

3 Blockchain Key Generation and Distribution Algorithms

3.1 System Architecture

The Blockchain key generation and distribution system is mainly divided into 4 parts: storage layer, network layer, consensus layer and distribution layer. The storage layer mainly uses the Merkel tree to preserve the relevant data structure of the public key distribution; the network layer is the client's network interaction module between servers; the consensus layer is through the improved PBFT consensus mechanism for the election of each node to jointly compute to elect the main node with the right to bookkeeping and modification rights, and mutual supervision between nodes through the consensus mechanism; the distribution layer is the server through the processing of requests for public key distribution initiated by the client module, while the client can query the Blockchain to verify the correctness of public key distribution.

To enable the successful exchange and updating of secret keys on the Blockchain, a key sharing system is built through a four-tier architecture (Fig. 3).

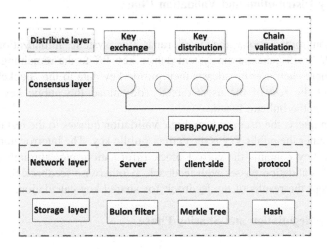

Fig. 3. The system framework of key sharing scheme

3.2 Description of the Blockchain Key Generation Algorithm

Assuming that the Blockchain is held by n user $P_1, P_2, \cdots, P_n$, where user P_i holds the bookkeeping rights of block BK_i, then in the key distribution system based on the Blockchain system described above, each user P_i generates its own key pair according to the following procedure.

1) Establish the key generation system and initialize the parameters. The parameters involved for the user include the user's address, the user's attributes, the block header hash value, the block timestamp, etc.
2) Calculates $H_i = Hash(ID_i\|IB_i\|Head_i\|Time_i)$, which is used to verify the existence and integrity of the public key.
3) The random number $x_i \leftarrow_R Z_p^*$ was generated by using a random number generator.
4) Generate a public-private key to (pk, sk), use user P_i to select the x_i on a finite domain, and calculate the $y_i = g^{x_i} \bmod q$.
5) Key storage and broadcast: where the private key is stored in the Merkle tree for the secret $sk = x_i$ and the public key is the $pk = (y_i, H_i)$ broadcast domain network.

3.3 Key Distribution and Key Exchange Methods

After key generation, the entire Blockchain system wants to share the key, then each user needs to broadcast their public key to each Blockchain node, after the Blockchain node receives the public key information from other users in the system, need to verify whether the received public key is the correct public key information, request verification to the sender, using the Blockchain Byzantine fault tolerance consensus mechanism for verification. The specific distribution and validation methods are as follows.

Phase 1: Key Distribution and Validation Phase

1) Distribution preparation: the user runs the system initialization algorithm $Setup(k, U)$, will generate the system public key PK to the remaining nodes. This can be where each user broadcasts their public key data to the Blockchain bulletin board, and the rest of the users directly download the public key information directory on the bulletin board.
2) Validation query: the user sends multiple validation queries to the rest of the user to verify whether the public key is the correct public key. The interrogator verifies that the public key contains the correct block information, etc., through a decryption algorithm. Validation passes with feedback 1, otherwise feedback 0.
3) Users accept the results of the feedback for shared key calculation.

Phase 2: Key Negotiation and Sharing Phase

1) Alice selects a random number $x_A (0 \leq x_A \leq q - 1)$ as the private key, Calculate $K_A = g^{x_A} \bmod q$ and broadcast K_A over the network.

2) Bob selects a random number $x_B(0 \le x_B \le q-1)$ as the private key, Calculate $K_B = g^{x_B}(\text{mod } q)$ and broadcast K_B over the network.

3) Alice and Bob download the public key information of other nodes from the Blockchain system bulletin board and perform key negotiation calculation, Alice Calculate $K_{AB} = (g^{x_B})^{x_A} \text{ mod } q = g^{x_A x_B} \text{ mod } q$, Bob Calculate $K_{BA} = (g^{x_A})^{x_B} \text{ mod} q = g^{x_B x_A} \text{ mod } q$, At this time, the Shared key is $K = K_{AB} = K_{BA}$.

4) The public key information of all nodes obtained by any user node N_i is $PK = (y_1, y_2, \cdots, y_n) = (g^{x_1}, g^{x_2}, \cdots, g^{x_n}) \text{ mod } q$. Thus, node N_i calculates that all Shared keys with other nodes are $K = (K_{i1}, K_{i2}, \cdots, K_{in}) = (g^{x_i x_1}, g^{x_i x_2}, \cdots, g^{x_i x_n}) \text{ mod } q$.

4 Threshold-Based Blockchain Key Sharing Scheme

Blockchain is a distributed data storage technology system that stores data in a Blockchain structure, while using cryptography to ensure secure transmission and multiple access. Blockchain has become a hotspot for experts to study because of its decentralized, tamper-proof, highly transparent and traceable features. But the open transparency of the Blockchain potentially leaks transaction privacy, and the data written to the chain cannot be changed, much less destroyed, making it difficult for administrators to effectively manage illegal data on the chain.

To solve the above problems, the key private key of each block is distributed stored and Shared by using Lagrange interpolation polynomial function. The specific plan is divided into three phases.

Phase 1: Key Decomposition
Let the Blockchain sequence be $BK = \{BK_1, BK_1, \cdots, BK_n\}$, The private key information for each block node BK_i is S_i, Then the private key for all blocks is $\{S_1, S_2, \cdots, S_n\}$. Block BK_i splits the private key S_i into n sub-key $S_i = \{s_{i1}, s_{i2}, \cdots, s_{in}\}$. Thus, the private key sub-key of all blocks forms a sub-key matrix

$$A = \begin{bmatrix} s_{11} & s_{12} & \cdots & s_{1n} \\ s_{21} & s_{22} & \cdots & s_{2n} \\ \vdots & \vdots & \ddots & \vdots \\ s_{n1} & s_{n2} & \cdots & s_{nn} \end{bmatrix}$$

Where s_{ij} represents the jth sub-key decomposed by the ith block node.

Phase 2: Key Distribution and Storage
The sub-keys for each block are exchanged and stored through a key exchange mechanism. In a key exchange, Block BK_i sends its sub-key share s_{ij} to Block BK_j, Block BK_j sends its sub-key share s_{ji} to Block BK_i, The key is exchanged among all nodes so that the key is distributed and distributed.

After the key exchange, Block node BK_i stores the sub-key of all block nodes as $(s_{1i}, s_{2i}, \cdots, s_{ni})$. Thus, the subkey sharing key matrix formed by all block nodes is as follows:

$$A^T = \begin{bmatrix} s_{11} & s_{21} & \cdots & s_{n1} \\ s_{12} & s_{22} & \cdots & s_{n2} \\ \vdots & \vdots & \ddots & \vdots \\ s_{1n} & s_{2n} & \cdots & s_{nn} \end{bmatrix}$$

According to the basic method of key sharing, the computational complexity of all key full node backup for all members is $n!$.

Phase 3: Key Sharing and Synthesis
Since each block node holds a sub-key for all other nodes, the following steps can be followed when the block node loses its own key for key reconstruction.

Step1. To the original decomposition of the stored sub-key $S_i = \{s_{i1}, s_{i2}, \cdots, s_{in}\}$, except for the locally stored s_{ii}, t keys are randomly selected from the remaining n − 1 sub-keys as key recovery preparations.

Step2. Initialize system parameters and set the threshold value t of key synthesis, and the key S_i is synthesized by using Lagrange interpolation function.

$$f(x) = \sum_{j=1}^{t} f(s_j) \prod_{\substack{l=1 \\ l \neq j}}^{t} \frac{(s - s_l)}{s_j - s_l} \pmod{q}$$

Where the key $S_i = f(0)$.

5 Block Chain Change Algorithm Based on Hash Trap Function

5.1 Blockchain Hash Trap Function

A hash function is simply a function that turns any length of input into a fixed-length output, which is called the hash value or hash of the original message. An ideal hash function produces different outputs for different inputs, and if two different inputs produce the same hash value it is called a collision. The hash function has the following characteristics: (1) collision resistance; (2) high sensitivity.

Unlike the traditional hash function is the chameleon hash function can be considered to set a trap, master the trap can easily find a hash collision. The hash function is just as collision resistant for users without trap gates. Define the chameleon hash function as follows.

A chameleon hash function consists of four algorithms Cham − hash = (Setup, KeyGen, Hash, Forge).

- *Setup*(λ) : Input safety parameter λ, output public parameter *pp*.
- *KeyGen*(*pp*) : Input public parameters *pp*, output public and private key pairs (HK, CK), which is the public key *HK*, the private key *CK* is trapped.
- *Hash*(HK, m, r) : Input public key *HK*, messeage *m* and random number *r*, chameleon hash value *CH*.
- *Forge*(CK, m, r, r') : Input private key *CK*, messeage *m*, random number *r* and messeage *m'*, output another chameleon hash value $CH = Hash(HK, m, r) = Hash(HK, m', r')$.

The chameleon hash function has the following safety features.

1) Collision resistance: there is no finite algorithm that can find (m_1, r_1) and (m_2, r_2) after inputting the public key *HK* makes $Hash(HK, m_1, r_1) = Hash(HK, m_2, r_2)$.
2) Trap collision: there is a finite algorithm after input trap *CK*, for any m_1, r_1, m_2, can find r_2 makes $Hash(HK, m_1, r_1) = Hash(HK, m_2, r_2)$.
3) Semantic security: for any two messages m_1, m_2, the probabilities of $Hash(HK, m_1, r_1)$ and $Hash(HK, m_2, r_2)$ are indistinguishable, especially when *r* is chosen randomly and no information about *m* is available from $Hash(HK, m, r)$.

5.2   Blockchain Update Algorithm Description

The chameleon hash function described above can be used directly to implement editable Blockchains, but from time to time only the user with the trap can modify the historical block, which depends on finding a reliable ear user to make the Blockchain modification. The algorithm is designed to decide whether to modify a historical block by a vote of all participants, with a more straightforward idea falling into secret sharing, and then if more than half of the participants agree to modify the block information, the process requires multiple interactions.

When there are unexpected circumstances that require block modifications, the scheme can be modified in three phases: the voting stage, the random selection stage and the change confirmation stage. The process is as follows.

Phase 1: Vote on Historical Messages that Need to be Modified

1) After the system runs, if a user P_i in the Blockchain initiates a change request R_i, requests that the content of *m* in a historical Blockchain be changed to *m'*, the user requests a signature σ_i and broadcasts (R_i, σ_i) to other users in the chain, opening the voting phase.
2) If other users in the chain receive the request and agree to change it, the user P_i signs the request and broadcasts it.
3) After User P_i collects more than half of the user's signatures, broadcast this t-signature.

Phase 2 Random Selection of Users to Change Blocks

1) All block nodes on the block chain are numbered and publicized by the system.

2) The system uses random number generator to automatically generate a random number, with the generated random number to select the block node.
3) Broadcast the selected block nodes and obtain the consensus of all nodes. Consensus formation through phase 1 selection, and the use of a randomly selected user at this phase.

Phase 3 Change and Confirm Phase

1) Generate trap gate parameters. The selected block node inputs the security parameter λ and the common parameter pp to obtain the trap parameter CK. The trap parameter CK is secretly stored.
2) Get the value of the chameleon function. By inputting the public key information HK and the random parameter r generated by the selected node, then outputting the chameleon hash value CH.
3) Complete the content modification and confirm. input the private key CK, message m, random number r, and message m', output other random number r' to satisfy $CH = Hash(HK, m, r) = Hash(HK, m', r')$.

6 Programme Analysis

Aiming at the key management problem in the Blockchain system, this paper uses Diffe-Hellman key exchange negotiation to form a Shared key between any two block nodes and conduct secret sharing. Diffe-Hellman key exchange negotiation has been proven to be secure.

This paper uses Lagrange interpolation polynomial to store the private key information of each node on the Blockchain in different places, so that the key can be safely stored in each block node, which has a good protection for the attack of malicious nodes and the loss of the key. The (t, n) threshold interpolation polynomial is used to calculate the Shared key. The synthesis of the key depends on the value of threshold value t. The secure sharing of the key can be fully guaranteed during the synthesis of the key.

Using chameleon hash function to modify the contents of diseased block nodes requires setting a hash back door, The Blockchain node update scheme proposed in this paper carries out consensus authentication for the contents that need to be modified according to the voting mechanism, and then use the random algorithm to select a block node to modify the diseased node. The data after the modification is finally verified and confirmed by all the Blockchain nodes.

This updating method makes full use of the security features of hash function and use the consensus mechanism of block chain to complete the verification and confirmation of modified data, which can resist the attack and tampering from malicious nodes and has high application value for completing the block chain system.

7 Conclusion

Sharing and updating in key management has always been one of the important issues of information security. The article proposes a Blockchain key sharing and updating scheme based on (t, n) thresholds. On the one hand, the generation and storage of Blockchain keys is realized using the Diffie-Hellman key exchange protocol, and the generation and distribution of node keys is completed. In addition, a Blockchain key sharing algorithm is designed based on Lagrange interpolation function for key sharing, and Blockchain key sharing is implemented. For dead and sick nodes, a Blockchain key update mechanism is designed using chameleon hash functions to fix node loss problems in Blockchain sharing.

In the future research work, the efficiency of the algorithm can be further studied to find a more efficient key sharing algorithm. On the other hand, other algorithms for key sharing of block chain can be strengthened to make full use of the superior performance of block chain and study key sharing schemes that meet application requirements.

Acknowledgments. Our research work is funded by National Natural Science Foun-dation of China (No. 61962009), Major Scientific and Technological Special Project of Guizhou Province (20183001), Talent project of Guizhou Big Data Academy. Guizhou Provincial Key Laboratory of Public Big Data ([2018]01), Foundation of Guizhou Provincial Key Laboratory of Public Big Data (2018BDKFJJ003). This work is supported by the National Key R&D Program of China project under Grant 2018YFF0212106.

References

1. Nakamoto, S.: Bitcoin: a peer-to-peer electronic cash system (2008). https://bitcoin.org/bitcoin.pdf
2. Asokan, N., Ginzboorg, P.: Key agreement in ad hoc networks. Comput. Commun. **23**(17), 1627–1637 (2000). https://doi.org/10.1016/S0140-3664(00)00249-8
3. Capkun, S., Buttyán, L., Hubaux, J.: Self-organized public-key management for mobile ad hoc networks. IEEE Trans. Mobile Comput. **2**(1), 52–64 (2003). https://doi.org/10.1109/tmc.2003.1195151
4. Kosba, A.E., Miller, A., Shi, E., et al.: Hawk: the Blockchain model of cryptography and privacy-preserving smart contracts. In: Proceedings of IEEE Symposium on Security and Privacy—SP 2016, pp. 839–858. IEEE Computer Society (2016). https://doi.org/10.1109/sp.2016.55
5. Yuan, Y., Wang, F.Y.: Current status and prospects of blockchain technology development. Acta Automatica Sinica **42**(4), 481–494 (2016)
6. Raman, R.K., Varshney, L.R.: Dynamic distributed storage for scaling blockchains. arXiv preprint arXiv:1711.07617 (2017)
7. Kosba, A., Miller, A., Shi, E., et al.: Hawk: the blockchain model of cryptography and privacy-preserving smart contracts. In: Security and Privacy, pp. 839–858. IEEE (2016)
8. Fukumitsu, M., Hasegawa, S., Iwazaki, J., et al.: A proposal of a secure P2P-type storage scheme by using the secret sharing and the blockchain. In: 2017 IEEE 31st International Conference on Advanced Information Networking and Applications (AINA), pp. 803–810. IEEE (2017)

9. Diffie, W., Hellman, M.: New directions in cryptography. IEEE Trans. Inf. Theory **22**(6), 644–654 (1976)

10. Joux, A.: A one round protocol for tripartite Diffie-Hellman. J. Cryptol. **17**(4), 263–276 (2004)

11. Krawczyk, H.M., Rabin, T.D.: Chameleon hashing and signatures. US 2000. US6108783 A

12. Ateniese, G., Magri, B., Venturi, D., et al.: Redactable Blockchain or Rewriting History in Bitcoin and Friends. In: 2017 IEEE European Symposium on Security and Privacy (EuroS&P). IEEE (2017)

13. Peili, L., Xu, H., Ma, T., Mu, Y.: Research on scalable block chain technology. Chinese J. Cryptogr. **5**(05), 501–509 (2015)

14. Yuan, Y., Wang, F.Y.: Blockchain: the state of the art and future trends. Acta Automatic Sinica **42**(4), 481–494 (2016)

15. Garg, A., Lee, T.: Secure key agreement for multi-device home IoT environment, vol. 11. Elsevier B.V. (2020)

16. Biswas, A.K., Dasgupta, M.: Two polynomials based (t, n) threshold secret sharing scheme with cheating detection, vol. 44, no. 4. Taylor & Francis (2020)

17. Chao, L., Yu, M., Liu, Y.: Secret image sharing scheme based on Lagrangian Interpolation polynomial. J. Huazhong Univ. Sci. Technol. (Nat. Sci. edn.) (S1), 285–288 (2005)

Attribute Propagation Enhanced Community Detection Model for Bitcoin De-anonymizing

Jiming Wang[2], Xueshuo Xie[1], Yaozheng Fang[2], Ye Lu[2], Tao Li[1,3(✉)], and Guiling Wang[4]

[1] College of Computer Science, Nankai University, Tianjin 300350, China
litao@nankai.edu.cn
[2] College of Cyber Science, Nankai University, Tianjin 300350, China
[3] Tianjin Key Laboratory of Network and Data Security Technology, Tianjin 300350, China
[4] New Jersey Institute of Technology, Newark, NJ 07102, USA

Abstract. Bitcoin is a kind of decentralized cryptocurrency on a peer-to-peer network. Anonymity makes Bitcoin widely used in online payment but it is a disadvantage for regulatory purposes. We aim to de-anonymize Bitcoin to assist regulation. Many previous studies have used heuristic clustering or machine learning to analyze historical transactions and identify user behaviors. However, the accuracy of user identification is not ideal. Heuristic clustering only uses the topological structure of the transaction graph and ignores many transaction information, and supervised machine learning methods are limited by the size of labeled datasets. To identify user behaviors, we propose a community detection model based on attribute propagation, combining the topological structure of the transaction graph and additional transaction information. We first parse the transaction data of public ledger and construct a bipartite graph to describe correlations between addresses and transactions. We also extract address attributes from historical transactions to construct an attributed graph with the previous bipartite graph. Then, we design an adaptive weighted attribute propagation algorithm named AWAP running on the attributed graph to classify bitcoin addresses, and further identify user behaviors. Extensive experiments highlight that the proposed detection model based on AWAP achieves 5% higher *accuracy* on average compared to state-of-the-art address classification methods in Bitcoin. AWAP also achieves 25% higher *F-score* on average compared to previous community detection algorithms on two datasets.

Keywords: Bitcoin anonymity · Community detection · Attribute propagation

1 Introduction

Bitcoin was proposed by Satoshi Nakamoto in 2008 [12]. As a global decentralized cryptocurrency, Bitcoin has received extensive attention because its anonymity

© Springer Nature Switzerland AG 2020
X. Chen et al. (Eds.): ML4CS 2020, LNCS 12486, pp. 607–622, 2020.
https://doi.org/10.1007/978-3-030-62223-7_53

can protect user privacy. In practice, users do not need any real-world identity registration information to join the bitcoin system, and each user is uniquely identified by a pseudonym. Bitcoin's anonymity ensures that the real identity of a trader is not revealed and thus attracts a large number of users for Bitcoin. However, anonymity also makes Bitcoin as circulating currency for many illegal activities. Bitcoin has been widely used in ransomware, thefts and scams [1,21], such as the black market Silk Road [3]. From the perspective of regulatory purposes, it is important and meaningful to understand the anonymity of the Bitcoin system. On the one hand, a healthy cryptocurrency system needs to support technical legal investigations to ensure the safety and legality of transactions. On the other hand, the cryptocurrency system should provide sufficient anonymity to protect user privacy. In this paper, we focus on the de-anonymization of Bitcoin to support regulation. The question we are exploring is how much anonymity the bitcoin system provides, and whether we can reveal user behaviors by analyzing their relationships through historical transactions.

In Bitcoin, a transaction is a transfer record between addresses. The transaction contains the connection between addresses and also some additional transaction information. Each transaction needs to be recorded on a public ledger to prove its validity. Therefore, a large number of transactions are published on the ledger. Using these public transactions, we can construct a transaction graph to track user transactions and further reveal user behaviors. Thus, the anonymity of the Bitcoin system is pseudo-anonymity. For Bitcoin de-anonymizing, graph-based classification methods of Bitcoin addresses can construct a transaction graph from public transaction records and use address heuristic clustering to complete address user mapping [18,29]. This mapping is conducive to transaction traceability and statistical feature analysis. But this method only considers the connection between addresses, ignoring many additional transaction information. Recently, some other methods use supervised learning [20] to classify bitcoin addresses. But these methods are limited by the size of the labeled dataset, so it is not suitable for large-scale analysis of historical transactions.

Furthermore, community detection based on graph is an important research topic in data mining. The goal of community detection is to classify closely connected nodes into a group, so that the nodes in the community are tightly connected, and the connections between the communities are sparse. Traditional community detection is based on the topological structure. In recent years, many studies have added node attributes to a graph to form an attributed graph. The community detection on attributed graph comprehensively considers the topological structure and node attributes, and widely used in user similarity analysis and content recommendation system in social networks. This work proposes a novel attribute propagation enhanced community detection method to complete the classification of Bitcoin addresses and further de-anonymize. Although promising, it is a challenging task to analyze the large-scale historical transactions in the Bitcoin system. One challenge is that we need to extract the features of a specific address from the massive historical transactions. Another challenge is that we need to comprehensively use topological structure and node attributes although attributes sometimes mismatch with topology and different types of attributes have different contributions to the result of community detection.

To address the above challenges, we design a novel model to de-anonymize in the bitcoin system based on attributed graph community detection. First, we parse the transaction data of public ledger and construct a bipartite graph [6] to describe correlations between addresses and transactions. We also extract address attributes from historical transactions and obtain an attributed graph. Then, we design an adaptive weighted attribute propagation algorithm named AWAP running on the attributed graph to classify bitcoin addresses. We treat the transaction attributed graph as a dynamic system. The attributes are transmitted between nodes using the topology as a medium to affect each other. We call the process *attribute propagation*. We use the propagation results to analyze the correlation between the nodes and further reveal user behaviors. Finally, we test the model on the benchmark labeled data set. The experimental results show that our method has higher accuracy and outperforms state-of-the-art methods. In summary, this paper makes the following contributions:

- We design a community detection model based on attribute propagation, comprehensively considering the topology of the graph and node attributes, and leveraging the attribute propagation to complete the node classification.
- We propose an adaptive weighted attribute propagation algorithm based on an attributed graph, which can maintain a dynamic attributed graph as the dynamic propagation of attributes in Bitcoin.
- We present a transaction parser to generate the features of bitcoin addresses and construct an attributed graph.

2   Background and Motivation

2.1   Bitcoin

The Bitcoin system can be viewed as a composition of large-scale transactions. Each transaction can hold multiple inputs and multiple outputs. When making a payment, a user signs the transaction with his private key to prove his ownership of the bitcoins. Transactions record relations between addresses and other information such as transaction fees and generation time of blocks. We can analyze the whole Bitcoin system by traversing all the transactions and extracting useful information including addresses relations and attributes from transactions .

The identities in Bitcoin are private keys. Each private key generates a public key and some addresses for public identification. These addresses assure user anonymity since they contain no links to a person. An address is called a pseudonym. According to [12], the pseudonym mechanism guarantees complete anonymity on two conditions. One is that the pseudonym has no connection with the real world, and the other is to use a new pseudonym for each transaction. But in fact, few people follow such rules [20]. In this way, using the information extracted from the Bitcoin transaction, we can potentially reveal the activities that the pseudonym participated in and eventually de-anonymize Bitcoin users.

2.2 Community Detection

Community detection is one of the major topics in data mining. Community detection helps discover the structural characteristics, such as functional modules of protein-protein interaction networks [16] or groups of people with similar interests in social networks [24]. Graph as a data structure is popularly used to model the structural relationship between objects in many applications. In addition to the topological structure, nodes are usually associated with attributes. We can add node attributes to a graph to form an attributed graph. Community detection on attributed graph aims to discover groups with common properties, such as similarity among group members or densely connected structure.

Most community detection methods only focus on graph topology or node attributes separately. Examples of topological structure-based methods include modularity [2], spectral clustering [10] and non-negative matrix factorization [8], while node attribute-based methods include k-SNAP [22]. Both topological structure and node attributes provide key information for community detection. It is unwise to ignore any of them. However, specified in [14], there is no evidence that topological structure and node attributes share the same characteristics in any case. In other words, node attributes may unexpectedly mismatch with topology. Different types of attributes have different degrees of contribution to community detection.

The Bitcoin system is dynamic, so we also treat attributed graph constructed from Bitcoin as a dynamic graph. The establishment of the connection between nodes is accompanied by the propagation of attributes. As connections increase, nodes receive attribute information from other nodes and send their own attribute to others. This process is similar to information propagation, which is a fundamental factor in the study of social networks [11].

2.3 Challenges and Goals

For the Bitcoin system, the data size of historical transactions is huge. It is time consuming to construct transaction graphs and extract address features. At the same time, the traditional bipartite address-transaction graph is not suitable for community detection. So the existing community detection algorithm is not ideal for de-anonymizing Bitcoin. Motivated by information propagation, we aim to address the following challenges:

- How to efficiently and accurately extract the features of a specific address from the massive bitcoin transaction history?
- How to construct an attributed graph that can be applied to community detection since bipartite address-transaction graph is not suitable for community detection?
- How to combine topological structure and node attributes together since node attributes sometimes mismatch with topology and different types of attributes have different contributions to community detection?

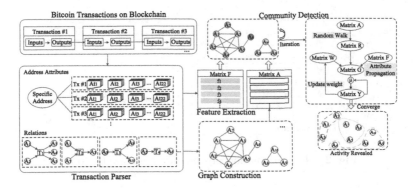

Fig. 1. An overview of our model.

3   System Model

3.1   Model Overview

In Fig. 1, our model starts with getting bitcoin transaction data on the blockchain. The transaction parser parses raw transaction data into the connections between addresses and some addresses attributes. The connections are described as a bipartite graph. In the graph construction stage, the bipartite graph is converted into a community graph suitable for community detection. In the feature extraction stage, we build a feature vector for a specific address based on the address attributes provided by the transaction parser. We then combine the community graph and the address features to form an attributed graph for community detection. The detection completes addresses classification and reveals user behaviors.

3.2   Transaction Parser

The size of Bitcoin data on the blockchain is huge. The transaction parser needs to efficiently obtain data and complete the parsing work. [18] employed a forked version of *bitcointools* using LevelDB. [5] used Armory to parse data on the blockchain. [7] designed a platform for parsing and analyzing blockchain. Taking into account the factors of time consumption and the specific information we need, we use the API provided by *blockchain.info* to implement our own parser. As mentioned in Background, there is lots of information in a transaction. Some information such as Transaction Hash, ScriptSig is not what we need. Parser needs to filter out useless information. Parser also extracts connections between addresses and constructs a bipartite address-transaction graph.

3.3   Graph Construction

The upper part of Fig. 2 shows the bipartite address-transactions graph constructed by the parser, where A represents an address and T represents a transaction. The bipartite graph can show the relationship between addresses and

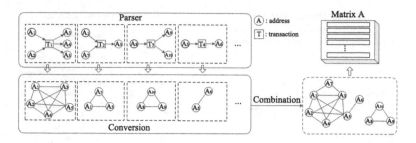

Fig. 2. The construction process of a community graph

transactions. However, it cannot be applied in community detection, because the nodes in a community graph should be of the same type. So we convert the bipartite graph to the lower part of Fig. 2. Our construction principle is to delete transaction nodes T and increase the edges between related nodes. We convert a directed bipartite graph into an undirected graph. So the process may lose some information. But our goal is to classify the nodes. The direction of the edges between the nodes is not important for the result, as long as the edges can reflect the connections between nodes.

We use a 2-tuple $G = (V, E)$ to represent a community graph, where $V = \{v_i | i \in [1, N]\}$ is the set of nodes, $E = \{(v_i, v_j) | v_i, v_j \in V, i \neq j\}$ is the set of edges. The graph here is an undirected graph. The adjacency matrix A of the graph G can be computed as:

$$A_{i,j} = \begin{cases} 1, & \text{if } (v_i, v_j) \in E, \text{ or } (v_j, v_i) \in E, \text{ or } i = j \\ 0, & \text{otherwise} \end{cases} \tag{1}$$

3.4 Features Extraction

In this part, we use the address attributes provided by the parser to generate address features vector. The process of feature extraction is shown in Fig. 3. What features we extract depends on the characteristics of different types of transactions. For example, mining pool transactions have no inputs, and gambling transactions often have many inputs, so we select the average number of inputs of transactions as an address feature. In other words, the address features we choose can reflect the transaction behaviors. Eventually, We select 22 features for each address. Some of these features are shown in Table 1.

Considering the attribute propagation process, we extend the feature value vector to a binary-valued vector to speed up the propagation. We record all the vectors in the feature matrix F, then a 3-tuple $G = (V, E, F)$ can be used to represent an attributed graph.

3.5 Community Detection

Next we define the process of attribute propagation. We calculate the probability that the attribute of a node propagates to another by random walk. The one

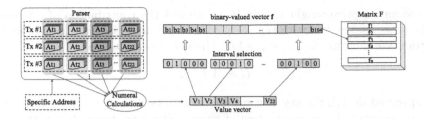

Fig. 3. The process of feature extraction

Table 1. Some features extracted from bitcoin transactions

Features	Description
n_{tx}	The number of transactions
n_{spent}	The number of spent transactions
BTC_{spent}	Total spent bitcoin
Fee	Transaction fee
$Balance$	The balance in an address
$Lifetime$	The duration between the first transaction and the last transaction
f_{tx}	The frequency of transactions

step transition probability P_{ij} denotes the probability of a node i arriving at node j at time $t = 1$ given that i started at time $t = 0$.

$$P_{ij} = P_{t=1|0}(j|i) = \frac{A_{ij}}{\sum_{a=1}^{N} A_{ia}} \tag{2}$$

Further, we treat t as a random variable from $[0, \infty)$ and follows a geometric distribution, then the t step transition probability:

$$P_{t|0}(j|i) = \sum_{s=0}^{\infty} P_{s|0}(j|i) \cdot P(t = s) = \sum_{s=0}^{\infty} P_{s|0}(j|i) \cdot \lambda(1 - \lambda)^s \tag{3}$$

We assume the start point of a random walk is chosen at random, the probability that node j receives attribute from node i can be calculated as:

$$P_{0|t}(i|j) = \frac{P_{t|0}(j|i)}{\sum_{a=1}^{N} P_{t|0}(j|a)} \tag{4}$$

We obtain matrix R where $R_{ij} = P_{0|t}(i|j)$. The attribute propagation can be written in matrix form G:

$$G = F^{\top} R \tag{5}$$

As mentioned in Sect. 2, attributes may mismatch with topology and different types of attributes have different degrees of contribution to community detection, we use an adaptive weight matrix W to control the contribution of attributes. W is a diagonal matrix with $W_{ii} = w_i$, $\forall i \in [1, m]$. m is the dimension of feature vectors. We initialize $w_1, ..., w_m = 1.0$. Then G is rewritten as:

$$G = WF^\top R \tag{6}$$

Specified in [11], the key element of community detection based on information propagation is the assumption of community consistency. When the propagation reaches stability, nodes in the same community are likely receive the same amount of attribute propagation. We use ϕ_i to denote the attribute node i receive. Then, we can get μ_k:

$$\mu_k = \frac{\sum_{i=1}^m \phi_i}{m} \tag{7}$$

μ_k denotes the expectation of attribute propagation received by nodes in the community C_k. m denotes the number of nodes in the community C_k. Considering a membership matrix Y and K is the number of communities, we have:

$$E[\phi_i] = \sum_{k=1}^K \mu_k \cdot Y_{ik}, \ where \ Y_{ik} = \begin{cases} 1, & i \in C_k \\ 0, & i \notin C_k \end{cases} \tag{8}$$

where $E[\phi_i]$ denotes the expectation of attribute propagation received by node i. We use g_i to denote the i-th row of matrix G, which represents the actual attribute propagation obtained by node i. Obviously, $g_i = \phi_i$. Then, community detection based on attribute propagation can be obtained by solving the following optimization:

$$\underset{Y, \mu_k}{\arg\min} \sum_{i=1}^N \| g_i - E[\phi_i] \|_2^2 \tag{9}$$

Y is the result we want, indicating the relationship between the node and the community. First, we solve μ_k with Y and (7):

$$\mu_k = \sum_{i=1}^N \frac{g_i \cdot Y_{ik}}{\sum_{j=1}^N Y_{jk}} \tag{10}$$

Take μ_k to (8) and (9), we can set matrix Y by calculating the first K eigenvectors of matrix $R^\top W F^\top F W^\top R$ according to [25].

Then, during the iteration, we update μ and Y with:

$$\mu_k^{t+1} = \sum_{i=1}^N \frac{g_i \cdot Y_{ik}^t}{\sum_{j=1}^N Y_{jk}^t} \tag{11}$$

$$Y_{ik}^{t+1} = \begin{cases} 1, & \forall m \in [1, K], \| \mu_k^t - g_i \| \leq \| \mu_m^t - g_i \| \\ 0, & otherwise \end{cases} \tag{12}$$

Finally, we use a vote mechanism, similar to [30], to adjust attribute weights. We assume $w_1^t, ... w_m^t$ are the attribute weights in the tth iteration. The weight of attribute a_i in the $(t+1)^{th}$ iteration is computed as:

$$w_i^{t+1} = \frac{1}{2}(w_i^t + \Delta w_i^t) \qquad (13)$$

We use a vote mechanism to accurately calculate Δw_i^t. If nodes in the same community share the same value of attribute a_i, it means attribute a_i can reflect the characteristics of the community, then the weight w_i of a_i increase. If nodes in the same community have a random distribution on values of attribute a_i, the weight w_i of a_i decrease. The vote process can be computed as:

$$vote_i(v_p, v_q) = \begin{cases} 1, & if \ v_p, v_q \ share \ the \ same \ value \ on \ a_i \\ 0, & otherwise \end{cases} \qquad (14)$$

and Δw_i^t is calculated as

$$\Delta w_i^t = \frac{\sum_{j=1}^{k} \sum_{v \in V_j} vote_i(c_j, v)}{\frac{1}{m} \sum_{p=1}^{m} \sum_{j=1}^{k} \sum_{v \in V_j} vote_p(c_j, v)} \qquad (15)$$

where V_j denotes the nodes in community j and c_j denotes a virtual node with expectation attributes of community j. The algorithm of community detection based on AWAP is summarized in Algorithm 1.

Algorithm 1. Adaptive Weighted Attribute Propagation

Input: adjacency matrix A; feature matrix F; number of clusters K;parameter λ;
Output: detected communities indicated by Y;
1: Initialize $w_1 = w_2 = ... = w_m = 1.0$;
2: Calculate R matrix with random walk(4) ;
3: Calculate G with (6);
4: Calculate the first K eigenvectors and initialize Y;
5: initialize μ with (10);
6: **while** not converged **do**
7:     update Y with μ and W by (12);
8:     update μ with Y by (11);
9:     update weights $w_1, w_2, ..., w_m$ with (13);
10: **end while**
11: Return Y;

---

4   Evaluation

In this section, we demonstrate the effectiveness of our proposed model in terms of bitcoin address classification and community detection. We choose 4 Bitcoin address classification methods and 7 previous community detection algorithms as the baselines. The evaluation is concerning the following questions:

- How does the Bitcoin address classification performance when using AWAP as the community detection compared with state-of-the-art methods?
- How does the AWAP performance in community detection compared with previous community detection algorithms?
- Why AWAP can increase the accuracy, F-score, and Jaccard?
- How do parameters and weight distribution influence performance?

4.1 Experimental Setup

Datasets. For Bitcoin de-anonymizing, our model can run directly on the raw Bitcoin transaction data. But in this paper, we select a labeled dataset to compare the performance of our model with other methods. We use a five categories bitcoin addresses dataset in [6]. And, we also use the parser to extract address feature vectors from historical transactions to further improve the dataset. Finally, our dataset consists: Exchange: 10413 addresses; Gambling: 10479 addresses; DarkNet Marketplace: 10593 addresses; Mining Pool: 10498 addresses; Service: 10597 addresses. For each address in the dataset, there is a 104-dimensional feature vector.

Measured Metrics. We use 3 metrics *F-score, Jaccard similarity* and *NMI* to evaluate the performance of the detected communities C using the ground-truth communities C^*, and 3 metrics *Accuracy, Precision* and F_1-score to evaluate the performance of bitcoin address classification.

$$F_{score}(C, C^*) = \sum_{C_i \in C} \frac{|C_i|}{\sum_{C_j \in C} |C_j|} \max_{C_j^* \in C^*} F_{score}(C_i, C_j^*) \qquad (16)$$

$$Jac(C, C^*) = \sum_{C_j^* \in C^*} \frac{\max_{C_i \in C} Jac(C_i, C_j^*)}{2|C^*|} + \sum_{C_i \in C} \frac{\max_{C_i^* \in C^*} Jac(C_i, C_j^*)}{2|C|} \qquad (17)$$

$$NMI(C, C^*) = \frac{\sum_{C_i, C_j^*} p(C_i, C_j^*)(log\ p(C_i, C_j^*) - log\ p(C_i)p(C_j))}{\max(H(C), H(C^*))} \qquad (18)$$

$H(C)$ is the entropy of the community C. *Accuracy* is the proportion of correct predictions to total predictions. *Precision* is the proportion of positive predictions to the total positive predictions. *Recall* represents a measure of the completeness of a classifier. F_1-score is the harmonic mean of *Precision* and *Recall*.

$$F_1 - score = 2 \cdot \frac{Precision \cdot Recall}{Precision + Recall} \qquad (19)$$

The 6 metrics all take values from $[0, 1]$, and larger values indicate better results.

Configuration. Our experiment is tested on the machine with Windows 10, Intel Core 2.20 GHz CPUs, and 16 GB of RAM. Our parser step is implemented in Python 3.7.2. and community detection algorithm is implemented in Matlab.

Table 2. Bitcoin address classification results

Algorithm	Accuracy	Precision	F_1-score
Logistic regression	0.85	0.87	0.85
LightGBM	0.92	**0.92**	**0.91**
BAGC	0.55	0.47	0.50
CP	0.89	0.71	0.79
AWAP	**0.94**	0.85	0.89

Table 3. Community quality comparison on Citeseer and Cora

Algorithm	Information	Citeseer			Cora		
		F-score	Jaccard	NMI	F-score	Jaccard	NMI
CNM	Topology	0.1735	0.1094	0.2290	0.4210	0.2315	0.1491
DeepWalk	Topology	0.2699	0.2481	0.0878	0.3917	0.3612	0.3270
Big-CLAM	Topology	0.5114	0.0872	0.2197	0.4829	0.2340	0.2919
Circles	Topology+Attributes	0.3405	0.1867	0.0024	0.3595	0.1810	0.0064
CP	Topology+Attributes	0.6918	0.4991	0.4314	0.6770	0.5168	0.4863
CODICIL	Topology+Attributes	0.5953	0.4041	0.3392	0.5857	0.3947	0.4254
CESNA	Topology+Attributes	0.5240	0.1158	0.1158	0.6059	0.3254	0.4671
AWAP	Topology+Attributes	**0.7134**	**0.4570**	**0.5205**	**0.7583**	**0.5875**	**0.5683**

4.2   Model Performance

Address Classification Performance. We summarize the address classification results of different methods in Table 2. We also use some other community detection algorithms BAGC [26] and CP [11] to classify bitcoin addresses. The results show that our method has higher accuracy, while precision and F_1-score are inferior to LightGBM. The reason why accuracy is high and precision is slightly lower may be because the classification of most addresses is correct, but one of the categories of addresses is wrong. We further analyze accuracy, precision, and F_1-score of the five address types, and find that some Services addresses are identified as DarkNet addresses, resulting in a decrease in the accuracy of Exchange and Mining, and precision of Exchange.

Community Detection Performance. We evaluate our model from the perspective of address classification above, and this part we evaluate the community detection results of our community detection algorithm (AWAP). We conduct investigation on Citeseer and Cora. We consider three metrics: *F-score, Jaccard similarity* and *NMI*. *F-score* mainly describes the accuracy of detected communities, while *Jaccard* is a statistic used for comparing the similarity of detected communities and the ground truth, and *NMI* offers an entropy measure of the overall matching. The results are shown in Table 3.

The results show that our AWAP outperforms the baselines. By comparison, it is shown that the algorithm that comprehensively considers the topology

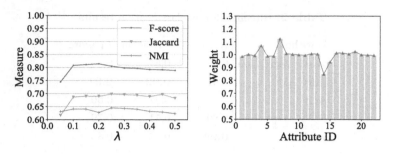

(a) Performance of AWAP with different values of λ

(b) Weight distribution of different
attributes

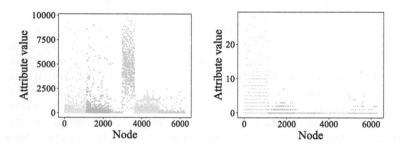

(c) the distribution of attribute Total Sent BTC in nodes

(d) the distribution of attribute
Transaction Fee in nodes

Fig. 4. The performance on: (a) different parameters; (b) weight distribution; (c) attribute distribution; (d) attribute distribution.

and node attributes is indeed superior to the algorithm that only considers the topology. Dynamically adjusting attribute weights can also improve the performance of community detection. Our method increases the contribution of specific attributes and reduces the contribution of attributes that mismatch with the topology or do not match the expected attributes of the community. We will analyze the distribution of values of different weighted attributes in different communities in the Discuss section. On the other hand, the method of attribute propagation is based on information propagation. The topology is used as a medium to transfer node attributes. Naturally, the topology structure and the node attributes are combined together. For the topologically independent node, the node attributes are automatically compared with the community expected attributes.

Discussion. In the experiment, we fixed the value of λ to 0.2. In this part, we first investigate the influence of λ on the performance of our AWAP. The value of λ is varied from 0.05 to 0.5 with step size of 0.05. The results are summarized in Fig. 4(a). We can observe that the three metrics all reach the maximum value when the value of λ is between 0.2 and 0.25 and then decrease slowly overall when λ get larger. This may be because when λ is at this interval, the attributes are more easily and thoroughly propagated in the topology, which is conducive to improve the effectiveness of community detection.

Next, we discuss the attribute weights determined by AWAP. Aggregating 104-dimensional feature weight vectors to calculate the weights of 22 attributes, we get Fig. 4(b). Two attributes with the highest weights are the number of payback transactions N_{pt} and bitcoins an address total sent BTC_{sent} while two attributes with the lowest are related to transaction fees Fee. Figure4(c) and Fig. 4(d) are the value distribution of BTC_{sent} and Fee in nodes respectively. Different colors indicate different communities, from left to right are Exchange, Gambling, DarkNet, Mining and Services. BTC_{sent} usually reflects the scale of transactions. We can observe that BTC_{sent} of DarkNet is concentrated in the high-value area, BTC_{sent} of Services is generally low, and the other three types of attribute values also have their own distributions. BTC_{sent} can distinguish DarkNet and Services very well which is a good basis for community detection. So its weight is high. Fee often has a fixed lower limit in a transaction, and few addresses are willing to pay higher fees to the miners. In the figure, 96% of nodes have a Fee less than 10. Different types of addresses have similar Fee. So it is not able to provide a basis for community detection.

5   Related Work

Bitcoin de-anonymization methods often use heuristic clustering to construct the one-to-many mapping from entities to addresses based on the properties of the Bitcoin protocol. [17] derive two topological structures from Bitcoin's public transaction history and combine these structures with external information to investigate an alleged theft of Bitcoins. [18] use multiple inputs heuristic clustering on the full bitcoin transaction graph and answer a variety of questions about the typical behavior of users. [23] use transaction-specific features to achieve 70% accuracy for classifying addresses into several types. [15] introduces the notion of transaction motifs and finally achieve more than 80% accuracy. [6] analyze the information revealed by the pattern of transactions in the neighborhood of a given entity transaction and achieve 85% accuracy for the Logistic Regression algorithm and 92% for LightGBM.

Based on the graph, the algorithm of community detection can be categorized into two types. One only considers the topology of the graph, while the other comprehensively considers the topological structure and node attributes. [2] uses a heuristic method to extract the community structure of large networks based on modularity optimization. [27] present BIGCLAM, an overlapping community detection method that scales to large networks of millions of nodes and edges based on topology. [4] presents a hierarchical agglomeration algorithm for detecting community structure. [13] proposes DeepWalk which is a structure-only representation learning method. DeepWalk uses local information obtained from truncated random walks to learn latent representations.

A model is proposed for detecting circles that combine network structure as well as user profile information [9]. They learn members and user profile similarity metric for each circle. A Bayesian probabilistic model (BAGC) for attributed graph clustering is proposed in [26]. The model provides a principled and natural framework for capturing both structural and attribute aspects of a graph, avoiding the artificial design of a distance measure. [28] develop CESNA for overlapping community detection which has a linear runtime in the network size. [11] treats a network with a dynamic system and uses the principle of information propagation to integrate the structure and contents in a network. [19] design a mechanism for fusing content and link similarity. They present a biased edge sampling procedure and finally get an edge set.

6   Conclusion

In this paper, we formulate the Bitcoin de-anonymity as a problem of Bitcoin addresses classification to explore user trading behaviors. To achieve this goal, we first construct an attributed graph based on bitcoin historical transactions. And then, we propose a community detection method based on attribute propagation that comprehensively uses the topological structure and node attributes of the attributed graph. The method also dynamically adjusts weights of different attributes. Our approach provides sound results on public datasets. Our proposed model can efficiently resolve the problems of bitcoin addresses classification and community detection. An interesting direction is to apply more community detection algorithms to explore bitcoin user behaviors and further contribute to the healthy development of Bitcoin.

References

1. Bartoletti, M., Pes, B., Serusi, S.: Data mining for detecting bitcoin Ponzi schemes. In: 2018 Crypto Valley Conference on Blockchain Technology (CVCBT), pp. 75–84. IEEE (2018)
2. Blondel, V.D., Guillaume, J.L., Lambiotte, R., Lefebvre, E.: Fast unfolding of communities in large networks. J. Stat. Mech. Theory Exp. **2008**(10), P10008 (2008)
3. Christin, N.: Traveling the silk road: a measurement analysis of a large anonymous online marketplace. In: Proceedings of the 22nd International Conference on World Wide Web, pp. 213–224 (2013)
4. Clauset, A., Newman, M.E., Moore, C.: Finding community structure in very large networks. Phys. Rev. E **70**(6), 066111 (2004)
5. Fleder, M., Kester, M.S., Pillai, S.: Bitcoin transaction graph analysis. arXiv preprint arXiv:1502.01657 (2015)
6. Jourdan, M., Blandin, S., Wynter, L., Deshpande, P.: Characterizing entities in the bitcoin blockchain. In: 2018 IEEE International Conference on Data Mining Workshops (ICDMW), pp. 55–62. IEEE (2018)
7. Kalodner, H., Goldfeder, S., Chator, A., Möser, M., Narayanan, A.: BlockSci: design and applications of a blockchain analysis platform. arXiv preprint arXiv:1709.02489 (2017)

8. Kamuhanda, D., He, K.: A nonnegative matrix factorization approach for multiple local community detection. In: 2018 IEEE/ACM International Conference on Advances in Social Networks Analysis and Mining (ASONAM), pp. 642–649. IEEE (2018)

9. Leskovec, J., Mcauley, J.J.: Learning to discover social circles in ego networks. In: Advances in Neural Information Processing Systems, pp. 539–547 (2012)

10. Li, X., Kao, B., Ren, Z., Yin, D.: Spectral clustering in heterogeneous information networks. In: Proceedings of the AAAI Conference on Artificial Intelligence, vol. 33, pp. 4221–4228 (2019)

11. Liu, L., Xu, L., Wangy, Z., Chen, E.: Community detection based on structure and content: a content propagation perspective. In: 2015 IEEE International Conference on Data Mining, pp. 271–280. IEEE (2015)

12. Nakamoto, S., Bitcoin, A.: A peer-to-peer electronic cash system (2008). https://bitcoin.org/bitcoin.pdf

13. Perozzi, B., Al-Rfou, R., Skiena, S.: DeepWalk: online learning of social representations. In: Proceedings of the 20th ACM SIGKDD International Conference on Knowledge Discovery and Data Mining, pp. 701–710 (2014)

14. Qin, M., Jin, D., Lei, K., Gabrys, B., Musial-Gabrys, K.: Adaptive community detection incorporating topology and content in social networks. Knowl. Based Syst. **161**, 342–356 (2018)

15. Ranshous, S., et al.: Exchange pattern mining in the bitcoin transaction directed hypergraph. In: Brenner, M., et al. (eds.) FC 2017. LNCS, vol. 10323, pp. 248–263. Springer, Cham (2017). https://doi.org/10.1007/978-3-319-70278-0_16

16. Ravasz, E., Somera, A.L., Mongru, D.A., Oltvai, Z.N., Barabási, A.L.: Hierarchical organization of modularity in metabolic networks. Science **297**(5586), 1551–1555 (2002)

17. Reid, F., Harrigan, M.: An analysis of anonymity in the bitcoin system. In: Altshuler, Y., Elovici, Y., Cremers, A., Aharony, N., Pentland, A. (eds.) Security and Privacy in Social Networks, pp. 197–223. Springer, New York (2013). https://doi.org/10.1007/978-1-4614-4139-7_10

18. Ron, D., Shamir, A.: Quantitative analysis of the full bitcoin transaction graph. In: Sadeghi, A.-R. (ed.) FC 2013. LNCS, vol. 7859, pp. 6–24. Springer, Heidelberg (2013). https://doi.org/10.1007/978-3-642-39884-1_2

19. Ruan, Y., Fuhry, D., Parthasarathy, S.: Efficient community detection in large networks using content and links. In: Proceedings of the 22nd International Conference on World Wide Web, pp. 1089–1098 (2013)

20. Shao, W., Li, H., Chen, M., Jia, C., Liu, C., Wang, Z.: Identifying bitcoin users using deep neural network. In: Vaidya, J., Li, J. (eds.) ICA3PP 2018. LNCS, vol. 11337, pp. 178–192. Springer, Cham (2018). https://doi.org/10.1007/978-3-030-05063-4_15

21. Sun Yin, H.H., Langenheldt, K., Harlev, M., Mukkamala, R.R., Vatrapu, R.: Regulating cryptocurrencies: a supervised machine learning approach to de-anonymizing the bitcoin blockchain. J. Manag. Inf. Syst. **36**(1), 37–73 (2019)

22. Tian, Y., Hankins, R.A., Patel, J.M.: Efficient aggregation for graph summarization. In: Proceedings of the 2008 ACM SIGMOD International Conference on Management of Data, pp. 567–580 (2008)

23. Toyoda, K., Ohtsuki, T., Mathiopoulos, P.T.: Multi-class bitcoin-enabled service identification based on transaction history summarization. In: 2018 IEEE International Conference on Internet of Things (iThings) and IEEE Green Computing and Communications (GreenCom) and IEEE Cyber, Physical and Social Computing (CPSCom) and IEEE Smart Data (SmartData), pp. 1153–1160. IEEE (2018)

24. Watts, D.J., Dodds, P.S., Newman, M.E.: Identity and search in social networks. Science **296**(5571), 1302–1305 (2002)
25. Xu, L., White, M., Schuurmans, D.: Optimal reverse prediction: a unified perspective on supervised, unsupervised and semi-supervised learning. In: Proceedings of the 26th Annual International Conference on Machine Learning, pp. 1137–1144 (2009)
26. Xu, Z., Ke, Y., Wang, Y., Cheng, H., Cheng, J.: A model-based approach to attributed graph clustering. In: Proceedings of the 2012 ACM SIGMOD International Conference on Management of Data, pp. 505–516 (2012)
27. Yang, J., Leskovec, J.: Overlapping community detection at scale: a nonnegative matrix factorization approach. In: Proceedings of the Sixth ACM International Conference on Web Search and Data Mining, pp. 587–596 (2013)
28. Yang, J., McAuley, J., Leskovec, J.: Community detection in networks with node attributes. In: 2013 IEEE 13th International Conference on Data Mining, pp. 1151–1156. IEEE (2013)
29. Zhao, C., Guan, Y.: A graph-based investigation of bitcoin transactions. In: Peterson, G., Shenoi, S. (eds.) DigitalForensics 2015. IAICT, vol. 462, pp. 79–95. Springer, Cham (2015). https://doi.org/10.1007/978-3-319-24123-4_5
30. Zhou, Y., Cheng, H., Yu, J.X.: Graph clustering based on structural/attribute similarities. Proc. VLDB Endow. **2**(1), 718–729 (2009)

A Secure and Moderate Data Synchronization Method Based on Network Isolation

Bing Zhang[1], Zhiyong Guo[1], Yangdan Ni[2], Meng Yang[1],
Ruiying Cheng[1], and Yu Xiao[3,4(✉)]

[1] State Grid Information and Telecommunication Co., Ltd., Beijing 100761,
China
[2] State Grid Zhejiang Electric Power Co., LTD., Hangzhou 310000, China
[3] Department of Computer Science and Technology, Shandong University
of Technology, Zibo 255022, Shandong, China
yuxiao8907118@163.com
[4] School of Computer Science and Technology, Beijing Institute of Technology,
Beijing 100081, China

Abstract. This paper discusses a secure and moderate data synchronization method based on network isolation. In this method, trigger method or shadow table method is used to monitor database and capture the changes of database. Thus, the distributed database system in different network domains, trusted network and non-trusted networks, is synchronized and the security of the database is guaranteed. We apply the method to water fee system and secondary system protection project in power plants, the experiment results show that the system is high performance and has more advantages in Security.

Keywords: Networks isolation · Database synchronization · Shadow table

1 Introduction

At present, database technology has developed into a third-generation database system with object-oriented model as its main feature, and the architecture has changed from the original centralized database to a distributed database based on client-server mechanism. With the maturity of technology, database applications become more and more important, data sharing and data security have attracted more and more attention.

The traditional practice of data backup is to achieve data security provision under the premise of network connectivity by database vendors or database researchers. However, in some secret-related networks, database synchronization must be realized in the security isolation environment, and the traditional method appears to be powerless. So a new technology is needed to complete the database synchronization between the isolated networks.

© Springer Nature Switzerland AG 2020
X. Chen et al. (Eds.): ML4CS 2020, LNCS 12486, pp. 623–633, 2020.
https://doi.org/10.1007/978-3-030-62223-7_54

2   Network Isolation Technology

Physical isolation technology is through the establishment of a network isolation device between the trusted intranet and non-trusted external network [1]. In order to achieve data transmission between the two networks, the device adopts a shared storage mechanism.

Normally, the isolation device is not connected to the two networks. When there is an information exchange request, the isolation device is connected to one of the external network or the internal network. The isolation device can be understood as pure storage media and a simple scheduling and control circuit. Figure 1 shows a physical isolation architecture used in the system.

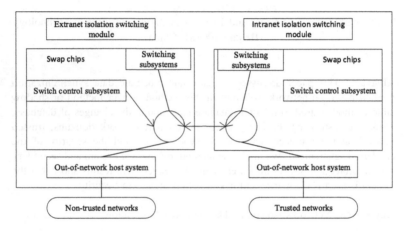

Fig. 1. Physical isolation system structure

Network isolation systems use a very secure network security technology [2]. TCP/IP protocol or other common network protocols are not adopted, but a dedicated protocol in accordance with a certain security policy is used to transmit specific data. Because there is no direct or indirect network connection between the internal and external network, physical isolation system effectively blocking the TCP/IP connection, completely eliminate the current TCP/IP network attack. With the help of the network isolation technology and special operating system, the network isolation system effectively reduces the threat of attacking by exploiting the vulnerability of the operating system.

3   Database Synchronization Strategy in Network Isolation Environment

Assume there are two databases needed to be synchronized in two isolated networks. The changed content of the source database needs to be synchronized to the target database. Figure 2 shows the structure of the synchronization.

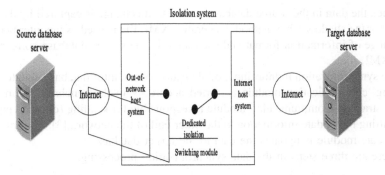

Fig. 2. Network structure of the synchronization

The synchronization process is mainly as follows. The changes of the source database are captured firstly, and then the data are distributed and updated to the target database. Figure 3 shows the overall structure to achieve database synchronization.

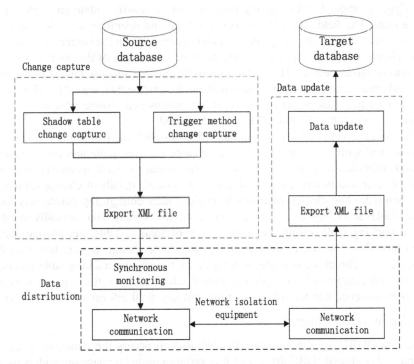

Fig. 3. Overall structure of database synchronization

The entire system is composed of several modules, such as change capture module, data distribution module, network communication module, synchronous monitoring module and data update module.

When the data in the source database changes, the change is captured by the trigger method or the shadow table method. Generally, XML file is used as the intermediary of the change of information format and each table in the source database corresponding to an XML file.

The synchronization monitoring module is used to monitor database updates. When updating, communication module is started according to the synchronization config-uration strategy. Communication module is responsible for sending (or receiving) data, transmitting the update information to the other end of the network [3]. The function of data update module is updates the data to the target database.

There are three steps in the data synchronization processing.

(1) Capture the changes

Capture the changes is a prerequisite for database synchronization. Its main function is to obtain the change sequence information that needs to be synchronized to the target database [4]. In order not to affect the operation of the original application system and reduce the impact on the performance of the source database, trigger and shadow table are always used.

Trigger method: Create tracking triggers such as insert, update and delete in the source table. The field information, operation type and operation sequence number of the new result after all insert, update and delete operations on the source table are saved in the change tracking table for incremental synchronization of the source table.

Shadow table method: The method needs to build a shadow table for the source table and create a new stored procedure to clear the change tracking table. Then, source table and shadow table are analyzed to get the incremental change information. Based on above method, the shadow table is synchronized.

No matter which synchronization method is adopted, the distribution module only needs to deal with the source table or the change tracking table and obtain synchro-nization information. Thus, the function of the module is well encapsulated into the database layer and hidden from the distribution module details of change capture [5].

When recording change capture information, after configuring parameters for the source table according to the synchronization, the system automatically creates a change tracking table, change tracking trigger or shadow table, net change analysis stored procedure and source table for the source table change capture based on these parameters synchronization mode. Among them, the change tracking table records all the field information of the operated source table, such as the type of operation, operation sequence number, operation time and key field information before change.

(2) Synchronous monitoring

JDBC and ODBC are the most popular methods to access the database by external programs. Java-based JDBC driver and Java programming language are widely used by developers because of their platform independence.

The synchronous monitoring module uses JDBC to connect to the database, and monitors the change of the data source according to the setting of the monitoring mode. When the source data changes, the network communication module will be started according to the synchronization mode.

(3) Data update

The data update is implemented at the target node. When the target node receives the XML file, it immediately extracts the SQL statement from the XML file. If it is a create operation, an initialization operation and a new synchronization table is created in the target database. If it is one of insert, delete or update operations, the SQL statement will be directly executed, and the target table will be updated.

4 Experiments

4.1 Water Fee System

Synchronization of Water Fee System
The synchronous technology based on SQL reduction method has been successfully applied in the water fee system [6]. The water fee system consists of internal and external networks. The internal network is a water fee information processing system, which has the functions of meter reading data entry, bill printing, business information management, etc., and realizes the automation of water fee copying, payment and settlement. The external network is a water fee Query Web site, which provides online water fee query to the public, so that users can master their own water situation in time.

Because the water fee data of internal and external application systems are placed on different databases, and they are not the same database. Therefore, in order to keep the consistency between the internal and external databases, it is necessary to synchronize the water fee data of the internal network to the external network in a timely manner, and the security of data transmission must be taken into account, and it is not allowed to invade the water fee processing system of the internal network from the external network, which is a typical problem of data synchronization between heterogeneous databases based on network isolation.

System Implementation
According to the demand of user's online water fee query, the system must extract three tables from the intranet database to the Internet database. One of the above mentioned tables records current month's meter reading, cancellation data and previous non cancellation data table. The second table records current month's meter reading and cancellation details data table and the third records user's basic information.

Because the real-time property of water fee information is not very oppressive, the timing synchronization strategy is selected for the system, that is, two or three times a day, which is generally selected when the internal network water fee processing system is idle, such as noon or night.

In order to ensure the security of the internal network water fee system and data transmission, PEGAP is used to isolate the internal network from the external network. The basic structure of the system is shown in Fig. 4. It can be seen from the system structure that the system is divided into two isolated networks, internal and external, which are connected through PEGAP.

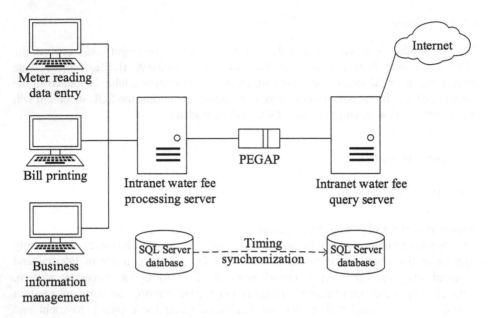

Fig. 4. Data synchronization structure of water fee system

Because the internal network database is a SQL Server database with powerful trigger function, and both the internal and external network servers use Microsoft Windows Server operating system, the water fee system uses trigger method and Winsock communication to realize data synchronization of the internal and external network application system database.

Operation Performance
The results show that with the increase of the number of records, the time complexity of SQL based restore method increases linearly ($o(n)$, where n is the number of records), and the space complexity is mainly memory consumption, which basically keeps constant ($o(1)$). Therefore, the performance of the internal network water fee treatment system is perfect.

However, adding triggers to each synchronized source table is bound to bring some efficiency problems to existing applications, especially when there is a large amount of data in the intranet database to be updated at the same time, the triggers are frequently triggered, and the efficiency of the system will be significantly reduced.

4.2   Database Synchronization of Secondary System Protection Project in Power Plant

Background of Power Plant Secondary System Protection Project
With the rapid development of power enterprises, the data network of power system is also expanding rapidly. There are more and more data exchanges among dispatching center, power plant, users, etc.

Remote control is widely used in power plants and substations, which poses a severe challenge to the security, reliability and real-time of power control system and data network [7, 8]. Some dispatching centers, power plants and substations do not pay enough attention to the network security when planning, designing, constructing and operating control systems or data networks, which makes the monitoring system with real-time control function interconnected with local MIS or even directly connected with the Internet without effective security protection.

The increasingly serious network intrusion, production safety problems and the leakage of internal confidential information on the network and many other facts, also give a warning to the safety production and management of power enterprises. So now the relevant departments of the power system have reached a consensus: like other secret related networks such as government and military, the information security of the internal network of power enterprises, especially the real-time data network and dispatching data network related to production, must be paid attention to and strengthened [9].

Special Network Isolation Device of Power System

Network isolation device designed for power system is adopted as network gate in power system. In addition to the basic firewall, proxy server and other security protection technologies, the device adopts the "dual computer non network" isolation technology, that is, the device can block the direct connection of the network, and the two networks are not connected to the equipment at the same time. It can block the logical connection of the network, that is, TCP/IP must be stripped and the original data will be transmitted in no network mode.

The isolated transmission mechanism is not programmable and data is controlled by two level agents. The function of data monitoring excludes data from attack. In addition, it has powerful management and control function that realize the one-way communication mode (UDP) and one way data 4-byte return mode (TCP) required by the national dispatching center for security protection.

Isolation Scheme of Telecontrol Network and MIS Network in Power Plant

The topology of telecontrol system (telecontrol network) and MIS network of power plant is shown in Fig. 5. It can be seen from the figure that if the network isolation is not implemented, the telecontrol system communicates with the production site and dispatching center. In addition, one end of the telecontrol system is directly connected with the MIS network, and the other end is connected with the Internet through the firewall. Once it is damaged by viruses or hackers, the consequences are unimaginable, which does not conform to the security protection provisions of the power secondary system.

In order to ensure the security of the remote control system intranet, it is necessary to implement the network isolation between the telecontrol system and the MIS network [10], so that the original network-based applications will be cut off. The connection between the original web system and the telecontrol database through ODBC will also be blocked at the same time, so a new image database of telecontrol database must be created in MIS network to replace the original telecontrol database to provide data service.

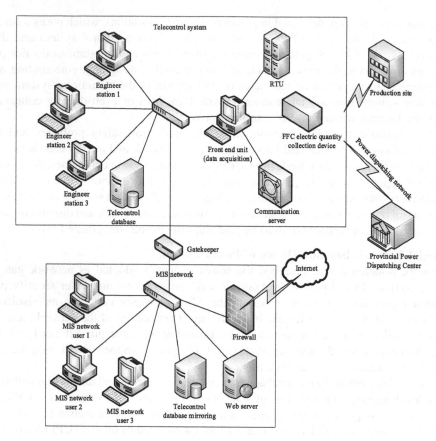

Fig. 5. Topology diagram of network isolation implementation.

Implementation of Database Synchronization

(1) Synchronous system deployment

The synchronization system is divided into sender and receiver. In order to save hardware resources, the sender is deployed on the remote database server and the receiver on the mirror database server [11].

(2) Synchronization table configuration

Because too many tables in the telecontrol database, most of the tables should be synchronized firstly. Here, we classify the tables in the telecontrol database from the perspective of data synchronization:

The tables that do not need to be synchronized are mainly the parameter tables related to the collections and operations of the front-end computer, the evaluation parameter setting table, the intermediate table for evaluation calculation, etc. The above mentioned tables are not used in external network, so synchronization is not required.

For the tables that need to be synchronized, we mainly focus on the size and update frequency of these tables to determine the appropriate synchronization method.

- Real time table. These tables are characterized by fewer records and faster updates. All records will be refreshed in about 3–6 s. Generally, the total number of records will not change. The incremental synchronization method is adopted, with a synchronization period of 3 s, and no triggers are added, so as to avoid frequent triggers causing database performance degradation. Such as analog real-time meter and state real-time meter.
- History table. These tables are characterized by a large number of records, only adding operations, updating every few minutes. The trigger synchronization method is used with a specific synchronization period.
- Electric quantity table. These tables are characterized by a large number of records and a batch of increase and update operations. The trigger synchronization method is same as history table.
- Appraisal result table. There are many records with increasing and updating operations.
- Alarm record table. It mainly refers to the record data in case of abnormal conditions in the production operation and front-end acquisition of the power plant. Characterized by a large number of records, accompanied by increase and update operations. The update time is random, with high real-time requirements. Trigger synchronization is adopted with more precise period.
- Browse display setting table. It is mainly used to define parameters such as content and style of display data with few changes. In intranet, it can be manually modified, or synchronized by manual snapshot.

System Operation

Create a new image database with the same name as the source database on the image database server. Run the synchronous receiver program, and monitor the network at port 9098 after connecting to the database successfully.

Run the receiver program on the source database server. After the synchronization table configuration is completed, change tracking table, change tracking trigger, shadow table and incremental changes analysis start. Then the system starts to perform a snapshot synchronization for each source table to complete the initialization of the target table. After normal operation, the system will read the change data of the source table according to the synchronization settings, and complete the synchronization update of the external network data. Generally, there is no need for manual intervention.

Performance Analysis

When the system is running the initialization of the target table, the synchronous SQL statements in every minute can reach 80000 records, and there are about 10 million records in the telecontrol database.

The initialization of the target database is completed in about 10 min, but during this period, the receiving program has been updating the target database, so the CPU occupation rate is high, about 50%. The memory occupation is about 170 MB. After the database initialization of the target table is completed, most of the tables are updated incrementally. At this time, the synchronous SQL statements have about

10000 records per minute. The CPU utilization of receiver is less than 10%, and the memory is about 110 MB.

The system has been stable and reliable since it was put into operation. The mirror database data is updated in real time, and the users of MIS can hardly feel the existence of network isolation. The original application based on telecontrol database runs as usual. It is easy for the system to deal with the damage of the database of the external network.

5   Conclusion

The database synchronization technology in the network isolation environment realizes the safe and moderate data exchange between databases in different trust network domains under the condition of physical isolation. This technology can not only fit for synchronization between isomorphic databases, but also synchronization between heterogeneous databases. In addition, because of the use of shadow table method, XML data exchange and other technologies, the database synchronization reduces the network transmission delay, improves the synchronization performance, and provides logging and error reporting functions to record and query all kinds of data synchronization information. We will further optimize synchronization performance and will continue to improve the system's ability to synchronize between non-mainstream databases while reducing the impact on other user applications.

Acknowledgments. This research is sponsored by State Grid Technology Project "Research and Application of Key Technologies in Enterprise-level Data Center Platform based on Full-Service Unified Data Center" under grants number 5211XT190033.

References

1. Elmasri, R., Navathe, S.B.: Database System Foundation. Shao P., Zhang K., translated, 3rd edn. People's Posts and Telecommunications Press, Beijing (2002)
2. Fan, Q., Tan, M., Luo, Y.: Security setting and security hardening of computer equipment in LAN. Inf. Secur. Commun. Confident. **07**, 31–39 (2008)
3. Dong, B.: Physical isolation technology for network security. Comput. Autom. **02**, 108–110 (2004)
4. Liu, W., Tong, L.: Design of Change Capture Scheme in Integration of Heterogeneous Databases. Figure 4 Workflow of database synchronization sending end Computer Application Research (07), pp. 213–215 (2005)
5. Wu, J., Li, N.: Design and application of safety isolation software for intelligent hydropower plant. Hydropower Plant Autom. **37**(04), 67–69 (2016)
6. Yu, H., Ding, Y., Gao, X., Geng, N., Huang, X., Lu, Y.: Data security transmission technology of water conservancy project standardization management based on one-way isolation gate. Zhejiang Water Sci. Technol. **44**(05), 48–50 (2016)
7. Cui, H., Feng, J., Ma, W., Zhang, Q., Pang, K., Yu, K.: Research and implementation of heterogeneous database synchronization technology based on isolation gateway. Softw. Eng. **19**(02), 10–13 (2016)

8. Dai, L., Zeng, F., Huang, H., Ji, X., Yang, T.: Establishment of hospital appointment diagnosis and treatment platform based on safety isolation network gate technology. China Med. Educ. Technol. **27**(04), 454–457 (2013)
9. Thomson Licensing; Patent Application Titled "Database Synchronization" Published Online (USPTO 20200142908). Politics & Government Week (2020)
10. Danijel, F., Danijel, S., Picek, R.: Bidirectional database synchronization to the cloud computing platform. In: ICISS 2020: 2020 The 3rd International Conference on Information Science and System (2020)
11. Marotta, A., Cassioli, D., Tornatore, M.: Reliable slicing with isolation in optical metro-aggregation networks. In: Optical Fiber Communication Conference (2020)

Secret Image Sharing Based on Chinese Remainder Theorem over a Polynomial Ring

Shuai Zhang and Fuyou Miao[(✉)]

School of Computer Science and Technology, University of Science and Technology of China, Hefei 230026, Anhui, China
709907153@qq.com, mfy@ustc.edu.cn

Abstract. Secret image sharing denotes a technique for apportioning secret images into n shadow images and preserving in n participants as the extension of secret sharing on images. Compared to Shamir's scheme-based secret image sharing, Chinese remainder theorem-based secret imaging has the advantages as lossless recovery, no further encryption, and low recovery computation complexity. However, traditional secret sharing schemes based on the Chinese remainder theorem have shortcomings including no (t, n) threshold, lossy recovery, ignoring image features or further encryption. In this paper, a (t, n) secret image sharing scheme is suggested based on Chinese remainder theorem over a polynomial ring realizing no further encryption and lossless recovery and making the pixel values of shadow images randomly distribute $[0, 255]$. The effectiveness of the suggested scheme will be demonstrated by experiments and analyses later.

Keywords: Secret image sharing · Secret sharing · Chinese remainder theorem · Polynomial rings · Lossless recovery

1 Introduction

Since image transmission is a relatively common phenomenon in current social information exchanges, securely transmitting secret images through an unsecured channel is an important research content. Furthermore, to guarantee the security of secret image transmission is typically investigated in terms of image encryption, image sharing, and image hiding. In either image hiding or image encryption, a single file is normally created to share the security of secret images. Moreover, the secret images will fail to be transmitted once the file is destroyed or lost in transmission. If many copies of the file are transmitted to overwhelm the above weakness, the security of the transmitted secret images will be diminished as well. Nevertheless, by the image sharing technique, this risk is avoided, hence, it is more worthy of research.

In (t, n) secret image sharing, a secret image is divided into n shadow images and independently preserved by n participants, moreover, the original secret image can be restored by t or more than t shadow images, however, it cannot be less than t shadow images. The majority of secret image sharing methods have been established based on Shamir's secret sharing scheme [1, 2] and Chinese remainder theorem [3–9].

X. Chen et al. (Eds.): ML4CS 2020, LNCS 12486, pp. 634–643, 2020.
https://doi.org/10.1007/978-3-030-62223-7_55

Secret image sharing is to apply and extend the secret-sharing on images. It was initially proposed as an outline for the security of cryptographic keys by Blakley [10] and Shamir [1]. A data block is divided by (t, n) secret sharing into n pieces, and the original data can be recovered by t or more than t pieces, not by less than t data shares. Using the original Shamir's scheme [1] based on (t, n) secret image sharing, each pixel value of a secret image is taken as a constant term of a $(t - 1)$ degree polynomial, then, n shadow images are obtained and further distributed into n participants. Furthermore, t or more than t shadow images can be utilized to reconstruct the secret image with high resolution through Lagrange interpolation. Shamir's scheme was extended by Thien and Lin [2] in 2002 and processed digital images. Specifically, using t coefficients of a $(t - 1)$ degree polynomial a secret image is shared, so that the size of each shadow image is $1/t$ of the original secret image. Later, some researchers put forward secret image sharing strategies with more features based on Shamir's scheme [11, 12]. Although the size of shadow images can be reduced by Shamir's scheme-based secret image sharing, the original secret image is generally lossy sometimes requiring further encryption during recovery.

Mignotte [4] firstly proposed secret sharing in terms of the Chinese remainder theorem in 1982 improved by Bloom and Asmuth in 1983 [3]. Some researchers also put forward secret image sharing schemes derived from Chinese remainder theorem-based secret sharing [5, 6, 8, 13, 14]. For instance, Yan et al. [5] first applied the Chinese remainder theorem to secret image sharing and found information distortion and leakage. Based on Mignotte's scheme, a (t, n) secret image sharing scheme was developed by Shyu et al. [6] utilizing a pseudo-random number generator, however, it requires further encryption. Ulutas et al. [8] presented an enhanced secret image sharing where the pixel values of grayscale images are divided into two intervals based on the secret sharing scheme of Asmuth and Bloom. Hu et al. [13] put forward an image sharing technique requiring further encryption in terms of chaotic mapping. Chuang et al. [14] reported a simple secret image sharing method and demonstrated the experimental results of $(3, 5)$ on RGB color images. In the scheme designated by Chuang et al., lossy recovery happens, and the least significant bit is stored for each pixel in advance. Hence, most of the present Chinese remainder theorem-based secret image sharing schemes have the problems of lossy recovery, no (t, n) threshold, ignoring image characteristics or further encryption.

Yan et al. [15] established a Chinese remainder theorem-based (t, n) secret sharing scheme realizing lossless recovery and requires no further encryption, however, in this scheme, not all the pixel values of shadow images can be distributed randomly within $[0, 255]$, and they should be split into two intervals for processing. Ning et al. [16] represented a secret sharing scheme based on the Chinese remainder theorem over a polynomial ring in 2018. Based on this scheme, a (t, n) secret image sharing scheme in terms of the Chinese remainder theorem over a polynomial ring is reported in this paper, hence, all pixel values of shadow images can distribute randomly in $[0, 255]$, without dividing into two intervals.

The structure of this paper is as follows: Some basic information is introduced in Sect. 1. Section 2 explains the (t, n) secret image sharing scheme based on the Chinese remainder theorem over a polynomial ring. The experimental results are demonstrated in Sect. 3, and the proposed scheme is analyzed and compared with other schemes in Sect. 4. Ultimately, a summary is made in Sect. 5.

2 Basic Information

In this section, some basic information on the present work is represented. (t, n) secret image sharing is implemented to split a secret image S into n shadow images $SC_1, SC_2, \ldots, SC_n$, and any $m(t \le m \le n)$ can be utilized to restore the original secret image S_0.

2.1 Chinese Remainder Theorem over a Polynomial Ring

Supposing that k is a field and $m_1(x), m_2(x), \ldots, m_n(x)$ are pairwise coprime polynomials for $k[x]$, then $f(x) \equiv f_1(x)M_1(x)M_1^{-1}(x) + f_2(x)M_2(x)M_2^{-1}(x) + \ldots + f_n(x)M_n(x) M_n^{-1}(x)$ [mod $m(x)$] is merely the solution for the following linear congruence equations, in which, $M(x) = \prod_{i=1}^{n} m_i(x)$, $M_i(x) = M(x)/m_i(x)$, $M_i(x)M_i^{-1}(x) \equiv 1(mod\ m_i(x))$.

$$\begin{cases} f(x) \equiv f_1(x)(\text{mod } m_1(x)) \\ f(x) \equiv f_2(x)(\text{mod } m_2(x)) \\ \quad\quad\cdots \\ f(x) \equiv f_n(x)(\text{mod } m_n(x)) \end{cases}$$

2.2 (t, n) Secret Sharing Scheme Proposed by Asmuth and Bloom

Secret sharing is made as follows: First, the distributor takes pairwise coprime positive integers $m_1, m_2, \ldots, m_n$, in which $m_0 < m_1 < m_2 < \ldots < m_n$ and $m_0 m_{n-t+2} \ldots m_n < m_1 \ldots m_t$. Then, a secret S is taken and an integer α is randomly selected, in which, $S \in [0, m_0 - 1]$ and $S + \alpha m_0 < m_1 \ldots m_t$. The share held by each participant is (s_i, m_i) where $s_i = S + \alpha m_0(mod\ m_i)$, $1 \le i \le n$.

Secret recovery is carried out as follows: Cooperating any t participants in restoring the secret will result in the following linear congruence equations.

$$\begin{cases} x \equiv s_{i_1}(mod\ m_{i_1}) \\ x \equiv s_{i_2}(mod\ m_{i_2}) \\ \quad\quad\cdots \\ x \equiv s_{i_t}(mod\ m_{i_t}) \end{cases}$$

Since $m_{i_1}, m_{i_2}, \ldots, m_{i_n}$ are co-prime in pair, S_0 represents the unique solution in $[0, m_{i_1} m_{i_2} \ldots m_{i_n} - 1]$ for the linear congruence equations, and the original secret is attained by determining $S \equiv S_0(mod\ m_0)$.

2.3 Analysis of Image Characteristics

Images are comprised of pixels correlated with each other, hence, the correlations between the original secret images pixels should be removed in secret image sharing.

Since the pixel values of grayscale images distribute in $[0, 255]$, it is supposed that the pixel values of the shadow images of the shared secret images also lie in $[0, 255]$.

3 (t, n) Secret Image Sharing Scheme

This section demonstrates the (t, n) secret sharing scheme based on the Chinese remainder theorem for $F_2[x]$ and its usage to images.

3.1 (t, n) Secret Sharing Outline Based on Chinese Remainder Theorem for $F_2[x]$

To perform the secret distribution a distributor selects $m_0(x) = x^8$, and a pairwise co-prime polynomial $m_i(x) \in F_2[x]$, in which $\deg(m_i) = 8$, $i \in [n]$. Furthermore, any $m_i(x)$ is co-prime to $m_0(x)$. Then, the distributor chooses a secret $S(x) \in \{g(x) \in F_2(x) | \deg(g(x)) < 8\}$ and randomly takes $\alpha(x) \in \{g(x) \in F_2(x) | \deg(g(x)) \le 8t - 8 - 1\}$. The share held by each participant is $(s_i(x), m_i(x))$, where $s_i(x) \equiv s(x) + \alpha(x)m_0(x)(mod\ m_i(x))$, $1 \le i \le n$.

Secret recovery is accomplished by taking part in any t participants in restoring the secret to obtain the following linear congruence equations.

$$\begin{cases} X(x) \equiv s_{i_1}(x)(mod\ m_{i_1}(x)) \\ X(x) \equiv s_{i_2}(x)(mod\ m_{i_2}(x)) \\ \qquad \cdots \\ X(x) \equiv s_{i_t}(x)(mod\ m_{i_t}(x)) \end{cases}$$

$m_{i_1}(x), m_{i_2}(x), \ldots, m_{i_t}(x)$ denote the pairwise co-prime polynomials for $F_2[x]$, hence, there exists the only solution $s_0(x)$ for the congruence equations if the degree is less than $8t$ based on the Chinese remainder theorem over a polynomial ring, and the original secret is calculated in terms of $s(x) \equiv s_0(x)(mod\ m_0(x))$.

3.2 (t, n) Secret Image Sharing Scheme Based on Chinese Remainder Theorem over a Polynomial Ring

Assume that $F_2[x](n) = \{f(x) \in F_2(x) | \deg(f(x)) \le n\}$, the two kinds of mappings are determined as:

$$\phi: F_2[x](7) \to [0, 255], \sum_{i=0}^{7} a_i x^i \mapsto \sum_{i=0}^{7} a_i 2^i$$

$$\tau: [0, 255] \to F_2[x](7), \sum_{i=0}^{7} a_i 2^i \mapsto \sum_{i=0}^{7} a_i x^i$$

Suppose that the size of a secret image S is H × W, each pixel value of the secret image is stated as $S(h, w)$, however, it is as $SC_i(h, w)$ for shadow images, where $1 \leq h \leq H$, $1 \leq w \leq W$, $1 \leq i \leq n$.

To perform secret image distribution, $s(x) = \tau(S(h, w))$, and $s(x)$ is processed as a secret for each pixel value of the secret image using the (t, n) secret sharing scheme based on Chinese remainder theorem for $F_2[x]$ (all the parameters are the same for each pixel value in the secret sharing scheme except for $\alpha(x)$) to enable $SC_i(h, w) = \phi(s_i(x))$. Ultimately, the corresponding shadow images preserved by each participant SC_i and polynomial $m_i(x)$ are obtained.

To perform the secret image recovery existing any t participants for restoring the secret image, each pixel value of shadow images is processed as follows: If $s_{i_j}(x) = \tau\big(SC_{i_j}(h, w)\big)$ and $1 \leq j \leq t$, then $S(h, w) = \phi(s(x))$ is realized utilizing the (t, n) secret sharing recovery algorithm based on the Chinese remainder theorem for $F_2[x]$. Ultimately, the original secret image S is restored.

4 Experimental Results

In this section, the experimental results of the $(3, 4)$ secret image sharing based on Chinese remainder theorem over a polynomial ring are revealed, with $m_1(x) = x^8 + x^4 + x^3 + x^2 + 1$, $m_2(x) = x^8 + x^7 + x^5 + x^4 + 1$, $m_3(x) = x^8 + x^6 + x^5 + x^4 + 1$ and $m_4(x) = x^8 + x^7 + x^2 + x + 1$.

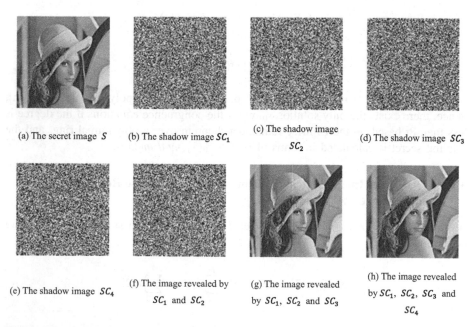

(a) The secret image S (b) The shadow image SC_1 (c) The shadow image SC_2 (d) The shadow image SC_3

(e) The shadow image SC_4 (f) The image revealed by SC_1 and SC_2 (g) The image revealed by SC_1, SC_2 and SC_3 (h) The image revealed by SC_1, SC_2, SC_3 and SC_4

Fig. 1. The experimental results of $(3, 4)$ secret image sharing based on Chinese remainder theorem over a polynomial ring.

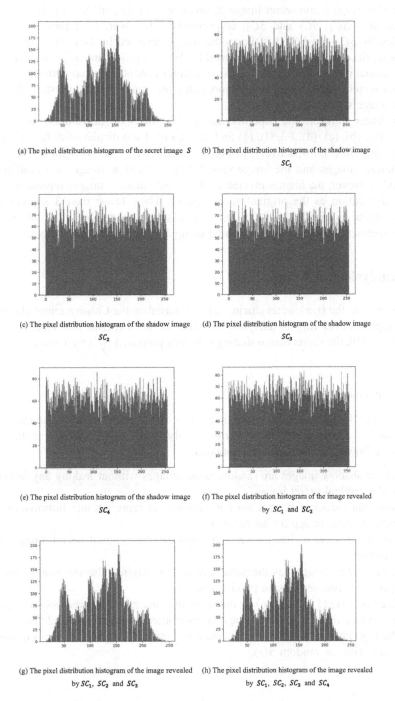

(a) The pixel distribution histogram of the secret image S

(b) The pixel distribution histogram of the shadow image SC_1

(c) The pixel distribution histogram of the shadow image SC_2

(d) The pixel distribution histogram of the shadow image SC_3

(e) The pixel distribution histogram of the shadow image SC_4

(f) The pixel distribution histogram of the image revealed by SC_1 and SC_2

(g) The pixel distribution histogram of the image revealed by SC_1, SC_2 and SC_3

(h) The pixel distribution histogram of the image revealed by SC_1, SC_2, SC_3 and SC_4

Fig. 2. The pixel distribution histograms of experimental results of $(3, 4)$ secret image sharing based on Chinese remainder theorem over a polynomial ring

In Fig. 1, (a) is the secret image S, however, (b), (c), (d) and (e) are the shadow images SC_1, SC_2, SC_3 and SC_4, respectively. Moreover, (f) represents the image revealed by SC_1 and SC_2, (g) shows the image revealed by SC_1, SC_2 and SC_3. Furthermore, (h) displays the image revealed by SC_1, SC_2, SC_3 and SC_4. According to the experimental results, fewer than 3 shadow images cannot reveal any information on the original secret image, however, 3 or more shadow images serve to restore the original secret image without distortion.

To better illustrate the experimental results, the pixel distribution histograms of images (a), (b), (c), (d), (e), (f), (g) and (h) in Fig. 1 are displayed as (a), (b), (c), (d), (e), (f), (g) and (h), respectively, in Fig. 2. According to the histograms, the pixels of the shadow images and the image revealed by 2 shadow images are randomly distributed, however, the images raveled by 3 or more shadow images represent the same pixel distribution as the original secret image. Thus, fewer than 3 shadow images cannot reveal any information on the original secret image, while the original secret image without distortion can be restored using 3 or more shadow images.

5   Analysis and Comparison

In this section, the (t, n) secret sharing scheme based on the Chinese remainder theorem over a polynomial ring is analyzed in terms of the experimental results, and it is compared with the secret image sharing schemes proposed by Thien and Lin as well as Yan et al.

5.1   Analysis

Considering the experimental results in Sect. 3, the (t, n) secret image sharing scheme based on Chinese remainder theorem over a polynomial ring is analyzed in this section, and the following conclusions are obtained:

(a)   All the shadow images are random noise images without leaking any information on the original secret image.
(b)   Less than t shadow images are not sufficient to represent any information on the original secret image during recovery.
(c) t or more shadow images serve to restore the original secret image without distortion.
(d)   Each shadow image has the same size as the original shadow image, hence, the algorithm proposed has no pixel expansion.
(e)   Since $m\_i\,(x)\;(1 \leq i \leq n)$ in the algorithm are all 8th degree polynomials, each pixel value of each shadow image is distributed randomly in [0, 255].
(f)   The algorithm can remove the correlations between the pixels of the original secret image with the random $\alpha(x)$.

5.2   Comparison

Based on Shamir's secret sharing scheme, t coefficients were replaced by Thien and Lin in the $(t - 1)$ degree polynomial with the pixel values of the original secret image, so that the size of each shadow image is $1/t$ of that of the original secret image. However, this method fails to eliminate the correlation within the pixels of the original secret image, hence, it requires pre-replacement of secret images. Since a prime number p is no higher than 251, the pixels greater than 250 cannot be restored by the scheme proposed by Thien and Lin leading to lossy recovery. On the other hand, a lossless recovery scheme was provided by Thien and Lin, nonetheless, the pixel value x larger than 250 needs to be truncated to 250 and $(x - 250)$ for processing. Therefore, the size of each shadow image will greatly vary with the original secret image's features.

Yan et al. put forward such a Chinese remainder theorem-based (t, n) secret sharing scheme making the possible lossless recovery and eliminating the correlations between the pixels of secret images, without further replacement. However, in this scheme, the pixel values need to be divided into two intervals and separately processed. Moreover, all the pixel values of each shadow image do not need to lie in $[0, 255]$.

In this paper, the proposed (t, n) secret image sharing scheme based on the Chinese remainder theorem over a polynomial ring realizes lossless recovery, without separating the pixels of secret images. Furthermore, with this scheme, all the pixel values of shadow images are distributed randomly in $[0, 255]$.

The comparison of the three schemes is shown in Table 1.

Table 1. The comparison of Thien's scheme, Lin's scheme, Yan's scheme and the scheme used in this paper

Scheme	Characteristic			
	Are replacement of secret images needed?	Are the pixels of secret images need to be separated?	Are the secret images distorted?	Are all the pixel values of shadow images are distributed randomly in $[0, 255]$?
Thien and Lin's schemes	Yes	No	Distorted images or the images with a pixel larger than 250 required a special treatment	No
Yan et al's scheme	No	Yes	No	No
Scheme used in this paper	No	No	No	Yes

6 Summary

In the present study, a (t, n) secret image sharing scheme is suggested based on the Chinese remainder theorem over a polynomial ring. By collecting t or more than t shadow images, an original secret image will be restored losslessly, or any information on the original secret image will not be revealed by this scheme. In addition, this scheme includes no pixel expansion making the shadow images' pixel values randomly distribute in $[0, 255]$.

Acknowledgments. The work was supported by the National Natural Science Foundation of China (No. 61572454, 61520106007). We thank the editors and anonymous reviewers for giving us many constructive comments that significantly improved the paper.

References

1. Shamir, A.: How to share a secret. Commun. ACM **22**(11), 612–613 (1979)
2. Thien, C.C., Lin, J.C.: Secret image sharing. Comput. Graph. **26**(1), 765–771 (2002)
3. Asmuth, C., Bloom, J.: A modular approach to key safeguarding. IEEE Trans. Inf. Theory **29**(2), 208–210 (1983)
4. Mignotte, M.: How to share a secret. In: Beth, T. (ed.) EUROCRYPT 1982. LNCS, vol. 149, pp. 371–375. Springer, Heidelberg (1983). https://doi.org/10.1007/3-540-39466-4_27
5. Yan, W., Ding, W., Dongxu, Q.: Image sharing based on Chinese remainder theorem. J. North China Univ. Tech. **12**(1), 6–9 (2000)
6. Shyu, S.J., Chen, Y.R.: Threshold secret image sharing by Chinese remainder theorem. In: IEEE Asia-Pacific Services Computing Conference, 9–12, pp. 1332–1337 (2008)
7. Stinson, D.: Cryptography: Theory and Practice. CRC Press, CRC Press LCC, Boca Raton (1995). ISBN 0849385210
8. Ulutas, M., Nabiyev, V.V., Ulutas, G.: A new secret sharing technique based on asmuth bloom's scheme. In: IEEE International Conference on Application of Information and Communication Technologies, 1–5, pp. 14–16 (2009)
9. Lambert, M.S., Miriam, T.T., Susan, F.M.: Secret Sharing Using the Chinese Remainder Theorem. Betascript Publishing,(2010)
10. Blakley, G.R.: Safeguarding Cryptographic Keys. In: AFIPS Conference Proceedings, vol. 48, pp. 313–317 (1979)
11. Yang, C.N., Ciou, C.B.: Image secret sharing method with two-decoding-options: lossless recovery and previewing capability. Image Vis. Comput. **28**(12), 1600–1610 (2010)
12. Li, P., Ma, P.J., Su, X.H., Yang, C.N.: Improvements of a two-in-one image secret sharing scheme based on gray mixing model. J. Vis. Commun. Image Represent. **23**(3), 441–453 (2012)
13. Hu, C., Liao, X., Xiao, D.: Secret image sharing based on chaotic map and chinese remainder theorem. Int. J. Wavelets Multiresolut. Inf. Process. **10**(3), 1250023 (2012)
14. Chuang, T.W., Chen, C.C., Chien, B.: Image sharing and recovering based on chinese remainder theorem. In: International Symposium on Computer, Consumer and Control (IS3C), pp. 817–820 (2016)

15. Yan, X., Lu, Y., Liu, L., Wan, S., Ding, W., Liu, H.: Chinese remainder theorem-based secret image sharing for (k, n) threshold. In: Sun, X., Chao, H.-C., You, X., Bertino, E. (eds.) ICCCS 2017. LNCS, vol. 10603, pp. 433–440. Springer, Cham (2017). https://doi.org/10.1007/978-3-319-68542-7_36
16. Ning, Y., Miao, F.Y., Huang, W.C., Meng, K.J., Xiong, Y., Wang, X.F.: Constructing ideal secret sharing schemes based on Chinese remainder theorem. In: Asiacrypt (2018)

Author Index

Printed in the United States
By Bookmasters